FUNDAMENTALS OF HUMAN RESOURCE MANAGEMENT SECOND EDITION

Gary Dessler

Florida International University

Prentice Hall

Boston   Columbus   Indianapolis   New York   San Francisco   Upper Saddle River
Amsterdam   Cape Town   Dubai   London   Madrid   Milan   Munich   Paris   Montreal   Toronto
Delhi   Mexico City   Sao Paulo   Sydney   Hong Kong   Seoul   Singapore   Taipei   Tokyo

Editorial Director: Sally Yagan
Editor-in-Chief: Eric Svendsen
Director of Editorial Services: Ashley Santora
Editorial Project Manager: Meg O'Rourke
Editorial Assistant: Carter Anderson
Director of Marketing: Patrice Lumumba Jones
Marketing Manager: Nikki Ayana Jones
Marketing Assistant: Ian Gold
Senior Managing Editor: Judy Leale
Production Project Manager: Kelly Warsak
Senior Operations Supervisor: Arnold Vila
Operations Specialist: Cathleen Petersen
Creative Director: Christy Mahon

Senior Art Director: Kenny Beck
Text Designer: LCI Design
Cover Designer: LCI Design
Cover Art: © Diana Ong/SuperStock
Manager, Rights and Permissions: Hessa Albader
Media Project Manager: Lisa Rinaldi
Media Assistant Editor: Denise Vaughn
Full-Service Project Management: Jennifer Welsch/BookMasters, Inc.
Composition: Integra Software Services
Printer/Binder: R.R. Donnelley/Willard
Cover Printer: Lehigh-Phoenix Color/Hagerstown
Text Font: 10/12 Times New Roman

Credits and acknowledgments borrowed from other sources and reproduced, with permission, in this textbook appear on appropriate page within text.

Microsoft® and Windows® are registered trademarks of the Microsoft Corporation in the U.S.A. and other countries. Screen shots and icons reprinted with permission from the Microsoft Corporation. This book is not sponsored or endorsed by or affiliated with the Microsoft Corporation.

Many of the designations by manufacturers and seller to distinguish their products are claimed as trademarks. Where those designations appear in this book, and the publisher was aware of a trademark claim, the designations have been printed in initial caps or all caps.

Library of Congress Cataloging-in-Publication Data
Dessler, Gary
   Fundamentals of human resource management/Gary Dessler.—2nd ed.
      p. cm.
   Includes bibliographical references and index.
   ISBN 978-0-13-255590-6 (pbk. : alk. paper)
   1. Personnel management.   I. Title.
   HF5549.D437884 2011
   658.3—dc22

                          2010032155

10 9 8 7 6 5 4 3 2 1

Prentice Hall
is an imprint of

www.pearsonhighered.com   ISBN 10:   0-13-255590-5
                          ISBN 13: 978-0-13-255590-6

Brief Contents

Contents

Preface

Fundamentals of Human Resource Management provides students in undergraduate and graduate human resource management courses and practicing managers with a comprehensive and modern review of the human resource management body of knowledge in a lively and manageable 14-chapter format. *Fundamentals* provides full coverage of human resource management, but with abbreviated treatment of research findings and advanced topics. *Fundamentals* merges the breadth of my 18-chapter *Human Resource Management, 12th edition* with the brevity of my 10-chapter *Framework for Human Resource Management, 6th edition*. As with those books, I also wrote *Fundamentals* to show students why human resource management is important, even if you never spend one day as an HR manager. Every day of your business career, you may have to interview and hire people, and train and appraise them, for instance. Studying this book should therefore help you as a manager, whatever your job title happens to be.

NEW TO THIS SECOND EDITION

This second edition of *Fundamentals* represents a substantial revision of the first. The book's chapter outline and topic coverage is basically the same, so moving from the first to the second edition should be fairly seamless for adopters. However, there are **six major changes**, as follows:

Change 1. Most importantly, *Fundamentals of Human Resource Management, 2nd edition* is **the first book in this market to build its core around the talent management process**. To that end, Part 2, Staffing and Talent Management, includes Chapter 4 Recruiting and Talent Management, Chapter 5 Selecting Employees, Chapter 6 Training and Developing Employees, Chapter 7 Performance and Talent Management, and Chapter 8 Compensating Employees. The traditional approach to staffing, appraisal, and compensation tends to be to treat these topics as a sequence of somewhat isolated steps, from personnel planning to recruiting, selecting, training, appraising, and compensating employees. This sequential approach makes sense, but may mask the fact that these activities should be interactive and integrated. For example, training and development should reflect both employee performance and the company's longer-term workforce planning needs.

Employers today therefore increasingly view all these staff—appraise—reward activities as part of a single integrated talent management process. We define talent management as the *goal-oriented* and *integrated* process of *planning, recruiting, developing, managing, and compensating* employees. Defining this system in terms of talent management isn't just semantics. We'll see throughout this book that five things set talent management apart from simply recruiting, selecting, training, appraising, and rewarding employees:

1. As we explain in Chapter 4, viewing the various talent management activities as parts of a single integrated process helps ensure that managers *consciously think through and focus on all the tasks required* for managing the company's talent.
2. An effective talent management process should *integrate the underlying talent management activities* such as workforce planning, recruiting, developing, and compensating employees. For example, performance appraisal results should prompt training for employees.
3. Talent management is *goal directed*. The aim is to (1) align the employees' competencies and (2) the firm's talent management activities with (3) the company's strategic goals. Managers should always be asking, "What type of recruiting or other actions should I be taking to get the employee competencies we need to achieve our company's strategic goals?"
4. Talent management is *proactive*. Taking a talent management approach requires that employers *actively manage* their employees' recruitment, selection, development, and rewards. For example, many employers are segmenting out their most "mission-critical" employees, and managing their development and rewards separately from the firms' other employees.
5. Talent management requires taking *formal steps to integrate* the underlying talent management activities, either via coordinative activities among HR professionals or via talent management software.

Change 2. New **Managing HR in Challenging Times** features show how managers are adjusting their human resource pay, promotion, selection, and other practices to improve performance in economically challenging times.

Change 3. New **HR APPS 4 U** features show how managers use iPhone-type applications to carry out human resource tasks such as record keeping and testing.

Change 4. I thoroughly **updated** all chapters, and added dozens of **new topics**, including, for instance, *Making the Selection Decision* in Chapter 5, and *Employee Retention* in the new Employee Retention, and Career Management Module at the end of the book.

Change 5. In the first edition, two boxed features showed how managers apply *Personal Competencies* (such as "*Building Your Cross-Cultural Sensitivity*") and *Business Knowledge* (such as "*Building Your Business Law Knowledge in Testing*") in doing their HR jobs. In this second edition, I **converted these features into end-of-chapter exercises**. Now readers can concentrate, in the body of the chapters, on the traditional human resource management knowledge and applications.

Change 6. I rewrote Chapter 14 (now titled Building High-Performance Work Systems and Improving Strategic Results) to focus it less on quantitative subjects and more on **how managers build high-performance work systems**.

TEACHING AND LEARNING SUPPORT

Fundamentals of Human Resource Management continues to be supported with an extensive supplement package for both students and faculty.

Instructor's Resource Center

www.pearsonhighered.com/educator is where instructors can access a variety of print, media, and presentation resources available with this text in downloadable, digital format.

Once you register, you will not have additional forms to fill out, or multiple usernames and passwords to remember to access new titles and/or editions. As a registered faculty member, you can log in directly to download resource files, and receive immediate access and instructions for installing Course Management content to your campus server.

Our dedicated Technical Support team is ready to assist instructors with questions about the media supplements that accompany this text. Visit http://247pearsoned.custhelp.com for answers to frequently asked questions and toll-free user support phone numbers. The following supplements are available to adopting instructors.

To download the supplements available with this text, please visit www.pearsonhighered. com/educator

Instructor's Manual
Test Item File
TestGen test generating software
PowerPoints

Videos on DVD

Video segments illustrate the most pertinent topics in human resource management today and highlight relevant issues that demonstrate how people lead, manage, and work effectively. Contact your Pearson representative for the DVD. Additional videos are available to mymanagementlab users at www.mymanagementlab.com.

mymanagementlab.com

www.mymanagementlab.com is an easy-to-use online tool that personalizes course content and provides robust assessment and reporting to measure individual and class performance. In each student chapter, mymanagementlab contains a study plan activity, a video activity, a critical thinking activity, along with end-of-chapter assessments. Further, student PowerPoint files and flash cards help students quickly review and prepare for class. Students can also choose to go completely digital, purchasing access to the Pearson eText version of the textbook directly from the website (an option for students to inexpensively "upgrade" to a print version after buying electronic access is also available). Further, instructors will also find access to their supplements, including an extensive video library featuring clips that illustrate the most pertinent topics in human resource management today.

CourseSmart eTextbook

CourseSmart is an exciting new choice for students looking to save money. As an alternative to purchasing the print textbook, students can purchase an electronic version of the same content for less than the suggested list price of the print text. With a CourseSmart e-textbook, students can search the text, make notes online, print out reading assignments that incorporate lecture notes, and bookmark important passages for later review. For more information, or to purchase access to the CourseSmart e-textbook version of this text, visit www.coursesmart.com.

Acknowledgments

I am indebted to many people for their assistance in creating this book. I appreciate the hard work and conscientious and useful suggestions from the reviewers of the first and second editions of *Fundamentals*, including Kristen Diehl-Olger, Montcalm Community College; Fred Dorn, University of Mississippi; Karen Ferguson, Franklin University; Laurie Giesenhagen, California State University–Fullerton; Sonia Goltz, Michigan Tech; Judith Grenkowicz, Kirtland Community College; Elaine Guertler, Wesley College–Dover; Gundy Kaupins, Boise State University; Jacqueline Landau, Salem State College; Alicia Maciel, California State University-Fullerton; David McGuire, Southern Utah University; Michelle Paludi, Union College; Quinetta Roberson, Villanova University; Carolyn Waits, Cincinnati State Technical and Community College; Scott Warman, ECPI Technical College; Thomas Zagenczyk, Clemson University; Lu Zhang, Pennsylvania State University-Harrisburg; David Zoogah, Morgan State University; Wesley A. Scroggins, Missouri State University; Deborah M. Wharff, University of North Carolina Pembroke and University of Massachusetts, Lowell; and David C. Jacobs, Morgan State University. At Pearson Prentice Hall, I want to thank the team I worked with on this book, including Editor-in-Chief Eric Svendsen, Director of Editorial Services Ashley Santora, Editorial Project Manager Meg O'Rourke, Editorial Assistant Carter Anderson, Senior Managing Editor Judy Leale, Production Project Manager Kelly Warsak, and Marketing Manager Nikki Jones, as well as the world-wide members of Pearson's sales team and Project Manager Jennifer Welsch of BookMasters. At home, I want to thank my wife Claudia for her support, my son Derek for his advice, and of course, Samantha and Taylor, for keeping things lively.

About the Author

Gary Dessler is a widely read author of textbooks in human resource management, and management. His best-selling *Human Resource Management, 12th edition* (Prentice Hall, 2010) is also available in 10 languages including Traditional and Simplified Chinese. Dessler's other books include *Managing Now* (Houghton Mifflin, 2008), *Framework for Human Resource Management, 6th edition* (Prentice Hall), and *Winning Commitment: How to Build and Keep a Competitive Workforce* (McGraw-Hill). His published articles and presentations include "Expanding into China? What Foreign Employers Entering China Should Know About Human Resource Management in China Today," SAM *Advanced Management Journal*, September 2006; "How to Fine-Tune Your Employees' Ethical Compasses," *Supervision*, April 2006; and "Business Models of China's Online Recruiting Sites: A Taxonomy and Implications," (co-author), paper presented at Rollins China Center Conference, December 2006. Dessler is a Founding Professor at Florida International University where he teaches courses in human resource management, strategic management, and management. He has degrees from New York University (B.S.), Rensselaer Polytechnic Institute (M.S.), and the Baruch School of Business of the City University of New York (Ph.D.). Dr. Dessler served for 3 years on the Institute of International Education's national selection committee for the Fulbright student awards; is a member of the Society for Human Resource Management, the Academy of Management, and the Authors Guild; and, as a board member for a chemical engineering and pollution control firm, serves as that firm's consulting human resource manager.

1 Managing Human Resources Today

- What Is Human Resource Management?
- The Trends Shaping Human Resource Management
- The Main Implications for Human Resource Managers
- The Plan of This Book

Source: © Andre Jenny/Alamy.

When you finish studying this chapter, you should be able to:

1. Answer the question "What is human resource management?"

2. Explain with at least five examples why "knowing HR management concepts and techniques is important to any supervisor or manager."

3. Explain with examples what we mean by "the changing environment of human resource management."

4. List, with examples, the main implications of the trends influencing human resource managers.

INTRODUCTION

Most L.L.Bean customers know it's a pleasure to deal with their staff, who usually are knowledgeable, courteous, and understanding. What might not be so obvious is that having staff like that is no accident. It's the product of a well-thought-out plan for recruiting, selecting, training, and rewarding employees. For one thing, the company knows just what it's looking for. L.L.Bean says candidates should be friendly, helpful, authentic, honest, experienced, outdoor oriented, and environmentally aware.[1] In return, L.L.Bean offers an outdoors-oriented working environment, competitive pay, and numerous benefits including (for instance) cash performance bonuses, medical and insurance plans, a pension program, and an advanced management program.[2] The company also offers something less tangible. For example, when the company's Web sales recently first exceeded its phone sales, L.L.Bean closed four call centers, but arranged for the 220 employees to work from their homes. And instead of sending jobs abroad, the company keeps them close to the town where Leon Leonwood Bean started out almost 100 years ago.[3] Like many smart employers today, this company knows that a great staff makes it more competitive, and that the better it treats its staff, the better the staff treats L.L.Bean's customers. ■

1 Answer the question "What is human resource management?"

organization
A group consisting of people with formally assigned roles who work together to achieve the organization's goals.

manager
Someone who is responsible for accomplishing the organization's goals, and who does so by managing the efforts of the organization's people.

managing
To perform five basic functions: planning, organizing, staffing, leading, and controlling.

management process
The five basic functions of planning, organizing, staffing, leading, and controlling.

human resource management (HRM)
The process of acquiring, training, appraising, and compensating employees, and of attending to their labor relations, health and safety, and fairness concerns.

WHAT IS HUMAN RESOURCE MANAGEMENT?

L.L.Bean is an *organization*. An **organization** consists of people (in this case, people like call-center employees, tailors, assembly workers, and managers) with formally assigned roles who work together to achieve the organization's goals. A **manager** is someone who is responsible for accomplishing the organization's goals, and who does so by managing the efforts of the organization's people. Most writers agree that **managing** involves performing five basic functions: planning, organizing, staffing, leading, and controlling. In total, these functions represent the **management process**. Some of the specific activities involved in each function include:

- *Planning.* Establishing goals and standards; developing rules and procedures; developing plans and forecasts.
- *Organizing.* Giving each subordinate a specific task; establishing departments; delegating authority to subordinates; establishing channels of authority and communication; coordinating the work of subordinates.
- *Staffing.* Determining what type of people should be hired; recruiting prospective employees; selecting employees; setting performance standards; compensating employees; evaluating performance; counseling employees; training and developing employees.
- *Leading.* Getting others to get the job done; maintaining morale; motivating subordinates.
- *Controlling.* Setting standards such as sales quotas, quality standards, or production levels; checking to see how actual performance compares with these standards; taking corrective action as needed.

In this book, we are going to focus on one of these functions—the staffing, personnel management, or *human resource management (HRM)* function. **Human resource management** is the process of acquiring, training, appraising, and compensating employees, and of attending to their labor relations, health and safety, and fairness concerns. The topics we'll discuss should therefore provide you with the concepts and techniques you'll need to perform the "people" or personnel aspects of management. These include:

- *Conducting job analyses* (determining the nature of each employee's job)
- *Planning labor needs* and *recruiting* job candidates
- *Selecting* job candidates
- *Orienting and training* new employees
- *Managing wages and salaries* (compensating employees)
- *Providing incentives and benefits*
- *Appraising performance*
- *Communicating* (interviewing, counseling, disciplining)
- *Training employees*, and *developing managers*
- *Building employee commitment*

And also what a manager should know about:

- Equal opportunity and affirmative action
- Employee health and safety
- Handling grievances and labor relations

Why Is Human Resource Management Important to All Managers?

Why are these concepts and techniques important to all managers? Perhaps it's easier to answer this by listing some of the personnel mistakes you don't want to make while managing. For example, you don't want

- To have your employees or company not performing at peak capacity
- To hire the wrong person for the job
- To experience high turnover
- To find employees not doing their best
- To have your company taken to court because of your discriminatory actions
- To have your company cited under federal occupational safety laws for unsafe practices
- To allow a lack of training to undermine your department's effectiveness
- To commit any unfair labor practices

2 Explain with at least five examples why "knowing HR management concepts and techniques is important to any supervisor or manager."

WHY STUDY THIS BOOK? Carefully studying this book can help you avoid mistakes like these. More important, it can help ensure that you get results—through people. Remember that you could do everything else right as a manager—lay brilliant plans, draw clear organization charts, set up modern assembly lines, and use sophisticated accounting controls—but still fail, for instance, by hiring the wrong people or by not motivating subordinates.

On the other hand, many managers—from presidents to generals to supervisors—have been successful even without adequate plans, organizations, or controls. They were successful because they had the knack for hiring the right people for the right jobs and motivating, appraising, and developing them. Remember as you read this book that getting results is the bottom line of managing and that, as a manager, you will have to get these results through people. This fact hasn't changed from the dawn of management. As one company president summed it up:

> For many years it has been said that capital is the bottleneck for a developing industry. I don't think this any longer holds true. I think it's the workforce and the company's inability to recruit and maintain a good workforce that does constitute the bottleneck for production. I don't know of any major project backed by good ideas, vigor, and enthusiasm that has been stopped by a shortage of cash. I do know of industries whose growth has been partly stopped or hampered because they can't maintain an efficient and enthusiastic labor force, and I think this will hold true even more in the future.[4]

Line and Staff Aspects of HRM

All managers are, in a sense, human resource managers, because they all get involved in activities such as recruiting, interviewing, selecting, and training. Yet most firms also have a separate human resource department with its own human resource (HR) manager. How do the duties of this departmental HR manager and his or her staff relate to line managers' human resource duties? Let's answer this by starting with short definitions of line versus staff authority.

Line Versus Staff Authority

authority
The right to make decisions, direct others' work, and give orders.

line manager
A manager who is authorized to direct the work of subordinates and is responsible for accomplishing the organization's tasks.

staff manager
A manager who assists and advises line managers.

Authority is the right to make decisions, to direct the work of others, and to give orders. In management, we usually distinguish between line authority and staff authority. Line authority gives managers the right (or authority) to issue orders to other managers or employees. It creates a superior–subordinate relationship. Staff authority gives a manager the right (authority) to advise other managers or employees. It creates an advisory relationship. **Line managers** have line authority. They are authorized to give orders. **Staff managers** have staff authority. They are authorized to assist and advise line managers.

In popular usage, managers associate line managers with managing functions (like sales or production) that the company must have to survive. Staff managers generally run departments that are advisory or supportive, like purchasing, human resource management, and quality control. This distinction makes sense as long as the "staff" department is, in fact, advisory. But in some companies, quality control, for instance, is so important that it is a line function, and directs how other departments control the quality of their activities. So, strictly speaking, it is not the type of department the person is in charge of or its name that determines if the manager in charge is line or staff. It is the nature of the relationship. The line manager can issue orders. The staff manager can advise.

Human resource managers are staff managers. They assist and advise line managers in areas like recruiting, hiring, and compensation. (However, we'll see that line managers also have human resource duties.)

LINE–STAFF HR COOPERATION HR and line managers share responsibility for most human resource activities. For example, human resource and line managers in about two-thirds of the firms in one survey shared responsibility for skills training.[5] (Thus, the supervisor might describe what training she thinks the new employee needs, HR might design the training, and the supervisors might then ensure that the training is having the desired effect.)

Line Managers' Human Resource Management Responsibilities

In any case, all supervisors spend much of their time on HR/personnel-type tasks. Indeed, the direct handling of people always has been an integral part of every line manager's responsibility, from president down to the first-line supervisor.

For example, one company outlines its line supervisors' responsibilities for effective human resource management under the following general headings:

1. Placing the right person in the right job
2. Starting new employees in the organization (orientation)
3. Training employees for jobs that are new to them
4. Improving the job performance of each person
5. Gaining creative cooperation and developing smooth working relationships
6. Interpreting the company's policies and procedures
7. Controlling labor costs
8. Developing the abilities of each person
9. Creating and maintaining departmental morale
10. Protecting employees' health and physical conditions

In small organizations, line managers may carry out all these personnel duties unassisted. But as the organization grows, line managers need the assistance, specialized knowledge, and advice of a separate human resource staff.

Moving from Line Manager to HR Manager

Which brings us to another reason to be familiar with this book's contents; you may well make a planned (or unplanned) stopover some day as a human resource manager. A survey by a team at the University of Southern California found that about one-fourth of large U.S. businesses appointed managers with no human resource management experience as their top human resource management executives. Reasons include that these people may give the firms' human resource management efforts a more strategic emphasis, and the possibility that they may sometimes be better equipped to integrate the firm's HR efforts with the rest of the business.[6] In any case, companies often promote their line managers through HR on their way up the corporate ladder. After General Motors emerged from Chapter 11 bankruptcy in 2009, it replaced its long-term human resource director with GM's vice president for global manufacturing engineering, someone with no human resource management experience.[7]

However, most top human resource executives do have prior human resource experience. About 80% of those in one survey worked their way up within HR.[8] About 17% of these HR executives had earned the Human Resource Certification Institute's senior professional in human resources (SPHR) designation, and 13% were certified professionals in human resources (PHR).

HR FOR ENTREPRENEURS And, here is another reason to study this book. You may well end up as your own human resource manager. More than half the people working in the United States work for small firms. Statistically speaking, therefore, most people graduating in the next few years either will work for small businesses or will create new small businesses of their own. Especially if you are managing your own small firm, you'll have to be skilled at human resource management.[9]

Organizing the Human Resource Department's Responsibilities

In larger firms the *human resource department* provides such specialized assistance. Figure 1.1 shows the human resource management jobs you might find in a large organization. Typical positions include compensation and benefits manager, employment and recruiting supervisor, training specialist, and employee relations executive. Examples of job duties include:

> *Recruiters:* Maintain contact within the community and perhaps travel extensively to search for qualified job applicants.
>
> *Equal employment opportunity (EEO) representatives or affirmative action coordinators:* Investigate and resolve EEO grievances, examine organizational practices for potential violations, and compile and submit EEO reports.
>
> *Job analysts:* Collect and examine detailed information about job duties to prepare job descriptions.
>
> *Compensation managers:* Develop compensation plans and handle the employee benefits program.
>
> *Training specialists:* Plan, organize, and direct training activities.
>
> *Labor relations specialists:* Advise management on all aspects of union–management relations.

HR IN SMALL BUSINESSES Human resource management in small firms is not just a shrunken version of big-company human resource management. Employers usually have about one HR professional per 100 employees. Small firms (say, those with less than 100 employees) generally don't have the critical mass required for a full-time human resource manager. Their human resource management therefore tends to be "ad hoc and informal." For example, one survey concludes that small firms tend to use "unimaginative" recruiting practices like relying on newspaper ads, walk-ins, and word-of-mouth, and to do little or no formal training.[10] However, that certainly does not need to be the case. Techniques like those throughout this book (and in Chapter 12) can boost the small business owner's "HR IQ."

NEW HUMAN RESOURCES ORGANIZATIONS Employers are also increasingly offering their human resource services in new ways. For example, rather than offering a "one size fits all" set

FIGURE 1.1

Human Resource Department Organization Chart Showing Typical HR Job Titles

Source: www.co.pinellas.fl.us/persnl/pdf/orgchart.pdf, accessed April 1, 2009.

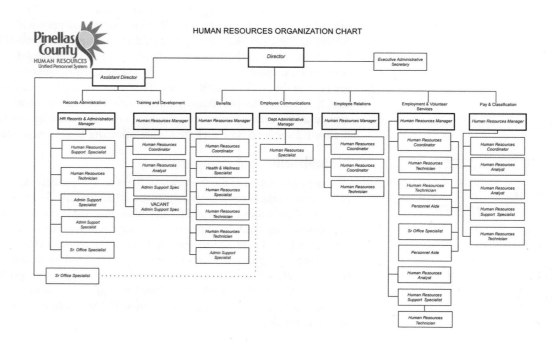

Randy MacDonald and IBM reorganized its human resource management group to focus on the needs of specific groups of IBM employees.

Source: Courtesy of IBM.

of recruitment, testing, and other services for all the firm's employees, some are tailoring their services to different types of employees. For instance, in some companies:[11]

- The *transactional HR* group focuses on using centralized call centers and vendors (such as benefits advisors) to provide employees with specialized support in day-to-day transactional HR activities (such as changing benefits plans) to the company's employees.
- The *corporate HR* group focuses on assisting top management in "top level" issues such as developing the company's long-term strategic plan.
- The *embedded HR* unit assigns HR generalists (also known as "relationship managers" or "HR business partners") to departments like sales and production, to provide the assistance the departments need.
- The *centers of expertise* are like specialized HR consulting firms within the company, for instance, providing specialized assistance in areas such as organizational change.

IBM EXAMPLE IBM's reorganized human resource management effort reflects such a new "tailor-made" approach to offering HR services. J. Randall (Randy) MacDonald, IBM's senior vice president of human resources, says the traditional human resource organization isolates HR functions into "silos" such as recruitment, training, and employee relations. This silo approach means there's no one team of human resource specialists focusing on the needs of specific groups of employees.

MacDonald therefore reorganized IBM's human resources function. He segmented IBM's 330,000 employees into three groups: executive and technical employees, managers, and rank and file. Separate human resource management teams (consisting of recruitment, training, and compensation specialists, for instance) now focus on each employee segment. These specialized teams help the employee/"talent" in each employee segment get precisely the testing, training, competencies, and rewards they require.[12] This new, segmented approach thereby helps IBM to more actively manage its talent.

THE TRENDS SHAPING HUMAN RESOURCE MANAGEMENT

Someone must staff the organization, so human resource (or "personnel") managers have long played important roles at work. Working cooperatively with line managers, they've helped administer benefits, screen employees, and recommend appraisal forms, for instance.

However, as at IBM, exactly what they do and how they do it is changing. Some of the reasons for these changes are obvious. For example, employers can now use intranets to let employees change their own benefits plans. That's something they obviously couldn't do 20 or so years ago. Some other trends shaping human resource management practices include globalization, deregulation, changes in demographics and the nature of work, and economic challenges.[13] Figure 1.2 sums up how such trends are affecting human resource management.

3 Explain with examples what we mean by "the changing environment of human resource management."

Globalization and Competition

Globalization refers to the tendency of firms to extend their sales, ownership, and/or manufacturing to new markets abroad. Examples are all around us. Toyota produces the Camry in Kentucky, while Dell produces and sells PCs in China. Free trade areas—agreements that reduce tariffs and barriers among trading partners—further encourage international trade. NAFTA (the North American Free Trade Agreement) and the EU (European Union) are examples.

More globalization means more competition, and more competition means more pressure to be "world class"—to lower costs, to make employees more productive, and to do things better and less expensively. As when the Spanish retailer Zara opens a new store in Manhattan, globalization pressures local employers and their HR teams to institute practices that get the best from their employees.

FIGURE 1.2

Trends Shaping Human Resource Management

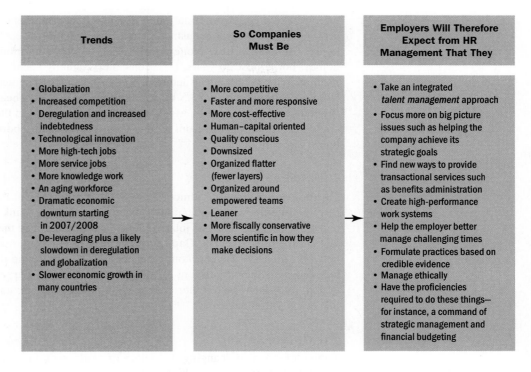

Trends	So Companies Must Be	Employers Will Therefore Expect from HR Management That They
• Globalization • Increased competition • Deregulation and increased indebtedness • Technological innovation • More high-tech jobs • More service jobs • More knowledge work • An aging workforce • Dramatic economic downturn starting in 2007/2008 • De-leveraging plus a likely slowdown in deregulation and globalization • Slower economic growth in many countries	• More competitive • Faster and more responsive • More cost-effective • Human–capital oriented • Quality conscious • Downsized • Organized flatter (fewer layers) • Organized around empowered teams • Leaner • More fiscally conservative • More scientific in how they make decisions	• Take an integrated *talent management* approach • Focus more on big picture issues such as helping the company achieve its strategic goals • Find new ways to provide transactional services such as benefits administration • Create high-performance work systems • Help the employer better manage challenging times • Formulate practices based on credible evidence • Manage ethically • Have the proficiencies required to do these things— for instance, a command of strategic management and financial budgeting

OFFSHORING The search for greater efficiencies is prompting employers to *offshore* (export more jobs to lower-cost locations abroad). For example, Dell offshored some call-center jobs to India. Figure 1.3 illustrates that in the next few years, many employers plan to offshore even highly skilled jobs such as sales managers, general managers—and HR managers.[14]

For fifty or so years, globalization boomed. For example, the total sum of U.S. imports and exports rose from $47 billion in 1960, to $562 billion in 1980, to about $3.4 *trillion* in 2009.[15] Changes in economic and political philosophies drove this boom. Governments dropped cross-border taxes or tariffs, formed economic "free trade areas" such as NAFTA, and took other steps to encourage the free flow of trade among countries. The fundamental economic rationale was that by doing so, all countries would gain. And indeed, economies around the world did grow rapidly.

Indebtedness ("Leverage") and Deregulation

Other trends contributed to this economic growth. Deregulation was one. In many countries, governments stripped away rules and regulations. In the U.S and Europe, for instance, the rules that prevented commercial banks from expanding into new businesses such as investment banking

FIGURE 1.3

Employment Exodus

Percent of employers who said they planned as of 2008 to offshore a number of these jobs.

Source: Created from data provided at http://img.icbdr.com/images/aboutus/pressroom/OffshoreStudyFinal.pdf, accessed April 29, 2009.

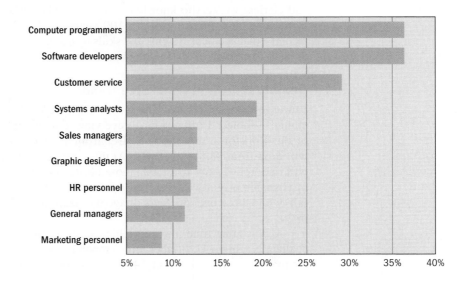

were relaxed. Giant, multinational "financial supermarkets" such as Citibank emerged. As economies boomed, more businesses and consumers went deeply into debt. Homebuyers bought homes, often with little money down. Banks freely lent money to developers to build more homes. For almost 20 years, U.S. consumers actually spent more than they earned. The U.S. itself increasingly became a debtor nation. Its balance of payments (exports minus imports) went from a healthy positive $3.5 billion in 1960, to a not-so-healthy *minus* $19 billion in 1980 (imports exceeded exports), to a huge $378 billion deficit in 2009.[16] The only way the country could keep buying more from abroad than it sold was by borrowing money. So, much of the boom was built on debt.

Technological Advances

Technology is changing almost everything businesses do. For example, technology (in the form of Internet communications) made it feasible for Bank of America's Merrill Lynch to outsource security analysis jobs to India. Zara doesn't need the expensive inventories that burden competitors like The Gap. Zara operates its own Internet-based worldwide distribution network, linked to the checkout registers at its stores around the world. Suppose its headquarters in Spain sees a garment "flying" out of a store? Zara's computerized manufacturing system dyes the required fabric, cuts and manufactures the item, and speeds new garments to that store within days.

The Nature of Work

Technology is also changing the nature of work, even factory work. In plants throughout the world, knowledge-intensive high-tech manufacturing jobs are replacing traditional factory jobs. Skilled machinist Chad Toulouse illustrates this. After an 18-week training course, this former college student became a team leader in a plant where about 40% of the machines are automated. In older plants, machinists would manually control machines that cut chunks of metal into things like engine parts. Today, Chad and his team spend much of their time typing commands into computerized machines that create precision parts for products, including water pumps.[17] Technology-based employees like these need new skills and training to excel at these more complex jobs.

SERVICE JOBS Technology is not the only trend driving this change from "brawn to brains." Today over two-thirds of the U.S. workforce is employed in producing and delivering services, not products. Between 2004 and 2014, almost all the 19 million new jobs added in the United States will be in services, not in goods-producing industries.[18]

HUMAN CAPITOL For employers, this all means a growing need for "knowledge workers" and human capital. *Human capital* refers to the knowledge, education, training, skills, and expertise of a firm's workers.[19] Today, "the center of gravity in employment is moving fast from manual and clerical workers to knowledge workers, who resist the command-and-control model that business took from the military 100 years ago."[20] Managers need new world-class human resource management systems and skills to select, train, and motivate these employees and to get them to work more like committed partners.

Demographic and Workforce Trends

DEMOGRAPHIC TRENDS The U.S. workforce is also fast becoming older and more multiethnic.[21] Table 1.1 offers a bird's eye view. For example, between 1998 and 2018, the percent of the workforce that the U.S. Department of Labor classifies as "white, non Hispanic" will drop from 83.8% to 79.4%. At the same time, the percent of the workforce that is black will rise from 11.6% to 12.1%, those classified Asian will rise from 4.6% to 5.6%, and those of Hispanic origin will rise from 10.4% to 17.6%. The percentages of younger workers will fall, while those over 55 years of age will leap from 12.4% of the workforce in 1998 to 23.9% in 2018.[22]

At the same time, demographic trends are making finding and hiring employees more challenging. In the U.S., labor force growth is not expected to keep pace with job growth, with an estimated shortfall of about 14 million college-educated workers by 2020.[23] One study of

TABLE 1.1 Demographic Groups as a Percent of the Workforce, 1998–2018

Age, race, ethnicity	1998	2008	2018
Age: 16–24	15.9%	14.3	12.7
25–54	71.7	67.7	63.5
55+	12.4	18.1	23.9
White, non-Hispanic	83.8	81.4	79.4
Black	11.6	11.5	12.1
Asian	4.6	4.7	5.6
Hispanic Origin	10.4	14.3	17.6

Source: Adapted from http://www.bls.gov/news.release/ecopro.t01.htm. Accessed May 10, 2010.

35 large global companies' senior human resource officers said "talent management"—in particular, the acquisition, development and retention of talent to fill the companies' employment needs—ranked as their top concern.[24]

"GENERATION Y" Furthermore, many younger Generation Y workers may have different work values than did their parents.[25] Also called "Millennials," Gen Y employees are roughly those born 1977 to 2002. They take the place of the labor force's previous new entrants, Generation X, those born roughly 1965 to 1976 and who themselves were the children of, and followed into the labor force, the Baby Boomers, born just after the Second World War (born roughly 1944–1950). Based on one study, older employees are more likely to be work-centric (to focus more on work than on family with respect to career decisions). Younger Gen Y workers tend to be more family-centric or dual-centric (balancing family and work life).[26]

Fortune magazine says that today's millennial or Generation Y employees bring challenges and strengths. They may be "the most high maintenance workforce in the history of the world."[27] Employers like Lands' End and Bank of America are therefore teaching their managers to give millennials quick feedback and recognition.[28] But, having grown up with computers and e-mail, their capacity for using information technology will also make them the most high-performing.[29]

RETIREES Many human resource professionals call "the aging workforce" the biggest demographic threat affecting employers. The basic problem is that there aren't enough younger workers to replace the projected number of baby boom–era older workers retiring.[30] One survey found that 41% of surveyed employers are bringing retirees back into the workforce.[31]

NONTRADITIONAL WORKERS At the same time, jobs are shifting to nontraditional workers. Nontraditional workers include those who hold multiple jobs, or who are "contingent" or part-time workers, or those working in alternative arrangements (such as a mother–daughter team sharing one clerical job). Others including former executives, lawyers, or other professionals serve as "independent contractors" for specific projects. Almost 10% of American workers—13 million people—fit this nontraditional workforce category.

Technological trends facilitate alternative work arrangements. For example, professional Web sites like LinkedIn (www.linkedin.com) enable free agent professionals to promote their services. Thanks to information technology, about 17 million people now work from remote locations at least once per month. Seeking the collaboration that's often missing when one works alone, "co-working sites" are springing up. These offer freelance workers and consultants office space and access to office equipment (and the opportunity to interact with other independents) for several hundred dollars per month.[32]

WORKERS FROM ABROAD With retirements triggering projected workforce shortfalls, many employers are hiring foreign workers for U.S. jobs. The country's H-1B visa program lets U.S. employers recruit skilled foreign professionals to work in the U.S. when they can't find qualified American workers. U.S. employers bring in about 181,000 foreign workers per year under these

FIGURE 1.4

Gross National Product, 1940–2010

Source: http://research.stlouisfed.org/
fred2/fredgraph?chart_type=line&s[1]
[id]=GNP&s[1][transformation]=ch1,
accessed April 18, 2009.

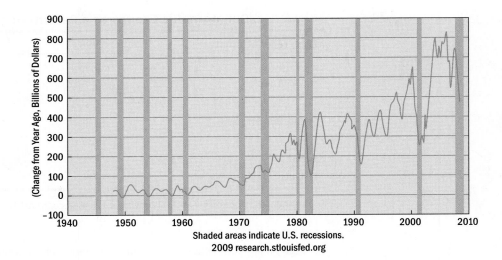

programs. Particularly with high unemployment, such programs face opposition. One study concluded that many workers brought in under these programs filled jobs that didn't actually demand specialized skills, often paying less than $15 an hour.[33]

Economic Challenges and Trends

All these trends are occurring in a context of challenge and upheaval. As you can see in Figure 1.4, Gross National Product (GNP)—a measure of the United States of America's total output—boomed between 2001 and 2007. During this period, home prices (see Figure 1.5) leaped as much as 20% per year. Unemployment remained docile at about 4.7%.[34] Then, around 2007/2008, all these measures seemingly fell off a cliff. GNP fell. Home prices dropped by 10% or more (depending on city). Unemployment nationwide rose to more than 10% in 2010.

Why did all this happen? That is a complicated question, but for one thing, all those years of accumulating debt ran their course. Banks and other financial institutions (such as hedge funds) found themselves owning trillions of dollars of worthless loans. Governments stepped in to try to prevent their collapse. Lending dried up. Many businesses and consumers stopped buying. The economy tanked.

Economic trends will undoubtedly turn positive again, perhaps even as you read these pages. However, they have certainly grabbed employers' attention. After what the world went through starting in 2007–2008, it's doubtful that the deregulation, leveraging, and globalization that drove economic growth for the previous 50 years will continue unabated. That may mean slower growth for many countries, perhaps for years. We'll use boxed "Managing HR in Challenging Times" features to illustrate the skills managers need to manage human resources in challenging times.

FIGURE 1.5

Case-Shiller Home Price Indexes

Source: www.clevelandfed.org/
research/trends/2009/0309/
04ecoact.cfm, accessed April 18, 2009.

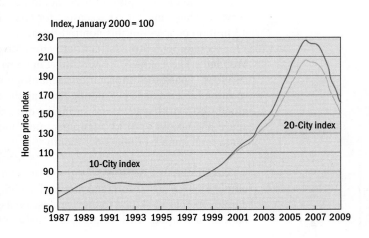

MANAGING HR IN CHALLENGING TIMES

Trends like these mean challenging times ahead for employers. They mean that for the foreseeable future—and even well after things turn positive—employers will have to be more frugal and creative in managing their human resources than they've been in the past. For example, in part due to the recent recession, HR administrative jobs are down from 5% to 14%, depending on the industry.[35] With HR staffing down, many employers are taking steps to simplify and consolidate their human resource management practices and costs.

Here are some examples. One employer had more than 50 sales incentive plans in place for its 5,000 salespeople. By simplifying that, it reduced its incentive plan's administrative costs. Many employers still "price" all their jobs by surveying what the market pays for similar jobs. Employers cut the costs of this expensive process by shifting to the wage curve–type compensation plans we explain in Chapter 8. This enables employers to survey just a few "benchmark" jobs, and then to adjust automatically all other jobs accordingly. In performance appraisal, some employers had multiple supervisors evaluate one employee. Now they've switched to having just the direct supervisor evaluate the employee. All this streamlines HR.

THE MAIN IMPLICATIONS FOR HUMAN RESOURCE MANAGERS

Trends like these prompted changes in what employers expect from human resource management. In the early 1900s, "personnel" took over hiring and firing from supervisors and began managing payroll and benefits. As testing technology improved, personnel departments played bigger roles in employee selection and training.[36] Union legislation in the 1930s expanded personnel's role to protecting the firm in its interaction with unions. Discrimination legislation in the 1960s and '70s expanded HR's "protector" role.[37]

Today, global competition puts a premium on using trained and committed employees to get a competitive edge. That has implications for human resource managers.

---

4 List, with examples, the main implications of the trends influencing human resource managers.

They Take a Holistic "Talent Management" Approach to Managing Human Resources

First, with employers competing vigorously, no one wants to lose any current high-potential employees, or to fail to attract, keep, or fully utilize top-caliber ones.[38] One survey of human resource executives found that "talent management" issues were among the most pressing ones they faced.[39] A survey of CEOs of big companies said they typically spent between 20% and 40% of their time on "talent management issues."[40] Human resource managers are therefore emphasizing talent management.

talent management
The end to end process of planning, recruiting, developing, managing, and compensating employees throughout the organization.

WHAT IS TALENT MANAGEMENT? **Talent management** "is the end to end process of planning, recruiting, developing, managing, and compensating employees throughout the organization."[41] It involves instituting a coordinated process for identifying, recruiting, hiring, and developing high-potential employees.

What does this mean in practice? For one thing, talent management means being proactive about how you manage your company's talent. Taking a talent management approach requires that employers actively manage their employees' recruitment, selection, development, and rewards. For example, we saw that IBM segmented its employees into three groups so that it could fine-tune the way it served the employees in each segment. As another example, many employers are segmenting out their most "mission-critical" employees, and managing their development and rewards separately from the firms' other employees. We'll look more closely at using talent management techniques and tools starting in Chapter 4.

They Emphasize Focus More on Big Picture Issues

Relatedly, human resource managers are also more focused on their companies' strategic, "big picture" issues. Top management, with HR management's help, formulates an overall strategy or plan for the company. The human resource manager then aligns his or her company's personnel

Like Signicast, Albertsons' Markets illustrates how HR managers help their companies implement their strategies. Albertsons sought to improve service while reducing costs. Its HR managers instituted new selection and training processes to improve service, while automating HR processes to reduce costs.

policies and practices to support the company's overall plan. (We'll look more closely at strategic planning in Chapter 3.)

EXAMPLE Several years ago, Wisconsin-based Signicast Corp.'s president, Terry Lutz, and his board decided to build a new, computerized plant. Signicast produces metal parts from a casting process. The firm needed the new, automated plant to stay competitive. Mr. Lutz and his team knew that "in the real world, new automation technology requires a new kind of employee." The computerized plant would be useless without employees who could work in teams, manage their own work, and run the computerized equipment. Lutz and his management team relied on Signicast's human resource managers to select, train, and organize the tech-friendly people the new plant required.[42] The HR team supported Signicast's new strategy by formulating and executing the hiring and other personnel practices that Signicast needed.

The bottom line is that today's human resource managers are more focused on strategic issues.[43] They are moving from focusing on transactional activities like signing on new employees and enrolling them in benefits plans. They are moving to being their firms' *internal consultants,* institutionalizing changes that help employees better contribute to the company's success.[44]

They Find New Ways to Provide Transactional Services

Focusing more on strategic issues means that today's human resource managers also must be skilled at offering traditional transactional HR services such as recruiting and benefits administration in new ways. For example, they *outsource* more services (such as benefits administration) to outside vendors.[45] They use *technology* (such as intranets) to enable employees to self-administer benefits plans. They set up *centralized call centers* to answer HR-related inquiries from employees and supervisors. (Table 1.2 lists some important ways employers use technology to support their human resource management activities.[46])

They Build High-Performance Work Systems

Competitive and economic challenges also mean that employers expect their human resource managers to institute practices that bolster *productivity and performance* improvement. Effective human resource management practices can translate into improved performance. For example, well-trained employees perform better than untrained ones, and safe workplaces produce fewer lost-time accidents. Better employee selection improves customer service.[47] Offering employees training opportunities boosts employee commitment and reduces voluntary early retirements.[48]

Dell put much of its HR services online.

TABLE 1.2 Some Technological Applications to Support HR

Technology	How Used by HR
Application service providers (ASPs) and technology outsourcing	ASPs provide software application, for instance, for processing employment applications. The ASPs host and manage the services for the employer from their own remote computers
Web portals	Employers use these, for instance, to enable employees to sign up for and manage their own benefits packages and to update their personal information
Streaming desktop video	Used, for instance, to facilitate distance learning and training or to provide corporate information to employees quickly and inexpensively
Internet- and network-monitoring software	Used to track employees' Internet and e-mail activities or to monitor their performance
Electronic signatures	Legally valid e-signatures that employers use to more expeditiously obtain signatures for applications and record keeping
Electronic bill presentment and payment	Used, for instance, to eliminate paper checks and to facilitate payments to employees and suppliers
Data warehouses and computerized analytical programs	Help HR managers monitor their HR systems. For example, they make it easier to assess things like cost per hire, and to compare current employees' skills with the firm's projected strategic needs

A *high-performance work system* is a set of human resource management policies and practices that together produce superior employee performance. For example, in one study, the "high-performance" plants paid more (median wages of $16 per hour compared with $13 per hour for all plants), trained more (83% offered more than 20 hours of training per year, compared with 32% for all plants), used more sophisticated recruitment and hiring practices (tests and validated interviews, for instance), and used more self-managing work teams. They also had the best overall performance, in terms of higher profits and lower employee turnover.[49]

They Use Evidence-Based Human Resource Management

Saying you have a "high-performance" organization assumes that you can measure how you're doing.[50] For example, "How much is that new testing program saving us in reduced employee turnover?" And, "In terms of HR staff per employee, how do we compare to our competitors?"[51]

Using evidence such as this is the heart of *evidence-based human resource management.* This is the use of data, facts, analytics, scientific rigor, critical evaluation, and critically evaluated research/case studies to support human resource management proposals, decisions, practices, and conclusions.[52] Put simply, evidence-based human resource management means using the best-available evidence in making decisions about the human resource management practices you are focusing on.[53] The evidence may come from *actual measurements* (such as, How did the trainees like this program?). It may come from *existing data* (such as, What happened to company profits after we installed this training program?). Or, it may come from published *research studies* (for instance, median HR expenses as a proportion of companies' total operating costs average about 0.8%).[54]

EXAMPLES An insurance firm was considering cutting costs by buying out highly paid senior underwriters. But after looking at the data, the human resource manager saw that these underwriters also accounted for a lopsided share of the company's revenue. The firm decided to eliminate certain call-center employees instead, replacing them with less expensive employees. As another example, the chemical company BASF Corp. analyzed employee data showing the relationship among stress, health, and productivity. Based on that evidence, the firm created stress-reduction programs that would more than pay for themselves in increased productivity.[55]

They Measure HR Performance

In today's performance-based environment, employers also expect their human resource managers to measure their effectiveness. For example, IBM's Randall MacDonald needed $100 million from IBM to reorganize its HR operations. He utilized human resource metrics. He told top management, "I'm going to deliver talent to you that's skilled and on time and ready to be deployed. I will be able to measure the skills, tell you what skills we have, what [skills] we don't have [and] then show you how to fill the gaps or enhance our training."[56]

SAMPLE METRICS To make claims like these, human resource managers need performance measures (or "metrics"). For example, median HR expenses as a proportion of companies' total operating costs average about 0.8%. There tends to be between 0.9 and 1.0 human resource staff persons per 100 employees.[57] Employers can obtain customized benchmarks from services such as the Society for Human Resource Management's Human Capital Benchmarking Service.[58]

THE HR SCORECARD Managers often use an *HR Scorecard* process to measure the human resource function's effectiveness. The *HR Scorecard* is a concise measurement system, often displayed in a desktop window showing the metrics in graphs and charts. It shows the metrics the firm uses to measure each HR activity (such as training), and to measure the employee behaviors (like better service) resulting from these activities, and to measure the organizational outcomes of those employee behaviors. (For example, more training leads to more productive employees, which leads to better profits.)

They Manage Ethics

Whether it's insider trading or Ponzi schemes, ethical misdeeds will torpedo even otherwise competent managers. Therefore, *managing ethics* is always a critical human resource management issue. **Ethics** refers to the standards one uses to decide what his or her conduct should be. Ethical decisions always involve matters of serious consequence to society's well-being, such as murder, lying, and stealing. Newspaper headlines regarding ethical lapses (like Ponzi schemes) never seem to end.

Congress passed the Sarbanes-Oxley Act in 2003 to help ensure that managers take their ethics responsibilities seriously. Sarbanes-Oxley (SOX) aims to curb erroneous corporate financial reporting. Among other things, it requires CEOs and CFOs to certify their companies' financial reports. It also prohibits personal loans to executive officers and directors, and requires CEOs and CFOs to reimburse their firms for bonuses and stock option profits if financial statements subsequently require restating.[59] Under SOX, every publicly listed company now needs a code of ethics, often promulgated by human resources.

Human resource management's ethics responsibilities don't end with Sarbanes-Oxley. One survey found that six of the ten most serious ethical issues—workplace safety, employee records, employee theft, affirmative action, "comparable work," and employee privacy rights—were human resource management related.[60] We'll address ethics in more detail in Chapter 9.

They Have New Proficiencies[61]

Activities such as strategizing, measuring, and dealing with Sarbanes-Oxley also means that HR managers must exhibit *new proficiencies*. Human resource managers still need skills in areas like employee selection and training. But now they must also command broader *business knowledge and competencies*. For example, to assist top management in strategic planning, human resource managers need to know strategic planning, marketing, production, and finance.[62] They must "speak the CFO's language" by explaining human resource needs in financially measurable terms.[63]

Partly as a result, human resource executives are increasingly well-paid.[64] For example, in 2009, the head of human resources and labor relations at Delta Air Lines earned about $5 million in total compensation, and the one at eBay earned over $4 million.[65]

HR Certification

HR managers are turning to certification as a way to illustrate their mastery of modern HR practices. Three levels of exams from the Society for Human Resource Management test the professional's knowledge of human resource management, including management practices, staffing, development, compensation, labor relations, and health and safety. Those who successfully complete all requirements earn the SPHR (senior professional in HR), PHR (professional in HR) certificate, or GHR (global professional in HR). The Human Resource Certification Institute also offers credential testing for California's human resource professionals.[66] Managers can take an online HRCI assessment exam at www.HRCI.org (or by calling 866-898-HRCI).

ethics
The principles of conduct governing an individual or a group; specifically, the standards you use to decide what your conduct should be.

THE PLAN OF THIS BOOK

The basic aim of this book is to provide all current and future managers (not just current and future *human resource* managers) with the concepts and skills they need to carry out the people or personnel aspects of their jobs.

The Chapters

We've organized the topics in the following chapters:

Part 1: Introduction

1. *Managing Human Resources Today*
2. *Managing Equal Opportunity and Diversity* What you'll need to know about equal opportunity laws as they relate to human resource management activities, such as interviewing, selecting employees, and evaluating performance appraisals.
3. *Strategic Human Resource Management* What is strategic planning, and how human resource management contributes to mergers, acquisitions, and strategy formulation and execution.

Part 2: Staffing and Talent Management

4. *Recruiting and Talent Management* What is talent management? How to analyze a job and how to determine the job's requirements, specific duties, and responsibilities, as well as what sorts of people need to be hired and how to recruit them.
5. *Selecting Employees* Techniques such as testing that you can use to ensure that you're hiring the right people.
6. *Training and Developing Employees* Providing the training and development necessary to ensure that your employees have the knowledge and skills required to accomplish their tasks.
7. *Performance and Talent Management* Techniques for managing and appraising performance.
8. *Compensating Employees* How to develop equitable pay plans, including incentives and benefits, for your employees.

Part 3: Employee and Labor Relations

9. *Ethics, Employee Rights, and Fair Treatment at Work* Ensuring ethical and fair treatment through discipline, grievance, and career management processes.
10. *Working with Unions and Resolving Disputes* Concepts and techniques concerning the relations between unions and management, including the union-organizing campaign, negotiating and agreeing on a collective bargaining agreement between unions and management, and managing the agreement.
11. *Improving Occupational Safety, Health, and Security* The causes of accidents, how to make the workplace safe, and laws governing your responsibilities in regard to employee safety and health.

Part 4: Special Issues in Human Resource Management

12. *Managing Human Resources in Entrepreneurial Firms* Special HRM methods small business managers can use to compete more successfully.
13. *Managing HR Globally* Applying human resource management policies and practices in a global environment.
14. *Building High-Performance Work Systems and Improving Results* How managers can measure, assess, and improve the effectiveness of their human resource practices.

REVIEW

SUMMARY

1. Staffing, personnel management, or human resource management includes activities such as recruiting, selecting, training, compensating, appraising, and developing.
2. HR management is a part of every line manager's responsibilities. These responsibilities include placing the right person in the right job and then orienting, training, and compensating the person to improve his or her job performance.
3. The HR manager and his or her department provide various staff services to line management, including assisting in the hiring, training, evaluating, rewarding, promoting, disciplining, and safety of employees at all levels.
4. Trends are requiring HR to play a more strategic role in organizations. These trends include workforce diversity, technological change, globalization, economic upheaval, and changes in the nature of work, such as the growing emphasis on education and human capital.
5. The consequence of such changes is that HR managers' jobs are increasingly strategic in nature. HR managers must also find new ways to deliver transactional services (such as benefits administration), focus more on providing internal consulting expertise with respect to improving employee morale and performance, build high-performance work organizations, manage talent, and be skilled at acting based on evidence and metrics.

KEY TERMS

organization   2
manager   2
managing   2
management process   2
human resource management   2

authority   3
line manager   3
staff manager   3
talent management   11
ethics   14

DISCUSSION QUESTIONS

1. What is human resource management?
2. Explain with at least five examples why "a knowledge and proficiency in HR management concepts and techniques is important to all supervisors or managers."
3. Explain with examples what we mean by "the changing environment of human resource management."
4. Give examples of how the HR manager's duties today are different from 30 years ago.
5. Discuss, with examples, four important issues influencing HR management today.
6. Explain HR management's role in relation to the firm's line management.
7. Compare the authority of line and staff managers. Give examples of each.
8. Why is it important for a company to make its human resources into a "competitive advantage"? How can HR contribute to doing so?
9. What is evidence-based management and why (with an example) is it important for HR managers to adopt such an approach?
10. Define High Performance Work System and illustrate some things that make them unique.

INDIVIDUAL AND GROUP ACTIVITIES

1. Working individually or in groups, contact the HR manager of a local bank. Ask the HR manager how he or she is working as a strategic partner to manage human resources, given the bank's strategic goals and objectives. Back in class, discuss the responses of the different HR managers.
2. Working individually or in groups, interview an HR manager. Based on that interview, write a short presentation regarding HR's role today in building competitive organizations.
3. Working individually or in groups, bring several business publications such as *BusinessWeek* and the *Wall Street*

Journal to class. Based on their contents, compile a list entitled "What HR Managers and Departments Do Today."

4. Based on your personal experiences, list 10 examples showing how you used (or could have used) human resource management techniques at work or school.

5. Laurie Siegel, senior vice president of human resources for Tyco International, took over her job just after numerous charges forced the company's previous board of directors and top executives to leave the firm. Hired by new CEO Edward Breen, Siegel had to tackle numerous difficult problems starting the moment she assumed office. For example, she had to help hire a new management team. She had to do something about what the outside world viewed as a culture of questionable ethics at her company. And she had to do something about the company's top management compensation plan, which many felt contributed to the allegations by some that former company officers had used the company as a sort of private ATM.

Siegel came to Tyco after a very impressive career. For example, she had been head of executive compensation at

AlliedSignal, and was a graduate of the Harvard Business School. But, as strong as her background was, she obviously had her work cut out for her when she took the senior vice president of HR position at Tyco.

Working individually or in groups, conduct an Internet search and library research to answer the following questions: What human resource management–related steps did Siegel take to help get Tyco back on the right track? Do you think she took the appropriate steps? Why or why not? What, if anything, do you suggest she do now?

6. Working individually or in groups, develop a list showing how trends such as workforce diversity, technological trends, globalization, and changes in the nature of work have affected the college or university you are now attending or the organization for which you work.

7. Working individually or in groups, develop several examples showing how the new HR management practices mentioned in this chapter (using technology, for instance) have or have not been implemented to some extent in the college or university you are now attending or in the organization for which you work.

WEB-e's (WEB EXERCISES)

1. Several years ago, Stanford's restaurant in Lake Oswego was written up for how well it used HR to keep good employees. What do customers at sites such as www.yelp.com/biz/stanfords-restaurant-and-bar-lake-oswego say about Stanford's and what implications do you think this has for Stanford's HR practices?

2. This chapter explained how Randy MacDonald, IBM's senior vice president of human resources, reorganized

IBM's human resources function. Use sites such as www-03.ibm.com/press/us/en/biography/10067.wss to help explain and illustrate the sorts of experiences that go into making a strong HR manager.

3. The Web site www.co.pinellas.fl.us/persnl/pdf/orgchart.pdf shows one example of an HR organization. Find two others and compare them.

APPLICATION EXERCISES

HR IN ACTION CASE INCIDENT 1
Jack Nelson's Problem

As a new member of the board of directors for a local bank, Jack Nelson was being introduced to all the employees in the home office. When he was introduced to Ruth Johnson, he was curious about her work and asked her what her machine did. Johnson replied that she really did not know what the machine was called or what it did. She explained that she had been working there for only 2 months. She did, however, know precisely how to operate the machine. According to her supervisor, she was an excellent employee.

At one of the branch offices, the supervisor in charge spoke to Nelson confidentially, telling him that "something was wrong," but she didn't know what. For one thing, she explained, employee turnover was too high, and no sooner had one employee been put

on the job than another one resigned. With customers to see and loans to be made, she explained, she had little time to work with the new employees as they came and went.

All branch supervisors hired their own employees without communication with the home office or other branches. When an opening developed, the supervisor tried to find a suitable employee to replace the worker who had quit.

After touring the 22 branches and finding similar problems in many of them, Nelson wondered what the home office should do or what action he should take. The banking firm was generally regarded as a well-run institution that had grown from 27 to 191 employees during the past 8 years. The more he thought about the matter, the more puzzled Nelson became. He couldn't quite put his finger on the problem, and he didn't know whether to report his findings to the president.

Questions

1. What do you think is causing some of the problems in the bank's home office and branches?
2. Do you think setting up an HR unit in the main office would help?

3. What specific functions should an HR unit carry out? What HR functions would then be carried out by the bank's supervisors and other line managers?

Source: Claude S. George, *Supervision in Action: The Art of Managing Others*, 4th ed., 1985. Electronically reproduced by permission of Pearson Education, Inc., Upper Saddle River, New Jersey.

HR IN ACTION CASE INCIDENT 2
Carter Cleaning Company

Introduction

A main theme of this book is that HR management—activities like recruiting, selecting, training, and rewarding employees—is not just the job of a central HR group but rather a job in which every manager must engage. Perhaps nowhere is this more apparent than in the typical small service business. Here the owner/manager usually has no HR staff to rely on. However, the success of his or her enterprise (not to mention his or her family's peace of mind) often depends largely on the effectiveness through which workers are recruited, hired, trained, evaluated, and rewarded. Therefore, to help illustrate and emphasize the front-line manager's HR role, throughout this book we will use a continuing case based on an actual small business in the southeastern United States. Each chapter's segment of the case will illustrate how the case's main player—owner/manager Jennifer Carter—confronts and solves personnel problems each day at work by applying the concepts and techniques of that particular chapter. Here is background information you will need to answer questions that arise in subsequent chapters. (We also present a second, unrelated case incident in each chapter.)

Carter Cleaning Centers

Jennifer Carter graduated from State University in June 2005, and, after considering several job offers, decided to do what she really always planned to do—go into business with her father, Jack Carter.

Jack Carter opened his first laundromat in 1998 and his second in 2001. The main attraction of these coin laundry businesses for him was that they were capital-intensive rather than labor-intensive. Thus, once the investment in machinery was made, the stores could be run with just one unskilled attendant and have none of the labor problems one normally expects from being in the retail service business.

The attractiveness of operating with virtually no skilled labor notwithstanding, Jack had decided by 1999 to expand the services in each of his stores to include the dry cleaning and pressing of clothes. He embarked, in other words, on a strategy of "related diversification" by adding new services that were related to and consistent with his existing coin laundry activities. He added these in part because he wanted to better utilize the unused space in the rather large stores he currently had under lease. But he also did so because he was, as he put it, "tired of sending out the dry cleaning and pressing work that came in from our coin laundry clients to a dry cleaner five miles away, who then took most of what should have been our profits." To reflect the new, expanded line of services he renamed each of his two stores Carter Cleaning Centers and was sufficiently satisfied with their performance to open four more of the same type of stores over the next five years. Each store had its own on-site manager and, on average, about seven employees and annual revenues of about $600,000. It was this six-store cleaning centers chain that Jennifer joined upon graduating from State University.

Her understanding with her father was that she would serve as a troubleshooter/consultant to the elder Carter with the aim of both learning the business and bringing to it modern management concepts and techniques for solving the business's problems and facilitating its growth.

Questions

1. Make a list of five specific HR problems you think Carter Cleaning will have to grapple with.
2. What would you do first if you were Jennifer?

EXPERIENTIAL EXERCISE

Helping "The Donald"

Purpose The purpose of this exercise is to provide practice in identifying and applying the basic concepts of human resource management by illustrating how managers use these techniques in their day-to-day jobs.

Required Understanding Be familiar with the material in this chapter, and with several episodes of shows like *The Apprentice*, with developer Donald Trump.

How to Set Up the Exercise/Instructions

1. Divide the class into teams of three to four students.
2. Read this: As you know by having watched "The Donald" as he organized his business teams for *The Apprentice*, human resource management plays an important role in what Donald Trump and the participants on his separate teams need to do to be successful. For example,

Donald Trump needs to be able to appraise each of the participants. And, for their part, the leaders of each of his teams need to be able to staff his or her teams with the right participants and then provide the sorts of training, incentives, and evaluations that help their companies succeed and that therefore make the participants themselves (and especially the team leaders) look like "winners" to Mr. Trump.

3. Watch several of these shows (or reruns of the shows), and then meet with your team and answer the following questions:

   a. What specific HR functions (recruiting, interviewing, and so on) can you identify Donald Trump using on this show? Make sure to give specific examples.

   b. What specific HR functions (recruiting, selecting, training, and so on) can you identify one or more of the team leaders using to help manage their teams on the show? Again, give specific examples.

   c. Provide a specific example of how HR functions (such as recruiting, selection, interviewing, compensating, appraising, and so on) contributed to one of the participants coming across as particularly successful to Mr. Trump. Can you provide examples of how one or more of these functions contributed to Mr. Trump telling a participant "You're fired"?

   d. Present your team's conclusions to the class.

4. Answer the question "What is human resource management?"

Two Special Exercises: *Personal Competencies Edu-Exercises* and *Business in Action Edu-Exercises*

SHRM, the Society for Human Resource Management, distributed its new *SHRM Human Resource Curriculum Guidebook* a few years ago. One point the *Guidebook* makes is that to do their jobs, it's not sufficient for human resource managers to be familiar with HR Content (such as equal employment law), or to have HR skills (such as how to appraise performance). Instead, human resource managers also need certain *business knowledge* and *personal skills* in order to best utilize their human resource management knowledge.

Among other things, the *Guidebook* therefore suggests teaching human resource management in a way that blends the *HR content* with these business and personal skills. For example, when discussing equal employment law, tie in discussions of relevant *personal competencies* (such as "ethical decision making") and *business knowledge applications* (such as "corporate social responsibility").

Because doing so makes sense even for managers who do not intend to be human resource managers, you'll find two special "Edu-Exercises" at the end of Chapters 2–14. We call them Edu-Exercises, because each provides useful background information about an important business policy or personal competence, as well as questions for you to apply and test your knowledge.

1. ***Personal Competencies Edu-Exercises*** The *Personal Competencies Edu-Exercises* highlight relevant managerial personal competencies (skills). So, for example, for the Managing Equal Opportunity and Diversity chapter (Chapter 2) the exercise will ask you to apply your *ethical decision-making* competencies to solving an equal employment issue.

2. ***Business in Action Edu-Exercises*** The *Business in Action Edu-Exercises* highlight relevant business/policy knowledge applications. Thus, for the Managing Equal Opportunity and Diversity chapter's *Business in Action* exercise, you'll apply business law and public policy skills in helping California's Longo Toyota auto dealership support its business policy goals by building a diverse workforce.

ENDNOTES

1. http://llbeancareers.com/culture.htm, accessed February 28, 2010.
2. http://llbeancareers.com/benefits.htm, accessed February 28, 2010.
3. Michael Arndt, "L.L.Bean Follows Its Shoppers to the Web," *Business Week* (March 1, 2010).
4. Quoted in Fred K. Foulkes, "The Expanding Role of the Personnel Function," *Harvard Business Review* (March/April 1975): 71–84. See also Dave Ulrich and Wayne Brockbank, *The HR Value Proposition* (Boston, Mass.: Harvard Business School Press, 2005).
5. "Human Resource Activities, Budgets & Staffs, 1999–2000," *BNA Bulletin to Management* 51, no. 25 (June 29, 2000): S1–S6.
6. Steve Bates, "No Experience Necessary? Many Companies Are Putting Non-HR Executives in Charge of HR with Mixed Results," *HR Magazine* 46, no. 11 (November 2001), 34–41.

See also Fay Hansen, "Top of the Class," *Workforce Management* (June 23, 2008): 1, 25–30.
7. Jeremy Smerd, "Outsider Thinking for GM HR," *Workforce Management* (August 17, 2009): 1–3.
8. "A Profile of Human Resource Executives," *BNA Bulletin to Management* (June 21, 2001): S5.
9. "Small Business: A Report of the President," (1998), www.SBA.gov/ADV/stats; see also "Statistics of U.S. Businesses and Non-Employer Status," www.SBA.gov/ADVoh/ research/data.html, accessed March 9, 2006.
10. Susan Mayson and Rowena Barrett, "The 'Science' and 'Practice' of HR in Small Firms," *Human Resource Management Review* 16 (2006): 447–455.

11. See Dave Ulrich, "The New HR Organization," *Workforce Management* (December 10, 2007): 40–44, and Dave Ulrich, "The 21st-Century HR Organization," *Human Resource Management* 47, no. 4 (Winter 2008): 829–850. Some writers distinguish among three basic human resource management subfields: *micro HRM* (which covers the HR subfunctions such as recruitment and selection), *strategic HRM*, and *international HRM*. Mark Lengnick Hall et al., "Strategic Human Resource Management: The Evolution of the Field," *Human Resource Management Review* 19 (2009): 64–85.

12. Robert Grossman, "IBM's HR Takes a Risk," *HR Management* (April 2007): 54–59.

13. For discussions of some other important trends see, for example, "Workplace Trends: An Overview of the Findings of the Latest SHRM Workplace Forecast," Society for Human Resource Management, *Workplace Visions* 3 (2008): 1–8, and Ed Frauenheim, "Future View," *Workforce Management* (December 15, 2008): 18–23.

14. "Study Predicts 4.1 Million Service Jobs Offshored by 2008," *BNA Bulletin to Management* (August 2, 2005): 247. See also Monica Belcourt, "Outsourcing—the Benefits and the Risks," *Human Resource Management Review* 16 (2006): 269–279.

15. www.census.gov/foreign-trade/statistics/historical/ gands.pdf, accessed May 27, 2010.

16. Ibid.

17. Timothy Appel, "Better Off a Blue-Collar," *Wall Street Journal* (July 1, 2003): B-1.

18. See "Charting the Projections: 2004–2014," *Occupational Outlook Quarterly* (Winter 2005–2006); and www.bls. gov/emp/optd/optd003.pdf, accessed July 13, 2008).

19. Richard Crawford, *In the Era of Human Capital* (New York: Harper Business, 1991): 26.

20. Peter Drucker, "The Coming of the New Organization," *Harvard Business Review* (January–February 1988): 45. See also James Guthime et al., "Correlates and Consequences of High Involvement Work Practices: The Role of Competitive Strategy," *International Journal of Human Resource Management* (February 2002): 183–197, and James Combs et al., "How Much Do High-Performance Work Practices Matter? A Meta-Analysis of Their Effects on Organizational Performance," *Personal Psychology* 59 (2006): 501–528.

21. "Charting the Projections: 2004–2014," *Occupational Outlook Quarterly* (Winter 2005–2006): 48–50, and www.bls.gov/emp/emplabor01.pdf, accessed October 20, 2008.

22. "Percent Growth in Labor Force by Race, Projected 2008–18," *Occupational Outlook Quarterly* (Winter 2009–2010): P35, and "Percent Growth in Labor Force by Ethnic Origin, Projected 2008 dish 2018," *Occupational Outlook Quarterly* (Winter 2009–2010): 36.

23. Tony Carneval, "The Coming Labor and Skills Shortage," *Training and Development* (January 2005): 39.

24. "Talent Management Leads in Top HR Concerns," *Compensation & Benefits Review* (May/June 2007): 12.

25. For example, see Kathryn Tyler, "Generation Gaps," *HR Magazine* (January 2008): 69–72.

26. Eva Kaplan-Leiserson, "The Changing Workforce," *Training and Development* (February 2005): 10–11. See also S. A. Hewlett, et al., "How Gen Y & Boomers Will Reshape Your Agenda," *Harvard Business Review* 87, no. 7/8 (July/August 2009): 71–76.

27. By one report, the economic downturn of 2008 made it more difficult for dissatisfied generation Y employees to change jobs, and is contributing to a buildup of "griping" among some of them. "Generation Y Goes to Work," *The Economist* (January 3, 2009): 47.

28. Nadira Hira, "You Raised Them, Now Manage Them," *Fortune* (May 28, 2007): 38–46; Katheryn Tyler, "The Tethered Generation," *HR Magazine* (May 2007): 41–46; Jeffrey Zaslow, "The Most Praised Generation Goes to Work," *Wall Street Journal* (April 20, 2007): W1, W7; Rebecca Hastings, "Millennials Expect a Lot from Leaders," *HR Magazine* (January 2008): 30.

29. To capitalize on this, more employers are using social networking tools to promote employee interaction and collaboration, particularly among generation Y employees. "Social Networking Tools Aimed at Engaging Newest Employees," *BNA Bulletin to Management* (September 18, 2007): 303.

30. "Talent Management Leads in Top HR Concerns," *Compensation & Benefits Review* (May/June 2007): 12.

31. Jennifer Schramm, "Exploring the Future of Work: Workplace Visions," *Society for Human Resource Management* 2 (2005): 6; Rainer Strack, Jens Baier, and Anders Fahlander, "Managing Demographic Risk," *Harvard Business Review* (February 2008): 119–128.

32. Adrienne Fox, "At Work in 2020," *HR Magazine* (January 2010): 18–23.

33. Rita Zeidner, "Does the United States Need Foreign Workers?" *HR Magazine* (June 2009): 42–44.

34. www.bls.gov/opub/ted/2006/may/wk2/art01.htm, accessed April 18, 2009.

35. Based on Sydney Robertson and Vic Dayal, "When Less Is More: Managing Human Resources with Reduced Staff," *Compensation & Benefits Review* (March/April 2009): 21–26.

36. "Immigrants in the Workforce," *BNA Bulletin to Management Datagraph* (August 15, 1996): 260–261. See also Shari Caudron et al., "80 People, Events and Trends that Shaped HR," *Workforce* (January 2002): 26–56.

37. See for example, "HR 2018: Top Predictions," *Workforce Management* 87, no. 20 (December 15, 2008): 20–21.

38. Paul Loftus, "Tackle Talent Management to Achieve High Performance," *Plant Engineering* 61, no. 6 (June 15, 2007): 29.

39. "Survey: Talent Management a Top Concern," *CIO Insight* (January 2, 2007).

40. Michael Laff, "Talent Management: From Hire to Retire," *Training and Development* (November 2006): 42–48.

41. www.talentmanagement101.com, accessed December 10, 2007.

42. Ben Nagler, "Recasting Employees into Teams," *Workforce* (January 1998): 101–106.

43. Boudreau and Ramstad, *Beyond HR: The New Science of Human Capital* (Boston: Harvard Business School Publishing Corporation, 2007): 9.

44. A recent survey found that HR managers referred to "strategic/critical thinking skills" as the top "most important factor in attaining next HR job." See "Career Development for HR Professionals," *Society for Human Resource Management Research Quarterly* (second quarter, 2008): 3.

45. For example, see Sandra Fisher et al., "Human Resource Issues in Outsourcing: Integrating Research and Practice," *Human Resource Management* 47, no. 3 (Fall 2008): 501–523; and "Sizing Up the HR Outsourcing Market," *HR Magazine* (November 2008): 78.

46. Studies suggest that information technology usage does support human resource managers' need to participate more in strategic

planning. See Victor Haines III and Genevieve LaFleur, "Information Technology Usage and Human Resource Roles and Effectiveness," *Human Resource Management* 47, no. 3 (Fall 2008): 525–540.

47. Chad van Iddekinge et al., "Effects of Selection and Training on Unit Level Performance Over Time: A Latent Growth Modeling Approach," *Journal of Applied Psychology* 94, no. 4 (2009): 829–843.

48. Olivier Herrbach et al., "Perceived HRM Practices, Organizational Commitment, and Voluntary Early Retirement Among Late-Career Managers," *Human Resource Management* 48, no. 6 (November/December 2009): 895–916.

49. "Super Human Resources Practices Result in Better Overall Performance, Report Says," *BNA Bulletin to Management* (August 26, 2004): 273–274. See also Wendy Boswell, "Aligning Employees with the Organization's Strategic Objectives: Out of Line of Sight, Out of Mind." *International Journal of Human Resource Management* 17, no. 9 (September 2006): 1014–1041. Another study suggests that it's not always necessary to implement the full range of high-performance HR practices to achieve improved results. Even implementing smaller "bundles" of HR-related practices (such as empowerment, motivation, and improving skills) can improve business outcomes if the activities themselves are synergistic. Mahesh Subramony, "A Meta-Analytic Investigation of the Relationship Between HRM Bundles and Firm Performance," *Human Resource Management* 48, no. 5 (September–October 2009): 745–758.

50. As one expert puts it, "A great deal of what passes as 'best practice' in HRM most likely is not. In some cases, there is simply no evidence that validates what are thought to be best practices, while in other cases there is evidence to suggest that what are thought to be best practices are inferior practices." Edward Lawler III, "Why HR Practices Are Not Evidence-Based," *Academy of Management Journal* 50, no. 5 (2007): 1033.

51. See, for example, www.personneltoday.com/blogs/hcglobal-human-capital-management/2009/02/theres-no-such-thing-as-eviden.html, accessed April 18, 2009.

52. Ibid.

53. The evidence-based movement began in medicine. In 1996, in an editorial published by the *British Medical Journal*, David Sackett, MD, defined "evidence-based medicine" as "use of the best-available evidence in making decisions about patient care," and urged his colleagues to adopt its tenets. "Evidence-Based Training™: Turning Research into Results for Pharmaceutical Sales Training," an AXIOM Whitepaper, © 2006 AXIOM Professional Health Learning LLC. All rights reserved.

54. Chris Brewster et al., "What Determines the Size of the HR Function? A Cross National Analysis," *Human Resource Management* 45, no. 1 (Spring 2006): 3–21. See also, "SHRM

Survey Report, 2006 Strategic HR Management," *Society for Human Resource Management,* pp. 18–19.

55. Bill Roberts, "How to Put Analytics on Your Side," *HR Magazine* (October 2009): 43–46.

56. Robert Grossman, "IBM's HR Takes a Risk," *HR Management* (April 2007): 54–59. See also Robert Grossman, "Close the Gap Between Research and Practice," *HR Magazine* (November 2009): 31–37.

57. Brewster, et al., "What Determines the Size of the HR Function? A Cross National Analysis," *Human Resource Management* 45, no. 1 (Spring 2006): 3–21.

58. Contact the Society for Human Resource Management, 703.535.6366.

59. Jonathon Segal, "The Joy of Uncooking: The New Corporate Accountability Law Puts New Burdens on HR in an Effort to Prevent Companies from Cooking the Books," *HR Magazine* (November 2002): 52–58.

60. Kevin Wooten, "Ethical Dilemmas in Human Resource Management," *Human Resource Management Review* 11 (2001): 161.

61. Except as noted, most of this section is based on Richard Vosburgh, "The Evolution of HR: Developing HR as an Internal Consulting Organization," *Human Resource Planning* 30, no. 3 (September 2007): 11–24.

62. See, for example, "Employers Seek HR Executives with Global Experience, SOX Knowledge, Business Sense," *BNA Bulletin to Management* (September 19, 2006): 297–298; and Robert Rodriguez, "HR's New Breed," *HR Magazine* (January 2006): 67–71.

63. Susan Wells, "From HR to the Top," *HR Magazine* (June 2003): 49. SHRM's 2008 *Managing Your HR Career Survey Report* concluded that HR professionals needed several key skills "to get to the top," including interpersonal communication, drive/ambition, reputation in the organization, and strategic/critical thinking skills. Kathy Gurchiek, "Survey: 'Key' Skills Advance HR Career," *HR Magazine* (April 2008): 38.

64. See also James Hayton et al., "Conversations on What the Market Wants from HR Graduates, and How Can We Institutionalize Innovation in Teaching," *Human Resource Management Review* 15 (2005): 238–245. For a contrary view, see, for example, P. J. Kiger, "Survey: HR Still Battling for Leaders' Respect," *Workforce Management* 87, no. 20 (December 15, 2008): 8.

65. Jessica Marquez, "As The Economy Goes," *Workforce Management* (August 17, 2009): 27–33.

66. "The Human Resource Certification Institute (HRCI) Announces the California Certification," www.hrci.org/HRCI_Files/_Items/HRCI-MR-TAB2-951/Docs/At_A_Glance.pdf, accessed December 28, 2007.

2 Managing Equal Opportunity and Diversity

SYNOPSIS

- Selected Equal Employment Opportunity Laws
- Defenses Against Discrimination Allegations
- Illustrative Discriminatory Employment Practices
- The EEOC Enforcement Process
- Diversity Management and Affirmative Action Programs

Source: David Young-Wolff/PhotoEdit Inc.

When you finish studying this chapter, you should be able to:

1. Summarize the basic equal employment opportunity laws regarding age, race, sex, national origin, religion, and handicap discrimination.

2. Explain the basic defenses against discrimination allegations.

3. Present a summary of what employers can and cannot legally do with respect to recruitment, selection, and promotion and layoff practices.

4. Explain the Equal Employment Opportunity Commission enforcement process.

5. List five strategies for successfully increasing diversity of the workforce.

INTRODUCTION

A Texas man recently filed a discrimination complaint against Hooters of America. He alleged that one of its franchisees would not hire him as a waiter because it " . . . merely wishes to exploit female sexuality as a marketing tool to attract customers and insure profitability."[1] Hooters defended its right to hire only women before reaching a confidential settlement with the man. ∎

SELECTED EQUAL EMPLOYMENT OPPORTUNITY LAWS

As you can see at sites such as eeoc.gov/eeoc/newsroom/index.cfm, hardly a day goes by without equal opportunity lawsuits at work. One survey of 300 corporate general counsels found that employment lawsuits like these were their biggest litigation fears.[2] Performing day-to-day supervisory tasks like hiring or transferring employees without understanding these laws is fraught with peril. Let us start with some background.

Background

1 Summarize the basic equal employment opportunity laws regarding age, race, sex, national origin, religion, and handicap discrimination.

American race relations were not always as tolerant as Barak Obama's inauguration might suggest. It took centuries of legislative action, court decisions, and evolving public policy to arrive at this point. The Fifth Amendment to the U.S. Constitution (ratified in 1791) states that "no person shall . . . be deprived of life, liberty, or property, without due process of the law."[3] Other laws as well as various court decisions made discrimination against minorities illegal by the early 1900s, at least in theory.[4]

But as a practical matter, Congress and presidents avoided dramatic action on implementing equal employment until the early 1960s. At that point, civil unrest among minorities and women and changing traditions prompted them to act. Congress passed a multitude of new civil rights laws.

Equal Pay Act of 1963

Equal Pay Act of 1963
The act requiring equal pay for equal work, regardless of sex.

The **Equal Pay Act of 1963** (amended in 1972) was one of the first new laws passed. It made it unlawful to discriminate in pay on the basis of sex when jobs involve equal work—equivalent skills, effort, and responsibility—and are performed under similar working conditions. However, differences in pay do not violate the act if the difference is based on a seniority system, a merit system, a system that measures earnings by quantity or quality of production, or a differential based on any factor other than sex.

Title VII of the 1964 Civil Rights Act

Title VII of the 1964 Civil Rights Act
The section of the act that says an employer cannot discriminate on the basis of race, color, religion, sex, or national origin with respect to employment.

Title VII of the 1964 Civil Rights Act was another of the new laws. Title VII (amended by the 1972 Equal Employment Opportunity Act) says an employer cannot discriminate based on race, color, religion, sex, or national origin. Specifically, it states that it shall be an unlawful employment practice for an employer:[5]

1. *To fail or refuse to hire or to discharge an individual or otherwise to discriminate against any individual* with respect to his or her compensation, terms, conditions, or privileges of employment, because of such individual's race, color, religion, sex, or national origin.
2. *To limit, segregate, or classify his or her employees or applicants for employment* in any way that would deprive or tend to deprive any individual of employment opportunities or otherwise adversely affect his or her status as an employee, because of such individual's race, color, religion, sex, or national origin.

Equal Employment Opportunity Commission (EEOC)
The commission, created by Title VII, is empowered to investigate job discrimination complaints and sue on behalf of complainants.

Title VII established the **Equal Employment Opportunity Commission (EEOC)**. It consists of five members, appointed by the president with the advice and consent of the Senate. Each member of the EEOC serves a term of 5 years. The EEOC has a staff of thousands to assist it in administering the Civil Rights law in employment settings.

Establishing the EEOC greatly enhanced the federal government's ability to enforce equal employment opportunity laws. The EEOC receives and investigates job discrimination complaints. When it finds reasonable cause that the charges are justified, it attempts (through conciliation) to reach an agreement. If this conciliation fails, the EEOC has the power to go directly to court. Under the Equal Employment Opportunity Act of 1972, discrimination charges may be filed by the EEOC on behalf of an aggrieved individual, as well as by the individuals themselves. We explain this procedure later in this chapter.

Executive Orders

affirmative action
Making an extra effort to hire and promote those in protected groups, particularly when those groups are underrepresented.

Under executive orders that U.S. presidents issued years ago, most employers who do business with the U.S. government have an obligation beyond that imposed by Title VII to refrain from employment discrimination. Executive Orders 11246 and 11375 don't just ban discrimination; they require that contractors take **affirmative action** to ensure equal employment opportunity (we explain affirmative action later in this chapter). These orders also established the **Office of Federal Contract Compliance Programs (OFCCP)**, which is responsible for ensuring the compliance of federal contracts. President Obama's administration recently directed more funds and staffing to the OFCCP.[6]

Office of Federal Contract Compliance Programs (OFCCP)
The office responsible for implementing the executive orders and ensuring compliance of federal contractors.

Age Discrimination in Employment Act of 1967

The **Age Discrimination in Employment Act (ADEA) of 1967**, as amended, makes it unlawful to discriminate against employees or applicants for employment who are 40 years of age or older, effectively ending most mandatory retirement.[7]

Age Discrimination in Employment Act (ADEA) of 1967
The act prohibiting arbitrary age discrimination and specifically protecting individuals over 40 years old.

Vocational Rehabilitation Act of 1973

The **Vocational Rehabilitation Act of 1973** requires employers with federal contracts over $2,500 to take affirmative action for the employment of disabled persons. The act does not require that an unqualified person be hired. It does require that an employer take steps to accommodate a disabled worker unless doing so imposes an undue hardship on the employer.

Vocational Rehabilitation Act of 1973
The act requiring certain federal contractors to take affirmative action for disabled persons.

Pregnancy Discrimination Act of 1978

Congress passed the **Pregnancy Discrimination Act (PDA)** in 1978 as an amendment to Title VII. The act prohibits using pregnancy, childbirth, and related medical conditions for discrimination in hiring, promotion, discharge, or any other term or condition of employment. Basically, the act says that if an employer offers its employees disability coverage, then pregnancy and childbirth must be treated like any other disability and must be included in the plan as a covered condition. Court decisions and more working mothers are prompting more—and more successful—PDA claims. Pregnancy claim plaintiff victories rose about 66% in one recent 10-year period, while pregnancy claims filed rose about 39%.[8]

Pregnancy Discrimination Act (PDA)
An amendment to Title VII of the Civil Rights Act that prohibits sex discrimination based on "pregnancy, childbirth, or related medical conditions."

Progressive human resource thinking notwithstanding, one firm, an auto dealership, recently fired an employee after she told them she was pregnant. The reason? Allegedly "in case I ended up throwing up or cramping in one of their vehicles. They said pregnant women do that sometimes, and I could cause an accident."[9]

Federal Agency Uniform Guidelines on Employee Selection Procedures

Initially, the federal agencies charged with ensuring compliance with the aforementioned laws and executive orders issued their own implementing guidelines. Subsequently, the EEOC, Civil Service Commission, Department of Labor, and Department of Justice adopted detailed, uniform guidelines for employers.[10] These guidelines explain, for instance, how and under what conditions to validate a selection procedure.[11] The OFCCP has its own *Manual of Guidelines*. The American Psychological Association published its own (non-legally binding) *Standards for Educational and Psychological Testing*.

Historically, these guidelines have fleshed out the procedures to use in complying with equal employment laws. For example, recall that the ADEA prohibited employers from discriminating against persons over 40 years old because of age. Subsequent guidelines stated that it was unlawful to discriminate in hiring (or in any way) by giving preference because of age even to individuals within the 40-plus age bracket. Thus, you can't reject a 58-year-old candidate based on age, and defend yourself by showing you hired a 46-year-old.[12] (Hiring, say, a 54-year-old may provide a defense, though.)

Selected Court Decisions Regarding Equal Employment Opportunity (EEO)

Several early court decisions helped to form the courts' interpretive foundation for EEO laws. We summarize some important decisions in this section.

Griggs v. Duke Power Company

Supreme Court case in which the plaintiff argued that his employer's requirement that coal handlers be high school graduates was unfairly discriminatory. In finding for the plaintiff, the Court ruled that discrimination need not be overt to be illegal, that employment practices must be related to job performance, and that the burden of proof is on the employer to show that hiring standards are job related.

protected class

Persons such as minorities and women protected by equal opportunity laws, including Title VII.

GRIGGS V. DUKE POWER COMPANY Griggs v. Duke Power Company (1971) was a landmark case because the Supreme Court used it to define unfair discrimination. In this case, a suit was brought against the Duke Power Company on behalf of Willie Griggs, an applicant for a job as a coal handler. The company required its coal handlers to be high school graduates. Griggs claimed that this requirement was illegally discriminatory because it wasn't related to success on the job and because it resulted in more blacks than whites being rejected for these jobs.

Griggs won the case. The decision of the Court was unanimous, and in his written opinion, Chief Justice Burger laid out three crucial guidelines affecting equal employment legislation. First, the court ruled that discrimination on the part of the employer need not be overt; in other words, the employer does not have to be shown to have intentionally discriminated against the employee or applicant—it need only be shown that discrimination took place. Second, the court held that an employment practice (in this case requiring the high school diploma) must be shown to be *job related* if it has an unequal impact on members of a **protected class**.

In the words of Justice Burger:

> The act proscribes not only overt discrimination but also practices that are fair in form, but discriminatory in operation. The touchstone is business necessity. If an employment practice which operates to exclude Negroes cannot be shown to be related to job performance the practice is prohibited.[13]

Third, Burger's opinion clearly placed the burden of proof on the employer to show that the hiring practice is job related. Thus, the *employer* must show that the employment practice (in this case, requiring a high school diploma) is needed to perform the job satisfactorily if it has a disparate impact on (unintentionally discriminates against) members of a protected class.

ALBEMARLE PAPER COMPANY V. MOODY In the *Griggs* case, the Supreme Court decided that a screening tool (such as a test) had to be job related or valid—that is, performance on the test must be related to performance on the job. The 1975 *Albemarle* case is important because it helped to clarify what the employer had to do to prove that the test or other screening tools are related to or predict performance on the job. For example, the Court ruled that before using a test to screen job candidates, the performance standards for the job in question should be clear and unambiguous, so the employer can identify which employees were performing better than others (and thus whether the screening tool was effective). In arriving at its decision, the Court also cited the EEOC guidelines concerning acceptable selection procedures and made these guidelines the "law of the land."[14]

The Civil Rights Act of 1991

Civil Rights Act of 1991 (CRA 1991)

The act that places burden of proof back on employers and permits compensatory and punitive damages.

Subsequent Supreme Court rulings in the 1980s actually had the effect of limiting the protection of women and minority groups under equal employment laws. For example, in *Price Waterhouse* v. *Hopkins*, the court ruled that an employer's unlawful actions may not be discriminatory if *lawful* actions (such as not promoting the employee due inferior performance) would have resulted in the same personnel decision. The net effect was that Congress passed the new **Civil Rights Act of 1991 (CRA 1991)**, and President George H. W. Bush signed it into law in November 1991. The effect of CRA 1991 was to roll back the clock to where it stood before the 1980s decisions. In some respects it placed even more responsibility on employers.

First, CRA 1991 addressed the issue of *burden of proof.* Today, after CRA 1991, the process of filing and responding to a discrimination charge goes something like this. The plaintiff (say, a rejected applicant) demonstrates that an employment practice (such as a test) has a disparate impact on a particular group. (**Disparate impact** means that "an employer engages in an employment practice or policy that has a greater adverse impact [effect] on the members of a protected group under Title VII than on other employees, regardless of intent."[15]) Requiring a college degree for a job would have an adverse impact on some minority groups, for instance.

disparate impact

An unintentional disparity between the proportion of a protected group applying for a position and the proportion getting the job.

Disparate impact claims do not require proof of discriminatory intent. Instead, the plaintiff must show two things. First, he or she must show that a significant disparity exists between the proportion of (say) women in the available labor pool and the proportion hired. Second, he or she must show that an apparently neutral employment practice, such as word-of-mouth advertising or a requirement that the job holder "be able to lift 100 pounds," is causing the disparity.[16]

Then, once the plaintiff shows such disparate impact, the *employer* has the *burden of proving* that the challenged practice is job related for the position in question. For example, the employer has to show that lifting 100 pounds is actually required for the position in question, and that the business could not run efficiently without the requirement—that it is a business necessity.

disparate treatment

An intentional disparity between the proportion of a protected group and the proportion getting the job.

CRA 1991 also makes it easier to sue for *money damages*. It provides that an employee who is claiming *intentional discrimination* (called **disparate treatment**) can ask for both compensatory damages and punitive damages, if he or she can show the employer engaged in discrimination "with malice or reckless indifference to the federally protected rights of an aggrieved individual." (See also the Global Issues in HR feature.)

Finally, under CRA 1991 an employer generally can't avoid liability by showing that because of say, poor performance, it would have taken the same action—such as terminating someone—even without a discriminatory motive. If there is any such motive, such as sex discrimination, the practice may be unlawful.[17]

Sexual Harassment

sexual harassment

Harassment on the basis of sex that has the purpose or effect of substantially interfering with a person's work performance or creating an intimidating, hostile, or offensive work environment.

EEOC guidelines define **sexual harassment** as unwelcome sexual advances, requests for sexual favors, and other verbal or physical conduct of a sexual nature that takes place under any of the following conditions:

1. Submission is either explicitly or implicitly a term or condition of an individual's employment.
2. Submission to or rejection of such conduct is the basis for employment decisions affecting such individual.
3. Such conduct has the purpose or effect of unreasonably interfering with an individual's work performance or creating an intimidating, hostile, or offensive work environment.

Sexual harassment is a violation of Title VII when such conduct has the purpose or effect of substantially interfering with a person's work performance or creating an intimidating, hostile, or offensive work environment. The EEOC's guidelines further assert that employers have a duty to maintain workplaces free of sexual harassment and intimidation. The Civil Rights Act of 1991 added teeth to this by permitting victims of intentional discrimination, including sexual harassment, to have jury trials and to collect compensatory damages for pain and suffering and punitive damages in cases in which the employer acted with "malice or reckless indifference" to the individual's rights.[18]

Sexual harassment laws don't just address harassment of women by men. They also cover those occasions when women harass men, as well as same-sex harassment. The U.S. Supreme Court held (in *ONCALE. v. Sundowner Offshore Services Inc.*) that "same-sex discrimination consisting of same-sex sexual harassment is actionable under Title VII." It said that same-sex subordinates, coworkers, or superiors are liable under the theory that they create a hostile work environment for the employee.[19] In one recent year, EEOC received 13,867 sexual harassment charges, 15.9% of which males filed.[20]

Proving Sexual Harassment

An employee can prove sexual harassment in three main ways.

QUID PRO QUO   The most direct is to prove that rejecting a supervisor's advances adversely affected what the EEOC calls a "tangible employment action" such as hiring, firing, promotion, demotion, undesirable assignment, benefits, compensation, and/or work assignment. Thus in one case the employee showed that continued advancement was dependent on her agreeing to her supervisor's sexual demands.

HOSTILE ENVIRONMENT CREATED BY SUPERVISORS   To qualify as harassment, the behavior need not have tangible consequences, such as a demotion or termination. For example, in one case the court found that a male supervisor's behavior had substantially affected a female employee's

Sexual harassment is unwelcome sexual advances, requests for sexual favors, and other verbal or physical conduct of a sexual nature.

Source: Bruce Ayres/Getty Images, Inc.—Liaison.

emotional and psychological ability to the point that she felt she had to quit her job. Although he made no direct threats or promises in exchange for sexual advances, the advances interfered with the woman's performance and created an offensive work environment. This was sufficient to prove that sexual harassment had occurred.

Distinguishing between harassment and flirting can be tricky. The courts do not interpret as sexual harassment any sexual relationships that arise during the course of employment but that do not have a substantial effect on that employment. In one decision, for instance, the U.S. Supreme Court held that sexual harassment law doesn't cover ordinary "intersexual flirtation." In his ruling, Justice Scalia said courts must carefully distinguish between "simple teasing" and truly abusive behavior.[21]

HOSTILE ENVIRONMENT CREATED BY COWORKERS OR NONEMPLOYEES The advances don't have to come from the person's supervisor to qualify as sexual harassment. An employee's coworkers or customers can cause the employer to be held responsible for sexual harassment. In one case, the court held that a sexually provocative uniform that the employer required led to lewd comments by customers toward the employee. When she complained that she would no longer wear the uniform, she was fired. Because the employer could not show there was a job-related necessity for requiring such a uniform (and because the uniform was required only for female employees), the court ruled that the employer, in effect, was responsible for the sexually harassing behavior. Such abhorrent client behavior is more likely when the clients are in positions of power, and when they have less reason to think they'll be penalized.[22]

Court Decisions

In the *Meritor Savings Bank, FSB* v. *Vinson* case, the U.S. Supreme Court broadly endorsed the EEOC's sexual harassment guidelines. Two more recent U.S. Supreme Court decisions further clarified the law on sexual harassment.

In the first, *Burlington Industries* v. *Ellerth*, the employee said her boss propositioned and threatened her with demotion if she did not respond. The threats were not carried out, and she was in fact promoted. In the second case, *Faragher* v. *City of Boca Raton*, the employee accused the employer of condoning a hostile work environment: She said she quit her lifeguard job after repeated taunts from other lifeguards. The Court ruled in favor of the employees in both cases.

The Court's decisions here have two implications for employers.

First, they make it clear that in a quid pro quo case it is *not* necessary for the employee to have suffered tangible job action (such as being demoted) to win the case.

Second, the decisions spell out an important defense against harassment suits. The Court said that an employer could defend itself against sexual harassment liability by showing two things: (1) that " . . . the employer exercised care to prevent and correct promptly any sexually harassing behavior"; and (2) that the plaintiff "unreasonably failed to take advantage of any preventive or corrective opportunities provided by the employer." The Supreme Court said that the employee's failing to use formal organizational reporting systems satisfied the second component.

Prudent employers promptly took steps to show they did take reasonable care.[23] The HR in Practice feature lists steps to take. A form such as the one illustrated in Figure 2.1 facilitates this process.[24]

HR IN PRACTICE

What Employers Should Do to Minimize Liability in Sexual Harassment Claims[25]

- *Take all complaints* about harassment seriously.
- *Encourage* the victim to inform the harasser directly that the conduct is unwelcome and must stop, and to use any employer complaint mechanism available.
- *Issue* a strong policy statement condemning such behavior. It should clearly describe the prohibited conduct; assure protection against retaliation; and describe a complaint process that provides confidentiality, accessible avenues of complaint, and prompt, thorough, impartial investigations and corrective action.
- *Inform* all employees about the policy and of their rights under the policy.
- *Take steps* to prevent sexual harassment from occurring. For example, communicate to employees that the employer will not tolerate sexual harassment, and take immediate action when someone complains.

(continued)

- *Establish* a management response system that includes an immediate reaction and investigation.
- *Train* supervisors and managers to increase their awareness of the issues.
- *Discipline* managers and employees involved in sexual harassment.
- *Keep thorough records* of complaints, investigations, and actions taken.
- *Conduct* exit interviews that uncover any complaints and that acknowledge by signature the reasons for leaving.

- *Re-publish* the sexual harassment policy periodically.
- *Encourage* upward communication, for instance through periodic written attitude surveys.
- *Do not retaliate* against someone who files a harassment (or other EEO) complaint.

Sources: Adapted from *Sexual Harassment Manual for Managers and Supervisors*, published in 1991, by CCH Incorporated, a WoltersKluwer Company, and from http://archive.eeoc.gov/types/sexual_harassment.html, accessed May 29, 2010.

FIGURE 2.1

Online Form to Facilitate Filing a Report of Sexual Harassment

Source: www.uiowa.edu/∼eod/policies/sexual%20harassment%20form.pdf, accessed April 28, 2009.

Print Form

The University of Iowa
Office of Equal Opportunity and Diversity
CONFIDENTIAL REPORT OF INFORMAL* SEXUAL HARASSMENT COMPLAINT RESOLUTION
Please complete this form and submit it to the Office of Equal Opportunity and Diversity, 202 Jessup Hall,
As soon as reasonably possible after resolution of the complaint
Due to confidentiality considerations, please do not e-mail these forms.

Date of Incident	Date complaint received

College/Organizational Unit	Department	Today's Date
Name of Individual Completing Report	Title	Campus Telephone #

Consistent with the UI Policy on Sexual Harassment, if the person charged in the complaint has been informed of the existence of the complaint, all parties' names shall be disclosed; if the person charged has not been informed of the existence of the complaint, the parties' names shall not be disclosed.

Name of Complainant(s)

Department   Gender ☐ Male ☐ Female ☐ Unknown
Status of Complaint(s): ☐ Academic or Administrative Officer ☐ Faculty ☐ Professional & Scientific ☐ Merit ☐ Student Employee ☐ Undergraduate Student ☐ Graduate Student ☐ Job Applicant ☐ Former Employee ☐ No current University affiliation ☐ Graduate Assistant ☐ Other _____
Ethnicity of Complainant(s): ☐ American Indian or Alaskan Native ☐ White, not of Hispanic Origin ☐ African American and Black, not of Hispanic Origin ☐ Asian or Pacific Islander ☐ Latino or Hispanic

Name of Victim(s) (if other than Complainant)

Department   Gender ☐ Male ☐ Female ☐ Unknown
Status of Victim(s): ☐ Academic or Administrative Officer ☐ Faculty ☐ Professional & Scientific ☐ Merit ☐ Student Employee ☐ Undergraduate Student ☐ Graduate Student ☐ Job Applicant ☐ Former Employee ☐ No current University affiliation ☐ Graduate Assistant ☐ Other _____
Ethnicity of Victim(s): ☐ American Indian or Alaskan Native ☐ White, not of Hispanic Origin ☐ African American and Black, not of Hispanic Origin ☐ Asian or Pacific Islander ☐ Latino or Hispanic

Name of Respondent(s)

Department   Gender ☐ Male ☐ Female ☐ Unknown
Status of Respondent(s): ☐ Academic or Administrative Officer ☐ Faculty ☐ Professional & Scientific ☐ Merit ☐ Student Employee ☐ Undergraduate Student ☐ Graduate Student ☐ Job Applicant ☐ Former Employee ☐ No current University affiliation ☐ Graduate Assistant ☐ Other _____
Ethnicity of Respondent(s): ☐ American Indian or Alaskan Native ☐ White, not of Hispanic Origin ☐ African American and Black, not of Hispanic Origin ☐ Asian or Pacific Islander ☐ Latino or Hispanic

DEFINITION: The University's Policy on Sexual Harassment defines sexual harassment as persistent, repetitive or egregious conduct directed at a specific individual or group of individuals that a reasonable person would interpret, in the full context in which the conduct occurs, as harassment of a sexual nature, when:

1. submission to such conduct is made or threatened to be made explicitly or implicitly a term or condition of an individual's employment, education, on campus living environment, or participation in a University activity;
2. submission to or rejection of such conduct is used or threatened to be used as a basis for a decision affecting an individual employment, education, on-campus living environment, or participation in a University activity; or
3. such conduct has the purpose or effect of unreasonably interfering with work or educational performance, or of creating an intimidating or offensive environment for employment, education, on-campus living, or participation in a University activity.

M:\KLast\Forms\sexual harassment form.doc, Page 1

FIGURE 2.1

(Continued)

For the purposes of this form, "informational complaints" are those handled by department or units outside the Office of Equal Opportunity and Diversity. Pursuant to the UI Policy on Sexual Harassment, any academic or administrative officer who becomes aware of allegations of sexual harassment by any means **must** consult with the Office of Equal Opportunity and Diversity regarding appropriate steps.

Forms of Sexual Harassment: (check all forms of unwelcome behavior that apply)

☐ **Verbal Harassment**	☐ **Physical Harassment**	☐ **Visual Harassment**
☐ comments of a sexual nature ☐ unwelcome advances ☐ derogatory sex based comments ☐ verbal threats ☐ other (explain)	☐ unwelcome contact ☐ physical gestures ☐ exhibitionism ☐ stalking ☐ assault ☐ other (explain)	☐ written ☐ pictures/photos ☐ posters ☐ electronic/computer ☐ other (explain)
☐ **Conditioning employment or educational benefits on submitting to sexual requests**	☐ **retaliation for complaining about sexual harassment**	☐ **Other (explain)**

Please provide summary of the nature of the allegations below (attach additional pages if necessary):

Outcome (check only one):

☐ Founded	☐ unfounded	☐ resolved/negotiated settlement
☐ complaint pending	☐ complaint withdrawn	☐ referred to another office
☐ Other		

Discipline (check all that apply):

☐ apology	☐ educational program	☐ counseling
☐ verbal reprimand	☐ written reprimand	☐ reassignment
☐ suspension	☐ no contact order	☐ termination
☐ other (explain)		
☐ **sanctions applied under the Code of Student Life** (explain)		

*To your knowledge, has this complaint been referred to another office? ☐ Yes ☐ No   If yes, please indicate where:
☐ Office of Equal Opportunity and Diversity ☐ Office of Student Services ☐ other (specify)

** For Office of Student Services use only: Date report Completed

Please return this form to the Office of Equal Opportunity and Diversity, 202 Jessup Hall.
Due to confidentiality considerations, please do not e-mail these forms.
Thank you for your assistance in resolving the complaint.

M:\KLast\Forms\sexual harassment form.doc, Page 2

What Causes Sexual Harassment?

Sexual harassment's causes are more varied than people realize. Perhaps the most important factor is a permissive social climate. For example, employees conclude there's a risk to victims for complaining, that complaints aren't taken seriously, or that there's a lack of sanctions against offenders.[26] Minority women are particularly at risk. One study found "women experienced more sexual harassment than men, minorities experienced more ethnic harassment than whites, and minority women experienced more harassment overall than majority men, minority men, and majority women."[27]

Most people probably assume that sexual motives drive sexual harassment, but that's not always so. Instead, *gender harassment* is the most common form of sexual harassment. **Gender harassment** is "a form of hostile environment harassment that appears to be motivated by hostility toward individuals who violate gender ideals." Thus in one case, bosses told a high-performing female accountant to "walk more femininely [and] dress more femininely."[28]

gender harassment
A form of hostile environment harassment that appears to be motivated by hostility toward individuals who violate gender ideals.

Adding to the causes is the unfortunate fact that most sexual harassment victims don't sue or complain. Instead, either due to fear of losing one's job, or a sense that complaining is futile, they quit or try to avoid their harassers. "The few women who do formally complain do so only after encountering frequent, severe sexual harassment; at that point, considerable damage may have already occurred."[29]

Furthermore, people differ in what they view as offensive. In one study, about 58% of employees reported experiencing at least some of the potentially harassment-type behaviors at work. Overall, about 25% found it fun and flattering and about half viewed it as benign. But on closer examination, about four times as many men as women found the behavior flattering or benign.[30] "Women perceive a broader range of socio-sexual behaviors as harassing."[31]

WHAT THE MANAGER/EMPLOYER SHOULD DO Given this, employers should do three things: They should take steps (as in the HR in Practice feature) to *ensure harassment does not take place*. Second, once becoming aware of such a situation, they should take immediate *corrective action*, even if the offending party is a nonemployee.[32]

Finally, we've seen that what is harassment to one person may be innocent to another. Furthermore, a harassment compliance procedure may be reasonable in the legal sense, but not so reasonable to the employees who must use it. Managers therefore (third) must *ensure that the organization's climate* (including management's real willingness to eradicate harassment), and not just its written rules, supports employees who feel harassed.[33]

WHAT THE EMPLOYEE CAN DO Prior to taking action, understand how courts define sexual harassment. For example, "hostile environment" sexual harassment generally means that the discriminatory intimidation was sufficiently severe or pervasive to alter the conditions of employment. Courts here look at whether the discriminatory conduct is frequent or severe; whether it is physically threatening or humiliating or a mere offensive utterance; and whether it unreasonably interferes with an employee's work performance. They also look at whether an employee welcomed the conduct, or instead immediately showed that the conduct was unwelcome. The steps an employee can take include:

1. Be aware of and follow the employer's harassment procedure.
2. File a verbal contemporaneous complaint with the harasser and the harasser's boss stating that the unwanted overtures should cease because the conduct is unwelcome.
3. Write and deliver a letter to the accused. This should provide a detailed statement of the facts as the writer sees them, describe his or her feelings and what damage the writer thinks the behavior caused, and state that he or she would like to request that the future relationship be on a purely professional basis.
4. If the unwelcome conduct does not cease, file verbal and written reports with the harasser's manager and/or the human resource director.
5. If the letters and appeals to the employer do not suffice, the accuser should turn to the local office of the EEOC to file the necessary claim.
6. If the harassment is of a serious nature, the employee can also consult an attorney about suing the harasser for assault and battery, intentional infliction of emotional distress, injunctive relief, and to recover compensatory and punitive damages.

The Americans with Disabilities Act

Americans with Disabilities Act (ADA)

The act requiring employers to make reasonable accommodations for disabled employees; it prohibits discrimination against disabled persons.

WHAT IS THE ADA? The **Americans with Disabilities Act (ADA)** of 1990 prohibits employment discrimination against qualified disabled individuals.[34] And, it requires that employers make "reasonable accommodations" for physical or mental limitations, unless doing so imposes an "undue hardship" on the business.

The ADA's key terms are important in understanding its impact. They provide that "impairment" includes any physiological disorder or condition, cosmetic disfigurement, or anatomical loss affecting one or more of several body systems, or any mental or psychological disorder.[35] However, the act doesn't list specific disabilities. Instead, the EEOC's implementing regulations provide that an individual is disabled if he or she has a physical or mental impairment that substantially limits one or more major life activities. On the other hand, the act does set forth certain conditions that are *not* to be regarded as disabilities. These include homosexuality, bisexuality, voyeurism, compulsive gambling, pyromania, and certain disorders resulting from the person currently using illegal drugs.[36] The ADA does protect employees with intellectual disabilities, including those with IQs below 70–75.[37] Mental disabilities account for the greatest number of claims brought under the ADA.[38]

Simply being disabled does not qualify someone for a job, of course. Instead, the act prohibits discrimination against qualified individuals—those who, with (or without) a reasonable accommodation, can carry out the essential functions of the job. This means that the individual must have the requisite skills, educational background, and experience to do the essential functions of the position. A job function is essential when, for instance, it is the reason the position exists, or because the function is so highly specialized that the person doing the job is hired for his or her expertise or ability to perform that particular function.[39]

REASONABLE ACCOMMODATION If the individual can't perform the job as currently structured, the employer is required to make a reasonable accommodation, unless doing so would present an undue hardship. *Reasonable accommodation* might include re-designing the job, modifying work schedules, or modifying or acquiring equipment or other devices (such as widening door openings).[40]

Court cases illustrate what "reasonable accommodation" means. For example, a Walmart door greeter was diagnosed with and treated for back problems. When she returned to work, she asked if she could sit on a stool while on duty. Walmart said no, contending that standing was an essential part of the greeter's job. She sued. The federal district court agreed with the employer that the door greeters must act in an "aggressively hospitable manner," which can't be done sitting on a stool.[41]

Improving Productivity through HRIS: Accommodating Disabled Employees

Technology facilitates accommodating disabled employees. For example, the National Federation of the Blind estimates that about 70% of working age blind adults are unemployed or underemployed, although they have the requisite education. Yet numerous technologies would enable most of these people to work successfully in numerous job functions. For example, a screen-reading program called Jaws converts text from the computer screen into Braille, while speaking it.[42] Employees with mobility impairments benefit from voice recognition software. Real-time translation captioning enables employees with hearing and/or speech impairments to participate in lectures and meetings. IBM created a disability-friendly Web site, "Arizona@YourService," to help link prospective employees and others to various Arizona agencies.[43]

THE ADA IN PRACTICE Workplace disabilities are on the rise, and employers need to accommodate increasing numbers of heavier and disabled employees.[44] ADA complaints therefore continue to flood the courts.

However, employers traditionally prevailed in almost all (96%) federal circuit court ADA decisions.[45] A main reason is that the employee must establish that he or she has a disability that fits under the ADA's definition.[46] Doing so is more complicated than proving that one is a particular age, race, or gender.

For example, an assembly-line worker sued Toyota, arguing that carpal tunnel syndrome and tendonitis prevented her from doing her job (*Toyota Motor Manufacturing of Kentucky, Inc. v. Williams*). The U.S. Supreme Court ruled that the ADA covers carpal tunnel syndrome and tendonitis if the impairments affect not only job performance but also daily living activities. Here, the employee admitted that she could perform personal tasks and chores such as washing her face, and fixing breakfast, and doing laundry. The court said the disability must be central to the employee's daily living (not just job) to qualify under the ADA.[47]

But employers don't win them all. For example, one U.S. Circuit Court of Appeals held that punctuality was not an essential job function for a disabled laboratory assistant who was habitually tardy. The court decided he could perform the job's 7 1/2 hours of data entry even if he arrived late.[48]

LEGAL OBLIGATIONS The ADA imposes numerous legal obligations on employers. These include (but are not limited to) the following:

● Employers may not make preemployment inquiries about a person's disability, although employers may ask about the person's ability to perform specific job functions.

- The timing and nature of any job offer are important. The central issue is this: In the event the employer rescinds an offer after the medical exam, the applicant must be able to identify the specific reason for the rejection. In one case the courts found that American Airlines had violated the ADA by not making a "real" offer to three candidates before requiring them to take their medical exams, because American still hadn't checked their background references. In this case, the medical exams showed the candidates had HIV and American rescinded their offers, thus violating the ADA.[49]
- Employers should review job application forms, interview procedures, and job descriptions for potentially discriminatory items, and identify the essential functions of the jobs in question.
- Employers must make a reasonable accommodation, unless doing so would result in undue hardship.

THE "NEW" ADA The era in which employers prevail in most ADA claims probably ended January 1, 2009. On that day, the ADA Amendments Act of 2008 (ADAAA) became effective. The new act's basic effect will be to make it easier for employees to show that their disabilities are "substantially limiting." For example, the new act makes it easier for an employee to show that his or her disability is influencing one of his or her "major life activities." It does this by adding examples like reading, concentrating, thinking, sleeping, and communicating to the list of ADA major life activities.[50] As another example, under the new act an employee is considered disabled even if he or she has been able to control his or her impairments through medical modifications. The bottom line is that employers must henceforth redouble their efforts to make sure they're complying with the ADA and providing reasonable accommodations.[51] Figure 2.2 summarizes some important ADA guidelines for managers and employers.

Many employers simply take a progressive approach. Research shows that common employer concerns about people with disabilities (for instance, that they can't perform physically demanding tasks, and have more accidents) are generally baseless.[52] So, for example, Walgreens has a goal of filling at least one-third of the jobs at its two large distribution centers with people with disabilities.[53]

Genetic Information Non-Discrimination Act of 2008 (GINA)

GINA prohibits discrimination by health insurers and employers based on someone's genetic information. Specifically, it prohibits the use of genetic information in employment, prohibits the intentional acquisition of genetic information about applicants and employees, and imposes strict confidentiality requirements.[54]

Technological innovations make it easier today for employers to accommodate disabled employees.

Source: Jim Cummins/Getty Images, Inc.–Taxi.

Sexual Orientation

The federal Employment Non-Discrimination Act (ENDA) would prohibit workplace discrimination based on sexual orientation and gender identity if Congress passes it.[55] Meanwhile, a federal appeals court recently decided that a homosexual man is not necessarily barred from filing a sexual discrimination claim under Title VII of the Civil Rights Act.[56] Many states do bar discrimination at work based on sexual orientation.[57]

State and Local Equal Employment Opportunity Laws

In addition to the federal laws, all states and many local governments also prohibit employment discrimination. State and local laws usually cover employers not covered by federal legislation (such as those with fewer than 15 employees). Similarly, some local governments extend protections to those not covered by federal law (such as to young people as well as to those over 40). For instance, it would be illegal to advertise for "mature" applicants because that might discourage some teenagers from applying. As two examples, State of Florida statutes prohibit wage rate discrimination based on sex by those employers not subject to the federal Fair Labor Standards Act.[58] The New York City Human Rights Law prohibits discrimination in employment based on arrest or conviction record and status as a victim of domestic violence.[59]

FIGURE 2.2

ADA Guidelines for Managers and Employers[60]

- *Do not* deny a job to a disabled individual if the person is qualified and able to perform the essential job functions.
- *Make* a reasonable accommodation unless doing so would result in undue hardship[61]
- *You need not* lower existing performance standards or stop using tests for a job. However, those standards or tests must be job related and uniformly applied to all employees and candidates.
- *Know* what you can ask applicants. In general, you may *not* make preemployment inquiries about a person's disability before making an offer conditioned on passing the medical exam and reference check.[62] However, you *may* ask questions about the person's ability to perform essential job functions.[63]
- *Remove from* the job application, interview procedures, and job descriptions illegal questions about health, disabilities, medical histories, or previous workers' compensation claims.[64]
- *Itemize* essential job functions on the job descriptions.
- *Do not* allow misconduct or erratic performance (including absences and tardiness), "even if that behavior is linked to the disability."[65]
- One expert advises, "*Don't treat employees as if they are disabled.*" If they can control their conditions (for instance, through medication), courts usually won't consider them disabled. But if you treat them as disabled, they'll normally be "regarded as" disabled and protected.[66]

State and local equal employment opportunity agencies (often called *human resources commissions, commissions on human relations,* or *fair employment commissions*) also play a role in the equal employment compliance process. When the EEOC receives a discrimination charge, it usually defers it for a limited time to the state and local agencies that have comparable jurisdiction.

The Global Issues in HR feature addresses some international aspects of equal employment.

GLOBAL ISSUES IN HR

Applying Equal Employment Law in a Global Setting

Globalization complicates the task of complying with equal employment laws. For example, Dell recently announced big additions to its workforce in India. Are U.S. citizens working for Dell abroad covered by U.S. equal opportunity laws? Are non-U.S. citizens covered? Are non-U.S. citizens working for Dell in the United States covered?

In practice, the answers depend on U.S. laws, international treaties, and the laws of the countries in which the U.S. firms are doing business. For example, the Civil Rights Act of 1991 specifically covers U.S. employees of U.S. firms working abroad. But in practice, the laws of the country in which the U.S. citizen is working may take precedence.[67]

Summary

Table 2.1 summarizes these and selected other equal employment opportunity legislation, executive orders, and agency guidelines.

TABLE 2.1 Summary of Important Equal Employment Opportunity Actions

Action	What It Does
Title VII of 1964 Civil Rights Act, as amended	Bars discrimination because of race, color, religion, sex, or national origin; instituted EEOC
Executive orders	Prohibit employment discrimination by employers with federal contracts of more than $10,000 (and their subcontractors); established office of federal compliance; require affirmative action programs

(continued)

TABLE 2.1 (Continued)

Federal agency guidelines	Indicate policy covering discrimination based on sex, national origin, and religion, as well as on employee selection procedures; for example, require validation of tests
Supreme Court decisions: *Griggs* v. *Duke Power Company, Albemarle Paper Company* v. *Moody*	Ruled that job requirements must be related to job success; that discrimination need not be overt to be proved; that the burden of proof is on the employer to prove the qualification is valid
Equal Pay Act of 1963	Requires equal pay for men and women for performing similar work
Age Discrimination in Employment Act of 1967	Prohibits discriminating against a person 40 or over in any area of employment because of age
State and local laws	Often cover organizations too small to be covered by federal laws
Vocational Rehabilitation Act of 1973	Requires affirmative action to employ and promote qualified disabled persons and prohibits discrimination against disabled persons
Pregnancy Discrimination Act of 1978	Prohibits discrimination in employment against pregnant women, or related conditions
Vietnam Era Veterans' Readjustment Assistance Act of 1974	Requires affirmative action in employment for veterans of the Vietnam War era
Americans with Disabilities Act of 1990 and ADA Amendments Act of 2008	Strengthens the need for most employers not to discriminate and to make reasonable accommodations for disabled employees at work
Civil Rights Act of 1991	Reverses several 1980s Court decisions; places burden of proof back on employer and permits compensatory and punitive money damages for discrimination
Genetic Information Non-Discrimination Act of 2008 (GINA)	Prohibits discrimination by health insurers and employers based on people's genetic information

DEFENSES AGAINST DISCRIMINATION ALLEGATIONS

What Is Adverse Impact?

To understand how employers defend themselves against employment discrimination claims, we should first briefly review some basic legal terminology.

Adverse impact plays a central role in discriminatory practice allegations. Under the Civil Rights Act of 1991, a person who believes he or she has been unintentionally discriminated against need only establish a prima facie case of discrimination; this means showing that the employer's selection procedures had an *adverse impact* on a protected minority group. **Adverse impact** "refers to the total employment process that results in a significantly higher percentage of a protected group in the candidate population being rejected for employment, placement, or promotion."[68] "Employers may not institute an employment practice that causes a disparate impact on a particular class of people unless they can show that the practice is job related and necessary."[69]

What does this mean? If a minority or other protected group applicant for the job feels he or she has been discriminated against, the applicant need only show that the selection procedures resulted in an adverse impact on his or her minority group. (There are several ways to do this. One is the "4/5ths rule"; this involves showing, for example, that 80% (4/5ths) of the white applicants passed the test, but only 20% of the black applicants passed; if this is the case, a black applicant has a prima facie case proving adverse impact.[70]) Then, it becomes the employer's task (its "burden of proof") to prove that its test, application form, interview, or the like is a valid predictor of performance on the job, and that the employer applied it fairly and equitably to both minorities and non-minorities.

adverse impact

The overall impact of employer practices that result in significantly higher percentages of members of minorities and other protected groups being rejected for employment, placement, or promotion.

Alas, such cases aren't ancient history. For example, a few years ago a U.S. Appeals Court upheld a $3.4 million jury verdict against Dial Corp. Dial allegedly rejected 52 women for entry-level jobs at a meat processing plant because they failed strength tests, although strength was not a job requirement.[71]

Discrimination law distinguishes between disparate *treatment* and disparate *impact*. *Disparate treatment* means intentional discrimination. It "requires no more than a finding that women (or protected minority group members) were intentionally treated differently . . . because of their gender (or minority status)." *Disparate impact* claims do not require proof of discriminatory intent. Instead, the plaintiff must show that there is a significant disparity between the proportion of (say) women in the available labor pool and the proportion hired, and that there's an apparently neutral employment practice (such as word-of-mouth advertising) causing the disparity.[72] Proving that there was a business necessity for the practice is usually the defense for disparate impact claims.

BRINGING A CASE OF DISCRIMINATION: SUMMARY Assume that an employer turns down a member of a protected group for a job based on a test score (or some other employment practice, such as interview questions). Further, assume that the person believes that he or she was discriminated against due to being in a protected class and decides to sue the employer.

All he or she has to do is show (to the court's satisfaction) that the employer's test had an adverse impact on members of his or her minority group. The burden of proof then shifts to the employer, which has the burden of defending itself against the charges of discrimination.

The employer can then use two defenses: the bona fide occupational qualification (BFOQ) defense and the business necessity defense. Either can be used to justify an employment practice that has been shown to have an adverse impact on the members of a minority group. (A third defense is that the decision was made on the basis of legitimate nondiscriminatory reasons, such as poor performance, having nothing to do with the alleged prohibited discrimination.)

Bona Fide Occupational Qualification

One approach an employer can use to defend against charges of discrimination is to claim that the employment practice is a **bona fide occupational qualification (BFOQ)** for performing the job. Specifically, Title VII provides that

> it should not be an unlawful employment practice for an employer to hire an employee . . . on the basis of religion, sex, or national origin in those certain instances where religion, sex, or national origin is a bona fide occupational qualification reasonably necessary to the normal operation of that particular business or enterprise.

For example, an employer can use age as a BFOQ to defend itself against a disparate treatment (intentional discrimination) charge when federal requirements impose a compulsory age limit, such as when the Federal Aviation Agency sets a ceiling of age 65 for pilots. Actors required for youthful or elderly roles suggest other instances when age may be a BFOQ. But the courts set the bar high: The reason for the discrimination must go to the essence of the business. The BFOQ defense is not explicitly allowed for race or color. Hooters used the BFOQ defense when the Texas man in the chapter opener filed his discrimination complaint.[73]

Business Necessity

The **business necessity** defense requires showing that there is an overriding business purpose for the discriminatory practice and that the practice is therefore acceptable. It's not easy to prove that a practice is a business necessity. The Supreme Court has made it clear that business necessity does not encompass such matters as avoiding inconvenience or expense. The Second Circuit Court of Appeals held that *business necessity* means an "irresistible demand" and that to be retained the practice "must not only directly foster safety and efficiency," but also be essential to these goals.[74]

Thus, it is not easy to prove that a practice is required for business necessity. For example, an employer cannot generally discharge employees whose wages have been garnished merely because garnishment (requiring the employer to divert part of the person's wages to pay his or her debts) creates an inconvenience for the employer. On the other hand, many employers have

bona fide occupational qualification (BFOQ)
Requirement that an employee be of a certain religion, sex, or national origin where that is reasonably necessary to the organization's normal operation. Specified by the 1964 Civil Rights Act.

2 Explain the basic defenses against discrimination allegations.

business necessity
Justification for an otherwise discriminatory employment practice, provided there is an overriding legitimate business purpose.

used this defense successfully. In *Spurlock* v. *United Airlines,* a minority candidate sued United Airlines, stating that its requirements that a pilot candidate have 500 flight hours and a college degree were unfairly discriminatory. The Court agreed that these requirements did have an adverse impact on members of the person's minority group. However, the Court held that in light of the cost of the training program and the tremendous human and economic risks involved in hiring unqualified candidates, the selection standards were required by business necessity and were job related.[75]

Attempts by employers to show that their selection tests or other screening practices are valid represent one example of the business necessity defense. Where the employer can establish such validity, the courts have often supported the use of the test or other practice as a business necessity. Used in this context, the word *validity* means the degree to which the test or other employment practice is related to or predicts performance on the job. We discuss validation in Chapter 5.

ILLUSTRATIVE DISCRIMINATORY EMPLOYMENT PRACTICES

A Note on What You Can and Cannot Do

In this section, we present several illustrations of what managers can and cannot do under equal employment laws. But before proceeding, keep in mind that most federal laws, such as Title VII, do not expressly ban preemployment questions about an applicant's race, color, religion, sex, age, or national origin. Similarly:

> With the exception of personnel policies calling for outright discrimination against the members of some protected group, it is not really the intrinsic nature of an employer's personnel policies or practices that the courts object to. Instead, it is the result of applying a policy or practice in a particular way or in a particular context that leads to an adverse impact on some protected group.[76]

For example, it is not illegal to ask a job candidate about marital status (although at first glance such a question might seem discriminatory). You can ask such a question as long as you can show either that you do not discriminate or that you can defend the practice as a BFOQ or business necessity.

In other words, illustrative inquiries and practices such as those summarized on the next few pages aren't illegal per se. But, in practice, there are two good reasons to avoid such questionable practices. First, although federal law may not bar such questions, many state and local laws do. Second, the EEOC has said that it disapproves of such practices as asking women their marital status or applicants their age. Employers who use such practices thus increase their chances of having to defend themselves against charges of discriminatory employment practices.

Recruitment

WORD OF MOUTH You cannot rely on word-of-mouth dissemination of information about job opportunities when your workforce is all (or substantially all) white or all members of some other class such as all female, all Hispanic, and so on. Doing so might reduce the likelihood that others will become aware of the jobs and thus apply for them.

MISLEADING INFORMATION It is unlawful to give false or misleading information to members of any group or to fail to refuse to advise them of work opportunities and the procedures for obtaining them.

HELP WANTED ADS "Help wanted—male" and "Help wanted—female" advertising classifieds are violations of laws forbidding sex discrimination in employment unless sex is a BFOQ for the job advertised.[77] Also, you cannot advertise in any way that suggests that applicants are being discriminated against because of their age. For example, you cannot advertise for a "young" man or woman.

---

3 Present a summary of what employers can and cannot legally do with respect to recruitment, selection, and promotion and layoff practices.

Selection Standards

EDUCATIONAL REQUIREMENTS An educational requirement may be held illegal when (1) it can be shown that minority groups are less likely to possess the educational qualifications (such as a high school diploma), and (2) such qualifications are also not required to perform the job.

TESTS According to former Chief Justice Burger:

> Nothing in the [Title VII] act precludes the use of testing or measuring procedures; obviously they are useful. What Congress has forbidden is giving these devices and mechanisms controlling force unless they are demonstrating a *reasonable measure of job performance.*

Thus, tests that disproportionately screen out minorities or women *and are not job related* are deemed unlawful by the courts.

PREFERENCE TO RELATIVES You cannot give preference to relatives of your current employees with respect to employment opportunities if your current employees are substantially nonminority.

HEIGHT, WEIGHT, AND PHYSICAL CHARACTERISTICS Maximum weight rules for employees don't usually trigger adverse legal rulings. Similarly, "few applicants or employees will be able to demonstrate an actual weight-based disability" (in other words, they are 100% above their ideal weight or there is a physiological cause for their disability). Few are thus entitled to reasonable accommodations under the ADA.

However, managers should be vigilant against stigmatizing obese people. First, you may adversely impact minority groups, some of whom have a higher incidence of obesity. Furthermore, studies leave little doubt that obese individuals are less likely to be hired, less likely to receive promotions, more likely to get less desirable sales assignments, and more likely to receive poor customer service as customers.[78]

HEALTH QUESTIONS Under the ADA, "Employers are generally prohibited from asking questions about applicants' medical history or requiring preemployment physical examinations." However, such questions and exams can be used once the job offer has been extended to determine that the applicant can safely perform the job.[79]

ARREST RECORDS You cannot ask about or use a person's arrest record to disqualify him or her automatically for a position because there is always a presumption of innocence until proof of guilt. In addition, arrest records in general have not been shown valid for predicting job performance, and a higher percentage of minorities than nonminorities have been arrested.

APPLICATION FORMS Employment applications generally shouldn't contain questions pertaining, for instance, to applicants' disabilities, workers' compensation history, age, arrest record, marital status, or U.S. citizenship. It's best to collect personal information required for legitimate reasons (such as who to contact in case of emergency) after the person has been hired.[80]

Sample Discriminatory Promotion, Transfer, and Layoff Procedures

Fair employment laws protect not just job applicants but current employees as well.[81] Therefore, any employment practices regarding pay, promotion, termination, discipline, or benefits that (1) are applied differently to different classes of persons, (2) have the effect of adversely affecting members of a protected group, and (3) cannot be shown to be required as a BFOQ or business necessity may be held to be illegally discriminatory. For example, the EEOC issued an enforcement guidance making it clear that employers may not discriminate against employees in connection with their benefits plans.[82]

UNIFORMS When it comes to discriminatory uniforms and suggestive attire, courts have frequently sided with the employee. For example, requiring female employees (such as waitresses) to wear sexually suggestive attire as a condition of employment has been ruled as violating Title VII in many cases.[83]

THE EEOC ENFORCEMENT PROCESS

There are several steps in the EEOC enforcement process.

4 Explain the Equal
Employment Opportunity
Commission enforcement
process.

Processing a Discrimination Charge

FILING OF CLAIM The EEOC enforcement process begins with someone filing a claim. Under CRA 1991, the discrimination claim must be filed within 300 days (when there is a similar state law) or 180 days (no similar state law) after the alleged incident took place (2 years for the Equal Pay Act).[84] The filing must be in writing and under oath, by (or on behalf of) either the aggrieved person or by a member of the EEOC who has reasonable cause to believe that a violation occurred. In practice the EEOC typically defers a person's charge to the relevant state or local regulatory agency; if the latter waives jurisdiction or cannot obtain a satisfactory solution to the charge, they refer it back to the EEOC. The EEOC received 93,277 private-sector discrimination charges in fiscal year 2009.[85]

EEOC INVESTIGATION After a charge is filed (or the state or local deferral period ends), the EEOC has 10 days to serve notice of the charge on the employer. The EEOC then investigates the charge to determine whether there is reasonable cause to believe it is true; it is expected to make this determination within 120 days. If no reasonable cause is found, the EEOC must dismiss the charge, in which case the person who filed the charge has 90 days to file a suit on his or her own behalf. If reasonable cause for the charge is found, the EEOC must attempt to conciliate. If this conciliation is not satisfactory, the EEOC may bring a civil suit in a federal district court or issue a notice of right to sue to the person who filed the charge. Figure 2.3 summarizes important questions an employer should ask after receiving notice from the EEOC of a bias complaint.

The Equal Employment Opportunity Commission tends to pursue changing initiatives (see for instance, http://eeoc.gov/eeoc/initiatives/e-race/index.cfm).[86] For example, for fiscal years 2008–2013, one initiative is Eradicating Racism And Colorism from Employment (E-RACE). In a suit apparently prompted by its previous "Eradicating Racism from Employment" campaign, the EEOC charged that Walgreens used race to determine who to assign to low-performing stores in African-American communities.[87]

VOLUNTARY MEDIATION The EEOC refers a fraction of its charges to a voluntary mediation mechanism.[88] If the plaintiff agrees to mediation, the employer is asked to participate. A mediation session usually lasts up to 4 hours. If no agreement is reached or one of the parties rejects participation, the charge is then processed through the EEOC's usual mechanisms.

FIGURE 2.3

Questions to Ask When an Employer Receives Notice that EEOC Has Filed a Bias Claim

Sources: Fair Employment Practices Summary of Latest Developments, January 7, 1983: 3, Bureau of National Affairs, Inc. (800-372-1033); Kenneth Sovereign, *Personnel Law* (Upper Saddle River, NJ: Prentice Hall, 1999): 36–37; "EEOC Investigations— What an Employer Should Know." Equal Employment Opportunity Commission www.eeoc.gov/ employers/investigations.html, accessed May 6, 2007.

1. Exactly what is the charge and is your company covered by the relevant statutes? (For example, Title VII and the American with Disabilities Act generally apply only to employers with 15 or more employees; the Age Discrimination in Employment Act applies to employers with 20 or more employees; but the Equal Pay Act applies to virtually all employers with one or more employee.) Did the employee file his or her charge on time, and was it processed in a timely manner by the EEOC?

2. What protected group does the employee belong to? Is the EEOC claiming disparate impact or disparate treatment?

3. Are there any obvious bases upon which you can challenge and/or rebut the claim? For example, would the employer have taken the action if the person did not belong to a protected group? Does the person's personnel file support the action taken by the employer?

4. If it is a sexual harassment claim, are there offensive comments, calendars, posters, screensavers, and so on, on display in the company?

5. In terms of the practicality of defending your company against this claim, who are the supervisors who actually took the allegedly discriminatory actions and how effective will they be as potential witnesses? Have you received an opinion from legal counsel regarding the chances of prevailing? Even if you do prevail, what do you estimate will be the out-of-pocket costs of taking the charge through the judicial process? Would you be better off settling the case, and what are the prospects of doing so in a way that will satisfy all parties?

Faced with an offer to mediate, three responses are generally possible: agree to mediate the charge, make a settlement offer without mediation, or prepare a "position statement" for the EEOC. If the employer does not mediate or make an offer, the position statement is required. It should include information relating to the company's business and the charging party's position, a description of any rules or policies and procedures that are applicable, and the chronology of the offense that led to the adverse action.[89]

The EEOC is expanding its mediation program. Under this program, the EEOC refers all eligible discrimination charges filed against these employers to the commission's mediation unit, rather than to the usual charge processing system.[90]

How to Respond to Employment Discrimination Charges

There are several things to keep in mind when confronted by a charge of illegal employment discrimination. We can summarize some of the more important items as follows:

1. Be meticulous. For example, is the charge signed, dated, and notarized by the person who filed it? Was it filed within the time allowed?[91]
2. Remember that EEOC investigators are not judges and aren't empowered to act as courts. If the EEOC eventually determines that an employer may be in violation of a law, its only recourse is to file a suit or issue a notice of right to sue to the person who filed the charge.
3. Some experts advise meeting with the employee who made the complaint to determine all relevant issues. For example, ask: *What happened? Who was involved? Were there any witnesses?* Then prepare a written statement summarizing the complaints, facts, dates, and issues involved and request that the employee sign and date this.[92]
4. Give the EEOC a position statement based on your own investigation of the matter. Say something like, "Our company has a policy against discrimination and we would not discriminate in the manner outlined in the complaint." Support your case with some statistical analysis of the workforce, copies of any documents that support your position, and an explanation of any legitimate business justification for the actions you took.
5. Ensure that there is information in the EEOC's file demonstrating lack of merit of the charge. Often the best way to do that is by providing a position statement (as in #4).
6. Limit the information supplied as narrowly as possible. For example, if the charge only alleges sex discrimination, do not provide a breakdown of employees by age and sex.
7. Seek as much information as possible about the charging party's claim, to ensure that you understand the claim and its ramifications.
8. Prepare for the EEOC's *fact-finding conferences*. These are supposed to be informal meetings held early in the investigatory process aimed at determining whether there is a basis for negotiation. However, the EEOC's emphasis is often on settlement. Its investigators therefore use the conferences to find weak spots. Therefore, thoroughly prepare witnesses who are going to testify, especially supervisors.
9. Finally, preventing claims is usually better than litigating them. Racism's causes are many and complex. However, when someone with racist attitudes works in a company where there's a climate supporting racism, there is more likelihood of racial discrimination.[93]

DIVERSITY MANAGEMENT AND AFFIRMATIVE ACTION PROGRAMS

To some extent, demographic changes and globalization are rendering moot the goals of equitable and fair treatment driving equal employment legislation. Today, as we've seen, white males no longer dominate the labor force, and women and minorities will represent the lion's share of labor force growth over the near future. Furthermore, globalization requires employers to hire people with the cultural and language skills to deal with customers abroad.

This means two things for employers. First, companies are increasingly striving for demographic balance, not just because the law says they must, but due to self-interest.[94] Second, since many American workplaces are already diverse, the focus increasingly is on managing diversity

With strong top-management support, IBM created several minority task forces focusing on groups such as women and Native Americans.

diversity
Having a workforce comprised of two or more groups of employees with various racial, ethnic, gender, cultural, national origin, handicap, age, and religious backgrounds.

rather than on "justifying" it.[95] **Diversity** means being diverse or varied, and at work means having a workforce comprised of two or more groups of employees with various racial, ethnic, gender, cultural, national origin, handicap, age, and religious backgrounds.[96]

Diversity's Potential Pros and Cons

The resulting workforce diversity produces both benefits and threats for employers.

SOME DOWNSIDES Diversity can produce behavioral barriers that undermine work team collegiality and cooperation. Potential problems include:

- *Stereotyping* is a process in which someone ascribes specific behavioral traits to individuals based on their apparent membership in a group.[97] For example, "older people can't work hard." *Prejudice* means a bias toward prejudging someone based on that person's traits. For example, "we won't hire him because he's old."

discrimination
Taking specific actions toward or against the person based on the person's group.

- *Discrimination* is prejudice in action. **Discrimination** means taking specific actions toward or against the person based on the person's group.[98]

  In the U.S. and many countries, we've seen that it's generally illegal to discriminate at work based on a person's age, race, gender, disability, or country of national origin. But in practice, discrimination is often subtle. For example, many argue that a "glass ceiling," enforced by an "old boys' network" (friendships built in places like golf clubs), effectively prevents women from reaching top management.

- *Tokenism* occurs when a company appoints a small group of women or minorities to high-profile positions, rather than more aggressively seeking full representation for that group.[99]

- *Ethnocentrism* is the tendency to view members of other social groups less favorably than one's own. For example, one study found that managers attributed the performance of some minorities less to their abilities and effort and more to help they received from others. The same managers attributed the performance of *non*-minorities to their own abilities and efforts.[100]

gender-role stereotypes
The tendency to associate women with certain (frequently non-managerial) jobs.

- Discrimination against women goes beyond glass ceilings. Working women also confront **gender-role stereotypes**, the tendency to associate women with certain (frequently non-managerial) jobs.

SOME DIVERSITY BENEFITS The key is properly managing these potential threats. For example in one study, researchers examined the diversity climate in 654 stores of a large U.S. retail chain. They defined "diversity climate" as the extent to which employees in the stores reported believing that the firm promotes equal opportunity and inclusion. They found the greatest sales growth in stores with the highest pro-diversity climate, and the lowest in stores where subordinates and managers reported less hospitable diversity climates.[101] The following Strategy and HR feature provides another example.

Strategy and HR: Boosting Minority Sales at IBM

Workforce diversity makes strategic sense. IBM created several minority task forces focusing on groups such as women and Native Americans. One effect of these teams has been internal: In the 10 or so years since forming them, IBM has boosted the number of U.S.-born ethnic minority executives by almost 2 1/2 times.[102]

However, the firm's diversity program also helped IBM's strategy of expanding its markets. For example, one task force decided to focus on expanding IBM's market among multicultural and women-owned businesses. They did this in part by providing "much-needed sales and service support to small and midsize businesses, a niche well populated with minority and female buyers."[103] As a direct result, this market grew from $10 million to more than $300 million in revenue in just 3 years.

Managing Diversity

Managing diversity means maximizing diversity's potential advantages while minimizing the potential barriers—such as prejudices and bias—that can undermine the functioning of a diverse workforce. Diversity management includes both required and voluntary actions. However, compulsory actions (including EEO compliance) alone can't guarantee a close-knit and thriving community. Diversity management therefore also relies on efforts to get employees to get along and work together productively.[104]

TOP-DOWN PROGRAMS Typically, this starts at the top. The employer institutes a diversity management program. A main aim is to make employees more sensitive to and better able to adapt to individual cultural differences. One diversity expert says these five activities are at the heart of the typical company-wide diversity management program:

Provide strong leadership. Companies with exemplary reputations in managing diversity typically have CEOs who champion the cause of diversity. Leadership means, for instance, becoming a role model for the behaviors required for the change.

Assess the situation. One study found that the most common tools for measuring a company's diversity include equal employment hiring and retention metrics, employee attitude surveys, management and employee evaluations, and focus groups.[105]

Provide diversity training and education. The most common starting point for a diversity management effort is usually some type of diversity consciousness education program.

Change culture and management systems. For example, change the performance appraisal procedure to appraise supervisors based partly on their success in reducing inter-group conflicts.

Evaluate the diversity management program. For example, do employee attitude surveys indicate an improvement in employees' attitudes toward diversity?

EXAMPLE Employers use various means to increase workforce diversity. Many companies, such as Baxter Healthcare Corporation, start by adopting strong company policies advocating the benefits of a culturally, racially, and sexually diverse workforce: "Baxter International believes that a multi-cultural employee population is essential to the company's leadership in healthcare around the world." Baxter then publicizes this philosophy throughout the company.

Next, Baxter takes concrete steps to foster diversity at work. These steps include evaluating diversity program efforts, recruiting minority members to the board of directors, and interacting with representative minority groups and networks. Diversity training is another concrete activity. It aims at sensitizing all employees about the need to value cultural differences, build self-esteem, and generally create a more smoothly functioning and hospitable environment for the firm's diverse workforce.

5 List five strategies for successfully increasing diversity of the workforce

Developing a Multi-Cultural Consciousness

In July 2009, after a heated exchange on his doorstep, Cambridge, Massachusetts, police arrested Professor Henry Louis Gates Jr., a nationally known African-American Harvard professor, for disorderly conduct. Professor Gates initially accused the police of racially profiling him. The arresting officer (whose department had appointed as a trainer to show fellow officers how to avoid racial profiling) denied any racial motives. President Obama, at a news conference, accused the Cambridge police of using less than good judgment. Whatever else one can say about the episode, it seems that three people who should know quite a bit about multicultural consciousness differed dramatically about how culturally sensitive the other person had been.

One moral is that being sensitive to and adapting to individual cultural differences is easier said than done. People tend to view the world through the prism of their own experiences. Sometimes it's not easy for even a well-meaning person to appreciate how people who are different from us may be feeling. This suggests that it's useful to take steps to develop a personal diversity consciousness. Figure 2.4 summarizes steps one expert suggests.[106]

Equal Employment Opportunity Versus Affirmative Action

Equal employment opportunity aims to ensure that anyone, regardless of race, color, disability, sex, religion, national origin, or age, has an equal chance for a job based on his or her qualifications. *Affirmative action* goes beyond equal employment opportunity by requiring the employer to make an extra effort to hire and promote those in a protected group. Affirmative action thus includes specific actions (in recruitment, hiring, promotions, and compensation) to eliminate the present effects of past discrimination.

Steps in an Affirmative Action Program

According to the EEOC, in an affirmative action program the employer ideally takes these steps:

1. Issues a written equal employment policy indicating that it is an equal employment opportunity employer, and indicating commitment to affirmative action.
2. Appoints a top official with responsibility and authority to direct and implement the program.
3. Publicizes the equal employment policy and affirmative action commitment.
4. Surveys present minority and female employment to determine locations where affirmative action programs are especially desirable.[107]
5. Develops goals and timetables to improve utilization of minorities, males, and females where need for improved utilization has been identified.
6. Develops and implements specific programs to achieve these goals. Here, review the entire human resource management system to identify equal employment barriers and to make needed changes.
7. Establishes an internal audit and reporting system to monitor and evaluate progress in each aspect of the program.
8. Develops support for the affirmative action program, both inside the company and outside the company in the community.[108]

FIGURE 2.4

Steps in Developing Diversity Consciousness

1. **Take an active role in educating yourself.** For example, develop diverse relationships, and widen your circle of friends.
2. **Put yourself in a learning mode in any multicultural setting.** For example, suspend judgment and view the person you're dealing with just as an individual and in terms of the experiences you've actually had with him or her.
3. **Move beyond your personal comfort zone.** For example, put yourself in more situations where you are an "outsider."
4. **Don't be too hard on yourself if misunderstandings arise.** As this expert says, "The important thing is to acknowledge our mistakes and learn from them."[109]
5. **Realize that you are not alone.** Remember that there are other people including colleagues, friends, and mentors at work who you can turn to for advice as you deal with diversity issues.

Affirmative Action Today

Affirmative action is still a significant workplace issue today. The incidence of major court-mandated programs is down. However, many employers still engage in voluntary programs. For example, Executive Order 11246 (issued in 1965) requires federal contractors to take affirmative action to improve employment opportunities for women and racial minorities. It covers about 26 million workers—about 22% of the U.S. workforce.

Avoiding an employee backlash to affirmative action programs is important. One review suggests several steps to increase employee support. Current employees need to see that the program is fair. *Transparent selection procedures* help in this regard. *Communication* is also crucial. Make clear that the program doesn't involve preferential selection standards. Provide details on the qualifications of all new hires (both minority and nonminority). *Justifications* for the program should emphasize redressing past discrimination and the practical value of diversity, not underrepresentation.[110]

Voluntary Programs

Affirmative action is still very much a workplace issue today (for example, Executive Order 11246 mandates it for federal contractors). As another example, in 2009, the U.S. Supreme Court decided an important "reverse discrimination" suit brought by Connecticut firefighters. In *Ricci* v. *DeStefano*, 19 white firefighters and one Hispanic said the city of New Haven should have promoted them based on their test scores. The city argued that certifying the tests would have left them vulnerable to lawsuits by minorities for violating Title VII.[111] The Court decided in favor of the white firefighters.

In implementing voluntary programs, the employer should ensure that its program does not conflict with the Civil Rights Act of 1991, which two experts say may "bar employers from giving any consideration whatsoever to an individual's status as a racial or ethnic minority or as a woman when making an employment decision."[112] To reduce this problem, employers should take steps to recruit and develop better qualified minority and female employees, "while basing employment decisions on legitimate criteria."[113]

REVIEW

SUMMARY

1. Legislation barring discrimination is not new. For example, the Fifth Amendment to the U.S. Constitution (ratified in 1791) states that no person shall be deprived of life, liberty, or property without due process of law.
2. Legislation barring employment discrimination includes Title VII of the 1964 Civil Rights Act (as amended), which bars discrimination because of race, color, religion, sex, or national origin; various executive orders; federal guidelines (covering procedures for validating employee selection tools, etc.); the Equal Pay Act of 1963; and the Age Discrimination in Employment Act of 1967. In addition, various Court decisions (such as *Griggs* v. *Duke Power Company*) and state and local laws bar various aspects of discrimination.
3. The EEOC was created by Title VII of the Civil Rights Act. It is empowered to try conciliating discrimination complaints, but if this fails, the EEOC has the power to go directly to court to enforce the law.
4. The Civil Rights Act of 1991 had the effect of revising several Supreme Court equal employment decisions and

"rolling back the clock." For example, it placed the burden of proof back on employers and held that a nondiscriminatory reason was insufficient to let an employer avoid liability for an action that also had a discriminatory motive.
5. The Americans with Disabilities Act prohibits employment discrimination against the disabled. Specifically, qualified persons cannot be discriminated against if the firm can make reasonable accommodations without undue hardship on the business.
6. A person who believes he or she has been discriminated against by a personnel procedure or decision must prove either that he or she was subjected to unlawful disparate treatment (intentional discrimination) or that the procedure in question has a disparate impact (unintentional discrimination) on members of his or her protected class. Once a prima facie case of disparate treatment is established, an employer must produce evidence that its decision was based on legitimate reasons (such as BFOQ). If the employer does that, the person claiming discrimination must prove that the

employer's reasons are only a pretext for letting the company discriminate. Once a prima facie case of disparate impact has been established, the employer must produce evidence that the allegedly discriminatory practice or procedure is job related and is based on a substantial business reason.

7. An employer should avoid various specific discriminatory human resource management practices:

a. *In recruitment.* An employer usually should not rely on word-of-mouth advertising or give false or misleading information to minority group members. Also (usually), an employer should not specify the desired sex in advertising or in any way suggest that applicants might be discriminated against.

b. *In selection.* An employer should avoid using any educational or other requirements where (1) it can be shown that minority-group members are less likely to possess the qualification and (2) such requirement is also not job related. Tests that disproportionately screen out minorities and women and that are not job related are deemed unlawful. Remember that you can use various tests and standards, but you must prove that they are job related or show that they are not used to discriminate against protected groups.

8. In practice, a person's discrimination charge to the EEOC is often first referred to a local agency. When the EEOC finds reasonable cause to believe that discrimination occurred, it may suggest the parties try to work out a conciliation. EEOC investigators can only make recommendations. Make sure to clearly document your position (as the employer).

9. An employer can use three basic defenses in the event of a discriminatory practice allegation. One is *business necessity.* Attempts to show that tests or other selection standards are valid is one example of this defense. *Bona fide occupational qualification* is the second defense. This is applied when, for example, religion, national origin, or sex is a bona fide requirement of the job (such as for actors or actresses). A third is that the decision was made on the basis of legitimate nondiscriminatory reasons (such as poor performance) having nothing to do with the prohibited discrimination alleged.

10. Steps in an affirmative action program (based on suggestions from the EEOC) are (1) issue a written equal employment policy, (2) appoint a top official, (3) publicize the policy, (4) survey present minority and female employees, (5) develop goals and timetables, (6) develop and implement specific programs to achieve goals, (7) establish an internal audit and reporting system, and (8) develop support of in-house and community programs.

11. Recruitment is one of the first activities to which EEOC laws and procedures are applied. We turn to this in Chapter 4.

KEY TERMS

Equal Pay Act of 1963   23
Title VII of the 1964 Civil Rights Act   23
Equal Employment Opportunity Commission (EEOC)   23
affirmative action   24
Office of Federal Contract Compliance Programs (OFCCP)   24
Age Discrimination in Employment Act (ADEA) of 1967   24
Vocational Rehabilitation Act of 1973   24
Pregnancy Discrimination Act (PDA)   24
Griggs v. *Duke Power Company*   25
protected class   25
Civil Rights Act of 1991 (CRA 1991)   25

disparate impact   25
disparate treatment   26
sexual harassment   26
gender harassment   29
Americans with Disabilities Act (ADA)   30
adverse impact   34
bona fide occupational qualification (BFOQ)   35
business necessity   35
diversity   40
discrimination   40
gender-role stereotypes   40

DISCUSSION QUESTIONS

1. Summarize the basic equal employment opportunity laws regarding age, race, sex, national origin, religion, and handicap discrimination.

2. Explain the basic defenses against discrimination allegations.

3. Present a summary of what employers can and cannot legally do with respect to recruitment, selection, and promotion and layoff practices.

4. Explain the Equal Employment Opportunity Commission enforcement process.

5. List five strategies for successfully increasing diversity of the workforce.

6. What is Title VII? What does it state?

7. What important precedents were set by the *Griggs* v. *Duke Power Company* case? The *Albemarle* v. *Moody* case?

8. What is adverse impact? How can it be proven?

9. Explain the defenses and exceptions to discriminatory practice allegations.

10. What is the difference between affirmative action and equal employment opportunity?

INDIVIDUAL AND GROUP ACTIVITIES

1. Working individually or in groups, respond to the following three scenarios based on what you learned in this chapter. Under what conditions (if any) do you think the following constitute sexual harassment? (a) A female manager fires a male employee because he refuses her requests for sexual favors. (b) A male manager refers to female employees as "sweetie" or "baby." (c) A female employee overhears two male employees exchanging sexually oriented jokes.

2. Working individually or in groups, discuss how you would set up an affirmative action program.

3. Compare and contrast the issues presented in recent court rulings on affirmative action. Working individually or in groups, discuss the current direction of affirmative action.

4. Working individually or in groups, write a paper entitled "What the manager should know about how the EEOC handles a person's discrimination charge."

5. Assume you are the manager in a small restaurant. You are responsible for hiring employees, supervising them, and recommending them for promotion. Working individually or in groups, compile a list of potentially discriminatory management practices you should avoid.

WEB-e's (WEB EXERCISES)

1. Citicorp recently faced a billion dollar discrimination suit. Use Web sites such as www.allbusiness.com/legal/legal-services-litigation/5062526-1.html to discuss what happened with these suits.

2. Using sites such as www.foxnews.com/story/0,2933,517334,00.html, discuss the details of the discrimination suit against Hooters.

3. What conclusions can you draw from sites such as www.usatoday.com/news/health/weightloss/2008-05-20-overweight-bias_N.htm about handling and avoiding discrimination against obese people?

APPLICATION EXERCISES

HR IN ACTION CASE INCIDENT 1

An Accusation of Sexual Harassment in Pro Sports

The jury in a sexual harassment suit brought by a former high-ranking New York Knicks basketball team executive recently awarded her over $11 million in punitive damages. They did so after hearing testimony during what the *New York Times* called a "sordid four-week trial." Officials of the Madison Square Garden (which owns the Knicks) said they would appeal the verdict. However, even if they were to win on appeal (which one University of Richmond Law School professor said was unlikely), the case still exposed the organization and its managers to a great deal of unfavorable publicity.

The federal suit pitted Anucha Browne Sanders, the Knicks' senior vice president of marketing and business operations (and former Northwestern University basketball star), against the team's owner, Madison Square Garden, and its president, Isiah Thomas. The suit charged them with sex discrimination and retaliation. Ms. Browne Sanders accused Mr. Thomas of verbally abusing and sexually harassing her over a 2-year period, and says the Garden fired her about a month after she complained to top management about the harassment. "My pleas and complaints about Mr. Thomas' illegal and offensive actions fell on deaf ears," she said. At the trial, the Garden cited numerous explanations for the dismissal, saying she had "failed to fulfill professional responsibilities." At a news conference, Browne Sanders said that Thomas "refused to stop his demeaning and repulsive behavior and the Garden refused to intercede." For his part, Mr. Thomas vigorously insisted he was innocent, and said, "I will not allow her or anybody, man or woman, to use me as a pawn for their financial gain." According to one report of the trial, her claims of harassment and verbal abuse had little corroboration from witnesses, but neither did the Garden's claims that her performance had been subpar. After the jury decision came in favor of the plaintiff, Browne Sanders' lawyers said, "this [decision] confirms what we've been saying all along, that [Browne Sanders] was sexually abused and fired for complaining about it." The Garden's statement said, in part, that "We look forward to presenting our arguments to an appeals court and believe they will agree that no sexual harassment took place."

Questions

1. Do you think Ms. Browne Sanders had the basis for a sexual harassment suit? Why or why not?

2. From what you know of this case, do you think the jury arrived at the correct decision? If not, why not? If so, why?

3. Based on the few facts that you have, what steps if any could Garden management have taken to protect themselves from liability in this matter?

4. Aside from the appeal, what would you do now if you were the Garden's top management?
5. "The allegations against the Madison Square Garden in this case raise ethical questions with regard to the employer's actions." Explain whether you agree or disagree with this statement, and why.

Sources: "Jury Awards $11.6 Million to Former Executive of Pro Basketball Team in Harassment Case," *BNA Bulletin to Management* (October 9, 2007): 323; Richard Sandomir, "Jury Finds Knicks and Coach Harassed a Former Executive," *The New York Times*, www.nytimes.com/2007/10/03/sports/basketball/03garden.html?em&ex=1191556800&en=41d47437f805290d&ei=5087%0A, accessed November 13, 2007; "Thomas Defiant in Face of Harassment Claims," http://espn.com, accessed November 13, 2007.

HR IN ACTION CASE INCIDENT 2
Carter Cleaning Company

A Question of Discrimination

One of the first problems Jennifer faced at her father's Carter Cleaning Centers concerned the inadequacies of the firm's current HR management practices and procedures.

One problem that particularly concerned her was the lack of attention to equal employment matters. Virtually all hiring was handled independently by each store manager, and the managers themselves had received no training regarding such fundamental matters as the types of questions that should not be asked of job applicants. It was therefore not unusual—in fact, it was routine—for female applicants to be asked questions such as, "Who's going to take care of your children while you are at work?" and for minority applicants to be asked questions about arrest records and credit histories. Nonminority applicants—three store managers were white males and three were white females, by the way—were not asked these questions, as Jennifer discerned from her interviews with the managers. Based on discussions with her father, Jennifer deduced that part of the reason for the laid-back attitude toward equal employment stemmed from (1) her father's lack of sophistication regarding the legal requirements and (2) the fact that, as Jack Carter put it, "Virtually all our workers are women or minority members anyway, so no one can really come in here and accuse us of being discriminatory, can they?"

Jennifer decided to mull that question over, but before she could, she was faced with two serious equal rights problems. Two women in one of her stores privately confided to her that their manager was making unwelcome sexual advances toward them, and one claimed he had threatened to fire her unless she "socialized" with him after hours. And during a fact-finding trip to another store, an older man—he was 73 years old—complained of the fact that although he had almost 50 years of experience in the business, he was being paid less than people half his age who were doing the very same job. Jennifer's review of the stores resulted in the following questions.

Questions

1. Is it true, as Jack Carter claims, that "we can't be accused of being discriminatory because we hire mostly women and minorities anyway"?
2. How should Jennifer and her company address the sexual harassment charges and problems?
3. How should she and her company address the possible problems of age discrimination?
4. Given the fact that each of its stores has only a handful of employees, is her company in fact covered by equal rights legislation?
5. And finally, aside from the specific problems, what other human resource management matters (application forms, training, and so on) have to be reviewed given the need to bring them into compliance with equal rights laws?

EXPERIENTIAL EXERCISE

The Interplay of Ethics and Equal Employment

If one accepts the proposition that equal employment is at least partly an ethical matter, then we should expect that real employers recognize and emphasize that fact, for instance, on their Web sites. Some do. For example, the Duke Energy Company (which, when known as Duke Power many years ago, lost one of the first and most famous equal employment cases) posts the following on its Web site:

Equal Employment Opportunity: Duke Energy's Code of Business Ethics Duke Energy seeks and values diversity. The dignity of each person is respected, and everyone's contributions are recognized. We expect Duke Energy employees to act with mutual respect and cooperation toward one another. We do not tolerate discrimination in the workplace.

We comply with laws concerning discrimination and equal opportunity that specifically prohibit discrimination on the basis of certain differences. We will recruit, select, train and compensate based on merit, experience and other work-related criteria.

Our Responsibilities Duke Energy employees are expected to treat others with respect on the job and comply with equal employment opportunity laws, including those related to discrimination and harassment.

Duke Energy employees must not:

- Use any differences protected by law as a factor in hiring, firing or promotion decisions.
- Use any differences protected by law when determining terms or conditions of employment, such as work assignments, employee development opportunities, vacation or overtime.
- Retaliate against a person who makes a complaint of discrimination in good faith, reports suspected unethical conduct, violations of laws, regulations, or company policies, or participates in an investigation.

Source: www.duke-energy.com/corporate-governance/code-of-business-ethics/equal-employment-opportunity.asp, accessed May 28, 2010. © Duke Energy Corporation. All Rights Reserved.

Purpose: Ethical decision-making is an important HR-related personal competency. The purpose of this exercise is to increase your understanding of how ethics and equal employment are interrelated.

Required Understanding: Be thoroughly familiar with the material presented in this chapter.

How to Set Up the Exercise/Instructions:

1. Divide the class into groups of three to five students.
2. Each group should use the Internet to identify and access at least five companies that emphasize how ethics and equal employment are interrelated.
3. Next, each group should develop answers to the following questions:
   a. Based on your Internet research, how much importance do employers seem to place on emphasizing the ethical aspects of equal employment?
   b. What seem to be the main themes these employers emphasize with respect to ethics and equal employment?
   c. Given what you've learned, explain how you would emphasize the ethical aspects of equal employment if you were creating an equal employment training program for new supervisors.

BUSINESS IN ACTION EDU-EXERCISE

Building Your *Public Policy* Knowledge in Equal Employment

Laws govern much of what we do and how we live. For example, traffic laws govern how fast we should drive; tax laws largely govern who pays what taxes; and equal employment laws state, with some precision, what managers can and cannot do when selecting, training, paying, and promoting and firing members of minority groups.

What may not be so obvious is that all laws invariably stem from public policy considerations. In other words, governments enact laws so as to further the government's public policy aims. Thus, if New York decides that it's in the best interests of its citizens to lower fuel consumption by getting everyone to drive slower, its legislature may lower New York's speed limit, say from 65 to 55 miles per hour. If the people elect a new U.S. president whose administration believes that lowering tax rates is a way to encourage entrepreneurs to start new businesses, it may encourage Congress to lower the taxes that business people pay.

According to a review of the term *public policy* at www.answers.com/topic/public-policy, there's no one definition of "public policy." But, to paraphrase one good definition on that site, *public policy* is a course of action or inaction that public authorities choose to pursue, in order to address a problem. Put another way, "public policy consists of political decisions for implementing programs to achieve societal goals." As with traffic and tax laws, governments express their chosen public policies by way of the laws and regulations they set, and

the other decisions they make (such as how they spend their tax revenues).

Public policy is thus important for several reasons. First, laws almost never spring up at random; instead, they flow out of the government's public policy agenda. Second, much of the political debate you see occurring around election time reflects the fact that one political party's public policy agenda is considerably different from the other's—one may believe in redistributing wealth, while the other believes in lowering the tax on wealthy people to encourage them to invest more, for instance. Third, "public policy" is not just some abstract concept. A government's public policy viewpoint drives its legislative agenda. The laws and the other decisions it makes then govern what its citizens can and cannot do. We can therefore best understand the notions of equitableness and nondiscrimination underlying equal employment laws as reflecting what our government over time saw as vital societal—and therefore public policy—goals.

Questions

1. Explain with examples how the evolution of equal employment law in the 1960s helps illustrate how public policy considerations drove the original EEO legislation.
2. Give at least three examples of how current EEOC policy reflects public policy decisions.

PERSONAL COMPETENCIES EDU-EXERCISE

Building Your *Ethical Decision-Making* Skills

Managers should understand that equal employment is also an ethical issue.

Ethics are "the principles of conduct governing an individual or a group"—they're the principles people use to decide what their conduct should be.[114] As such, how to treat employees who may be disabled, or of a different age, race, gender, or national origin than you, is almost always as much of an ethical question as a purely legal one.

Consider this incident. A jury in Central Islip, New York, ordered Walmart to pay Patrick Brady $7.5 million for violating the Americans with Disabilities Act. Walmart hired Patrick, who has cerebral palsy, to work as a pharmacist's assistant in one of its stores. According to the complaint, he worked as an assistant for just one day before the store reassigned him to collect carts and pick up trash. The complaint claims that the pharmacist didn't think the disabled man was "fit for the pharmacy job."[115]

Questions

1. What (if anything) is the ethical issue here?
2. In terms of any moral or ethical code that you'd like to apply, do you think the pharmacist did the ethically right thing?
3. Can you think of anything the pharmacist could have done that would change your opinion?
4. Do you think the pharmacist's actions were legal?
5. Could the pharmacist's actions have been legal but still unethical? How?

ENDNOTES

1. http://www.foxnews.com/story/0,2933,517334,00.html, accessed January 7, 2010.
2. Betsy Morris, "How Corporate America Is Betraying Women," *Fortune* (January 10, 2005): 64–70.
3. Note that private employers are not bound by the U.S. Constitution.
4. Based on or quoted from *Principles of Employment Discrimination Law, International Association of Official Human Rights Agencies,* Washington, D.C. See also Bruce Feldacker, *Labor Guide to Labor Law* (Upper Saddle River, NJ: Prentice Hall, 2000); and "EEOC Attorneys Highlight How Employers Can Better Their Nondiscrimination Practices," *BNA Bulletin to Management* (July 20, 2008): 233; and www.eeoc.gov, accessed June 27, 2009. Employment discrimination law is a changing field, and the appropriateness of the rules, guidelines, and conclusions in this chapter and book may also be affected by factors unique to the employer's operation. They should be reviewed by the employer's attorney before implementation.
5. The Equal Employment Opportunity Act of 1972, Subcommittee on Labor or the Committee of Labor and Public Welfare, United States Senate, March 1972, p. 3. In general, it is not discrimination, but unfair discrimination against a person merely because of that person's race, age, sex, national origin, or religion that is forbidden by federal statutes. In the federal government's *Uniform Employee Selection Guidelines,* unfair discrimination is defined as follows: "unfairness is demonstrated through a showing that members of a particular interest group perform better or poorer on the job than their scores on the selection procedure (test, etc.) would indicate through comparison with how members of the other groups performed." For a discussion of the meaning of fairness, see James Ledvinka, "The Statistical Definition of Fairness in the Federal Selection Guidelines and Its Implications for Minority Employment," *Personnel Psychology* 32 (August 1979): 551–562. In summary, a selection device (such as a test) may discriminate—for example, between low performers and high performers. However, unfair discrimination—discrimination that is based solely on the person's race, age, sex, national origin, or religion—is illegal.
6. "Restructured, Beefed Up OFCCP May Shift Policy Emphasis, Attorney Says," *BNA Bulletin to Management* (August 18, 2009): 257.
7. Note that the U.S. Supreme Court (in *General Dynamics Land Systems Inc.* v. *Cline, 2004*) held that the ADEA does *not* protect younger workers from being treated worse than older ones. "High Court: ADEA Does Not Protect Younger Workers Treated Worse Than Their Elders," *BNA Bulletin to Management* 55, no. 10 (March 4, 2004): 73–80. The U.S. Supreme Court recently held that the plaintiff must show that age was the determining factor in the employer's personnel action. See "Justices, 5-4, Reject Burden Shifting," *BNA Bulletin to Management* (June 23, 2009): 199.
8. John Kohl, Milton Mayfield, and Jacqueline Mayfield, "Recent Trends in Pregnancy Discrimination Law," *Business Horizons* 48, no. 5 (September 2005): 421–429.
9. Nancy Woodward, "Pregnancy Discrimination Grows," *HR Magazine* (July 2005): 79.
10. www.uniformguidelines.com/uniformguidelines.html, accessed November 23, 2007.
11. Ibid.
12. See, for example, Gillian Flynn, "The Maturing of the ADEA," *Workforce Management* (October 2002): 86–87.
13. *Griggs* v. *Duke Power Company,* 3FEP cases 175.
14. IOFEP cases 1181.
15. Bruce Feldacker, *Labor Guide to Labor Law* (Upper Saddle River, NJ: Prentice Hall, 2000): 513.
16. "The Eleventh Circuit Explains Disparate Impact, Disparate Treatment," *BNA Fair Employment Practices* (August 17, 2000): 102. See also Kenneth York, "Disparate Results in Adverse Impact Tests: The 4/5ths Rule and the Chi Square Test," *Public Personnel Management* 31, no. 2 (Summer 2002): 253–262. A recent analysis based on mathematical simulations concluded that employee selection effectiveness in general, and the potential weaknesses of applying the 4/5 rule in particular, can be ameliorated by formulating and using a multistage selection

strategy, for instance basing the initial screen, say for conscientiousness, on paper-and-pencil tests, and then one or two subsequent screens on other selection procedures including interviews. See David Finch et al., "Multistage Selection Strategies: Simulating the Effects on Adverse Impact and Expected Performance for Various Predictor, Nations," *Journal of Applied Psychology* 94, no. 2 (2009): 318–340.

17. www.eeoc.gov/policy/cra91.html, accessed November 11, 2007.
18. Larry Drake and Rachel Moskowitz, "Your Rights in the Workplace," *Occupational Outlook Quarterly* (Summer 1997): 19–20.
19. Richard Wiener et al., "The Fit and Implementation of Sexual Harassment Law to Workplace Evaluations," *Journal of Applied Psychology* 87, no. 4 (2002): 747–764. The Federal Violence Against Women Act of 1994 provides another avenue that women can use to seek relief for violent sexual harassment. It provides that someone who commits a crime of violence motivated by gender and thus deprives another of her rights shall be liable to the party injured. Congress and the president renewed this in 2005. http://www.ovw.usdoj.gov/regulations.htm, accessed November 1, 2010.
20. http://www.eeoc.gov/types/sexual_harassment.html, accessed April 24, 2009.
21. Edward Felsenthal, "Justice's Ruling Further Defines Sexual Harassment," *Wall Street Journal* (March 5, 1998): B1, B5. Similarly, a series of compliments and "requests for a hug" were not sufficient to rise to the level of sexual harassment in one case involving a female supervisor and her female subordinate. "Compliments, Request for Hug Were Not Harassment by Female Supervisor, Court Says," *Human Resources Report, BNA* (November 20, 2003): 1193.
22. Hilary Gettman and Michele Gelfand, "When the Customer Shouldn't Be King: Antecedents and Consequences of Sexual Harassment by Clients and Customers," *Journal of Applied Psychology* 92, no. 3 (2007): 757–770.
23. See Mindy D. Bergman et al., "The (Un)reasonableness of Reporting: Antecedents and Consequences of Reporting Sexual Harassment," *Journal of Applied Psychology* 87, no. 2 (2002), 230–242; see also W. Kirk Turner and Christopher Thrutchley, "Employment Law and Practices Training: No Longer the Exception—It's the Rule," *Society for Human Resource Management Legal Report* (July–August 2002): 1–2.
24. See the discussion in "Examining Unwelcome Conduct in a Sexual Harassment Claim," *BNA Fair Employment Practices* (October 19, 1995): 124. See also Molly Bowers et al., "Just Cause in the Arbitration of Sexual Harassment Cases," *Dispute Resolution Journal* 55, no. 4 (November 2000): 40–55.
25. The EEOC says, "Prevention is the best tool to eliminate sexual harassment in the workplace. Employers are encouraged to take steps necessary to prevent sexual harassment from occurring. They should clearly communicate to employees that sexual harassment will not be tolerated. They can do so by providing sexual harassment training to their employees and by establishing an effective complaint or grievance process and taking immediate and appropriate action when an employee complains." www.eeoc.gov/, accessed November 11, 2007.
26. Chelsea Willness et al., "A Meta-Analysis of the Antecedents and Consequences of Workplace Sexual Harassment," *Personnel Psychology* 60, no. 60 (2007): 127–162.
27. Jennifer Berdahl and Celia Moore, "Workplace Harassment: Double Jeopardy for Minority Women," *Journal of Applied Psychology* 91, no. 2 (2006): 426–436.

28. Jennifer Berdahl, "The Sexual Harassment of Uppity Women," *Journal of Applied Psychology* 92, no. 2 (2007): 425–437.
29. Lilia Cortina and S. Arzu Wasti, "Profile to Coping: Response to Sexual Harassment Across Persons, Organizations, and Cultures," *Journal of Applied Psychology* 90, no. 1 (2005): 182–192.
30. Jennifer Berdahl and Karl Aquino, "Sexual Behavior at Work: Fun or Folly?" *Journal of Applied Psychology* 94, no. 1 (2009): 34–47.
31. Maria Rotundo et al., "A Meta-Analytic Review of Gender Differences in Perceptions of Sexual Harassment," *Journal of Applied Psychology* 86, no. 5 (2001): 914–922. See also Nathan Bowling and Terry Beehr, "Workplace Harassment from the Victim's Perspective: A Theoretical Model and Meta Analysis," *Journal of Applied Psychology* 91, no. 5 (2006): 998–1012.
32. See the discussion in "Examining Unwelcome Conduct in Sexual Harassment Claim," *BNA Fair Employment Practices* (October 19, 1995): 124. See also Molly Bowers et al., "Just Cause in the Arbitration of Sexual Harassment Cases," *Dispute Resolution Journal* 55, no. 4 (November 2000): 40–55.
33. Mindy D. Bergman et al., op cit., 237.
34. Elliot H. Shaller and Dean Rosen, "A Guide to the EEOC's Final Regulations on the Americans with Disabilities Act," *Employee Relations* 17, no. 3 (Winter 1991–1992), and www.eeoc.gov/ada/, accessed November 20, 2007.
35. Elliot H. Shaller and Dean Rosen, "A Guide to the EEOC's Final Regulations on the Americans with Disabilities Act," *Employee Relations* 17, no. 3 (Winter 1991–1992): 408. The ADEA does not just protect against intentional discrimination (disparate treatment). Under the Supreme Court's *Smith* v. *Jackson, Miss* decision, it also covers employer practices that seem neutral but which actually bear more heavily on older workers (disparate impact). "Employees Need Not Show Intentional Bias to Bring Claims under ADEA, High Court Says," *BNA Bulletin to Management* 56, no. 14 (April 5, 2005): 105.
36. Ibid., 409.
37. "EEOC Guidance on Dealing with Intellectual Disabilities," *Workforce Management* (March 2005): 16.
38. James McDonald, Jr., "The Americans with Difficult Personalities Act," *Employee Relations Law Journal* 25, no. 4 (Spring 2000): 93–107.
39. See, for example, Paul Starkman, "The ADA's 'Essential Job Function' Requirements: Just How Essential Does an Essential Job Function Have to Be?" *Employee Relations Law Journal* 26, no. 4 (Spring 2001): 43–102.
40. www.ada.gov/reg3a.html#Anchor-Appendix-52467, accessed January 23, 2009.
41. "No Sitting for Store Greeter," *BNA Fair Employment Practices* (December 14, 1995): 150.
42. Martha Frase, "And Underestimated Talent Pool," *HR Magazine* (April 2009): 55–58.
43. IOFEP cases 1181. See also Joe Mullich, "Hiring Without Limits," *Workforce Management* (June 2004): 52–58.
44. M. P. McQueen, "Workplace Disabilities Are on the Rise," *Wall Street Journal* (May 1, 2007): A1.
45. For example, A U.S. circuit court recently found that a depressed former kidney dialysis technician could not claim ADA discrimination after the employer fired him for attendance problems. The court said he could not meet the essential job function of predictably coming to work. "Depressed Worker Lacks ADA Claim, Court Decides," *BNA Bulletin to*

Management (December 18, 2007): 406. See also www.eeoc.gov/press/5-10-01-b.html, accessed January 8, 2008.

46. "Odds Against Getting Even Are Long in ADA Cases," *BNA Bulletin to Management* (August 20, 2000): 229; "Determining Employers' Responsibilities Under ADA," *BNA Fair Employment Practices* (May 16, 1996): 57. See also Barbara Lee, "The Implications of ADA Litigation for Employers: A Review of Federal Appellate Court Decisions," *Human Resource Management* 40, no. 1 (Spring 2001): 35–50.

47. "Supreme Court Says Manual Task Limitation Needs Both Daily Living, Workplace Impact," *BNA Fair Employment Practices* (January 17, 2002): 8.

48. "Differing Views: Punctuality as Essential Job Function," *BNA Fair Employment Practices* (April 27, 2000): 56. As another example, Walmart recently had to reinstate hearing-impaired workers and pay a $750,000 fine for discrimination under the ADA.www.eeoc.gov/press/5–10–01-b.html, accessed January 8, 2008.

49. "Airline Erred in Giving Test Before Making Formal Offer," *BNA Bulletin to Management* (March 15, 2005): 86.

50. The EEOC's recent implementing of rules add sitting, reaching, and interacting with others to the number of major life activities. "EEOC OKs Proposed Rule to Implement ADA Amendments Act," *BNA Bulletin to Management* (September 22, 2009): 303.

51. Lawrence Postol, "ADAAA Will Result in Renewed Emphasis on Reasonable Accommodations," *Society for Human Resource Management Legal Report* (January 2009): 1–3.

52. Mark Lengnick-Hall et al., "Overlooked and Underutilized: People with Disabilities Are an Untapped Human Resource," *Human Resource Management* 47, no. 2 (Summer 2008): 255–273.

53. Susan Wells, "Counting on Workers with Disabilities," *HR Magazine* (April 2008): 45. Similarly, Verizon Wireless has a formal program aimed at assisting current employees to better manage a transition from healthy to disabled. For example, they train supervisors to identify potentially disability-related deterioration in their employees' performance and to speak with these employees to try to identify what the issues are. If it becomes necessary for an employee to take a disability leave, the program encourages the employee to remain in contact with Verizon's HR professionals and to work with them to set realistic return dates. J. Adam Shoemaker, "A Welcome Back for Workers with Disabilities," *HR Magazine* (October 2009): 30–32.

54. www.eeoc.gov/press/2-25-09.html, accessed April 3, 2009.

55. Bill Leonard, "Bill to Ban Sexual Orientation Bias Introduced," *HR Magazine* 54, no. 8 (August 2009): 18.

56. Judy Greenwald, "Ruling Opens Door to Gender Stereotyping Suits," *Business Insurance* 43, no. 31 (September 7, 2009): 3.

57. employment.findlaw.com/employment/employment-employee-discrimination-harassment/employment-employee-gay-lesbian-discrimination.html, accessed May 29, 2010.

58. www.leg.state.fl.us/Statutes/index.cfm?App_mode=Display_Statute&Search_String=&URL=Ch0448/SEC07.HTM&Title=-%3E2009-%3ECh0448-%3ESection%2007#0448.07, accessed May 29, 2010.

59. www.nyc.gov/html/cchr/, accessed May 29, 2010.

60. Unless otherwise noted, these are adapted from Wayne Barlow and Edward Hane, "A Practical Guide to the Americans with Disabilities Act," *Personnel Journal* 72 (June 1992): 59.

61. "Tips for Employers with Asymptomatic HIV-Positive Employees," *BNA Fair Employment Practices* (November 27, 1997): 141.

62. The timing of any medical test is important: In the event the hiring employer rescinds an offer after the medical exam, the applicant must be able to unambiguously identify the reason for the rejection as being medical. In one case, the courts found that American Airlines had not made a "real" offer to three candidates before requiring them to take their medical exams, because (even if they passed the medical exam) the offer was still contingent on American checking their references. The medical exams showed the candidates had HIV, and American rescinded their offers. This left open the question of whether it was the exams or the reference checks that torpedoed the offer, and American lost the case. "Airline Erred in Giving Test Before Making Formal Offer," *BNA Bulletin to Management* (March 15, 2005): 86.

63. Similar limitations apply to medical exams for *current* employees. In one case, superiors ordered a Chicago police officer to take a blood test to determine if the level of Prozac his physician prescribed would seriously impair his ability to do his job. At the time, the officer had not engaged in any behavior that suggested any performance problems. The court said the blood test was therefore not job related and violated the ADA's prohibition against inquiries into the nature or severity of an individual's disability. *Krocka v. Bransfield*, DC N111, #95C627, 6/24/97; reviewed in "Test for Prozac Violates ADA," *BNA Fair Employment Practices* (August 7, 1997): 91. See also Sue Willman, "Tips for Minimizing Abuses of the Americans with Disabilities Act," *Society for Human Resource Management Legal Report* (January–February 2003): 8.

64. Elliot Shaller, "Reasonable Accommodation Under the Americans with Disabilities Act: What Does It Mean," *Employee Relations Law Journal* 16, no. 4 (Spring 1991), 445–446.

65. Barbara Lee, "The Implications of ADA Litigation for Employers: A Review of Federal Appellate Court Decisions," *Human Resource Management* 40, no. 1 (Spring 2001): 35–50.

66. Timothy Bland, "The Supreme Court Focuses on the ADA," *HR Magazine* (September 1999): 42–46. See also James Hall and Diane Hatch, "Supreme Court Decisions Require ADA Revision," *Workforce* (August 1999): 60–66. Note also that courts traditionally defined "disabilities" quite narrowly. Employers may therefore require that the employee provide documentation of the disorder, and assess what effect that disorder has on the employee's job performance. Employers should therefore ask questions such as: Does the employee have a disability that substantially limits a major life activity? Is the employee qualified to do the job? Can the employee perform the essential functions of the job? Can any reasonable accommodation be provided without creating an undue hardship on the employer?

67. "Expansion of Employment Laws Abroad Impacts US Employers," *BNA Bulletin to Management* (April 11, 2006): 119; Richard Posthuma, Mark Roehling, and Michael Campion, "Applying US Employment Discrimination Laws to International Employers: Advice for Scientists and Practitioners," *Personnel Psychology* 59 (2006): 705–739.

68. John Klinefelter and James Thompkins, "Adverse Impact in Employment Selection," *Public Personnel Management* (May/June 1976): 199–204. For a recent discussion, see, for example, www.hr-guide.com/data/G702.htm, accessed November 21, 2007.

69. John Moran, *Employment Law* (Upper Saddle River, NJ: Prentice Hall, 1997): 168. A recent study found that using the so-called 4/5ths rule often resulted in false-positive ratings of

adverse impact, and that incorporating tests of statistical significance could improve the accuracy of applying the 4/5ths rule. See Philip Roth, Philip Bobko, and Fred Switzer, "Modeling the Behavior of the 4/5ths Rule for Determining Adverse Impact: Reasons for Caution," *Journal of Applied Psychology* 91, no. 3 (2006): 507–522.

70. A recent analysis based on mathematical simulations concluded that employee selection effectiveness in general, and the potential weaknesses of applying the 4/5ths rule in particular, can be ameliorated by formulating and using a multistage selection strategy, for instance, basing the initial screen, say for conscientiousness, on paper-and-pencil tests, and then one or two subsequent screens on other selection procedures including interviews. See David Finch et al., "Multistage Selection Strategies: Simulating the Effects on Adverse Impact and Expected Performance for Various Predictor, Nations," *Journal of Applied Psychology* 94, no. 2 (2009): 318–340.

71. "Eighth Circuit OKs $3.4 Million EEOC Verdict Relating to Pre-Hire Strength Testing Rules," *BNA Bulletin to Management* (November 28, 2006): 377.

72. "The Eleventh Circuit Explains Disparate Impact, Disparate Treatment," *BNA Fair Employment Practices* (August 17, 2000): 102.

73. www.foxnews.com/story/0,2933,517334,00.html, accessed January 7, 2010.

74. *U.S.* v. *Bethlehem Steel Company,* 3FEP cases 589.

75. *Spurlock* v. *United Airlines,* 5FEP cases 17.

76. James Ledvinka and Robert Gatewood, "EEO Issues with Preemployment Inquiries," *Personnel Administrator*, 22, no. 2 (February 1997): 22–26.

77. Howard Anderson and Michael D Levin-Epstein, *Primer of Equal Employment Opportunity* (Washington, D.C.: The Bureau of National Affairs, 1982): 28.

78. Jenessa Shapiro et al., "Expectations of Obese Trainees: How Stigmatized Trainee Characteristics Influence Training Effectiveness," *Journal of Applied Psychology* 92, no. 1 (2007): 239–249. See also Lisa Finkelstein et al., "Bias Against Overweight Job Applicants: Further Explanations of When and Why," *Human Resource Management* 46, no. 2 (Summer 2007): 203–222; and Svetlana Shkolnikova, "Weight Discrimination Could Be as Common as Racial Bias," www.usatoday.com/news/health/weightloss/2008-05-20-overweight-bias_N.htm, accessed January 21, 2009.

79. "American Airlines, Worldwide Flight Sued by EEOC Over Questioning of Applicants," *BNA Fair Employment Practices* (October 12, 2000): 125.

80. See, for example, www.eeoc.gov/policy/docs/guidanceinquiries. html, accessed June 28, 2009.

81. This is based on *Anderson* and *Levin-Epstein, Primer of Equal Opportunity*, 93–97.

82. "EEOC Issues New Enforcement Guidance on Discrimination in Employee Benefits," *BNA Fair Employment Practices* (October 12, 2000): 123.

83 Matthew Miklaue, "Sorting Out a Claim of Bias," *Workforce* 80, no. 6 (June 2001): 102–103. Dress codes are a different matter. For example, the U.S. Court of Appeals for the Third Circuit recently upheld the city of Philadelphia's decision to refuse to relax its dress code to permit a female Muslim police officer to wear a headscarf while in uniform. "City Can Bar Muslim Police Woman from Wearing Scarf," *BNA Bulletin to Management* (April 21, 2009): 126.

84. In 2007, the U.S. Supreme Court, in *Ledbetter* v. *Goodyear Tire & Rubber Company* held that employees claiming Title VII pay discrimination must file their claims within 180 days of when they first receive the allegedly discriminatory pay. In 2009, Congress formulated and the president signed new legislation enabling employees to file claims anytime, as long as the person is still receiving a paycheck.

85. "Record Monetary Results at EEOC," *BNA Bulletin to Management* (November 24, 2009): 375.

86. eeoc.gov/eeoc/initiatives/e-race/index.cfm, accessed May 29, 2010.

87. Mark Schoef, "Walgreens Suit Reflects EEOC's Latest Strategies," *Workforce Management* (March 26, 2007): 8.

88. www.eeoc.gov/mediate/facts.html, accessed June 29, 2009.

89. Timothy Bland, "Sealed Without a Kiss," *HR Magazine* (October 2000): 85–92.

90. "EEOC Has 18 Nationwide, 300 Local Accords with Employers to Mediate Job Bias Claims Charges," *BNA Human Resources Report* (October 13, 2003): H-081; www.eeoc.gov/mediate/index.html, accessed April 12, 2008.

91. Bland, "Sealed Without a Kiss," 85–92.

92. "Conducting Effective Investigations of Employee Bias Complaints," *BNA Fair Employment Practices* (July 13, 1995): 81.

93. Jonathan Zeigert and Paul Hangies, "Employment Discrimination: The Role of Implicit Attitudes, Motivation, and a Climate for Racial Bias," *Journal of Applied Psychology* 90, no. 3 (2005): 553–562.

94. See, for example, "Diversity Is Used as Business Advantage by Three Fourths of Companies, Survey Says," *BNA Bulletin to Management* (November 7, 2006): 355.

95. Brian O'Leary and Bart Weathington, "Beyond the Business Case for Diversity in Organizations," *Employee Responsibilities and Rights* 18, no. 4 (December 2006): 283–292.

96. See for example, Michael Carrell and Everett Mann, "Defining Work-Force Diversity in Public Sector Organizations," *Public Personnel Management* 24, no. 1 (Spring 1995): 99–111; Richard Koonce, "Redefining Diversity," *Training and Development Journal* (December 2001): 22–33; Kathryn Canas and Harris Sondak, *Opportunities and Challenges of Workplace Diversity* (Upper Saddle River, NJ: Pearson, 2008), 3–27. One writer lists race and ethnicity diversity, gender diversity, age diversity, disability diversity, sexual orientation diversity, and cultural and national origin diversity as examples. Lynn Shore et al., "Diversity in Organizations: Where Are We Now and Where Are We Going?" *Human Resource Management Review* 19 (2009): 117–133.

97. Cox, op cit., 88.

98. Taylor Cox, Jr., *Cultural Diversity in Organizations* (San Francisco, CA: Berrett Kohler Publishers, Inc., 1993): 64.

99. Ibid., 179–180.

100. J. H. Greenhaus and S. Parasuraman, "Job Performance Attributions and Career Advancement Prospects: An Examination of Gender and Race Affects," *Organizational Behavior and Human Decision Processes* 55 (July 1993): 273–298.

101. Patrick McKay et al., "A Tale of Two Climates: Diversity Climate from Subordinates and Managers Perspectives and Their Role in Store Unit Sales Performance," *Personnel Psychology* 62 (2009): 767–791.

102. David Thomas, "Diversity as Strategy," *Harvard Business Review* (September 2004): 98–104; See also J. T. Childs Jr., "Managing Global Diversity at IBM: A Global HR Topic that Has Arrived," *Human Resource Management* 44, no. 1 (Spring 2005): 73–77.

103. Thomas, op. cit., 99.

104. As another example, leaders who facilitated high levels of power sharing within their groups helped to reduce the frequently observed positive relationship between increased diversity and increased turnover. But, leaders who were inclusive of only a select few followers "may actually exacerbate the relationship between diversity and turnover." (1422) Lisa Nishii and David Mayer, "Do Inclusive Leaders Help to Reduce Turnover in Diverse Groups? The Moderating Role of a Leader–Member Exchange in the Diversity to Turn over Relationship," *Journal of Applied Psychology* 94, no. 6 (2009): 1412–1426.

105. Patricia Digh, "Creating a New Balance Sheet: The Need for Better Diversity Metrics," *Mosaics*, Society for Human Resource Management (September/October 1999): 1. For diversity management steps see Taylor Cox, Jr., *Cultural Diversity in Organizations: Theory, Research and Practice* (San Francisco: Berrett-Koehler, 1993): 236; see also Richard Bucher, "Diversity Consciousness" (Upper Saddle River, NJ: 2004): 109–137.

106. Richard Bucher, *Diversity Consciousness: Opening Our Minds to People, Cultures, and Opportunities* (Upper Saddle River, NJ: Pearson Prentice Hall, 2004): 132–133.

107. Frank Jossi, "Reporting Race," *HR Magazine* (September 2000): 87–94.

108. U.S. Equal Employment Opportunity Commission, *Affirmative Action and Equal Employment* (Washington, D.C.: January 1974). See also David Kravitz and Steven Klineberg, "Reactions to Two Versions of Affirmative-Action Among Whites, Blacks, and Hispanics," *Journal of Applied Psychology* 85, no. 4 (2000): 597–611.

109. Ibid, 133.

110. David Harrison et al., "Understanding Attitudes toward Affirmative Action Programs in Employment: Summary and Meta-Analysis of 35 Years of Research," *Journal of Applied Psychology* 91, no. 5 (2006): 1031–1036.

111. http://newsfeedresearcher.com/data/articles_n17/tests-city-court.html, accessed April 24, 2009.

112. James Coil, III and Charles Rice, "Managing Work-Force Diversity in the Nineties: The Impact of the Civil Rights Act of 1991," *Employee Relations Law Journal* 18 (Spring 1993): 548. See also Norma Carr-Ruffino, *Making Diversity Work* (Upper Saddle River, NJ: Prentice Hall, 2006): 2–28.

113. Coil and Rice, 562–563.

114. Manuel Velasquez, *Business Ethics: Concepts and Cases* (Upper Saddle River, NJ: Prentice Hall, 1992): 9. See also Kate Walter, "Ethics Hot Lines Tap into More Than Wrongdoing," *HR Magazine* (September 1995): 79–85; Skip Kaltenheuser, "Bribery Is Being Outlawed Virtually Worldwide," *Business Ethics* (May 1998): 11.

115. Lauren Weber, "Jury Awards Worker $7.5 Million in Wal-Mart Disability Discrimination," *Knight-Ridder/Tribune Business News* (February 25, 2005).

3

Strategic Human Resource Management

SYNOPSIS

- What Is Strategic Human Resource Management?
- Why Strategic Planning Is Important to All Managers
- The Strategic Management Process

- Human Resource Manager's Role in Strategic Planning
- Strategic HR in Action: Human Resource Management's Role in Mergers and Acquisitions

Source: Xiang Sheren/Newscom.

When you finish studying this chapter, you should be able to:

1. Outline the steps in the strategic management process.
2. Explain and give examples of each type of company-wide and competitive strategy.
3. Explain how employers create competitive advantage through human resource management.
4. Define and give several examples of strategic human resource management.
5. Learn how to devise human resource practices to support the employer's business strategy.

INTRODUCTION

A few years ago, Shanghai China's Portman Shangri-La Hotel was a very good but not extraordinary property. Employee and guest satisfaction ratings averaged around 75%. Financial results were not exceptional.[1] When it took over managing the hotel, The Ritz-Carlton Hotel Company installed a new general manager, and the hotel was renamed The Portman Ritz-Carlton, Shanghai. Together the new management team set out to turn the hotel into a premier property. They built their strategy for doing so partly around superior customer service. A Ritz-Carlton Company motto is, "We are Ladies and Gentlemen serving Ladies and Gentlemen." Management knew the hotel's employees were crucial to their effort: "We're a service business, and service comes only from people." Management introduced the Ritz-Carlton Company's human resource system, including new employee selection standards and training. The efforts paid off. Since then, The Portman Ritz-Carlton, Shanghai, was named the "Best Employer in Asia" and the "best business hotel in China," and the China National Tourism Administration recognized it as Shanghai's only Platinum Five-Star winner.[2] ■

strategic human resource management

Formulating and executing human resource policies and practices that produce the employee competencies and behaviors the company needs to achieve its strategic aims.

WHAT IS STRATEGIC HUMAN RESOURCE MANAGEMENT?

The Portman Ritz-Carlton's turnaround illustrates what managers mean by "strategic human resource management." We'll see in this chapter that **strategic human resource management** means *formulating and executing human resource policies and practices that produce the employee competencies and behaviors the company needs to achieve its strategic aims.* The basic idea behind strategic human resource management is simple but easily missed. The basic idea is this: "in formulating human resource management policies and activities, the manager's goal must be to produce the employee skills and behaviors that the company needs to achieve its strategic aims." We can summarize the process as follows: First, *decide what the strategic goals are,* then *identify the employee skills and behaviors that achieving these goals require,* and then *formulate human resource management policies and practices that will produce these required employee skills and behaviors.*

The Portman Ritz-Carlton, Shanghai Example

The Portman Shangri-La's new management team followed this strategic human resource management process. Here's how:

- *Strategically,* they aimed to make the renamed Portman Ritz-Carlton, Shanghai, an outstanding property by offering superior customer service.
- To achieve this, the hotel's employees would have to exhibit new *skills and behaviors.* For example, they would have to be proactive about providing superior customer service.
- To produce these employee skills and behaviors, management introduced the Ritz-Carlton Hotel Company's *human resource system and practices.* For example, even the hotel's top executive personally interviewed each candidate. Managers delved deeply into each candidate's values. They hired only employees who cared for and respected others: "our selection focuses on talent and personal values because these are things that can't be taught . . . it's about caring for and respecting others."[3]

This new human resource strategy, plus other changes such as a major renovation, helped turn The Portman Ritz-Carlton, Shanghai, into an extraordinary hotel.

In this chapter, we'll focus on what managers need to know about strategic planning and its relationship to human resource management policies and practices. We'll turn first to a quick overview of why strategic planning is important.

WHY STRATEGIC PLANNING IS IMPORTANT TO ALL MANAGERS

You may not realize it when you're managing, but your company's strategic plan is guiding much of what you do. Management expert Peter Drucker once said that management " . . . is the responsibility for execution." What he meant is that as a manager you'll be judged on at least one thing—on the extent to which you accomplished your unit's goals. Organizations exist to achieve some purpose, and if they fail to achieve their ends, to that extent they have failed. As Drucker also said, "there has to be something to point to and say, [we] have not worked in vain." Those aims or goals—and the hard work you put into accomplishing them—all depend on your company's plan. All your personnel and other decisions—what sorts of people you hire and how you hire them, what you train them to do, and how you appraise and reward them, for instance—depend on the goals that trickled down to you from your firm's overall plan. We'll look more closely at your role in strategic planning in this chapter.

The Hierarchy of Goals

For now, it will suffice to give you just a bird's-eye view of why strategic planning is important to you. It is important because in well-run companies the goals from the very top of the organization chart down to where you're working form a more-or-less unbroken chain (or "hierarchy") of goals. These goals should be guiding what you do.

We can use a hierarchy of goals diagram as in Figure 3.1 to summarize this. At the top of the company, the president and his or her staff set strategic goals (such as to "Double sales revenue to $16 million in fiscal year 2011"). Lower-level managers (in this case, vice presidents) then set goals (such as to "Add one production line at plant"). These goals should flow from and make sense in terms of the goals at the next level up. (In other words, "What must I as production head do to help make sure that the company accomplishes its 'double sales' goal?") Then the vice presidents' subordinates set their own goals, and so on down the line.

In this way, the company creates a hierarchy or chain of departmental goals, from the top down to the lowest-ranked managers, and even employees. Then, if every one does his or her job—if each salesperson sells his or her quota, and the sales manager hires enough good salespeople, and the HR manager creates the right incentive plan, and the purchasing head buys enough raw materials—the company and the CEO should also accomplish the overall, company-wide strategic goals. You could therefore say with great certainty that without a clear plan at the top, no one in the company (including you and the other managers) would have the foggiest notion of what to do. At best, you'd all be working at cross-purposes. This hierarchy of goals flows from the company's basic planning process.

The Planning Process

People make plans every day, often without giving it a thought. We plan our routes to school or work, what courses to take, and what to do on Saturday night. Underlying all those plans, however, is an often unstated planning process.

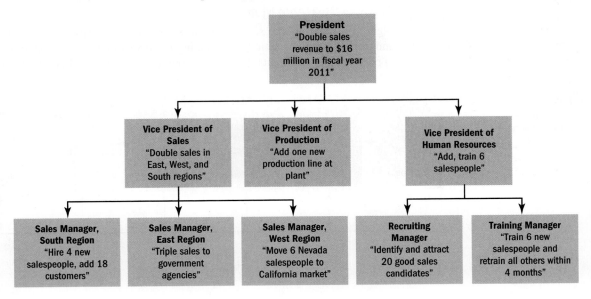

FIGURE 3.1

Sample Hierarchy of Goals Diagram for a Company

Consider how you might create a plan for your career. You might:

1. Tentatively *set an objective,* such as "to work as a management consultant."
2. *Make forecasts* (for instance, of industry trends and to check your basic assumptions about things like your strengths and weaknesses) to determine your consulting prospects.
3. *Determine what your alternatives are for getting from where you are now to where you want to be.* The point here is to help you identify what courses of action (including college major, summer experiences, etc.) will get you to your goal best.
4. *Evaluate your alternatives.*
5. Finally, implement and evaluate *your plan.*

That is all there is to the planning process. It hardly matters whether you're planning your career, a trip abroad, or how to sell your company's new product. The basic planning process always involves setting objectives, forecasting and assessing your basic planning "premises" or assumptions, determining alternative courses of action, evaluating which options are best, and then choosing and implementing your plan.

The process is the same when managers plan for their firms, with one small complication. We saw that there is usually a *hierarchical aspect* to managerial planning. First top management approves a long-term or strategic plan. Then each department, working with top management, creates its own subsidiary budgets, goals, and other plans to fit and to contribute to the company's overall strategic plan.

THE STRATEGIC MANAGEMENT PROCESS

A **strategic plan** is the company's plan for how it will match its internal strengths and weaknesses with external opportunities and threats in order to maintain a competitive advantage. The essence of **strategic planning** is to ask, "Where are we now as a business, where do we want to be, and how should we get there?" The manager then formulates specific (human resources and other) strategies to take the company from where it is now to where he or she wants it to be. When Yahoo! tries to figure out whether to sell its search business to Microsoft, or Citibank ponders whether to get out of the brokerage business, they're engaged in strategic planning. A **strategy** is a course of action. If Yahoo! decides it must raise money and focus more on applications like Yahoo! Finance, one strategy might be to sell Yahoo! Search. **Strategic management** is "the process of identifying and executing the organization's strategic plan, by matching the company's capabilities with the demands of its environment."

Steps in Strategic Management

Figure 3.2 sums up the strategic management process. This includes (1) defining the business and developing a mission, (2) evaluating the firm's internal and external strengths, weaknesses, opportunities, and threats, (3) formulating a new business direction, (4) translating the mission

---

strategic plan
The company's plan for how it will match its internal strengths and weaknesses with external opportunities and threats in order to maintain a competitive advantage.

strategic planning
The manager formulates specific strategies to take the company from where it is now to where he or she wants it to be.

strategy
The company's long-term plan for how it will balance its internal strengths and weaknesses with its external opportunities and threats to maintain a competitive advantage.

strategic management
The process of identifying and executing the organization's mission by matching its capabilities with the demands of its environment.

---

1 Outline the steps in the strategic management process.

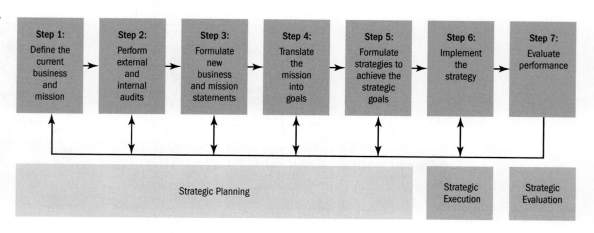

FIGURE 3.2
The Strategic Management Process

into strategic goals, and (5) formulating strategies or courses of action. Step (6) and step (7) then entail implementing and then evaluating the strategic plan. Let's look at each step.

Step 1: **Define the Current Business** A logical place to start is by defining one's current business. Specifically, what products do we sell, where do we sell them, and how do our products or services differ from our competitors? For example, Rolex and Casio both sell watches. But there the similarity ends. Rolex sells a limited line of expensive watches. Casio sells a variety of relatively inexpensive but innovative specialty watches with features like compasses and altimeters.

Step 2: **Perform External and Internal Audits** The next step is to ask, "Are we heading in the right direction?" No one is immune to competitive pressures. Yahoo!'s search tool was on top of the world until Google came along. Amazon's Kindle Reader launch forced even more bookstores to close, and then the iPad gave the Kindle its own competition. Prudent managers periodically assess what's happening in their environments.

You can use two tools to help here. The *environmental scanning worksheet* in Figure 3.3 is a simple guide for compiling relevant information about the company's environment. This includes things like economic, competitive, and political trends that may affect the

FIGURE 3.3

Worksheet for Environmental Scanning

Economic Trends
(such as recession, inflation, employment, monetary policies)
_____
_____
_____
_____

Competitive and Market Trends
(such as market/customer trends, entry/exit of competitors, new products from competitors)
_____
_____
_____
_____

Political Trends
(such as legislation and regulation/deregulation)
_____
_____
_____
_____

Technological Trends
(such as introduction of new production/distribution technologies, rate of product obsolescence, trends in availability of supplies and raw materials)
_____
_____
_____
_____

Social Trends
(such as demographic trends, mobility, education, evolving values)
_____
_____
_____
_____

Geographic Trends
(such as opening/closing of new markets, factors affecting current plant/office facilities location decisions)
_____
_____
_____
_____

POTENTIAL STRENGTHS	**POTENTIAL WEAKNESSES**
• Market leadership • Strong research and development • High-quality products • Cost advantages • Patents	• Large inventories • Excess capacity for market • Management turnover • Weak market image • Lack of management depth
POTENTIAL OPPORTUNITIES	**POTENTIAL THREATS**
• New overseas markets • Failing trade barriers • Competitors failing • Diversification • Economy rebounding	• Market saturation • Threat of takeover • Low-cost foreign competition • Slower market growth • Growing government regulation

company. The *SWOT chart* in Figure 3.4 is the 800-pound guerrilla of strategic planning; everyone uses it. Managers use it to compile and organize the company's strengths, weaknesses, opportunities, and threats. The idea, of course, is to create a strategy that makes sense in terms of the company's strengths, weaknesses, opportunities, and threats.

LEVERAGING In creating a new strategy, strategy experts counsel against blindly avoiding strategies that may seem to be beyond the company's capabilities. They argue there are times when, to pursue great opportunities, you should underplay the firm's weaknesses, and instead capitalize on ("leverage") your unique company strength.

For example, strategy experts Hamel and Prahalad say that if modest resources were an insurmountable deterrent, relatively small firms like Honda could not have put GM and Ford on the defensive. And, Apple—competing against giants like Microsoft—capitalized on its competitive strengths (including very creative employees) in innovating new products like the iPhone and iPad.

Step 3: **Formulate a New Direction** The question now is, based on the environmental scan and SWOT analysis, what should our new business be, in terms of three things—what products we will sell, where we will sell them, and how our products or services will differ from those of our competitors?

Managers sometimes formulate a *vision statement* to summarize how they see the essence of their business down the road. The **vision statement** is a general statement of the firm's intended direction and shows, in broad terms, "what we want to become."[4] Rupert Murdoch, chairman of News Corporation (which owns MySpace.com, the Fox network, and many newspapers and satellite TV businesses), has a vision of an integrated, global

vision statement
A general statement of the company's intended direction that evokes emotional feelings in organization members.

Rupert Murdoch, chairman and chief executive officer of News Corp., has a vision for News Corporation.

Indra C. Nooyi, Chairman and CEO, PepsiCo.

Source: Pepsi-Cola North America.

satellite-based news-gathering, entertainment, and multimedia firm. PepsiCo's latest vision is "Performance with Purpose." PepsiCo's CEO Indra Nooyi says the company's executives choose businesses to be in and make decisions based on Performance with Purpose's three pillars, namely human sustainability, environmental sustainability, and talent sustainability.[5]

Whereas vision statements usually describe in broad terms what the business should be, the company's **mission statement** summarizes what the company's main tasks are now. Before the recent downturn, Ford pursued and then strayed from a remarkably successful mission, summed up by the phrase, "Where Quality Is Job One."

Step 4: **Translate the Mission into Strategic Goals** Saying the mission is "to make quality job one" is one thing; operationalizing that mission for your managers is another. The company and its managers need strategic goals. At Ford, for example, what exactly did "Quality Is Job One" mean for each department in terms of how they would boost quality? The answer is that its managers had to meet strict goals such as "no more than 1 initial defect per 10,000 cars."

Step 5: **Formulate Strategies to Achieve the Strategic Goals** Next, the manager chooses strategies—courses of action—that will enable the company to achieve its strategic goals. For example, what strategies could Ford pursue to hit its goal of no more than 1 initial defect per 10,000 cars? Perhaps open two new high-tech plants, reduce the number of car lines to better focus on just a few, and pursue a partnership with a firm known for quality cars, like Honda.

mission statement
Spells out who the company is, what it does, and where it's headed.

Step 6: **Implement the Strategies** Strategy implementation (or execution) means translating the strategies into action. The company's managers do this by actually hiring (or firing) people, building (or closing) plants, and adding (or eliminating) products and product lines.

Step 7: **Evaluate Performance** Things don't always turn out as planned. For example, a few years before the recent recession, Ford bought Jaguar and Land Rover to reduce reliance on lower-profit cars. With auto competition brutal, Ford announced in 2009 it was selling Jaguar and Land Rover (to Tata, a company in India). It wants to focus its scarce resources on modernizing and turning around its struggling North American operations. Like all companies, Ford continually needs to assess its strategic decisions.

Improving Productivity through HRIS: Using Computerized Business Planning Software

Business planning software packages are available to assist the manager in writing strategic and business plans. CheckMATE (www.checkmateplan.com) uses strategic planning tools such as SWOT analysis to enable even users with no prior planning experience to develop sophisticated strategic plans.[6] Business Plan Pro from Palo Alto Software contains all the information and planning aids you need to create a business plan. It contains 30 sample plans, step-by-step instructions (with examples) for creating each part of a plan (executive summary, market analysis, and so on), financial planning spreadsheets, easy-to-use tables (for instance, for making sales forecasts), and automatic programs for creating color 3-D charts for showing things like monthly sales and yearly profits.

2 Explain and give examples of each type of company-wide and competitive strategy.

Types of Strategies

Managers formulate three types of strategic plans, depending on the level of their companies for which they are formulating plans (see Figure 3.5, page 60). There is corporate-wide planning, business unit (or competitive) planning, and functional (or departmental) planning. We'll look at each.

corporate strategy
Identifies the sorts of businesses that will comprise the company and the ways in which these businesses relate to each other.

CORPORATE STRATEGY First, every company needs a *corporate strategy*. At the overall corporate level, a company's **corporate strategy** identifies the sorts of businesses that will comprise the company and the ways in which these businesses relate to each other. For example, PepsiCo doesn't just make Pepsi. Instead, PepsiCo is comprised of four main businesses: Frito-Lay North America, PepsiCo Beverages North America, PepsiCo International, and Quaker Oats North America.[7] PepsiCo thus bases its corporate strategy on expanding abroad, and on diversifying into food businesses related to its famous Pepsi brand beverages.

FIGURE 3.5

Type of Strategy at Each Company Level

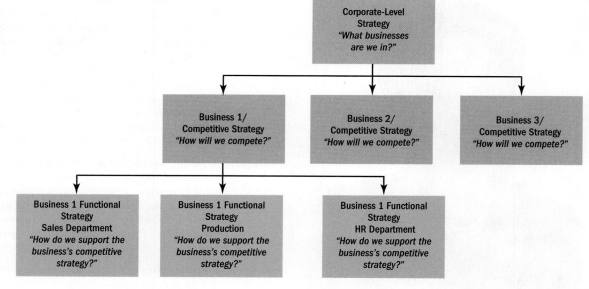

Companies can pursue several generic (or standard) corporate strategic options when deciding on what basis to build their business portfolio:

- A *diversification* corporate strategy implies that the firm will expand by adding new product lines.
- A *vertical integration* strategy means the firm expands by, perhaps, producing its own raw materials, or selling its products direct.
- A *consolidation* strategy means reducing the company's size.
- *Geographic expansion* means expanding the firm into new locations, for example, taking the business abroad.
- A *concentration* strategy means the firm opts to limit itself to one line of business—McDonald's is an example of such a "one business" business.

competitive strategy
Identifies how to build and strengthen the business's long-term competitive position in the marketplace.

competitive advantage
Any factors that allow an organization to differentiate its product or service from those of its competitors to increase market share.

COMPETITIVE STRATEGY At the next level down, each of these businesses (such as Frito-Lay) needs its own *business-level/competitive strategy*. A **competitive strategy** identifies how to build and strengthen the business's long-term competitive position in the marketplace.[8] It identifies, for instance, how Pizza Hut will compete with Papa John's or how Walmart competes with Target. Companies try to achieve competitive advantages for each business they are in. We can define **competitive advantage** as any factors that allow a company to differentiate its product or service from those of its competitors to increase market share. Companies use several generic competitive strategies to achieve competitive advantage:

- *Cost leadership* means the enterprise aims to become the low-cost leader in an industry. Dell is an example. It maintains its competitive advantage through its Internet-based sales-processing and distribution system, and by selling direct.
- *Differentiation* is a second example of a competitive strategy. In a differentiation strategy, a firm seeks to be unique in its industry along dimensions that are widely valued by buyers.[9] Thus, Papa John's Pizza stresses fresh ingredients, Target sells somewhat more upscale brands than Walmart, and Mercedes-Benz emphasizes reliability and quality. Like Mercedes-Benz, firms can charge a premium if they stake a claim to being substantially different from competitors in some coveted way.
- *Focusers* carve out a market niche (like Ferrari). They compete by providing a product or service customers can get in no other way.

FUNCTIONAL STRATEGY Finally, each individual business (like Frito-Lay or Quaker Oats) is composed of departments, such as manufacturing, sales, and human resource management.

functional strategies
Identify the basic courses of action that each department will pursue in order to help the business attain its competitive goals.

Functional strategies identify the basic courses of action that each department will pursue in order to help the business attain its competitive goals.

The firm's functional strategies should make sense in terms of its business/competitive strategy. For example, consider The Portman Ritz-Carlton Hotel's human resource management strategies (interviewing each candidate, screening based on values, and so on). These aim to support management's efforts to offer premier customer service as the hotel's competitive advantage.

3 Explain how employers create competitive advantage through human resource management.

How Human Resource Management Creates Competitive Advantage

Every successful company needs a competitive advantage if it is to differentiate its product or service from those of its competitors, and many companies today build their competitive advantages around their employees. For example, Apple has creative engineers producing innovative products. Southwest Airlines keeps costs low in part because its personnel policies produce motivated workers doing things like turning planes around quickly.

As another example, computerized factories might seem to run themselves, but even here, "human capital"—highly trained and motivated employees—sets successful plants apart. A Harvard production expert studied manufacturing firms that installed computer-integrated manufacturing systems to boost efficiency. He summed his findings as follows:

> All the data in my study point to one conclusion: Operational flexibility is determined primarily by a plant's operators and the extent to which managers cultivate, measure, and communicate with them. Equipment and computer integration are secondary.[10]

Throughout this book you'll find examples of how human resource departments help to create such employee-based competitive advantages. Longo Toyota in El Monte, California, provides one example.

LONGO TOYOTA EXAMPLE Some employers assume that workforce diversity always creates conflict and higher cost. But the Longo Toyota dealership in El Monte, California, uses human resource policies and practices to actually encourage hiring and developing salespeople who speak everything from Spanish and Korean to Tagalog. Workforce diversity is Longo's big competitive advantage.

Because of that human resource strategy, Longo is a top-grossing auto dealer. With a 60-person sales force that speaks more than 20 languages, Longo's staff offers a powerful competitive advantage for serving El Monte's highly diverse customer base. While other dealerships lose half of their salespeople each year, Longo retains 90% of its staff; it does this in part by emphasizing a promotion-from-within policy (more than two-thirds of its managers are minorities). It also

Workforce diversity is Longo Toyota's big competitive advantage.

Source: Tony Freeman/PhotoEdit Inc.

took steps to attract more women. For instance, Longo assigned a sales management person to provide the training that inexperienced salespeople need.

The bottom line is that in a business in which competitors can easily imitate products and showrooms, Longo built a competitive advantage based on employee diversity.

Strategic Human Resource Management

4 Define and give several examples of strategic human resource management.

Longo and other effective employers use strategic human resource management to build the employee skills and behaviors that they need to achieve their strategic goals. We saw that strategic human resource management means *formulating and executing human resource policies and practices that produce the employee competencies and behaviors the company needs to achieve its strategic aims.* The basic process of strategic human resource management is simple. First, *decide what the strategic goals are,* then *identify the employee skills and behaviors that achieving these goals require,* and then *formulate human resource management policies and practices that will produce these required employee skills and behaviors.*

HUMAN RESOURCE STRATEGIES Managers use the term *human resource strategies* to refer to the specific human resource management functional policies and practices the company uses to help achieve its strategic aims.[11] For example, Longo hires, trains, and rewards a diverse workforce. One of FedEx's strategic aims is to achieve superior levels of customer service through a highly committed workforce. FedEx's human resource strategies stem from this aim. They include building two-way communications, screening out potential managers whose values are not people-oriented, guaranteeing fair treatment and employee security, and utilizing promotion-from-within to give employees opportunities to realize their potential. Figure 3.6 illustrates this idea.

SOUTHWEST AIRLINES EXAMPLE Most of the passengers boarding Southwest Airlines' flight 172 from Salt Lake City to Las Vegas probably aren't thinking about how Southwest keeps its prices low. Those who are may assume it's Southwest's new planes, or fuel-buying policies—but those aren't the main reasons. If they were, American and United could just copy Southwest.

Southwest's real secret is its human resource management strategies. Strategic human resource management means formulating and executing human resource management policies and practices that produce the employee competencies and behaviors the company needs to achieve its strategic aims. Let's see how Southwest does this.

- What are Southwest's aims? Its basic aim is to deliver low-cost, convenient service on short-haul routes.
- How does it do this? One big way is by getting fast, 15-minute turnarounds at the gate, thus keeping planes flying longer hours than rivals do.

FIGURE 3.6

Linking Company-Wide and HR Strategies

Source: © Gary Dessler, Ph.D., 2010.

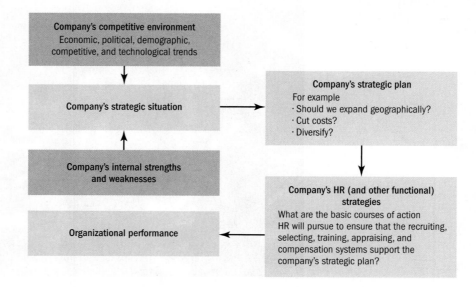

- What employee competencies and skills does Southwest need for these fast turnarounds? Ground crews, gate employees, and even pilots who all pitch in and do what it takes to get planes turned around.
- And what human resource management policies and practices would produce such employee competencies and behaviors? Ones built on high compensation, flexible job assignments, cross training, and employee stock ownership.
- We can outline this as follows: (1) high compensation, flexible work assignments, and so forth, *lead to* (2) motivated flexible ground crews and employees, *who do whatever it takes to* (3) turn the planes around in 15 minutes, *so that* (4) Southwest achieves its strategic aims of delivering low-cost, convenient service.

Challenging times mean that employers must adjust their human resource management plans and policies to reduce costs and improve efficiencies. The Managing HR in Challenging Times feature illustrates this.

MANAGING HR IN CHALLENGING TIMES

Adjusting HR Policies to Challenging Times

As the economy tanked in 2008, the HR consulting firm Watson Wyatt asked human resource managers, "Given the events in 2008 in the economy and financial markets, what changes have you made or do you expect to make in HR policies?" They surveyed the managers in October 2008 and in December 2008. It was clear that between October and December HR managers accelerated their policy changes. By December 2008, for instance, 48% were restricting company travel, 47% implemented a hiring freeze, 39% were laying off workers, 35% had downgraded or cancelled the holiday party, and 28% had eliminated or reduced hiring of temporary workers.

Source: Watson Wyatt, *Effect of Economic Crisis on HR Programs, Update* (December 2008): p. 5.

HUMAN RESOURCE MANAGER'S ROLE IN STRATEGIC PLANNING

Human resource manager's role in strategic planning is growing but still limited. Only about half of employers in one survey said senior human resource managers were involved in developing their companies' plans.[12] A survey by the Society for Human Resource Management demonstrates the current situation regarding employers' use of strategic human resource management.[13] About 75% of the human resource managers surveyed said their companies had strategic plans. However, only about 56% of the firms with strategic plans in place said their human resources departments had their own HR department strategic plans.

Table 3.1 summarizes these latter results. As you can see, 56% of the HR managers say "to a large extent" they work closely with senior management in creating strategic plans; 68% say they do so with respect to actually implementing the plans. We'll look next at exactly how employers use HR managers to develop and execute their strategies.

TABLE 3.1 Extent of HR's Involvement in Strategic Planning (According to HR Managers)

(*n* = 236)	To a Large Extent	To Some Extent	To No Extent
HR works closely with senior management in implementing organizational strategies	68%	29%	3%
HR works closely with senior management in *creating* organizational strategies	56%	38%	6%
HR *implements* strategies and processes to drive business results	46%	49%	6%
The role of HR is increasingly more focused on strategic interests	43%	49%	8%
HR is involved in the development of the business goals	31%	55%	14%
HR is involved in monitoring the achievement of business goals	30%	49%	21%

Note: Percentages within each category may not total 100% due to rounding.
Source: Adapted from Society for Human Resource Management, 2006. www.shrm.org, accessed May 10, 2007.

HR's Strategy Execution Role

Strategy execution is traditionally the heart of the human resource manager's role in strategic planning. Top management formulates the company's corporate and competitive strategies. Then the human resource manager creates and implements human resource management policies and practices that make sense in terms of the company's goals. For example, The Portman Ritz-Carlton's human resource policies and practices helped improve customer service and thus make the hotel a premier property. Longo's human resource policies align the firm's diverse workforce with the needs of its equally diverse market area.

HR's Strategy Formulation Role

Beyond their traditional strategy execution role, human resource managers also increasingly help formulate the company's strategic plan.

EXTERNAL OPPORTUNITIES AND THREATS For example, the human resource manager is in a position to supply competitive intelligence for strategic planning. Details regarding competitors' incentive plans, opinion survey data from employees that elicit information about customer complaints, and information about pending legislation such as labor laws and mandatory health insurance are some examples. Furthermore:

> From public information and legitimate recruiting and interview activities, you ought to be able to construct organization charts, staffing levels, and group missions for the various organizational components of each of your major competitors. Your knowledge of how brands are sorted among sales divisions and who reports to whom can give important clues as to a competitor's strategic priorities. You may even know the record of accomplishment and characteristic behavior of the executives.[14]

INTERNAL STRENGTHS AND WEAKNESSES Human resource managers can also provide strategically useful insights regarding the company's own human strengths and weaknesses. For example, several years ago, Signicast Corp. of Wisconsin decided that to compete effectively, it had to move its operations to a new highly automated plant. However, doing so required that production workers exhibit a new set of skills. These included using computers, reading technical manuals, working in teams, and so on. Therefore, before the CEO could continue his strategic planning, he needed input from HR on his employees' competencies and skills. How many were computer literate? How many had the educational background to assimilate the new training? What math competencies did they have? And could the company provide the necessary training, on time, or would it have to turn to hiring all new workers?

Some firms, thanks to such input, even build new strategies around human resource strengths. For example, in the process of automating its factories, farm equipment manufacturer John Deere developed a workforce that was exceptionally expert in factory automation. This prompted the firm to start a new-technology division to offer automation services to other companies.

Offshoring (see the Global Issues in HR feature) illustrates an area in which human resource managers play both a strategic planning and execution role.

GLOBAL ISSUES IN HR

Dealing with Offshoring

In the film *Slumdog Millionaire,* the hero works in an Indian call center. Here hundreds of his colleagues spend their days juggling calls from client companies' users around the world. The client companies *offshored* this call-handling task to the call center's relatively low-paid employees.

Offshoring increasingly plays a role in employers' competitive strategies. **Offshoring** "is the exporting of jobs from developed countries to countries where labor and other costs are lower."[15] When a pharmaceutical company decides to have its drugs produced in China, or you find yourself on the phone with a call center employee in Bangalore, India, offshoring is taking place.

Historically, offshoring involved mostly lower skilled manufacturing jobs, as, say, clothing manufacturers chose to assemble their garments abroad. Increasingly however, employers—seeking to reduce costs and stay competitive—are offshoring thousands of higher skilled jobs, for instance, in financial, legal, and security analysis.

offshoring
Having local employees abroad do jobs that the firm's domestic employees previously did in-house.

The human resource manager plays a role at each stage of the offshoring decision. For example, the CEO should have the human resource team involved in the earliest stages of gathering information about things like the educational and pay levels of the countries to which the firm is thinking of offshoring jobs. However, HR's main involvement usually occurs once the company decides to offshore. For example, the human resource management team needs to establish policies governing things like compliance with ethical safety and work standards, and pay levels. Human resource management's involvement back home may be even more crucial. Current home-country employees and their unions may well resist the transfer of work. Maintaining employee commitment and maintaining open communications with employees is therefore important.[16]

Strategic Management Tools

Human resource (and other) managers use several tools to help them translate the company's strategic goals into specific human resource management policies and activities. Three important tools include the strategy map, the HR Scorecard, and the digital dashboard.

strategy map

A graphical tool that summarizes the chain of activities that contribute to a company's success.

STRATEGY MAP The **strategy map** is a graphical tool that summarizes the chain of activities that contribute to a company's success. It thus shows the "big picture" of how each department's performance contributes to achieving the company's overall strategic goals. It also helps the manager visualize the role his or her department plays in helping to execute the company's strategic plan.

Figure 3.7 presents a strategy map example, in this case for Southwest Airlines. Recall that Southwest has a low-cost leader strategy. The strategy map for Southwest succinctly lays out the hierarchy of major activities required for Southwest Airlines to succeed. At the top is achieving company-wide, strategic financial goals. Then the strategy map shows the chain of activities that help Southwest Airlines achieve these goals. For example, as we saw earlier in this chapter, to boost revenues and profitability Southwest needs to fly fewer planes (to keep costs down), maintain low prices, and maintain on-time flights, for instance.

In turn (further down the strategy map), on-time flights and low prices require fast turnaround. And, fast turnaround requires motivated ground and flight crews. The strategy map helps each department (including HR) visualize what it needs to do to support the company's low-cost strategy.

FIGURE 3.7

Strategy Map for Southwest Airlines

Source: Adapted from "Creating a Strategy Map," Ravi Tangri: Team @ TeamCHRYSALIS.com.

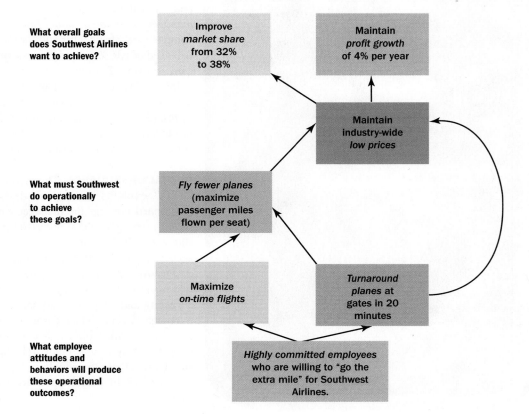

balanced scorecard

A process for assigning financial and nonfinancial goals to the chain of activities required for achieving the company's strategic aims and for continuously monitoring results.

HR Scorecard

A process for assigning financial and nonfinancial goals or *metrics* to the human resource management–related chain of activities required for achieving the company's strategic aims and for monitoring results.

digital dashboard

Presents the manager with desktop graphs and charts, so he or she gets a computerized picture of where the company stands on all those metrics from the HR Scorecard process.

THE BALANCED SCORECARD Many employers quantify and computerize this mapping approach, by answering, for example, "what do we mean by faster turnaround time?" and "what do we mean by on-time flights?"

The *balanced scorecard process* helps the manager do this. The **balanced scorecard** is not actually a scorecard; instead, it refers to a process for assigning financial and nonfinancial goals to the chain of activities required for achieving the company's strategic aims and for continuously monitoring results. Simply put, the idea is to take the strategy map and to quantify it. Specifically, the balanced scorecard process involves:

- Assigning financial and nonfinancial goals to the activities in the strategy map,
- Informing all employees of their goals,
- Monitoring and assessing performance, and
- Taking corrective action as required.

The "balanced" in balanced scorecard refers to a balance of goals. It includes a balance of financial and nonfinancial goals or measures, of short-term and long-term goals, and of external goals (for instance, what the customer thinks) and internal goals (for instance, airplane turnaround time). For example, Southwest might measure turnaround time in terms of "improve turnaround time from an average of 30 minutes per plane to 26 minutes per plane this year." It might measure customer satisfaction with periodic surveys.

The great advantage of the balanced scorecard process is that it is predictive. Traditional financial goals such as budgets are better at telling managers how they've done in the past than how they'll do tomorrow. On the other hand, continuously monitoring a balanced set of measures can signal problems ahead. For example, it might prompt a Southwest Airlines manager to say, "Our customer service ratings dipped, and, since customer service leads to more customers and in turn to future revenues, we should take corrective action now."

Human resource managers may want to focus not on the company's overall financial, marketing, and operational goals, but exclusively on those measures (or "metrics") that pertain to human resource management. The *HR Scorecard* helps them to do so. The **HR Scorecard** refers to a process for assigning financial and nonfinancial goals or metrics to *the human resource management–related chain of activities* required for achieving the company's strategic aims and for monitoring results.[17] For either a balanced or HR scorecard process, managers can use special scorecard software. For example, the computerized scorecard process helps the HR manager visualize and quantify the relationships between (1) the HR activities (amount of testing, training, and so forth), (2) the resulting employee behaviors (customer service, for instance), and (3) the resulting firm-wide strategic outcomes and performance (such as customer satisfaction and profitability).[18]

DIGITAL DASHBOARDS The saying "a picture is worth a thousand words" explains the digital dashboard's purpose. A **digital dashboard** presents the manager with desktop graphs and charts, so he or she gets a computerized picture of where the company stands on all those metrics from the HR Scorecard process (see accompanying illustration, page 67). For example, a top manager's dashboard for Southwest Airlines might display on the PC screen real-time trends for strategy map activities such as fast turnaround, attracting and keeping customers, and on-time flights. This gives the manager time to take corrective action. For example, if ground crews are turning planes around slower today, financial results tomorrow may decline unless the manager takes action. Figure 3.8 summarizes these three tools.

The HR in Practice feature summarizes the strategic HR process.

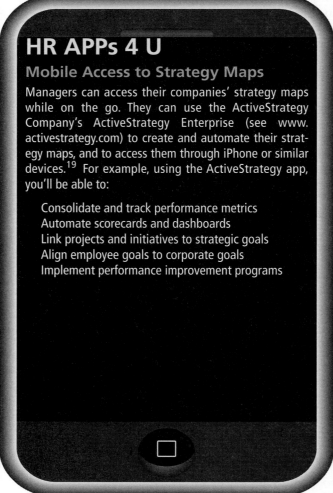

HR APPs 4 U

Mobile Access to Strategy Maps

Managers can access their companies' strategy maps while on the go. They can use the ActiveStrategy Company's ActiveStrategy Enterprise (see www.activestrategy.com) to create and automate their strategy maps, and to access them through iPhone or similar devices.[19] For example, using the ActiveStrategy app, you'll be able to:

Consolidate and track performance metrics
Automate scorecards and dashboards
Link projects and initiatives to strategic goals
Align employee goals to corporate goals
Implement performance improvement programs

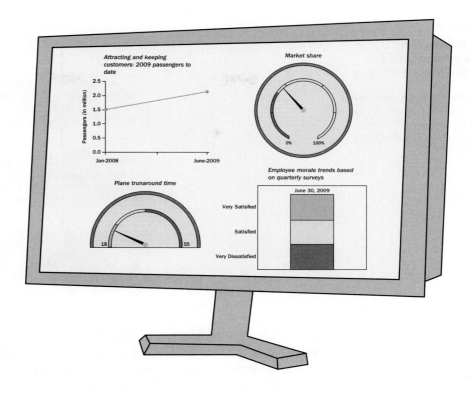

How to Translate Strategy into Human Resource Policy and Practice

How can a human resource manager translate the company's strategic plan into HR policies and practices?[20] Figure 3.9, page 68, outlines the basic process.

1. Management formulates a *strategic plan.*
2. The strategic plan implies certain *workforce requirements* in terms of the employee skills, attributes, and behaviors that the human resource management team must deliver to enable the business to achieve its strategic goals. (For example, must our employees improve customer service?[21] Do we need more computer-literate employees?)

3. Given these workforce requirements, formulate specific *HR strategies, policies, and practices* you believe will produce the desired workforce skills, attributes, and behaviors. (New selection, training, and compensation policies and practices, for instance.)[22]
4. Finally, identify measures you can use to gauge the extent to which your new policies and practices are actually producing the required employee competencies and skills, and thus supporting management's strategic goals. (For example, how many weeks of training per year do our employees receive?)

Strategy Map	HR Scorecard	Digital Dashboard
Graphical tool that summarizes the chain of activities that contribute to a company's success, and so shows employees the "big picture" of how their performance contributes to achieving the company's overall strategic goals.	A process for managing employee performance and for aligning all employees with key objectives, by assigning financial and nonfinancial goals, monitoring and assessing performance, and quickly taking corrective action.	Presents the manager with desktop graphs and charts, so he or she gets a picture of where the company has been and where it's going, in terms of each activity in the strategy map.

FIGURE 3.8

Three Important Strategic HR Tools

FIGURE 3.9

How to Align HR Strategy and Actions with Business Strategy

Source: Adapted from Garrett Walker and J. Randall MacDonald, "Designing and Implementing an HR Scorecard," *Human Resources Management* 40, no. 4 (2001): 370.

Formulate business strategy
"What are the strategic goals of the business?"

↓

Identify workforce requirements
"What employee competencies and behaviors must HR deliver to enable the business to reach its goals?"

↓

Formulate HR strategic policies and activities
"Which HR strategies and practices will produce these employee competencies and behaviors?"

↓

Develop detailed HR scorecard measures
"How can HR measure whether it is executing well for the business, in terms of producing the required workforce competencies and behaviors?"

---

5 Learn how to devise human resource practices to support the employer's business strategy.

Strategic Human Resource Management in Action: Einstein Medical Example

When a new CEO took over Einstein Medical Hospital in New York City, it was a single acute-care hospital, treating the seriously ill.[23] Technological changes, the growth of managed care, and significant cuts in Medicare meant that his company needed a new strategic plan. He and his management team followed the strategic human resource management process in formulating and executing a human resource management strategy for Einstein Medical:

1. They identified Einstein Medical's new strategy and goals
2. They identified the employee competencies required to support these aims
3. They installed the required HR policies and practices to produce these competencies
4. They achieved the medical center's strategic goals

Source: Paul Burns/Jupiter Images Royalty Free.

Einstein Medical's human resource manager had to ask, "What specific HR policies and practices will enable Einstein to create a dedicated, accountable, generative, and resilient workforce?"

EINSTEIN MEDICAL'S NEW STRATEGY AND GOALS The essence of the CEO's new strategy was to turn Einstein Medical into a multiple facility health care network, offering a range of health care services in several local markets. He knew that moving from a single acute-care hospital to a network of full-care facilities would require changes in how Einstein Medical's employees did things. For example, they'd have to help Einstein Medical *produce new services, capitalize on opportunities,* and offer consistently *high-quality services.*

NEW EMPLOYEE COMPETENCIES AND BEHAVIORS The CEO then asked, "What employee competencies, skills, and behaviors will Einstein Medical employees have to exhibit to help us to produce new services, capitalize on new opportunities, and offer high quality services?" He and his HR managers decided the employees would need to be *dedicated, accountable, generative, and resilient:*

1. They would have to be *dedicated* to Einstein's need to adapt.
2. They would have to take personal *accountability* for their results.
3. They would have to be *generative,* which means able and willing to apply new knowledge in a constant search for innovative solutions.
4. And they would have to be *resilient,* for instance, in terms of moving from job to job, as the company's needs changed.

NEW HUMAN RESOURCE POLICIES AND PRACTICES Einstein Medical's human resource manager then asked, "What specific HR policies and practices will enable us to create a dedicated, accountable, generative, and resilient workforce?" This led to several new human resource programs:

- New *training and communications programs* ensured that employees understood the company's new vision and what it would require of them.
- *Enriching work* involved providing employees with flexible assignments and team-based work.
- New *training and benefits programs* encouraged employees to take personal responsibility for their own improvement and personal development.
- New pay plans tied employees' rewards to Einstein Medical's results.
- *Improved selection, orientation, and dismissal procedures* helped Einstein find and keep a more dedicated, resilient, accountable, and generative workforce.

ACHIEVE STRATEGIC AIMS Combined with other actions, these human resource management activities helped Einstein Medical achieve its strategic aim of becoming a multiple location facility.

STRATEGIC HR IN ACTION: HUMAN RESOURCE MANAGEMENT'S ROLE IN MERGERS AND ACQUISITIONS

In one recent year, giant corporations or private equity firms acquired 42 of the Fortune 1000 corporations. (Private equity firms attract investor capital, which they then use to buy and improve companies, so as to sell them in several years at a profit.) For example, in 2010, Liberty Media acquired Live Nation. Thousands of smaller firms were similarly merged or acquired.[24]

The logic driving most of these strategic acquisitions is simple, and summed up by the word *synergy*. Synergy means cutting costs or boosting revenues (or both) by combining operations. Thus, when HP merged with Compaq some years ago, the idea was to enable the new HP to sell the same or more computers than did HP and Compaq alone (boost revenues), while eliminating duplicate accounting, advertising, sales, and other departments (cut expenses). Management gurus therefore sometimes define the synergy idea by saying it means "2 + 2 = 5." The plan is often to achieve such results by reducing the workforce.

Unfortunately, even with such layoffs (or, some would say, because of them), many mergers and acquisitions (M&As) fail to achieve their financial goals. Estimates vary, but, until recently, it appears that only about half of all mergers and acquisitions achieved their anticipated outcomes.[25] Some put the success rate at 40% or less.[26]

Why Should Human Resource Managers Be Involved in Mergers and Acquisitions?

Which brings us to an important point. When mergers and acquisitions fail, it's often not due to financial or technical issues (like inadequate financing) but to personnel-related ones. These may include, for example, employee resistance, mass exits by high-quality employees, declining morale and productivity, inadequate financial incentives, and unexpectedly high benefits expenses. Related problems include product development delays and customer defections.[27] As one study concluded some years ago, mergers and acquisitions often fail due to "a lack of adequate preparation of the personnel involved and a failure to provide training which fosters self-awareness, cultural sensitivity, and a spirit of cooperation."[28]

INVOLVEMENT BY HR It's therefore ironic that until recently CEOs rarely involved their human resource managers in planning the merger or acquisition. Surveys found that prior to 2000, HR executives usually just got involved at the post-merger integration stage. Today, by contrast, "close to two-thirds of the [survey] participants are involved in M&A due diligence now, and fully three-quarters expect a high degree of involvement in due diligence and future deals."[29]

Even private equity firms, known for their hard-nosed financial approach, increasingly tap human resource management expertise early on. For example, "because they are looking to sell the company for a profit within a few years, private equity investors turn to HR to create incentive plans with short-term goals of generating cash." HR can also provide critical early information (for instance, regarding which employees and executives to keep), as well as guidance in installing employee retention and incentive plans.[30] As the head of the M&A practice at one consulting firm put it, "there is a growing understanding that people issues can make or break a deal."[31]

HR INVOLVEMENT AND M&A RESULTS So, it may not be a coincidence that surveys show (1) a rise in M&A success as (2) employers have involved their human resource experts earlier. Prior to 2000, HR tended to be less involved, and (as noted) about half of all mergers and acquisitions failed to meet their shareholders expectations.[32]

In contrast, a more recent survey concluded that almost 80% of recent mergers and acquisitions had satisfactory results. The reason, in part, "is that HR functions now have far greater involvement in the process than in the past—at earlier stages as well . . ." and believe they are increasingly well-prepared to identify and address the many issues that might derail a merger.[33] Another survey of 1,310 human resource management professionals found that mergers in which top management asked human resource management to apply its expertise consistently outperformed those in which human resources was less involved.[34] Figure 3.10 summarizes the findings.

Examples of Human Resource Management's Specific Merger and Acquisition Roles

Companies benefit from human resource managers' expertise at the M&A *planning, due diligence,* and *integration* stages.

PLANNING STAGE In *planning* its initial offer, the acquiring team needs information about the acquisition target on matters such as total headcount, benefits and pension obligations, and pending litigation—all HR-related topics generally accessible via public sources.

DUE DILIGENCE STAGE Before finalizing a deal, it is usual for the acquirer (or merger partners) to perform due diligence reviews. These ensure they know what they're getting into. For human resource teams, due diligence reviews include reviewing, for instance, organizational structure, employee compensation and benefits, industrial relations, pending employee litigation, human resource policies and procedures, and key talent analysis.[35]

Employee benefits are another area for personnel due diligence. For example, do the target firm's health insurance contracts have termination clauses that could eliminate coverage for all employees if too many are laid off after the acquisition? How much do you estimate it will cost in separation benefits—severance, continuing health benefits, and higher unemployment compensation charges, for instance? [36]

INTEGRATION STAGE The human resource team also has responsibilities as the merger or acquisition moves into the integration stage. These include choosing the management team, communicating effectively with employees, retaining key talent, and aligning the cultures of the organizations.[37]

FIGURE 3.10

Percent of Successful Mergers in Which HR Manager Was Involved

Source: HR Magazine by Jeffrey Schmidt. Copyright 2001 by Society for Human Resource Management (SHRM). Reproduced with permission of Society for Human Resource Management (SHRM) in the format Textbook via Copyright Clearance Center.

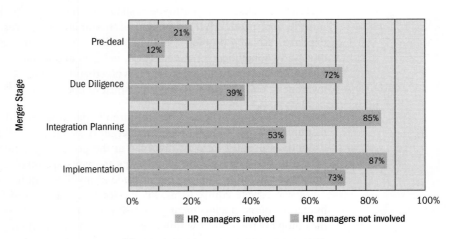

Percent of Successful Mergers

SHAW'S EXAMPLE Shaw's Supermarkets acquired Star Markets. At the time, Shaw's had 126 stores and Star had 54.[38] The acquisition prompted the two firms' human resource management teams to tackle numerous tasks. These included developing preliminary organizational designs and identifying the top three levels of management, assessing critical players and critical managers and employees in the new company, retention of key people, and planning for and executing the separation of redundant staff. They also had to develop a total rewards strategy for the combined company, develop and implement a communication strategy to inform employees about the acquisition, and integrate the payroll benefits and human resource information systems.[39]

REVIEW

SUMMARY

1. There are seven basic steps in the strategic management process: (1) Define the business and its mission, (2) perform an external and internal audit, (3) formulate new business and mission statements, (4) translate the mission into strategic goals, (5) formulate a strategy to achieve the strategic goals, (6) implement the strategy, and (7) evaluate performance.

2. There are three main types of strategic plans. The company's corporate strategy identifies the portfolio of businesses that in total comprise the company and includes diversification, vertical integration, consolidation, and geographic expansion. Each business needs a business level/competitive strategy: Differentiation and cost leadership are two examples. Finally, each individual business is composed of departments that require functional strategies. The latter identify the basic courses of action each department will pursue in order to help the business attain its strategic goals.

3. A strategy is a course of action. It shows how the enterprise will move from the business it is in now to the business it wants to be in, given its opportunities and threats and its internal strengths and weaknesses.

4. Strategic human resource management means formulating and executing HR systems that produce the employee competencies and behaviors the company requires to achieve its strategic aims.

5. The basic process of aligning human resource strategies and actions with business strategy entails four steps: (1) Formulate the business strategy, (2) identify the workforce (employee) behaviors needed to produce the outcomes that will help the company achieve its strategic goals, (3) formulate human resources strategic policies and actions to produce these employee behaviors, and (4) develop measures (metrics) to evaluate the human resources department's performance.

6. There's been a rise in M&A success as employers have involved their human resource experts earlier.

7. Top management requires HR expertise at the M&A *planning, due diligence,* and *integration* stages. In *planning* its initial offer, for example, the acquiring team will benefit from having information about the acquisition target on matters such as total headcount. Before finalizing a deal, HR due diligence reviews include reviewing, for instance, employee compensation and benefits, industrial relations, and pending employee litigation. As the merger or acquisition moves into the *integration* stage, critical HR team issues include ensuring effective top management leadership.

KEY TERMS

strategic human resource management   54
strategic plan   56
strategic planning   56
strategy   56
strategic management   56
vision statement   58
mission statement   59
corporate strategy   59

competitive strategy   60
competitive advantage   60
functional strategies   61
offshoring   64
strategy map   65
balanced scorecard   66
HR Scorecard   66
digital dashboard   66

DISCUSSION QUESTIONS

1. Outline the steps in the strategic management process.
2. Explain and give examples of each type of company-wide and competitive strategy.
3. Explain how employers create competitive advantage through human resource management.
4. Define and give several examples of strategic human resource management.
5. Give two examples of how a banker could use human resource practices to support his or her bank's business strategy.
6. Give an example of hierarchical planning in an organization.
7. List the main components of a business plan, and describe each briefly.
8. How would you suggest using human resource managers in deciding whether to pursue a particular merger or acquisition?
9. What is the difference between a strategy, a vision, and a mission? Give one example of each.
10. Define and give examples of the cost leadership competitive strategy and the differentiation competitive strategy.
11. Explain how human resource management can be instrumental in helping a company create a competitive advantage.
12. What do you think is meant by "HR adding value"? Provide several examples of how HR managers add value to their companies.
13. Define what an HR Scorecard is, and briefly explain its use.

INDIVIDUAL AND GROUP ACTIVITIES

1. With three or four other students, form a strategic management group for your college or university. Your assignment is to develop the outline of a strategic plan for the college or university. It should include mission and vision statements; strategic goals; and corporate, competitive, and functional strategies. In preparing your plan, make sure to show the main strengths, weaknesses, opportunities, and threats the college faces, and identify which prompted you to develop your particular strategic plans.
2. Using the Internet or library resources, analyze the annual reports of five companies. Bring to class examples of how those companies say they are using their HR processes to help the company achieve its strategic goals.
3. Interview an HR manager and write a short report on "The Strategic Roles of the HR Manager at XYZ Company."
4. Using the Internet or library resources, bring to class and discuss at least two examples of how companies are using an HR Scorecard to help create HR systems that support the company's strategic aims. Do all managers seem to mean the same thing when they refer to "HR Scorecards"? How do they differ?
5. It is probably safe to say that your career plan is one of the most important plans you'll ever create. Unfortunately, most people never lay out such a plan, or they don't realize they need one until it's too late. Using the concepts and techniques in this chapter, develop an outline of a career plan for yourself, one that has sufficient detail to provide direction for your career decisions over the next five years. Make sure to include measurable goals and/or milestones.

WEB-e's (WEB EXERCISES)

1. From Internet sources such as http://travel.nytimes.com/travel/guides/asia/china/shanghai/34221/portman-ritz-carlton-hotel/hotel-detail.html and www.tripadvisor.com, how does The Portman Ritz-Carlton, Shanghai, seem to be doing today? What specific information can you find that relates the Portman's HR practices to the quality of service at the hotel?
2. In 2009, Comcast Cable announced it was buying NBC/Universal to combine its own cable delivery business with NBC's content. Many thought the acquisition was ill-conceived, in part because the "content" employees' culture might differ from that of the cable employees' culture. Some of the concerns are illustrated at http://arstechnica.com/tech-policy/news/2010/02/congress-told-that-comcastnbc-merger-a-big-crapshoot.ars. Use other Internet sources to answer this question: How different are the two companies' cultures and how would you as CEO overcome those differences?

APPLICATION EXERCISES

HR IN ACTION CASE INCIDENT 1
Siemens Builds a Strategy-Oriented HR System

Siemens is a 150-year-old German company, but it's not the company it was even a few years ago. Until recently, Siemens focused on producing electrical products. Today the firm has diversified into software, engineering, and services, and is also global, with over 400,000 employees working in 190 countries. In other words, Siemens became a world leader by pursuing a corporate strategy that emphasized diversifying into high-tech products and services, and doing so on a global basis.

With a corporate strategy like that, human resource management plays a big role at Siemens. Sophisticated engineering and services require more focus on employee selection, training, and compensation than in the average firm, and globalization requires delivering these services globally. Siemens sums up the basic themes of its human resource strategy in several points. These include:

1. *A living Company is a learning Company.* The high-tech nature of Siemens's business means that employees must be able to learn on a continuing basis. Siemens uses its system of combined classroom and hands-on apprenticeship training around the world to help facilitate this. It also offers employees extensive continuing education and management development.
2. *Global teamwork is the key to developing and using all the potential of the firm's human resources.* Because it is so important for employees throughout Siemens to feel free to work together and interact, employees have to understand the whole process, not just bits and pieces. To support this, Siemens provides extensive training and development. It also ensures that all employees feel they're part of a strong, unifying corporate identity. For example, HR uses cross-border, cross-cultural experiences as prerequisites for career advances.
3. *A climate of mutual respect is the basis of all relationships— within the Company and with society.* Siemens contends that the wealth of nationalities, cultures, languages, and outlooks represented by its employees is one of its most valuable assets. It therefore engages in numerous HR activities aimed at building openness, transparency, and fairness, and in supporting diversity.

Questions

1. Based on the information in this case, provide examples, for Siemens, of at least four strategically required organizational outcomes and four required workforce competencies and behaviors.
2. Identify at least four strategically relevant HR system policies and activities that Siemens has instituted in order to help human resource management contribute to achieving Siemens' strategic goals.
3. Provide a brief illustrative outline of a strategy map for Siemens.

HR IN ACTION CASE INCIDENT 2
The Carter Cleaning Company: The High-Quality Work System

As a recent graduate and person who keeps up with the business press, Jennifer is familiar with the benefits of programs such as total quality management and high-quality work systems. She believes quality must be a cornerstone of Carter's competitive strategy.

Jack has installed a total quality program of sorts at Carter, and it has been in place for about 5 years. This program takes the form of employee meetings. Jack holds employee meetings periodically, but particularly when there is a serious problem in a store—such as poor-quality work or machine breakdowns. When problems like these arise, instead of trying to diagnose them himself or with Jennifer, he contacts all the employees in that store and meets with them as soon as the store closes. Hourly employees get extra pay for these meetings. The meetings have been fairly useful in helping Jack to identify and rectify several problems. For example, in one store all the fine white blouses were coming out looking dingy. It turned out that the cleaner-spotter had been ignoring the company rule that required cleaning ("boiling down") the perchloroethylene cleaning fluid before washing items like these. As a result, the fine white blouses were being washed in cleaning fluid that had residue from other, earlier washes.

Jennifer now wonders whether these employee meetings should be expanded to give the employees an even bigger role in managing the Carter stores' quality. "We can't be everywhere watching everything all the time," she said to her father. "Yes, but these people only earn about $8 per hour. Will they really want to act like mini-managers?" he replied.

Questions

1. Would you recommend that the Carters expand their quality program? If so, specifically what form should it take?
2. What specific sorts of HR policies and practices should Carter institute to execute successfully the new quality program?
3. Assume the Carters want to institute strategic human resource management practices as a test program in one of their stores. Write a one-page outline summarizing what such a program would consist of.

EXPERIENTIAL EXERCISE

Developing an HR Strategy for Starbucks

By 2009, Starbucks was facing serious challenges. Sales per store were stagnant or declining, and its growth rate and profitability were down. Many believed that its introduction of breakfast foods had diverted its "baristas" from their traditional jobs as coffee-preparation experts. McDonald's and Dunkin' Donuts were introducing lower priced but still high-grade coffees. Starbucks' former CEO stepped back into the company's top job. You need to help him formulate a new direction for his company.

Purpose: The purpose of this exercise is to give you experience in developing an HR strategy, in this case by developing one for Starbucks.

Required Understanding: You should be thoroughly familiar with the material in this chapter, including the "Einstein Medical" HR strategy example and Figure 3.6.

How to Set Up the Exercise/Instructions: Set up groups of three or four students for this exercise. You are probably already quite familiar with what it's like to have a cup of coffee or tea in a Starbucks coffee shop, but if not, spend some time in one prior to this exercise. Meet in groups and develop an outline for an HR strategy for Starbucks Corp. Your outline should include four basic elements, as follows: a basic business/competitive strategy for Starbucks, workforce requirements (in terms of employee competencies and behaviors) this strategy requires, specific HR policies and the activities necessary to produce these workforce requirements, and suggestions for metrics to use to measure the success of the HR strategy.

BUSINESS IN ACTION EDU-EXERCISE

Achieving Strategic Fit

Strategic planning expert Michael Porter says managers should ensure that their firms' functional department strategies make sense in terms of the business's competitive strategy. For example, Southwest Airlines pursues a low-cost leader strategy. It therefore tailors its functional activities to deliver low-cost, convenient service on its short-haul routes. It gets fast, 15-minute turnarounds at the gate, so it can keep its planes flying longer hours than rivals and have more departures with fewer aircraft. It also shuns frills like meals, assigned seats, and premium classes of service on which other full-service airlines build their competitive strategies.

Various Southwest Airlines sub-activities and decisions support each of these activities. For example, limited passenger service means no seat assignments, no baggage transfers, and limited use of travel agents. Highly productive ground crews mean high compensation, flexible union contracts, and a high level of employee stock ownership.

Questions

1. As this exercise does for Southwest Airlines, explain what activities at each level would support The Portman Ritz-Carlton, Shanghai's strategy.
2. How does Porter's strategic fit idea relate to the strategy mapping process we discussed in this chapter? Draw a strategy map for Southwest Airlines.

PERSONAL COMPETENCIES EDU-EXERCISE

Building Your *Organizational Culture* Skills

Sometimes, the most challenging aspect of a merger is blending the two firms' *organizational cultures*—the basic values its employees share and the ways in which these values manifest themselves in the companies' ways of doing things and in their employees' behavior. For example, one writer described Motorola's culture in the early 2000s as "stifling bureaucracy, snail-paced decision making . . . and internal competition so fierce that [former CEO] Galvin himself has referred to it as a 'culture of warring tribes.'"[40]

So, there you are. You take over a merged but struggling company. Backbiting, bureaucratic behavior, and disdain for clients are rampant. Having sized up the situation, what should you do to change the culture? The thing to keep in mind is that it is the manager's behavior, not just what he or she says, that molds what employees come to see as the firm's real values. Experts suggest taking the following actions.[41]

The first step is to understand the culture now. To do this:[42]

- *Observe the physical surroundings.* Look at how the employees dress, the openness among offices, the furniture and its placement, and any signs (such as a long list of activities that are "prohibited here").
- *Sit in on a team meeting.* How do the employees treat each other? Are the communications open or one-sided?
- *Listen to the language.* Is there a lot of talk about "quality," "perfection," and "going the extra mile"? Or is there more emphasis on "don't rock the boat," or "don't tell those people what we're doing"?
- *Note to whom you are introduced and how they act.* Is the person casual or formal, laid-back or serious?
- *Get the views of outsiders, including vendors, customers, and former employees.* What do they think of the firm? Do you get responses like "they're so bureaucratic that it takes a year to get an answer"?

Next, take steps to change the culture. Specifically:

- *Make it clear to your employees what you pay attention to, measure, and control.*
- *React appropriately* to critical incidents and organizational crises. For example, if you want to emphasize the value that "we're all in this together," don't react to declining profits by saying "it's their fault."
- *Use signs, symbols, stories, rites, and ceremonies* to signal your values. JCPenney prides itself on tradition. To support this, the firm inducts new management employees into the "Penney Partnership" at conferences where they commit to Penney's values of "honor, confidence, service, and cooperation."
- *Deliberately role model, teach, and coach the values you want to emphasize.* For example, Walmart founder Sam Walton lived the values "hard work, honesty, neighborliness, and thrift." He explained driving a pickup truck by saying, "If I drove a Rolls-Royce, what would I do with my dog?"
- *Communicate your priorities by how you appraise employees and allocate rewards.* For example, General Foods reoriented its strategy from cost control to diversification and sales growth. It supported these new priorities by linking bonuses to sales volume and new product development, rather than just increased earnings.

Questions

1. Given their strategy, what cultural values would you suggest that the management of The Portman Ritz-Carlton, Shanghai, aspire to? Why?
2. List four concrete things they can do to cultivate those values.

PART I VIDEO CASES APPENDIX
VIDEO 1: INTRODUCTION TO HUMAN RESOURCE MANAGEMENT AND STRATEGIC HUMAN RESOURCE MANAGEMENT

Video Title: Showtime

Showtime Networks operates cable networks and pay-per-view cable channels across the United States and in several countries abroad. As this video illustrates, its HR function supports corporate strategy by helping to determine what kind of employees are needed to keep the company in peak performance, and then by providing the company and its employees with the HR activities that these employees need to do their jobs. For example, you'll see that Showtime offers many development and training programs, as well as personal development–type activities including mentoring programs and career-oriented development activities. The firm's performance management process (which the employees helped develop) focuses specifically on the work activities and results that help achieve departmental and corporate goals. In this video, Matthew, the firm's CEO, emphasizes that it's essential to use human resources as a strategic partner, and the video then goes on to provide something of a summary of the basic human resource management functions.

Discussion Questions

1. What concrete evidence do you see in this video that HR at Showtime helps the company achieve its strategic goals?
2. What specific HR functions does the video mention, at least in passing?
3. Why do you think management at Showtime places such a heavy emphasis on personal development and quality of work issues such as open door policies, mentoring programs, and allowing employees to swap jobs?

VIDEO 2: MANAGING EQUAL OPPORTUNITY AND DIVERSITY

Video Title: IQ Solutions

IQ Solutions is in the business of providing health care system services. It says one of its aims is lessening the inequality that it believes exists in America's health care system, and the company uses its diverse employee base to better serve and attract a broad client base. Employees at IQ Solutions work together in teams to achieve the company's goals. As we see in this video, the company itself is indeed very diverse: for example, employees speak about 18 languages. The company capitalizes on this diversity in many ways. For example, it lets its employees share their ethnically unique holidays, and provides special training and other benefits that support diversity.

Discussion Questions

1. To what extent does diversity management at IQ Solutions contribute to the company achieving its strategic goals?
2. Based upon what you read in this part of the book, which diversity management programs can you identify in use at IQ Solutions?

ENDNOTES

1. Arthur Yeung, "Setting Up for Success: How the Portman Ritz-Carlton Hotel Gets the Best from Its People," *Human Resource Management* 45, no. 2 (Summer 2006): 67–75.
2. http://travel.nytimes.com/travel/guides/asia/china/shanghai/34221/portman-ritz-carlton-hotel/hotel-detail.html, accessed February 28, 2010.
3. Ibid.
4. See, for example, Fred David, *Strategic Management* (Upper Saddle River, NJ: Prentice Hall, 2007): 11.
5. Tony Bingham and Pat Galagan, "PepsiCo," *Training and Development* (June 2008): 33.
6. www.checkmateplan.com, accessed April 24, 2009.
7. www.pepsico.com/PEP_Company/Overview, accessed December 7, 2007.
8. Paul Nutt, "Making Strategic Choices," *Journal of Management Studies* (January 2002): 67–96.
9. Michael Porter, *Competitive Strategy* (New York: The Free Press, 1980): 14.
10. David Upton, "What Really Makes Factories Flexible?" *Harvard Business Review* (July–August 1995): 75.
11. See, for example, Evan Offstein, Devi Gnyawali, and Anthony Cobb, "A Strategic Human Resource Perspective of Firm Competitive Behavior," *Human Resource Management Review* 15 (2005): 305–318.
12. "Strategic HR Means Translating Plans into Action," *HR Magazine* 48, no. 3 (March 2003): 8; and "Closer to Becoming a Strategic Partner? HR Moves Forward but Faces Obstacles," *BNA Bulletin to Management* (July 15, 2005): 225.
13. SHRM Research, "2006 Strategic HR Management," *Society for Human Resource Management* (2006): 5–19, www.SHRM.org, accessed May 10, 2007.
14. Samuel Greengard, "You're Next! There's No Escaping Merger Mania!" *Workforce* (April 1997): 52–62. See also E. E. Lawler et al., "What Makes HR a Strategic Partner?" *People & Strategy* 32, no. 1 (2009): 14.
15. "Offshoring," *Workplace Visions* (No. 2-2004, SHRM Research): 1.
16. Ibid, 7.
17. When focusing on the HR activities, managers call this an HR Scorecard. When applying the same process broadly to all the

company's activities, including, for example, sales, production, and finance, managers call it the *balanced scorecard* process.

18. The idea for the HR Scorecard derives from a broader measurement tool managers call the balanced scorecard. This does for the company as a whole what the HR Scorecard does for HR, summarizing instead the impact of various functions including HRM, sales, production, and distribution. The "balanced" in balanced scorecard refers to a balance of goals—financial and nonfinancial.

19. www.activestrategy.com/solutions/strategy_mapping.aspx, accessed March 24, 2009.

20. See, for example, Maria Fleurie and Lenne Fleurie, "In Search of Competence: Aligning Strategy and Competencies in the Telecommunications Industry," *International Journal of Human Resource Management* 16, no. 9 (September 2005): 1640–1655.

21. Garrett Walker and J. Randall MacDonald, "Designing and Implementing an HR Scorecard," *Human Resource Management* 40, no. 4 (2001): 365–377.

22. See, for example, James Werbel and Samuel DeMarie, "Aligning Strategic Human Resource Management and Person–Environment Fit," *Human Resource Management Review* 15 (2005): 247–262.

23. Richard Shafer et al., "Crafting a Human Resource Strategy to Foster Organizational Agility: A Case Study," *Human Resource Management* 40, no. 3 (Fall 2001): 197–211.

24. www.marketwatch.com/news/story/layoff-plans-rise-16-november/story.aspx?guid=%7BC201E82C%2DCAA3%2D46BE%2D952D%2D4985C49E4F8A%7D&dist=msr_10, accessed December 5, 2007, and http://Money.CNN.com/ magazines/fortune, accessed December 5, 2007.

25. Bou-Wen Lin et al., "Mergers and Acquisitions as a Human Resource Strategy," *International Journal of Manpower* 27, no. 2 (2006): 127.

26. "Mergers & Acquisitions—Managing the HR Issues," *The M&A Spotlight* (January 1, 2007), www.accessmylibrary.com/coms2/summary_0286–29399891_ITM, accessed December 3, 2007.

27. Andy Cook, "Make Sure You Get a Prenup," *EVCJ* (December/January 2007): 76. See also www.accessmylibrary.com/coms2/summary_0286-29140938_ITM, accessed June 29, 2009.

28. Bou-Wen Lin et al., "Mergers and Acquisitions as a Human Resource Strategy," *International Journal of Management* 27, no. 2 (2006): 135–142.

29. www.towersPerrin.com, accessed December 4, 2007.

30. Jessica Marquez, "HR's Rising Equity," *Workforce Management* (September 24, 2007): 16–22.

31. Ann Pomeroy, "A Fitting Role: HR Is Helping Businesses Puzzle Through the Difficult Process of a Successful Merger or Acquisition," *HR Magazine* 50, no. 6 (June 2005): 54–61.

32. Ibid.

33. www.towersPerrin.com, accessed December 4, 2007.

34. Jeffrey Schmidt, "The Correct Spelling of M&A Begins with HR," *HR Magazine* (June 2001): 102–108. See also Wendy Boswell, "Aligning Employees with the Organization's Strategic Objectives: Out of Line of Sight, Out of Mind," *International Journal of Human Resource Management* 17, no. 9 (September 2006): 1014–1041.

35. "Mergers & Acquisitions—Managing the HR Issues," *The M&A Spotlight* (January 1, 2007), www.accessmylibrary.com/coms2/summary_0286–29399891_ITM, accessed December 3, 2007.

36. Leah Carlson, "Smooth Transition: HR Input Can Prevent Benefits Blunders During M&A's," *Employee Benefit News* (June 1, 2005).

37. www.towersPerrin.com, accessed December 4, 2007. See also Ingmar Bjorkman, "The HR Function in Large-Scale Mergers and Acquisitions: The Case of Nordea," *Personnel Review* 35, no. 6 (2006): 654–671, and Elina Antila, "The Role of HR Managers in International Mergers and Acquisitions: A Multiple Case Study," *The International Journal of Human Resource Management* 17, no. 6, issue 6 (June 2006): 999–1020.

38. "Mergers & Acquisitions—Managing the HR Issues," *The M&A Spotlight* (January 1, 2007).

39. Ibid; see also Ruth Bramson, "HR's Role in Mergers and Acquisitions," *Training and Development* 54, no. 10 (October 2000): 59–66.

40. John Kador, "Shall We Dance?" *Electronic Business* 28, no. 2 (February 2002): 56.

41. Edgar Schein, *Organizational Culture and Leadership* (San Francisco: Jossey-Bass, 1985): 224–237. Peter Wright, Mark Kroll, and John Parnell, *Strategic Management Concepts* (Upper Saddle River, NJ: Prentice Hall, 1996): 233–236; and Benjamin Schneider et al., "Creating a Climate and Culture for Sustainable Organizational Change," *Organizational Dynamics* 24, no. 4 (1996): 7–19. See also John S. Oakland and Steve J. Tanner "Quality Management in the 21st Century: Implementing Successful Change," *International Journal of Productivity and Quality Management* 1, no. 1/2 (December 12, 2005): 69.

42. This checklist is based on Philip Hunsaker, *Training in Management Skills* (Upper Saddle River, NJ: Prentice Hall, 2001): 323.

4 Recruiting and Talent Management

SYNOPSIS

- The Talent Management Process
- Conducting Job Analysis and Creating Success Profiles
- Workforce Planning and Predictive Workforce Monitoring
- Recruiting Job Candidates
- Developing and Using Application Forms

Source: Robert Galbraith/CORBIS-NY.

When you finish studying this chapter, you should be able to:

1. Explain the talent management process.
2. Describe the basic methods of collecting job analysis information.
3. Outline and briefly discuss each step in the recruitment and selection process.
4. Explain the process of forecasting personnel requirements.
5. Compare eight methods for recruiting job candidates.
6. Explain how to use application forms to predict job performance.

INTRODUCTION

As one might expect from a company founded by mathematicians, Google recently devised a new way to determine which applicants and employees were most likely to succeed or to quit. Google created a mathematical algorithm, a sort of mathematical roadmap, similar to the approach they take to helping people search the Web. Google scientists scrutinized data from employee reviews and promotion and pay histories to build a mathematical formula Google says can identify which of its 20,000 employees are most likely to succeed or to quit. They hope their new approach will take much of the guesswork out of recruiting, selecting, training, appraising, and rewarding employees. For example, it will help Google fine-tune exactly what sorts of recruiting media and appeals would be best for attracting high-potential applicants. It would also make it easier to identify during appraisals which employees are most likely to quit, so Google can adjust the rewards of those it does not want to lose. ■

THE TALENT MANAGEMENT PROCESS

This chapter begins Part 2 of the book, **Staffing and Talent Management**, which covers the following topics:

Chapter 4   Recruiting and Talent Management
Chapter 5   Selecting Employees
Chapter 6   Training and Developing Employees
Chapter 7   Performance and Talent Management
Chapter 8   Compensating Employees

Although most employers still staff their companies the traditional way, some, like Google, are taking a more modern approach. The traditional approach to staffing, appraisal, and compensation is to treat these topics as a logical sequence of steps:

1. Decide what positions to fill, through *personnel planning and forecasting.*
2. Build a pool of candidates for these jobs, by *recruiting* internal or external candidates.
3. Have candidates complete *application forms* and perhaps undergo initial screening interviews.
4. Use *selection tools* like tests, interviews, background checks, and physical exams to identify viable candidates.
5. Decide to whom to *make an offer.*
6. *Orient, train and develop employees* to provide them with the competencies they need to do their jobs.
7. *Appraise employees* to assess how they're doing.
8. *Reward and compensate* employees to maintain their motivation.

This sequential approach certainly makes sense. For example, you usually don't test applicants before you recruit them, and you usually can't reward them until they're hired and trained.

However, viewing this staff—appraise—compensate process as just a sequence of steps has several drawbacks. For one thing, doing so may mask the fact that these activities should be interactive and integrated. For example, the training and development that an employee requires should reflect not just his or her performance but the company's longer term workforce planning needs. Similarly, as at Google, knowing which employees perform best can help you do a better job of deciding who to recruit and how to recruit them. Why recruit if you're not sure who you're looking for?

Therefore, employers today increasingly view all these staff—appraise—reward activities as part of a single integrated *talent management* process. One survey of human resource executives found that "talent management" issues were among the most pressing ones they faced.[1] Another survey, of CEOs of big companies, said they typically spent between 20% and 40% of their time on "talent management issues."[2]

talent management
The end to end process of planning, recruiting, developing, managing, and compensating employees throughout the organization.

What Is Talent Management?

We can define **talent management** as the *goal-oriented* and *integrated* process of *planning, recruiting, developing, managing, and compensating* employees.[3] In one respect, there's nothing new about talent management, since in simplest terms it involves getting the right people (in terms of competencies) in the right jobs, at the right time, doing their jobs correctly. But in fact, five things set talent management apart from simply recruiting, selecting, training, appraising, and rewarding employees.

1. **Ensure that all talent management functions are goal-directed.** First, all talent management tasks must be ***goal directed***. This starts with identifying the workforce profiles (in terms of *competencies, knowledge, traits,* and *experiences*) that the firm will need to achieve its strategic goals. For example, a planned factory automation should produce new "profiles" of the worker knowledge and skills required for each role in the new plant. To manage talent effectively, managers should always be asking, "What recruiting, testing, or other actions should I be taking to produce the employee competencies we need to achieve our strategic goals?" Figure 4.1 summarizes this idea.

2. **Management focuses on all the functions required for managing the firm's talent.** Second, viewing the talent management tasks (such as recruiting, training, and paying employees) as parts of a single talent management process helps ensure that managers ***consciously think through and focus on all the tasks required*** for managing the company's talent. For example, having employees with the right competencies depends as much on recruiting and training as it does on applicant testing.

3. **Use the same set of competencies for all talent management functions.** Third, talent management means ***consistently using*** the same profile of competencies, traits, knowledge and experience for formulating recruitment plans for the employee as you do for making selection, training, appraisal, and payment decisions for him or her. For example, use selection interview questions to determine if the candidate has the knowledge and skills the job requires; then appraise and develop the employee based on whether he or she shows mastery of the required knowledge and skills.

4. **Actively manage each employee segment.** Talent management is ***proactive***. Taking a talent management approach requires that employers ***actively manage*** their employees' recruitment, selection, development, and rewards. For example, IBM segmented its employees into three main groups so that it could fine-tune the way it served the employees in each segment. As another example, many employers are identifying their "mission-critical" employees, and managing their development and rewards separately from the firms' other employees.

5. **Integrate/coordinate all the talent management functions.** An effective talent management process should ***integrate the underlying talent management activities*** such as workforce planning, recruiting, developing, and compensating employees. For example, performance appraisal results should prompt the required employee training. The point is that

FIGURE 4.1

Building Blocks of the Talent Management Process

talent management always requires taking formal steps to integrate the underlying talent management activities. One way to do this is just to have HR managers meet as a team to visualize and discuss how to coordinate activities like testing, appraising, and training. (For instance, to make sure the firm is using the same profile to recruit, select, train, and appraise for a particular job.) However, in practice, integrating these activities often means using information technology.

- For example, Talent Management Solutions' (www.talentmanagement101.com) talent management suite includes e-recruiting software, employee performance management, a learning management system, and compensation management. Among other things, Talent Management Solutions' suite of programs "relieves the stress of writing employee performance reviews by automating the task," and ensures "that all levels of the organization are aligned—all working for the same goals."[4]

- SilkRoad Technology's talent management solution includes applicant tracking, onboarding, performance management, compensation, and an employee intranet. Its talent management Life Suite "helps you recruit, manage, and retain your best employees."[5]

- Info HCM Talent Management "includes several upgrades including tracking and monitoring performance metrics, interactive online training via WebEx, support for e-commerce integration to enable training . . . , and full localization for additional languages including Spanish, French, and Chinese."[6]

CONDUCTING JOB ANALYSES AND CREATING SUCCESS PROFILES

Staffing and talent management typically start with determining what each job entails in terms of duties and required competencies. The traditional way to determine this is job analysis.

What Is Job Analysis?

Job analysis is the procedure through which you determine the duties of the company's jobs and the characteristics of the people who should perform them. The manager then uses this information for developing **job descriptions** (what the job entails) and **job specifications** (what kind of people to hire for the job).[7]

A supervisor or HR specialist normally does the job analysis, perhaps using a questionnaire like the one in the chapter appendix (Figure A4.3 on pages 113–114). The questionnaire typically includes information on the work activities performed (such as cleaning, selling, teaching, or painting) and about matters like physical working conditions and work schedule.[8]

Job analysis is the basis for many human resource management decisions.[9] For example, you'll need information about the job's duties to create training programs and to compute pay rates.

JOB ANALYSIS AND EQUAL EMPLOYMENT OPPORTUNITY (EEO) Job analysis is crucial for validating all major personnel activities. Employers must be able to show that their screening tools and appraisals relate to performance on the job in question. To do this, the manager must know what duties and skills the job entails.

Methods of Collecting Job Analysis Information

Managers use various techniques to do a job analysis. Some of the more popular techniques follow.

INTERVIEWS Interviews are probably the most widely used method for determining a job's duties and responsibilities. Typical interview questions include "What is the job being performed?" "What are the major duties of your position?" "What exactly do you do?" and "What activities do you participate in?"

This is a simple and straightforward method. Interviewing also lets workers report activities and behavior that might not otherwise surface, such as important relationships that would not be obvious from the organization chart.

Interviewing's major problem is distortion of information. A job analysis is often a prelude to changing a job's pay rate. Employees therefore sometimes exaggerate some responsibilities and minimize others.[10]

job analysis
The procedure for determining the duties and skill requirements of a job and the kind of person who should be hired for it.

job description
A list of a job's duties, responsibilities, reporting relationships, working conditions, and supervisory responsibilities—one product of a job analysis.

job specification
A list of a job's "human requirements," that is, the requisite education, skills, personality, and so on—a product of a job analysis.

Managers use direct observation with jobs such as assembly-line worker, that consist mainly of observable physical activity.

Source: Blend Images/Alamy Images.

QUESTIONNAIRES Many firms have employees fill out questionnaires to describe their job-related duties and responsibilities.

Some questionnaires present employees with an inventory of perhaps hundreds of specific tasks (such as "change and splice wire"). Each employee indicates whether he or she performs each task and, if so, how much time is spent on each. At the other extreme, some questionnaires are open-ended. They simply ask each employee to "describe the major duties of your job."

In practice, the best questionnaire often falls between these two extremes. Again as in Figure A4.3, it might have several open-ended questions (such as "Is the incumbent performing duties he/she considers unnecessary?") as well as structured questions (concerning, for instance, previous experience required).

OBSERVATION Managers use direct observation when jobs consist mainly of observable physical activity. Jobs such as janitor, assembly-line worker, and accounting clerk are examples.

PARTICIPANT DIARY/LOGS Here you ask workers to keep a diary/log of what they do during the day. For each activity he or she engages in, the person records the activity and time in a log. This can produce a very complete picture of the job, especially when supplemented with subsequent interviews. Some employees compile their logs by periodically dictating what they're doing into a handheld dictating machine.

USING THE INTERNET Face-to-face interviews and observations can be time-consuming. Collecting the information from internationally dispersed employees is particularly challenging.[11]

Internet-based job analysis is a good solution.[12] The human resource department distributes job analysis questionnaires via the company intranet, with instructions to complete and return them by a particular date.

EXPEDITING THE JOB ANALYSIS PROCESS The job analysis process might take several days to explain, and then to interview several employees and their managers. However, it's possible to reduce the process to just 3 or 4 hours.[13] The abbreviated steps include:

1. Greet participants and conduct very brief introductions.
2. Briefly explain the job analysis process and the participants' roles in this process.
3. Spend about 15 minutes determining the scope of the job you're about to analyze by getting agreement on the job's basic summary.
4. Identify the job's broad functional or duty areas, such as "administrative" and "supervisory."
5. Identify tasks within each duty area, using a flip chart or collaboration software.
6. Print the task list and get the group to sign off on it.

OTHER JOB ANALYSIS METHODS You may encounter several other job analysis methods, most notably those in the chapter appendix.

Writing Job Descriptions

The job analysis should provide the information required for writing a job description. A job description is a written statement of *what* the jobholder does, *how* he or she does it, and under *what conditions* the job is performed. The manager in turn uses this information to write a job specification. This lists the knowledge, abilities, and skills needed to perform the job satisfactorily. Figure 4.2 presents a typical job description. As is usual, it contains several types of information:

JOB TITLE: Telesales Representative	**JOB CODE:** 100001
RECOMMENDED SALARY GRADE:	**EXEMPT/NONEXEMPT STATUS:** Nonexempt
JOB FAMILY: Sales	**EEOC:** Sales Workers
DIVISION: Higher Education	**REPORTS TO:** District Sales Manager
DEPARTMENT: In-House Sales	**LOCATION:** Boston
	DATE: April 2010

SUMMARY (Write a brief summary of job.)

The person in this position is responsible for selling college textbooks, software, and multimedia products to professors, via incoming and outgoing telephone calls, and to carry out selling strategies to meet sales goals in assigned territories of smaller colleges and universities. In addition, the individual in this position will be responsible for generating a designated amount of editorial leads and communicating to the publishing groups product feedback and market trends observed in the assigned territory.

SCOPE AND IMPACT OF JOB

Dollar responsibilities (budget and/or revenue)

The person in this position is responsible for generating approximately $2 million in revenue, for meeting operating expense budget of approximately $4000, and a sampling budget of approximately 10,000 units.

Supervisory responsibilities (direct and indirect)

None

Other

REQUIRED KNOWLEDGE AND EXPERIENCE (Knowledge and experience necessary to do job)

Related work experience

Prior sales or publishing experience preferred. One year of company experience in a customer service or marketing function with broad knowledge of company products and services is desirable.

Formal education or equivalent

Bachelor's degree with strong academic performance or work equivalent experience.

Skills

Must have strong organizational and persuasive skills. Must have excellent verbal and written communications skills and must be PC proficient.

Other

Limited travel required (approx 5%)

FIGURE 4.2

Sample Job Description, Pearson Education

JOB IDENTIFICATION As in Figure 4.2, the job identification section contains the job title, such as marketing manager or inventory control clerk. It also usually contains department, date, and similar information.

JOB SUMMARY The job summary should portray the general nature of the job, listing only its major functions or activities.

RELATIONSHIPS A relationships statement may show the jobholder's relationships with others inside and outside the organization. It might look like this for a human resource manager:

> *Reports to:* Vice president of employee relations
> *Supervises:* Human resource clerk, test administrator, labor relations director, and one secretary
> *Works with:* All department managers and executive management
> *Outside the company:* Employment agencies, executive recruiting firms, union representatives, state and federal employment offices, and various vendors

RESPONSIBILITIES AND DUTIES This section would present a full list of the job's duties. Each of the job's major duties should be listed and described. For instance, you might further define the duty "selects, trains, and develops subordinate personnel" as follows: "develops spirit of cooperation and understanding," "ensures that work group members receive specialized training as necessary," and "directs training involving teaching, demonstrating, and/or advising."

AUTHORITY This section details the job's authority. For example, the jobholder might have authority to approve purchase requests up to $5,000, grant time off or leaves of absence, discipline department personnel, and interview and hire new employees.[14]

STANDARDS OF PERFORMANCE The job description may contain a "standards of performance" section. This lists the standards the employee is to achieve in each of the job description's main duties and responsibilities.

WORKING CONDITIONS AND PHYSICAL ENVIRONMENT The working conditions section might include noise level, hazardous conditions, heat, and other conditions.

INTERNET-BASED JOB DESCRIPTIONS Most employers use Internet-based services to help write their job descriptions. For example, on www.jobdescription.com, search by alphabetical title, key word, or industry to find the desired job title. This leads you to a generic job description for that title—say, "Computers & EDP systems sales representative." You can then use the wizard to customize the generic description with job title, department, and preparation date. You can also choose from a number of possible desirable competencies and experience levels.

The U.S. Department of Labor's *Occupational Information Network*, or O*NET (http://online.onetcenter.org), is an invaluable (and free) resource. Its wizards allow users to see the duties and responsibilities of thousands of jobs, as well as the training, experience, and education and knowledge each job requires. Figure 4.3 presents part of one O*NET job description. The appendix to this chapter illustrates how to use O*NET.

WRITING JOB DESCRIPTIONS THAT COMPLY WITH THE ADA Most ADA lawsuits revolve around the question, "What are the essential functions of the job?" *Essential job functions* are those job duties that employees must be able to perform, with or without reasonable accommodation. Without a job description listing these functions, it is difficult to convince a court that the functions are essential.[15] The job description should therefore list the essential functions as "essential."[16]

Writing Job Specifications

The job specification starts with the job description and then answers the question, "What human traits and experience are required to do this job well?" It shows what kind of person to recruit and for what qualities that person should be tested.

TRAINED EMPLOYEES It's usually not too difficult to determine the human traits for placing experienced people such as trained bookkeepers on a job. You may reasonably assume that past

FIGURE 4.3

O*Net Job Description

Source: http//online.onetcenter.org/
link/summary11-2202.00, accessed
March 1, 2010.

Summary Report for:

11-2022.00 - Sales Managers

Direct the actual distribution or movement of a product or service to the customer. Coordinate sales distribution by establishing sales territories, quotas, and goals and establish training programs for sales representatives. Analyze sales statistics gathered by staff to determine sales potential and inventory requirements and monitor the preferences of customers.

Sample of reported job titles: Sales Manager, Vice President of Sales, Director of Sales, District Sales Manager, Regional Sales Manager, Sales Supervisor, General Manager, Sales and Marketing Vice President, Sales Representative, Store Manager

View report: Summary Details Custom

Tasks | Tools & Technology | Knowledge | Skills | Abilities | Work Activities | Work Context | Job Zone | Interests | Work Styles | Work Values | Related Occupations | Wages & Employment | Additional Information

Tasks

- Resolve customer complaints regarding sales and service.
- Oversee regional and local sales managers and their staffs.
- Plan and direct staffing, training, and performance evaluations to develop and control sales and service programs.
- Determine price schedules and discount rates.
- Review operational records and reports to project sales and determine profitability.
- Monitor customer preferences to determine focus of sales efforts.
- Prepare budgets and approve budget expenditures.
- Confer or consult with department heads to plan advertising services and to secure information on equipment and customer specifications.
- Direct and coordinate activities involving sales of manufactured products, services, commodities, real estate or other subjects of sale.
- Confer with potential customers regarding equipment needs and advise customers on types of equipment to purchase.

performance is a good predictor of how the person will do. Your job specifications might focus on traits such as education, length of previous service, and previous job performance.

UNTRAINED EMPLOYEES It's not as simple when you're filling jobs with untrained people. Here you must specify qualities such as physical traits or sensory skills that imply some potential for performing the job or for having the ability to do the job. For example, suppose the job requires detailed work on a circuit board assembly line. You might want to ensure that the person scores high on a test of finger dexterity. Identifying such human requirements is accomplished either through a subjective, judgmental approach or through statistical analysis.

O*NET JOB SPECIFICATIONS The O*NET system provides job specification information. As an example, the O*NET sales manager report lists required sales manager skills such as "Active Listening—Giving full attention to what other people are saying, taking time to understand the points being made, and not interrupting at inappropriate times"[17]

The Role of Profiles in Talent Management

To manage their talent more actively, more employers, such as Google, are creating *profiles* for each job. According to the human resource management consulting firm DDI, the aim of creating profiles (or "success profiles") is to develop detailed definitions of what is required for exceptional performance in a given role or job, in terms of required Competencies (necessary behaviors), Personal Attributes (traits, personality, etc.), Knowledge (technical and/or professional), and Experience (necessary educational and work achievements). Each job's profile then becomes the benchmark for creating recruitment, selection, training, and evaluation and development plans for each job.[18] Figure 4.4 illustrates a type of profile, this one in the form of what HR experts call a competency model.

IBM EXAMPLE For example, IBM recently identified every one of the possible 490 roles that workers, managers, and executives might fill. All IBM employees play at least one role (leader, and so on.) IBM analysts studied what people do in each role and what skill sets each role requires.

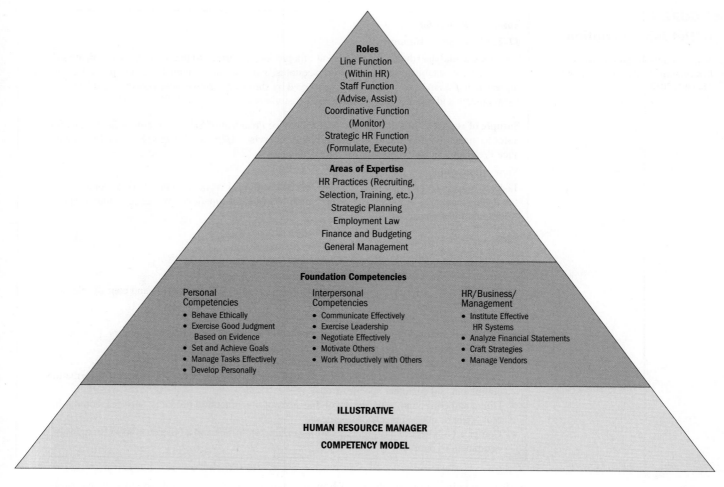

Roles
Line Function
(Within HR)
Staff Function
(Advise, Assist)
Coordinative Function
(Monitor)
Strategic HR Function
(Formulate, Execute)

Areas of Expertise
HR Practices (Recruiting,
Selection, Training, etc.)
Strategic Planning
Employment Law
Finance and Budgeting
General Management

Foundation Competencies

Personal Competencies	Interpersonal Competencies	HR/Business/ Management
• Behave Ethically	• Communicate Effectively	• Institute Effective HR Systems
• Exercise Good Judgment Based on Evidence	• Exercise Leadership	• Analyze Financial Statements
• Set and Achieve Goals	• Negotiate Effectively	• Craft Strategies
• Manage Tasks Effectively	• Motivate Others	• Manage Vendors
• Develop Personally	• Work Productively with Others	

ILLUSTRATIVE

HUMAN RESOURCE MANAGER

COMPETENCY MODEL

FIGURE 4.4

Example of Competency Model for Human Resource Manager

For these 490 roles, there are 4,000 possible skill sets. IBM rates employees' skills on a continuum from Zero—"You have not demonstrated a significant mastery of the skill set," to Three—"You have achieved a mastery level demonstrated by the fact that you're not only proficient, but that you're developing others around it." Now IBM will be able to tell each employee "where we see your skill sets, which skills you have that will become obsolete and what jobs we anticipate will become available down the road. . . . We'll direct you to training programs that will prepare you for the future."[19]

BP EXAMPLE Several years ago, British Petroleum's (BP's) exploration division executives decided their unit needed a more efficient, faster acting organization.[20] To help accomplish this, they felt they had to shift employees from a job duties–oriented "that's-not-my-job" attitude to one that motivated them to obtain the skills required to accomplish their broader responsibilities.

Their solution was a skills matrix like that in Figure 4.5. BP created skills matrices for each job or job family (such as drilling managers) within two groups of employees: those on a management track and those whose aims lay elsewhere (such as in engineering). As in Figure 4.5, each matrix listed (1) the basic skills required to do that job (such as technical expertise) and (2) the minimum level of each skill required for that job or job family. Now, with these matrices, the exploration division's focus is on recruiting, hiring, and developing people with the skills these employees need. Talent management in this BP unit now means recruiting, hiring, training, appraising and rewarding employees based on the competencies they need to perform their ever-changing jobs, with the overall aim of creating a faster-acting, more flexible organization.

FIGURE 4.5

The Skills Matrix for One Job at BP

Note: The shaded boxes (D, C, B, E, D, D, C) indicate the minimum level of skill required for the job.

Level	Technical expertise	Business awareness	Communication and interpersonal	Decision making and initiative	Leadership and guidance	Planning and organizational ability	Problem solving
H	H	H	H	H	H	H	H
G	G	G	G	G	G	G	G
F	F	F	F	F	F	F	F
E	E	E	E	**E**	E	E	E
D	**D**	D	D	D	**D**	**D**	D
C	C	**C**	C	C	C	C	**C**
B	B	B	**B**	B	B	B	B
A	A	A	A	A	A	A	A

Why use profiles? Traditionally, a job is a set of closely related activities carried out for pay, but the concept of a job is changing. Globalized competition means more pressure for performance. Employers are therefore instituting high-performance work policies and practices. These include management systems (such as organizing around multi-function work teams) that require flexible, multiskilled employees.

In situations like these, compiling a list of job duties for jobs that change daily can be counterproductive.[21] The better option is often to create profiles that list the competencies, traits, knowledge, and experience that employees in these multi-skilled jobs *must be able to exhibit.* Then hire, train, appraise, and reward employees based on these profiles, rather than on a list of static job duties.

COMPETENCY-BASED JOB ANALYSIS Employers use competency-based job analysis to create the profiles. *Competencies* are observable and measurable behaviors of the person that make performance possible. To determine what a job's required competencies are, ask, "In order to perform this job competently, the employee should be able to: . . . ?" Competencies are typically skills. Examples of competencies include "program in HTML," "produce a lesson plan," and "engineer the struts for a bridge." *Competency-based job analysis* means describing the job in terms of measurable, observable, behavioral competencies (knowledge, skills, and/or behaviors) that an employee doing that job must exhibit.[22] Traditional job analysis is more job-focused (What are this job's duties?). Competency-based analysis is more worker-focused (What must employees be competent at to do this multi-skilled job?).

WORKFORCE PLANNING AND PREDICTIVE WORKFORCE MONITORING

Talent management requires having the right people in the right jobs at the right time, doing their jobs the right way. It therefore depends on knowing what your job requirements and needs are going to be. For example, when Dan Hilbert became staffing manager at Valero Energy Corp., he analyzed the firm's demographic and turnover data and discovered that Valero faced critical employment shortages. The projected shortfalls were four times higher than Valero could fill with its current recruitment procedures. The solution was to start developing specific employment plans.[23]

workforce (or employment or personnel) planning
The process of formulating plans to fill the employer's future openings, based on (1) projecting open positions, and (2) deciding whether to fill these with inside or outside candidates.

Workforce (or employment or personnel) planning is the process of periodically reviewing what positions the firm will have to fill and how to fill them. Workforce planning embraces all future positions, from maintenance clerk to CEO. However, we'll see that most firms call the process of deciding how to fill executive jobs *succession planning.*

STRATEGY AND WORKFORCE PLANNING The firm's strategy should determine its workforce needs. For example, in terms of IBM's strategic needs, "in three years, 22 percent of our workforce will have obsolete skills. Of the 22 percent, 85 percent have fundamental competencies that we can build on to get them ready for skills we'll need years from now." The remaining 15 percent will either self-select out of IBM or be let go.[24]

FIGURE 4.6

**Linking Employer's
Strategy to Plans**

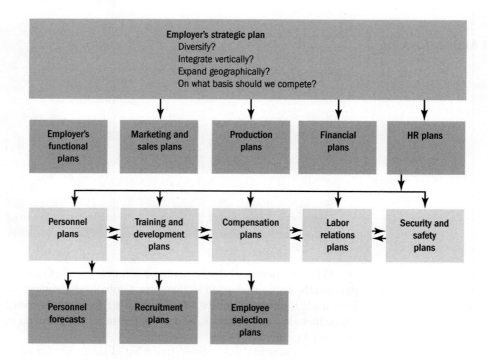

Ideally, as at IBM, workforce planning should entail thinking through the skills and competencies the firm needs to execute its overall strategy. At IBM, for instance, human resource executives review with finance and other executives the personnel ramifications of their company's strategic plans.[25] Figure 4.6 summarizes the link between strategic and personnel planning.

How does a manager like Dan Hilbert at Valero Energy decide how many employees he or she needs over the next few years? In planning for employment requirements, you'll need to forecast (given your company's strategic plans) three things: personnel needs, the supply of inside candidates, and the supply of outside candidates. We'll start with personnel needs.

How to Forecast Personnel Needs

Initially, managers traditionally use simple tools like *trend analysis, ratio analysis, and scatter plots* to estimate staffing future needs. The usual process is to first forecast revenues. Then estimate the size of the staff required to achieve this volume, for instance, by using historical ratios.

TREND ANALYSIS   **Trend analysis** involves studying your firm's employment levels (perhaps by department) over the past 5 years or so to predict future needs. The aim is to identify employment trends you think might continue into the future.

RATIO ANALYSIS   **Ratio analysis** means making forecasts based on the ratio between some causal factor (such as sales volume) and the number of employees required. For example, suppose you find that a salesperson traditionally generates $500,000 in sales. Then, if the sales revenue-to-salespeople ratio remains the same, you would require six new salespeople next year (each of whom produces an extra $500,000 in sales) to produce, say, an extra $3 million in sales.

SCATTER PLOTS   The **scatter plot** method shows graphically how two variables are related. If they are related, then if you can forecast the level of one variable (for example, hospital size) you should also be able to estimate your personnel requirements (for example, nurses).

For example, assume a 1,000-bed hospital expects to expand to 1,500 beds over the next 5 years. The director of nursing and the human resource director want to forecast the requirement for registered nurses. The human resource director decides to determine the relationship between *size of hospital* (in terms of number of beds) and *number of nurses required*. She calls several hospitals of various sizes and gets the following figures:

trend analysis
Study of a firm's past employment needs over a period of years to predict future needs.

ratio analysis
A forecasting technique that involves analyzing and extrapolating the ratio of a dependent variable, such as salespersons required, with an independent variable, such as sales.

scatter plot
A graphical method used to help identify the relationship between two variables.

Size of Hospital (Number of Beds)	Number of Registered Nurses
200	240
300	260
400	470
500	500
600	620
700	660
800	820
900	860

Figure 4.7 shows the hospital size (in beds) on the horizontal axis. The number of nurses is shown on the vertical axis. If the two factors are related, then the points will tend to fall along a straight line, as they do here. If you carefully draw a line to minimize the squared distances between the line and each of the plotted points, you will be able to estimate (forecast) the number of nurses needed for each given hospital size. Thus, for a 1,500-bed hospital, the human resource director would assume she needs about 1,100 nurses.

MANAGERIAL JUDGMENT Numerical analysis aside, managerial judgment always plays a role in employment planning. It's rare that any historical trend will continue unchanged. Important factors that may influence your forecasts include:

1. Projected turnover (as a result of resignations or terminations)
2. Quality and skills needed (in relation to the changing needs of your organization)
3. Strategic decisions to upgrade the quality of products or services or enter new markets
4. Technological and other changes resulting in increased productivity
5. The financial resources available

Forecasting the Supply of Outside Candidates

The preceding forecast answers half the staffing equation, namely "How many employees will we need?" Next, the manager must estimate the projected supply of both internal and external candidates. We'll start with external candidates.

This step may require forecasting economic conditions, local market conditions, and occupational market conditions. Usually, the lower the rate of unemployment, the lower the labor supply and the harder it is to recruit personnel. Thus, unemployment rates of almost 10% in the United States in 2010 signaled to HR managers that finding good candidates would be easier.[26] Look for economic

FIGURE 4.7

Using a Scatter Plot to Estimate Relationship Between Hospital Size and Number of Nurses

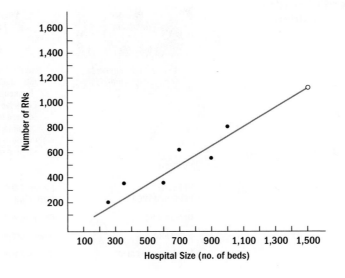

projections online, for instance, from the U.S. Congressional Budget Office (CBO) (www.cbo.gov/showdoc.cfm?index=1824&sequence=0) and the Bureau of Labor Statistics (BLS) www.bls.gov/news.release/ecopro.toc.htm. For hard-copy formats, *Bloomberg BusinessWeek* presents a weekly snapshot of the economy on its Outlook page, as well as a yearly forecast in December.

Local labor market conditions are also important. For example, the growth of computer and semiconductor firms recently prompted lower unemployment in cities like Seattle, quite aside from general economic conditions in the country.

Finally, forecast the availability of potential job candidates in specific target occupations. For example, jobs for network systems and data communications analysts are among the most in-demand occupations for the period 2006–2016 (see http://www.bls.gov/opub/ooq/2010/spring/art02.pdf).[27]

Forecasting the Supply of Inside Candidates

Can we fill our expected future job openings internally? In practice, as at Valero and IBM, managers here ask questions such as "How many current employees are due to retire?" "What is our usual yearly turnover?" and "What are our current employees' competency levels?"

A qualifications inventory facilitates forecasting internal candidates. **Qualifications inventories** contain summary data such as each current employee's performance record, educational background, age, and promotability, compiled either manually or in a computerized system. **Personnel replacement charts** (see Figure 4.8) show the present performance and promotability for each potential replacement for important positions. Alternatively, you can develop a *position replacement card* for each position, showing possible replacements as well as present performance, promotion potential, and training required by each possible candidate.

COMPUTERIZED INFORMATION SYSTEMS Large employers can't maintain qualifications inventories manually. They therefore computerize this information, and packaged systems are available for accomplishing this task.

Typically, employees fill out a Web-based survey in which they describe their background, experience, and performance appraisals. When a manager needs a qualified person to fill a position, he or she describes the position (for instance, in terms of skills) and then enters this information online. After scanning its database, the program presents a list of candidates. Longer term, systems like these enable firms like IBM to identify employee competency development needs, and to create plans for rectifying deficiencies and needs.

qualifications inventories
Manual or computerized records listing employees' education, career and development interests, languages, special skills, and so on to be used in identifying inside candidates for promotion.

personnel replacement charts
Company records showing present performance and promotability of inside candidates for the firm's most important positions.

FIGURE 4.8

Management Replacement Chart Showing Development Needs of Potential Future Divisional Vice Presidents

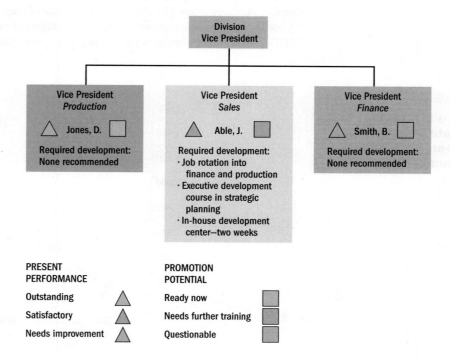

SUCCESSION PLANNING Forecasting the availability of inside candidates is particularly important in succession planning. *Succession planning* is "the process of ensuring a suitable supply of successors for current and future key jobs arising from business strategy, so that the careers of individuals can be planned and managed to optimize the organization's needs and the individuals' aspirations."[28] For example, the company might route potential successors for top management through the top jobs at several key divisions as well as overseas, and through the Harvard Business School's Advanced Management Program. Succession planning includes these activities:

- Analysis, based on the strategic plan, of the projected need for managers and professionals by company level, function, and skill
- Audit of existing executives and projection of likely future supply from internal and external sources
- Planning of individual career paths based on objective appraisals and estimates of future needs
- Accelerated promotions, with development targeted against the future needs of the business
- Performance-related training and development to prepare individuals for future roles
- Planned strategic recruitment, not only to fill short-term needs but also provide people to develop to meet future needs[29]
- Integration—of the companies planning to change their succession management practices, three-fourths recently cited the need to "integrate succession management with other talent management processes [such as testing, appraisal, and development]."[30]

Improving Productivity through HRIS: Succession Planning Systems

More companies are therefore relying on software to integrate the succession planning process. For example, Dole Food Co. Inc.'s separate operating companies used to handle most of their own succession planning. Dole's new strategy focused on improving financial performance by reducing redundancies and centralizing activities.[31] Dole decided to use special succession planning software from Pilat NAI to do this.

Dole's managers access the program via the Web using a password. They fill out online résumés for themselves, including career interests, and assess themselves on four competencies. When a manager completes his or her succession planning input, the program automatically notifies the manager's boss. The latter then assesses his or her subordinate's potential and indicates whether the person should be promoted. Dole's senior vice president for HR for North America then uses the information to create a career development plan for each manager, including training.[32]

Talent Management and Predictive Workforce Monitoring

Traditionally, employers engage in workforce planning only periodically, perhaps once every year or two. This may not always provide enough time to take corrective action, for instance to gear up a new employee development plan. Proactively managing talent *requires paying continuous attention* to workforce planning issues. The newer, continuous approach to workforce planning is called predictive workforce monitoring. Some examples follow.

INTEL CORPORATION EXAMPLE Intel conducts semi annual "Organization Capability Assessments." The staffing department works with the firm's business heads twice a year to assess workforce needs—immediate and up to two years out.[33]

AMERADA HESS EXAMPLE Amerada Hess uses its Organizational Capability (OC) group to monitor workforce attrition (such as retirement age, experience with Hess, education, etc.) and prospective talent requirements. It "then works with the lines of business to better prepare them for meeting changing global talent demands. The group considers how each line of business is evolving, examines what jobs at Hess will look like in the future, identifies sources for procuring the best talent, and assists in developing current and newly hired employees."[34]

VALERO ENERGY EXAMPLE Valero created a *labor supply chain* for monitoring steps in recruiting and hiring. It includes an analytic tool that predicts Valero's labor needs based on past experience. It also includes computer screen "dashboards" that show how components in the chain, such as ads placed on job boards, are performing according to cost, speed, and quality. In 2002, it took 41 pieces of paper to hire an employee and more than 120 days to fill a position. Each hire cost about $12,000. Today, with the labor supply chain in place, little paper is needed to bring an employee on board; the time-to-fill figure is below 40 days and cost per hire dropped to $2,300.[35]

ABB EXAMPLE ABB's Talent Management process allows talent information to be stored on a global IT platform. For example, it stores performance appraisals, career plans, and training and development information. It also shows a global overview of key management positions, including who holds them, and their potential successors. Potential successors get two kinds of assessments: by line managers, and against externally benchmarked leadership competency profiles.[36]

RECRUITING JOB CANDIDATES

Once authorized to fill a position, the next step is to develop an applicant pool.

Recruiting is important because the more applicants you have, the more selective you can be in your hiring. With baby boomers now retiring and fewer young people entering the labor pool, some estimate that the longer-term shortage of workers will grow from almost nothing today to about 20 million workers by 2020.[37]

Effective recruiting is more complex than just placing ads and calling agencies. For one thing, recruitment should *make sense in terms of your company's strategic plans.* For example, Valero found that executing its strategy required thinking through what employees they'd need and how they'd do the recruiting. Recruiting effectiveness also reflects various *nonrecruitment issues.*[38] For example, paying 10% more than competitors should make recruiting easier. There are also legal constraints. For example, with a nondiverse workforce, relying on word-of-mouth referrals may be a barrier to equal employment opportunity.[39]

Rationally, one would expect most employers to try to assess which of their recruiting tactics are working best. Is it more cost-effective for us to advertise for applicants on the Web or in Sunday's paper? Should we use this employment agency or that one? Yet one survey found that only about 44% of the 279 firms surveyed make formal attempts to evaluate the outcomes of their recruitment efforts.[40]

job posting
Posting notices of job openings on company bulletin boards as a recruiting method.

Internal Sources of Candidates

Although *recruiting* may bring to mind employment agencies and online ads, filling open jobs with current employees (internal recruiting) is often an employer's best bet. To be effective, this approach requires using **job posting,** personnel records, and skill banks.[41] *Job posting* means posting the open job—on company bulletin boards and/or on the Web— and listing its attributes, such as qualifications, supervisor, working schedule, and pay rate. Some union contracts require such postings. Yet posting is also good practice in nonunion firms if it facilitates the transfer and promotion of qualified inside candidates. Personnel records are also useful. Examining personnel records (including qualifications inventories) may reveal persons who have potential for further training or those who already have the right background for the open jobs in question.

Recruiting via the Internet

Internal candidates may not be sufficient to fill your recruiting needs. And many firms, including GE, cap the proportion of jobs they fill from within, in order to inject new ideas into the firm. In that case, the manager turns to outside sources. Most firms start with Web-based recruiting and with their own Web sites.

HOME PAGES Many firms attract employment applications via their own Web sites. GE's home page (www.ge.com) includes a link to www.ge.com.careers. It provides useful information about working for GE, and includes numerous useful job-seeker aids, such as separate buttons titled "University Students" and "U.S. Military Veterans." The accounting firm Deloitte & Touche created one global recruitment site, thus eliminating the need to maintain 35 separate local recruiting Web sites.[42]

Making the employer's Web site user-friendly is important.[43] For example, make it easy to get from the home page to the jobs section in one or two clicks. Keep pre-screening questions simple. And, let job seekers apply online and

Source: Peter Dazeley/Getty Images, Inc.—Liaison.

Job posting means posting the open job—on company bulletin boards and/or on the Web—and listing its attributes, such as qualifications, supervisor, working schedule, and pay rate.

via fax or e-mail.[44] In addition, job applicants view ads with more specific job information as more attractive and more credible.[45] Studies also suggest that employers should include employee testimonials on their recruitment Web sites; video and audio testimonials have the most impact.[46]

JOB BOARDS Others post positions on Internet job boards such as CareerBuilder.com, or on the sites of professional associations (such as the American Institute of Chemical Engineers) or on local newspapers' sites. Figure 4.9 lists some top online recruiting job sites.

Employers are shifting from general job board sites to niche sites. For example, recently the unique visitors to CareerBuilder.com dropped about 2%, while those to technology site Dice.com jumped 34%.[47]

Some job boards capitalize on social networking. Users register and supply their name, location, and the kind of work they do on social networking/recruitment sites like Monster Network and LinkIn.com. These sites enable members to develop personal relationships for networking, hiring, and employee referrals.[48] To benefit from YouTube-type networking sites, the accounting

FIGURE 4.9

Some Top Online Recruiting Job Boards

Source: www.quintcareers.com/ top_10_sites.html, accessed April 28, 2009. Used with permission of QuintCareers.com.

HR APPs 4 U

Posting and Accessing Job Openings

CareerBuilder.com iPhone App—'Jobs'[50]

The CareerBuilder.com iPhone application offers a way to search nearly 2 million jobs on America's largest job site. Users may search for jobs by keyword, read job descriptions and salaries, save jobs to a list of favorites, and e-mail job links to anyone on their contact list. The application also takes advantage of the iPhone's geo-location capabilities—users may specify that it search only for jobs in their region.

firm Deloitte & Touche asked employees to make short videos describing their experiences with the firm. Deloitte then took the 14 best (of the 400 videos that employees submitted) and posted them on YouTube.[49]

THE DOT-JOBS DOMAIN The .jobs domain gives job seekers a simple, one-click conduit for finding jobs at the employers who registered at .jobs (employers register at www.goto.jobs). For example, applicants seeking a job at Disneyland can go to www.Disneyland.jobs. This takes them to Disney's recruiting Web site for Disneyland.

VIRTUAL JOB FAIRS Virtual (fully online) job fairs are another option. For example, the magazine *PR Week* organized a virtual job fair for public relations employers. At a virtual job fair, "online visitors see a very similar setup to a regular job fair. They can listen to presentations, visit booths, leave résumés and business cards, participate in live chats, and get contact information from recruiters, HR managers, and even hiring managers."[51] At *PR Week*'s fair, one employer included short videos in its virtual "booth" introducing its company and talking about the firm. Several of its recruiters were online from 9 A.M. to 9 P.M. to chat with the hundreds of prospective applicants who visited its virtual job booth.[52]

Other Web Recruiting Practices

Recruiters are also seeking passive candidates (people not actively looking for jobs) by using social networking sites such as LinkedIn to find potential candidates.[53] One Massachusetts staffing firm uses its Facebook and LinkedIn pages to announce openings. Other firms use Twitter to announce job openings to jobseekers who subscribe to their twitter feeds.[54] ResumePal, from the career site JobFox (www.jobfox.com/), is an online standard universal job application. Jobseekers submit it to participating employers, who can then use the standardized application's keywords to identify viable candidates more easily.[55] McDonald's Corp. posted a series of employee testimonials on social networking sites like Second Life to attract applicants.[56] Other employers simply screen through job boards' resume listings.[57]

Job boards account for about 12.3% of hires. Other major sources include company Web sites (20.1%), referrals (27.3%), plus others such as temp to hire, rehires, and employment agencies. For example, The Cheesecake Factory uses four recruiting sources: employee referrals, promotions of current employees, search firms, and online job postings. The firm's head of HR says the Web has become "our No. 1 source of recruitment, with between 30% and 35% of our new managers coming through it." For most jobs, it posts the entire job description.[58] This helps screen out people who see that the job is not for them. (The server's description on CareerBuilder.com includes a 765-word list of duties, for instance.)[59]

APPLICANT TRACKING SYSTEMS Some employers cite a flood of responses as one downside of Internet recruiting. The problem is that the relative ease of responding to Internet ads encourages unqualified or geographically remote job seekers to apply. **Applicant tracking systems** (such as the recruitsoft.com and Itrack-IT solutions) are software systems that help employers screen and keep track of their applicants by performing various services such as collecting application information, prescreening applicants, scheduling interviews, and letting employers easily do searches (such as by skill) to match candidates with positions. The systems also help employers compile reports, such as "EEO-applicants by reject reason."[60]

The applicant tracking system should also (but often doesn't) help the employer identify and compare recruiting sources.[61] If the employer can't identify which recruiting sources are producing which hires, it's impossible to determine which source is most effective, or to allocate the recruitment budget efficiently.

applicant tracking systems
Online systems that help employers attract, gather, screen, compile, and manage applications.

APPLICATION SERVICE PROVIDERS While many employers manage their own applicant tracking software, others outsource that processing work to *application service providers* (ASPs). Then, when applicants log on to the "jobs" page of the employer's Web site, they actually go to the servers of the **application service provider**. These use their own systems to compile application information, prescreen applicants, and help the employer rank applicants and set interview appointments. Major suppliers of e-recruiting services include Automatic Data Processing (www.ADP.com), HRSmart (www.hrsmart.com), Silkroad Technology (www.silkroad.com), and Monster (www.monster.com).[62]

application service provider
An online vendor that uses its own servers and systems to manage tasks for employers, such as recruitment or training. In recruitment, they compile application information, prescreen applicants, and help the employer rank applicants and set interview appointments.

Advertising as a Source of Candidates

Using help wanted ads successfully requires addressing two issues: the media and the ad's construction. The selection of the best media depends on the positions for which you're recruiting. Your local newspaper is usually a good source of blue-collar help, clerical employees, and lower-level administrative employees. For specialized employees or professionals, you can advertise in trade and professional journals such as the *American Psychologist, Sales Management, Chemical Engineering,* and *American Banker.*

Help wanted ads in papers such as the *Wall Street Journal* are good sources of middle- or senior-management personnel. For instance, the *Wall Street Journal* has several regional editions so that you can target the entire country or the appropriate geographic area for coverage. Other employers turn to the Internet for faster turnaround.

CONSTRUCTING THE AD Experienced advertisers use the acronym AIDA (attention, interest, desire, action) to construct ads. You must attract attention to the ad, or readers may just miss or ignore it. Figure 4.10 shows an ad from one paper's classified section. Why does this ad attract *attention*? The phrase "next key player" helps. Employers usually advertise key positions in separate display ads like this one.

Next, develop *interest* in the job. You can create interest by the nature of the job itself, with lines such as "Are you looking to make an impact?" You can also use other aspects of the job, such as its location, to create interest.

Create *desire* by spotlighting the job's interest factors with words such as *travel* or *challenge.* As an example, having a graduate school nearby may appeal to engineers and professional people.

FIGURE 4.10

Help Wanted Ad That Draws Attention

Source: As published in *The New York Times,* May 13, 2007, Business p. 18. Reprinted by permission of Giombetti Associates.

Are You Our Next Key Player?

PLANT CONTROLLER | Northern New Jersey

Are you looking to make an impact? Can you be a strategic business partner and team player, versus a classic, "bean counter"? Our client, a growing **Northern New Jersey** manufacturer with two locations, needs a high-energy, self-initiating, technically competent Plant Controller. Your organizational skills and strong understanding of general, cost, and manufacturing accounting are a must. We are not looking for a delegator, this is a hands-on position. If you have a positive can-do attitude and have what it takes to drive our accounting function, read oh!

Responsibilities and Qualifications:
- Monthly closings, management reporting, product costing, and annual budget.
- Accurate inventory valuations, year-end physical inventory, and internal controls.
- 4-year Accounting degree, with 5–8 years experience in a manufacturing environment.
- Must be proficient in Microsoft Excel and have general computer skills and aptitude.
- Must be analytical and technically competent, with the leadership ability to influence people, situations, and circumstances.

If you have what it takes to be our next key player, tell us in your cover letter, *"Beyond the beans, what is the role of a Plant Controller?"* **Only cover** letters addressing that question will be considered. Please indicate your general salary requirements in your cover letter and email or fax your resume and cover letter to:

Rich Frigon
Giombetti Associates
2 Allen Street, P.O. Box 720
Hampden, MA 01036
Email: rfrigon@giombettiassoc.com
Fax: (413) 566-2009

Finally, the ad should prompt *action*, with a statement like "Call today," or "Please forward your résumé." (And, of course, the ad should comply with equal employment laws, avoiding features like "man wanted.")

In general, job applicants view ads with more specific job information as more attractive and more credible.[63] If the job has big drawbacks, then consider a realistic ad. When the New York City Administration for Children's Services was having problems with employee retention, it began using these ads: "Wanted: men and women willing to walk into strange buildings in dangerous neighborhoods, [and] be screamed at by unhinged individuals . . . " Realism reduces applicants, but improves employee retention.[64]

Employment Agencies as a Source of Candidates

There are three basic types of employment agencies: (1) those operated by federal, state, or local governments; (2) those associated with nonprofit organizations; and (3) privately owned agencies.

Public, state employment service agencies exist in every state. They are aided and coordinated by the U.S. Department of Labor. The latter also maintains a nationwide computerized job bank to which state employment offices are connected. Public agencies are a major source of blue-collar and often white-collar workers.

Beyond just filling jobs, agency counselors will visit an employer's work site, review the employer's job requirements, and even assist the employer in writing job descriptions. And most states have turned their local state employment service agencies into "one-stop career centers." Under a single roof, employers and job seekers can access an array of services such as recruitment services, employee training programs, and access to local and national labor market information.

Other employment agencies are associated with *nonprofit organizations*. For example, most professional and technical societies have units that help their members find jobs. Similarly, many public welfare agencies try to place people who are in special categories, such as those who are physically disabled or who are war veterans.

Private employment agencies are important sources of clerical, white-collar, and managerial personnel. They charge a fee, usually set by state law, for each applicant they place. The trend is toward "fee-paid jobs." Here the employer pays the fee.

Some reasons to use an agency include:

- Your firm found it difficult in the past to generate a pool of qualified applicants.
- You must fill an opening quickly.
- You want to attract a greater number of minority or female applicants.
- You want to reach individuals who are currently employed, and who might feel more comfortable dealing with employment agencies than with competitors directly.

However, employment agencies are no panacea. For example, the agency's screening may let unqualified applicants go directly to the supervisors responsible for hiring, who may in turn naïvely hire them.

Temporary Workers

Many employers supplement their permanent employee base by hiring contingent or temporary workers, often through temporary help agencies. Also called *part-time* or *just-in-time* workers, the *contingent workforce* is big and growing. The contingent workforce is not limited to clerical or maintenance staff. Each year, more than 100,000 people find temporary work just in engineering, science, or management support occupations.

Today's desire for higher productivity contributes to temp workers' growing popularity. Employers pay temp workers only for hours worked, not for the hours that some non-temp workers may spend sitting around. Temp workers often aren't paid benefits, another saving for the employer. And using temp workers lets employers readily expand and contract with changes in demand. Many firms use temporary hiring to give prospective employees a trial before hiring them as regular employees.[65]

Employers hire temp workers either directly or through temporary staff agencies. Direct hiring involves simply hiring workers and placing them on the job. The employer usually pays these people directly, as it does all its employees, but classifies them separately from regular employees.[66] The employer generally classifies these workers as casual, seasonal, or temporary employees, and often awards few if any benefits (such as pension benefits).

Another approach is to have a temp agency supply the employees. In this case the agency usually pays the employees' salaries and any benefits. Nike Inc. signed a multimillion dollar deal with Kelly Services to manage Nike's contingent workforce (temporary hires).[67]

Several years ago, federal immigration agents rounded up about 250 illegal store cleaning contract workers in 60 Walmart stores. This underscores the need for employers to understand the status and source of the contract employees who work on their premises under the auspices of outside staffing firms.[68]

ALTERNATIVE STAFFING Temporary employees are examples of alternative staffing—basically, the use of nontraditional recruitment sources. The use of alternate staffing sources is widespread and growing. About 1 of 10 U.S. employees works in some alternative work arrangement. They include, for example, in-house temporary employees (people employed directly by the company, but on an explicit short-term basis) and contract technical employees (highly skilled workers like engineers, who are supplied for long-term projects under contract from an outside technical services firm).

Executive Recruiters as a Source of Candidates

Executive recruiters (also called *headhunters*) are special employment agencies retained by employers to seek out top-management talent for their clients. They fill jobs in the $80,000 and up category, although $120,000 is often the lower limit. The percentage of your firm's positions filled by these services might be small. However, these jobs include the most crucial executive and technical positions. For top executive positions, headhunters may be your *only* source. The employer pays their fees.

Most of these firms now have Internet-linked databases, which can help create a list of potential candidates at the push of a button. Top recruiters include Heidrick & Struggles, Egon Zehnder International, Russell Reynolds Associates, and Spencer Stuart.[69]

PROS AND CONS Headhunters have many contacts and are especially adept at contacting qualified candidates who are not actively looking to change jobs. They can also keep your firm's name confidential until late in the search process. The recruiter can save top management time by doing the preliminary work of advertising for and screening applicants.

But the employer must explain fully what sort of candidate is required and why. Sometimes, what clients say or think they want isn't really what they need. Therefore, be prepared for some in-depth dissecting of your request. Also make sure to meet the person who will be handling your search, nail down exactly what the charges will be, and always make sure to check (or re-check) the final candidates' references yourself.

CANDIDATES' CAVEATS As a job candidate, keep several things in mind. Some of these firms may present an unpromising candidate to a client simply to make their other one or two proposed candidates look better. Some eager clients may also jump the gun, checking your references and undermining your present position prematurely. Finally, do not confuse executive search firms with the many executive assistance firms that help out-of-work executives find jobs. The latter charge the job seekers handsome fees to assist with things like résumé preparation and interview skills. They rarely actually reach out to prospective employers to find their clients jobs.

College Recruiting and Interns as a Source of Candidates

College recruiting is an important source of management trainees, as well as of professional and technical employees. However, the recent recession reduced, dramatically, the number of firms recruiting on college campuses. Between 2008 and 2009, about 52% of employers surveyed said they decreased such activities.[70]

There are two main problems with on-campus recruiting. First, it is expensive. Schedules must be set, brochures printed, records of interviews kept, and much time spent on campus. Second, recruiters themselves are sometimes ineffective. Some recruiters are unprepared, show little interest in candidates, and act superior. Others don't effectively screen their student candidates.

Campus recruiters should have two goals. The main one is determining whether a candidate is worthy of further consideration. The traits to assess usually include motivation, communication skills, education, appearance, and attitude.

While the main goal is to find good candidates, the other is to attract them to your firm. A sincere and informal attitude, respect for the applicant, and prompt follow-up letters can help to sell the employer to the interviewee.

INTERNSHIPS Many college students get their jobs through college internships, a recruiting approach that has grown dramatically in recent years.

Internships can be win–win situations. For students, an internship may mean being able to hone business skills, check out potential employers, and learn more about their career likes (and dislikes). Employers can use the interns to make useful contributions while evaluating them as possible full-time employees. One survey found that employers offer jobs to over 70% of their interns.[71]

Partnering with a college or university's career center can thus be useful.[72] It provides recruiters with relatively quick and easy access to a good source of applicants. And it can provide useful advice to recruiters regarding things like labor market conditions and the effectiveness of one's recruiting ads.[73] Employers who send effective recruiters to campuses and build relationships with opinion leaders such as career counselors and professors have better recruiting results.[74]

Recruiting is increasingly global, as the Global Issues in HR feature explains.

GLOBAL ISSUES IN HR

The Global Talent Search

As companies expand globally, they must tap overseas recruiting sources. For example, Gillette (part of Procter & Gamble) has an international graduate training program aimed at identifying and developing foreign nationals. Gillette subsidiaries overseas hire outstanding business students from top local universities. These foreign nationals are then trained for 6 months at the Gillette facility in their home countries.

However, you don't have to be a multinational to have to recruit abroad. Desperate for qualified nurses, many hospitals (such as Sinai and Northwest hospitals in the Baltimore, Maryland, area) are recruiting in countries like the Philippines, India, and China.[75]

Furthermore, when employers hire "global" employees, they're not just hiring employees to work abroad. As one article recently put it, "Cube dwellers increasingly need to work, often virtually, across borders with people whose first language is not English, who don't have the same cultural touch points as U.S. employees do, and who don't approach business in the same way that Americans do."[76]

As a result, many employers want their recruiters to look for evidence of global awareness early in the interview process. International experience (including internships and considerable travel abroad) as well as language proficiency are two of the things employers such as these often look for.

Referrals and Walk-ins as a Source of Candidates

With *employee referrals* campaigns, the firm posts announcements of openings and requests for referrals on its intranet and bulletin boards. It may offer prizes for referrals that end in hirings. As one head of recruiting said, "Quality people know quality people. If you give employees the opportunity to make referrals, they automatically suggest high-caliber people because they are stakeholders."[77] The new employees may also have more realistic views of what the firm is really like.

But the success of the campaign depends on your employees' morale. And the campaign can backfire if you reject an employee's referral. Using referrals exclusively may also be discriminatory if most of your current employees (and their referrals) are male or white.

Employee referral programs are popular. Employee referrals have been the source of almost half of all hires at AmeriCredit since the firm kicked off its "you've got friends, we want to meet them" employee referrals program. Employees making a referral receive $1,000 awards, with the payments spread over a year.

WALK-INS Particularly for hourly workers, *walk-ins*—direct applications made at your office—are a major source of applicants, one you can even encourage by posting "Hiring" signs on your property.

Many employers give every walk-in a brief interview with someone in the HR office, even if it is only to get information on the applicant in case a position should open in the future. Good business practice also requires answering all letters of inquiry from applicants promptly and courteously.

The Container Store trains its employees to recruit new employees from among the firm's customers.

Other Recruiting Sources

CUSTOMERS AS CANDIDATES The Container Store uses a successful variant of the employee referrals campaign. It trains its employees to recruit new employees from among the firm's customers. For example, if an employee sees that a customer seems interested in the Container Store, the employee might say, "If you love shopping here, you'd love working here."[78]

TELECOMMUTERS Hiring telecommuters is another option. For example, JetBlue Airways uses at-home agents who are JetBlue employees to handle its reservation needs. These "crewmembers" all live in the Salt Lake City area and work out of their homes. They use JetBlue-supplied computers and technology, and receive JetBlue training.[79]

MILITARY PERSONNEL Returning and discharged U.S. military personnel provide an excellent source of trained recruits. Several military branches have programs to facilitate soldiers finding jobs. For example, the U.S. Army's Partnership for Youth Success enables someone entering the Army to select a post-Army corporate partner for an employment interview, as a way to help soldiers find jobs after leaving the Army.[80]

OUTSOURCING AND OFFSHORING Rather than bringing people in to do the company's jobs, outsourcing and offshoring send the jobs out. *Outsourcing* means having outside vendors supply services (such as benefits management or manufacturing) that the company's own employees previously did in-house. *Offshoring* is a narrower term. It means having outside vendors *abroad* supply services that the company's own employees previously did in-house.

Outsourcing and offshoring are both contentious. Particularly in challenging economic times (see accompanying feature), employees, unions, legislators, and even many business owners feel that "shipping jobs out" (particularly overseas) is ill-advised. That notwithstanding, employers are sending more jobs out, and not just blue-collar jobs. Current projections show that about 3 million white-collar jobs ranging from call center employee to radiologist moved abroad in the past few years. But rising overseas wages (call center hourly wages in India rose from $2 an hour in 1998 to $6 in 2008, for instance) and quality issues are prompting more U.S. employers to bring their jobs back home.[81]

Summary of Current Recruitment Practices

An SHRM survey provides a useful overview of current recruitment practices.[82] For most employers, national online job boards (such as CareerBuilder.com) produced the *most* applicants, followed by employee referrals and the employer's own Web site. Employee referrals, followed by national online job boards and internal job postings, generated by far the highest *quality* of job

MANAGING HR IN CHALLENGING TIMES

Reducing Recruitment Costs

Challenging economic times are prompting employers to rethink how they recruit, with an emphasis on cost cutting. For those using traditional job boards, one expert says employers "should be proactive about asking for deals with recruitment sites." For example, negotiate a one-year discount on a shorter contract. Employers are also turning to free (or almost free) recruitment options. For example, free or low-cost recruitment resources include craigslist.org and jobbing.com. More employers are also focusing more on their states' one-stop career centers, not just for nonexempt employees, but for professional and administrative employees as well.[83]

candidates. Employee referrals, national online job boards, and internal job postings produced the *best return* on these employers' recruiting dollars. Figure 4.11 presents information on recruiting source usage, based on one survey. Overall, employers most often used employee referrals and large job boards (such as Monster).[84] The accompanying Managing HR in Challenging Times feature provides another perspective.

Table 4.1 summarizes practical information about using various recruiting sources.

Recruiting a More Diverse Workforce

The composition of the U.S. workforce is becoming more diverse. This means taking special steps to recruit older workers, minorities, and women. In general, the important thing is to take the steps that "say" this is a good place for diverse employees to work. Doing so might include using minority-targeted media outlets; highly diverse ads; emphasizing inclusiveness in policy statements; and using minority, female, and/or older recruiters.[85] Many commonsense factors contribute to successful minority/female recruiting. For example, flexible hours make it easier to attract and keep single parents.

Creative recruiting can boost the numbers of qualified minority applicants.[86] The basic aim is to unearth applicants with the desired qualities (such as cognitive ability and conscientiousness). So, for example, you might seek out candidates based on academic achievement information such as Dean's lists. Google posted math puzzles on large signs in subway stations in major cities. When people who solved the puzzles followed a Web link, Google encouraged them to submit resumes.

OLDER WORKERS AS A SOURCE OF CANDIDATES   The number of workers aged 55–64 is growing faster than just about all other demographic groups.[87] As many of these workers retire, employers are having difficulty replacing them with younger workers. Fortuitously, because of buyouts and downsizing-related early retirements, many workers retired early and want to reenter the workforce.[88] One survey concluded that about 70% of baby boomers expect to work after retirement, at least part-time.[89]

FIGURE 4.11

Relative Recruiting Source Use Based on New Hires

Source: © Staffing.org, Inc., 2007. All Rights Reserved. The 2007 Recruiting Metrics and Performance Benchmark Report, 2nd Ed., is sponsored by NAS Recruitment Communications. Used with permission of Staffing.org, Inc.

Note: Internet job boards continue to be the most *effective* sources followed by employee referral programs and professional and trade media and associations.

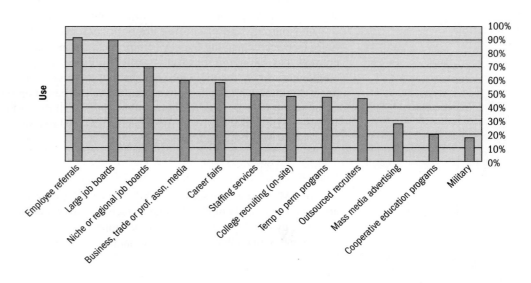

TABLE 4.1 Recruitment: Practical Applications for Managers

Research Finding[a]	Practical Applications for Managers
The recruitment source affects the characteristics of applicants you attract.	Use sources such as referrals from current employees, which yield applicants more likely to be better performers.
Recruitment materials have a more positive impact if they contain more specific information.	Provide applicants with more information on aspects of the job, such as salary, location, and diversity.
Organizational image influences applicants' initial reactions.	Ensure all communications regarding an organization provide a positive message regarding attractiveness as a place to work.
Applicants with a greater number of job opportunities are more attentive to early recruitment activities.	Ensure initial recruitment activities (e.g., Web site, brochure, on-campus recruiting) are attractive to candidates.
Realistic job previews that highlight both the advantages and the disadvantages of the job reduce subsequent turnover.	Provide applicants with a realistic picture of the job, not just the positives.
Applicants will infer (perhaps erroneous) information about the job and company if the information is not clearly provided by the company.	Provide clear, specific, and complete information in recruitment materials.
Recruiter warmth has a large and positive effect on applicants.	Choose individuals who have contact with applicants for their interpersonal skills.
Recruitment source has a significant effect on reducing turnover.	Individuals recruited through personal recruitment sources such as employee referral programs are less likely to terminate their employment early.

[a]Selected research principles from M. S. Taylor & C. J. Collins "Organizational recruitment: Enhancing the intersection of theory and practice." In C. L. Cooper & E. A. Locke (Eds.), *Industrial and Organizational Psychology: Linking Theory and Practice* (2000): 304–334, Oxford, UK: Blackwell.

Sources: Adapted from Ann Marie Ryan and Nancy Tippins, "Attracting and Selecting: What Psychological Research Tells Us," *Human Resource Management* 43, no. 4 (Winter 2004): 311, and Ingo Weller et al., "Level and Time Effects of Recruitment Sources on Early Voluntary Turnover," *Journal of Applied Psychology* 94, no. 5 (2009): 1146–1162. Reprinted by permission of Society for Human Resource Management via Copyright Clearance Center.

Recruiting and attracting older workers generally requires a comprehensive effort to make the company an attractive place in which the older worker can work. For example, AARP published its list of "The Top 15" best companies for older workers. A sampling of what sets these employers apart for older workers follows:[90]

- Baptist Health System South Florida, Stanley Group, and Hartford Financial Services Group offer flexible work arrangements including phased retirement. Hartford actually offers eight flexible work arrangements.
- New York Life Insurance Company opens its child care center to grandchildren.
- The most effective ads for attracting older workers emphasize schedule flexibility and accentuate the firm's equal opportunity employment statement.[91]

RECRUITING SINGLE PARENTS Formulating an intelligent program for attracting and keeping single parents starts with understanding the problems they encounter. In one early survey, working single parents (the majority single mothers) stated that their work responsibilities interfered significantly with their family life. They described as a no-win situation the challenge of having to do a good job at work and being a good parent.

Given such concerns, the first step in attracting and keeping single parents is to make the workplace as user-friendly for single parents as practical. Organizing regular, ongoing support groups and other forums at which single parents can share their concerns is useful. So is teaming human resource employees with out-of-work single parents to mentor them in interviewing and résumé writing.[92]

However, the main aim should be to make the workplace more family friendly. Many firms' family friendly programs may not be extensive enough. For example, *flextime* programs provide employees some flexibility (such as 1-hour windows at the beginning or end of the day) around which to build their workdays. The problem is that for many single parents this limited flexibility may not be enough to make a difference in the face of the "patchwork child care" pressures that many face.[93]

Flexible work schedules and child care benefits are thus two main single-parent magnets. In addition, surveys suggest that a supportive attitude on the supervisor's part is crucial.

RECRUITING MINORITIES AND WOMEN   Again, employers have to formulate comprehensive plans for attracting minorities and women. Thus, to the extent that many minority applicants may not meet the educational or experience standards for a job, many companies (such as Aetna Life & Casualty) offer remedial training in basic arithmetic and writing. Using online diversity data banks or minority-focused recruiting publications and offering flexible work hours are other options.

Sometimes the easiest way to recruit women and minorities is to make sure that they don't quit in the first place. For example, at the accounting firm KPMG, when an expectant mother tells HR that she's going to take maternity leave, the company sends her a basket containing a description of its parental leave benefits as well as a baby bottle, a rattle, and a tiny T-shirt that says, "My mom works at KPMG."[94]

THE DISABLED   The EEOC estimates that nearly 70% of the disabled are jobless, but it certainly doesn't have to be that way.[95] For some managers it may require a new mindset, one that welcomes disabled employees as an excellent source of competent labor for jobs ranging from information technology to creative advertising to receptionist. Complying with the Americans with Disabilities Act is another sensible strategy, but it's also important to go beyond this. For instance, actively seek out and make available the sorts of voice recognition and other technologies that can ensure the disabled worker is a productive one. For instance, a receptionist, Mr. Janz, greets customers visiting Volkswagen's Wolfsburg plant in Germany. Mr. Janz is blind, and a sign on his desk tells visitors to speak directly to him so he knows they are there.[96] Volkswagen recruited Mr. Janz because the company has a policy of integrating people with disabilities into its workforce.

DEVELOPING AND USING APPLICATION FORMS

Purpose of Application Forms

application form

The form that provides information on education, prior work record, and skills.

Once you have a pool of applicants, the selection process can begin. For most employers the application form is the first step in this process. (Some firms first require a brief, prescreening interview.) The **application form** provides verifiable historical data from the candidate.

A filled-in form provides five types of information. First is data on *substantive matters*, such as does the applicant have the education and experience to do the job? Second, you can draw some conclusions about the applicant's *career progress*. Third, you can draw tentative conclusions regarding the applicant's *stability* based on previous work record. (However, be careful not to assume that an unusual number of job changes necessarily reflects on the applicant's stability; for example, the person's two most recent employers may have had to lay off large numbers of employees.) Fourth, it provides information to check *references* and to assess the veracity of the applicant's answers.

Finally, employers can use analyses of application information ("biodata") to predict employee tenure and performance. Thus in one study, the researchers found that applicants who had longer tenure with previous employers were less likely to quit, and also had higher performance within six months after hire.[97] Examples of biodata items might include "quit a job without giving notice," "graduated from college," and "traveled considerably growing up."[98]

In practice, most organizations need several application forms. For technical and managerial personnel, for example, the form may require answers to questions concerning such areas as the applicant's education. The form for hourly factory workers might focus on tools and equipment the applicant has used.

Equal Opportunity and Application Forms

Employers should carefully review their application forms to ensure compliance with equal employment laws. Questions concerning race, religion, age, sex, or national origin are generally not illegal per se under federal laws (but are under certain state laws). However, the EEOC views them with disfavor. If the applicant shows that a disproportionate number of protected group applicants is screened out, then the burden of proof will be on the employer to prove that the potentially discriminatory items are both job-related and not unfairly discriminatory. One survey of 41 Internet-based applications found that over 97% contained at least one inadvisable question. Questions regarding the applicant's past salary, age, and driver's license information led the list.[99]

FEDERAL BUREAU OF INVESTIGATION

FIELD OFFICE USE ONLY
Right Thumb Print

Preliminary Application for
Special Agent Position
(Please Type or Print in Black Ink)

Div: Program:

Date: _____

I. PERSONAL HISTORY

Name in Full   (Last, First, Middle) | List College Degree(s) Already Received or Pursuing, Major, School, and Month/Year:

Marital Status: ☐ Single ☐ Engaged ☐ Married ☐ Separated ☐ Legally Separated ☐ Widowed ☐ Divorced

Birth Date (Month, Day, Year)
Birth Place: | Social Security Number: (Optional) | Do you understand FBI employment requires availability for assignment anywhere in the U.S.?

Current Address

Street   Apt. No. | Home Phone _____
| Area Code   Number

City   State   Zip Code | Work Phone _____
| Area Code   Number

Are you: CPA ☐ Yes ☐ No   Licensed Driver ☐ Yes ☐ No   U. S. Citizen ☐ Yes ☐ No

Have you served on active duty in the U. S. Military? ☐ Yes ☐ No If yes, indicate branch of service and dates (month/year) of active duty. Include military school attendance (month/year):

How did you learn or become interested in FBI employment as a Special Agent? | Have you previously applied for FBI employment? ☐ Yes ☐ No If yes, location and date:

Do you have a foreign language background? ☐ Yes ☐ No   List proficiency for each language on reverse side.

Have you ever been arrested for any crime (include major traffic violations such as Driving Under the Influence or While Intoxicated, etc.)? ☐ Yes ☐ No If so, list all such matters on a continuation sheet, even if not formally charged, or no court appearance or found not guilty, or matter settled by payment of fine or forfeiture of collateral. Include date, place, charge, disposition, details, and police agency on reverse side.

II. EMPLOYMENT HISTORY

Identify your most recent three years FULL-TIME work experience, after high school (excluding summer, part-time and temporary employment).

From Month/Year	To Month/Year	Title of Position and Description of Work	# of hrs. Per week	Name/Location of Employer

III. PERSONAL DECLARATIONS

Persons with a disability who require an accommodation to complete the application process are required to notify the FBI of their need for the accommodation.

Have you used marijuana during the last three years or more than 15 times? ☐ Yes ☐ No

Have you used any illegal drug(s) or combination of illegal drugs, other than marijuana, more than 5 times or during the last 10 years? ☐ Yes ☐ No

All Information provided by applicants concerning their drug history will be subject to verification by a preemployment polygraph examination.

Do you understand all prospective FBI employees will be required to submit to an urinalysis for drug abuse prior to employment? ☐ Yes ☐ No

Please do not write below this line.

I am aware that willfully withholding information or making false statements on this application constitutes a violation of Section 1001. Title 18, U.S. Code and if appointed, will be the basis for dismissal from the Federal Bureau of Investigation. I agree to these conditions and I hereby certify that all statements made by me on this application are true and complete, to the best of my knowledge.

_____
Signature of applicant as usually written (**Do Not Use Nickname**)

FIGURE 4.12

FBI Employment Application

Source: www.fbijobs.gov/employment/fd646c.pdf, accessed April 28, 2009.

Figure 4.12 presents the approach one employer—the FBI—uses to collect application form information. The Employment History section requests information on each prior employer, including job title, duties, name of supervisor, and whether the employment was involuntarily terminated. Also note that in signing the application, the applicant certifies his or her understanding of several things: that falsified statements may be cause for dismissal; that investigation of credit, employment, and driving records is authorized; that a medical examination may be required; that drug screening tests may be required; and that employment is for no definite period of time.

Video Résumés More candidates are submitting video résumés. About half of responding employers in one survey thought video résumés might give employers a better feel for the candidate's professional demeanor, presentation skills, and job experience. The danger is that a video résumé makes it more likely rejected candidates may claim discrimination.[100]

MANDATORY DISPUTE RESOLUTION More employers are requiring applicants to sign mandatory alternative dispute resolution forms as part of the application process. But while mandatory arbitration is on the rise, it is also under attack. Courts, the EEOC, and even arbitrators are concerned that binding arbitration strips away too many employees' rights (*voluntary* arbitration is not under attack).[101] Mandatory arbitration can also have a significantly negative impact on the attractiveness to the subjects of the company as a place to work.[102]

Mandatory dispute resolution is generally enforceable, with some caveats.[103] For example, the agreement should be a signed and dated separate agreement. Use simple wording. Provide for reconsideration and judicial appeal if there is an error of law.[104] The employer must absorb most of the cost of the arbitration process. The arbitration process should be reasonably swift. The employee, if he or she prevails, should be eligible to receive the full remedies that he or she would have had if he or she had had access to the courts.

After You Receive the Application

After you receive the application, the job of screening the applicants begins, so we turn to selection and screening in Chapter 5. Before turning to selection, however, there are two points to keep in mind.

COURTESY First, some employers institute recruiting programs and then drop the ball. A survey by Monster.com illustrates this. What interviewer behaviors most annoyed job seekers? Seventy percent of job seekers listed "acting as if there is no time to talk to me." Fifty-seven percent listed "withholding information about position." About half listed "turning interview into cross examination" and "showing up late."[105]

STAYING IN TOUCH Second, given recruiting's costs, it pays to maintain contact with candidates who, while not hirable today, may be of interest tomorrow. Some employers use "candidate relationship management" systems for this. *Candidate relationship management* systems aim to nurture relationships with prospective candidates by periodically informing past candidates about potentially interesting job openings.[106]

REVIEW

SUMMARY

1. *Talent management* is the *goal-oriented* and *integrated* process of *planning, recruiting, developing, managing, and compensating* employees.[107] In one respect, there's nothing new about talent management, since in simplest terms it involves getting the right people (in terms of competencies) in the right jobs, at the right time, doing their jobs correctly.

2. Job analysis is the procedure through which you find out (1) what the job entails and (2) what kinds of people should be hired for the job. It involves six steps: (1) Determine the use of the job analysis information, (2) collect background information, (3) select the positions to be analyzed, (4) collect job analysis data,

(5) review information with participants, and (6) develop a job description and job specification.

3. The job specification supplements the job description to answer the question "What human traits and experience are necessary to do this job well?" It tells what kind of person to recruit and for what qualities that person should be tested. Job specifications are usually based on the educated guesses of managers; however, a more accurate statistical approach to developing job specifications can also be used.

4. *Traditional job analysis* focuses on "what" a job is in terms of job duties and responsibilities. *Competency analysis* focuses more on "how" the worker meets the

job's objectives or actually accomplishes the work. Traditional job analysis is more job focused. Competency-based analysis is worker focused—specifically, what must he or she be competent to do?

5. Developing personnel plans requires three forecasts: one for personnel requirements, one for the supply of outside candidates, and one for the supply of inside candidates. To predict the need for personnel, first project the demand for the product or service. Next project the volume of production required to meet these estimates. Finally, relate personnel needs to these production estimates.

6. Once personnel needs are projected, the next step is to build a pool of qualified applicants. We discussed several sources of candidates, including internal sources (or promotion from within), advertising, employment agencies, executive recruiters, college recruiting, the Internet, referrals, and walk-ins.

7. Once you have a pool of applicants, the work of selecting the best can begin. We turn to employee selection in the following chapter.

KEY TERMS

DISCUSSION QUESTIONS

1. Describe the basic methods of collecting job analysis information.
2. Explain how you would conduct a job analysis.
3. Explain the process of forecasting personnel requirements.
4. Compare the eight methods for recruiting job candidates.
5. Explain how to use application forms to predict job performance.
6. What items are typically included in a job description? What items are not shown?
7. What is job analysis? How can you make use of the information it provides?
8. What types of information can an application form provide?

INDIVIDUAL AND GROUP ACTIVITIES

1. Bring to class several classified and display ads from the Sunday help wanted ads. Analyze the effectiveness of these ads using the guidelines discussed in this chapter.
2. Working individually or in groups, develop a 5-year forecast of occupational market conditions for five occupations such as accountant, nurse, and engineer.
3. Working individually or in groups, visit the local office of your state employment agency. Come back to class prepared to discuss the following questions: What types of jobs seem to be available through this agency, predominantly? To what extent do you think this particular agency would be a good source of professional, technical, and/or managerial applicants? What sorts of paperwork are applicants to the state agency required to complete before their applications are processed by the agency? What other services does the office provide? What other opinions do you form about the state agency?

4. Working individually or in groups, find at least five employment ads, either on the Internet or in a local newspaper, that suggest that the company is family friendly and should appeal to women, minorities, older workers, and single parents. Discuss what they're doing to be family friendly.
5. Working individually or in groups, interview a manager between the ages of 25 and 35 at a local business who manages employees age 40 or older. Ask the manager to describe three or four of his or her most challenging experiences managing older employees.
6. Working individually or in groups, review help wanted ads placed over the past few Sundays by local employment agencies. Do some employment agencies seem to specialize in some types of jobs? If you were an HR manager seeking a relationship with an employment agency for each of the following types of jobs, which local agencies would you turn to first, based on their help wanted ad

history: engineers, secretaries, data-processing clerks, accountants, and factory workers?

7. Working individually or in groups, obtain copies of job descriptions for clerical positions at the college or university you attend or the firm where you work. What types of information do they contain? Do they give you enough information to explain what the job involves and how to do it? How would you improve the descriptions?

WEB-e's (WEB EXERCISES)

1. What can you tell from Web sites such as www.cakecareers.com about how the Cheesecake Factory recruits and selects employees?
2. Use http://online.onetcenter.org to answer the question, "How I can use O*NET OnLine to do a better job of selecting employees for my department?"
3. Your boss has asked you to find an executive recruiter who can help your company hire a sales manager for a chemical engineering company. Use sites such as www.onlinerecruitersdirectory.com/ to suggest three such recruiters.

APPLICATION EXERCISES

HR IN ACTION CASE INCIDENT 1
Finding People Who Are Passionate About What They Do

Trilogy Enterprises Inc., of Austin, Texas, is a fast-growing software company that provides software solutions to giant global firms for improving sales and performance. It prides itself on its unique and unorthodox culture. Many of its approaches to business practice are unusual, but in Trilogy's fast-changing and highly competitive environment they seem to work.

There is no dress code and employees make their own hours—often very long. They tend to socialize together (the average age is 26), both in the office's well-stocked kitchen and on company-sponsored events and trips to places like local dance clubs and retreats in Las Vegas and Hawaii. An in-house jargon has developed, and the shared history of the 16-year-old firm has taken on the status of legend. Responsibility is heavy and comes early, with a "just do it now" attitude that dispenses with long apprenticeships. New recruits are given a few weeks of intensive training, known as Trilogy University and described by participants as "more like boot camp than business school." Information is delivered as if with "a fire hose," and new employees are expected to commit their expertise and vitality to everything they do. Jeff Daniel, director of college recruiting, admits the intense and unconventional firm is not the employer for everybody. "But it's definitely an environment where people who are passionate about what they do can thrive."

The firm employs about 700 such passionate people. Trilogy's managers know the rapid growth they seek depends on having a staff of the best people they can find, quickly trained and given broad responsibility and freedom as soon as possible. Founder and CEO Joe Liemandt says, "At a software company, people are everything. You can't build the next great software company, which is what we're trying to do here, unless you're totally committed to that. Of course, the leaders at every company say, 'People are everything.' But they don't act on it."

Trilogy makes finding the right people (it calls them "great people") a company-wide mission. Recruiters actively pursue the freshest, if least experienced, people in the job market, scouring college career fairs and computer science departments for talented over-achievers with ambition and entrepreneurial instincts. Top managers conduct the first rounds of interviews, letting prospects know they will be pushed to achieve but will be well rewarded. Employees take top recruits and their significant others out on the town when they fly into Austin for the standard, 3-day preliminary visit. A typical day might begin with grueling interviews but end with mountain biking, rollerblading, or laser tag. Executives have been known to fly out to meet and woo hot prospects who couldn't make the trip.

One year, Trilogy reviewed 15,000 résumés, conducted 4,000 on-campus interviews, flew 850 prospects in for interviews, and hired 262 college graduates, who account for over a third of its current employees. The cost per hire was $13,000; recruiter Jeff Daniel believes it was worth every penny.

Questions
1. Identify some of the established recruiting techniques that underlie Trilogy's unconventional approach to attracting talent.
2. What particular elements of Trilogy's culture most likely appeal to the kind of employees it seeks? How does it convey those elements to job prospects?
3. Would Trilogy be an appealing employer for you? Why or why not? If not, what would it take for you to accept a job offer from Trilogy?
4. What suggestions would you make to Trilogy for improving its recruiting processes?

Sources: Chuck Salter, "Insanity, Inc.," *Fast Company* (January 1999): 101–108; and http://trilogy.com/careers.php, accessed May 31, 2010.

HR IN ACTION CASE INCIDENT 2

Carter Cleaning Company: A Tight Labor Market for Cleaners

While most of the publicity about "tight" labor markets usually revolves around systems engineers, nurses, and chemical engineers, some of the tightest markets are found in some surprising places. For example, if you were to ask Jennifer Carter, the head of her family's chain of dry cleaning stores, what the main problem was in running their firm, the answer would be quick and short: hiring good people. The typical dry cleaning store is heavily dependent on hiring good managers, cleaner-spotters, and pressers. Employees generally have no more than a high school education (many have less), and the market is very competitive. Over a typical weekend, literally dozens of want ads for cleaner-spotters or pressers can be found in area newspapers. These people are generally paid about $12 an hour, and they change jobs frequently.

Why so much difficulty finding good help? The work is hot and uncomfortable; the hours are often long; the pay is often the same or less than the typical applicant could earn working in an air-conditioned environment, and the fringe benefits are usually nonexistent, unless you count getting your clothes cleaned for free.

Complicating the problem is the fact that Jennifer and other cleaners are usually faced with the continuing task of recruiting and hiring qualified workers out of a pool of individuals who are almost nomadic in their propensity to move around. The turnover in her stores and the stores of many competitors is often 400% per year. The problem, Jennifer says, is maddening: "On the one hand, the quality of our service depends on the skills of the cleaner-spotters, pressers, and counter staff. People come to us for our ability to return their clothes to them spotless and crisply pressed. On the other hand, profit margins are thin and we've got to keep our stores running, so I'm happy just to be able to round up enough live applicants to be able to keep my stores fully manned."

Questions

1. Recruiting for cleaning store employees obviously presents quite a challenge. Provide a detailed list of recommendations concerning how Jennifer should go about increasing the number of acceptable job applicants, so that her company need no longer hire just about anyone who walks in the door. Specifically, your recommendations should include:
   - Completely worded classified ads
   - Recommendations concerning any other recruiting strategies you would suggest she use
2. What practical suggestions could you make that might help reduce turnover and make the stores an attractive place in which to work, thereby reducing recruiting problems?

EXPERIENTIAL EXERCISE

The Nursing Shortage

As of 2010, employers were obviously holding back on their hiring. However, while many people were unemployed, that was not the case with nurse professionals. Virtually every hospital was aggressively recruiting nurses. Many were turning to foreign-trained nurses, for example, by recruiting nurses in the Philippines. Experts expected nurses to be in very short supply for years to come.

Purpose: The purpose of this exercise is to give you experience creating a recruitment program.

Required Understanding: You should be thoroughly familiar with the contents of this chapter, and with the nurse recruitment program of a hospital such as Lenox Hill Hospital in New York (see for example, www.lenoxhillhospital.org/jobs.aspx?id=728%5D).[108]

How to Set Up the Exercise/Instructions: Set up groups of four to five students for this exercise. The groups should work separately and should not converse with each other. Each group should address the following tasks:

1. Based on information available on the hospital's Web site, create a hard-copy ad for the hospital to place in the Sunday edition of *The New York Times*. Which (geographic) editions of the *Times* would you use and why?
2. Analyze and critique the hospital's current online nurses' ad. How would you improve it?
3. Prepare in outline form a complete nurses' recruiting program for this hospital, including all recruiting sources your group would use

BUSINESS IN ACTION EDU-EXERCISE

Building Your *Marketing* Knowledge

Attracting applicants is more important than most managers realize. As we said in this chapter, the more applicants you have, the more selective you can be in your hiring. The converse is that with, say, just one or two applicants for one or two positions, your only real decision is to "take them or leave them." You can't be very selective.

That's why attracting applicants relies (or should rely) on good marketing skills. *Marketing* doesn't just mean selling. Marketing means enabling people *to get what they need and want by creating something that's of value to them.*[110] Employers can therefore view recruiting partly in terms of marketing. You want to attract applicants. You do this by signaling that working for you will create value for the prospective applicants. And you do that by appealing, with your recruitment efforts, to their *needs* (for things like security, affection, camaraderie, or self expression) or to their *wants* (for culturally determined things like particular items such as designer clothes). It's therefore no accident

that some high-fashion retail stores like Saks prominently emphasize employee shopping discounts when they write their help wanted ads! The bottom line is that you should take a marketing "how can we create value for prospective applicants" approach when creating your recruitment campaign.

Questions

1. Obtain a selection of five online and hard-copy newspaper recruiting ads. Review these ads and evaluate them in terms of how good a job they do appealing to prospective applicants' needs and wants, and sending the signal that working for the employer would create something of value for them.
2. Check the jobs or careers sections of three employers' Web sites. How good a job of "marketing" does each do to prospective employees? Why?

PERSONAL COMPETENCIES EDU-EXERCISE

Building Your *Vendor Management* Skills

Vendor management is an important skill when dealing with suppliers like employment and temp agencies. Delegating too much authority to them, without retaining sufficient oversight, can lead to problems, such as bringing employees on board who don't meet your firm's normal screening standards. When working with temporary agencies, effective vendor management means taking steps and precautions such as:

- *Invoicing.* Get a sample copy of the agency's invoice. Make sure it fits your company's needs.
- *Time sheets.* With temps, the time sheet is not just a verification of hours worked. Once the worker's supervisor signs it, it's usually an agreement to pay the agency's fees.
- *Temp-to-perm policy.* What is the policy if the client wants to hire one of the agency's temps as a permanent employee?
- *Recruitment of and benefits for temp employees.* Find out how the agency plans to recruit employees and what sorts of benefits it pays.
- *Dress code.* Specify the appropriate attire at each of your offices or plants.

- *Equal employment opportunity statement.* Get a document from the agency stating that it is not discriminating when filling temp orders.
- *Job description information.* Have a procedure whereby you can ensure the agency understands the job to be filled and the sort of person, in terms of skills and so forth, you want to fill it.
- *Selection standards.* Make sure you and the agency fully understand and agree on the selection procedures and standards the agency will use in selecting employees for your positions.[109]

Questions

Assume you are the HR manager for Apex Electronics, and that you want to retain an employment agency to recruit candidates for the job of bookkeeper.

1. Use online or other means to compile a sample of policies governing matters such as invoicing, time sheets, and temp-to-perm from employment agencies in your geographic area.
2. Create a procedure whereby you can ensure the agency understands the job to be filled and the sort of person, in terms of skills and so forth, you want to fill it.

APPENDIX

ENRICHMENT TOPICS IN JOB ANALYSIS: ADDITIONAL JOB ANALYSIS METHODS

Job Analysis Record Sheet

The U.S. Civil Service Commission has a standardized procedure for comparing and classifying jobs. Information here is compiled on a *job analysis record sheet* (Figure A4.1). Identifying information (such as job title) and a brief summary of the job are listed first. Next, the job's specific tasks are listed in order of importance. Then, for each task, the analyst specifies such things as the knowledge required (for example, the facts or principles the worker must be acquainted with to do his or her job), skills required (for example, the skills needed to operate machines or vehicles), and abilities required (for example, mathematical, reasoning, problem solving, or interpersonal abilities).

Position Analysis Questionnaire

The *position analysis questionnaire (PAQ)* is a very structured job analysis questionnaire.[111] The PAQ is filled in by a job analyst, a person who should be acquainted with the particular job to be analyzed. The PAQ contains 194 items, each of which (such as "written materials") represents a basic element that may or may not play an important role in the job. The job analyst decides whether each item plays a role on the job and, if so, to what extent. In Figure A4.2 on page 112, for example, "Written materials" might receive a rating of 4, indicating that written materials (such as books, reports, and office notes) play a considerable role in this job.

JOB ANALYSIS RECORD SHEET

IDENTIFYING INFORMATION

Name of Incumbent:	A. Adler
Organization/Unit:	Welfare Services
Title:	Welfare Eligibility Examiner
Date:	11/12/09
Interviewer:	E. Jones

BRIEF SUMMARY OF JOB

Conducts interviews, completes applications, determines eligibility, provides information to community sources regarding food stamp program; refers noneligible food stamp applicants to other applicable community resource agencies.

TASKS

1. Decide (determine) eligibility of applicant in order to complete client's application for food stamps using regulatory policies as guide.

Knowledge Required

– Knowledge of contents and meaning of items on standard application form
– Knowledge of Social-Health Services food stamp regulatory policies
– Knowledge of statutes relating to Social-Health Services food stamp program

Skills Required

– None

(continued)

FIGURE A4.1

Portion of a Completed Civil Service Job Analysis Record Sheet

Note: This job might typically involve five or six tasks. For *each* task, list the knowledge, skill abilities, physical activities, environmental conditions, typical work incidents, and interest areas.

Abilities Required

—Ability to read and understand complex instructions such as regulatory policies
—Ability to read and understand a variety of procedural instructions, written and oral, and convert these to proper actions
—Ability to use simple arithmetic: addition and subtraction
—Ability to translate requirements into language appropriate to laypeople

Physical Activities

—Sedentary

Environmental Conditions

—None

Typical Work Incidents

—Working with people beyond giving and receiving instructions

Interest Areas

—Communication of data
—Business contact with people
—Working for the presumed good of people

2. Decides upon, describes, and explains other agencies available for client to contact in order to assist and refer client to appropriate community resources using worker's knowledge of resources available and knowledge of client's needs.

Knowledge Required

—Knowledge of functions of various assistance agencies
—Knowledge of community resources available and their locations
—Knowledge of referral procedures

Skills Required

—None

Abilities Required

—Ability to extract (discern) persons' needs from oral discussion
—Ability to give simple oral and written instructions to persons

Physical Activities

—Sedentary

Environmental Conditions

—None

Typical Work Incidents

—Working with people beyond giving and receiving instructions

Interest Areas

—Communication of data
—Business contact with people
—Abstract and creative problem solving
—Working for the presumed good of people

FIGURE A4.1
(Continued)

The advantage of the PAQ is that it provides a quantitative score or profile of any job in terms of how that job rates on five basic job traits such as "having decision-making/communications/social responsibilities." The PAQ lets you assign a single quantitative score or value to each job. You can therefore use the PAQ results to compare jobs relative to one another; this information can then be used to assign pay levels for each job.

U.S. Department of Labor Procedure

The *U.S. Department of Labor (DOL) procedure* also aims to provide a standardized method by which different jobs can be quantitatively rated, classified, and compared. Although largely displaced by the Department of Labor's newer O*NET

system, it still provides a useful approach.[112] The heart of this analysis is a rating of each job in terms of an employee's specific functions with respect to *data, people,* and *things.* As illustrated in Table A4.1, a set of basic activities called *worker functions* describes what a worker can do with respect to data, people, and things. With respect to *data,* for instance, the basic functions include synthesizing, coordinating, and copying. Note also that each worker function has been assigned an importance level. Thus, "coordinating" is 1 and "copying" is 5. If you were analyzing the job of a receptionist/clerk, for example, you might label the job 5, 6, 7, which would represent copying data, speaking/signaling people, and handling things.

TABLE A4.1 **Basic Department of Labor Worker Functions**

	Data	People	Things
Basic Activities	0 Synthesizing	0 Mentoring	0 Setting up
	1 Coordinating	1 Negotiating	1 Precision working
	2 Analyzing	2 Instructing	2 Operating/controlling
	3 Compiling	3 Supervising	3 Driving/operating
	4 Computing	4 Diverting	4 Manipulating
	5 Copying	5 Persuading	5 Tending
	6 Comparing	6 Speaking/signaling	6 Feeding/offbearing
		7 Serving	7 Handling
		8 Taking instructions/helping	

Note: Determine employee's job "score" on data, people, and things by observing his or her job and determining, for each of the three categories, which of the basic functions illustrates the person's job. "0" is high; "6," "8," and "7" are lows in each column.

A Practical Job Analysis Method

Many managers and small business owners face two hurdles when doing job analyses and job descriptions. First, they need a streamlined approach for developing a job description. Second, they fear that they will overlook duties that subordinates should be assigned.

Web sites like www.jobdescription.com provide customizable descriptions by title and industry. We'll focus here on how you can write a job description using O*NET (http://online.onetcenter.org).[113]

Step 1. Decide on a Plan Ideally, the jobs you need should flow from your departmental or company plans. Therefore, you may want to review your plan. What do you expect your sales to be next year, and in the next few years? What areas or departments do you think will have to be expanded or reduced? What kinds of new positions do you think you'll need?

Step 2. Develop an Organization Chart You may want to develop an organization chart. Start with the organization as it is now. Then (depending upon how far you're planning), produce a chart showing how you'd like your chart to look in

the future (say, in a year or two). Microsoft's MS Word includes an organization charting function. Software packages such as OrgPublisher from TimeVision of Irving, Texas, are another option.[114]

Step 3. Use a Simplified Job Analysis Questionnaire Next, gather preliminary information about the job's duties. (You can use one of the more comprehensive job analysis questionnaires, such as that shown in Figure A4.3 on page 113. But the questionnaire shown in Figure A4.4 on page 115 is simpler and satisfactory for our purposes here.) Fill in the required information. This includes the job's duties divided into daily duties, periodic duties, and duties performed at irregular intervals.

Step 4. Obtain Job Duties from O*NET The list of job duties you uncovered in the previous step may or may not be complete. We'll therefore use O*NET to compile a more complete list. Refer to the visual examples as you read along.

Start by going to http://online.onetcenter.org (A), shown on page 116. Here, click on *Find Occupations.* Assume you want to create job descriptions for a retail salesperson. Type in *Retail Sales* for the occupational titles, and *Sales and Related* from the "job families" drop-down box.

The PAQ Answer Sheet

The PAQ answer sheet is a two-sided computer-scorable answer sheet designed for optical scanning. The first side is for administrative use and should be filled out by the job analyst, simply coding in the information requested and providing in the upper left corner a brief job description of the job being analyzed. Refer to the PAQ *Job Analysis Manual* for explicit instructions on completing the information fields shown on side 1. The second side is reserved for item responses. Use only a No. 2 pencil for marking responses, filling in response bubbles completely and erasing carefully any changed responses and/or stray marks. Please do not fold or staple the answer sheet.

When entering responses to PAQ items, make sure to use the response scale that is clearly indicated in the outer narrow margin. After deciding which is the most appropriate response, darken the corresponding response bubble for the item on the answer sheet. Once you have responded to all of the items on the PAQ, please review the answer sheet to ensure that all information entered is complete and accurate. Refer to the PAQ *Job Analysis Manual* for specific instructions regarding the completion of the Pay or Income items found in section F10.

A. Information Input

A1. Visual Sources of Job Information

Using the response scale at the left, rate each of the following items on the basis of the extent to which it is used by the worker as a source of information in performing the job.

Extent of Use

0 Does not apply
1 Nominal/very infrequent
2 Occasional
3 Moderate
4 Considerable
5 Very substantial

1. Written materials
E.g., books, reports, office notes, articles, job instructions, or signs

2. Quantitative materials
Materials that deal with quantities or amounts, e.g., graphs, accounts, specifications, or tables of numbers

3. Pictorial materials
Pictures or picture-like materials used as sources of information, e.g., drawings, blueprints, diagrams, maps, tracings, photographic films, x-ray films, or TV pictures

4. Patterns or related devices
E.g., templates, stencils, or patterns used as sources of information when observed during use (Do not include materials described in item 3.)

5. Visual displays
E.g., dials, gauges, signal lights, radarscopes, speedometers, or clocks

6. Measuring devices
E.g., rules, calipers, tire pressure gauges, scales, thickness gauges, pipettes, thermometers, or protractors used to obtain visual information about physical measurements (Do not include devices described in item 5.)

7. Mechanical devices
E.g., tools, equipment, or machinery that are sources of information when observed during use or operation

FIGURE A4.2

Portions of a Completed Page from the Position Analysis Questionnaire

Source: Reprinted by permission of PAQ Services, Inc.

Job Analysis Information Sheet

Job Title _____ Date _____

Job Code _____ Dept. _____

Superior's Title _____

Hours worked _____ AM to _____ PM

Job Analyst's Name _____

1. **What is the job's overall purpose?**

_____

2. **If the incumbent supervises others,** list them by job title; if there is more than one employee with the same title, put the number in parentheses following the title.

_____

3. **Check those activities** that are part of the incumbent's supervisory duties.

☐ Training

☐ Performance appraisal

☐ Inspecting work

☐ Budgeting

☐ Coaching and/or counseling

☐ Others (please specify) _____

4. **Describe the type and extent of supervision** received by the incumbent.

_____

5. **JOB DUTIES:** Describe briefly WHAT the incumbent does and, if possible, HOW he/she does it. Include duties in the following categories:

   a. Daily duties (those performed on a regular basis every day or almost every day)

   _____

   b. Periodic duties (those performed weekly, monthly, quarterly, or at other regular intervals)

   _____

   c. Duties performed at irregular intervals

   _____

6. Is the incumbent performing duties he/she considers unnecessary? If so, describe.

_____

7. Is the incumbent performing duties not presently included in the job description? If so, describe.

_____

8. **EDUCATION:** Check the box that indicates the educational requirements for the job (not the educational background of the incumbent).

☐ No formal education   ☐ Eighth grade education

☐ High school diploma (or equivalent)   ☐ 2-year college degree (or equivalent)

☐ 4-year college degree (or equivalent) (specify)   ☐ Graduate work or advanced degree

☐ Professional license (specify)

9. **EXPERIENCE:** Check the amount of experience needed to perform the job.

☐ None   ☐ Less than one month

☐ One to six months   ☐ Six months to one year

☐ One to three years   ☐ Three to five years

☐ Five to ten years   ☐ More than ten years

(continued)

FIGURE A4.3

Job Analysis Questionnaire for Developing Job Descriptions. *Use a questionnaire like this to interview job incumbents, or have them fill it out.*

Source: Reprinted from HR.BLR.com with the permission of BLR. © 2007. Business & Legal Reports, Inc., 141 Mill Rock Rd East, Old Saybrook, CT 06475.

10. **LOCATION:** Check location of job and, if necessary or appropriate, describe briefly.

☐ Outdoor   ☐ Indoor

☐ Underground   ☐ Pit

☐ Scaffold   ☐ Other (specify)

11. **ENVIRONMENTAL CONDITIONS:** Check any objectionable conditions found on the job and note afterward how frequently each is encountered (rarely, occasionally, constantly, etc.).

☐ Dirt   ☐ Dust

☐ Heat   ☐ Cold

☐ Noise   ☐ Fumes

☐ Odors   ☐ Wetness/humidity

☐ Vibration   ☐ Sudden temperature changes

☐ Darkness or poor lighting   ☐ Other (specify)

12. **HEALTH AND SAFETY:** Check any undesirable health and safety conditions under which the incumbent must perform and note how often they are encountered.

☐ Elevated workplace   ☐ Mechanical hazards

☐ Explosives   ☐ Electrical hazards

☐ Fire hazards   ☐ Radiation

☐ Other (specify)

13. **MACHINES, TOOLS, EQUIPMENT, AND WORK AIDS:** Describe briefly what machines, tools, equipment, or work aids the incumbent works with on a regular basis.

_____

14. Have concrete work standards been established (errors allowed, time taken for a particular task, etc.)? If so, what are they?

_____

15. Are there any personal attributes (special aptitudes, physical characteristics, personality traits, etc.) required by the job?

_____

16. Are there any exceptional problems the incumbent might be expected to encounter in performing the job under normal conditions? If so, describe.

_____

17. Describe the successful completion and/or end results of the job.

_____

18. What is the seriousness of error on this job? Who or what is affected by errors the incumbent makes?

_____

19. To what job would a successful incumbent expect to be promoted?

[**Note:** This form is obviously slanted toward a manufacturing environment, but it can be adapted quite easily to fit a number of different types of jobs.]

FIGURE A4.3

(Continued)

Click *Find Occupations* to continue, which brings you to the *Find Occupations Search Result* (B), shown on page 116.

Clicking on *Retail Salespersons*-summary produces the job summary and specific occupational duties for retail salespersons (C), shown on page 116. For a small store, you might want to combine the duties of the "retail salesperson" with those of "first-line supervisors/managers of retail sales workers."

Step 5. List the Job's Human Requirements from O*NET Next, return to the *Snapshot* (summary) *for Retail Salesperson* (C).

Here, instead of choosing occupation-specific information, click, for example, *Worker Experiences, Occupational Requirements,* and *Worker Characteristics*. Use this information to help develop a job specification for your job. Use this for recruiting, selecting, and training your employees.

Step 6. Finalize the Job Description Finally, write an appropriate job summary for the job. Then use the information obtained in Steps 4 and 5 to create a complete listing of the tasks, duties, and human requirements of each of the jobs you will need to fill.

Background Data
for Job Description

Job Title _____   Department_____

Job Number _____   Written By _____

Today's Date_____   Applicable Codes_____

I. Applicable job titles from O*NET:

II. Job Summary:
(List the more important or regularly performed tasks)

III. Reports To:

IV. Supervises:_____

V. Job Duties: _____
(Briefly describe, for each duty, what employee does and, if possible, how employee does it. Show in parentheses at end of each duty the approximate percentage of time devoted to duty.)

A. Daily Duties:

B. Periodic Duties:
(Indicate whether weekly, monthly, quarterly, etc.)

C. Duties Performed at Irregular Intervals:

FIGURE A4.4
Job Description Questionnaire

(A)

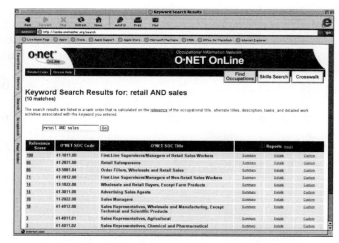

(B)

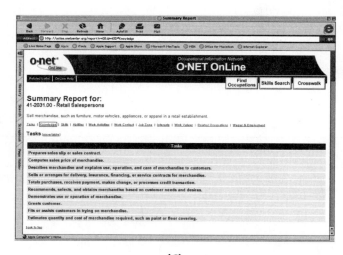

(C)

Shown in the three screen captures, O*Net easily allows the user to develop job descriptions.

Source: Reprinted by permission of O*NET OnLine.

ENDNOTES

1. "Survey: Talent Management a Top Concern," *CIO Insight* (January 2, 2007).
2. Michael Laff, "Talent Management: From Hire to Retire," *Training and Development* (November 2006): 42–48.
3. www.talentmanagement101.com, accessed December 10, 2007.
4. www.talentmanagement101.com, accessed December 10, 2007.
5. www.silkroadtech.com, accessed December 10, 2007.
6. "Software Facilitates Talent Management," *Product News Network* (May 18, 2007).
7. Frederick Morgeson and Michael Campion, "Accuracy in Job Analysis: Toward an Inference Based Model," *Journal of Organizational Behavior* 21, no. 7 (November 2000): 819–827. See also Frederick Morgeson and Stephen Humphrey, "The Work Design Questionnaire (WDQ): Developing and Validating a Comprehensive Measure for Assessing Job Design and the Nature of Work," *Journal of Applied Psychology* 91, no. 6 (2006): 1321–1339; and "Job Analysis," www.paq.com/index.cfm?FuseAction=bulletins.job-analysis, accessed February 3, 2009.

8. See, for example, T. A. Stetz et al., "New Tricks for an Old Dog: Visualizing Job Analysis Results," *Public Personnel Management* 38, no. 1 (Spring 2009): 91–100.
9. One writer recently called job analysis "The hub of virtually all human resource management activities necessary for the successful functioning organizations." See Parbudyal Singh, "Job Analysis for a Changing Workplace," *Human Resource Management Review* 18 (2008): 87.
10. Frederick Morgeson et al., "Self Presentation Processes in Job Analysis: A Field Experiment Investigating Inflation in Abilities, Tasks, and Competencies," *Journal of Applied Psychology* 89, no. 4 (November 4, 2004): 674–686.
11. Roni Reiter-Palmon et al., "Development of an O*NET Web Based Job Analysis and Its Implementation in the U.S. Navy: Lessons Learned," *Human Resource Management Review* 16 (2006): 294–309.
12. Ibid, 294.
13. Darin Hartley, "Job Analysis at the Speed of Reality," *Training and Development* (September 2004): 20–22.

14. Op. cit., 18.

15. Deborah Kearney, *Reasonable Accommodations: Job Descriptions in the Age of ADA, OSHA, and Workers Comp* (New York: Van Nostrand Reinhold, 1994): 9.

16. Ibid.

17. http://online.onetcenter.org/link/summary/11–2022.00, accessed April 18, 2008.

18. "Nine Best Practices for Effective Talent Management," DDI Development Dimensions International, Inc

19. Robert Grossman, "IBM'S HR Takes a Risk," *HR Magazine*, April 27, 2007, p. 57.

20. See, for example, Carol Spicer, "Building a Competency Model," *HR Magazine* (April 2009): 34–36.

21. Jeffrey Shippmann et al., "The Practice of Competency Modeling," *Personnel Psychology* 53, no. 3 (2000): 703.

22. Ibid.

23. Carolyn Hirschman, "Putting Forecasting in Focus," *HR Magazine* (March 2007): 44–49.

24. Robert Grossman, "IBM'S HR Takes a Risk," *HR Magazine*, April 27, 2007, p. 57.

25. "More Companies Turn to Workforce Planning to Boost Productivity and Efficiency," The Conference Board, press release/news (August 7, 2006); Carolyn Hirschman, "Putting Forecasting in Focus," *HR Magazine* (March 2007): 44–49.

26. See for example, "HR's Insight into the Economy," *Society for Human Resource Management Workplace Visions* 4 (2008): 5; D. Mattioli, "Only the Employed Need Apply," *Wall Street Journal* (Eastern Edition) (June 30, 2009): D1.

27. See http://www.bls.gov/opub/ooq/2010/spring/art02.pdf, assessed May 30, 2010. See also, Benjamin Wright, "Employment, Trends, and Training in Information Technology," *Occupational Outlook Quarterly* (Spring 2009): 34–36.

28. This is a modification of a definition found in Peter Wallum, "A Broader View of Succession Planning," *Personnel Management* (September 1993): 45. See also Michelle Harrison et al., "Effective Succession Planning," *Training and Development* (October 2006): 22–23.

29. Wallum op. cit., 43–44.

30. "Succession Planning: A Never-Ending Process That Must Mesh with Talent Management," *HR Focus* 84, no. 5 (May 2007): 8.

31. Bill Roberts, "Matching Talent with Tasks," *HR Magazine* (November 2002): 91–96.

32. Ibid.

33. "Next Generation Talent Management," http://www.hewittassociates.com/_MetaBasicCMAssetCache_/Assets/Articles/next_generation.pdf, accessed November 9, 2010.

34. Ibid.

35. Ed Frauenheim, "Valero Energy," *Workforce Management* March 13, 2006.

36. Gunter Stahl et al., "Global Talent Management: How Leading Multinationals Build and Sustain their Talent Pipelines," Faculty & Research Working Paper, INSEAD, 2007.

37. Tony Carnevale, "The Coming Labor and Skills Shortage," *Training and Development* (January 2005): 36–41. "Report Says More Companies Focus on Workforce Planning to Heighten Productivity," *Training and Development* (October 2006): 10–12. See also "Employers Responding to a Potential Exodus with Recruitment, Retention, Training," *BNA Bulletin to Management* 58, no. 31 (July 31, 2007): 241.

38. Paul Loftus, "Tackle Talent Management to Achieve High Performance," *Plant Engineering* 61, no. 6 (June 15, 2007): 29.

39. Jonathan Segal, "Land Executives, Not Lawsuits," *HR Magazine* (October 2006): 123–130.

40. Kevin Carlson et al., "Recruitment Evaluation: The Case for Assessing the Quality of Applicants Attracted," *Personnel Psychology* 55 (2002): 461–490. For a recent survey of recruiting source effectiveness, see "The 2007 Recruiting Metrics and Performance Benchmark Report, 2nd ed.," Staffing.org, Inc. (2007).

41. Arthur R. Pell, *Recruiting and Selecting Personnel* (New York: Regents, 1969): 10–12.

42. Jessica Marquez, "A Global Recruiting Site Helps Far-Flung Managers at the Professional Services Company Acquire the Talent They Need—and Saves One Half-Million Dollars a Year," *Workforce Management* (March 13, 2006): 22.

43. Dawn Onley, "Improving Your Online Application Process," *HR Magazine* 50, no. 10 (October 2005): 109.

44. Martha Frase-Blunt, "Make a Good First Impression," *HR Magazine* (April 2004): 81–86. See also "Corporate Recruiting Web Sites Luring Workers, But Could Be Improved, Experts Say," *BNA Bulletin to Management* (March 14, 2006): 81–82.

45. James Breaugh, "Employee Recruitment: Current Knowledge and Important Areas for Future Research," *Human Resource Management Review* 18 (2008): 111.

46. H. Jack Walker et al., "Displaying Employee Testimonials on Recruitment Websites: Effects of Communication Media, Employee Race, and Jobseeker Race on Organizational Attraction and Information Credibility," *Journal of Applied Psychology* 94, no. 5 (2009): 1354–1364.

47. Emily Steel, "Job Search Sites Face a Nimble Threat," *Wall Street Journal*, http://online.wsj.com/public/article/SB119189368160253014-ZQlBizIzas3h1_yL_eRq5Yc4_kI_20071108.html?mod=tff_main_tff_top, accessed April 18, 2008.

48. Jennifer Berkshire, "Social Network Recruiting," *HR Magazine* (April 2005): 95–98. See also S. DeKay, "Are Business-Oriented Social Networking Web Sites Useful Resources for Locating Passive Jobseekers? Results of a Recent Study," *Business Communication Quarterly* 72, no. 1 (March 2009): 101–105.

49. Josee Rose, "Recruiters Take Hip Path to Fill Accounting Jobs," *Wall Street Journal* (September 18, 2007): 38. See also Karen Donovan, "Law Firms Go a Bit Hollywood to Recruit the YouTube Generation," *New York Times* (September 28, 2007).

50. Reprinted from www.careerbuilder.com/MarketingWeb/iPhone/CBJobsApplication.aspx?cbRecursionCnt=1&cbsid=7fd458dafd4a444fb192d9a24ceed771-291142537-wx-6&ns_siteid=ns_us_g_careerbuilder_iphone, accessed March 23, 2009.

51. Elizabeth Agnvall, "Job Fairs Go Virtual," *HR Magazine* (July 2007): 85.

52. Ibid.

53. Ed Frauenheim, "Logging Off of Job Boards," *Workforce Management* (June 22, 2009): 25–27.

54. Jennifer Arnold, "Twittering at Face Booking While They Were," *HR Magazine* (December 2009): 54.

55. "ResumePal: Recruiter's Friend?" *Workforce Management* (June 22, 2009): 28.

56. "Innovative HR Programs Cultivate Successful Employees," *Nation's Restaurant News* 41, no. 50 (December 17, 2007): 74.

57. J. De Avila, "Beyond Job Boards: Targeting the Source," *Wall Street Journal* (Eastern Edition) (July 2, 2009): D1, D5.

58. "Help Wanted—and Found," *Fortune* (October 2, 2006): 40.

59. Ibid.

60. Jim Meade, "Where Did They Go?" *HR Magazine* (September 2000): 81–84.

61. Gino Ruiz, "Special Report: Talent Acquisition," *Workforce Management* (July 23, 2007): 39.

62. "E-recruiting Software Providers," *Workforce Management* (June 22, 2009): 14.

63. James Breaugh, "Employee Recruitment: Current Knowledge and Important Areas for Future Research," *Human Resource Management Review* 18 (2008): 111.

64. Ibid., 113.

65. "John Zappe, "Temp-to-Hire Is Becoming a Full-Time Practice at Firms," *Workforce Management* (June 2005): 82–86.

66. Robert Bogner Jr. and Elizabeth Salasko, "Beware the Legal Risks of Hiring Temps," *Workforce* (October 2002): 50–57.

67. Fay Hansen, "A Permanent Strategy for Temporary Hires," *Workforce Management* (February 26, 2007): 27.

68. Carolyn Hirschman, "Are Your Contractors Legal?" *HR Magazine* (March 2004): 59–63.

69. "Leading Executive Search Firms," *Workforce Management* (June 25, 2007): 24.

70. Donna Owens, "College Recruiting in a Downturn," *HR Magazine* (April 2009): 52.

71. "Internships Growing in Popularity Among Companies Seeking Fresh Talent and Ideas," *BNA Bulletin to Management* (March 20, 2007): 89–90.

72. Joel Mullich, "Finding the Schools that Yield the Best Job Applicant ROI," *Workforce Management* (March 2004): 67–68.

73. Lisa Munniksma, "Career Matchmakers," *HR Magazine* (February 2005): 93–96.

74. Greet Van Hoye and Filip Lievens, "Tapping the Grapevine: A Closer Look at Word-of-Mouth as a Recruitment Source," *Journal of Applied Psychology* 94, no. 2 (2009): 341–352.

75. Scott Graham, "Hospitals Recruiting Overseas," *Baltimore Business Journal* (June 1, 2001): 1.

76. Martha Frase, "Show All Employees a Wider World," *HR Magazine* (June 2007): 99–102.

77. Michelle Martinez, "The Headhunter Within," *HR Magazine* (August 2001): 48–56.

78. Jennifer Taylor Arnold, "Customers as Employees," *HR Magazine* (April 2007): 77–82.

79. Martha Frase-Blunt, "Call Centers Come Home," *HR Magazine* (January 2007): 85–90.

80. Theresa Minton-Eversole, "Mission: Recruitment," *HR Magazine* (January 2009): 43–45.

81. See, for example, "Economics of Offshoring Shifting, as Some Reconsider Ventures," *BNA Bulletin to Management* (September 23, 2008): 311.

82. "2007 Advances in E-Recruiting: Leveraging the .jobs Domain," *Society for Human Resource Management* (June 2007).

83. See, for example, Rita Zeigner, "Strategies for Saving in a Down Economy," *HR Magazine* (February 2009): 31.

84. Gina Ruiz, "Special Report: Talent Acquisition," *Workforce Management* (July 23, 2007): 39.

85. Derek Avery and Patrick McKay, "Target Practice: An Organizational Impression Management Approach to Attracting Minority and Female Job Applicants," *Personnel Psychology* 59 (2006): 157–187.

86. Daniel Newman and Julia Lyon, "Recruitment Efforts to Reduce Adverse Impact: Targeted Recruiting for Personality, Cognitive Ability, and Diversity," *Journal of Applied Psychology* 94, no. 2 (2009): 298–317.

87. "Workforce Trends," *AARP*, www.AARP.org/money/careers, accessed December 23, 2007.

88. Sandra Block and Stephanie Armour, "Many Americans Retire Years Before They Want To," *USA Today* (July 26, 2006), http://usatoday.com, accessed December 23, 2007.

89. Ibid.

90. Ed Shanahan, "The Top 15," www.aarpmagazine.org/ lifestyle, accessed December 23, 2007.

91. Gary Adams and Barbara Rau, "Attracting Retirees to Apply: Desired Organizational Characteristics of Bridge Employment," *Journal of Organizational Behavior* 26, no. 6 (September 2005): 649–660.

92. "Barclaycard Helps Single Parents to Find Employment," *Personnel Today* (November 7, 2006).

93. Susan Glairon, "Single Parents Need More Flexibility at Work, Advocates in Denver Says," *Daily Camera* (February 8, 2002).

94. Allison Wellner, "Welcoming Back Mom," *HR Magazine* (June 2004): 77–78.

95. Linda Moore, "Firms Need to Improve Recruitment, Hiring of Disabled Workers, EEO Chief Says," *Knight Ridder/Business News* (November 2003): Item 03309094. See also "Recruiting Disabled More Than Good Deed, Experts Say," *BNA Bulletin to Management* (February 27, 2007): 71.

96. Richard Donkin, "Making Space for a Wheelchair Worker," *Financial Times* (November 13, 2003): 9.

97. Murray Barrick and Ryan Zimmerman, "Hiring for Retention and Performance," *Human Resource Management* 48, no. 2 (March/April 2009): 183–206.

98. James Breaugh, "The Use of Biodata for Employee Selection: Test Research and Future Directions," *Human Resource Management Review* 19 (2009): 219–231. Utilizing biodata items presumes that the employer can show that the items predict performance. Biodata items such as "graduated from college" may have an adverse impact on minorities but studies suggest that employers can avoid that problem through judicious choice of biodata items (p. 229).

99. J. Craig Wallace et al., "Applying for Jobs Online: Examining the Legality of Internet-Based Application Forms," *Public Personnel Management* 20, no. 4 (Winter 2000): 497–504.

100. Kathy Gurchiek, "Video Resumes Spark Curiosity, Questions," *HR Magazine* (May 2007): 28–30; and "Video Resumes Can Illuminate Applicants Abilities, But Pose Discrimination Concerns," *BNA Bulletin to Management* (May 20, 2007): 169–170.

101. *Ryan's Family Steakhouse Inc.* v. *Floss*, "Supreme Court Let Stand Decision Finding Prehire Arbitration Agreements Unenforceable," *BNA Bulletin to Management* (January 11, 2001): 11.

102. Douglas Mahoney et al., "The Effects of Mandatory Employment Arbitration Systems on Applicants' Attraction to Organizations," *Human Resource Management* 44, no. 4 (Winter 2005): 449–470.

103. "Supreme Court Denies Circuit City's Bid for Review of Mandatory Arbitration," *BNA Bulletin to Management* (June 6, 2002): 177.

104. "Supreme Court Gives the Employers Green Light to Hold Most Employees to Arbitration Pacts," *BNA Bulletin to Management* (March 29, 2001): 97–98.

105. Scott Erker, "What Does Your Hiring Process Say About You?" *Training and Development* (May 2007): 67–70.

106. Martha Frase, "Stocking Your Talent Pool," *HR Magazine* (April 2007): 67–74.

107. www.talentmanagement101.com, accessed December 10, 2007.

108. Accessed April 18, 2008.

109. This is adapted from Nancy Howe, "Match Temp Services to Your Needs," *Personnel Journal* (March 1989): 45–51. See also Richard Vosburgh, "The Evolution of HR: Developing HR as an Internal Consulting Organization," *Human Resource Planning* 30, no. 3 (September 2007): 11–12; and Stephen Miller, "Collaboration Is Key to Effective Outsourcing," *HR Magazine* 58 (supp Trendbook 2008): 60–61.

110. See, for example, Phillip Kotler and Gary Armstrong, *Principles of Marketing* (Upper Saddle River, NJ: Prentice Hall, 2001): 6–8.

111. Note that the PAQ (and other quantitative techniques) can also be used for job evaluation, which is explained in Chapter 8.

112. See, for example, Sidney A. Fine, "Fifty Years of Things, Data, People: Whither Job Analysis?" http://www.siop.org/TIP/backissues/Oct04/07fiine.aspx, accessed April 18, 2008.

113. O*Net™ is a trademark of the U.S. Department of Labor, Employment and Training Administration.

114. Jorgen Sandberg, "Understanding Competence at Work," *Harvard Business Review* (March 2001): 28. Other organization chart software vendors include Nakisa, Aquire, and HumanConcepts. See "Advanced Org Charting," *Workforce Management* (May 19, 2008): 34.

5 Selecting Employees

When you finish studying this chapter, you should be able to:

1. Define basic testing concepts, including validity and reliability.

2. Discuss at least four basic types of personnel tests.

3. Explain the factors and problems that can undermine an interview's usefulness, and techniques for eliminating them.

4. Explain the pros and cons of background investigations, reference checks, and preemployment information services.

Source: photosindia/Getty Images, Inc.–Liaison.

INTRODUCTION

It seemed a good idea at the time. Many retailers, seeking to reduce expenses, automated their hiring processes. The retailers teamed with special online application service providers. The latter linked their sites to the retailers' sites, and posted special tests. The idea was to use the online tests to prescreen job candidates, thus reducing the time that store managers spent interviewing applicants. Theory hasn't translated too well into practice, however. As the *Wall Street Journal* recently noted, ". . . the test is also creating a culture of cheating and raising questions for applicants about its fairness, even as it becomes a critical determinant of who gets a job and who doesn't in a stressful era of rising unemployment." Many retailers are understandably wondering if they should change their employee testing and selection processes.[1] ■

THE BASICS OF TESTING AND SELECTING EMPLOYEES

With a pool of applicants, your next step is to select the best person for the job. This usually means whittling down the applicant pool by using tests, interviews, and background and reference checks.

Why Careful Selection Is Important

Selecting the right employees is important for several reasons.

- First, carefully testing and screening job candidates should lead to *improved employee and organizational performance*. No one wants to hire an incompetent. Few things are more important to a manager than putting the right person in the right job.
- Second, *your own performance* always depends partly on your subordinates. Hire employees without the necessary skills or who are obstructionist and your own performance and the firm's will suffer.
- Third, screening can help reduce *dysfunctional behaviors* at work. By one account, about 30% of all employees say they've stolen from their employers; about 41% are managers.[2] In retail, employers apprehended about 1 out of every 28 workers for stealing.[3] The time to screen out such undesirables is before they are in the door.
- Fourth, effective screening is important because it's *costly* to recruit and hire employees. Hiring and training even a clerk can cost $10,000 or more in fees and supervisory time. That's money wasted if the person doesn't work out.

LEGAL IMPLICATIONS AND NEGLIGENT HIRING Finally, careful selection is important because of the *legal implications* of inept selection.

There are two issues here. First, we saw in Chapter 2 that EEO laws require that you ensure that you're not unfairly discriminating against any protected group.[4]

Negligent hiring is a second legal issue. Courts will find employers liable when employees with criminal records or other problems use their access to customers' homes or similar opportunities to commit crimes. Hiring workers with such backgrounds without proper safeguards is **negligent hiring**. For example, after lawyers sued Walmart alleging that several of its employees with criminal convictions for sexually-related offenses had assaulted young girls, Walmart instituted a new program of criminal background checks.[5] Among other things, employers "must make a systematic effort to gain relevant information about the applicant, verify documentation, follow up on missing records or gaps in employment, and keep a detailed log of all attempts to obtain information, including the names and dates for phone calls or other requests."[6]

negligent hiring
Hiring workers with criminal records or other such problems without proper safeguards.

Reliability

Effective screening depends to a large degree on the basic testing concepts of reliability and validity. **Reliability** refers to the test's consistency. It is "the consistency of scores obtained by the same person when retested with the identical tests or with an equivalent form of a test."[7] Test reliability is essential: If a person scored 90 on an intelligence test on Monday and 130 when retested on Tuesday, you wouldn't have much faith in the test.

reliability
The characteristic that refers to the consistency of scores obtained by the same person when retested with the identical or equivalent tests.

1 Define basic testing concepts, including validity and reliability.

There are several ways to estimate a test's consistency or reliability. You could administer the same test to the same people at two different points in time, comparing their test scores at Time 2 with their scores at Time 1; this would be a *retest estimate*. Or you could administer a test and then administer what experts believe to be an equivalent test later; this would be an *equivalent-form estimate*. The Scholastic Aptitude Test is an example of the latter.

A test's internal consistency is another measure of its reliability. For example, assume you have 10 items on a test of vocational interest. These items all aim to measure in various ways the person's interest in working outdoors. You administer the test and then statistically analyze the degree to which responses to these items vary together. This would provide a measure of the internal reliability of the test; psychologists refer to it as an *internal comparison estimate*. Internal consistency is one reason you often find questions that apparently are repetitive on some test questionnaires.

Validity

Any test is a sample of a person's behavior, but some tests more clearly reflect the behavior you're sampling. For example, a typing test clearly corresponds to an on-the-job behavior—typing. At the other extreme, there may be no apparent relationship between the items on the test and the behavior. For example, in the Rorschach test item in Figure 5.1, the person is asked to explain how he or she interprets the somewhat eerie picture. The psychologist then uses that interpretation to draw conclusions about the person's personality and behavior. With such tests, it is harder to "prove" that the tests are measuring what they are purported to measure—that they are *valid*.

Test validity answers the question "Does this test measure what it's supposed to measure?" Stated differently, "validity refers to the confidence one has in the meaning attached to the scores."[8] With respect to employee selection tests, the term *validity* often refers to evidence that the test is job related—in other words, that performance on the test is a *valid predictor* of subsequent performance on the job. A selection test must be valid because, without proof of its validity, there is no logical or legally permissible reason to continue using it to screen job applicants.

In employment testing, there are two main ways to demonstrate a test's validity: **criterion validity** and **content validity**. Demonstrating *criterion* (or criterion-related) *validity* means demonstrating that those who do well on the test also do well on the job, and that those who do poorly on the test do poorly on the job. In psychological measurement, a

test validity

The accuracy with which a test, interview, and so on measures what it purports to measure or fulfills the function it was designed to fill.

criterion validity

A type of validity based on showing that scores on the test (*predictors*) are related to job performance (*criterion*).

content validity

A test that is *content valid* is one in which the test contains a fair sample of the tasks and skills actually needed for the job in question.

FIGURE 5.1

A Slide from the Rorschach Test

Source: http://en.wikipedia.org/wiki/File:Rorschach1.jpg, accessed July 27, 2009.

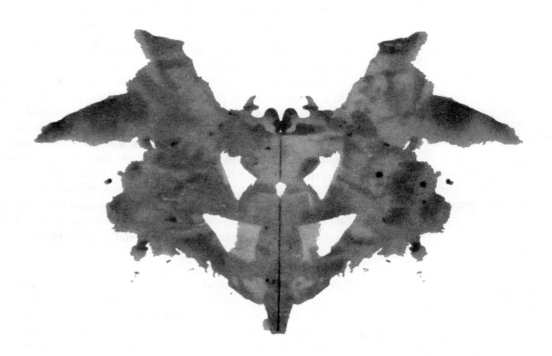

predictor is the measurement (in this case, the test score) that you are trying to relate to a criterion, such as job performance (perhaps as measured by supervisors' appraisals of the employee). In criterion validity, the criterion and predictor should be closely related. The term *criterion validity* comes from that terminology.

The employer demonstrates the *content validity* of a test by showing that the test constitutes a fair sample of the content of a job. A typing test illustrates this. If the content of the typing test is a representative sample of the typist's job, then the test is probably content valid.

How to Validate a Test

What makes a test such as the Graduate Record Examination (GRE) useful for graduate school admissions directors? What makes a mechanical comprehension test useful for managers hiring machinists?

The answer to both questions is usually that people's scores on these tests are predictive of how people perform. Thus, other things being equal, students who score high on the GRE also do better in graduate school. Applicants who score higher on a mechanical comprehension test perform better as machinists. Employers would use statistical means to determine the degree of correlation between mechanical comprehension scores and machinists' performance. The validation process (see Figure 5.2) usually requires the expertise of an industrial psychologist.

GENERALIZABILITY The question often is, can you generalize the validity of the test from one setting to another? It often turns out that one cannot. For example, suppose everyone who took the test in Company one was a college graduate, and the test was shown to validly predict

FIGURE 5.2

How to Validate a Test

> **Step 1: Analyze the Job.** First, analyze the job descriptions and specifications. Specify the human traits and skills you believe are required for adequate job performance. For example, must an applicant be aggressive? Must the person be able to assemble small, detailed components? These requirements become your predictors. They are the human traits and skills you believe to be predictive of success on the job.
>
> In this first step, you must also define what you mean by "success on the job" because it is this success for which you want predictors. The standards of success are called *criteria*. You could focus on production-related criteria (quantity, quality, and so on), personnel data (absenteeism, length of service, and so on), or judgments (of worker performance by persons such as supervisors). For an assembler's job, predictors for which to test applicants might include manual dexterity and patience. Criteria that you would hope to predict with your test might then include quantity produced per hour and number of rejects produced per hour.
>
> **Step 2: Choose the Tests.** Next, choose tests that you think measure the attributes (predictors) important for job success. This choice is usually based on experience, previous research, and best guesses, and you usually won't start off with just one test. Instead, you choose several tests, combining them into a test battery aimed at measuring a variety of possible predictors, such as aggressiveness, extroversion, and numeric ability.
>
> **Step 3: Administer Tests.** Administer the selected test(s) to employees. *Predictive validation* is the most dependable way to validate a test. The test is administered to applicants before they are hired. Then these applicants are hired using only existing selection techniques, not the results of the new test you are developing. After they have been on the job for some time, you measure their performance and compare it to their performance on the earlier test. You can then determine whether their performance on the test could have been used to predict their subsequent job performance.
>
> **Step 4: Relate Scores and Criteria.** Next, determine whether there is a significant relationship between scores (the predictor) and performance (the criterion). The usual way to do this is to determine the statistical relationship between scores on the test and performance through correlation analysis, which shows the degree of statistical relationship.
>
> **Step 5: Cross-Validate and Revalidate.** Before putting the test into use, you may want to check it by cross-validating, by again performing steps 3 and 4 on a new sample of employees. At a minimum, an expert should validate the test periodically.

subsequent job performance. Now you want to use the same test in Company two, but most of your applicants will not be college grads. Can you still generalize that the test will validly predict performance for them too? Perhaps not.[9] Tests you buy "off the shelf" should include validity information.[10] Ideally, employers should revalidate the tests for the job(s) at hand.

UTILITY *Utility* refers to the practical value of the test or other selection tool. It is possible for a test to be reliable and valid but to have little or no practical value (utility) to an employer. For example, there usually is considerable variability in how people perform. However, if for some reason there were little or no practical difference in how well people perform a particular job, then testing for that job would have little or no practical value.[11]

TESTING AND EQUAL EMPLOYMENT OPPORTUNITY   At best, invalid tests (tests not related to employee performance) are a waste of time. At worst, they may be discriminatory. We've seen that various federal and state laws bar discrimination on the basis of race, color, age, religion, sex, disability, and national origin. With respect to testing, these laws boil down to two things: (1) You must be able to prove that your tests are related to success or failure on the job, and (2) you must prove that your tests don't unfairly discriminate against either minority or nonminority subgroups. If confronted by a legitimate discrimination charge, the burden of proof rests with you. Once the plaintiff shows that one of your selection procedures has an adverse impact on his or her protected class, you must demonstrate the validity and selection fairness of the allegedly discriminatory test or item. *Adverse impact* means there is a significant discrepancy between rates of rejection of members of the protected groups and others. For example, a federal court ruled that Dial Corp. discriminated against female job applicants at a meatpacking facility by requiring employees to take a preemployment strength test. The test had an adverse impact on women. Furthermore, there appeared to be no compelling need for strength on the job.[12]

You can't avoid EEO laws by not using tests, by the way. The same burden of proving job relatedness falls on interviews and other techniques (including performance appraisals) that fall on tests.

INDIVIDUAL RIGHTS OF TEST TAKERS AND TEST SECURITY   Under the American Psychological Association's standard for educational and psychology tests (which guide professional psychologists but are not legally enforceable), test takers have the right to the confidentiality of the test results and the right to informed consent regarding the use of these results. They have the right to expect that only people qualified to interpret the scores will have access to them or that sufficient information will accompany the scores to ensure their appropriate interpretation. They have the right to expect that the test is secure; no person taking the test should have prior information concerning the questions or answers.

USING TESTS AS SUPPLEMENTS   Tests aren't infallible. Even in the best cases, the test score usually accounts for only about 25% of the variation in the measure of performance. Therefore, don't use tests as your only selection technique; instead, use them to supplement other techniques such as interviews and background checks.

USING TESTS AT WORK

Tests can be effective. For example, researchers administered an aggression questionnaire to high school hockey players prior to the season. Preseason aggressiveness as measured by the questionnaire predicted the amount of minutes they subsequently spent in the penalty box for penalties such as fighting, slashing, and tripping.[13] Try the test in Figure 5.3 to see how prone you might be to on-the-job accidents.

How Do Employers Use Tests at Work?

Employers use tests to measure a wide range of candidate attributes, including cognitive (mental) abilities, motor and physical abilities, personality and interests, and achievement. Many firms such as FedEx have applicants take computerized tests—sometimes online, and sometimes by phone using the touchtone keypad—to quickly prescreen applicants prior to more in-depth interviews and background checks. Barclays Capital gives graduate and undergraduate job candidates aptitude tests instead of first-round interviews.[14]

CHECK YES OR NO   YES   NO

1. You like a lot of excitement in your life.
   _____

2. An employee who takes it easy at work
   is cheating on the employer.
   _____

3. You are a cautious person.
   _____

4. In the past three years you have found yourself
   in a shouting match at school or work.
   _____

5. You like to drive fast just for fun.
   _____

Analysis: According to John Kamp, an industrial psychologist, applicants who answered no, yes, yes, no, no to questions 1, 2, 3, 4, and 5 are statistically likely to be absent less often, to have fewer on-the-job injuries, and, if the job involves driving, to have fewer on-the-job driving accidents. Actual scores on the test are based on answers to 130 questions.

FIGURE 5.3

Sample Selection Test

Source: Courtesy of *The New York Times*.

EXAMPLE Outback Steakhouse has used preemployment testing since just after the company started. Outback is looking for employees who are highly social, meticulous, sympathetic, and adaptable. It uses a personality assessment test as part of its preemployment interview process. Applicants take the test, and the company then compares the results to the profile for Outback Steakhouse employees. Those who score low on certain traits (like compassion) don't move to the next step. Two managers interview those who score high. They ask "behavioral" questions, such as "What would you do if a customer asked for a side dish we don't have on the menu?"[15]

Outback Steakhouse has used preemployment testing since just after the company started.

2 Discuss at least four basic
types of personnel tests.

Types of Tests

We discuss the basic types of tests next.

TESTS OF COGNITIVE ABILITIES Employers often want to assess a candidate's cognitive or mental abilities. For example, you may be interested in determining whether a supervisory candidate has the intelligence to do the job's paperwork or a bookkeeper candidate has the required numeric aptitude.

Intelligence tests, such as IQ tests, are tests of general intellectual abilities. They measure not a single intelligence trait, but rather a range of abilities, including memory, vocabulary, and numeric ability. Psychologists often measure intelligence with individually administered tests such as the Stanford-Binet test or the Wechsler Adult Intelligence Scale. Employers use other IQ tests such as the Wonderlic test to provide quick measures of IQ for both individuals and groups of people.

There are also measures of specific mental abilities. Tests in this category are often called *aptitude tests* because they aim to measure the applicant's aptitude for the job. For example, the Test of Mechanical Comprehension in Figure 5.4 tests the applicant's understanding of basic mechanical principles. It may therefore reflect a person's aptitude for jobs such as an engineer.

TESTS OF MOTOR AND PHYSICAL ABILITIES There are many motor or physical abilities you might want to measure, such as finger dexterity, strength, and manual dexterity. The Stromberg Dexterity Test is an example. It measures the speed and accuracy of simple judgment as well as the speed of finger, hand, and arm movements.

MEASURING PERSONALITY A person's mental and physical abilities alone seldom explain his or her job performance. Other factors, such as motivation and interpersonal skills, are important, too. As one consultant put it, most people are hired based on qualifications, but most are fired for nonperformance. And *nonperformance* (or *performance*) "is usually the result of personal characteristics, such as attitude, motivation, and especially, temperament."[16] Employers such as Outback Steakhouse use personality and interests tests (or "inventories") to measure and predict such intangibles. Acxiom Corp. uses tests like the Birkman Method® (www.birkman.com/) personality assessment to help new employees better understand the tasks at which they're best.[17]

Personality tests measure basic aspects of an applicant's personality, such as introversion, stability, and motivation. A sample personality inventory item is:

It does not make sense to work hard on something if no one will notice.

   a. Definitely true.
   b. Somewhat true.
   c. Neither true nor false.
   d. Somewhat false.
   e. Definitely false.[18]

Of course, personality testing isn't limited to employment settings. Some online dating services, like eHarmony.com, have prospective members take online personality tests, and reject those its software judges as unmatchable. Figure 5.5 shows a sample page from one online personality inventory.

Many personality tests are projective, meaning that the person taking the test must interpret an ambiguous stimulus such as an inkblot or clouded picture. Because the pictures are ambiguous, the person supposedly projects into the picture his or her own emotional attitudes. Thus, a

FIGURE 5.4

Type of Question Applicant Might Expect on a Test of Mechanical Comprehension

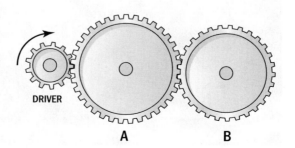

DRIVER

A   B

Which gear will turn the same way as the driver?

FIGURE 5.5

Sample Online Personality Test Questions

Source: Elaine Pulakos, "Selection Assessment Methods," SHRM Foundation (2005): 9. Reprinted with permission of the Society for Human Resource Management (www.shrm.org), Alexandria, VA, publisher of *HR Magazine.* © SHRM.

HumanMetrics

Jung Typology Test™

After completing the questionnaire, you will obtain:

- Your type formula according to Carl Jung and Isabel Myers-Briggs typology along with the strengths of the preferences
- The description of your personality type
- The list of occupations and educational institutions where you can get relevant degree or training, most suitable for your personality type - Jung Career Indicator™

For Organizations and Professionals

Organizations and specialists interested in Jung personality assessments for team building, candidate assessment, leadership, career development, psychographics - visit **HRPersonality**™ for practical and validated instruments and professional services.

1. You are almost never late for your appointments
   ○ YES ○ NO
2. You like to be engaged in an active and fast-paced job
   ○ YES ○ NO
3. You enjoy having a wide circle of acquaintances
   ○ YES ○ NO
4. You feel involved when watching TV soaps
   ○ YES ○ NO
5. You are usually the first to react to a sudden event: the telephone ringing or unexpected question
   ○ YES ○ NO
6. You are more interested in a general idea than in the details of its realization
   ○ YES ○ NO
7. You tend to be unbiased even if this might endanger your good relations with people
   ○ YES ○ NO
8. Strict observance of the established rules is likely to prevent a good outcome
   ○ YES ○ NO
9. It's difficult to get you excited
   ○ YES ○ NO
10. It is in your nature to assume responsibility
    ○ YES ○ NO
11. You often think about humankind and its destiny
    ○ YES ○ NO
12. You believe the best decision is one that can be easily changed
    ○ YES ○ NO
13. Objective criticism is always useful in any activity
    ○ YES ○ NO
14. You prefer to act immediately rather than speculate about various options
    ○ YES ○ NO
15. You trust reason rather than feelings
    ○ YES ○ NO
16. You are inclined to rely more on improvisation than on careful planning
    ○ YES ○ NO
17. You spend your leisure time actively socializing with a group of people, attending parties, shopping, etc.
    ○ YES ○ NO
18. You usually plan your actions in advance
    ○ YES ○ NO
19. Your actions are frequently influenced by emotions
    ○ YES ○ NO
20. You are a person somewhat reserved and distant in communication
    ○ YES ○ NO
21. You know how to put every minute of your time to good purpose
    ○ YES ○ NO
22. You readily help people while asking nothing in return
    ○ YES ○ NO
23. You often contemplate about the complexity of life
    ○ YES ○ NO
24. After prolonged socializing you feel you need to get away and be alone
    ○ YES ○ NO
25. You often do jobs in a hurry
    ○ YES ○ NO
26. You easily see the general principle behind specific occurrences
    ○ YES ○ NO
27. You frequently and easily express your feelings and emotions
    ○ YES ○ NO
28. You find it difficult to speak loudly
    ○ YES ○ NO

security-oriented person might describe the image in Figure 5.1 (page 122) as "A giant bug coming to get me." Other projective techniques include Make a Picture Story (MAPS), House-Tree-Person (H-T-P), and the Forer Structured Sentence Completion Test. Some personality tests are *self-reported*: applicants fill them out themselves. For example, the Guilford-Zimmerman survey measures personality traits like emotional stability versus moodiness, and friendliness versus criticalness. The Minnesota Multiphasic Personality Inventory (MMPI) taps traits like hypochondria and paranoia. Available online,[19] the Myers-Briggs test provides a personality type classification useful for decisions such as career selection and planning. The DiSC® Profile learning instrument enables the user to gain insight into and better understand the strengths and challenges of his or her behavioral style.[20]

Personality tests—particularly the projective type—are difficult to evaluate and use. An expert must analyze the test taker's interpretations and reactions and infer from them his or her personality. The usefulness of such tests for selection then assumes that you find a relationship between a measurable personality trait (such as extroversion) and success on the job. Because they are personal in nature, employers should always use personality tests with caution. Rejected candidates may (validly) claim that the results are false, or that they violate the Americans with Disabilities Act (ADA).

PERSONALITY TEST EFFECTIVENESS The difficulties notwithstanding, personality tests can help companies hire effective workers. Industrial psychologists often study the "big five" personality dimensions: extroversion, emotional stability, agreeableness, conscientiousness, and openness to experience.[21]

One study focused on how these five personality dimensions predicted performance for professionals, police officers, managers, sales workers, and skilled/semiskilled workers. Conscientiousness showed a consistent relationship with all job performance criteria for all the occupations. Extroversion was a valid predictor of performance for managers and sales employees. Openness to experience and extroversion predicted training proficiency for all occupations.[22]

Recently, a panel of distinguished industrial psychologists raised the question of whether *self-report* personality tests (which applicants fill out themselves) predict performance at all.[23] They said that if you carefully conduct predictive validation studies with actual job candidates validity is low.[24] Other experts call such concerns "unfounded."[25]

Overall, the evidence on personality testing suggests the following: Employers are increasingly using personality tests. The weight of evidence is that personality measures contribute to predicting job performance. Employers can reduce personality test faking by warning applicants that faking may reduce the chance of being hired.[26] And, make sure that any personality tests you use—particularly self-report types—actually do predict performance.[27]

INTEREST INVENTORIES *Interest inventories* compare one's interests with those of people in various occupations. Thus, when a person takes the Strong-Campbell Interest Inventory, he or she receives a report comparing his or her interests to those of people already in occupations such as accounting and medical technology.

ACHIEVEMENT TESTS An *achievement test* is a measure of what a person has learned. Most of the tests you take in school are achievement tests. They measure your knowledge in areas such as economics, marketing, or accounting. In addition to job knowledge, achievement tests can measure applicants' abilities; a typing test is one example.[28] The Global Issues in HR feature addresses testing for assignments abroad.

GLOBAL ISSUES IN HR

Testing for Assignments Abroad

Living and working abroad requires some special talents. Not everyone can easily adapt to having one's family far away, and to dealing with colleagues whose cultural values may be strikingly different from one's own. Doing so requires high levels of adaptability and interpersonal skills.[29]

Employers often use special inventories such as the Global Competencies Inventory (GCI) here. The report focuses on three aspects of intercultural adaptability.

- The Perception Management Factor assesses people's tendency to be rigid in their view of cultural differences, their tendency to be judgmental about those differences, and their ability to deal with complexity and uncertainty.
- The Relationship Management Factor scales assess a person's orientation toward the importance of relationships, and one's awareness of the impact he or she is having on others.
- The Self Management Factor assumes that being successful in an assignment abroad starts with having a stable sense of self, and being mentally and emotionally healthy.

Computerized and Online Testing

Computerized and online testing (see, for example, Figure 5.6, a sample of the Wonderlic personnel test) is increasingly replacing conventional paper-and-pencil and manual tests. Most of the types of tests we described are available in both computerized and paper form. Studies of

Sample Questions for WPT-R
The following questions are similar, but not identical, to those presented on the actual WPT-R forms.

Question 1
Which of the following is the earliest date?

A) Jan. 16, 1898   B) Feb. 21, 1889   C) Feb. 2, 1898   D) Jan. 7, 1898   E) Jan. 30, 1889

Question 2
LOW is to HIGH as EASY is to_____?

J) SUCCESSFUL   K) PURE   L) TALL   M) INTERESTING   N) DIFFICULT

Question 3
One word below appears in color. What is the OPPOSITE of that word?

She gave a complex answer to the question and we all agreed with her.

A) long   B) better   C) simple   D) wrong   E) kind

Answers
1. E   2. N   3. C

FIGURE 5.6

Sample Items from Wonderlic Personnel Test

Source: www.wonderlic.com/products/selection/wptr/sampleQuestions.asp.

tests like the Test of Workplace Essential Skills (a test of adult literacy) suggest that paper and computerized test version scores are equivalent.[30] Test vendors such as PreVisor (www.previsor.com) now offer online adaptive personality tests. As a candidate answers each question, these tests adapt the next question to each test taker's answers to the previous question. In addition to improving test validity, adaptive testing may reduce cheating. For example, it makes it less likely that candidates can share test questions (since each candidate gets what amounts to a customized test).[31]

CITY GARAGE COMPUTERIZED TESTING EXAMPLE Texas-based City Garage knew it couldn't implement its growth strategy without a dramatic change in how it tested and hired employees.[32] Its old hiring process consisted of a paper-and-pencil application and one interview, followed by a hire/don't hire decision. While that might work for a slow-growth operation, it was unsatisfactory for a fast-growing operation like City Garage. For one thing, local shop managers didn't have the time to evaluate every applicant, so "if they had been shorthanded too long, we would hire pretty much anybody who had experience," said the firm's training director. Furthermore, City Garage competitively differentiates itself with an "open garage" arrangement, where customers interact directly with technicians. Therefore, finding mechanics that not only tolerate but also react positively to customer inquiries is essential.

City Garage purchased the Personality Profile Analysis (PPA) online test from Dallas-based Thomas International USA. Now, after a quick application and background check, likely candidates take the 10-minute, 24-question PPA. City Garage staff then enter the answers into the PPA Software system and receive test results in about 2 minutes. These show whether the applicant is high or low in four personality characteristics. It also produces follow-up questions about areas that might cause problems. For example, applicants might be asked how they've handled possible weaknesses such as lack of patience. If candidates answer those questions satisfactorily, they're asked back for extensive, all-day interviews, after which hiring decisions are made.

HR APPs 4 U

Testing via the iPhone

Vendors are making tests available for applicants to take via their iPhones. For example, the accompanying screen grab illustrates one app, in this case for an online typing test you can take on an iPhone.[33]

Source: http://www.iphonetypingtest.com, accessed March 23, 2009.

---

management assessment center
A facility in which management candidates are asked to make decisions in hypothetical situations and are scored on their performance.

Situational Judgment Tests

Situational judgment tests are personnel tests that "are designed to assess an applicant's judgment regarding a situation encountered in the workplace." As an example, "you are facing a project deadline and are concerned that you may not complete the project by the time it is due. It is very important to your supervisor that you complete a project by the deadline. It is not possible to get anyone to help you with the work. You would

A. Ask for an extension of the deadline
B. Let the supervisor know that you may not meet the deadline
C. Work as many hours as it takes to get the job done by the deadline
D. Explore different ways to do the work so it can be completed by the deadline
E. On the date the project is due, hand in what you have done so far
F. Do the most critical parts of the project by the deadline and complete the remaining parts after the deadline
G. Tell your supervisor that the deadline is unreasonable
H. Give your supervisor an update and express your concern about your ability to complete the project by the deadline
I. Quit your job" [34]

Situational judgment tests are effective and widely used.[35]

Management Assessment Centers

In a **management assessment center**, management candidates take tests and make decisions in simulated situations, while trained assessors grade their performance.[36] The center may be a plain conference room, but often it is a room with a one-way mirror to facilitate unobtrusive observations. Examples of the simulated but realistic exercises included in a typical assessment center are as follows:

- ● *The in-basket*. In this exercise, the candidate faces an accumulation of reports, memos, notes of incoming phone calls, letters, and other materials. The candidate takes appropriate action on each of these materials.
- ● *The leaderless group discussion*. A leaderless group receives a discussion question and must arrive at a group decision. The raters then evaluate each group member's interpersonal skills, acceptance by the group, leadership ability, and individual influence.
- ● *Individual presentations*. A participant's communication skills and persuasiveness are evaluated by having the person make an oral presentation on an assigned topic.

In practice, employers use assessment centers for selection, promotion, and development. Supervisor recommendations usually play a big role in choosing participants. Line managers usually act as assessors and typically arrive at their ratings through consensus.[37] Centers are expensive to set up, but usually worth the cost. In one study (of 40 police candidates) the researchers concluded: "assessment center performance shows a unique and substantial contribution to the prediction of future police work success, justifying the usage of such method."[38]

GOOGLE EXAMPLE Having to add thousands of new employees each year, Google's top managers revamped their employee selection process. Google no longer requires most candidates to endure multiple interviews. It has streamlined the process. It did this in part by testing all its current employees to see what makes them successful. Then Google tests job candidates to see if they have these "Google success" traits.

INTERVIEWING CANDIDATES

interview
A procedure designed to solicit information from a person's oral responses to oral inquiries.

While not all employers use tests or assessment centers, it's very unusual for a manager not to interview a prospective employee. An **interview** is a procedure designed to solicit information from a person's oral responses to oral inquiries. A *selection interview* is "a selection procedure designed to predict future job performance on the basis of applicants' oral responses to oral inquiries."[39]

Types of Selection Interviews

As you probably know from your own experience, there are several ways to conduct selection interviews. For example, some interviewers are open-ended and perhaps even rambling in what they cover, while others follow a checklist of questions. In practice, interviews have three main features—structure, questions, and administration.

STRUCTURE First, most interviews vary in the degree to which the interviewer structures or standardizes the interview.[40] In more *nonstructured* interviews, the interviewer asks questions as they come to mind, generally with no set format. In a more structured or directive interview, the questions and perhaps even acceptable responses are specified in advance, and the responses may be rated for appropriateness. Figure 5.7 presents one example of a structured interview.

TYPES OF QUESTIONS Interviewers can also ask different types of questions. *Situational* questions focus on the candidate's ability to explain what his or her behavior *would be* in a given situation.[41] For example, you might ask a candidate for a supervisor position how he or she would react to a subordinate coming to work late 3 days in a row.

With *behavioral* questions you ask interviewees how they behaved *in the past* in some situation. Thus, an interviewer might ask "Did you ever have a situation in which a subordinate came in late? If so, how did you handle the situation?" For example, when Citizen's Banking Corporation in Flint, Michigan, found that 31 of the 50 people in its call center quit in 1 year, the center's head switched to behavioral interviews. Many of those who left did so because they didn't enjoy dealing with irate clients. So she no longer tries to predict how candidates will act based on asking them if they want to work with angry clients. Instead, she asks behavioral questions like "Tell me about a time you were speaking with an irate person, and how you turned the situation around." Only four people left her center in the following year.[42]

Knowledge and background questions probe candidates' job-related knowledge and experience, as in, "What math courses did you take in college?"

HOW TO ADMINISTER We can also classify interviews based on how we administer them. For example, most interviews are *one-on-one:* Two people meet alone and one interviews the other. In a *sequential interview* several people interview the applicant in sequence before a selection decision is made. In a *panel interview* the candidate is interviewed simultaneously by a group (or panel) of interviewers, rather than sequentially.

Some conduct interviews by *video* or *phone*. Phone interviews can actually be more accurate than face-to-face ones for judging things like interpersonal skills. Perhaps because neither side need worry about things like clothing or handshakes, the phone interview may let both focus more on substantive answers. In one study, interviewers tended to evaluate applicants more favorably in telephone versus face-to-face interviews. The interviewers came to about the same conclusions regarding the interviewees whether the interview was face-to-face or by videoconference. Applicants preferred face-to-face interviews.[43]

For better or worse, some employers are using a speed dating approach to interviewing applicants. One employer sent e-mails to all applicants for an advertised position. Of the 800 applicants contacted, 400 showed up. Over the next few hours, applicants first mingled with employees, and then (in a so-called "speed dating area") had one-on-one contacts with employees for a few minutes. Based on this, the recruiting team chose 68 candidates for follow-up interviews.[44]

FIGURE 5.7

Structured Interview Guide

Source: Copyright 1992. The Dartnell Corporation, Chicago, IL. Adapted with permission.

What did you do before you took your last job? _____

Where were you employed? _____

Location _____ Job title _____

Duties _____

Did you hold the same job throughout your employment with that company? _____ Yes _____ No. If not, describe the jobs you held, when you held them, and the duties of each. _____

_____

What was your starting salary? _____ What was your final salary? _____

Name of your last supervisor _____

May we contact that company? _____ Yes _____ No

What did you like most about that job? _____

What did you like least about that job? _____

Why did you leave that job? _____

Would you consider working there again? _____

Interviewer: If there is any gap between the various periods of employment, the applicant should be asked about them. _____

Interviewer's comments or observations _____

_____

What did you do prior to the job with that company? _____

What other jobs or experience have you had? Describe them briefly and explain the general duties of each.

_____

Have you been unemployed at any time in the last five years? _____ Yes _____ No. What efforts did you make to find work? _____

What other experience or training do you have that would help qualify you for the job applied for? Explain how and where you obtained this experience or training. _____

_____

Educational Background

What education or training do you have that would help you in the job for which you have applied? _____

_____

Describe any formal education you have had. (Interviewer may substitute technical training, if relevant.) _____

Off-Job Activities

What do you do in your off-hours? ___ Part-time job ___ Athletics ___ Spectator sports ___ Clubs ___ Other

Please explain. _____

Interviewer's Specific Questions

Interviewer: Add any questions to the particular job for which you are interviewing, leaving space for brief answers.

(Be careful to avoid questions that may be viewed as discriminatory.)

_____

_____

_____

Personal

Would you be willing to relocate? _____ Yes _____ No

Are you willing to travel? _____ Yes _____ No

MANAGING THE NEW WORKFORCE

Bias Against Working Mothers

Would you hire someone's mother? As silly as that question seems, managers should be aware of a sad fact: employers tend to view working mothers negatively.[45]

Here's an example. Researchers gave 100 MBA students (34% female, and all of whom worked full time) copies of a job description summary. The job was assistant vice president of financial affairs. The MBA students also got a "promotion applicant information form" to evaluate for each fictitious "applicant." These included researcher-created information such as marital status and supervisor comments. Some "applicants" were mothers.

The student-evaluators were biased against the mothers. They viewed them as less competent, and were less likely to recommend them for the job. As the researchers say, these data are consistent with mounting evidence that women suffer disadvantages in the workplace when they are mothers, a problem that has been termed "the maternal wall."[46]

How Useful Are Interviews?

While virtually all employers use interviews, the statistical evidence regarding their validity is mixed.[47] The key is that the interview's usefulness depends on how you do the interview itself.[48] In summary:

- For predicting job performance, *situational interviews* yield a higher mean (average) validity than do behavioral interviews.
- *Structured interviews*, regardless of content, are more valid and reliable (consistently applied) than unstructured interviews for predicting job performance.[49]
- *One-on-one interviews* tend to be more valid than panel interviews.[50]

In summary, structured situational interviews (in which you ask the candidates what they would do in a particular situation) conducted one-on-one seem to be the most useful for predicting job performance.

How to Avoid Common Interviewing Mistakes

Most people think they're better interviewers than they really are.[51] Actually, several common interviewing mistakes often undermine an interview's usefulness.

3 Explain the factors and problems that can undermine an interview's usefulness, and techniques for eliminating them.

SNAP JUDGMENTS Interviewers tend to jump to conclusions—make snap judgments—about candidates during the first few minutes of the interview. In fact, this often occurs before the interview begins, based on test scores or résumés. One London-based psychologist interviewed the chief executives of 80 top companies. She came to this conclusion about snap judgments in selection interviews:

Really, to make a good impression, you don't even get time to open your mouth. . . . An interviewer's response to you will generally be preverbal—how you walk through the door, what your posture is like, whether you smile, whether you have a captivating aura, whether you have a firm, confident handshake. You've got about half a minute to make an impact and after that all you are doing is building on a good or bad first impression. . . . It's a very emotional response.[52]

If you're the interviewee, such findings show why it's important to start right. Interviewers usually make up their minds about you during the first few minutes of the interview. What happens past this point usually adds little to change their decisions. From the interviewer's point of view, the findings highlight the importance of keeping an open mind until the interview is over.

NEGATIVE EMPHASIS Jumping to conclusions is especially troublesome given three interviewing facts: (1) Interviews are often mostly searches for negative information; (2) Interviewers are generally more influenced by unfavorable than favorable information; and (3) Interviewers' impressions are more likely to change from favorable to unfavorable than from unfavorable to favorable.

As an interviewer, the implication is, remember to keep an open mind and consciously work against unwarranted negative impressions. As an interviewee, remember the old saying that "You only have one chance to make a good first impression." If you start with a poor initial impression, you'll find it almost impossible to overcome that first, bad impression.

NOT KNOWING THE JOB Interviewers who don't know precisely what the job entails and what sort of candidate is best suited for it usually enter the interview with incorrect stereotypes about the ideal applicant. They then erroneously match interviewees against these incorrect stereotypes. Studies therefore have long shown that more interviewer knowledge about the job translates into better interviews.[53]

PRESSURE TO HIRE Being under pressure to hire undermines interview validity. In one study, managers were told that they were behind in their recruiting quota. A second group was told that they were ahead. Those behind evaluated the same recruits much more highly than did those ahead.[54]

CANDIDATE ORDER (CONTRAST) ERROR Candidate order (or contrast) error means that the order in which you see applicants affects how you rate them. In one study, researchers asked managers to evaluate a candidate who was "just average" after first evaluating several "unfavorable" candidates. The average candidate was evaluated more favorably than he might otherwise have been, because in contrast to the unfavorable candidates the average one looked better than he actually was.[55]

INFLUENCE OF NONVERBAL BEHAVIOR How the candidate behaves influences the interviewer's ratings. Interviewers rate applicants who demonstrate more eye contact, head moving, smiling, and similar nonverbal behaviors higher; such behavior can account for over 80% of the applicant's rating.[56] In one study, vocal cues (such as the interviewee's pitch, speech rates, and pauses) and visual cues (such as physical attractiveness, smile, and body orientation) correlated with evaluators' judgments of interviewee credibility.[57] Similarly, candidate self-promotion is strongly related to the interviewer's perceptions of candidate–job fit.[58]

ATTRACTIVENESS In general, individuals ascribe more favorable traits and more successful life outcomes to attractive people.[59] In one study, researchers asked subjects to evaluate candidates for promotability based on photographs. Men were perceived to be more suitable for hire and more likely to advance to the next executive level than were equally qualified women, and more attractive candidates, especially men, were preferred over less attractive ones.[60] These stereotypes are changing. However, women still account for only about 16% of corporate officers and 1% of CEOs at Fortune 500 companies.[61]

INGRATIATION Interviewees can boost their chances for job offers through self-promotion and ingratiation. *Ingratiation* means, for example, agreeing with the recruiter's opinions and thus signaling that they share similar beliefs. *Self-promotion* means promoting one's own skills and abilities to create the impression of competence.[62]

NON-VERBAL IMPLICATIONS Otherwise inferior candidates who "act right" in interviews often get higher ratings than do more competent applicants who lack nonverbal interviewing skills. Interviewers should thus look beyond the behavior to who the person is and what he or she is saying. Furthermore, since attributes such as attractiveness, sex, or race are generally irrelevant to job performance, interviewers should anticipate the potential impact of such biases and guard against letting them influence the ratings they give.

Steps in Conducting an Effective Interview

There are two ways to avoid interview errors. First, keep them in mind (don't make snap judgments, for instance). Second, structure the interview around job-related situational and behavioral questions. We'll look next at how to do this.

Step 1: **Structure the Interview**   The chapter appendix presents a precise way to create a structured interview. However there are also several simple ways to increase the standardization (structure) of the interview:[63]

1. It is essential to focus on how well the person can do the job. Therefore, first, compose your questions based on actual job duties from the job description.[64]
2. Next, use mostly job knowledge, situational, or behavioral questions. Questions that ask for opinions and attitudes, goals and aspirations, and self-descriptions and self-evaluations encourage self-promotion and let candidates avoid revealing weaknesses.

   Question examples include (1) *situational* questions like "Suppose you were giving a sales presentation and a difficult technical question arose that you could not answer. What would you do?" (2) *past behavior* questions like "Can you provide an example of a specific instance where you developed a sales presentation that was highly effective?" (3) *background* questions like "What work experiences, training, or other qualifications do you have for working in a teamwork environment?" and (4) *job knowledge* questions like "What factors should you consider when developing a TV advertising campaign?"
3. Train interviewers. For example, train interviewers to avoid potentially discriminatory questions. Doing so boosts their effectiveness.[65]
4. Use the same questions with all candidates. This can reduce bias by giving all candidates the same opportunity.
5. Use rating scales. For each question, try to have a range of sample ideal answers and a quantitative score for each. Then rate each candidate's answers against this scale.
6. Use multiple interviewers. Doing so can reduce bias by diminishing the importance of one interviewer's idiosyncratic opinions.
7. If possible, use a structured interview form. Interviews based on structured guides, as in Figure 5.7, usually result in superior interviews.[66]

Step 2: **Review Background**   Begin by reviewing the candidate's application and résumé, and note any vague areas. Review the job specification and start the interview with a clear picture of the traits of an ideal candidate.

Step 3: **Establish Rapport**   The point of the interview is to find out about the applicant. To do this, start by putting the person at ease. As a rule, all applicants—even unsolicited drop-ins—should receive friendly, courteous treatment, not only on humanitarian grounds but also because your reputation is on the line.

Step 4: **Ask Questions**   Try to follow your structured interview form, or questions you wrote out ahead of time. You'll find an additional menu of questions (such as "Describe a situation which best illustrates your leadership ability") in Figure 5.8.

One way to get candid answers is to make it clear you're going to conduct reference checks. Ask, "If I were to ask your boss, what's your best guess as to what he or she would say are your strengths, weak points, and overall performance?"[67] The HR in Practice feature presents some question guidelines.

HR IN PRACTICE

Dos and Don'ts of Interview Questions

- **Don't** ask questions that can be answered yes or no.
- **Don't** telegraph the desired answer, for instance, by nodding or smiling when the right answer is given.
- **Don't** interrogate the applicant as if the person is a criminal.
- **Don't** monopolize the interview by rambling, nor let the applicant dominate the interview.
- **Do** ask open-ended questions.
- **Do** listen to the candidate to encourage him or her to express thoughts fully.

- **Do** draw out the applicant's opinions and feelings by repeating the person's last comment as a question (e.g., "You didn't like your last job?").
- **Do** ask for examples.[68] For instance, if the candidate lists specific strengths or weaknesses, follow up with, "What are specific examples that demonstrate each of your strengths?"

WHAT *NOT* TO ASK   As a rule, avoid questions that might eliminate applicants based on age, race, gender, national origin, handicap, or other prohibited criteria. Can you pick out the inappropriate questions in the list on page 137?[69]

Organization and Planning Skills

1. Describe a specific situation which illustrates how you set objectives to reach a goal.
2. Tell me about a time when you had to choose between two or more important opportunities. How did you go about deciding which was most important to you?
3. Tell me how you normally schedule your time in order to accomplish your day-to-day tasks.
4. Describe a situation where you had a major role in organizing an important event. How did you do it?
5. Think about a lengthy term paper or report that you have written. Describe how you organized, researched and wrote that report.
6. Give an example of how you organized notes and other materials in order to study for an important exam.
7. Describe a time when you reorganized something to be more efficient. How did you do it?
8. Think of a time when you made important plans that were fouled up. How did you react? What did you do?

Interaction and Leadership

1. Tell me about an event in your past which has greatly influenced the way you relate to people.
2. Give a specific example that best illustrates your ability to deal with an uncooperative person.
3. Some people have the ability to "roll with the punches." Describe a time when you demonstrated this skill.
4. Tell me when you had to work with someone who had a negative opinion of you. How did you overcome this?
5. Recall a time when you participated on a team. Tell me an important lesson you learned that is useful to you today.
6. Describe an instance when you reversed a negative situation at school, work, or home. How did you do it?
7. Describe a situation which best illustrates your leadership ability.
8. Think about someone whose leadership you admire. What qualities impress you?

Assertiveness and Motivation

1. Describe several work standards that you have set for yourself in past jobs. Why are these important to you?
2. Tell me a time when you have experienced a lack of motivation. What caused this? What did you do about it?
3. Describe a situation where you had to deal with someone whom you felt was dishonest. How did you handle it?
4. Describe a situation that made you extremely angry. How did you react?
5. Tell me about a time that best illustrates your ability to "stick things out" in a tough situation.
6. Describe a time when you motivated an unmotivated person to do something you wanted them to do.
7. Give me an example of a time when you were affected by organizational politics. How did you react?
8. Give me an example of when someone tried to take advantage of you. How did you react?

Decision Making and Problem Solving

1. Give an example that illustrates your ability to make a tough decision.
2. Tell me about a decision you made even though you did not have all the facts.
3. Describe a situation where you have had to "stand up" for a decision you made, even though it was unpopular.
4. Describe a situation where you changed your mind, even after you publicly committed to a decision.
5. Describe a situation that illustrates your ability to analyze and solve a problem.
6. Tell me about a time where you acted as a mediator to solve a problem between two other people.
7. Describe a problem that seemed almost overwhelming to you. How did you handle it?
8. Tell me about a time where you have used a creative or unique approach to solve a tough problem.

The following general questions will also help you prepare for employment interviews:

1. Tell me a little about yourself.
2. Why did you attend Indiana State University?
3. What led you to choose your major or career field?
4. What college subjects did you like best/least? What did you like/dislike about them?
5. What has been your greatest challenge in college?
6. Describe your most rewarding college experience.
7. Do you think that your grades are a good indication of your academic abilities?
8. If you could change a decision you made while at college, what would you change? Why?
9. What campus involvements did you choose? What did you gain/contribute?
10. What are your plans for continued or graduate study?
11. What interests you about this job? What challenges are you looking for in a position?
12. How have your educational and work experiences prepared you for this position?
13. What work experiences have been most valuable to you and why?
14. Why are you interested in our organization? In what way do you think you can contribute to our company?
15. How would you describe yourself?
16. What do you consider to be your greatest strengths? Weaknesses? Give examples.
17. If I asked the people who know you for one reason why I shouldn't hire you, what would they say?
18. What accomplishments have given you the most satisfaction? Why?
19. What are your long-range career objectives? How do you plan to achieve these?
20. How would you describe your ideal job?
21. What two or three things are most important to you in your job?
22. Do you have a geographical preference? Why?

FIGURE 5.8

Sample Interview Questions

Source: Used with permission of the Indiana State University Career Center. All rights reserved.

- What kinds of things do you look for in a job?
- What types of interests or hobbies are you involved in?
- Do you have any handicaps?
- What university subjects do you like the most?
- What qualities should a successful manager possess?
- Do you have any future plans for marriage and children?
- What do you think you have to offer a company like Dandy Toys?
- What is your date of birth?
- What is the nature of your previous work experience?
- What kinds of things do you look for in a job?
- Have you ever been arrested for a crime?
- What do you consider to be your greatest strengths?

Step 5: **Close the Interview**   Leave time to answer any questions the candidate may have and, if appropriate, to advocate your firm to the candidate. Try to end all interviews on a positive note. Tell the applicant whether there is an interest and, if so, what the next step is. Similarly, make rejections diplomatically (for instance, with a statement such as "Thank you but there are other candidates whose experience is closer to our requirements").

Step 6: **Review the Interview**   After the candidate leaves, review your interview notes and fill in the structured interview guide (if any, and if you didn't do so during the interview). Then make your decision.

MANAGING HR IN CHALLENGING TIMES

Acing the Skype Interview

With employers cutting their recruitment budgets, and with free applications like Skype so widely used, there's no reason for not doing initial interviews via Skype.

Holding Skype job interviews requires few special preparations for the employer. However, Career FAQs (www.careerfaqs.com.au) says there are things that interviewees should keep in mind. Here's what they suggest:[70]

- Make sure you look presentable.
- Clean up the room, whether the interview is from your own home or a busy office environment.
- Do a dry run. Try recording yourself before the interview to try answering some imaginary questions.
- Relax. Treat it like any other face to-face meeting. Smile, look confident and enthusiastic, try to make eye contact, and don't shout, but do speak clearly.

Talent Management: Profiles and Employee Interviews

Talent management is the goal-oriented and integrated process of planning for, recruiting, selecting, developing, and compensating employees. Among other things, talent management involves using the same profile (competencies, traits, knowledge and experience) for recruiting as for selecting, training, appraising, and paying the employee.

Profiles can play an important role in employee selection. For example, we saw that IBM identified 490 possible roles employees might play, given IBM's strategic aims. IBM can then identify the skill sets each role requires. IBM then rates employees' skills from Zero to Three.

Managers can use a job's profile to formulate job-related situational, behavioral, and knowledge interview questions when selecting someone for a job or set of roles. Consider a simple example. Table 5.1 summarizes illustrative competency, knowledge, trait, and experience elements for a chemical engineer, along with sample interview questions. Selecting engineers based on this profile helps to ensure that you focus your questions on the things that someone must be proficient at to do this job successfully. The same profile would similarly provide guidance for determining how to recruit candidates for this position, and on what basis to train, appraise, and pay him or her.

TABLE 5.1 Asking Profile-Oriented Interview Questions

Profile Component	Example	Sample Interview Question
Competency	Able to use computer drafting software	Tell me about a time you used CAD Pro computerized design software.
Knowledge	How extreme heat affects hydrochloric acid (HCL)	Suppose you have an application where HCL is heated to 400 degrees fahrenheit at 2 atmospheres of pressure; what happens to the HCL?
Trait	Willing to travel abroad at least 4 months per year visiting facilities	Suppose you had a big affair that you had to attend next week and our company informed you that you had to leave for a job abroad immediately, and stay 3 weeks. How would you handle that?
Experience	Designed pollution filter for acid-cleaning facility	Tell me about a time when you designed a pollution filter device for an acid-cleaning facility. How did it work? What particular problems did you encounter? How did you address them?

USING OTHER SELECTION TECHNIQUES

Employers of course also use other selection techniques. These include the biodata method we discussed in Chapter 4, and those to which we now turn.

Background Investigations and Reference Checks

About 82% of HR managers report checking applicants' backgrounds, 80% do criminal convictions searches, and 35% do credit history reports.[71] There are two key reasons for checking backgrounds. One is to verify the accuracy of facts the applicant provided; the other is to uncover damaging background information such as criminal records. In Chicago, for instance, a pharmaceutical firm discovered that it had hired gang members in its mail delivery and computer repair departments. The gang members were stealing computer parts and then using the mail department to ship them to a nearby computer store they owned.[72]

Here's another reason for careful reference checking: Some enterprising individuals have created fake job reference services. For a fee, these services create fake work histories and references for job seekers.[73]

4 Explain the pros and cons of background investigations, reference checks, and preemployment information services.

WHAT TO VERIFY The most commonly verified background areas are legal eligibility for employment (to comply with immigration laws), dates of prior employment, military service (including discharge status), education, and identification (including date of birth and address). Other items should include county criminal records (current residence, last residence), motor vehicle record, credit, licensing verification, Social Security number, and reference checks.[74]

The position determines how deeply you search. For example, a credit and education check is more important for hiring an accountant than a groundskeeper. In any case, also periodically check, say, the credit ratings of employees who have easy access to company assets, and the driving records of employees who routinely use company cars.

COLLECTING BACKGROUND INFORMATION[75] Most employers try to verify directly an applicant's current position, salary, and employment dates with his or her current employer by phone (assuming that the candidate has cleared doing so). Others call the applicant's current and previous supervisors to try to discover more about the person's motivation, technical competence, and ability to work with others.

Many employers use commercial credit rating companies or employment screening services. These provide information about an applicant's credit standing, indebtedness, reputation, character, lifestyle, and the truthfulness of the person's application data. There are also thousands of online databases and sources for obtaining background information, including sex offender registries; workers compensation histories; nurses aid registries; and sources for criminal, employment, and educational histories.[76] Major employment screening providers include ADP (www.ADP.com), First Advantage (www.FADV.com/employer), and HireRight (www.hireright.com).[77]

CHECKING SOCIAL NETWORKING SITES More employers are checking candidates' social networking site postings. One employer went to Facebook.com and found that a top candidate described his interests as smoking marijuana and shooting people. Perhaps the student was joking. However, he did not get the offer.[78] After conducting such informal online reviews, recruiters found that 31% of applicants had lied about their qualifications and 19% had posted information about their drinking or drug use, according to one survey.[79] Similarly, as a *Wall Street Journal* article titled "Job references you can't control" noted, social networking sites can also help prospective employers identify an applicant's former colleagues, and thus contact them.[80] The caveat for employers is to avoid subterfuge, for instance, using a fictitious login name.

REFERENCE CHECK EFFECTIVENESS Handled correctly, background checks are an inexpensive and straightforward way to verify facts (such as current and previous job titles). Unfortunately, getting candid replies can be tricky. For one thing, it is not easy for the reference to prove that the bad reference was warranted. The rejected applicant thus has various legal remedies, including suing the reference for defamation. This can understandably inhibit former employers.[81] In one case, a man was awarded $56,000 after being turned down for a job because, among other things, a former employer called him a "character."

It is not just the fear of legal reprisal that can lead to useless or misleading references. Many supervisors don't want to diminish a former employee's chances for a job. Others give incompetent employees good reviews to get rid of them.

MAKING REFERENCE CHECKS MORE USEFUL You can do several things to make your reference checking more useful.

First, have the candidate sign a release (usually, on the application) authorizing the background check.[82]

Second, always obtain two forms of identification.

Third, ensure that applicants complete the applications fully. Always compare the application to the résumé (people tend to be more creative on their résumés than on their application forms, where they must certify the information).[83]

Fourth, use a structured reference-checking form as in Figure 5.9. This helps ensure that you don't overlook important questions.

Finally, use the references offered by the applicant as merely a source for other people who may know of the applicant's performance. Thus, you might ask each reference, "Could you give me the name of another person who might be familiar with the applicant's performance?" In that way, you begin getting information from references that may be more objective. Try to contact at least two previous superiors, two peers, and two subordinates.

Companies fielding reference requests should ensure that only authorized managers give them. Centralize the task within HR. Former employees may even hire reference-checking firms and take legal action for defamatory references. There are dozens of reference-checking firms like Allison & Taylor Reference Checking Inc. in Jamestown, New York.[84] Charging as little as $80, many use certified court reporters to manually transcribe what the reference is saying.[85] One supervisor, describing a former city employee, reportedly "used swear words, said he was incompetent and said that he almost brought the city down on its knees."[86]

USING PREEMPLOYMENT INFORMATION SERVICES Numerous employment screening services such as HireCheck (www.hirecheck.com) use databases to conduct background checks for employers.

Although such screening services are valuable, the employer should make sure its service does not violate EEO laws. For example, as we discussed in Chapter 2, under the ADA, employers should avoid preemployment inquiries into the existence, nature, or severity of a disability.

The employer should also make sure the firm requires an applicant-signed release authorizing the background check, complies with relevant laws such as the Fair Credit Reporting Act, and uses only legal data sources. A basic criminal check might cost $25, while a comprehensive background check costs about $200.[87]

Honesty Testing

Employers can use various tools to assess candidates' and employees' honesty.

POLYGRAPH TESTS The *polygraph* (or "*lie detector*") machine is a device that measures physiological changes such as increased perspiration. The assumption is that such changes reflect changes in the emotional stress that accompanies lying.

FIGURE 5.9

Reference Checking Form

Source: Society for Human Resource Management, © 2004, Reproduced with permission of Society for Human Resource Management in the Format Textbook via Copyright Clearance Center.

(Verify that the applicant has provided permission before conducting reference checks.)

Candidate
Name _____

Reference
Name _____

Company
Name _____

Dates of Employment
From: _____ To: _____

Position(s)
Held _____

Salary
History _____

Reason for
Leaving _____

Explain the reason for your call and verify the above information with the supervisor (including the reason for leaving)
_____
_____
_____

1. Please describe the type of work for which the candidate was responsible.
_____
_____

2. How would you describe the applicant's relationships with coworkers, subordinates (if applicable), and with superiors?
_____
_____

3. Did the candidate have a positive or negative work attitude? Please elaborate.
_____
_____

4. How would you describe the quantity and quality of output generated by the former employee?
_____
_____

5. What were his/her strengths on the job?
_____
_____

6. What were his/her weaknesses on the job?
_____
_____

7. What is your overall assessment of the candidate?
_____
_____

8. Would you recommend him/her for this position? Why or why not?
_____
_____

9. Would this individual be eligible for rehire? Why or why not?
_____
_____

Other comments?
_____
_____
_____

The polygraph (or "lie detector") machine is a device that measures physiological changes such as increased perspiration.

Complaints about offensiveness as well as doubts about the polygraph's accuracy culminated in the Employee Polygraph Protection Act of 1988. With few exceptions, the law prohibits most employers from conducting polygraph examinations of all applicants and most employees.

PAPER-AND-PENCIL HONESTY TESTS The virtual elimination of the polygraph triggered a burgeoning market for other honesty testing devices. Honesty tests are psychological tests designed to predict job applicants' proneness to dishonesty. Most of these tests measure attitudes regarding things such as tolerance of others who steal, and admission of theft-related activities. (See, for example, http://testyourself. psychtests.com/testid/2100.)

Psychologists have some concerns about paper-and-pencil honesty tests. For example, the tests may be prone to producing a high percentage of false positives, and are susceptible to coaching.[88] However, studies tend to support these tests' validity. One focused on 111 employees hired by a major retail convenience store chain to work at convenience store or gas station outlet counters.[89] The researchers found that scores on an honesty test successfully predicted theft, as measured by termination for theft.

In practice, detecting dishonest candidates (see the HR in Practice feature) involves not just tests but a comprehensive screening procedure.

HR IN PRACTICE

How to Spot Dishonesty

One expert suggests following these steps:

- Ask blunt questions.[90] For example, there is probably nothing wrong with asking, "Have you ever stolen anything from an employer?" and "Is any information on your application falsified?"
- Listen, rather than talk. You want to learn as much as possible about the person.
- Ask for a credit check. Include a clause in your application form that gives you the right to background checks, including credit checks and motor vehicle reports.
- Check all references.
- Consider using a paper-and-pencil honesty test.
- Test for drugs. Devise a drug testing program and give each applicant a copy of the policy.

- Conduct searches and establish a search-and-seizure policy. The policy should state that all lockers, desks, and similar property remain the property of the company and may be inspected. Give each applicant a copy of the policy and require a signed copy.
- Communicate with employees. Make clear that any failures to follow protocols or falsification of records will not be tolerated and will result in disciplinary action that may include immediate dismissal.[91]
- Use caution. Being rejected for dishonesty carries with it more stigma than does being rejected for, say, poor mechanical comprehension. Furthermore, some states, such as Massachusetts and Rhode Island, limit paper-and-pencil honesty testing.

Graphology

The use of graphology (handwriting analysis) is based on the assumption that the writer's basic personality traits will be expressed in his or her handwriting. Handwriting analysis thus has some resemblance to projective personality tests.

Although some writers estimate that more than 1,000 U.S. companies use handwriting analysis to assess applicants, the validity of handwriting analysis is questionable. One reviewer says, "There is essentially no evidence of a direct link between handwriting analysis and various measures of job performance . . . "[92] Why so many employers use it is thus a matter of debate. Perhaps it's because it seems, to many people, to have face validity. Or perhaps in some specific situations it can be shown to predict performance.[93]

Medical Exams

Medical exams are often the next step in the selection process. Such exams can confirm that the applicant qualifies for the physical requirements of the position and can unearth any medical limitations to take into account in placing the applicant. The examination can also detect communicable diseases. Under the ADA, a person with a disability can't be rejected for the job if he or she is otherwise qualified and if the person could perform the essential job functions with reasonable accommodation. According to the ADA, a medical exam is permitted during the period *between the job offer and the commencement of work*, if such exams are standard for all applicants for that job.[94]

Drug Screening

Employers generally conduct drug tests. The most common practice is to test new applicants just before formally hiring them. Many firms also test current employees when there is reason to believe an employee has been using drugs, such as after a work accident. Some firms administer drug tests on a random basis, while others do so when transferring an employee.[95] Most employers that conduct such tests use urine sampling. Numerous vendors provide workplace drug testing services.[96]

PROBLEMS Unfortunately, drug testing is problematical.[97] Although Breathalyzers and blood tests for alcohol (like those police give roadside to inebriated drivers) do correlate closely with impairment levels, urine and blood tests for other drugs only show whether drug residues are present. They can't measure impairment or, for that matter, habituation or addiction.[98] Furthermore, "there is a swarm of products that promise to help employees (both male and female) beat [urine analysis] drug tests."[99] However, hair follicle testing and newer oral fluid samples are much less subject to tampering.

Drug testing therefore raises several issues. Without strong evidence linking blood or urine drug levels to impairment, some argue that drug testing violates peoples' rights to privacy and due process, and that the procedures themselves are degrading and intrusive. Others argue that workplace drug testing might identify one's use of drugs during leisure hours, but have little or no relevance to the job.[100] It's also not clear that drug testing improves safety or performance. At least one study concluded that other than alcohol, there is no clear evidence that drugs diminish safety or job performance.[101]

LEGAL ISSUES Several federal laws affect workplace drug testing. Under the ADA, courts might well view a former drug user (one who no longer uses illegal drugs and successfully completed or is participating in a rehabilitation program) as a qualified applicant with a disability.[102] U.S. Department of Transportation regulations require firms with more than 50 eligible employees in transportation industries to conduct alcohol testing on workers with sensitive or safety-related jobs. These include mass-transit workers, air traffic controllers, train crews, and school bus drivers.[103] Particularly where safety-sensitive jobs are concerned, courts appear to side with employers when questions arise.

Realistic Job Previews

Sometimes, a dose of realism makes the best screening tool. For example, Walmart found that associates who quit within the first 90 days often did so because of conflict in their schedules or because they preferred to work in another geographic area. The firm then began explicitly explaining and asking about work schedules and work preferences.[104] One study even found that some applicants accepted jobs with the intention to quit, a fact that more realistic interviewing might have unearthed.[105]

Tapping Friends and Acquaintances

Testing and interviewing aside, don't ignore tapping the opinions of people you trust who have direct personal knowledge of the candidate. It may be an exaggeration, but as a former Continental Airlines CEO said, "the best possible interview is miniscule in value compared to somebody who's got even a couple of months of work experience with somebody."[106]

Making the Selection Decision

Once you've done all your testing and checking the question arises, How do you combine all this information and make a selection decision? Of course, if you're only using one predictor (such as one test score) then the decision is straightforward. For example, an applicant for an engineering position should score at least 30 answers correct on the Wonderlic test in order to be appointable as an engineer. If your applicant scores lower, you probably wouldn't hire him or her, and if it's higher, you probably would.

But, in reality, things are not so simple. For one thing, you'll probably not make your decision based on a single predictor (in this case, one test score). You'll also want to factor in the person's references, his or her interview and application information (such as school attended), and perhaps the results of other tests. In other words, you'll have not one but *multiple predictors* to juggle. Furthermore, you'll probably have more than one candidate.[107] Will you simply choose the one with the highest Wonderlic score? Probably not. So again, you'll need some way to weigh all the sources of information you have about each candidate.

How do you weigh all the input in reaching a selection decision? In simplest terms, you have three choices. You could use, first, a clinical (or intuitive or judgmental) approach. You're already probably most familiar with this one. Here you intuitively weigh all the evidence you have from the various sources about the candidate, and make your decision. Second, you could take a statistical or "mechanical" approach. In its purest sense, the mechanical approach involves quantifying all the information you collect about the candidate (including, for example subjective information from references). You then combine all this quantified information, perhaps using a formula that predicts the candidate's likely job success. And third, of course, you could take a hybrid approach, one that combines the mechanical results you obtained from your formula with judgment. Technically speaking, the mechanical/statistical approach is usually the most defensible.[108]

THREE STATISTICAL APPROACHES Unfortunately, taking a statistical approach doesn't fully solve your problem. For example, do you simply add up the candidates' test and other scores and hire the one with the highest total score? Or do you only hire candidates who obtain certain minimum scores on each test?

In practice, employers can use one of three statistical approaches. One, the *multiple regression* approach, assumes that your selection score is a function of the sum of the weighted predictor scores (such as 0.8 times his or her Wonderlic score plus 0.2 times his or her mechanical comprehension score). This approach makes the most sense when you are willing to trade off one thing for another. For example, if the person doesn't do well on the mechanical comprehension test, but does very well on the Wonderlic test, her total score might still be high, so you might still hire her.

Alternatively, with the *multiple cutoff* approach, you only hire the person if *every one* of the person's predictor scores exceeds the cutoff score you chose for each predictor.[109] If the person fails to pass the cutoff score on even one test, you would not make a job offer. This approach makes most sense when an ideal candidate must in fact exceed the cutoff scores on every predictor. For example, a police officer candidate requires a certain minimum required score in eyesight, hearing, and strength.

Finally, with the *multiple hurdle* approach, the candidate must exceed the cutoff score for each test or other selection device, *in sequence*. For example, if our police officer candidate doesn't have acceptable eyesight, he or she does not move on to take the hearing test. This approach takes longer—you need to administer the screening tools in sequence. But you avoid the expense of administering multiple tests to people who don't make the first cut.

A PRACTICAL APPROACH At the end of the day, you have a job to fill and the question is, how should you proceed? Three suggestions are in order.[110]

First, whichever approach you use, use it systematically. For example, don't use a multiple cutoff approach for one candidate, and a multiple hurdle approach for the others.

Second, two experts say that if you can create, using the multiple regression statistical approach, a formula that relates your criterion score (such as on-the-job performance) with scores on several weighted predictor scores (such as tests), that would be very helpful.[111]

Finally, while it's ideal to use a statistical approach such as multiple regression, a more informal approach is still usually better than nothing. For example, suppose you have a job opening for an engineer.[112] First ask yourself what specific tasks (like drafting, and computing stress indices) this engineer will have to perform and the standards of performance on which you will measure that performance. Next, think of several activities you can ask your candidates to perform that would be similar to these specific job tasks. After identifying several of these activities, think about the weights you'd attach to each activity based on its relative importance. Then have each candidate perform each activity, and award each activity he or she performs a score using some simple rating system (such as 1 to 5, from low to high). Then multiply each candidate's score on each activity with the weight you assigned for that activity, and sum up the results to determine which candidate scores highest.

Evaluating the Selection Process

More employers today take the time to evaluate how effective their recruitment and screening processes are. Thus, the consulting firm Bernard Hodes worked with one client to create phantom applicants, complete with résumés. These phantoms then applied to the client employer and reported on the effectiveness of the employer's recruitment and selection processes.[113] Table 5.2 summarizes the validity, cost, and potential adverse impact of some popular selection methods.

Complying with Immigration Law

Under the Immigration Reform and Control Act of 1986, people must prove that they are eligible to work in the United States. A person does not have to be a U.S. citizen to be employed under this act. However, employers should ask a candidate who is about to be hired whether he or she is a U.S. citizen or an alien lawfully authorized to work in the United States.

HOW TO COMPLY There are two ways prospective employees can show their eligibility for employment. One is to show a document such as a U.S. passport or alien registration card containing a photograph that proves *both* identity and employment eligibility. However, many prospective employees do not have either of these documents. Therefore, the other way to verify employment eligibility is to see one document that proves the person's identity, along with a separate document showing the person's employment eligibility, such as a work permit.

TABLE 5.2 Evaluation of Assessment Methods Based on Four Criteria

Assessment Method	Validity	EEO Adverse Impact	Costs (Develop/Administer)	Applicant Reactions
Cognitive ability test	High	High (against minorities)	Low/low	Somewhat favorable
Job knowledge test	High	High (against minorities)	Low/low	More favorable
Personality test	Low to moderate	Low	Low/low	Less favorable
Biographical data inventory	Moderate	Low to high for different types	High/low	Less favorable
Integrity test	Moderate to high	Low	Low/low	Less favorable
Structured interview	High	Low	High/high	More favorable
Physical fitness test	Moderate to high	High (against females and older workers)	High/high	More favorable
Situational judgment test	Moderate	Moderate (against minorities)	High/low	More favorable
Assessment center	Moderate to high	Low to moderate, depending on exercise	High/high	More favorable
Physical ability test	Moderate to high	High (against females and older workers)	High/high	More favorable

Note: There was limited research evidence available on applicant reactions to situational judgment tests and physical ability tests. However, because these tests tend to appear very relevant to the job, it is likely that applicant reactions to them would be favorable.
Source: Elaine Pulakos, *Selection Assessment Methods,* SHRM Foundation (2005): 17. Reprinted by permission of Society for Human Resource Management via Copyright Clearance Center.

Employers run the risk of accepting fraudulent documents, but can protect themselves. Preemployment screening should include employment verification, criminal record checks, drug screens, and reference checks. You can verify Social Security cards by calling the Social Security Administration.

More employers are using the federal government's voluntary electronic employment verification program, E-Verify.[114] This is " . . . an Internet-based system that allows an employer, using information reported on an employee's Form I-9, Employment Eligibility Verification, to determine the eligibility of that employee to work in the United States." For most employers, it is voluntary, but it's mandatory for some employers, such as those with certain federal contracts. There is no charge to employers to use E-Verify.[115]

The requirement to verify eligibility does not provide any basis to reject an applicant just because he or she is a foreigner, not a U.S. citizen, or an alien residing in the United States. But, the applicant must be able to prove his or her identity and employment eligibility. Employers can avoid accusations of discrimination by verifying the documents of all applicants, not just those they think may be suspicious.[116]

Improving Productivity through HRIS:
Comprehensive Applicant Tracking and Screening Systems

The applicant tracking systems we introduced in Chapter 4 do more than track online applicants. The new systems also help companies screen applicants.

First, most employers use their applicant tracking systems (ATSs) to "knock out" applicants who do not meet minimum, nonnegotiable job requirements, like holding driver's licenses.

Second, employers use them to test and screen applicants online. This includes Web-based skills tests (in arithmetic, for instance), cognitive tests (such as for mechanical comprehension), and even psychological tests. Recreation Equipment, Inc., needed a system to match applicant skills with the company's culture (specifically, to identify applicants who were inclined to work in teams). The company worked with its ATS vendor to customize its system to do that.[117]

Third, the newer systems don't just screen out candidates, but discover "hidden talents." The ATS can identify talents in the resume that lend themselves to job matches at the company that even the applicant didn't know existed.[118]

REVIEW

SUMMARY

1. In this chapter we discuss several techniques for screening and selecting job candidates: The first is testing.

2. Test validity answers the question "What does this test measure?" Criterion validity means demonstrating that those who do well on the test do well on the job. Content validity is demonstrated by showing that the test constitutes a fair sample of the content of the job.

3. As used by psychologists, the term *reliability* always means "consistency." One way to measure reliability is to administer the same (or equivalent) tests to the same people at two different points in time. Or you could focus on internal consistency, comparing the responses to roughly equivalent items on the same test.

4. There are many types of personnel tests in use, including intelligence tests, tests of physical skills, tests of achievement, aptitude tests, interest inventories, and personality tests.

5. Under equal opportunity legislation, an employer may have to prove that his or her tests are predictive of success or failure on the job. This usually requires a predictive validation study, although other means of validation are often acceptable.

6. Management assessment centers are screening devices that expose applicants to a series of real-life exercises. Performance is observed and assessed by experts, who then check their assessments by observing the participants when they are back at their jobs. Examples of such real-life exercises include a simulated business game, an in-basket exercise, and group discussions.

7. Several factors and problems can undermine the usefulness of an interview: making premature decisions, letting unfavorable information predominate, not knowing the requirements of the job, being under pressure to hire, not allowing for the candidate order effect, and nonverbal behavior.

8. The five steps in the interview include plan, establish rapport, question the candidate, close the interview, and review the data.

9. Other screening tools include reference checks, background checks, physical exams, and realistic previews.

10. Once you've selected and hired your new employees, they must be trained. We turn to training in the following chapter.

KEY TERMS

negligent hiring   121
reliability   121
test validity   122
criterion validity   122

content validity   122
management assessment center   130
interview   131
structured situational interview   149

DISCUSSION QUESTIONS

1. Explain what is meant by *reliability* and *validity*. What is the difference between them? In what respects are they similar?
2. Discuss at least four basic types of personnel tests.
3. Explain the factors and problems that can undermine an interview's usefulness, and techniques for eliminating them.
4. Explain the shortcomings of background investigations, reference checks, and preemployment information services, and how to overcome them.

5. Why is it important to conduct preemployment background investigations? How would you go about doing so?
6. For what sorts of jobs do you think computerized interviews are most appropriate? Why?
7. Briefly discuss and give examples of several common interviewing mistakes. What recommendations would you give for avoiding these interviewing mistakes?

INDIVIDUAL AND GROUP ACTIVITIES

1. Working individually or in groups, develop a list of specific selection techniques that you would suggest your dean use to hire the next HR professor at your school. Explain why you chose each selection technique.
2. Working individually or in groups, contact the publisher of a standardized test such as the Scholastic Assessment Test and obtain from it written information regarding the test's validity and reliability. Present a short report in class discussing what the test is supposed to measure and the degree to which you think the test does what it is supposed to do, based on the reported validity and reliability scores.

3. Give a short presentation titled "How to Be Effective as an Interviewer."
4. Write a short essay discussing some of the ethical and legal considerations in testing.
5. Give some examples of how interest inventories could be used to improve employee selection. In doing so, suggest several examples of occupational interests that you believe might predict success in various occupations, including college professor, accountant, and computer programmer.

WEB-e's (WEB EXERCISES)

1. What can you learn from www.google.com/intl/en/jobs/ about how Google goes about recruiting applicants and how Google screens and selects candidates?
2. What does www.siop.org/workplace/employment%20testing/ information_to_consider_when_cre.aspx suggest you consider when purchasing a selection test?

3. Could an employer actually use a typing test like that in www.iphonetypingtest.com/ to help select employees? If so, how exactly?

APPLICATION EXERCISES

HR IN ACTION CASE INCIDENT 1
Ethics and the Out-of-Control Interview

Ethics are "the principles of conduct governing an individual or a group"—they are the principles people use to decide what their conduct should be.[119]

Fairness is important in employee selection. For example, "If prospective employees perceive that the hiring process does not treat people fairly, they may assume that ethical behavior is not important in the company, and that 'official' pronouncements about the importance of ethics can be discounted."[120]

That's one reason why the situation Maria Fernandez ran into is disturbing. Maria is a bright, popular, and well-informed mechanical engineer who graduated with an engineering degree from State University in June 2010. During the spring preceding her graduation, she went out on many job interviews, most of which she thought were conducted courteously and were reasonably useful in giving both her and the prospective employer a good impression of where each of them stood on matters of importance to both of them. It was, therefore, with great anticipation that she looked forward to an interview with the one firm where she most wanted to work: Apex Environmental. She had always had a strong interest in cleaning up the environment and firmly believed she could best use her training and skills in a firm like Apex, where she thought she could have a successful career while making the world a better place.

The interview, however, was a disaster. Maria walked into a room in which a panel of five men—the president of the company, two vice presidents, the marketing director, and another engineer—began throwing questions at her that she felt were aimed primarily at tripping her up rather than finding out what she could offer through her engineering skills. The questions ranged from unnecessarily discourteous ("Why would you take a job as a waitress in college if you're such an intelligent person?") to irrelevant and sexist ("Are you planning on settling down and starting a family anytime soon?"). Then, after the interview, she met with two of the gentlemen individually (including the president), and the discussions focused almost exclusively on her technical expertise. She

thought that these later discussions went fairly well. However, given the apparent aimlessness and even mean-spiritedness of the panel interview, she was astonished when several days later she received a job offer from the firm.

The offer forced her to consider several matters. From her point of view, the job itself was perfect—she liked what she would be doing, the industry, and the firm's location. And, in fact, the president had been quite courteous in subsequent discussions, as had been the other members of the management team. She was left wondering whether the panel interview had been intentionally tense to see how she'd stand up under pressure, and, if so, why they would do such a thing.

Questions

1. How would you explain the nature of the panel interview Maria had to endure? Specifically, do you think it reflected a well-thought-out interviewing strategy on the part of the firm or carelessness (or worse) on the part of the firm's management? If it was carelessness, what would you do to improve the interview process at Apex Environmental?
2. Do you consider the managers' treatment of Maria ethical? Why? If not, what specific steps would you take to make sure the interview process is ethical from now on?
3. Would you take the job offer if you were Maria? If you're not sure, is there any additional information that would help you make your decision, and if so, what is it?
4. The job of applications engineer for which Maria was applying requires (a) excellent technical skills with respect to mechanical engineering, (b) a commitment to working in the area of pollution control, (c) the ability to deal well and confidently with customers who have engineering problems, (d) a willingness to travel worldwide, and (e) a very intelligent and well-balanced personality. List 10 questions you would ask when interviewing applicants for the job.

HR IN ACTION CASE INCIDENT 2
Honesty Testing at Carter Cleaning Company

Jennifer Carter, president of Carter Cleaning Centers, and her father have what the latter describes as an easy but hard job when it comes to screening job applicants. It is easy because for two important jobs—the people who actually do the pressing and those who do the cleaning-spotting—the applicants are easily screened with about 20 minutes of on-the-job testing. As with typists, as Jennifer points out, "Applicants either know how to press clothes fast enough or how to use cleaning chemicals and machines, or they don't, and we find out very quickly by just trying them out on the job." On the other hand, applicant screening for the stores can also be frustratingly hard because of the nature of some of the other qualities that Jennifer would like to screen for.

Two of the most critical problems facing her company are employee turnover and employee honesty. Jennifer and her father sorely need to implement practices that will reduce the rate of employee turnover. If there is a way to do this through employee testing and screening techniques, Jennifer would like to know about it because of the management time and money that are now being wasted by the never-ending need to recruit and hire new employees. Of even greater concern to Jennifer and her father is the need to institute new practices to screen out those employees who may be predisposed to steal from the company.

Employee theft is an enormous problem for Carter Cleaning Centers, and one that is not just limited to employees who handle the cash. For example, the cleaner-spotter and/or the presser often open the store themselves, without a manager present, to get the day's work started, and it is not unusual to have one or more of these people steal supplies or "run a route." Running a route means that an employee canvasses his or her neighborhood to pick up people's clothes for cleaning and then secretly cleans and presses them in the Carter store, using the company's supplies, gas, and power. It would also not be unusual for an unsupervised person (or his or her supervisor, for that matter) to accept a one-hour rush order for cleaning or laundering, quickly clean and press the item, and return it to the customer for payment without making out a proper ticket for the item posting the sale. The money, of course, goes into the worker's pocket instead of into the cash register.

The more serious problem concerns the store manager and the counter workers who actually handle the cash. According to Jack Carter, "You would not believe the creativity employees use to get around the management controls we set up to cut down on employee theft." As one extreme example of this felonious creativity, Jack tells the following story: "To cut down on the amount of money my employees were stealing, I had a small sign painted and placed in front of all our cash registers. The sign said: YOUR ENTIRE ORDER FREE IF WE DON'T GIVE YOU A CASH REGISTER RECEIPT WHEN YOU PAY. CALL 552–0235. It was my intention with this sign to force all our cash-handling employees to place their receipts into the cash register where they would be recorded for my accountants. After all, if all the cash that comes in

is recorded in the cash register, then we should have a much better handle on stealing in our stores, right? Well, one of our managers found a diabolical way around this. I came into the store one night and noticed that the cash register this particular manager was using just didn't look right, although the sign was dutifully placed in front of it. It turned out that every afternoon at about 5:00 P.M. when the other employees left, this character would pull his own cash register out of a box that he hid underneath our supplies. Customers coming in would notice the sign and of course the fact that he was meticulous in ringing up every sale. But unknown to them and us, for about five months the sales that came in for about an hour every day went into his cash register, not mine. It took us that long to figure out where our cash for that store was going."

Jennifer would like you to answer the following questions.

Questions

1. What would be the advantages and disadvantages to Jennifer's company of routinely administering honesty tests to all its employees?
2. Specifically, what other screening techniques could the company use to screen out theft-prone and turnover-prone employees, and how exactly could these be used?
3. How should her company terminate employees caught stealing, and what kind of procedure should be set up for handling reference calls about these employees when they go to other companies looking for jobs?

EXPERIENTIAL EXERCISE

The Most Important Person You'll Ever Hire

Purpose: The purpose of this exercise is to give you practice using some of the interview techniques you learned from this chapter.

Required Understanding: You should be familiar with the information presented in this chapter, and read this:

For parents, children are precious. It's therefore interesting that parents who hire nannies to take care of their children usually do little more than ask several interview questions and conduct what is often, at best, a perfunctory reference check. Given the often questionable validity of interviews, and the (often) relative inexperience of the father or mother doing the interviewing, it's not surprising that many of these arrangements end in disappointment. You know from this chapter that it is difficult to conduct a valid interview unless you know exactly what you're looking for and, preferably, also how to structure the interview. Most parents simply aren't trained to do this.

How to Set Up the Exercise/Instructions:

1. Set up groups of five or six students. Two students will be the interviewees, while the other students in the group will serve as panel interviewers. The interviewees will develop a form for assessing the interviewers, and the panel interviewers will develop a structured situational interview for a nanny.
2. Instructions for the interviewees: The interviewees should leave the room for about 20 minutes. While out

of the room, the interviewees should develop an interviewer assessment form based on the information presented in this chapter regarding factors that can undermine the usefulness of an interview. During the panel interview, the interviewees should assess the interviewers using the interviewer assessment form. After the panel interviewers have conducted the interview, the interviewees should leave the room to discuss their notes. Did the interviewers exhibit any of the factors that can undermine the usefulness of an interview? If so, which ones? What suggestions would you (the interviewees) make to the interviewers on how to improve the usefulness of the interview?

3. Instructions for the interviewers: While the interviewees are out of the room, the panel interviewers will have 20 minutes to develop a short structured situational interview form for a nanny. The panel interview team will interview two candidates for the position. During the panel interview, each interviewer should be taking notes on a copy of the structured situational interview form. After the panel interview, the panel interviewers should discuss their notes. What were your first impressions of each interviewee? Were your impressions similar? Which candidate would you all select for the position and why?

BUSINESS IN ACTION EDU-EXERCISE

Building Your *Business Law* Knowledge in Testing

We've seen that various federal and state laws bar discrimination on the basis of race, color, age, religion, sex, disability, and national origin. With respect to testing, these laws boil down to two things: (1) You must be able to prove that your tests were related to success or failure on the job, and (2) you must be able to prove that your tests don't unfairly discriminate against either minority or nonminority subgroups.

Questions

Use the website www.EEOC.gov to answer the following questions:

1. What are the steps the EEOC uses in investigating a charge?
2. What specific types of discrimination does U.S. EEO law address?
3. List five employment practices EEO law essentially prohibits.

PERSONAL COMPETENCIES EDU-EXERCISE

Building Your *Cross-Cultural Sensitivity*: Gender Issues in Testing

Employers using selection tests should know that gender issues might distort the results. Parents and others often socialize girls into traditionally female roles and boys into traditionally male roles. Thus, there is a continuing underrepresentation of women in traditional male areas such as top management and in engineering and the sciences. Such stereotypes are changing. One recent study found that both male and female managers "are rating women more as leaders than they did 15 and 30 years ago."[121]

Yet gender-role socialization does influence men and women's test results. For example, it can influence the occupational interests for which candidates express a preference. Males tend to score higher on aptitude tests in what some view as male fields (such as mechanical reasoning). The test results may thus ironically perpetuate the narrowing of females' career options.

Questions

1. Do you agree that gender-role socialization is a continuing reality? Give some examples of why you answered yes or no.
2. List five questions that you believe job interviewers would more likely ask of women than of men applicants.

APPENDIX
THE STRUCTURED SITUATIONAL INTERVIEW

There is little doubt that the **structured situational interview**—a series of job-relevant questions with predetermined answers that interviewers ask of all applicants for the job—produces superior results.[122] The basic idea is to write situational (what would you do), behavioral (what did you do), or job knowledge questions, *and* have job experts (like those supervising the job) also write sample answers for these questions, rated from good to poor. The people who interview and rate the applicants then use rating sheets anchored with examples of good or bad answers to rate the interviewees' answers.[123]

In creating structured situational interviews, people familiar with the job develop questions based on the job's actual duties. They then reach consensus on what are and are not acceptable answers. The procedure is as follows.[124]

structured situational interview
A series of job-relevant questions with predetermined answers that interviewers ask of all applicants for the job.

Step 1: **Job Analysis**   Write a job description with a list of job duties and required knowledge, skills, abilities, and other worker qualifications.

Step 2: **Rate the Job's Main Duties**   Identify the job's main duties. To do so, rate each job duty based on its importance to job success and on the time required to perform it compared to other tasks.

Step 3: **Create Interview Questions**   Create interview questions based on actual job duties, with more questions for the important duties. Recall that *situational questions* pose a hypothetical job situation, such as "What would you do if the machine suddenly began heating up?" *Job knowledge questions* assess knowledge essential to job performance, such as "What is HTML?" *Willingness questions* gauge the applicant's willingness and motivation to meet the job's requirements—to do repetitive physical work or to travel, for instance. *Behavioral questions* of course ask candidates how they've handled similar situations.

The people who create the questions usually write them in terms of critical incidents. For example, for a supervisory candidate, the interviewer might ask this situational question:

> Your spouse and two teenage children are sick in bed with colds. There are no relatives or friends available to look in on them. Your shift starts in three hours. What would you do in this situation?

Step 4: **Create Benchmark Answers** Next, *for each question*, develop ideal (benchmark) answers for good (a 5 rating), marginal (a 3 rating), and poor (a 1 rating). For example, consider the preceding situational question, where the spouse and children are sick. Three benchmark answers (from low to high) for the example question might be, "I'd stay home—my spouse and family come first" (1); "I'd phone my supervisor and explain my situation" (3); and "Since they only have colds, I'd come to work" (5).

Step 5: **Appoint the Interview Panel and Conduct Interviews** Employers generally conduct structured situational interviews using a panel, rather than one-on-one. The panel usually consists of three to six members, preferably the same ones who wrote the questions and answers. It may also include the job's supervisor and/or incumbent, and a human resources representative. The same panel interviews all candidates for the job.[125]

The panel members generally review the job description, questions, and benchmark answers before the interview. One panel member introduces the applicant, and asks all questions of all applicants in this and succeeding candidates' interviews (to ensure consistency). However, all panel members record and rate the applicant's answers on the rating scale sheet. They do this by indicating where the candidate's answer to each question falls relative to the ideal poor, marginal, or good answers. At the end of the interview, someone answers any questions the applicant has.[126]

Web-based programs help interviewers design and organize behaviorally based selection interviews. For example, SelectPro (www.selectpro.net) enables interviewers to create behavior-based selection interviews, custom interview guides, and automated online interviews.

ENDNOTES

1. Vanessa O'Connell, "Test for Dwindling Retail Jobs Spawns a Culture of Cheating," *Wall Street Journal* (January 7, 2009): A1, A10.
2. Kevin Hart, "Not Wanted: Thieves," *HR Magazine* (April 2008): 119.
3. Sarah Needleman, "Businesses Say Theft By Their Workers Is Up," *Wall Street Journal* (December 11, 2008): B8.
4. For an example, see C. Tuna et al., "Job-Test Ruling Cheers Employers," *Wall Street Journal* (July 1, 2009): B1-2.
5. "Wal-Mart to Scrutinize Job Applicants," *CNN Money* (August 12, 2004), http://money.cnn.com/2004/08/12/News/fortune500/walmart_jobs/index.htm, accessed August 8, 2005.
6. Fay Hansen, "Taking 'Reasonable' Action to Avoid Negligent Hiring Claims," *Workforce Management* (September 11, 2006): 31.
7. Anne Anastasi, *Psychological Patterns* (New York: Macmillan, 1968). See also Kevin Murphy and Charles David Shafer, *Psychological Testing* (Upper Saddle River, NJ: Prentice Hall, 2001): 108–124.
8. M. Guion, "Changing Views for Personnel Selection Research," *Personnel Psychology* 40, no. 2 (Summer 1987): 199–213. The Standards for Educational and Psychological Testing define validity as "the degree to which accumulated evidence and theories support specific interpretations of test scores entailed by proposed uses of a test." Deborah Whetzel and Michael McDaniel, "Situational Judgment Tests: An Overview of Current Research," *Human Resource Management Review* 19 (2009): 191.
9. See for example, Daniel A. Biddle and Patrick M. Nooren, "Validity Generalization vs. Title VII: Can Employers Successfully Defend Tests Without Conducting Local Validation Studies?" *Labor Law J* 57, no. 4, Winter 2006.
10. The Society for Industrial and Organizational Psychology says that "Experienced and knowledgeable test publishers have (and are happy to provide) information on the validity of their testing products." www.siop.org/workplace/employment%20testing/information_to_consider_when_cre.aspx, accessed March 22, 2009.
11. Frank Schmidt and John Hunter, "The Validity and Utility of Selection Methods in Personnel Psychology: Practical and Theoretical Implications of 85 Years of Research Findings," *Psychological Bulletin* 1198, 124, no. 2, 262–274.
12. "Hiring Based on Strength Test Discriminates Against Women," *BNA Bulletin to Management* (February 22, 2005): 62.
13. Brad Bushman and Gary Wells, "Trait Aggressiveness and Hockey Penalties: Predicting Hot Tempers on the Ice," *Journal of Applied Psychology* 83, no. 6 (1998): 969–974.
14. For some other examples see William Shepherd, "Increasing Profits by Assessing Employee Work Styles," *Employment Relations Today* 32, no.1 (Spring 2005): 19–23; and Eric Krell, "Personality Counts," *HR Magazine* (November 2005): 47–52.
15. Sarah Gale, "Three Companies Cut Turnover with Tests," *Workforce* (April 2002): 66–69.
16. William Wagner, "All Skill, No Finesse," *Workforce* (June 2000): 108–16. See also, for example, James Diefendorff and Kajal Mehta, "The Relations of Motivational Traits with Workplace Deviance," *Journal of Applied Psychology* 92, no. 4 (2007): 967–977.
17. Toddi Gutner, "Applicants' Personalities Put to the Test," *Wall Street Journal* (August 26, 2008): D4.
18. Elaine Pulakos, *Selection Assessment Methods*, SHRM Foundation (2005): 9.
19. www.myersbriggsreports.com/?gclid=CK71m6rEh6ACFVZS2g odDEjgkw, accessed February 22, 2010.
20. www.myersbriggsreports.com/?gclid=CK71m6rEh6ACFVZS2g odDEjgkw, accessed February 22, 2010.
21. See, for example, Douglas Cellar et al., "Comparison of Factor Structures and Criterion-Related Validity Coefficients for Two Measures of Personality Based on the Five Factor Model," *Journal of Applied Psychology* 81, no. 6 (1996): 694–704; Jesus Salgado, "The Five Factor Model of Personality and Job

Performance in the European Community," *Journal of Applied Psychology* 82, no. 1 (1997): 30–43; Joyce Hogan et al., "Personality Measurement, Faking, and Employee Selection," *Journal of Applied Psychology* 92, no. 5 (2007): 1270–1285.

22. Murray Barrick and Michael Mount, "The Big Five Personality Dimensions and Job Performance: A Meta Analysis," *Personnel Psychology* 44, no. 1 (Spring 1991): 1–26. See also Robert Schneider, Leatta Hough, and Marvin Dunnette, "Broad-Sided by Broad Traits: How to Sink Science in Five Dimensions or Less," *Journal of Organizational Behavior* 17, no. 6 (November 1996): 639–655; and Paula Caligiuri, "The Big Five Personality Characteristics as Predictors of Expatriate's Desire to Terminate the Assignment and Supervisor Rated Performance," *Personnel Psychology* 53 (2000): 67–68.

23. Frederick Morgeson et al., "Reconsidering the Use of Personality Tests in Personnel Selection Contexts," *Personnel Psychology* 60 (2007): 683.

24. Frederick Morgeson et al., "Are We Getting Fooled Again? Coming to Terms with Limitations in the Use of Personality Tests for Personnel Selection," *Personnel Psychology* 60 (2007): 1046.

25. Robert Tett and Neil Christiansen, "Personality Tests at the Crossroads: A Response to Morgeson, Campion, Dipboye, Hollenbeck, Murphy, and Schmitt" (2007), *Personnel Psychology* 60 (2007): 967. See also Deniz Ones et al., "In Support of Personality Assessment in Organizational Settings," *Personnel Psychology* 60 (2007): 995–1027. Part of the problem with self-report personality tests is that some applicants will see through to the aim of the test and provide answers they think the employer is looking for (they "fake" the test). The problem here of course is that less worthy candidates may actually succeed in earning higher test scores than more worthy candidates. In one study, researchers extensively studied this question. They concluded that one way to minimize the effects of faking was to compute "pass/fail" cut points by having non-applicants such as supervisors and existing employees take the test (rather than applicants). It remains a tricky problem, however. Christopher Berry and Paul Sackett, "Faking in Personnel Selection: Trade-Offs in Performance versus Fairness Resulting from Two Cut Score Strategies," *Personnel Psychology* 62 (2009) 835–863.

26. Mitchell Rothstein and Richard Goffin, "The Use of Personality Measures in Personnel Selection: What Does Current Research Support?" *Human Resource Management Review* 16 (2006): 155–180.

27. See, for example, W. A. Scroggins et al., "Psychological Testing in Personnel Selection, Part III: The Resurgence of Personality Testing," *Public Personnel Management* 38, no. 1 (Spring 2009): 67–77.

28. Kathryn Tyler, "Put Applicants' Skills to the Test," *HR Magazine* (January 2000): 75–79.

29. Adapted from www.kozaigroup.com/inventories.php, accessed March 3, 2008.

30. Hal Whiting and Theresa Kline, "Assessment of the Equivalence of Conventional versus Computer Administration of the Test of Workplace Essential Skills," *International Journal of Training and Development* 10, no. 4 (December 2006): 285–290.

31. Ed Frauenheim, "Personality Tests Adapt to the Times," *Workforce Management* (February 2010): 4.

32. Gilbert Nicholson, "Automated Assessments for Better Hires," *Workforce* (December 2000): 102–107.

33. www.iphonetypingtest.com/, accessed March 23, 2009.

34. Quoted from Deborah Whetzel and Michael McDaniel, "Situational Judgment Tests: An Overview of Current Research," *Human Resource Management Review* 19 (2009): 188–202.

35. Ibid.

36. George Thornton III and Alyssa Gibbons, "Validity of Assessment Centers for Personnel Selection," *Human Resource Management Review* 19 (2009): 169–187.

37. Annette Spychalski, Miguel Quinones, Barbara Gaugler, and Katja Pohley, "A Survey of Assessment Center Practices in Organizations in the United States," *Personnel Management* 50, no. 10 (Spring 1997): 71–90. See also Winfred Arthur Jr. et al., "A Meta Analysis of the Criterion Related Validity of Assessment Center Data Dimensions," *Personnel Psychology* 56 (2003): 124–154.

38. Kobi Dayan et al., "Entry-Level Police Candidate Assessment Center: An Efficient Tool or a Hammer to Kill a Fly?" *Personnel Psychology* 55 (2002): 827–848. A recent review concluded "the [assessment center method] has a long history of demonstrating strong predictive relationships between AC ratings and criteria . . . such as promotions, performance evaluations, [and] salary progress." George Thornton III and Alyssa Gibbons, "Validity of Assessment Centers for Personnel Selection," *Human Resource Management Review* 19 (2009): 169–187.

39. Michael McDaniel et al., "The Validity of Employment Interviews: A Comprehensive Review and Meta-Analysis," *Journal of Applied Psychology* 79, no. 4 (1994): 599. See also Richard Posthuma et al., "Beyond Employment Interview Validity: A Comprehensive Narrative Review of Recent Research and Trends over Time," *Personnel Psychology* 55 (2002): 1–81.

40. Therese Macan, "The Employment Interview: A Review of Current Studies and Directions for Future Research," *Human Resource Management Review* 19 (2009): 203–218.

41. Michael McDaniel et al., "The Validity of Employment Interviews: A Comprehensive Review and Meta-Analysis," *Journal of Applied Psychology* 79, no. 4 (1994): 601. See also Allen Huffcutt et al., "Comparison of Situational and Behavior Description Interview Questions for Higher Level Positions," *Personnel Psychology* 54 (Autumn 2001): 619–644; Stephen Maurer, "A Practitioner Based Analysis of Interviewer Job Expertise and Scale Format as Contextual Factors in Situational Interviews," *Personnel Psychology* 55 (2002): 307–327.

42. Bill Stoneman, "Matching Personalities with Jobs Made Easier with Behavioral Interviews," *American Banker* 165, no. 229 (November 30, 2000): 8a.

43. Susan Strauss et al., "The Effects of Videoconference, Telephone, and Face-to-Face Media on Interviewer and Applicant Judgments in Employment Interviews," *Journal of Management* 27, no. 3 (2001): 363–381. If the employer records a video interview with the intention of sharing it with hiring managers who don't participate in the interview, it's advisable to first obtain the candidate's written permission. Matt Bolch, "Lights, Camera . . . Interview!" *HR Magazine* (March 2007): 99–102.

44. Emily Maltby, "To Find the Best Hires, Firms Become Creative," *Wall Street Journal* (November 17, 2009): B6.

45. Madeline Heilman and Tyler Okimoto, "Motherhood: A Potential Source of Bias in Employment Decisions," *Journal of Applied Psychology* 93, no. 1 (2008): 189–198.

46. Ibid., 196.

47. See, for example, M. M. Harris, "Reconsidering the Employment Interview: A Review of Recent Literature and Suggestions for Future Research," *Personnel Psychology* 42 (1989): 691–726; Richard Posthuma et al., "Beyond Employment Interview Validity: A Comprehensive Narrative Review of Recent Research and Trends Over Time," *Personnel Psychology* 55, no. 1 (Spring 2002): 1–81.

48. Timothy Judge et al., "The Employment Interview: A Review of Recent Research and Recommendations for Future Research," *Human Resource Management* 10, no. 4 (2000): 392. There is disagreement regarding the relative superiority of individual versus panel interviews. See, for example, Marlene Dixon et al., "The Panel Interview: A Review of Empirical Research and Guidelines for Practice," *Public Personnel Management* (Fall 2002): 397–428. For an argument against holding selection interviews, see D Heath et al., "Hold the Interview," *Fast Company* 136 (June 2009): 51–52.

49. Frank Schmidt and Ryan Zimmerman, "A Counterintuitive Hypothesis About Employment Interview Validity and Some Supporting Evidence," *Journal of Applied Psychology* 89, no. 3 (2004): 553–561.

50. The validity discussion and these findings are based on Michael McDaniel et al., "The Validity of Employment Interviews: A Comprehensive Review and Meta-Analysis," *Journal of Applied Psychology* 79, no. 4 (1994): 607–610. See also Robert Dipboye et al., "The Validity of Unstructured Panel Interviews," *Journal of Business & Strategy* 16, no. 1 (Fall 2001): 35–49; and Marlene Dixon et al., "The Panel Interview: A Review of Empirical Research and Guidance," *Public Personnel Management* 3, no. 3 (Fall 2002): 397–428. See also Todd Maurer and Jerry Solamon, "The Science and Practice of a Structured Employment Interview Coaching Program," *Personnel Psychology* 59 (2006): 433–456.

51. Derek Chapman and David Zweig, "Developing a Nomological Network for Interview Structure: Antecedents and Consequences of the Structured Selection Interview," *Personnel Psychology* 58 (2005): 673–702.

52. Anita Chaudhuri, "Beat the Clock: Applying for a Job? A New Study Shows that Interviewers Will Make Up Their Minds about You Within a Minute," *The Guardian* (June 14, 2000): 2–6.

53. Don Langdale and Joseph Weitz, "Estimating the Influence of Job Information on Interviewer Agreement," *Journal of Applied Psychology* 57 (1973): 23–27.

54. R. E. Carlson, "Selection Interview Decisions: The Effects of Interviewer Experience, Relative Quota Situation, and Applicant Sample on Interview Decisions," *Personnel Psychology* 20 (1967): 259–280.

55. R. E. Carlson, "Effects of Applicant Sample on Ratings of Valid Information in an Employment Setting," *Journal of Applied Psychology* 54 (1970): 217–222.

56. See, for example, Scott Fleischmann, "The Messages of Body Language in Job Interviews," *Employee Relations* 18, no. 2 (Summer 1991): 161–176. See also James Westpall and Ithai Stern, "Flattery Will Get You Everywhere (Especially if You're a Male Caucasian): How Ingratiation, Board Room Behavior, and a Demographic Minority Status Affect Additional Board Appointments at US Companies," *Academy of Management Journal* 50, no. 2 (2007): 267–288.

57. Tim DeGroot and Stephen Motowidlo, "Why Visual and Vocal Interview Cues Can Affect Interviewer's Judgments and Predicted Job Performance," *Journal of Applied Psychology* (December 1999): 968–984.

58. Amy Kristof-Brown et al., "Applicant Impression Management: Dispositional Influences and Consequences for Recruiter Perceptions of Fit and Similarity," *Journal of Management* 28, no. 1 (2002): 27–46. See also Linda McFarland et al., "Impression Management Use and Effectiveness Across Assessment Methods," *Journal of Management* 29, no. 5 (2003): 641–661.

59. See, for example, Cynthia Marlowe, Sondra Schneider, and Carnot Nelson, "Gender and Attractiveness Biases in Hiring Decisions: Are More Experienced Managers Less Biased?" *Journal of Applied Psychology* 81, no. 1 (1996): 11–21; see also Shari Caudron, "Why Job Applicants Hate HR," *Workforce* (June 2002): 36.

60. Ibid., 18. See also Timothy Judge, Charlice Hurst, and Lauren Simon, "Does It Pay to Be Smart, Attractive, or Confident (Or All Three)? Relationships Among General Mental Ability, Physical Attractiveness, Core Self-Evaluations, and Income," *Journal of Applied Psychology* 94, no. 3 (2009): 742–755.

61. Emily Duehr and Joyce Bono, "Men, Women, and Managers: Are Stereotypes Finally Changing?" *Personnel Psychology* 59 (2006): 837.

62. Chad Higgins and Timothy Judge, "The Effect of Applicant Influence Tactics on Recruiter Perceptions of Fit and Hiring Recommendations: A Field Study," *Journal of Applied Psychology* 89, no. 4 (2004): 622–632.

63. Laura Gollub Williamson et al., "Employment Interview on Trial: Linking Interview Structure with Litigation Outcomes," *Journal of Applied Psychology* 82, no. 6 (1996): 901; Michael Campion, David Palmer, and James Campion, "A Review of Structure in the Selection Interview," *Personnel Psychology* 50 (1997): 655–702.

64. Unless otherwise specified, the following are based on Williamson et al., "Employment Interview on Trial," 901–902.

65. Todd Maurer and Jerry Solamon, "The Science and Practice of a Structured Employment Interview Coaching Program," *Personnel Psychology* 59 (2006): 433–456.

66. R. E. Carlson, "Selection Interview Decisions: The Effects of Interviewer Experience, Relative Quota Situation, and Applicant Sample on Interview Decisions," *Personnel Psychology* 20 (1967): 259–280.

67. "Looking to Hire the Very Best? Ask the Right Questions. Lots of Them," *Fortune* (June 21, 1999): 192–194.

68. Panel Kaul, "Interviewing Is Your Business," *Association Management* (November 1992): 29. See also Nancy Woodward, "Asking for Salary Histories," *HR Magazine* (February 2000): 109–112. Gathering information about specific interview dimensions such as social ability, responsibility, and independence (as is often done with structured interviews) can improve interview accuracy, at least for more complicated jobs. See also Andrea Poe, "Graduate Work: Behavioral Interviewing Can Tell You If an Applicant Just Out of College Has Traits Needed for the Job," *HR Magazine* 48, no. 10 (October 2003): 95–96.

69. These are from Alan M. Saks and Julie M. McCarthy, "Effects of Discriminatory Interview Questions and Gender On Applicant Reactions," *Journal of Business and Psychology* 21, no. 2 (Winter 2006).

70. These are quoted or adapted from www.careerfaqs.com.au/getthatjob_video_interview.asp, accessed March 2, 2009.

71. "Are Your Background Checks Balanced? Experts Identify Concerns Over Verifications," *BNA Bulletin to Management* (May 13, 2004): 153.

72. Based on Samuel Greengard, "Have Gangs Invaded Your Workplace?" *Personnel Journal* (February 1996): 47–57. See also Carroll Lachnit, "Protecting People and Profits with Background Checks," *Workforce* (February 2002): 52.

73. "Fake Job Reference Services Add New Wrinkle to Screening," *HR Magazine* (January 2010): 9.

74. Carroll Lachnit, "Protecting People and Profits with Background Checks," *Workforce* (February 2002): 52. See also Robert Howie and Lawrence Shapero, "Preemployment Criminal Background Checks: Why Employers Should Look Before They Leap," *Employee Relations Law Journal* (Summer 2002): 63–77.

75. See, for example, A. M. Forsberg et al., "Perceived Fairness of a Background Information Form and a Job Knowledge Test," *Public Personnel Management* 38, no. 1 (Spring 2009): 33–46.

76. Ibid, 50ff.

77. "Employment Related Screening Providers," *Workforce Management* (February 16, 2009): 14.

78. Alan Finder, "When A Risqué Online Persona Undermines a Chance for a Job," *New York Times* (June 11, 2006): 1.

79. "Vetting via Internet Is Free, Generally Legal, But Not Necessarily Smart Hiring Strategy," *BNA Bulletin to Management* (February 20, 2007): 57–58.

80. Anjali Athavaley, "Job References You Can't Control," *Wall Street Journal* (September 27, 2007): B1.

81. For example, see Lawrence Dube Jr., "Employment References and the Law," *Personnel Journal* 65, no. 2 (February 1986): 87–91. See also Mickey Veich, "Uncover the Resume Ruse," *Security Management* (October 1994): 75–76; Mary Mayer, "Background Checks in Focus," *HR Magazine* (January 2002): 59–62.

82. Diane Cadrain, "Job Detectives Dig Deep for Defamation," *HR Magazine* 49, no. 10 (October 2004): 34FF.

83. Carroll Lachnit, "Protecting People and Profits with Background Checks," *Workforce* (February 2002): 54; Shari Caudron, "Who Are You Really Hiring?" *Workforce* (November 2002): 31.

84. Kris Maher, "Reference Checking Firms Flourish, but Complaints About Some Arise," *Wall Street Journal* (March 5, 2002): B8.

85. Diane Cadrain, "Job Detectives Dig Deep for Defamation," *HR Magazine* 49, no. 10 (October 2004): 34FF.

86. "Undercover Callers Tip Off Job Seekers to Former Employers' Negative References," *BNA Bulletin to Management* (May 27, 1999): 161.

87. Carroll Lachnit, "Protecting People and Profits with Background Checks," *Workforce* (February 2002): 52.

88. Ronald Karren and Larry Zacharias, "Integrity Tests: Critical Issues," *Human Resource Management Review* 17 (2007): 221–234.

89. John Bernardin and Donna Cooke, "Validity of an Honesty Test in Predicting Theft Among Convenience Store Employees," *Academy of Management Journal* 36, no. 5 (1993): 1097–1108. HR in Practice suggestions adapted from "Divining Integrity Through Interviews," *BNA Bulletin to Management* (June 4, 1987): 184; and "Ideas and Trends," *Commerce Clearing House* (December 29, 1998): 222–223. Note that some suggest that by possibly signaling mental illness, integrity tests may conflict with the Americans with Disabilities Act, but one review concludes

that such tests pose little legal risk to employers. Christopher Berry et al., "A Review of Recent Developments in Integrity Test Research," *Personnel Psychology* 60 (2007): 271–301.

90. Based on "Divining Integrity Through Interviews," *BNA Bulletin to Management* (June 4, 1987), and "Ideas and Trends," Commerce Clearing House (December 29, 1998): 222–223.

91. Christopher S. Frings, "Testing for Honesty," *Medical Laboratory Observer* 35, no. 12 (December 2003): 27(1).

92. Steven L. Thomas and Steve Vaught, "The Write Stuff: What the Evidence Says About Using Handwriting Analysis in Hiring," *Advanced Management Journal* 66, no. 4 (August 2001): 31–35.

93. Ibid.; Kevin Murphy and Charles David Shafer, op. cit., 438–439.

94. See Bridget A. Styers and Kenneth S Shultz, "Perceived Reasonableness of Employment Testing Accommodations for Persons with Disabilities," *Public Personnel Management* 38, no. 3 (Fall 2009): 71–91.

95. Peter Cholakis, "How to Implement a Successful Drug Testing Program," *Risk Management* 52, no. 11 (November 2005): 24–28; Elaine Davis and Stacie Hueller, "Strengthening the Case for Workplace Drug Testing: The Growing Problem of Methamphetamines," *Advanced Management Journal* 71, no 3 (Summer 2006): 4–10.

96. For example, www.infolinkscreening.com/InfoLink/ DrugTesting/DrugTesting. aspx?s=buscom3a, accessed April 19, 2008.

97. Scott MacDonald et al., "The Limitations of Drug Screening in the Workplace," *International Labor Review* 132, no. 1 (1993): 100.

98. Ibid., 103.

99. Diane Cadrain, "Are Your Employees' Drug Tests Accurate?" *HR Magazine* (January 2003): 40–45. See also Ari Nattle, "Drug Testing Impaired," *Traffic World* 271, no. 45 (November 12, 2007): 18.

100. MacDonald et al., "The Limitations of Drug Screening in the Workplace," 105–106.

101. Lewis Maltby, "Drug Testing: A Bad Investment," *Business Ethics* 15, no. 2 (March 2001): 7.

102. Ann O'Neill, "Legal Issues Presented by Hair Follicle Testing," *Employment Relations Today* (December 22, 1991): 411.

103. Richard Lisko, "A Manager's Guide to Drug Testing," *Security Management* 38, no. 8 (August 1994): 92; www.dol.gov/ dol/topic/safety-health/drugfreeworkplace.htm, accessed April 19, 2008; and www.fmcsa.dot.gov/rules-regulations/topics/ drug/engtesting.htm, accessed April 19, 2008.

104. Coleman Peterson, "Employee Retention: The Secrets Behind Wal-Mart's Successful Hiring Policies," *Human Resource Management* 44, no. 1 (Spring 2005): 85–88.

105. Murray Barrick and Ryan Zimmerman, "Reducing Voluntary, Avoidable Turnover Through Selection," *Journal of Applied Psychology* 90, no. 1 (2005): 159–166.

106. Lawrence Kellner, "Corner Office," *New York Times* (September 27, 2009).

107. There may be other complications as well. For example, you may want to decide which of several possible potential jobs is best for your candidate.

108. See, for example, Frank Landy and Don Trumbo, *Psychology of Work Behavior* (Homewood, IL: Dorsey Press, 1976): 131–169. There are many other possibilities. See, for example, Robert Gatewood and Hubert Feild, *Human Resource Selection* (Fort Worth, TX: Dryden Press, 1994): 278–279.

109. Ibid. See also Panagiotis V. Polychroniou and Ioannis Giannikos, "A Fuzzy Multicriteria Decision-Making Methodology for Selection of Human Resources in a Greek Private Bank," *Career Development International* 14, no. 4 (2009): 372–387.

110. Robert Gatewood and Hubert Feild, *Human Resource Selection* (Fort Worth, TX: Dryden Press, 1994): 278–279.

111. Ibid.

112. Based on ibid.

113. Diane Cadrain, "Mystery Shoppers Can Improve Recruitment," *HR Magazine* (November 2006): 26.

114. "Conflicting State E-Verify Laws Troubling for Employers," *BNA Bulletin To Management* (November 4, 2008): 359.

115. www.dhs.gov/files/programs/gc_1185221678150.shtm, accessed February 21, 2010.

116. Russell Gerbman, "License to Work," *HR Magazine* (June 2000): 151–160. Recently the department of Homeland Security announced it was inspecting about 652 businesses nationwide as part of its new I-9 audit program. "I-9 Used to Conduct High Nine Audits at 652 Businesses as Focus of Enforcement Ships to Employers," *BNA Bulletin to Management* (July 7, 2009): 211. The employment and training administration agency of the U.S. Department of Labor installed a new system called iCERT to make it easier for employers to receive labor condition applications for the H1B program. "EPA Announces Electronic Portal to Receive Applications for H1B, Perm Certifications, "*BNA Bulletin to Management* (April 21, 2009): 123.

117. Note that unproctored Internet tests raise serious questions in employment settings. Nancy Tippins et al., "Unproctored Internet Testing in Employment Settings," *Personnel Psychology* 59 (2006): 189–225.

118. From Bob Neveu, "Applicant Tracking's Top 10: Do You Know What to Look for in Applicant Tracking Systems?" *Workforce* (October 2002): 10.

119. Manuel Velasquez, *Business Ethics: Concepts and Cases* (Upper Saddle River, NJ: Prentice Hall, 1992): 9. See also O. C. Ferrell, John Fraedrich, and Linog Ferrell, *Business Ethics* (Boston: Houghton Mifflin, 2008).

120. Gary Weaver and Linda Trevino, "The Role of Human Resources in Ethics/Compliance Management: A Fairness Perspective," *Human Resource Management Review* 11 (2001): 123. See also Linda Andrews, "The Nexus of Ethics," *HR Magazine* (August 2005): 53–58.

121. Dirk Steiner and Stephen Gilliland, "Fairness Reactions to Personnel Selection Techniques in France and the United States," *Journal of Applied Psychology* 81, no. 2 (1996): 134–141; Emily Duehr and Joyce Bono, "Men, Women, and Managers: Are Stereotypes Finally Changing?" *Personnel Psychology* 59 (2006): 815–846.

122. This section is based on Elliot Pursell et al., "Structured Interviewing: Avoiding Selection Problems," *Personnel Journal* 59 (November 1980): 907–912; and G. Latham et al., "The Situational Interview," *Journal of Applied Psychology* 65 (1980): 422–427. See also Jeff Weekley and Joseph Gier, "Reliability and Validity of the Situational Interview for a Sales Poisiton," *Journal of Applied Psychology*, August 1987, 484–487.

123. P. Taylor and B. Small, "Asking Applicants What They Would Do Versus What They Did Do: A Meta-Analytic Comparison of Situational and Past-Behavior Employment Interview Questions," *Journal of Occupational and Organizational Psychology* 75, no. 3 (September 2002): 277–295. Structured employment interviews using either situational questions or behavioral questions tend to yield high validities. However, structured interviews with situational question formats yield the higher ratings. This may be because interviewers get more consistent (reliable) responses with situational questions (which force all applicants to apply the same scenario) than they do with behavioral questions (which require each applicant to find applicable experiences). However there is some evidence that for higher-level positions, situational question–based interviews are inferior to behavioral question–based ones, possibly because the situations are "just too simple to allow any real differentiation among candidates for higher level positions." Alan Huffcutt et al., "Comparison of Situational and Behavioral Description Interview Questions for Higher Level Positions," *Personnel Psychology* 54, no. 3 (2001): 619.

124. See also Phillip Lowry, "The Structured Interview: An Alternative to the Assessment Center?" *Public Personnel Management* 23, no. 2 (Summer 1994): 201–215; Steven Maurer, "The Potential of the Situational Interview: Existing Research and Unresolved Issues," *Human Resource Management Review* 7, no. 2 (Summer 1997): 185–201; and Todd Maurer and Jerry Solamon, "The Science and Practice of a Structured Employment Interview Coaching Program," *Personnel Psychology* 59, no. 2 (Summer 2006): 433–456.

125. Pursell et al., "Structured Interviewing," 910.

126. From a speech by industrial psychologist Paul Green and contained in *BNA Bulletin to Management* (June 20, 1985): 2–3.

6

Training and Developing Employees

SYNOPSIS

- The Basic Orientation and Training Process
- Traditional Training Techniques
- Managerial Development and Training
- Organizational Change
- Evaluating the Training and Development Effort

Source: Jeff Greenberg/PhotoEdit Inc.

When you finish studying this chapter, you should be able to:

1. Describe the basic orientation and training process.
2. Explain the pros and cons of at least five training techniques.
3. Explain what management development is and why it is important.
4. Summarize the process of organizational change.
5. Explain how and why to evaluate a training program.

INTRODUCTION

After working as a chef and then head chef in several restaurants, Alex was thrilled to finally get the funding he needed to open his new French restaurant, Alex's Bistro, not far from the new "Mid-Town Miami" complex close to downtown Miami. For his kitchen staff he hired people with whom he'd worked closely at other restaurants, because he knew they were trained and competent and that they knew what to do. Hiring the wait staff was another thing. He had no personal experience with actually running the "front end" of a restaurant. So, he posted a *Help Wanted—Wait Staff* sign on the window, and hired six people who seemed to exhibit in interviews the conscientiousness and people orientation that he was looking for. He spent about an hour before opening day explaining to the wait staff details (such as how to use the computerized order input system), and how he wanted them to behave ("supportive and helpful; and keep your hands clean"). Unfortunately, opening day was a disaster. The wait staff couldn't answer basic questions such as "What's in this dish?" They got almost half the orders wrong, and when they finally did bring the orders to the tables, they didn't remember who ordered what dish, so the customers themselves ended up passing their dishes around. Later that night, Alex went home and asked his former boss what he thought had gone wrong. "Are you telling me you hardly trained your wait staff at all before letting them loose on your customers? That's unbelievable, Al." ■

THE BASIC ORIENTATION AND TRAINING PROCESS

After selecting new employees, management turns to orienting and training them for their new jobs. **Employee orientation** provides new employees with the basic background information they need to perform their jobs satisfactorily, such as information about company rules. Orientation (often called *onboarding* today) is one component of the employer's new-employee socialization process. *Socialization* is the continuing process of instilling in employees the attitudes, standards, values, and patterns of behavior that the organization expects.[1] Fostering such an appreciation for the company's culture and values distinguishes onboarding from traditional orientation.[2] For example, the Mayo Clinic's "heritage and culture" orientation covers Mayo's core principles, history, work atmosphere, teamwork, personal responsibility, integrity, and mutual respect.[3]

employee orientation
A procedure for providing new employees with basic background information about the firm.

---

1 Describe the basic orientation and training process.

Types of Programs

Orientation programs range from brief, informal introductions to lengthy, formal programs of a half day or more. In either case, new employees usually receive printed or Web-based handbooks covering matters such as working hours, performance reviews, getting on the payroll, and vacations. Other information might cover employee benefits, personnel policies, the employee's daily routine, company organization and operations, and safety measures and regulations.[4] Because the courts may find that your employee handbook's contents represent a contract with the employee, employers often include disclaimers. These make it clear that statements of company policies, benefits, and regulations do not constitute an employment contract. New employees are normally also taken on a tour of the facilities.

Purposes

A successful orientation accomplishes four things. The new employee should feel welcome. He or she should understand the organization in a broad sense (its past, present, culture, and vision of the future), as well as key facts such as policies and procedures. The employee should be clear about what the firm expects in terms of work and behavior. And, hopefully, the employee should begin the process of becoming socialized into the firm's preferred ways of acting and doing things.[5]

The HR specialist usually performs the initial orientation and explains such matters as working hours and vacation. The employee then meets his or her new supervisor. The latter continues the orientation by explaining the exact nature of the job, introducing the person to his or her new colleagues, and familiarizing the new employee with the workplace and the job.

HR APPs 4 U

Mobile Company Directory

With Workday's iPhone app, employers can provide their employees easy mobile access to their employee directories (www.workday.com/mobile). Users can search their company's worker directory for names, images, and contact information; call or e-mail coworkers directly; and view physical addresses on Google Maps.[7] For example, having the Workday app on your iPhone provides you with continuous, anytime access to your company's corporate directory. That way, finding a colleague's phone number or email is easy—you don't have to go plodding through your firm's Web site or voicemail systems. With Workday for iPhone, anyone can browse their corporate directory right from their iPhone. That way, calling or emailing the right person is just one touch away.

training
The process of teaching new employees the basic skills they need to perform their jobs.

Technology

Technology facilitates orientation. For example, some firms provide incoming managers with preloaded personal digital assistants. These contain information such as key contact information, main tasks to undertake, and even images of employees the new manager needs to know.[6] Some firms provide all new employees with disks containing discussions of corporate culture, videos of corporate facilities, and welcoming addresses from top managers. Others create orientation Web sites. Particularly for new managers, these cover information such as the company's approaches to hiring, ethics, procurement policies, and performance management.

VIRTUAL ORIENTATION IBM uses virtual environments like Second Life to support orientation, particularly for employees abroad. The new employees choose virtual avatars, which then interact with other company avatars for themselves, for instance, to learn how to enroll for benefits.[8]

After orientating the employee, training is next. **Training** means the methods and process employers use to give new or present employees the knowledge and skills they need to perform their jobs.

Training Today

Companies spent about $826 per employee for training in one recent year and offered each about 28 hours of training.[9] Training has an impressive record of influencing organizational effectiveness, scoring higher than appraisal and feedback and just below goal setting in its effect on productivity.[10]

Three things characterize training today. First, we'll see that training is increasingly *technology based.* Most employees today get at least some of their training online and/or via computers.

Second, trainers tend to focus more on *improving organizational performance* than they have in the past. A survey found that "establishing a linkage between learning and organizational performance" was the number one issue facing training professionals.[11] As one trainer said, "We sit down with management and help them identify strategic goals and objectives and the skills and knowledge needed to achieve them. Then we work together to identify whether our staff has the skills and knowledge, and when they don't, that's when we discuss training needs."[12] (Training experts today therefore sometimes use the phrase "workplace learning and performance" in lieu of training, to underscore training's dual aims of improving both employee learning and organizational performance.)[13]

Third, training's focus is broader today than it was years ago. People used to associate training with teaching technical skills, such as training assemblers to solder wires. Today's team-based companies demand a different type of employee and a different type of training. For example, employees today may require team-building, decision-making, and communication skills training.[14]

The Training and Development Process

Most training and development processes today still reflect the basic analysis-design-develop-implement-evaluate (ADDIE) model that evolved after World War II.[15] To simplify things, we can envision the training process as including four steps:

1. In the first, *needs analysis* step, you identify the specific knowledge and skills the job requires, and compare these with the prospective trainees' knowledge and skills.
2. In the *instructional design* step you formulate specific, measurable knowledge and performance training objectives, review possible training program content (including workbooks, exercises, and activities), and estimate a budget for the training program.[16]
3. In the *implementation* step, you implement the program by actually training the targeted employee group using methods such as on-the-job or online training.
4. Finally, in the *evaluation* step, you assess the program's success (or failures).

NEEDS ANALYSIS The first step in training is to determine what training, if any, the employee requires. Some call this "skills gapping." Employers determine the skills each job requires, and the skills of the job's current or prospective employee. Then they design a training program to eliminate the skills gap.[17]

There are two traditional ways to identify training needs. Assessing *new* employees' training needs usually involves *task analysis*—breaking the job into subtasks, and then teaching each to the new employee. Needs analysis for *current* employees is more complex: Is training the solution, or is performance down because the person isn't motivated? Here *performance analysis* is required. We'll look at each.

TASK ANALYSIS Managers use *task analysis* for identifying new employees' training needs. With inexperienced personnel, your aim is to provide the new employees with the skills and knowledge required for effective performance. **Task analysis** is a detailed study of the job to determine what specific skills—like Java (in the case of a Web developer) or interviewing (in the case of a supervisor)—the job requires. Job descriptions and job specifications are helpful here. These list the job's specific duties and skills and thus provide a basic reference point in determining the training required. You can also uncover training needs by reviewing performance standards, performing the job, and questioning current job holders and their supervisors.[18]

PERFORMANCE ANALYSIS For current employees whose performance is deficient, task analysis is usually not enough. Here, requests for training often start with supervisors expressing concerns, such as "we're getting too many complaints from call center clients."[19] **Performance analysis** means verifying that there is a performance deficiency and determining whether to rectify the deficiency through training or through some other means (such as transferring the employee or changing the compensation plan).

You can use several methods to identify employees' performance deficiencies and training needs. The first step is usually to appraise the employee's performance.[20] Examples of specific performance deficiencies are:

> I expect each salesperson to make 10 new contracts per week, but John averages only six.
> Other plants our size average no more than two serious accidents per month; we're averaging five.

Other methods for identifying performance deficiencies include:

- Analyzing job-related performance data (including productivity, absenteeism and tardiness, accidents, short-term sickness, grievances, waste, late deliveries, product quality, downtime, repairs, equipment utilization, and customer complaints)
- Observation by supervisors or other specialists
- Interviews with the employee or his or her supervisor
- Tests of things like job knowledge, skills, and attendance
- Attitude surveys
- Individual employee daily diaries
- Assessment centers
- Management-by-objective evaluations

Distinguishing between "can't do" and "won't do" problems is the heart of performance analysis. First, determine whether it's a "can't do" problem and, if so, its specific causes. Training won't solve all "can't do" problems. For example, perhaps the employees don't know what to do or what your standards are, or there are obstacles such as lack of tools or supplies. Perhaps job aids are needed, such as color-coded wires that show assemblers what wire goes where, or poor screening results in hiring people who haven't the skills to do the job. Or, perhaps inadequate training is the issue.

On the other hand, it might be a won't do problem; here employees *could* do a good job if they wanted to. Training won't help here. Instead, the manager may have to change the reward system, perhaps by implementing an incentive plan.

SETTING TRAINING OBJECTIVES After uncovering the training needs, trainers set measurable training objectives. Training, development, or (more generally) *instructional objectives* "specify the

---

task analysis
A detailed study of a job to identify the skills required so that an appropriate training program may be instituted.

performance analysis
Verifying that there is a performance deficiency and determining whether that deficiency should be rectified through training or through some other means (such as transferring the employee).

employee and organizational outcomes that should be achieved as a result of the training."[21] In other words, the objectives should specify what the trainee should be able to accomplish after successfully completing the training program. They thus provide a focus for the efforts of both the trainee and the trainer and a benchmark for evaluating the success of the training program. For example:

> The technical service representative will be able to adjust the color guidelines on this HP Officejet All-in-One printer copier within 10 minutes according to the device's specifications.

TALENT MANAGEMENT: PROFILES AND COMPETENCY MODELS We saw that talent management is the goal-oriented and integrated process of planning for, recruiting, selecting, developing, and compensating employees. Among other things, talent management involves using the same competencies profile for recruiting the employee as for selecting, training, appraising, and paying him or her. For training, we can summarize this as follows:

> Strategy>>>Workforce Competencies>>Training and Development Needs>>Training Evaluation.

competency model
A graphic model that consolidates, usually in one diagram, a precise overview of the competencies (the knowledge, skills, and behaviors) someone would need to do a job well.

Many employers (including Sharp Electronics and IBM) therefore use competency models to help compile and summarize a job's training needs. The **competency model** consolidates, usually in one diagram, a precise overview of the competencies (the knowledge, skills, and behaviors) someone would need to do a job well.

As an example, Figure 6.1 repeats the competency model for a human resource manager from Chapter 4. The top of the pyramid shows four main roles the human resource manager

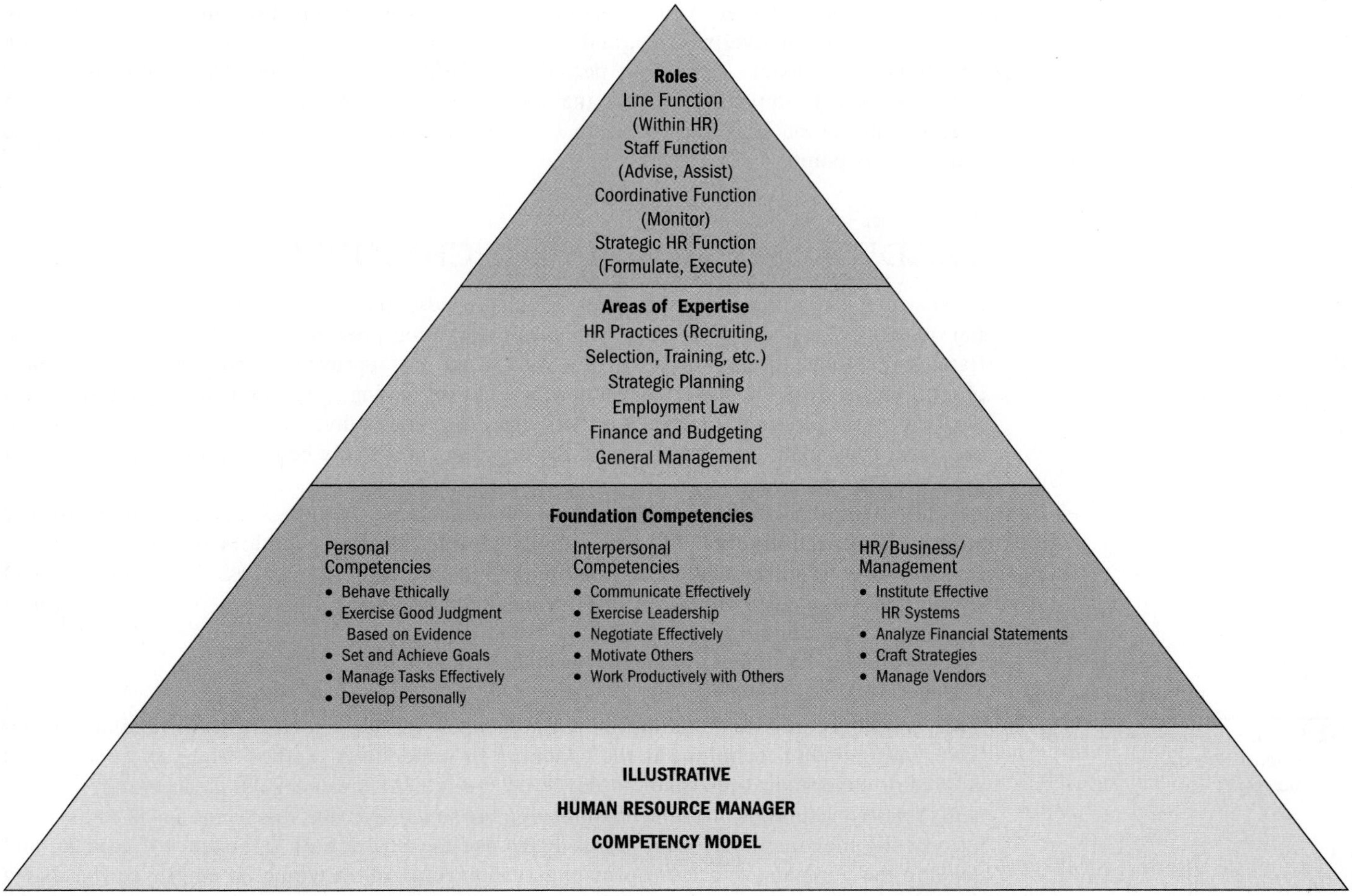

FIGURE 6.1

Example of Competency Model for Human Resource Manager

needs to fill. Beneath that are the areas of expertise such as selection and training, in which he or she must be expert in order to carry out these roles. Beneath are the HR manager's essential, "foundation" competencies, such as communicating effectively.[22]

The model's aim is to identify and compile in one place the competencies that are crucial for executing the job. At Sharp, training managers first interview senior executives to identify the firm's strategic objectives and to infer what competencies those objectives will require. Trainers also interview the job's top performers to identify the competencies (such as "focuses on the customer") the latter believe comprise the job's core competencies. Subsequent training then aims, in part, to develop these competencies.[23]

The employer can use the competency model in Figure 6.1 to support all its talent management functions, such as selection and training. Thus *selecting* employees based on this model helps to ensure that you focus your questions on the things that someone must be proficient at to do this job successfully. (For instance, the candidate's recruitment and testing knowledge.) The same model would help you to formulate training objectives. Thus a training objective for "testing knowledge" might be, "By completion of the ABC Company's HR manager training program, the trainee will be fully skilled at using the five testing tools that ABC uses to test its job applicants."

MOTIVATION AND THE LEARNING ENVIRONMENT Trainers and educators understand that the environment or context in which the learning takes place affects how well people learn.[24] Many steps here just aim to facilitate learning, such as posting "No Talking" signs in libraries. Others aim to ensure that the trainees are motivated to learn.[25] The employer can take several steps to increase trainee's motivation. Providing a graphic illustration of what can go wrong is one technique. For instance, ticketed drivers attending driving school often start class by watching filmed accidents. Other useful techniques to improve motivation include building in opportunities for active practice, and letting the trainee make errors and explore alternate solutions.[26] Feedback—including periodic performance assessments and frequent verbal critiques—is also important.[27] Also, make the material meaningful. For example, provide an overview of the material, and ensure that the program uses familiar examples and concepts to illustrate key points.[28]

TRADITIONAL TRAINING TECHNIQUES

After you've determined the employees' training needs, created a perceived need, and set training objectives, you can design and implement a training program. For all but the most trivial training programs, the employer will also want to see and approve a *training budget* for the program. Typical costs include the development costs (of having, say, a human resource specialist working on the program for a week or two), the direct and indirect (overhead) costs of the trainers' time, participant compensation (for the time they're actually being trained), and the cost of evaluating the program.

The budget will guide the program's instructional design. Many employers simply choose packaged on- and off-line training programs from vendors like the American Society for Training and Development.[29] Many other vendors, including HRDQ (www.hrdqstore.com/) also provide turnkey training packages.[30] We'll look at popular training techniques next.

On-the-Job Training

2 Explain the pros and cons of at least five training techniques.

Every employee gets some on-the-job training when starting a job. The most familiar on-the-job training (OJT) technique is the coaching or understudy method. Here an experienced worker or supervisor trains the employee on the job. At lower levels, trainees may acquire skills for, say, running a machine by observing the supervisor. But this technique is also widely used at top management levels. Some firms use the position of "assistant to" to train and develop the company's future top managers. Job rotation, in which an employee (usually a management trainee) moves from job to job at planned intervals, is another on-the-job training technique. Special assignments similarly give lower-level executives firsthand experience in working on actual problems.

The Men's Wearhouse uses on-the-job training. It has few full-time trainers. Instead, the Men's Wearhouse has a formal process of "cascading" responsibility for training: Every manager is formally accountable for the development of his or her direct subordinates.[31]

coaching
Educating, instructing, and training subordinates.

EFFECTIVE COACHING On-the-job training requires effective coaching skills. **Coaching** means educating, instructing, and training subordinates. Supervisors have coached employees from the dawn of management. But with more managers leading self-managing teams, supporting and coaching are fast replacing the manager's formal authority for getting things done. We can best think of coaching in terms of a four-step process: *preparation, planning, active coaching,* and *follow-up*.[32]

PREPARING TO COACH *Preparation* means understanding the problem, the employee, and the employee's skills. Your aim here is to formulate a hypothesis about what the problem is.

Preparation is partly an observational process. You'll watch the employee to see what he or she is doing, and observe the workflow and how coworkers interact with the employee. In addition to observation, you may review (as we saw) objective data on things like productivity, absenteeism, and tardiness.

PLANNING Perhaps the most powerful way to get someone to change is to obtain his or her enthusiastic agreement on what change is required. This requires reaching consensus on the problem and on what to change. In practice, you'll then lay out a change plan in the form *Steps to Take, Measures of Success,* and *Date to Complete*.

ACTIVE COACHING With agreement on a plan, you can start the actual "educating, instructing, and training"—namely, coaching. Here you are, in essence, in the role of a teacher. Your toolkit will include what you learned here about on-the-job training. However, interpersonal communications skills are the heart of effective coaching. As one writer says, "[a]n effective coach offers ideas and advice in such a way that the subordinate can hear them, respond to them, and appreciate their value."[33]

FOLLOW-UP Bad habits sometimes reemerge. It's therefore necessary to reobserve the person's progress periodically.

Informal Learning

Surveys estimate that as much as 80% of what employees learn on the job they learn not through formal training programs but through informal means, including performing their jobs in collaboration with their colleagues.[34] Although managers don't arrange informal learning, there's a lot they can do to ensure that it occurs. For example, Siemens Power Transmission and Distribution in Raleigh, North Carolina, places tools in cafeteria areas to capitalize on the work-related discussions taking place. Sun Microsystems implemented an informal online learning tool it called Sun Learning eXchange. This has evolved into a platform containing more than 5,000 informal learning items addressing topics ranging from sales to technical support.[35] Informal learning is one inexpensive training method for challenging times; the Managing HR in Challenging Times feature presents some others.

MANAGING HR IN CHALLENGING TIMES

Free Training Alternatives

When the economy sours, training and development are often the first human resource management activities to face the ax.[36] Recently, for instance, "morale and team building," "professional development," and "all staff training" (on issues like diversity) were the three most likely cuts HR managers were going to make.

Managers can, however, turn to no-cost training alternatives. For example, some states, including Pennsylvania, have free training programs for in-state employers. In Pennsylvania, the Workforce and Economic Development Network of Pennsylvania (WEDnetPA) provides in-state employers with grants of up to $450 per employee for basic skills training (www.wednetpa.com). Web sites such as free-training.com (www.free-training.com) are another option. The federal

(continued)

government's Small Business Administration (www.SBA.gov/training) provides a virtual campus that offers online courses, workshops, publications, and learning tools aimed at supporting entrepreneurs.[37]

Other employers turn to grants and other sources of support. For example, Titus, a heating and cooling manufacturing firm in Texas, received over $218,000 in grants from the Texas Workforce Commission to retrain employees. To find sources of training funds, check first with your local state unemployment agency since they're often the conduits for federal and state training funds. Also, many community colleges have workforce development or resource development officers who are familiar with funding sources.[38]

Apprenticeship Training

More employers are going "back to the future" by implementing apprenticeship training programs, an approach that began in the Middle Ages. Apprenticeship training is a structured process by which individuals become skilled workers through a combination of formal instruction and on-the-job training, usually under the guidance of an expert. It's especially popular for learning professional trades, such as plumber.

As an example, when steelmaker Dofasco discovered that many of its employees would be retiring during the next 5 to 10 years, it decided to revive its apprenticeship training program. Applicants are prescreened; new recruits then spend about 32 months in an internal training program that emphasizes apprenticeship training, learning various jobs under the tutelage of experienced craftspersons.[39]

The U.S. Department of Labor's National Apprenticeship System promotes apprenticeship programs. Over 460,000 apprentices participate in about 28,000 programs, and registered programs can receive federal and state contracts and other assistance.[40] Figure 6.2 lists popular recent apprenticeships.

Vestibule Training

vestibule/simulated training
A method in which trainees learn on the actual or simulated equipment they would use on the job, but are actually trained off the job.

With **vestibule training**, trainees learn on the actual or simulated equipment they will use on the job but receive their training off the job. Such training is necessary when it's too costly or dangerous to train employees on the job. Putting new assembly-line workers right to work could slow production, for instance. And, when safety is a concern—as with airline pilots—simulated training may be the only practical option.

Vestibule training (other words for vestibule are "foyer" or "entrance hall") may just occur in a separate room using the equipment the trainees will actually be using on the job. However, it often involves the use of equipment simulators. In pilot training, for instance, simulators let

FIGURE 6.2

Some Popular Apprenticeships

Source: www.doleta.gov/oa, accessed July 3, 2009.

The U.S. Department of Labor's Registered Apprenticeship program offers access to 1,000 career areas, including the following top occupations:

- Able seaman
- Carpenter
- Chef
- Child care development specialist
- Construction craft laborer
- Dental assistant
- Electrician
- Elevator constructor
- Fire medic
- Law enforcement agent
- Over-the-road truck driver
- Pipefitter

crews practice flight maneuvers in a controlled environment. UPS uses a life-size learning lab to provide a 46-hour, 5-day realistic training program for driver candidates.[41]

Behavior Modeling

behavior modeling
A training technique in which trainees are first shown good management techniques in a video, are then asked to play roles in a simulated situation, and are then given feedback and praise by their supervisor.

Behavior modeling involves (1) showing trainees the right (or "model") way of doing something, (2) letting trainees practice that way, and then (3) giving feedback on the trainees' performance. This is "one of the most widely used, well researched, and highly regarded psychologically based training interventions."[42] The procedure is as follows:

1. *Modeling.* First, trainees watch live or video examples that show models behaving effectively in a problem situation. The video might show a supervisor effectively disciplining a subordinate, if teaching how to discipline is the aim of the training program.
2. *Role playing.* Next, the trainees are given roles to play in a simulated situation; here they practice and rehearse the effective behaviors demonstrated by the models.
3. *Social reinforcement.* The trainer provides reinforcement in the form of praise and constructive feedback based on how the trainees perform in the role-playing situation.
4. *Transfer of training.* Finally, trainees are encouraged to apply their new skills when they are back on their jobs.

Behavior modeling is quite popular. By one estimate, firms spend more of their training dollars on behavioral computer skills training than they do on sales training, supervisory training, or communication training.[43] Studies suggest that behavioral modeling results in significant improvements in knowledge and skill learning, but its effect on actual job behavior is less clear.[44]

Videoconference Distance Learning

Videoconferencing is a popular way to train geographically dispersed employees. It is "a means of joining two or more distant groups using a combination of audio and visual equipment."[45] The communication often involves sending compressed audio and video signals over cable broadband lines, the Internet, or via satellite. Vendors such as Cisco offer videoconference products such as Webex and TelePresence (www.cisco.com/en/US/products/ps10352/index.html). These make it easy to create Web-based videoconference training programs.

Computer and Internet-Based Training

computer-based training (CBT)
Trainees use a computer-based system to interactively increase their knowledge or skills.

In **computer-based training (CBT)**, trainees use computer-based systems to increase their knowledge or skills interactively. This may mean presenting trainees with computerized simulations and using virtual reality to help the trainees learn the job.[46] But often, computer-based training is less complex. For example, it may simply involve reviewing PowerPoint slides online and passing a quiz.

In one computer-based training program, a trainee for a job as a recruiter sits before a computer screen. The screen shows the "applicant's" employment application, as well as information about the job. The trainee then begins a simulated interview by typing in questions that a prerecorded video-based "applicant" answers, using responses to dozens of questions experts previously programmed into the computer. At the end of the session, the computer tells the trainee where he or she went wrong (perhaps asking discriminatory questions, for instance) and offers instructional material to correct these mistakes.

DVD-Based Training

Many packaged training programs are available on DVDs. For example, McDonald's developed a number of computer disk–based courses for its franchises' employees. The programs consist of graphics-supported lessons, and require trainees to make choices to show their understanding.[47] Specialist multimedia software houses like Graphic Media of Portland, Oregon, produce much of the content for CBT programs like these. They produce both custom titles and generic programs, like a package for teaching workplace safety.

Orlando-based Environmental Tectonics Corporation created an Advanced Disaster Management simulation for emergency medical response trainees.

Source: David McNew/Getty Images, Inc.–Liaison.

Simulated Learning

"Simulated learning" means different things to different people. A survey asked training professionals what experiences qualified as simulated learning. The percentages of trainers choosing each experience were:

- Virtual reality–type games, 19%
- Step-by-step animated guide, 8%
- Scenarios with questions and decision trees overlaying animation, 19%
- Online role-play with photos and videos, 14%
- Software training including screenshots with interactive requests for responses, 35%
- Other, 6%[48]

EXAMPLES Employers increasingly rely on computerized simulations to inject more realism into their training programs. For example, Orlando-based Environmental Tectonics Corporation created an Advanced Disaster Management simulation for emergency medical response trainees. One simulated scenario involves a passenger plane crashing onto a runway. So realistic that it's "unsettling," trainees including firefighters and airport officials respond to the simulated crash's sights and sounds via pointing devices and radios.[49] IBM's IBM@Play uses videogame technology and three-dimensional virtual environments to facilitate training.[50] When Cisco Systems needed a better way to train the thousands of Cisco trainees around the world sitting for Cisco certification exams it hired a game developer. That person embedded the necessary learning within a videogame-like atmosphere that included music, graphics, and sound effects.[51] At ConAgra foods, managers use a simulation called The Executive Challenge to make realistic business decisions while rotating through various (simulated) functional jobs and fighting for market share. Top executives decide which teams won, based not just on financial results but also "on how well the business teams work and make decisions together."[52]

Other employers capitalize on virtual environments such as Second Life. For example, British Petroleum uses Second Life to train new gas station employees. The aim here is to show new gas station employees how to use the safety features of gasoline storage tanks. BP built three-dimensional renderings of the tank systems in Second Life. Trainees could use these to see "underground and observe the effects of using the safety devices."[53]

Training simulations are expensive, but, particularly for larger companies, the cost per employee is usually reasonable. For example, a "branching story" simulation challenges students to make a series of decisions as they move through a multiple-choice interface. Such a simulation usually ranges in cost from $30,000 to $500,000.[54]

Internet-Based Training

As in most colleges today, employers use Internet-based learning to deliver training. The training itself may simply include posting videos, written lectures, or PowerPoint slides, or may involve sophisticated simulations.

There are several ways to make online courses available to employees. The employer can encourage and/or facilitate having its employees take relevant online courses from the hundreds of online training vendors on the Web. For example, the employer might arrange with PureSafety (www.puresafety.com) to let its employees take one or more occupational safety courses from those PureSafety offers. Other online course providers include SkillSoft (www.skillsoft.com) and Click2Learn.com. Delta Air Lines' customer service personnel receive about 70% of their annual required FAA training via their intranet. Delta likes it because "prior to online training, employees had to travel to one of five training centers, keeping them away from their jobs for at least the day."[55] Other employers make their courses available via their intranet-based learning portals.

LEARNING PORTALS A *learning portal* is a section of an employer's Web site that offers employees online access to many or all of the training courses they need to succeed at their jobs. Most often, the employer contracts with training applications service providers (ASPs) like those in Figure 6.3. When employees go to their firm's learning portal, they actually access the server and menu of courses that the ASP company contracted with the employer to offer.

FIGURE 6.3

Partial List of E-Learning/ Training Applications Service Provider Vendors

Source: Google. www.google.com/ permissions/index.html, accessed January 19, 2008.

E-learning Companies
Reference > Education > Distance Learning > Online Teaching and Learning > E-learning Companies   Go to Directory Home

Categories

Course Authoring (71)
E-learning Portals (60)
E-learning Research (23)
Learning Management Systems (73)
Online Classrooms (18)

Related Categories:
Computers > Education > Commercial Services > Training Companies > Self-Study (49)
Reference > Education > Distance Learning > Online Courses (281)
Reference > Education > Distance Learning > Services (34)
Reference > Knowledge Management > Business and Companies (124)

Web Pages   Viewing in Google PageRank order   View in alphabetical order

Skillsoft - http://www.skillsoft.com
Providers of enterprise e-learning, a fully integrated student environment and courseware to support e-Learning initiatives in enterprises.

Plateau Systems - http://www.plateau.com
Corporate learning solutions deployed at enterprises across the world enabling global organizations to increase productivity and save millions of training dollars.

Academee - http://www.academee.com
Integrated learning programmes, blending consultancy, online e-learning and face-to-face classroom courses for management and professional development.

Enspire Learning - http://www.enspire.com
Enspire Learning develops custom e-learning courses that include interactive multimedia, simulations, and engaging scenarios.

Ninth House Network - http://www.ninthhouse.com/
A leading e-learning broadband environment for organizational development, delivering to the desktop experiential, interactive programs that leverage the world's foremost business thinkers.

Futurate Ltd - http://www.futurate.com/
Developers of eLearning content and systems that are engaging and accessible to all. They offer a 'full service' from consultancy to implementation and maintenance.

PrimeLearning - http://www.primelearning.com
E-learning company that specialises in business and professional skills courses provided off the self or can be custom made.

Intellinex - http://www.intellinex.com
Provider of e-Learning solutions for workers in Global 2000 companies, government, and educational institutions. Courseware covers PC and business skills applications.

Allen Communication - http://www.allencomm.com
Provides e-Learning solutions including learning portals, strategic planning for training, courseware development and authoring / design tools.

The Learning House, Inc. - http://www.learninghouse.com
Learning House, Inc. is an eLearning services company that creates off the shelf and custom online degree and professional development courses.

DefiniTion - http://www.definition.be
DefiniTion design and development e-learning courses for companies. The company is based in Belgium and their services include consultancy and support.

Intrac Design Inc - http://www.intrac.biz
The development and delivery of customizable training programs for live classroom and e-learning delivery.

Seward, Inc. - http://www.sewardinc.com
Seward, Inc. provide engaging, instructionally sound, cost-effective training solutions ranging from soft skills involved in sales to the most technically exacting fields of medicine, engineering, and finance.

Silverchair Learning Systems - http://www.silverchairlearning.com
Online employee education exclusively for the Senior Care industry.

Tata Interactive Systems - http://www.tatainteractivesystems.com
Developer of custom e-learning solutions for corporate, educational and governmental organizations.

Little Planet Learning - http://www.littleplanet.com
Provides design and development of learning experiences delivered live and through elearning, computer and web based training (CBT and WBT), and multimedia programs.

Employment Law Learning Technologies - http://www.elt-inc.com
Online compliance training for managers and employees on critical US employment law / HR topics, including harassment, discrimination, privacy and diversity.

Improving Productivity through HRIS:
Learning Management Systems

Learning management systems (LMSs) help employers identify training needs, and in scheduling, delivering, and managing the online training itself. For example, General Motors uses an LMS to help its dealers in Africa and the Middle East deliver high-quality training programs. The Internet-based LMS includes a course catalog, two-step enrollment (supervisor approved self enrollment), facilities and training schedule management, and assessment systems (including pre- and post-course tests). Dealers, supervisors, and employees can review the list of courses on the LMS. They then choose courses based upon their needs, for instance, in specific areas such as automobile transmissions and sales management. The system then automatically schedules the individual's training.[56] Colleges use Blackboard and WebCT, two familiar learning management systems.

In terms of talent management, employers are moving toward integrating the e-learning system with the company's enterprise-wide information systems. In that way, for instance, employers can automatically update skills inventories and succession plans as employees complete their training.[57]

The Virtual Classroom

Conventional Web-based learning tends to be limited to the sorts of online learning with which college students are already familiar—reading PowerPoint presentations, and taking online exams, for instance.

The virtual classroom takes online learning to a new level. A **virtual classroom** uses collaboration software to enable multiple remote learners, using their PCs or laptops, to participate in live audio and visual discussions, communicate via written text, and learn via content such as PowerPoint slides.

The virtual classroom combines the best of Web-based learning offered by systems like Blackboard and WebCT, with live video and audio. For example, Elluminate Inc. makes one popular virtual classroom system, Elluminate Live! It enables learners to communicate with clear, two-way audio; build communities with user profiles and live video; collaborate with chat and shared whiteboards; and learn with shared applications such as PowerPoint slides.[58]

Improving Web-Based Learning

Having already had some experience with Web learning, most students know it can be effective. In one review of the evidence, Web-based instruction was a bit more effective than classroom instruction for teaching memory of facts and principles. Web-based instruction and classroom instruction were equally effective for teaching information about how to perform a task or action. Trainees were equally satisfied with Web-based instruction and classroom instruction. Web-based instruction was superior when the program enabled the trainees to control the pace and selection of the content.[59] However, the need to teach large numbers of students remotely, or to enable students to study at their leisure, often makes e-learning so much more efficient that the small differences in effectiveness don't matter.[60]

IMPROVING E-LEARNING In establishing e-learning programs, there are three things to keep in mind. First, there are still many learning situations where conventional *in-class work is usually preferable*—a chemical engineering lab session, for instance. Second, the employer needs to *balance the extra cost* of creating the online learning against the advantages of being able to use it to offer courses 24/7, and remotely. Third and finally, the trainer should keep e-learning's *limitations* in mind. For example, allow for the fact that learners tend to be slower taking online exams than they are paper-and-pencil ones. (This is because the Web page tends to have fewer questions in a larger font than do paper quizzes, and because going back and reviewing one's answers tends to take longer online.) Also make sure to explain to trainees what control they have and how they can use it, such as how to change the learning sequence.[61]

In practice, the trend is toward blended learning, wherein the trainee uses several delivery methods (for instance, manuals, in-class lectures, self-guided e-learning programs, and Web-based seminars or "webinars") to learn the material.[62] Intuit (which makes software such as TurboTax) uses instructor-led classroom training for bringing in new distributors and getting them up to speed. Then it uses its virtual classroom systems to provide additional training, for monthly meetings with distributors, and for short classes on special software features.[63]

virtual classroom
Special collaboration software used to enable multiple remote learners, using their PCs or laptops, to participate in live audio and visual discussions, communicate via written text, and learn via content such as PowerPoint slides.

Mobile Learning

Mobile learning (or "on-demand learning") means delivering learning content on demand via mobile devices like cell phones, laptops, and iPhones, wherever and whenever the learner wants to access it.[64] For example, using dominKnow's (www.dominknow.com/) iPod touch and iPhone-optimized Touch Learning Center Portal, trainees can log in and take full online courses.[65]

MOBILE LEARNING EXAMPLES Capital One Bank purchased 3,000 iPods for trainees enrolled in one of 20 instructor-led courses at its Capital One University.[66] The training department then had an Internet audio book provider create an audio learning site within Capital One's firewall. Employees used it to download the instructor-requested books and other materials to their iPods.[67] IBM uses mobile learning to deliver just-in-time information (for instance about new product features) to its sales force. IBM's training department often breaks up, say, an hour program into 10-minute pieces.[68] Some employers, including J.P. Morgan, encourage employees to use instant messaging as a quick learning device. Employers also use instant messaging to supplement classroom training, for instance, by using IM for group chats. One training manager sends a short personal development idea or quote each day for others to access via his Twitter account.[69] A new Microsoft Word add-on enables someone to convert instantly any Word document into multimedia content that one can play on a portable MP3 player.[70]

Training for Special Purposes

Training today does more than prepare employees to perform their jobs. Training for special purposes—dealing with diversity, for instance—is required, too. A sampling of such special-purpose training programs follows.

lifelong learning
Providing employees with continuing learning experiences over their tenure with the firm, with the aim of ensuring they have the opportunity to obtain the knowledge and skills they need to do their jobs effectively.

PROVIDING LIFELONG LEARNING Lifelong learning means providing employees with continuing learning experiences over their tenure with the firm, with the aim of ensuring they have the opportunity to obtain the knowledge and skills they need to grow professionally and to do their jobs effectively. Such training may range from basic remedial skills to advanced decision-making techniques throughout employees' careers. Programs may include, as appropriate, training in such things as English as a second language, basic literacy, arithmetic, and computer literacy; college course work; and job-related training sessions. For example, one senior waiter at Rhapsody restaurant in Chicago received his undergraduate degree and began work towards a master of social work using the *lifelong learning account* (LiLA) program his employer offers. Somewhat similar to 401(k) plans, employers and employees contribute to LiLA plans (without the tax advantages of 401(k) plans), and employees can use these funds to better themselves.[71]

Many employers embrace lifelong learning because they're not satisfied with the basic learning skills their employees got in elementary and high school. Functional illiteracy—the inability to handle basic reading, writing, and arithmetic—is a serious problem at work. By one estimate, about 39 million people in the United States have a learning disability that makes it challenging to read, write, or do arithmetic.[72] Yet literacy is crucial. Today's emphasis on teamwork and quality requires employees to have the ability to adequately read, write, and understand numbers. Employers often turn to private firms like Education Management Corporation to provide the requisite postsecondary education.[73]

Another simple approach is to have supervisors teach basic skills by giving employees writing and speaking exercises.[74] One way to do this is to convert materials used in the employee's job into instructional tools. For example, if an employee needs to use a manual to find out how to change a part, teach that person how to use an index to locate the relevant section. Another approach is to bring in outside professionals (such as teachers from a local high school) to teach, say, remedial reading or writing. Having employees attend adult education or high school evening classes is another option.

DIVERSITY TRAINING With an increasingly diverse workforce, many firms employ diversity training programs. *Diversity training* refers to "techniques for creating better cross-cultural sensitivity among supervisors and nonsupervisors with the aim of creating more harmonious working relationships among a firm's employees." For example, Adams Mark Hotel & Resorts conducted a diversity training seminar for about 11,000 employees. It combined lectures, video, and employee role-playing to emphasize sensitivity to race and religion.[75]

There are many training programs aimed at counteracting potential problems associated with a diverse workforce. These include packaged programs for improving interpersonal skills, understanding/valuing cultural differences, improving technical skills, socializing into corporate culture, indoctrinating recent immigrants into the U.S. work ethic, and improving bilingual skills for English-speaking employees.

TRAINING FOR TEAMWORK AND EMPOWERMENT Teamwork is not something that always comes naturally. Companies like Toyota therefore devote many hours to training new employees to listen to each other and to cooperate. Toyota's training process stresses dedication to teamwork. For example, the program uses short exercises to illustrate examples of good and bad teamwork, and to mold new employees' attitudes regarding good teamwork.

Some firms use outdoor "adventure" training such as Outward Bound programs to build teamwork. Outdoor training usually involves taking a firm's management team out into rugged, mountainous terrain. For example, the chief financial officer for one large banking company helped organize a retreat for 73 of his firm's financial officers and accountants. As he said: "They are very individualistic in their approach to their work . . . . What I have been trying to do is get them to see the power of acting more like a team."[76] The accompanying Global Issues in HR feature illustrates another special type of training.

GLOBAL ISSUES IN HR

Exporting Values

Values—basic beliefs we have about what is right and wrong and what we should and shouldn't do—play an important role in training abroad. For example, Gap Inc. asked a World Bank affiliate to provide supervisory training for line managers in Gap's vendors' Cambodian garment factories.[77] Gap's goal was to improve labor relations at their vendors abroad. Gap's supervisory training program therefore covers matters such as how to handle worker complaints, and conflict resolution.

Bringing about value-based changes like these isn't easy. For example, Professor Geert Hofstede found that people in different cultures differ in the degree to which they accept that less powerful members of organizations expect power to be distributed unequally. (He calls this "power distance.")[78] In some countries, employees may thus find unilateral discipline to be less egregious than it might be in the United States.[79] Understanding the trainees' cultural heritage is thus essential for designing the training program.

MANAGERIAL DEVELOPMENT AND TRAINING

management development
Any attempt to improve current or future management performance by imparting knowledge, changing attitudes, or increasing skills.

Management development is any attempt to improve managerial performance by imparting knowledge, changing attitudes, or increasing skills. It thus includes in-house programs such as courses, coaching, and rotational assignments; professional programs such as SHRM seminars; and university programs such as executive MBA programs.

The ultimate aim of such development programs is, of course, to enhance the future performance of the organization itself. For this reason, the overall management development process consists of *assessing* the company's needs (for instance, to fill future executive openings, or to make the firm less bureaucratic), *appraising* the managers' performance, and then *developing* the managers themselves.[80]

3 Explain what management development is and why it is important.

Trends in Management Development

Globalization and increased competitiveness mean it's more important today for leadership development programs to be organizationally relevant. This means three things. First, the program should flow from and make sense in terms of the company's *strategy and goals*. This means involving top management in formulating the program's aims, and also specifying concrete competencies and knowledge outcomes. Thus Caterpillar Inc. created Caterpillar University to oversee its training and development programs. The University has a board of directors comprised of company executives. They set the university's policies, and oversee "the alignment of the corporation's learning needs with the enterprises' business strategy."[81]

Second, there should be emphasis on supplementing traditional development methods (such as lectures, case discussion groups, and simulations) with *realistic methods* like action learning; here trainees solve actual company problems.[82] The most popular development methods include classroom-based learning, executive coaching, action learning, 360-degree feedback (discussed in Chapter 7), experiential learning, off-site retreats, mentoring, and job rotation.[83]

Third, *trainee assessment* usually should precede manager development programs. For example, at frozen foods manufacturer Schwan's, a pre-development committee of senior executives first whittles 40 or more candidates down to 10 or less. Then the program begins with a one-day assessment by outside consultants of each manager's leadership strengths and weaknesses. This assessment becomes the basis for each manager's individual development plan. Action-learning projects then supplement individual and group training activities.[84]

Figure 6.4 summarizes several principles for designing leadership development programs (such as "involve top management"). Management development methods (many equally useful for first-line supervisors, too) are described next.

Managerial On-the-Job Training

On-the-job training isn't just for nonsupervisory employees. It is also a popular manager development method. **Job rotation** means moving management trainees from department to department to broaden their understanding of all parts of the business. The trainee may spend several months in each department; this helps not only broaden his or her experience, but also discover the jobs he or she prefers. The person learns the department's business by actually doing it, whether it involves sales, production, finance, or some other function. With the **coaching/understudy method**, the new manager, of course, receives ongoing advice, often from the person he or she is scheduled to replace.

Action Learning

Action learning programs give groups of managers released time to work full-time analyzing and solving problems in departments other than their own. The basics include carefully selected teams of 5 to 25 members, assigning teams real-world business problems that extend beyond their usual areas of expertise, and structured learning through coaching and feedback. The employer's senior managers usually choose the projects and decide whether to accept the teams' recommendations.[85] Many major firms around the world, from GE to Samsung and Deutsche Bank, use action learning.[86]

job rotation
A management training technique that involves moving a trainee from department to department to broaden his or her experience and identify strengths and weaknesses.

coaching/understudy method
An experienced worker or supervisor trains the employee on the job.

action learning
A training technique by which management trainees are allowed to work full time analyzing and solving problems in other departments.

FIGURE 6.4

Management and Leadership Development Guidelines

1. Design the program so that it flows from and makes sense in terms of the company's strategy and goals.
2. Involve the top management team in formulating the program's aims.
3. Make sure to design the program to improve managers' deficiencies and needs that you identify ahead of time.
4. Aim for practicality rather than just theory.
5. Specify concrete competencies and skills outcomes, not just knowledge and attitude changes, and use realistic learning methods like action learning projects where trainees solve real company problems.
6. Aim for short, high-involvement, 3- to 4-day programs rather than longer immersion programs.

Sources: Adapted from P. Nick Blanchard and James Thacker, *Effective Training* (Upper Saddle River, NJ: Pearson, 2007): 439–467; Jack Zenger, Dave Ulrich, and Norm Smallwood, "The New Leadership Development," *Training & Development* (March 2000): 22–27; W. David Patton and Connie Pratt, "Assessing the Training Needs of High Potential Managers," *Public Personnel Management* 31, no. 4 (Winter 2002): 465–474; and Ann Locke and Arlene Tarantino, "Strategic Leadership Development," *Training & Development* (December 2006): 53–55.

The Case Study Method

case study method
A development method in which the manager is presented with a written description of an organizational problem to diagnose and solve.

The **case study method** presents a trainee with a written (or sometimes online or video) description and history of an organizational problem. The trainee reads and analyzes the case, diagnoses the problem, and presents his or her findings and solutions in an interactive discussion with other trainees. The basic idea is to simulate an actual managerial situation, and so to give trainees realistic experience in identifying and analyzing complex problems, in an environment in which a trained discussion leader guides their progress.

The usefulness of the case study method depends largely on the trainer's (or professor's) case analysis skills. The trainer should at least:[87]

- Guide the trainees in examining the possible alternatives and consequences.
- Keep in mind that his or her analysis of the case situation and action plan may hinder the group's discussion and learning.
- Keep the aim of the training in mind; for instance, if the overall aim is building decision-making skills, interject in the discussion practical suggestions about decision-making skills.
- Make sure to facilitate the group discussion, for instance, by encouraging everyone to participate, discouraging harsh criticism, and encouraging everyone to consider each other's suggestions.

Management Games

management game
A development technique in which teams of managers compete by making computerized decisions regarding realistic but simulated situations.

In computerized **management games**, trainees split into five- or six-person companies, each of which has to compete with the others in a simulated marketplace. For example, the group may be allowed to decide how much to spend on advertising, how much to produce, how much inventory to maintain, and how many of which product to produce. Usually, the game compresses a 2- or 3-year period into days, weeks, or months. As in the real world, each company usually can't see what decisions the other firms have made, although these decisions affect their own sales. For example, if a competitor decides to increase its advertising expenditures, that firm may end up increasing its sales at the expense of the others.[88]

improvisation
A form of management training in which the trainees learn skills such as openness and creativity by playing games that require that they improvise answers and solutions.

Improvisation is a recent variant. For example, Nike Corporation asked Second City Communications, the consulting arm of the comedy improvisational group Second City, to help prepare some Nike engineers for an assignment. The engineers were to spend a month watching kids in playgrounds, so as to design new Nike shoes. Second City trainers put the engineers through an improvisational game called "word ball." Here trainees pass a make-believe ball to one another, each time calling out one word. (Thus, the first person might pass the ball and call out

Second City trainers put Nike engineers through an improvisational game called "word ball."

Source: Getty Images Inc.–PhotoDisc.

"cat," the second catches, then passes on the make-believe ball, and calls out "furry," and so on.) The aim was to get the Nike engineers "to instantly react without thinking . . . to be unafraid to look foolish."[89]

The Myers-Briggs Type Indicator

The Myers-Briggs Type Indicator (MBTI) is a popular development tool in the work setting. The MBTI classifies people as extraverted or introverted (E or I), sensing or intuitive (S or N), thinking or feeling (T or F), and perceiving or judging (P or J). The MBTI questionnaire classifies people into 16 different personality types (a 4 × 4 matrix); these 16 types are, in turn, classified into one of four cognitive (thinking or problem-solving) styles:

- Sensation–thinking (ST)
- Intuition–thinking (NT)
- Sensation–feeling (SF)
- Intuition–feeling (NF)

Classifying personality types and cognitive styles in this way has several applications. Some employers match the MBTI styles to particular occupations. Thus, people with the ST approach to problem solving are often well suited to occupations like auditor and safety engineer, for instance.

In addition, learning about one's MBTI style is useful for employee development purposes, for instance in terms of understanding how to fine-tune your reactions to co-workers. As the Myers-Briggs organization points out, "Knowledge of [MBTI] type can help you deal with the culture of the place you work, the development of new skills, understanding your participation on teams, and coping with change in the workplace."[90]

Outside Seminars

Many vendors offer management development seminars and conferences. The selection of short, (1- to 3-day) training programs offered by the American Management Association illustrates what's available. Recently, for instance its offerings ranged from "developing your emotional intelligence" to "assertiveness training for managers," "assertiveness training for women in business," "dynamic listening skills for successful communication," and "fundamentals of cost accounting."[91] SHRM—the Society for Human Resource Management—offers numerous courses for HR professionals.

Most such programs offer continuing education units (CEUs) for course completion. CEUs generally can't be used to obtain degree-granting credit at most colleges or universities. They do provide a record of the fact that the trainee participated in and completed a conference or seminar and may count toward professional certification.

University-Related Programs

Many universities provide executive education and continuing education programs in leadership, supervision, and the like. These can range from 1- to 4-day programs to executive development programs lasting 1 to 4 months. An increasing number of these are online.

The Advanced Management Program of the Graduate School of Business Administration at Harvard University is a well-known example.[92] Students consist of experienced managers from around the world. The program uses cases and lectures to provide them with the latest management skills, and with practice analyzing complex organizational problems.

University-based executive education is becoming more realistic, relying more on active learning, business simulations, and experiential learning.[93] Employers are also more sophisticated in how they select and manage university-related development programs. For example, Home Depot created a "preferred network" of university partners. Home Depot arranges for employees who take courses at an in-network university to get discount course prices.[94]

EXAMPLES Joint employer/university partnerships can be effective here. For example, when Hasbro Inc. needed to improve its top executives' creativity skills, it turned to the Amos Tuck business school at Dartmouth University. It wanted "a custom approach to designing a program that would be built from the ground up to suit Hasbro's specific needs."[95]

Hasbro and Tuck's executive program faculty directors designed a program with four basic elements. First, when participants arrive, they receive sealed envelopes containing their confidential performance assessment reports. Second, managers receive both group and individual coaching from special "executive coaches." The goal is to help Hasbro executives identify "blind spots" that may be hampering their performance and to develop plans to address these issues. Third, they participate in "MBA-type" courses, selected to be relevant for them, based on their and Hasbro's strategic needs. Finally, the executives work in action learning/project teams, under the guidance of Hasbro's in-house coaches.

In-House Learning and Development Centers

in-house development centers

A company-based facility for exposing current or prospective managers to exercises to develop improved management skills.

Many firms have **in-house development centers**, or "universities"; these usually combine classroom learning with other techniques such as assessment centers and online learning opportunities to help develop employees and other managers. For example, at General Electric's (GE) Leadership Institute, the courses range from entry-level programs in manufacturing and sales to a business course for English majors. However, in general, corporate universities seem to be moving from offering large catalogs of courses to more focused offerings on topics like strategy and performance management.[96]

LEARNING PORTALS For many firms, their online learning portals are their virtual in-house development centers. Bain & Company, a management consulting firm, is one example. Its Web-based virtual university provides a means for conveniently coordinating all the company's training efforts, and for delivering Web-based modules on topics from strategic management to mentoring.[97]

LEARNING ACCOUNTS IBM recently established 401(k)-type "learning accounts" to encourage its employees to further their training. An employee can put up to $1,000 a year into his or her account, and IBM contributes an additional $0.50 for every dollar the employee contributes. The accounts are interest-bearing, and the employees can use the funds as they prefer, or take the funds with them if they leave IBM.[98]

EXECUTIVE COACHES Many firms use executive coaches to develop their top managers' effectiveness. An *executive coach* is an outside consultant who questions the executive's boss, peers, subordinates, and (sometimes) family in order to identify the executive's strengths and weaknesses, and to counsel the executive so he or she can capitalize on those strengths and weaknesses. Coaches come from a variety of backgrounds, including teaching and counseling. Becton Dickinson & Co. encourages professional and management employees to coach each other.[99]

Executive coaching can be effective. Participants in one study included about 1,400 senior managers who had received 360-degree performance feedback from bosses, peers, and subordinates. About 400 worked with an executive coach to review the feedback. Then, about a year later, these 400 managers and about 400 who did not receive coaching again received multiscore feedback. Managers who received executive coaching were more likely to set more effective, specific goals for their subordinates, and to have received improved ratings from subordinates and supervisors.[100] Because executive coaching can cost as much as $50,000 per executive, experts recommend using formal assessments prior to coaching to provide more focus for the coaching.[101]

Talent Management and Mission-Critical Employees: Differential Development Assignments

Probably the most distinctive talent management best practice is to *actively manage employees*. In today's competitive environment, the traditional HR practice of allocating pay raises, development opportunities, and other scarce resources more-or-less across the board or based mostly on performance is no longer viable. Employers need to think through how to allocate those resources in a way that makes the most sense given their strategic aims. It therefore makes sense that talent management-oriented employers focus more of their development resources on their "mission-critical employees," those deemed critical to the companies' future growth.

We'll look at how employers do this in the following chapter. However, it is useful here to illustrate how employers implement this "differential" approach with several training-and-development examples:

- A telecommunications firm previously spread pay and development money evenly over its 8,000 employees. When the recent recession came, company leaders began segmenting their talent into four groups: business impact, high performers, high potentials, and critical skills. Then they shifted their dollars away from low performers and those not making an impact. "While the company lost some low performers, the high performers and high potentials felt like they finally received recognition . . . " [102]
- One large manufacturer gives "rising stars" special access to online discussion boards, led by the CEO, that are dedicated to the company's biggest challenges. It encourages emerging leaders to visit the board daily to share ideas and opinions and to apply for assignments. [103]
- High potential participants in Johnson & Johnson's special "LeAD" leadership development program receive advice and regular assessments from coaches brought in from outside the company. As special projects, they also must develop a new product or service, or a new business model, intended to create value for their individual units. [104]
- Some companies share future strategies on a privileged basis with rising leaders. For example, these high-potentials receive e-mail updates detailing firm performance and strategic changes. Some invite them to quarterly meetings with high-level executives; and some provide access to an online portal where the rising leaders can review the company's strategy and critical metrics. [105]

ORGANIZATIONAL CHANGE

International competition means companies have to change fast, perhaps changing their strategies to enter new businesses, or their organization charts, or their employees' attitudes and values. Major organizational changes like these are never easy, but perhaps the hardest part of leading a change is overcoming the resistance to it. Individuals, groups, and even entire organizations may resist the change, perhaps because they're accustomed to the usual way of doing things or because of perceived threats to their influence, or some other reason. [106] Several years ago Intel Corp. carried out a major reorganization that one writer says "may have badly damaged employee development, morale and the company's culture of innovation." [107]

Lewin's Process for Overcoming Resistance

Psychologist Kurt Lewin formulated a model of change to summarize what he believed was the basic process for implementing a change with minimal resistance. To Lewin, all behavior in organizations was a product of two kinds of forces: those striving to maintain the status quo and those pushing for change. Implementing change thus meant either reducing the forces for the status quo or building up the forces for change. Lewin's process consisted of three steps:

1. *Unfreezing* means reducing the forces that are striving to maintain the status quo, usually by presenting a provocative problem or event to get people to recognize the need for change and to search for new solutions.
2. *Moving* means developing new behaviors, values, and attitudes, perhaps by reorganizing the company, or by using other management development techniques like those we discussed.
3. *Refreezing* means building in the reinforcement to make sure the organization doesn't slide back into its former ways of doing things. Institute new incentive plans, for instance.

Of course, the challenge is in the details. Actually implementing the change in the face of employee resistance is the difficult part. You'll find an eight-step process for leading organizational change in the accompanying HR in Practice feature.

HR IN PRACTICE

A Process for Leading Organizational Change[108]

Unfreezing Stage

1. Establish a sense of urgency. This often takes creativity. For example, the CEO might present executives with an analyst's report describing the firm's lack of competitiveness.
2. Mobilize commitment through joint diagnosis of problems. Having established a sense of urgency, the leader may then create one or more task forces to diagnose the problems facing the company. Such teams can produce a shared understanding of what they can and must improve, and thereby mobilize commitment.

Moving Stage

3. Create a guiding coalition. No one can implement major organizational changes alone. Most CEOs create a guiding coalition of influential people. They work together as a team to act as missionaries and implementers.
4. Develop and communicate a shared vision. Organizational renewal requires a new leadership vision, "a general statement of the organization's intended direction that evokes emotional feelings in organization members." For example, when Barry Gibbons became CEO of Spec's Music some years ago, his vision of a leaner Spec's offering a diversified blend of concerts and retail music helped provide this direction.
5. Help employees make the change. Are there impediments to change? Does a lack of skills stand in the way? Do policies and procedures make it difficult to act? Do intransigent

managers discourage employees from acting? If so, address these impediments. When he was CEO at the former AlliedSignal, Lawrence Bossidy put all of his 80,000 people through quality improvement training.

6. Consolidate gains and produce more change. Aim for attainable short-term accomplishments, and use the credibility from these to change all the systems, structures, and policies that don't fit well with the company's new vision. Leaders produce more change by hiring and promoting new people, by identifying selected employees to champion the continuing change, and by providing additional opportunities for short-term wins by employees.[109]

Refreezing Stage

7. Reinforce the new ways of doing things with changes to the company's systems and procedures. Use new appraisal systems and incentives to reinforce the desired behaviors. Change the culture by ensuring that the firm's managers communicate the company's new values.
8. Finally, the leader must monitor and assess progress. In brief, this involves comparing where the company is today with where it should be. For example, several years ago, Avon's CEO knew the firm had to increase its new products dramatically. She instituted many changes. Then she asked, How many new products has the company introduced? How many new door-to-door sales reps has the firm added?

Organizational Development

4 Summarize the process of organizational change.

organizational development (OD)
A development method aimed at changing the attitudes, values, and beliefs of employees so that employees can improve the organization.

There are many ways to reduce the resistance associated with organizational change. Among the many suggestions are that managers impose rewards or sanctions that guide employee behaviors, explain why the change is needed, negotiate with employees, give inspirational speeches, or ask employees to help design the change.[110] Organizational development taps into the latter. **Organizational development (OD)** is a change process through which employees diagnose and formulate the change that's required and implement it, often with the assistance of trained consultants.

Action research is the foundation of most OD programs (or "interventions"). It means

- Gathering data about the organization and its operations and attitudes, with an eye toward solving a particular problem (for example, conflict between the sales and production departments).
- Feeding back these data to the employees involved.
- Having the employee team plan solutions to the problems.

survey feedback
A method that involves surveying employees' attitudes and providing feedback to facilitate problems being solved by the managers and employees.

sensitivity training
A method for increasing employees' insights into their own behavior through candid discussions in groups led by special trainers.

Specific examples of OD programs include survey feedback, sensitivity training, and team building. **Survey feedback** uses questionnaires to survey employees' attitudes and to provide feedback. Its aim is usually to crystallize for the managers the fact that there's a problem to address. Then they can use the results to turn to the job of discussing and solving it.

Sensitivity training aims to increase participants' insights into their behavior and the behavior of others by encouraging an open expression of feelings in the trainer-guided "T-group laboratory" (the "T" is for training). Sensitivity training seeks to accomplish its aim of increasing interpersonal sensitivity by requiring frank, candid discussions of each other in the small, off-site T-group, specifically discussions of participants' personal feelings, attitudes, and behavior. As a result, this is a controversial method surrounded by heated debate and is used much less today than in the past.

team building
Improving the effectiveness of teams through the use of consultants and team-building meetings.

Finally, **team building** refers to a group of OD techniques aimed at improving the effectiveness of teams at work. The typical team-building program begins with the consultant interviewing each of the group members prior to the group meeting. He or she asks what their problems are, how they think the group functions, and what obstacles are in the way of the group performing better.[111] The consultant then categorizes the interview or attitude survey data into themes and presents the themes to the group at the beginning of the meeting. They might include, for example, "Not enough time to get my job done," or "I can't get any cooperation around here." The group then ranks the themes by importance. The most important ones form the agenda for the meeting. The group examines and discusses the issues, examines the underlying causes of the problem, and begins work on a solution to the problems.

WEB-BASED TOOLS Employers use Web-based tools to facilitate organizational development programs. For example, there are Web-based organizational surveys, including ones at www.surveymonkey.com, www.Zoomerang.com, and www.brainbench.com. The manager will also find OD-related self-assessment tools at Web sites such as www.CPP.com.[112]

EVALUATING THE TRAINING AND DEVELOPMENT EFFORT

There are two basic issues in evaluating a training program. The first is how to design the evaluation study and, in particular, whether to use controlled experimentation. The second is what training effect to measure.

controlled experimentation
Formal methods for testing the effectiveness of a training program, preferably with before-and-after tests and a control group.

Controlled experimentation is the method of choice in evaluating training programs. A controlled experiment uses both a training group and a control group (which receives no training). Data (for instance, on quantity of production or quality of soldered junctions) are obtained both before and after the training effort in the group exposed to training, and before and after a corresponding work period in the control group. It is thus presumably possible to determine the extent to which any change in performance in the training group resulted from the training itself rather than from some organization-wide change such as a raise in pay; we assume that the latter would have equally affected employees in both groups. This controlled approach is feasible and is sometimes used.[113] In terms of current practices, however, few firms use this approach. Most simply measure trainees' reactions to the program; some also measure the trainees' job performance before and after training.

5 Explain how and why to evaluate a training program.

Training Effects to Measure

Four basic categories of training outcomes can be measured:

1. *Reaction.* First, evaluate trainees' reactions to the program. Did they like the program? Did they think it worthwhile?
2. *Learning.* Second, test the trainees to determine whether they learned the principles, skills, and facts they were supposed to learn.
3. *Behavior.* Next, ask whether the trainees' behavior on the job changed because of the training program. For example, are employees in the store's complaint department more courteous toward disgruntled customers than previously?
4. *Results.* Finally, but most importantly, ask what final results were achieved in terms of the training objectives previously set. Did the number of customer complaints about employees drop? Did the reject rate improve? Did scrappage cost decrease? Was turnover reduced?

EVALUATION IN PRACTICE In today's metrics-oriented business environment, employers increasingly demand quantified training evaluations of reactions, learning, behavior, results, or some combination of these. In one survey, most responding employers said they set formal response-rate goals (in terms of number of trainees responding) for end-of-training class evaluations. In general, the actual response rate depended on the method the employer used to obtain the response. The response rate of trainees was about 82% with paper-and-pencil end-of-class evaluation surveys, 59% with online surveys, and 53% with e-mail surveys. Response rates for delayed, follow-up surveys were only about 38%. Most firms collecting end-of-class evaluation data—about 90%—use paper-and-pencil surveys.[114] Figure 6.5 shows one survey.

FIGURE 6.5

Online Training Evaluation Form

Source: http://support.pearsonschool. com/surveys/index.cfm?fuseaction= Home.Survey, assessed August 2010. Used with permission of Pearson.

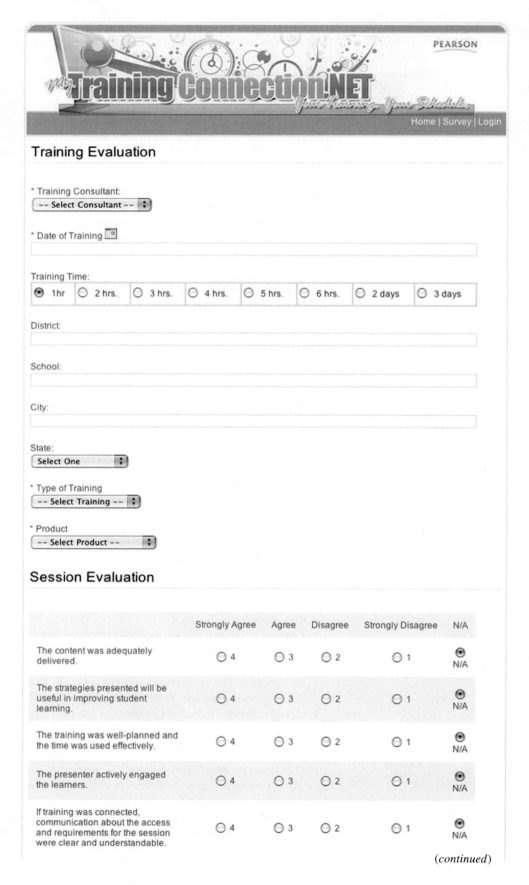

(*continued*)

FIGURE 6.5
(Continued)

Describe the portions of the training/consulting that were the **MOST** effective or useful for you?

Describe the portions of the training/consulting that were the **LEAST** effective or useful for you?

What recommendations do you have for changing the training/consulting you received?

As you begin using this product with students, what is the one aspect of your teaching that will change as a result of this session?

Submit   Reset

© 2010 - Pearson LLC

Computerization is facilitating the evaluation process. For example, Bovis Lend Lease in New York City offers its 625 employees numerous courses in construction and other subjects. The firm uses learning management software to monitor which employees are taking which courses, and the extent to which employees are improving their skills.[115]

TRANSFER OF TRAINING Evaluations show that only about 10% to 35% of trainees are transferring what they learn to their jobs a year after training. Managers can improve this.

- Prior to training, get trainee and supervisor input in designing the program, institute a training attendance policy, and encourage employees to participate.
- During training, provide trainees with training experiences and conditions (surroundings, equipment) that resemble the actual work environment.
- After training, reinforce what trainees learned, for instance, by appraising and rewarding employees for using new skills, and by ensuring that they have the tools and materials they need to use their new skills.[116]

One training expert suggests asking the questions in the HR in Practice feature prior to designing and implementing the new training event:[117]

Questions to Ask When Designing and Implementing a Training Program

- What organizational need will the requested training address?
- What organization or industry issues are driving the training request?
- Is training the solution?
- How will participants' performance improve because of the training?

- Of our suppliers and customers, who will be affected by the training?
- What can the organization expect as a return on its investment?
- What is the value of the results?
- How will we measure the value?

MCDONALD'S EXAMPLE To support McDonald's strategy of product and service consistency, its managers attend its Hamburger University. Employees at "seed stores" in each local area then provide employees from surrounding stores with hands-on training. These seed store–trained employees then train their own stores' teams.

McDonald's measures training effectiveness in several ways. It asks trainees to evaluate classes, and tests them on what they've learned. McDonald's also speaks with the employees' supervisors about how the trainees did before and after the training to try to determine the extent to which the trainees changed their behavior.[118]

REVIEW

SUMMARY

1. The training process consists of five steps: needs analysis, instructional design, validation, implementation, and evaluation.
2. Vestibule training combines the advantages of on- and off-the-job training.
3. On-the-job training might take the form of the coaching/understudy method, job rotation, or special assignments and committees. Other training methods include audiovisual techniques, lectures, and apprenticeship training.
4. Computer-based training includes simulated training, DVD/CD-ROM- and Internet-based training, and learning portals. *Mobile learning* (or "on-demand learning") means delivering learning content on demand via mobile devices like cell phones, laptops, and iPhones, wherever and whenever the learner has the time and desire to access it.
5. Management development is aimed at preparing employees for future managerial jobs with the organization, or at solving organization-wide problems concerning, for instance, inadequate interdepartmental communication.
6. On-the-job experience is the most popular form of management development.
7. Managerial on-the-job training methods include job rotation, coaching, and action learning. Case studies, management games, outside seminars, university-related programs, behavior modeling, and in-house development centers are other methods.
8. Organizational development is an approach to instituting change in which employees themselves play a major role in the change process by providing data, obtaining feedback on problems, and team-planning solutions. There are several OD methods, including sensitivity training, team development, and survey feedback.
9. Overcoming employee resistance is a crucial aspect of implementing organizational change.

KEY TERMS

employee orientation   156
training   157
task analysis   158
performance analysis   158
competency model   159
coaching   161
vestibule/simulated training   162
behavior modeling   163
computer-based training (CBT)   163
virtual classroom   166
lifelong learning   167
management development   168

job rotation   169
coaching/understudy method   169
action learning   169
case study method   170
management game   170
improvisation   170
in-house development centers   172
organizational development (OD)   174
survey feedback   174
sensitivity training   174
team building   175
controlled experimentation   175

DISCUSSION QUESTIONS

1. List and describe each step in the basic training process.
2. Discuss at least two techniques used for assessing training needs.
3. Explain the pros and cons of at least five training techniques.
4. Explain what management development is and why it is important.
5. Describe the main development techniques.
6. Explain how you would go about developing a training program for teaching this course.

INDIVIDUAL AND GROUP ACTIVITIES

1. You're the supervisor of a group of employees whose task is to assemble disk drives that go into computers. You find that quality is not what it should be and that many of your group's devices have to be brought back and reworked. Your boss says, "You'd better start doing a better job of training your workers."
   a. What are some of the "staffing" factors that could be contributing to this problem?
   b. Explain how you would go about assessing whether it is in fact a training problem.
2. Pick out some task with which you are familiar—mowing the lawn, making a salad, or studying for a test—and develop a job instruction sheet for it.
3. Working individually or in groups, develop a short, programmed learning program on the subject "Guidelines for Giving a More Effective Lecture."
4. Find a provider of management development seminars. Obtain copies of its recent listings of seminar offerings. At what levels of managers are the offerings aimed? What

seem to be the most popular types of development programs? Why do you think that's the case?
5. Working individually or in groups, develop several specific examples to illustrate how a professor teaching human resource management could use at least four of the techniques described in this chapter in teaching his or her HR course.
6. Working individually or in groups, develop an orientation program for high school graduates entering your university as freshmen.
7. A well-thought-out orientation program is especially important for employees (such as recent graduates) who have had little or no work experience. Explain why you agree or disagree with this statement.
8. John Santos is an undergraduate business student majoring in accounting. He just failed Accounting 101, and is upset. Explain how you would use performance analysis to identify what, if any, are Santos's training needs.

WEB-e's (WEB EXERCISES)

1. Describe in one page or less with examples how you would use www.secondlife.com to help orient or train employees in your company.
2. Use sites such as www.HRDQ.com to list three programs you could use to develop a project management training program for a company.
3. Based on www.cisco.com/en/US/products/ps10352/index.html, how would you use Cisco products to build a worldwide training program for employees in a company?

APPLICATION EXERCISES

HR IN ACTION CASE INCIDENT 1
Reinventing the Wheel at Apex Door Company

Jim Delaney, president of Apex Door Company, has a problem. No matter how often he tells his employees how to do their jobs, they invariably "decide to do things their way," as he puts it, and arguments ensue between Delaney, the employee, and the employee's supervisor. One example is in the door-design department. The designers are expected to work with the architects to design doors that meet the specifications. Although it's not "rocket science," as Delaney puts it, the designers often make mistakes, such as designing in too much steel—a problem that can cost Apex tens of thousands of wasted dollars, especially considering the number of doors in, say, a 30-story office tower.

The order processing department is another example. Although Jim has a specific, detailed way he wants each order written up, most of the order clerks don't understand how to use the multipage order form, and they improvise when it comes to a question such as whether to classify a customer as "industrial" or "commercial."

The current training process is as follows. None of the jobs have training manuals per se, although several have somewhat out-of-date job descriptions. The training for new employees is all on the job. Usually, the person leaving the company trains the new person during the 1- or 2-week overlap period, but if there's no overlap, the new person is trained as well as possible by other employees who have occasionally filled in on the job in the past. The training is basically the same throughout the company—for machinists, secretaries, assemblers, and accounting clerks, for example.

Questions
1. What do you think of Apex's training process? Could it help explain why employees "do things their way," and if so, how?
2. What role do job descriptions play in training?
3. Explain in detail what you would do to improve the training process at Apex. Make sure to provide specific suggestions.

HR IN ACTION CASE INCIDENT 2
Carter Cleaning Company: The New Training Program

At the present time Carter Cleaning Centers have no formal orientation or training policies or procedures, and Jennifer believes this is one reason why the standards to which she and her father would like employees to adhere are generally not followed.

The Carters would prefer that certain practices and procedures be used in dealing with the customers at the front counters. For example, all customers should be greeted with what Jack refers to as a "big hello." Garments they drop off should immediately be inspected for any damage or unusual stains so these can be brought to the customer's attention, lest the customer later return to pick up the garment and erroneously blame the store. The garments are then supposed to be immediately placed together in a nylon sack to separate them from other customers' garments. The ticket also has to be carefully written up, with the customer's name and telephone number and the date precisely and clearly noted on all copies. The counterperson is also supposed to take the opportunity to try to sell the customer additional services such as waterproofing, or simply notify the customer that "Now that people are doing their spring cleaning, we're having a special on drapery cleaning all this month." Finally, as the customer leaves, the counterperson is supposed to make a courteous comment like "Have a nice day" or "Drive safely." Each of the other jobs in the stores—pressing, cleaning and spotting, periodically maintaining the coin laundry equipment, and so forth—similarly contain certain steps, procedures, and most importantly, standards the Carters would prefer to see upheld.

The company has had problems, Jennifer feels, because of a lack of adequate employee training and orientation. For example, two new employees became very upset last month when they discovered that they were not paid at the end of the week, on Friday, but instead were paid (as are all Carter employees) on the following Tuesday. The Carters use the extra two days in part to give them time to obtain everyone's hours and compute their pay. The other reason they do it, according to Jack, is that "frankly, when we stay a few days behind in paying employees it helps to ensure that they at least give us a few days' notice before quitting on us. While we are certainly obligated to pay them anything they earn, we find that psychologically they seem to be less likely to just walk out on us Friday evening and not show up Monday morning if they still haven't gotten their pay from the previous week. This way they at least give us a few days' notice so we can find a replacement."

Other matters that could be covered during orientation and training, says Jennifer, include company policy regarding paid holidays, lateness and absences, health and hospitalization benefits (there are none, other than workers' compensation), and general matters like the maintenance of a clean and safe work area, personal appearance and cleanliness, time sheets, personal telephone calls and mail, company policies regarding matters like substance abuse, and eating or smoking on the job (both forbidden).

Jennifer believes that implementing orientation and training programs would help to ensure that employees know how to do their jobs the right way. And she and her father further believe that it is only when employees understand the right way to do their jobs that there is any hope their jobs will in fact be accomplished the way the Carters want them to be accomplished.

Questions

1. Specifically what should the Carters cover in their new employee orientation program and how should they convey this information?
2. In the HR management course Jennifer took, the book suggested using a job description sheet to identify tasks performed by an employee. Should Carter use a form like this for the counterperson's job, and if so, what would the filled-in form look like?
3. Which specific training techniques should Jennifer use to train her pressers, her cleaner-spotters, her managers, and her counter people, and why?

EXPERIENTIAL EXERCISE

The Interplay of Strategy and Training: Flying the Friendlier Skies

Purpose: The purpose of this exercise is to give you practice in developing a training program for the job of airline reservations clerk for a major airline.

Required Understanding: You should be fully acquainted with the material in this chapter and should read the following introduction and description of an airline reservations clerk's duties.

Its founders started JetBlue Airlines with a unique combination of competitive strategies: JetBlue would (1) pursue a low-cost strategy by hiring non-union employees and having many reservations and clerical people work from their homes, while (2) providing high-quality service, for instance, by emphasizing clean new planes, free in-flight food, and very friendly service. JetBlue knew that just low cost was not enough. Passengers wanted and demanded high-quality service, too. That obviously had implications for JetBlue's reservations clerk training programs.

Customers contact JetBlue's airlines reservations clerks to obtain flight schedules, prices, and itineraries. The reservations clerks use their online access tools to look up the requested information on our airline's online flight schedule system, which is updated continuously. The reservations clerk must deal courteously and expeditiously with the customer and be able to quickly find alternative flight arrangements in order to provide the customer with the itinerary that fits his or her needs. Alternative flights and prices must be found quickly, so that the customer is not kept waiting, and so that the reservations operations group maintains its efficiency standards. It is often necessary to look under various routings, since there may be a dozen or more alternative routes between the customer's starting point and destination.

You may assume that JetBlue just hired 30 new clerks, and that you must create a 3-day training program. Just about all clerks work out of their homes, although they meet periodically at local JetBlue centers.

How to Set Up the Exercise/Instructions: Divide the class into teams of five or six students. Airline reservations clerks obviously need numerous skills to perform their jobs. JetBlue Airlines has asked you to quickly develop the outline of a training program for its new reservations clerks. You may want to start by listing the job's main duties. In any case, produce the requested outline, making sure to be very specific about (1) what you want to teach the new clerks, (2) what the trainees should keep in mind regarding why they should do things in a particular way, and (3) specifically what methods and aids you suggest using to train them.

BUSINESS IN ACTION EDU-EXERCISE

Building Your *Strategic Management* Knowledge

Wisconsin-based Signicast produces metal parts from a casting process. The basic process is very old, although Signicast has improved it dramatically. For Signicast to vie with world-class competitors, it needs a new, automated plant. Many of its employees have little formal education, and lack the mathematical and computer skills the new plant will require of its employees. The question is, How should Signicast train the new plant's employees, so the computerized plant will have the tech-friendly employees it requires to succeed?[119] The firm's president, Terry Lutz, knew his plans for growing his company hinged on human resource management.[120]

Terry Lutz's experience illustrates why managers say that human resource management needs to be "strategic." Computerized machines like Signicast's are useless without competent employees to run them. The purpose of human resource management is for the company's human resource processes—screening, training, and appraising, for instance—*to produce the employee behaviors the company needs to achieve its strategic goals.* Signicast needs employees who can run the automated, computerized equipment for its new plant. With jobs that are increasingly knowledge- and technology-based, selecting the right employees, and getting them trained and performing satisfactorily, is crucial.

We discussed strategic planning in Chapter 3. Strategic human resource management means aligning the firm's human resource management policies and practices with the company's strategic goals, so that the company's HR policies and practices produce the employee behaviors the company needs to achieve its strategic goals.

Questions

1. What is Signicast's new strategy and what implications does it have for the workforce competencies the company will need?

2. Describe in detail four specific training programs and other programs the HR department can put in place to support Signicast's new strategy.

PERSONAL COMPETENCIES EDU-EXERCISE

Building Your *Leadership* Skills

Effective leadership is often the "secret ingredient" in successful organizational changes. For example, several years ago Avon Products was in trouble. Few people were signing on as Avon sales reps. It was taking the firm's research and development department 3 years to develop new products. The firm's whole "back end" operation—buying from suppliers, taking orders, and distributing products to local sales reps—lacked automation. The sales rep still took orders by hand. The company's board of directors knew it had to do something. What it did was appoint Andrea Jung as CEO. In 20 months, Avon's new CEO had turned her company around. She did it by overhauling "everything about the way Avon does business: how it advertises, manufactures, packages, and even sells its products."[121]

Major Avon-type transformations require special leaders. James McGregor Burns wrote a book in which he addressed this issue. He argued for a new type of leadership style.[122] Burns said all leadership behavior is either "transactional" or "transformational." Leaders act *transactional* when they focus on accomplishing the tasks at hand and at maintaining good relations.[123] Burns said that Avon-type changes require transformational leaders.[124] *Transformational* leaders inspire their followers to want to make the change and to throw themselves into doing so. They encourage and obtain performance beyond expectations, by formulating visions and inspiring subordinates to pursue them. Transformational leaders come across as charismatic, inspirational, considerate, and stimulating. Specifically, they are:[125]

- **Charismatic.** Employees often idolize and develop strong emotional attachments to these leaders. A typical transformational leadership questionnaire answer is, "I am ready to trust him or her to overcome any obstacle."
- **Inspirational.** Transformational leaders have the knack for passionately communicating a future idealistic organization that can be shared.
- **Considerate.** Transformational leaders treat employees as individuals. They stress helping these employees become all that they are capable of becoming.
- **Stimulating.** Transformational leaders encourage employees to approach familiar problems in new ways.

Questions

1. We discussed an eight-step process for implementing an organizational change. How exactly and in which steps will a leader find it useful to exhibit charisma, inspiration, considerateness, and stimulation?
2. Is it possible for a single leader to exhibit all these behaviors? Why or why not?

ENDNOTES

1. For a good discussion of socialization see, for example, George Chao et al., "Organizational Socialization: Its Content and Consequences," *Journal of Applied Psychology* 79, no. 5 (1994): 730–743. See also Talya Bauer et al., "Newcomer Adjustment During Organizational Socialization: A Meta-analytic Review of Antecedents, Outcomes, and Methods," *Journal of Applied Psychology* 92, no. 3 (2007): 707–721.
2. Charlotte Garvey, "The Whirlwind of a New Job," *HR Magazine* (June 2001): 111. See also Talya Bauer et al., "Newcomer Adjustment During Organizational Socialization: A Meta-analytic Review of Antecedents, Outcomes, and Methods," *Journal of Applied Psychology* 92, no. 3 (2007): 707–721.
3. Sheila Hicks et al., "Orientation Redesign," *Training and Development* (July 2006): 43–46.
4. John Kammeyer-Mueller and Connie Wanberg, "Unwrapping the Organizational Entry Process: Disentangling Multiple Antecedents and Their Pathways to Adjustments," *Journal of Applied Psychology* 88, no. 5 (2003): 779–794.
5. Sabrina Hicks, "Successful Orientation Programs," *Training & Development* (April 2000): 59. See also Howard Klein and Natasha Weaver, "The Effectiveness of an Organizational Level Orientation Program in the Socialization of New Hires," *Personnel Psychology* 53 (2000): 47–66; and Laurie Friedman, "Are You Losing Potential New Hires at Hello?" *Training and Development* (November 2006): 25–27.
6. This section based on Darin Hartley, "Technology Kicks Up Leadership Development," *Training and Development* (March 2004): 22–24.
7. www.workday.com/company/news/workday_mobility.php, accessed March 24, 2009.
8. Ed Frauenheim, "IBM Learning Programs Get a 'Second Life,'" *Workforce Management* (December 11, 2006): 6. See also J. T. Arnold, "Gaming Technology Used To Orient New Hires," *HRMagazine* (2009 HR Trendbook supp): 36, 38.
9. "Companies Invested More in Training Despite Economic Setbacks, Survey Says," *BNA Bulletin to Management* (March 7, 2002): 73. See also Andrew Paradise, "The 2008 ASTD State of the Industry Report Shows Sustained Support for Corporate Learning," *Training and Development* (November 2008): 45–51.

10. Winfred Alfred Jr. et al., "Effectiveness of Training in Organizations: A Meta Analysis of Design and Evaluation Features," *Journal of Applied Psychology* 88, no. 2 (2003): 242.

11. Nancy DeViney and Brenda Sugrue, "Learning Outsourcing: A Reality Check," *Training and Development* (December 2004): 41. See also "How Are Organizations Training Today?" *HR Focus* 86, no. 7 (July 2009): S2–S3.

12. Christine Ellis and Sarah Gale, "A Seat at the Table," *Training* (March 2001): 90–96.

13. Brenda Sugrue et al., "What in the World Is WLP?" *Training and Development* (January 2005): 51–54.

14. Harley Frazis, Diane Herz, and Michael Horrigan, "Employer-Provided Training: Results from a New Survey," *Monthly Labor Review* (May 1995): 3–17. See also Anders Gronstedt, "The Changing Face of Workplace Learning," *Training and Development* (January 2007): 20–24.

15. W. Clayton Allen, "Overview and Evolution of the ADDIE Training System" *Advances in Developing Human Resources* 8 no. 4 (November 2006): 430–441.

16. Employers increasingly utilize learning content management systems (LCMS) to compile and author training content. See, for example, Bill Perry, "Customized Content at Your Fingertips," *Training and Development* (June 2009): 29–30.

17. Marcia Jones, "Use Your Head When Identifying Skills Gaps," *Workforce* (March 2000): 118.

18. P. Nick Blanchard and James Thacker, *Effective Training: Systems, Strategies and Practices* (Upper Saddle River, NJ: Prentice Hall, 2007): 100–143.

19. Jay Bahlis, "Blueprint for Planning Learning," *Training and Development* (March 2008): 64–67.

20. Blanchard and Thacker, *Effective Training: Systems, Strategies and Practices* (Upper Saddle River, NJ: Prentice Hall, 2007): 106.

21. P. Nick Blanchard and James Thacker, *Effective Training: Systems, Strategies, and Practices* (Upper Saddle River, NJ: Prentice Hall, 2007): 8.

22. See, for example, Jennifer Salopek, "The Power of the Pyramid," *Training and Development* (May 2009): 70–73.

23. Richard Montier et al., "Competency Models Develop Top Performance," *Training and Development* (July 2006): 47–50. See also Jennifer Salopek, "The Power of the Pyramid," *Training and Development* (May 2009): 70–73.

24. See for example, Tom Krueger, "An Engaging Learning Environment," *Math Teaching* no. 217 (March 2010) 24–25.

25. Kenneth Wexley and Gary Latham, *Development and Training Human Resources in Organizations* (Upper Saddle River, NJ: Prentice Hall, 2002): 107.

26. Ibid., 82.

27. Ibid., 87.

28. Ibid., 90.

29. The American Society for Training & Development (ASTD) offers thousands of packaged training programs, such as "Be a Better Manager," "Strategic Planning 101," "12 Habits of Successful Trainers," "Mentoring," and "Using Job Aids." American Society for Training & Development, Spring and Fall Line Catalog 2007; American Society for Training and Development 2007 Buyers Guide, American Society for Training & Development, 1640 King St., Box 1443, Alexandria, VA 22313.

30. See, for example, the HRDQ catalog, www.HRDQ.com, accessed July 2010.

31. Donna Goldwaser, "Me a Trainer?" *Training* (April 2001): 60–66.

32. This is based on Richard Luecke, *Coaching and Mentoring* (Boston: Harvard Business School Press, 2004): 8–9.

33. Ibid., 9.

34. Robert Weintraub and Jennifer Martineau, "The Just in Time Imperative," *Training and Development* (June 2002): 52.

35. Aparna Nancherla, "Knowledge Delivered in Any Other Form Is . . . Perhaps Sweeter," *Training and Development* (May 2009): 54–60.

36. The recession that began around 2008 prompted a downturn in training expenditures. For example, one study estimates that total training spending in U.S. firms dropped from about $56 billion in 2008 to $48 billion in 2009. Garry Kranz, "Study: Training More Targeted Amid-Downturn," *Workforce Management* (November 16, 2009): 6.

37. Rita Zeidner, "Strategies for Saving in a Down Economy," *HR Magazine* (February 2009): 33. See also Katharine Giacalone, "Making New Employees Successful in Any Economy," *Training and Development* (June 2009): 37–39.

38. Kathryn Tyler, "Mining for Training Treasure," *HR Magazine* (September 2009): 99–102.

39. Cindy Waxer, "Steelmaker Revives Apprentice Program to Address Graying Workforce, Forge Next Leaders," *Workforce Management* (January 30, 2006): 40.

40. Kermit Kaleba, "New Changes to Apprenticeship Program Could Be Forthcoming," *Training and Development* (February 2008): 14.

41. Paula Ketter, "What Can Training Do for Brown?" *Training and Development* (May 2008): 30–36.

42. Paul Taylor et al., "A Meta-Analytic Review of Behavior Modeling Training," *Journal of Applied Psychology* 90, no. 4 (2005): 692–719.

43. See Tom Barron, "The Link Between Leadership Development and Retention," *Training and Development* (April 2004): 58–65.

44. Paul Taylor et al., "A Meta-Analytic Review of Behavior Modeling Training," *Journal of Applied Psychology* 90, no. 4 (2005): 692–719.

45. Michael Emery and Margaret Schubert, "A Trainer's Guide to Videoconferencing," *Training* (June 1993): 60. See also Mark Van Buren, "Learning Technologies: Can They or Can't They?" *Training and Development* (April 2000): 62.

46. See, for example, Kim Kleps, "Virtual Sales Training Scores a Hit," *Training and Development* (December 2006): 63–64.

47. Dina Berta, "Computer-Based Training Clicks with Both Franchisees and Their Employees," *Nation's Restaurant News* (July 9, 2001): 1, 18; See also Daniel Cable and Charles Parsons, "Socialization Tactics and Person-Organization Fit," *Personnel Psychology* 54 (2001): 1–23.

48. Michael Laff, "Simulations: Slowly Proving Their Worth," *Training and Development* (June 2007): 30–34.

49. Jenni Jarventaus, "Virtual Threat, Real Sweat," *Training and Development* (May 2007): 72–78.

50. Ed Frauenheim, "IBM Learning Programs Get a 'Second Life,'" *Workforce Management* (December 11, 2006): 6.

51. Clark Aldrich, "Engaging Mini-Games Find Niche in Training," *Training and Development* (July 2007): 22–24.

52. Dave Zielinski, "Training Games," *HR Magazine* (March 2010): 64–65.

53. Pat Galagan, "Second That," *Training and Development* (February 2008): 34–37. See also David Wilkins, "Learning 2.0 and Workplace Communities," *Training and Development* (April 2009): 28–31.

54. "What Do Simulations Cost?" *Training and Development* (June 2007): 88. See also Paul Harris, "Immersive Learning Seeks a Foothold," *Training and Development* (January 2009): 40–45.

55. Ellen Zimmerman, "Better Training Is Just a Click Away," *Workforce* (January 2001): 36–42.

56. John Zonneveld, "GM Dealer Training Goes Global," *Training and Development* (December 2006): 47–51.

57. "The Next Generation of Corporate Learning," *Training and Development* (June 2003): 47.

58. Traci Sitzmann et al., "The Comparative Effectiveness of Web-Based and Classroom Instruction: A Meta-Analysis," *Personnel Psychology* 59 (2006): 623–664.

59. Ibid.

60. For a list of guidelines for using e-learning, see, for example, Mark Simon, "E-learning Know How," *Training and Development* (January 2009): 34–39.

61. Renee DeRouin et al., "Optimizing E-Learning: Research-Based Guidelines for Learner Controlled Training," *Human Resource Management* 43, no. 2 (Summer/Fall 2004): 147–162.

62. "The Next Generation of Corporate Learning," *Training and Development* (June 2004): 47.

63. Ruth Clark, "Harnessing the Virtual Classroom," *Training and Development* (November 2005): 40–46.

64. Jennifer Taylor Arnold, "Learning on-the-Fly," *HR Magazine* (September 2007): 137.

65. www.dominknow.com/, accessed March 23, 2009.

66. Elizabeth Agnvall, "Just-in-Time Training," *HR Magazine* (May 2006): 67–78.

67. Ibid.

68. For a similar program, and Accenture, see Don Vanthournout and Dana Koch, "Training at Your Fingertips," *Training and Development* (September 2008): 52–57.

69. Marcia Conner, "Twitter 101: Are You Reading?" *Training and Development* (August 2009): 24–26.

70. Paul Harris, "A New Era for Accessibility," *Training & Development* (April 2009): 58–61.

71. Susan Ladika, "When Learning Lasts a Lifetime," *HR Magazine* (May 2008): 57.

72. Paula Ketter, "The Hidden Disability," *Training and Development* (June 2006): 34–40.

73. Jennifer Salopek, "The Growth of Succession Management," *Training and Development* (June 2007): 22–24; and Kermit Kalleba, "Businesses Continue to Push for Lifelong Learning," *Training and Development* (June 2007): 14.

74. Rita Zeidner, "One Workforce—Many Languages," *HR Magazine* (January 2009): 33–37.

75. "Adams Mark Hotel & Resorts Launches Diversity Training Program," *Hotel and Motel Management* 216, no. 6 (April 2001): 15.

76. Douglas Shuit, "Sound of the Retreat," *Workforce Management* (September 2003): 40.

77. "For Gap, Management Training Doesn't Stop at the Border," *BNA Bulletin to Management* (February 2005): 63.

78. www.geert-hofstede.com/geert_hofstede_resources.shtml, accessed February 3, 2010.

79. See, for example, Baiyin Yang et al., "Does It Matter Where to Conduct Training? Accounting for Cultural Factors," *Human Resource Management Review* 19 (2009): 324–333.

80. See for example, Jeff Kristick, "Filling the Leadership Pipeline," *Training and Development* (June 2009): 49–51.

81. Christopher Glynn, "Building a Learning Infrastructure," *Training and Development* (January 2008): 38–43.

82. Jack Zenger, Dave Ulrich, and Norm Smallwood, "The New Leadership Development," *Training and Development* (March 2000): 22–27. See also W. David Patton and Connie Pratt, "Assessing the Training Needs of High Potential Managers," *Public Personnel Management* 31, no. 4 (Winter 2002): 465–474; and Ann Locke and Arlene Tarantino, "Strategic Leadership Development," *Training and Development* (December 2006): 53–55.

83. Mike Czarnowsky, "Executive Development," *Training and Development* (September 2008): 44–45.

84. Ann Pomeroy, "Head of the Class," *HR Magazine* (January 2005): 57.

85. "Thrown into Deep End, Workers Surface as Leaders," *BNA Bulletin to Management* (July 11, 2002): 223.

86. Michael Marquardt, "Harnessing the Power of Action Learning," *Training and Development* (June 2004): 26–32.

87. Following quoted or paraphrased from P. Nick Blanchard and James Thacker, *Effective Training: Systems, Strategies and Practices* (Upper Saddle River, NJ: Prentice Hall, 2007): 233–234.

88. See, for example, Michael Laff, "Serious Gaming: The Trainer's New Best Friend," *Training and Development* (January 2007): 52–56.

89. Jean Thilmany, "Acting Out," *HR Magazine* (January 2007): 95–100.

90. http://www.myersbriggs.org/type-use-for-everyday-life/mbti-typeatwork/, accessed July 2010.

91. "AMA Seminars," October 2009–2010, the American Management Association, www.AMA seminars.org.

92. For a list of Harvard programs see, for example, their intensive two-day conferences in the brochure from their center for management research, "Programs on Leadership for Senior Executives," www.execseminars.com, accessed July, 2010.

93. Chris Musselwhite, "University Executive Education Gets Real," *Training and Development* (May 2006): 57.

94. Jeanne Meister, "Universities Put to the Test," *Workforce Management* (December 11, 2006): 27–30.

95. Ann Pomeroy, "Head of the Class," *HR Magazine* (January 2005): 57.

96. "Corporate Universities Getting a Refresher," *Workforce Management* (June 11, 2007): 23.

97. Russell Gerbman, "Corporate Universities 101," *HR Magazine* (February 2000): 101–106. Before creating an in-house university, the employer needs to ensure that the corporate university's vision, mission, and programs support the company's strategic goals. See Michael Laff, "Centralized Training Leads to Nontraditional Universities," *Training and Development* (January 2007): 27–29.

98. "Corporate Universities Getting a Refresher," *Workforce Management* (June 11, 2007): 23.

99. Joseph Toto, "Untapped World of Peer Coaching," *Training and Development* (April 2006): 69–72.

100. James Smither et al., "Can Working with an Executive Coach Improve Multiscore Feedback Ratings Over Time?" *Personnel Psychology* 56, no. 1 (Spring 2003): 23–44.

101. "As Corporate Coaching Goes Mainstream, Key Prerequisite Overlooked: Assessment," *BNA Bulletin to Management* (May 16, 2006): 153. See also Joyce Bono et al., "A Survey of Executive Coaching Practices," *Personnel Psychology* 62 (2009): 361–364.

102. Quoted and abstracted from, "Five Rules for Talent Management in the New Economy," TowersWatson.com.

103. Quoted and abstracted from, Martin and Conrad Schmidt, "How to Keep Your Top Talent," *Harvard Business Review* (May 2010): 53–61.

104. Quoted and abstracted from ibid.

105. Quoted and abstracted from ibid.

106. See, for example, John Austin, "Mapping Out a Game Plan for Change," *HR Magazine* (April 2009): 39–42.

107. Ed Frauenheim, "Lost in the Shuffle," *Workforce Management* (January 14, 2008): 13.

108. The steps are based on Michael Beer, Russell Eisenstat, and Burt Spector, "Why Change Programs Don't Produce Change," *Harvard Business Review* (November–December 1990): 158–166; Thomas Cummings and Christopher Worley, *Organization Development and Change* (Minneapolis, MN: West Publishing Company, 1993); John P. Kotter, "Leading Change: Why Transformation Efforts Fail," *Harvard Business Review* (March–April 1995): 59–66; and John P. Kotter, *Leading Change* (Boston: Harvard Business School Press, 1996). Change doesn't necessarily have to be painful. See, for example, Eric Abrahamson, "Change Without Pain," *Harvard Business Review* (July–August 2000): 75–79; and Michael Beer and Nitin Nohria, "Cracking the Code of Change," *Harvard Business Review* (June 2000): 133–141. See also David Herold et al., "Beyond Change Management: A Multilevel Investigation of Contextual and Personal Influences on Employee's Commitment to Change," *Journal of Applied Psychology* 92, no. 4 (2007): 949.

109. Michael Beer, Russell Eisenstat, and Burt Spector, "Why Change Programs Don't Produce Change," *Harvard Business Review* (November–December 1990): 164. See also Remco Schimmel and Dennis Muntslag, "Learning Barriers: A Framework for the Examination of Structural Impediments to Organizational Change," *Human Resource Management* 48, no. 3 (May–June 2009): 399–416.

110. Stacie Furst and Daniel Cable, "Employee Resistance to Organizational Change: Managerial Influence Tactics and Leader Member Exchange," *Journal of Applied Psychology* 3, no. 2 (2008): 453.

111. Wendell French and Cecil Bell Jr., *Organization Development* (Upper Saddle River, NJ: Prentice Hall, 1999): 155–190. See also P. Nick Blanchard and James Thacker, *Effective Training* (Upper Saddle River NJ: Pearson, 2007): 38–46.

112. Darin Hartley, "OD Wired," *Training and Development* (August 2004): 20–24.

113. See, for example, Charlie Morrow, M. Quintin Jarrett, and Melvin Rupinski, "An Investigation of the Effect and Economic Utility of Corporate-Wide Training," *Personnel Psychology* 50 (1997): 91–119. See also Antonio Aragon-Sanchez et al., "Effects of Training on Business Results," *International Journal of Human Resource Management* 14, no. 6 (September 2003): 956–980.

114. Jeffrey Berk, "Training Evaluations," *Training and Development* (September 2004): 39–45.

115. Todd Raphel, "What Learning Management Reports Do for You," *Workforce* 80, no. 6 (June 2001): 56–58. See also Jack Phillips and Patti Phillips, "Measuring What Matters: How CEOs View Learning Success," *Training and Development* (August 2009): 45–49.

116. Alan Saks and Monica Belcourt, "An Investigation of Training Activities and Transfer of Training in Organizations," *Human Resource Management* 45, no. 4 (Winter 2006): 629–648. See also K. Lee, "Implement Training Successfully," *Training* 46 no. 5 (June 2009): 16.

117. Elaine Biech, "Learning Eye To Eye: Aligning Training to Business Objectives," *Training and Development* (April 2009): 50–53.

118. Tony Bingaman and Pat Galagan, "Training: They're Lovin' It," *Training and Development* (November 2006): 30.

119. Ben Nagler, "Recasting Employees Into Teams," *Workforce* (January 1998): 101–106.

120. Ibid., p. 103.

121. "Avon Sees China Operation as a Sole Business Unit," *China Business Daily News* (December 13, 2005): 1; and "Avon, the Net, and Glass Ceiling," *Business Week* (February 6, 2005): 104; Katrina Brooker, "It Took a Lady to Save Avon," *Fortune* (October 15, 2001): 203–208.

122. J. M. Burns, *Leadership* (New York: Harper, 1978).

123. See, for example, Bernard Bass, "Theory of Transformational Leadership Redux," *Leadership Quarterly* (Winter 1995): 463–478.

124. Gary Yukl, *Leadership in Organizations* (Upper Saddle River, NJ: Prentice Hall, 1998): 324.

125. Bernard Bass, *Leadership and Performance Beyond Expectations* (New York: The Free Press, 1985); and Gary Yukl, *Leadership in Organizations* (Upper Saddle River, NJ: Prentice Hall, 1998): 298–299.

7

Performance and Talent Management

SYNOPSIS

- Basic Concepts in Performance Appraisal
- Appraisal Methods
- Dealing with Appraisal Problems and the Appraisal Interview
- Performance Management
- Talent Management Practices and Employee Appraisal

Source: Servais Mont/Newscom.

When you finish studying this chapter, you should be able to:

1. Explain the purpose of performance appraisal.
2. Answer the question, "Who should do the appraising?"
3. Discuss the pros and cons of at least eight performance appraisal methods.
4. Give examples of five potential appraisal problems.
5. Explain how to conduct an appraisal feedback interview.
6. Explain how to install a performance management program.
7. Illustrate the effects of segmenting and actively managing a company's talent.

INTRODUCTION

If you're planning to work for Google, be prepared for some tough and candid performance appraisals.[1] Google uses a technique called "360-degree feedback." This means several people (usually above, at, and below your level, as well as outside customers and suppliers) will appraise you. And Google's system uses special software to gather information, not just about your performance, but also about how you're interacting with just about everyone you deal with on the job. Although the system works very well at Google, that sort of pressure might not go over well at many other firms. But it can keep employees focused on providing great service. ▪

BASIC CONCEPTS IN PERFORMANCE APPRAISAL

Few things supervisors do are fraught with more peril than appraising subordinates' performance. Employees tend to be overly optimistic about what their ratings will be. And, they know that their raises, careers, and peace of mind may hinge on how you rate them. As if that's not enough, few appraisal processes are as fair and above-board as employers think they are. Hundreds of obvious and not-so-obvious problems (such as bias, and the tendency for supervisors to rate everyone "average") undermine the process. However, the perils notwithstanding, performance appraisal plays a central role in human resource management.

The Performance Appraisal Cycle

performance appraisal

Evaluating an employee's current and/or past performance relative to his or her performance standards.

Performance appraisal means evaluating an employee's current and/or past performance relative to his or her performance standards. You may equate appraisal forms like Figure 7.1 with "performance appraisal," but appraisal involves more than forms. Effective appraisal also requires that the supervisor set performance standards. And it requires that the employee receives the training, feedback, and incentives required to eliminate performance deficiencies.

Stripped to its essentials, performance appraisal always involves (1) setting work standards, (2) assessing the employee's actual performance relative to those standards, and (3) providing feedback to the employee with the aim of helping him or her to eliminate performance deficiencies or to continue to perform above par. As Figure 7.2 summarizes, managers call these three steps the *performance appraisal cycle*.

1 Explain the purpose of performance appraisal.

Why Appraise Performance?

There are five reasons to appraise subordinates' performance.

- First, most employers still base pay, promotion, and retention decisions on the employee's appraisal.[2]
- Second, appraisals play an central role in the employer's *performance management* process. Performance management means continuously making sure that each employee's performance makes sense in terms of the company's overall goals.
- Third, the appraisal lets you and the subordinate develop a plan for correcting any deficiencies, and to reinforce the things the subordinate does right.
- Fourth, appraisals should serve a useful career planning purpose. They provide an opportunity to review the employee's career plans in light of his or her exhibited strengths and weaknesses. The special career management module at the end of this book (pages 427–437) discusses career issues.
- Finally, supervisors use appraisals to identify employees' training and development needs. Conducted correctly, the appraisal should enable the supervisor to identify if there is a "performance gap" between the employee's performance and his or her standards. And it should help identify the cause of any such gap, and the remedial steps required.

The Importance of Continuous Feedback

For accomplishing several of these aims, traditional annual or semi-annual appraisal reviews make sense. For example, promotions and raises tend to be periodic decisions. Similarly, you probably wouldn't want to make career decisions without at least several months of data gathering and introspection.

FIGURE 7.1

**Online Faculty
Evaluation Form**

Source: Used with permission of
Central Oregon Community College.

CENTRAL OREGON
community college

EMPLOYEES
Benefits 2008-09
Faculty Resources
Forms
Policies & Procedures
Resources
Risk Management
Services
Wellness

COCC Home > Employees > Faculty Resources > Faculty Guidelines > Faculty Evaluation Standards > Faculty Evaluation Form

Faculty Evaluation Form

INSTRUCTIONS FOR COMPLETING STUDENT EVALUATION FORM

Today you are being asked to evaluate this course and the instructor. Please read and answer each question thoughtfully and honestly.

Evaluations are helpful to faculty in improving their teaching and their courses. They are also an important element in the College's ongoing evaluation of faculty for tenure and promotion.

Your answers are anonymous and confidential. Comments will be typed so that the instructor cannot identify your handwriting. Your answers will be returned to the instructor only after final grades for this course have been recorded.

Your written comments on the last page are especially helpful.

CRN _____   Course_____

Instructor_____   Term_____

STUDENT EVALUATION OF INSTRUCTION

Student Information: (Please circle your answers).

1. I had completed the recommended preparation (prerequisites) for this course before beginning the course. *(Select NA if the course has no prerequisites.)*

All   Most   Some   Very Few   Don't Know   NA

2. I attended classes.

All   Most   Some   Very Few   NA

3. To be adequately prepared for this class, I feel I need to spend this many hours per week outside of class, studying and preparing assignments:

15+ hours   12-14 hours   9-11 hours   7-8 hours   4-6 hours   1-3 hours

4. For this course, I expect to receive a grade of:

A   B   C   D   F

Evaluation of Instruction: (7 = *strongly agree..................... 1 = strongly disagree).*

1. The learning objectives (competencies) of this course have been made clear.

7   6   5   4   3   2   1

2. The course activities are related to the learning objectives (competencies).

7   6   5   4   3   2   1

3. The instructor is well-prepared for class.

7   6   5   4   3   2   1

4. The instructor is available during posted office hours or by appointment.

7   6   5   4   3   2   1

5. Feedback on my work is timely, constructive, and clear enough to benefit my learning.

7   6   5   4   3   2   1

6. My grades accurately measure my learning in this class.

7   6   5   4   3   2   1

7. The instructor creates a learning environment in which diverse points of view are respected and can be freely expressed.

7   6   5   4   3   2   1

8. Based on what I have learned, I would recommend this course to other students.

7   6   5   4   3   2   1

COMMENTS

Your written comments are especially helpful. Comments will be typed so that the instructor cannot identify your handwriting. Your answers will be returned to the instructor only after final grades for this course have been recorded.

1. What are the most valuable aspects of this course and/or the way the course was taught?

2. Even excellent courses can be improved. Can you give some constructive suggestions for making the course better?

3. Do you wish to comment on any of your ratings in the "Evaluation of Instruction" section on the

Previous page? If so, please state the item number to which your comment refers.

FIGURE 7.2

The Three-Step Performance Appraisal Cycle

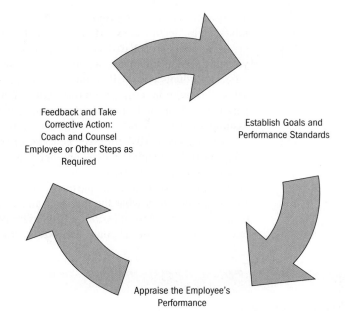

Feedback and Take Corrective Action: Coach and Counsel Employee or Other Steps as Required

Establish Goals and Performance Standards

Appraise the Employee's Performance

However, it's usually a mistake to wait until the actual "appraisal" to let employees know what they're doing wrong and doing right. Aligning the employee's efforts with the job's standards should be a continuous process. When you see a performance problem, the time to take action is immediately—there is no substitute for nudging your employee's performance back into line continuously and incrementally. Similarly, when someone does something well, the best reinforcement comes immediately, not six months later.

Performance Management

Recognizing this, many employers today take a more continuous (and often automated) approach to the performance appraisal cycle. For example, at Toyota Motor's Lexington, Kentucky Camry plant, the supervisors don't sit with individual employees to fill out forms and appraise them. Instead, teams of employees monitor their own results, even posting individual daily performance metrics. In frequent meetings they continuously align those results with the work team's standards and with the plant's overall quality and productivity needs. They do this by continuously adjusting how they and their team members do things. Team members who need coaching and training receive it, and procedures that need changing are changed. This is performance management in action. **Performance management** is the *continuous* process of identifying, measuring, and developing the performance of individuals and teams and *aligning* their performance with the organization's *goals*.[3] We'll discuss it more fully, later in the chapter.

Defining the Employee's Goals and Performance Standards

In any case, most employees need and expect to know ahead of time on what basis their employers will appraise them.[4] Ideally, each employee's goals should derive from and contribute to the company's overall aims. However, setting useful goals is not as simple as it may appear. There is an art to setting effective goals.

First the supervisor must decide what to measure. In practice, many employers simply use packaged employee appraisal forms, similar to that in Figure 7.1. The appraisal form shows what will be measured, for instance, "The instructor is well prepared." We'll see that other firms use a management by objectives approach. Thus the CEO may have a goal to double sales this year. Then her vice president of sales has his or her own sales goals, and each salesperson has his or her sales goal, set in discussions with his or her supervisor.

TALENT MANAGEMENT: BASING APPRAISAL STANDARDS ON REQUIRED COMPETENCIES
Another option is to appraise employees based on the competencies and skills the job requires. For example, at Sharp Electronics, skills in miniaturizing components are particularly valued for engineers because of the firm's miniaturization strategy; similarly, BP's exploration division appraises

performance management
The process through which companies ensure that employees are working toward organizational goals. It includes practices through which the manager defines the employee's goals and work, develops the employee's skills and capabilities, evaluates the person's goal-directed behavior, and then rewards him or her in a fashion consistent with the company's and the person's needs.

and rewards employees based on a skills matrix that shows (1) the basic skills required to do that job (such as "technical expertise") and (2) the minimum level of each skill that job requires.

Another approach to deciding what to measure is to set measurable goals for each expectation you have for the employee. Suppose you expect your sales manager to "handle the company's three biggest accounts personally," and to "manage the sales force." You might measure the "personal selling" activity in terms of a money goal—how many dollars of sales the manager is to generate personally. You might measure "managing the sales force" in terms of a turnover goal (on the assumption that less than 10% of the sales force will quit in any given year if morale is high).

But is, say, a 10% turnover goal reasonable? Managers soon find that setting goals is one thing; setting effective goals is another. One way to think of this is to remember that the goals you set should be "SMART." They are *specific*, and clearly state the desired results. They are *measurable*, and answer the question "How much?" They are *attainable*. They are *relevant*, and clearly derive from what the manager and company want to achieve. And they are *timely*, and reflect deadlines and milestones.[5] Behavioral science research studies provide useful insights into setting motivational goals. The HR in Practice feature summarizes these findings.

HR IN PRACTICE

How to Set Effective Goals

Behavioral science research studies suggest four guidelines for setting performance goals:

1. *Assign Specific Goals.* Employees who receive specific goals usually perform better than those who do not.
2. *Assign Measurable Goals.* Put goals in quantitative terms and include target dates or deadlines. If measurable results will not be available, then "satisfactory completion"—such as "satisfactorily attended workshop" or "satisfactorily completed his or her degree"—is the next best thing. In any case, always set target dates or deadlines.
3. *Assign Challenging but Doable Goals.* Goals should be challenging, but not so difficult that they appear impossible or unrealistic.

4. *Encourage Participation.* Throughout your management career, you'll be faced with this question: Should I just tell my employees what their goals are, or should I let them participate with me in setting their goals? The evidence suggests that participatively set goals do not consistently result in higher performance than assigned goals, nor do assigned goals consistently result in higher performance than participatively set ones. It is only when the participatively set goals are more difficult (are set higher) than the assigned ones that the participatively set goals produce higher performance. Because it tends to be easier to set higher standards when your employees participate in the process, participation tends to facilitate standards setting and performance.[6]

In practice, as we said, it's not unusual to have supervisors appraise employees not relative to goals, but based on generic, subjective (but still *carefully defined* and *previously discussed*) criteria such as "teamwork" and "quality" on an appraisal form. But again, with or without numerical goals, employees should always know ahead of time how and on what basis you're going to appraise them.[7]

Who Should Do the Appraising?

Appraisals by the immediate supervisor are still the heart of most appraisal processes. Getting a supervisor's appraisal is relatively straightforward and also makes sense. The supervisor should be and usually is in the best position to observe and evaluate his or her subordinate's performance. The supervisor is also responsible for that person's performance.

Yet, although widely used, supervisors' ratings are no panacea, and relying only on them is not always advisable. For example, an employee's supervisor may not understand or appreciate how customers and colleagues who interact with the employee rate his or her performance. Furthermore, there is always some danger of bias for or against the employee. If so, managers have several options.

PEER APPRAISALS With more firms using self-managing teams, appraisal of an employee by his or her peers—peer appraisal—is more popular. Typically, an employee due for an annual appraisal chooses an appraisal chairperson. The latter then selects one supervisor and three peers to evaluate the employee's work.

Research indicates that peer appraisals can be effective. One study involved undergraduates placed into self-managing work groups. The researchers found that peer appraisals had "an immediate positive impact on [improving] perception of open communication, task motivation,

2 Answer the question, "Who should do the appraising?"

A rating committee is usually composed of the employee's immediate supervisor and three or four other supervisors.

social loafing, group viability, cohesion, and satisfaction."[8] Employees, in other words, seem to be motivated to meet their colleagues' expectations.

RATING COMMITTEES Some companies use rating committees. A rating committee is usually composed of the employee's immediate supervisor and three or four other supervisors.[9]

Using multiple raters is advantageous. It can help cancel out problems such as bias on the part of individual raters.[10] It can also provide a way to include in the appraisal the different facets of an employee's performance observed by different appraisers. Multiple raters often see different facets of an employee's performance. Studies often find that the ratings obtained from different sources rarely match.[11] It's therefore advisable to at least obtain ratings from the supervisor, his or her boss, and perhaps another manager who is familiar with the employee's work.[12] At a minimum, most employers require that the supervisor's boss sign off on any appraisals the supervisor does.

SELF-RATINGS Some employers obtain employees' self-ratings, usually in conjunction with supervisors' ratings. The basic problem, of course, is that employees usually rate themselves higher than do their supervisors or peers.[13] One study found that, when asked to rate their own job performances, 40% of employees in jobs of all types placed themselves in the top 10%, and virtually all remaining employees rated themselves at least in the top 50%.[14] In another study, subjects' self-ratings actually correlated negatively with their subsequent performance in an assessment center—the higher they appraised themselves, they worse they did in the center. In contrast, an average of the person's supervisor, peer, and subordinate ratings predicted the subjects' assessment center performance.[15]

APPRAISAL BY SUBORDINATES Many employers have subordinates rate their managers, usually for developmental rather than for pay purposes. Anonymity affects such upward feedback. Managers who get feedback from subordinates who identify themselves view the upward feedback process more positively than do managers who get anonymous feedback. However, subordinates prefer giving anonymous responses (not surprisingly), and those who must identify themselves tend to give inflated ratings.[16]

Upward feedback can improve a manager's performance. One study focused on 252 managers during five annual administrations of an upward feedback program. Managers who were initially rated poor or moderate "showed significant improvements in [their] upward feedback ratings over the five-year period." And, managers who met with their subordinates to discuss their upward feedback improved more than the managers who did not.[17]

360-DEGREE FEEDBACK With 360-degree feedback, the employer collects performance information all around an employee—from his or her supervisors, subordinates, peers, and internal or external customers—generally for developmental rather than pay purposes.[18] The usual process is to have the raters complete online appraisal surveys on the ratee. Computerized systems then compile all this

FIGURE 7.3

Online 360-Degree Feedback

Source: www.hr-survey.com/sd3609q.htm, accessed April 28, 2009. Used with permission of HR-Survey.com, LLC.

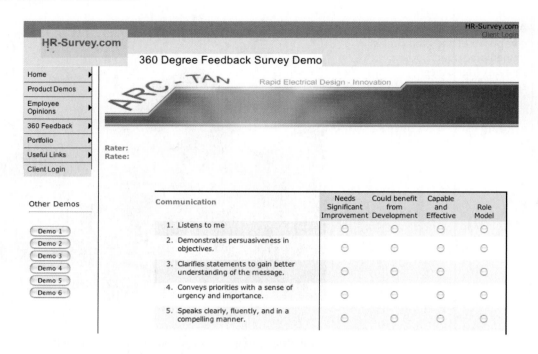

feedback into individualized reports to ratees (see the sample in Figure 7.3). The person may then meet with his or her supervisor to develop a self-improvement plan.

Results are mixed. Participants seem to prefer this approach, but one study concluded that multisource feedback led to "generally small" improvements in subsequent ratings by supervisors, peers, and subordinates. Improvement was most likely to occur when the feedback the person received indicated that change was necessary, and when the recipients believed that change was necessary and had a positive view of the change process.[19] Also, 360-degree appraisals are more candid when subordinates know rewards or promotions are not involved.

There are several ways to improve 360-degree appraisals.

- Anchor the 360-degree rating dimensions (such as "conflict management") with specific behavioral examples (such as "effectively deals with conflicts").[20]
- Carefully train the people who are giving and receiving the feedback.[21]
- With so many appraisers involved, each potentially with his or her own ax to grind, make sure that the feedback the person receives is productive, unbiased, and development oriented.[22]
- Reduce the administrative costs associated with collecting multisource feedback by using a Web-based system such as the one in Figure 7.3. This lets the rater log in, open a screen with a rating scale, and rate the person along a series of competencies with ratings such as "capable and effective."[23]

APPRAISAL METHODS

The manager usually conducts the actual appraisal using one or more of the formal methods we describe in this section.

Graphic Rating Scale Method

3 Discuss the pros and cons of at least eight performance appraisal methods.

A graphic rating scale lists a number of traits and a range of performance for each. As in Figure 7.4, a typical scale lists traits (such as teamwork) and a range of performance standards (in Figure 7.4, Below Expectations, Meets Expectations, and Role Model) for each trait. The supervisor rates each subordinate by circling or checking the score that best describes the subordinate's performance for each trait, and then totals the scores for all traits.

Alternation Ranking Method

Ranking employees from best to worst on a trait or traits is another popular appraisal method. Because it is usually easier to distinguish between the worst and best employees than to rank

Sample Performance Rating Form

Employee's Name _____   Level: Entry-level employee

Manager's Name _____

Key Work Responsibilities	Results/Goals to be Achieved
1. _____	1. _____
2. _____	2. _____
3. _____	3. _____
4. _____	4. _____

Communication

1	2	3	4	5

Below Expectations	Meets Expectations	Role Model
Even with guidance, fails to prepare straight-forward communications, including forms, paperwork, and records, in a timely and accurate manner; products require minimal corrections. Even with guidance, fails to adapt style and materials to communicate straightforward information.	With guidance, prepares straightforward communications, including forms, paperwork, and records, in a timely and accurate manner; products require minimal corrections. With guidance, adapts style and materials to communicate straightforward information.	Independently prepares communications, such as forms, paperwork, and records, in a timely, clear, and accurate manner; products require few, if any, corrections. Independently adapts style and materials to communicate information.

Organizational Know-How

1	2	3	4	5

Below Expectations	Meets Expectations	Role Model
<performance standards appear here>	<performance standards appear here>	<performance standards appear here>

Personal Effectiveness

1	2	3	4	5

Below Expectations	Meets Expectations	Role Model
<performance standards appear here>	<performance standards appear here>	<performance standards appear here>

Teamwork

1	2	3	4	5

Below Expectations	Meets Expectations	Role Model
<performance standards appear here>	<performance standards appear here>	<performance standards appear here>

Achieving Business Results

1	2	3	4	5

Below Expectations	Meets Expectations	Role Model
<performance standards appear here>	<performance standards appear here>	<performance standards appear here>

(continued)

FIGURE 7.4

Sample Graphic Rating Form with Behavioral Examples

Source: Sample Performance Rating Form from Elaine D. Pulakos, *Performance Management: A Roadmap for Developing, Implementing and Evaluating Performance Management Systems* (SHRM Foundation, 2004): 16–17.

Results Assessment

Accomplishment 1: _____

1	2	3	4	5
Low Impact		**Moderate Impact**		**High Impact**
The efficiency or effectiveness of operations remained the same or improved only minimally. The quality of products remained the same or improved only minimally.		The efficiency or effectiveness of operations improved quite a lot. The quality of products improved quite a lot.		The efficiency or effectiveness of operations improved tremendously. The quality of products improved tremendously.

Accomplishment 2: _____

1	2	3	4	5
Low Impact		**Moderate Impact**		**High Impact**
The efficiency or effectiveness of operations remained the same or improved only minimally. The quality of products remained the same or improved only minimally.		The efficiency or effectiveness of operations improved quite a lot. The quality of products improved quite a lot.		The efficiency or effectiveness of operations improved tremendously. The quality of products improved tremendously.

Narrative

_____

_____

_____

_____

_____

Areas to be Developed	Actions	Completion Date

Manager's Signature _____ Date _____

Employee's Signature _____ Date _____

The above employee signature indicates receipt of, but not necessarily concurrence with, the evaluation herein.

FIGURE 7.4

(Continued)

FIGURE 7.5

Alternation Ranking Method

ALTERNATION RANKING SCALE

Trait: _____

For the trait you are measuring, list all the employees you want to rank. Put the highest-ranking employee's name on line 1. Put the lowest-ranking employee's name on line 20. Then list the next highest ranking on line 2, the next lowest ranking on line 19, and so on. Continue until all names are on the scale.

Highest-ranking employee

1. _____	11. _____
2. _____	12. _____
3. _____	13. _____
4. _____	14. _____
5. _____	15. _____
6. _____	16. _____
7. _____	17. _____
8. _____	18. _____
9. _____	19. _____
10. _____	20. _____

Lowest-ranking employee

them, an alternation ranking method is useful. With this method the supervisor uses a form like that in Figure 7.5 to specify the employee who is highest on the trait being measured and also the one who is the lowest. He or she alternates between highest and lowest until all employees to be rated have been ranked.

Paired Comparison Method

With the paired comparison method, every subordinate to be rated is paired with and compared to every other subordinate on each trait. For example, suppose there are five employees to be rated. With this method, a chart such as that in Figure 7.6 shows all possible pairs of employees

FIGURE 7.6

Paired Comparison Method

Note: + means "better than," – means "worse than." For each chart, add up the number of +'s in each column to get the highest ranked employee.

FOR THE TRAIT "QUALITY OF WORK"

Employee rated:

As Compared to:	A Art	B Maria	C Chuck	D Diane	E José
A Art		+	+	–	–
B Maria	–		–	–	–
C Chuck	–	+		+	–
D Diane	+	+	–		+
E José	+	+	+	–	

↑ Maria ranks highest here

FOR THE TRAIT "CREATIVITY"

Employee rated:

As Compared to:	A Art	B Maria	C Chuck	D Diane	E José
A Art		–	–	–	–
B Maria	+		–	+	+
C Chuck	+	+		–	+
D Diane	+	–	+		–
E José	+	–	–	+	

↑ Art ranks highest here

for each trait. Then for each trait, the supervisor indicates (with a plus or minus) who is the better employee of the pair. Next, the number of times an employee is rated better is added up. In Figure 7.6 employee Maria ranked highest (has the most plus marks) for "quality of work," and Art ranked highest for "creativity."

Forced Distribution Method

With the forced distribution method, the manager places predetermined percentages of subordinates in performance categories, as when a professor "grades on a curve." About a fourth of Fortune 500 companies, including Sun, Microsoft, Conoco, and Intel, use forced distribution.[24] The advantages are that forced distribution (1) prevents supervisors from leniently rating most employees "satisfactory," and (2) makes top and bottom performers stand out.

EXAMPLES   For many years, Sun Microsystems managers appraised employees in groups of about 30 (Oracle Corporation acquired Sun in 2009). There was a top 20%, a middle 70%, and a bottom 10%. The bottom 10% could either take a quick exit package or embark on a 90-day performance improvement plan. If still in the bottom 10% in 90 days, they got a chance to resign and take severance pay. Some decided to stay, but "if it doesn't work out" the firm fired them without severance.[25] GE, which first popularized forced ranking, has been injecting more flexibility into its system. For instance, it no longer strictly adheres to its famous 20/70/10 split, and tells managers to use more common sense in assigning rankings.[26]

DRAWBACKS   While widely used, some balk at forced distribution appraisals. As most students know, forced distribution grading is unforgiving. With forced distribution, you're either in the top 5% or 10% (and thus get that "A"), or you're not. And, if you're in the bottom 5% or 10%, you get an "F," no questions asked. Your professor hasn't much wiggle room. In one survey 77% of responding employers were at least "somewhat satisfied" with forced ranking, while the rest were dissatisfied with it. The biggest complaints: 44% said it damages morale, and 47% said it creates interdepartmental inequities, since "high-performing teams must cut 10% of their workers while low-performing teams are still allowed to retain 90% of theirs."[27] Some writers refer unkindly to forced ranking as "Rank and Yank."[28]

Given this, employers need to be vigilant to protect these appraisal plans from managerial abuse. Office politics and managerial bias can taint ratings. To protect against bias claims, employers should take several steps.[29] Appoint a review committee to review any employee's low ranking. Train raters to be objective. And consider using multiple raters in conjunction with the forced distribution approach.

Critical Incident Method

The critical incident method entails keeping an anecdotal record of good or undesirable examples of an employee's work-related behavior and reviewing it with the employee at predetermined times. Employers often compile such incidents to supplement a rating or ranking method. Keeping a running list of critical incidents provides concrete examples of what specifically the subordinates can do to eliminate any performance deficiencies. It also provides opportunities for mid-year corrections if required. Compiling incidents all year also helps reduce supervisors' tendencies to focus unduly on just the last few weeks when appraising subordinates' performance.

Behaviorally Anchored Rating Scales

A behaviorally anchored rating scale (BARS) is an appraisal method that combines the benefits of critical incidents and quantitative ratings by anchoring a quantified scale with specific narrative examples of good and poor performance ("behavioral competencis" to psychologists). Figure 7.7 is an example of a BARS. It shows the behaviorally anchored rating scale for the trait "salesmanship skills" used for an automobile salesperson. Note how the various performance levels, from 10 (high) to 1 (low), are anchored with specific behavioral examples such as "The

FIGURE 7.7

Behaviorally Anchored Rating Scale

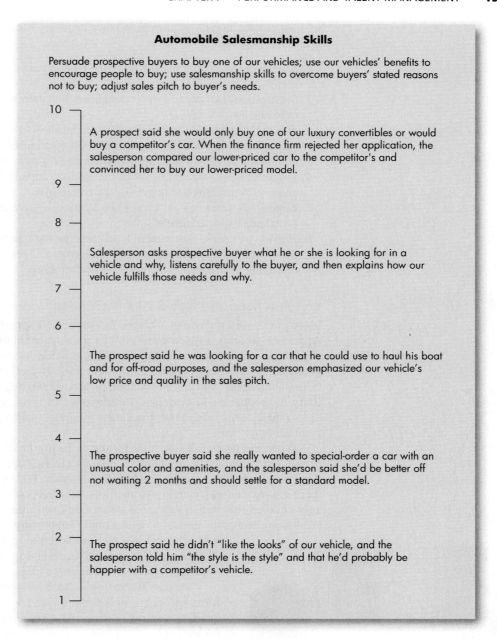

Automobile Salesmanship Skills

Persuade prospective buyers to buy one of our vehicles; use our vehicles' benefits to encourage people to buy; use salesmanship skills to overcome buyers' stated reasons not to buy; adjust sales pitch to buyer's needs.

10 —

A prospect said she would only buy one of our luxury convertibles or would buy a competitor's car. When the finance firm rejected her application, the salesperson compared our lower-priced car to the competitor's and convinced her to buy our lower-priced model.

9 —

8 —

Salesperson asks prospective buyer what he or she is looking for in a vehicle and why, listens carefully to the buyer, and then explains how our vehicle fulfills those needs and why.

7 —

6 —

The prospect said he was looking for a car that he could use to haul his boat and for off-road purposes, and the salesperson emphasized our vehicle's low price and quality in the sales pitch.

5 —

4 —

The prospective buyer said she really wanted to special-order a car with an unusual color and amenities, and the salesperson said she'd be better off not waiting 2 months and should settle for a standard model.

3 —

2 —

The prospect said he didn't "like the looks" of our vehicle, and the salesperson told him "the style is the style" and that he'd probably be happier with a competitor's vehicle.

1 —

prospect said he didn't 'like the looks' of our vehicle, and the salesperson told him 'the style is the style' and that he'd probably be happier with a competitor's vehicle."

Appraisal Forms in Practice

In practice, appraisal forms often blend several approaches. For example, Figure 7.4 (pages 193–194) is basically a graphic rating scale supported with specific behavioral competency expectations (examples of good or poor performance). These expectations pinpoint what raters should look for. Even without using the more elaborate behaviorally anchored appraisal approach, behaviorally anchoring a rating scale, as in Figure 7.7, can improve the reliability and validity of the appraisal scale.

The Management by Objectives Method

The term *management by objectives (MBO)* usually refers to a multi-step company-wide goal-setting and appraisal program. MBO requires the manager to set specific measurable organizationally relevant goals with each employee, and then periodically discuss the latter's progress toward these goals. The steps are:

1. *Set the organization's goals.* Establish a company-wide plan for next year and set goals.
2. *Set departmental goals.* Department heads and their superiors jointly set goals for their departments.
3. *Discuss departmental goals.* Department heads discuss the department's goals with their subordinates and ask them to develop their own individual goals. They should ask, How could each employee help the department attain its goals?
4. *Define expected results (set individual goals).* Department heads and their subordinates set short-term performance targets for each employee.
5. *Conduct performance reviews.* After a period, department heads compare each employee's actual and expected results.
6. *Provide feedback.* Department heads hold periodic performance review meetings with subordinates. Here they discuss the subordinates' performance and make any plans for rectifying or continuing the person's performance.

Computerized and Web-Based Performance Appraisals

More employers today use Web- or PC-supported appraisal tools. For example, Employee Appraiser presents a menu of more than a dozen evaluation dimensions, including dependability, initiative, communication, decision making, leadership, judgment, and planning and productivity.[30] Within each dimension are various performance factors. For example, under "Communication" you'll find separate factors for writing, verbal communication, and receptivity to feedback and criticism. Employees and managers using Employee Appraiser can access the system year-round, track their progress against goals in real time, and enter significant accomplishments.[31]

When the user clicks on a performance factor, he or she sees a comprehensive graphic rating scale. However, instead of ratings (from, say, poor to outstanding), Employee Appraiser uses behaviorally anchored examples. For example, for *verbal communication* there are six choices, ranging from "presents ideas clearly" to "lacks structure." The manager chooses the phrase that most closely describes the worker. Then Employee Appraiser produces a complete appraisal, with sample supporting text (for instance, describing briefly how the person's written communication occasionally lacks structure). The eAppraisal system from Halogen Software is another example.[32] Figure 7.8 presents an example of an online appraisal tool.

Seagate Technology chose "Enterprise Suite" for managing the performance of its 39,000 employees online.[33] Early in Seagate's first fiscal quarter, employees enter the system and set goals and development plans for themselves that make sense in terms of Seagate's corporate objectives. Employees update their plans quarterly, and then do self-evaluations at the end of the year, with follow-up reviews by their supervisors.

Electronic Performance Monitoring

Electronic performance monitoring (EPM) systems use computer technology to allow managers to monitor their employees' rate, accuracy, and time spent working online or just on their computers.[34]

EPM can improve productivity. For example, for more routine tasks, highly skilled and monitored subjects keyed in more data entries than did highly skilled unmonitored participants. However, EPM can also backfire. In this same study, low-skilled but highly monitored participants did more poorly than low-skilled, unmonitored participants. EPM also seems to raise employee stress.[35]

The Global Issues in HR feature discusses some special challenges in appraising employees abroad.

Source: Getty Images, Inc.–Liaison.

More employers today use Web- or PC-supported appraisal tools.

FIGURE 7.8
Online Appraisal Tool

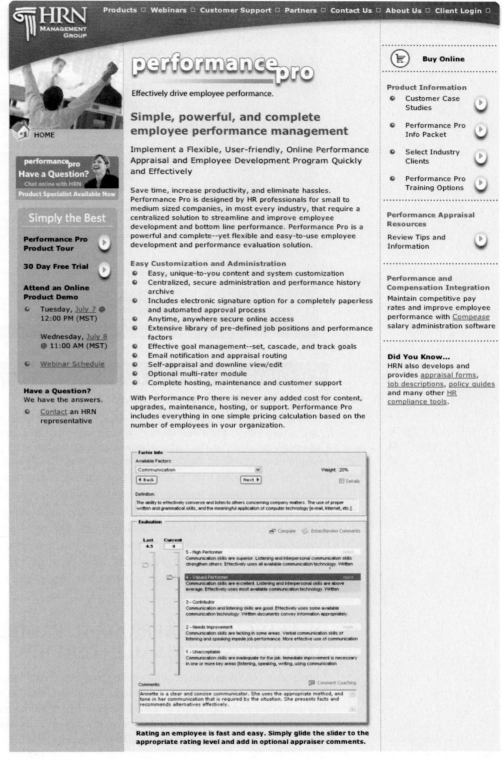

(continued)

FIGURE 7.8
(Continued)

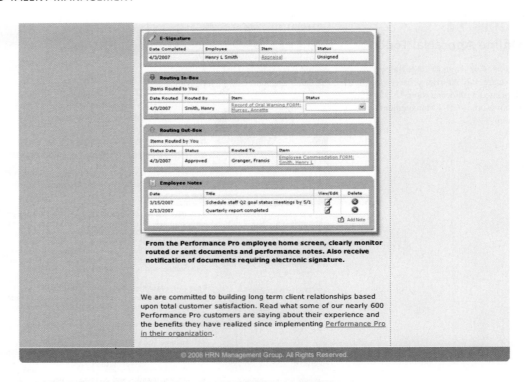

From the Performance Pro employee home screen, clearly monitor routed or sent documents and performance notes. Also receive notification of documents requiring electronic signature.

We are committed to building long term client relationships based upon total customer satisfaction. Read what some of our nearly 600 Performance Pro customers are saying about their experience and the benefits they have realized since implementing Performance Pro in their organization.

GLOBAL ISSUES IN HR

Appraising Employees Abroad

Appraising someone with whom you work everyday is challenging enough. Installing a process for appraising expatriate employees (who move temporarily abroad) is even more challenging. For example, do you use the same appraisal process as the local subsidiary, or the one by which you would have appraised the person if he or she was still working at home?

One study found that, at least for large multinational companies, employers used the same forms and procedures abroad that they do at headquarters. The researchers interviewed expatriate employees and human resource managers of five MNE (multinational enterprise) subsidiaries of information technology firms Applied Material (American), Philips (Dutch), Hitachi (Japanese), Samsung (Korean), and Winbond (Taiwan). In brief, each of the five firms used standardized performance forms set by headquarters, and did not adapt them to local operating situations. They therefore tried to maintain some comparability in both the appraisals and in the conclusions they could draw from those appraisals.[36]

DEALING WITH APPRAISAL PROBLEMS AND THE APPRAISAL INTERVIEW

A long-term NASA employee smuggled a revolver into the space center and, after speaking with his former supervisor for several minutes, said, "You're the one who's going to get me fired" and shot him. The supervisor had apparently given the shooter a poor job review, and the person feared dismissal.[37]

While such reactions aren't the norm, few supervisory tasks are fraught with more peril than appraising subordinates' performance.[38] Employees tend to be overly optimistic about what their ratings are. They also know that their raises, career progress, and peace of mind may hinge on how you rate them. This alone should make it somewhat difficult to rate performance. Even more problematic, however, are the numerous structural problems (unfairness, for instance, discussed next) that can cast doubt on just how fair the process is.[39] Fortunately, we'll see there are also ways to avoid these problems.

Ensure Fairness

The first task is to make sure that the subordinate views the appraisal as fair. Studies confirm that, in practice, some managers ignore accuracy and honesty in performance appraisals. Instead, they

- Base the performance review on duties and standards from a job analysis.
- Employees must be aware of how their performance will be assessed before the review, and their goals should be set effectively.
- Ensure that the employee's goals align with organizational objectives.
- To the extent possible, base the performance review on objective performance data.
- Use a standardized procedure for all employees.
- Gather information from several sources, preferably multiple raters; at least have the rater's supervisor review the appraisal ratings.
- Ensure an ongoing process, specifically, continuous feedback.
- Document the appraisal results.
- Indicate what the employee needs to do to improve his or her ratings.
- Include an appeals mechanism.

FIGURE 7.9

Selected Best Practices for Fair Performance Appraisals

Source: Based on Richard Posthuma, "Twenty Best Practices for Just Employee Performance Reviews," *Compensation & Benefits Review* (January/February 2008): 47–54; http://www.employee-performance.com/PerformanceManagement Resources/BestPracticesforPerformanceAppraisals.php, accessed July, 2010; and http://www.successfactors.com/articles/optimize-performance-management, accessed July, 2010. Reprinted with permission of the Society for Human Resource Management (www.shrm.com), Alexandria, VA, Publisher of *HR Magazine*, © SHRM.

use the process for political purposes (such as encouraging employees with whom they don't get along to leave the firm).[40] The employees' standards should be clear, employees should understand the basis on which you're going to appraise them, and the appraisals should be objective and fair.[41] Figure 7.9 summarizes some best practices for administering fair performance appraisals.

4 Give examples of five potential appraisal problems.

Clarify Standards

Often, the appraisal scale is too open to interpretation. As in Figure 7.10, this rating scale may seem objective, but would probably result in unfair appraisals because the traits and degrees of merit are open to interpretation. For example, different supervisors would probably define "good" performance differently. The same is true of traits such as "quality of work." The best way to rectify this problem is to develop and include descriptive phrases that define each trait and degree of merit.

Avoid Halo Effect Ratings

The halo effect means that the rating you give a subordinate on one trait (such as "gets along with others") influences the way you rate the person on other traits (such as "quantity of work"). Thus, you might rate an unfriendly employee unsatisfactory for all traits, rather than just for the trait "gets along with others." Being aware of this problem is a step toward avoiding it.

Avoid the Middle

The "central tendency" problem refers to a tendency to rate all employees as being about average, or in the middle. For example, if the rating scale ranges from 1 to 7, a supervisor may tend to avoid the highs (6 and 7) and lows (1 and 2) and rate most of his or her employees between

	Excellent	Good	Fair	Poor
Quality of work				
Quantity of work				
Creativity				
Integrity				

FIGURE 7.10

A Graphic Rating Scale with Unclear Standards

Note: For example, what exactly is meant by "good," "quantity of work," and so forth?

3 and 5. Such restriction can make the evaluations less useful for promotion, salary, and counseling purposes. Ranking employees instead of using a graphic rating scale can eliminate this problem. When you rank employees, they can't all be rated average.[42]

Don't Be Lenient or Strict

Conversely, some supervisors tend to rate all their subordinates consistently high or low, a problem referred to as the strictness/leniency problem. Again, one solution is to insist on ranking subordinates, because that forces the supervisor to distinguish between high and low performers.

The appraisal you do may be less objective than you realize. One study focused on how personality influenced the peer evaluations students gave their peers. Raters who scored higher on "conscientiousness" tended to give their peers lower ratings; those scoring higher on "agreeableness" gave higher ratings.[43]

Avoid Bias

Unfortunately, ratees' personal characteristics (such as age, race, and gender) can affect ratings, often quite apart from each person's actual performance. Studies suggest that "Rater idiosyncratic biases account for the largest percentage of the observed variances in performance ratings."[44]

EXAMPLE For example, one study found that raters penalized successful women for their success.[45] Earlier studies had found that raters tend to demean women's performance, particularly when they excel at what seems like male-typical tasks, and that is exactly what happened here. In this new study, the researchers told the subject-raters that they'd be viewing information about someone who was one of 30 people who had just finished a year-long management training program. The researchers were careful to make it seem that the training program was mostly for male employees. For instance, they emphasized that most of the trainees were men. The researchers found,

> There are many things that lead an individual to be disliked, including obnoxious behavior, arrogance, stubbornness, and pettiness, [but] it is only women, not men, for whom a unique propensity toward dislike is created by success in a nontraditional ["male-type"] work situation.[46]

Table 7.1 summarizes how the most popular appraisal methods rate in addressing these problems.

TABLE 7.1 Important Similarities, Differences, and Advantages and Disadvantages of Appraisal Tools

Tool	Similarities/Differences	Advantages	Disadvantages
Graphic rating scale	These scales both aim at measuring an employee's *absolute* performance based on objective criteria as listed on the scales.	Simple to use; provides a quantitative rating for each employee.	Standards may be unclear; halo effect, central tendency, leniency, bias can also be problems.
BARS		Provides behavioral "anchors." BARS is very accurate.	Difficult to develop.
Alternation ranking	These are both methods for judging the *relative* performance of employees relative to each other, but still based on objective criteria.	Simple to use (but not as simple as graphic rating scales); avoids central tendency and other problems of rating scales.	Can cause disagreements among employees and may be unfair if all employees *are*, in fact, excellent.
Forced distribution method		End up with a predetermined proportion of people in each group.	Appraisal results depend on the adequacy of your original choice of cutoff points (for top 10%, and so on).
Critical incident method	These are both subjective, narrative methods for appraising performance.	Helps clarify what exactly is "right" and "wrong" about the employee's performance; forces supervisor to size up subordinates on an ongoing basis.	Difficult to rate or rank employees relative to one another.
MBO		Tied to agreed-upon performance objectives.	Time consuming.

Addressing Legal Issues in Appraisal

Performance appraisals affect raises, promotions, training opportunities, and other HR actions. If the manager is inept or biased in making the appraisal, how can one defend the promotion decisions that stem from the appraisal? In one case, a 36-year-old supervisor ranked a 62-year-old subordinate at the bottom of the department's rankings, and then terminated him. The U.S. Court of Appeals for the 10th Circuit determined that the discriminatory motives of the younger boss might have influenced the appraisal and termination.[47] The HR in Practice feature summarizes some steps to make appraisals legally defensible.

HR IN PRACTICE

Making Appraisals Legally Defensible

Steps to ensure your appraisals are legally defensible include:

- Base the performance appraisal criteria on a job analysis.
- At the start of the period, communicate performance standards to employees in writing.
- Base your appraisals on separate evaluations of each performance dimension (such as quality, quantity, and gets along with others). Using a single "overall" rating of performance or ranking of employees is not acceptable to the courts.[48] Courts often characterize such systems as vague.
- Include an employee appeals process. Employees should have the opportunity to review and make comments, written or verbal, about their appraisals before they become final, and should have a formal appeals process through which to appeal their ratings.
- One appraiser should never have absolute authority to determine a personnel action.
- Document all information bearing on a personnel decision in writing. "Without exception, courts condemn informal performance evaluation practices that eschew documentation."[49]
- Train supervisors to use the appraisal tools. If formal rater training is not possible, at least provide raters with written instructions on how to use the rating scale.[50]

Handling the Appraisal Interview

A performance appraisal usually culminates in an appraisal interview. Here, you and your subordinate discuss the appraisal and formulate plans to remedy deficiencies and reinforce strengths. Few people like to receive or give negative feedback.[51] Adequate preparation and effective implementation are therefore essential.

PREPARING FOR THE APPRAISAL INTERVIEW Adequate preparation involves three things. First, give the subordinate at least *a week's notice* to review his or her work, and to compile questions and comments. Second, *compare the employee's performance to his or her standards*, and review the person's previous appraisals. Finally, find *a private area* for the interview where you won't be interrupted. Set a mutually agreeable time for the interview and leave enough time—perhaps a half-hour for lower-level personnel such as clerical workers and an hour or so for management employees.

CONDUCTING THE INTERVIEW There are several things to keep in mind when actually conducting appraisal interviews.

5 Explain how to conduct an appraisal feedback interview.

1. Remember that the interview's main aim is to reinforce satisfactory performance or to diagnose and improve unsatisfactory performance. Therefore, be direct and specific. Talk in terms of objective work data, using examples such as quality records and tardiness.
2. Get agreement before the subordinate leaves on how things will improve and by when. An action plan showing steps and expected results is essential. If a formal written warning is required, it should identify the standards under which the employee is judged, make it clear that the employee was aware of the standard, specify any violation, and show that the employee had an opportunity to correct his or her behavior.
3. Ensure that the process is fair. Letting the employee participate in the appraisal process by letting his or her opinions be heard is essential.[52]
4. Be prepared to deal with defensiveness. For example, when a person is accused of poor performance, the first reaction is usually denial—a defense mechanism. Attacking the person's defenses (for instance, by saying things like, "You know the real reason you're using that excuse is that you can't bear to be blamed for anything") is usually counterproductive. One approach is to postpone action. For instance, give the person a few minutes to cool down after being informed of unsatisfactory performance. Then focus on performance ("sales are down") rather than on the person (you're being defensive").

PERFORMANCE MANAGEMENT

Earlier in this chapter we said that performance management is the continuous process of identifying, measuring, and developing the performance of individuals and teams and aligning their performance with the organization's goals.[53] We look at performance management more closely in this section.

Performance Management vs. Performance Appraisal

In comparing performance management and performance appraisal, "the distinction is the contrast between a year-end event—the completion of the appraisal form—and a process that starts the year with performance planning and is integral to the way people are managed throughout the year."[54] Three main things distinguish performance management from performance appraisal.

1. First, performance management never means just meeting with a subordinate once or twice a year to "review your performance." It means *continuous, daily, or weekly* interactions and feedback to ensure continuous improvement.[55]
2. Second, performance management is always *goal-directed*. The continuing performance reviews always involve comparing the employee's or team's performance against goals that specifically stem from and link to the company's strategic goals.
3. Third, performance management means continuously re-evaluating and (if need be) *modifying how the employee and team get their work done*. Depending on the issue, this may mean additional training, changing work procedures, or instituting new incentive plans, for instance.

Furthermore, performance management systems increasingly use information technology to help managers automatically track employee performance and take immediate corrective action as required. By comparison, performance *appraisal* systems usually rely on paper forms, or perhaps online or computerized appraisal forms.

We can summarize performance management's six basic elements as follows:[56]

6 Explain how to install a performance management program.

- Direction sharing means communicating the company's goals throughout the company and then translating these into doable departmental, team, and individual goals.
- Goal alignment means having a method that enables managers and employees to see the link between the employees' goals and those of their department and company.
- Ongoing performance monitoring usually includes using computerized systems that measure and then email progress and exception reports based on the person's progress toward meeting his or her performance goals.
- Ongoing feedback includes both face-to-face and computerized feedback regarding progress toward goals.
- Coaching and developmental support should be an integral part of the feedback process.
- Recognition and rewards provide the consequences needed to keep the employee's goal-directed performance on track.

Using Information Technology to Support Performance Management

Performance management needn't be high-tech. For example, in many production facilities, work teams simply meet daily to review their performance and to get their efforts and those of their members aligned with their performance standards and goals.

On the other hand, information technology enables management to automate performance management and to monitor and correct deviations in real time. We can sum up this IT-supported performance management process as follows:

- *Assign financial and nonfinancial goals* to each team's activities along the strategy map chain of activities leading from the team's activities up to the company's overall strategic goals. (For example, an airline measures ground crew aircraft turnaround time in terms of "improve turnaround time from an average of 30 minutes per plane to 26 minutes per plane this year.")
- *Inform all employees* of their goals.
- *Use IT-supported tools* like scorecard software and digital dashboards to continuously display, monitor, and assess each team's and employee's performance. (We discussed this in Chapter 3.) Special performance management software then shows management a real-time overview of each team's performance, enabling the team to,
- *Take corrective action* before things swing out of control. Figure 7.11 presents an example of an online performance management report for an employee.

FIGURE 7.11
Summary of Performance-Management Process Report

Source: Performance Management Report from http://www.active strategy.com/images/7.2/PGM.jpg, accessed April 29, 2009. Used with permission of ActiveStrategy, Inc.

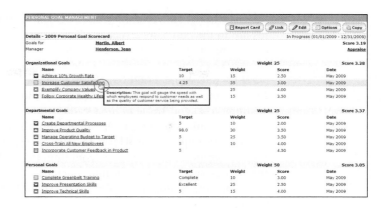

TALENT MANAGEMENT PRACTICES AND EMPLOYEE APPRAISAL

In Chapter 4, we defined talent management as the goal-oriented and integrated process of planning, recruiting, developing, appraising, and compensating employees. By way of review, we said five sets of practices distinguish talent management from merely recruiting, selecting, training, appraising, and paying employees. It requires:

1. Identifying the workforce profiles (competencies, knowledge, traits, and experiences) that the firm needs to achieve its strategic goals;
2. Consciously thinking through and focusing on all the tasks (recruiting and so on) required for managing the company's talent;
3. Consistently using the same profile for formulating recruitment plans for the employee as you do for making the selection, training, appraisal, and payment decisions;
4. Actively managing different employees' recruitment, selection, development, and rewards; and
5. Integrating the underlying talent management activities (planning for, recruiting, developing, appraising, and compensating employees).

Appraising and Actively Managing Employees

Performance appraisal traditionally plays a predictable role when managers make pay raise and related decisions. Perhaps with the exception of selected "fast-track" employees, managers tend to allocate resources such as compensation and development opportunities either across-the-board or based on the employee's appraisal ratings (or both).

In contrast, talent management requires *actively managing* decisions like these. The point is that in today's competitive environment, the traditional practice of allocating pay raises, development opportunities, and other scarce resources across the board or based just on performance makes less sense then it used to. Today, employers need to focus their attention and resources on their company's mission-critical employees, those who are critical to the firm's strategic needs. Simply allocating awards across the board obviously does not fill that requirement. And, even allocating, say, pay based solely on performance leaves something to be desired. For example, is an employer really actively managing its employees if it gives the same percentage pay raise to every employee who rates "excellent," regardless of how important that employee is to the company's future success?

Increasingly, the answer from employers is "no." They continue to use performance appraisal to evaluate how their employees

---

HR APPs 4 U

Mobile Performance Management

A new iPhone app enables managers and employees to monitor their performance management goals and progress while on the go. ActiveStrategy (www.activestrategy.com) recently demonstrated what they call "the first enterprise performance management application for the iPhone," ActiveStrategy Mobile™. Linked in to this vendor's ActiveStrategy Enterprise software, the new application "allows business users to keep in close touch with the strategic performance of their business, making it an ideal enterprise application for the iPhone."[57]

are performing. However, they also segment their employees based on how critical the employees are to the company's success. The point again is to focus your attention and resources on your company's mission-critical employees.

7 Illustrate the effects of segmenting and actively managing a company's talent.

HOW TO SEGMENT EMPLOYEES Figure 7.12 illustrates one way to do this. Accenture uses a 4×4 Strategic Role Assessment matrix to plot employees by *Performance* (exceptional, high, medium, low) and *Value to the Organization* (mission-critical, core, necessary, nonessential). As an example, consider a chemical engineering company that designs sophisticated pollution control equipment. Here, the firm's experienced engineers may be mission-critical, engineer-trainees core, sales, accounting, (and HR) necessary, and peripheral, outsource-able employees such as those in maintenance non-essential. The company would then tie pay, development, dismissal, and other personnel decisions to each employee's position in the matrix.

Segmenting and Actively Managing Employees in Practice

Several actual examples can illustrate how employers implement this active-management segmented approach in practice.

- Compass Group PLC identifies top performers. Then Compass assesses them for promot-ability, promotability time-frame, and leadership potential. Top employees then get special coaching and feedback, and development opportunities. Compass monitors their progress. GE prioritizes jobs and focuses on what it calls its employee, "game changers."[58]
- Tesco PLC segments employees according to personal and professional goals to better communicate and motivate its employees.[59]
- McKinsey & Co. recommends limiting the "high potential group in whom the company invests heavily to no more than 10 to 20% of managerial and professional staff."[60]
- Unilever includes 15% of employees per management level in its high potential list each year, and expects these people to move to the next management level within five years.[61]
- Shell China appoints "career stewards" to meet regularly with "emerging leaders." They assess their level of engagement, help them set realistic career expectations, and make sure they're getting the right development opportunities.[62]

Performance

	Exceptional	High	Average	Low
Mission-critical				
Core				
Necessary				
Non-essential				

Value to the organization

▬▬▬ Provide additional rewards and experiences and provide development opportunities to benefit individual and organization

▬▬▬ Provide training and experiences to prepare for mission-critical roles

▬▬▬ Identify as at risk: Provide additional training and performance management attention to improve motivation and performance, and/or to move into necessary or core roles

▬▬▬ Divest/seek alterative sourcing

FIGURE 7.12

Accenture's Strategic Role Assessment Matrix

Source: This information originally appeared in "The New Talent Equation" from the June 2009 issue of *Outlook*, an Accenture publication. © 2009 Accenture. All rights reserved. Chart reprinted by permission.

REVIEW

SUMMARY

1. Performance appraisal means evaluating an employee's current or past performance relative to his or her performance standards. Performance management is the process through which companies ensure that employees are working toward organizational goals, and includes defining goals, developing skills, appraising performance, and rewarding the employee.

2. Managers appraise their subordinates' performance to obtain input on which promotion and salary raise decisions can be made, to develop plans for correcting performance deficiencies, and for career planning purposes. Supervisory ratings are still at the heart of most appraisal processes.

3. The appraisal is generally conducted using one or more popular appraisal methods or tools. These include graphic rating scales, alternation ranking, paired comparison, forced distribution, critical incidents, behaviorally anchored rating scales, MBO, computerized performance appraisals, and electronic performance monitoring.

4. An appraisal typically culminates in an appraisal interview. Adequate preparation, including giving the subordinate notice, reviewing his or her job description and past performance, choosing the right place for the interview, and leaving enough time for it, is essential. In conducting the interview, the aim is to reinforce satisfactory performance or to diagnose and improve unsatisfactory performance. A concrete analysis of objective work data and development of an action plan are therefore advisable. Employee defensiveness is normal and needs to be dealt with.

5. The appraisal process can be improved, first, by eliminating chronic problems that often undermine appraisals and graphic rating scales in particular. These common problems include unclear standards, halo effect, central tendency, leniency or strictness, and bias.

6. Care should also be taken to ensure that the performance appraisal is legally defensible. For example, appraisal criteria should be based on documented job analyses, employees should receive performance standards in writing, and multiple performance dimensions should be rated.

7. Performance management is a *continuous* process of identifying, measuring, and developing the performance of individuals and teams and *aligning* their performance with the organization's *goals*. Unlike performance appraisal, performance management never just means meeting with a subordinate once or twice a year to "review your performance." It means *continuous, daily, or weekly* interactions and feedback to ensure continuous improvement in the employee's and team's capacity and performance.

8. At its core, talent management means actively managing decisions like these. In today's competitive environment, the traditional HR practice of allocating pay raises, development opportunities, and other scarce resources more-or-less across the board or based only on performance is no longer viable. Employers need to focus their attention and resources on their company's mission-critical employees, those who are critical to the firm's strategic needs

KEY TERMS

performance appraisal   187

performance management   189

DISCUSSION QUESTIONS

1. Explain the purpose of performance appraisal.
2. Answer the question, "Who should do the appraising?"
3. Discuss the pros and cons of at least eight performance appraisal methods.
4. Explain how to conduct an appraisal feedback interview.
5. Give examples of five potential appraisal problems.
6. Explain how to install a performance management program.
7. Explain how to design a career management program.
8. Explain how you would use the alternation ranking method, the paired comparison method, and the forced distribution method.
9. Discuss the pros and cons of using various potential raters to appraise an employee's performance.
10. Compare and contrast performance appraisal and performance management, using specific examples.

INDIVIDUAL AND GROUP ACTIVITIES

1. Working individually or in groups, develop a graphic rating scale for the following jobs: secretary, professor, directory assistance operator.
2. Working individually or in groups, describe the advantages and disadvantages of using the forced distribution appraisal method for college professors.
3. Working individually or in groups, develop, over the period of a week, a set of critical incidents

covering the classroom performance of one of your instructors.
4. Working individually or in groups, evaluate the rating scale in Figure 7.1. Discuss ways to improve it.
5. Create an Accenture-type grid for your place of work or college, showing how you would segment employees into four groups.

WEB-e's (WEB EXERCISES)

1. Use sites such as www.factorytour.com/tours/toyota.cfm to illustrate how Toyota appraises employees, and why that approach is important for the goals Toyota has for its cars.
2. Use sites such as www.hr-software.net/pages/209.htm to make a summary list of 10 appraisal software suppliers, including a summary of what each offers.

3. According to http://careercompass.berkeley.edu/perfmgmt/resources/evalforms.html, how does Berkeley appraise supervisors? What do you think of the form it uses?

APPLICATION EXERCISES

HR IN ACTION CASE INCIDENT 1
Appraising the Secretaries at Sweetwater U

Rob Winchester, newly appointed vice president for administrative affairs at Sweetwater State University, faced a tough problem shortly after his university career began. Three weeks after he came on board in September, Sweetwater's president, Rob's boss, told Rob that one of his first tasks was to improve the appraisal system used to evaluate secretarial and clerical performance at Sweetwater U. Apparently the main difficulty was that the performance appraisal was traditionally tied directly to salary increases given at the end of the year. So most administrators were less than accurate when they used the graphic rating forms that were the basis of the clerical staff evaluation. In fact, what usually happened was that each administrator simply rated his or her clerk or secretary as "excellent." This cleared the way for all support staff to receive a maximum pay increase every year.

But the current university budget simply did not include enough money to fund another "maximum" annual increase for every staffer. Furthermore, Sweetwater's president felt that the custom of providing invalid feedback to each secretary on his or her year's performance was not productive, so he had asked the new vice president to revise the system. In October, Rob sent a memo to all administrators telling them that in the future no more than half the secretaries reporting to any particular administrator could be appraised as "excellent." This move, in effect, forced each supervisor to begin ranking his or her secretaries for quality of performance. The vice president's memo met widespread resistance immediately—from administrators, who were afraid that many of

their secretaries would begin leaving for more lucrative jobs in private industry; and from secretaries, who felt that the new system was unfair and reduced each secretary's chance of receiving a maximum salary increase. A handful of secretaries had begun quietly picketing outside the president's home on the university campus. The picketing, caustic remarks by disgruntled administrators, and rumors of an impending slowdown by the secretaries (there were about 250 on campus) made Rob Winchester wonder whether he had made the right decision by setting up forced ranking. He knew, however, that there were a few performance appraisal experts in the School of Business, so he decided to set up an appointment with them to discuss the matter.

He met with them the next morning. He explained the situation as he had found it: The present appraisal system had been set up when the university first opened 10 years earlier, and the appraisal form had been developed primarily by a committee of secretaries. Under that system, Sweetwater's administrators filled out forms similar to the one shown in Figure 7.10. This once-a-year appraisal (in March) had run into problems almost immediately, since it was apparent from the start that administrators varied widely in their interpretations of job standards, as well as in how conscientiously they filled out the forms and supervised their secretaries. Moreover, at the end of the first year it became obvious to everyone that each secretary's salary increase was tied directly to the March appraisal. For example, those rated "excellent" received the maximum increases, those rated "good" received smaller increases, and those given neither rating received only the standard across-the-board, cost-of-living increase. Since universities in general—and Sweetwater in particular—have paid secretaries somewhat lower salaries than those prevailing in private industry, some secretaries left in a huff that first year. From that time on, most administrators simply rated all secretaries excellent in order to reduce staff turnover, thus ensuring each a maximum increase. In the process, they also avoided the hard feelings aroused by the significant performance differences otherwise highlighted by administrators.

Two Sweetwater School of Business experts agreed to consider the problem, and in two weeks they came back to the vice president with the following recommendations. First, the form used to rate the secretaries was grossly insufficient. It was unclear what "excellent" or "quality of work" meant, for example. They recommended instead a form like that in Figure 7.4. In addition, they recommended that the vice president rescind his earlier memo and no longer attempt to force university administrators to arbitrarily rate at least half their secretaries as something less than excellent. The two consultants pointed out that this was, in fact, an unfair procedure since it was quite possible that any particular administrator might have staffers who were all or virtually all excellent—or conceivably, although less likely, all below standard. The experts said that the way to get all the administrators to take the appraisal process more seriously was to stop tying it to salary increases. In other words, they recommended that every administrator fill out a form like that in Figure 7.4 for each secretary at least once a year and then use this form as the basis of a counseling session. Salary

increases would have to be made on some basis other than the performance appraisal, so that administrators would no longer hesitate to fill out the rating forms honestly.

Rob thanked the two experts and went back to his office to ponder their recommendations. Some of the recommendations (such as substituting the new rating form for the old) seemed to make sense. Nevertheless, he still had serious doubts as to the efficacy of any graphic rating form, particularly if he were to decide in favor of his original forced ranking approach. The experts' second recommendation—to stop tying the appraisals to automatic salary increases—made sense but raised at least one very practical problem: If salary increases were not to be based on performance appraisals, on what were they to be based? He began wondering whether the experts' recommendations weren't simply based on ivory tower theorizing.

Questions

1. Do you think that the experts' recommendations will be sufficient to get most of the administrators to fill out the rating forms properly? Why? Why not? What additional actions (if any) do you think will be necessary?
2. Do you think that Vice President Winchester would be better off dropping graphic rating forms, substituting instead one of the other techniques discussed in this chapter, such as a ranking method? Why?
3. What performance appraisal system would you develop for the secretaries if you were Rob Winchester? Defend your answer.

HR IN ACTION CASE INCIDENT 2
Carter Cleaning Company: The Performance Appraisal

After spending several weeks on the job, Jennifer was surprised to discover that her father had not formally evaluated any employee's performance for all the years that he had owned the business. Jack's position was that he had "a hundred higher-priority things to attend to," such as boosting sales and lowering costs, and, in any case, many employees didn't stick around long enough to be appraisable anyway. Furthermore, contended Jack, manual workers such as those doing the pressing and the cleaning did periodically get positive feedback in terms of praise from Jack for a job well done, or criticism, also from Jack, if things did not look right during one of his swings through the stores. Similarly, Jack was never shy about telling his managers about store problems so that they, too, got some feedback on where they stood.

This informal feedback notwithstanding, Jennifer believes that a more formal appraisal approach is required. She believes that there are criteria such as quality, quantity, attendance, and punctuality that should be evaluated periodically even if a worker is paid based on how much they produce. Furthermore, she feels quite strongly that the managers need to have a list of quality standards for matters such as store cleanliness, efficiency, safety, and adherence to budget on which they know they are to be formally evaluated.

Questions

1. Is Jennifer right about the need to evaluate the workers formally? The managers? Why or why not?
2. Develop a performance appraisal method for the workers and managers in each store.

EXPERIENTIAL EXERCISE

Setting Goals for and Appraising an Instructor

Purpose: The purpose of this exercise is to give you practice in developing and using a performance appraisal form.

Required Understanding: You are going to develop a performance appraisal form for an instructor and should therefore

be thoroughly familiar with the discussion of performance appraisals in this chapter.

How to Set Up the Exercise/Instructions: Divide the class into groups of four or five students.

1. First, based on what you now know about performance appraisals, do you think Figure 7.1 is an effective scale for appraising instructors? Why or why not?
2. Next, your group should develop its own tool for appraising the performance of an instructor. Decide which of the appraisal tools (graphic rating scales, alternation ranking, and so on) you are going to use, and then design the instrument itself. Apply what you learned in this chapter about goal-setting to provide the instructor with practical goals.

3. Next, have a spokesperson from each group put his or her group's appraisal tool on the board. How similar are the tools? Do they all measure about the same factors? Which factor appears most often? Which do you think is the most effective tool on the board? Can you think of any way of combining the best points of several of the tools into a new performance appraisal tool?

PERSONAL COMPETENCIES EDU-EXERCISE

Building Your Communications Skills

Few supervisory situations demand interpersonal communication skills more than does appraising employees' performance. People don't like giving or receiving negative feedback, and appraisals thus tend to be tense, unproductive affairs. Clear, unambiguous, effective, communication is vital.

Start by understanding the barriers to effective communication. These include ambiguous messages; emotions, anger, or frustration; and misperceptions—for instance, if the employee is concerned about his or her job, he or she may be so preoccupied as to not be listening to what you say.

Given this, methods for improving interpersonal communications include:

1. Pay attention. You are unlikely to create such a common understanding if you don't listen attentively, and make it clear that the person has your undivided attention.
2. Make yourself clear. For example, if you mean immediately, say "immediately," not "as soon as you can."
3. Be an active listener. Communication pioneer Carl Rogers says that active listeners don't just listen to what the

speaker says; they also try to understand and respond to the feelings underlying the words. Suggestions include listen for total meaning (try to understand the feelings underlying what the person is saying), reflect feelings (for instance, by replying with something like "they're pushing you pretty hard, aren't they?"), and watch for all cues (not all communication is verbal; facial expressions and gestures reveal feelings too).

Questions

1. List three specific aspects of performance appraisal and career development for which interpersonal communications skills are essential, and explain why they are essential for these activities.
2. Many colleges have students "appraise" professors with forms like the one in Figure 7.1. Create a feedback process, based on good communications methods, that you think the college should use in feeding back this information to the professor.

ENDNOTES

1. Aliah D. Wright, "At Google, It Takes a Village to Hire an Employee," *HR Magazine* (2009 HR Trendbook supp.): 56–57.
2. Experts debate the pros and its six cons of tying appraisals to pay decisions. One side argues that doing so distorts the appraisals. A recent study concludes the opposite. Based on an analysis of surveys from over 24,000 employees in more than 6000 workplaces in Canada, the researchers concluded: (1) linking the employees' pay to their performance appraisals contributed to improved pay satisfaction; (2) even when appraisals are *not* directly linked to pay, they apparently contributed to pay satisfaction, "probably through mechanisms related to perceived organizational justice"; and (3) whether or not the employees received performance pay, "individuals who do not receive performance appraisals are significantly less satisfied with their pay." Mary Jo Ducharme et al., "Exploring the Links Between Performance Appraisals and Pay Satisfaction," *Compensation and Benefits Review* (September/October 2005): 46–52. See also

Robert Morgan, "Making the Most of Performance Management Systems," *Compensation and Benefits Review* (September/October 2006): 22–27.
3. Peter Glendinning, "Performance Management: Pariah or Messiah," *Public Personnel Management* 31, no. 2 (Summer 2002): 161–178. See also Herman Aguinis, *Performance Management* (Upper Saddle River, NJ: Prentice Hall 2007): 2.
4. Vesa Suutari and Marja Tahbanainen, "The Antecedents of Performance Management among Finnish Expatriates," *Journal of Human Resource Management* 13, no. 1 (February 2002): 53–75.
5. "Get SMART about Setting Goals," *Asia Africa Intelligence Wire* (May 22, 2005).
6. See, for example, Robert Renn, "Further Examination of the Measurement of Properties of Leifer & McGannon's 1996 Goal Acceptance and Goal Commitment Scales," *Journal of Occupational and Organizational Psychology* (March 1999): 107–114.

7. See, for example, Doug Cederblom and Dan Pemerl, "From Performance Appraisal to Performance Management: One Agency's Experience," *Personnel Management* 31, no. 2 (Summer 2002): 131–140.

8. Vanessa Druskat and Steven Wolf, "Effects and Timing of Developmental Peer Appraisals in Self-Managing Work-Groups," *Journal of Applied Psychology* 84, no. 1 (1999): 58–74.

9. See, for example, Brian Hoffman and David Woehr, "Disentangling the Meaning of Multisource Performance Rating Source and Dimension Factors," *Personnel Psychology* 62 (2009): 735–765.

10. As one study recently concluded, "Far from being a source of non-meaningful error variance, the discrepancies among ratings from multiple perspectives can in fact capture meaningful variance in multilevel managerial performance." In-Sue Oh and Christopher Berry, "The Five Factor Model of Personality and Managerial Performance: Validity Gains through the Use of 360° Performance Ratings," *Journal of Applied Psychology* 94, no. 6 (2009): 1510.

11. Jeffrey Facteau and S. Bartholomew Craig, "Performance Appraisal Ratings from Different Rating Scores," *Journal of Applied Psychology* 86, no. 2 (2001): 215–227.

12. See also Kevin Murphy et al., "Raters Who Pursue Different Goals Give Different Ratings," *Journal of Applied Psychology* 89, no. 1 (2004): 158–164.

13. Such findings may be culturally related. One study compared self and supervisor ratings in "other-oriented" cultures (as in Asia, where values tend to emphasize teams). It found that self and supervisor ratings were related. M. Audrey Korsgaard et al., "The Effect of Other Orientation on Self: Supervisor Rating Agreement," *Journal of Organizational Behavior* 25, no. 7 (November 2004): 873–891. See also Heike Heidemeier and Klaus Mosar, "Self Other Agreement in Job Performance Ratings: A Meta-Analytic Test of a Process Model," *Journal of Applied Psychology* 94, no. 2 (2009): 353–370.

14. Forest Jourden and Chip Heath, "The Evaluation Gap in Performance Perceptions: Illusory Perceptions of Groups and Individuals," *Journal of Applied Psychology* 81, no. 4 (August 1996): 369–379. See also Sheri Ostroff, "Understanding Self-Other Agreement: A Look at Rater and Ratee Characteristics, Context, and Outcomes," *Personnel Psychology* 57, no. 2 (Summer 2004): 333–375.

15. Paul Atkins and Robert Wood, "Self versus Others Ratings as Predictors of Assessment Center Ratings: Validation Evidence for 360 Degree Feedback Programs," *Personnel Psychology* 55, no. 4 (Winter 2002): 871–904.

16. David Antonioni, "The Effects of Feedback Accountability on Upward Appraisal Ratings," *Personnel Psychology* 47 (1994): 349–355.

17. Alan Walker and James Smither, "A Five-Year Study of Upward Feedback: What Managers Do with Their Results Matters," *Personnel Psychology* 52 (1999): 393–423.

18. See, for example, "360-Degree Feedback on the Rise Survey Finds," *BNA Bulletin to Management* (January 23, 1997): 31; Leanne Atwater et al., "Multisource Feedback: Lessons Learned and Implications for Practice," *Human Resource Management* 46, no. 2 (Summer 2007): 285. However, a small number of employers are beginning to use 360-degree feedback for performance appraisals, rather than just development. See, for example, Tracy Maylett, "360° Feedback Revisited: The Transition from Development to Appraisal," *Compensation & Benefits Review* (September/October 2009): 52–59.

19. James Smither et al., "Does Performance Improve Following Multi-Score Feedback? A Theoretical Model, Meta Analysis, and Review of Empirical Findings," *Personnel Psychology* 58 (2005): 33–36.

20. Christine Hagan et al., "Predicting Assessment Center Performance with 360 Degree, Top-Down, and Customer-Based Competency Assessments," *Human Resource Management* 45, no. 3 (Fall 2006): 357–390.

21. Bruce Pfau, "Does a 360-Degree Feedback Negatively Affect the Company Performance?" *HR Magazine* (June 2002): 55–59.

22. Jim Meade, "Visual 360: A Performance Appraisal System That's 'Fun,'" *HR Magazine* (July 1999): 118–119.

23. www.sumtotalsystems.com/performance/index.html?e=001&sitenbr=156896193&keys=visual+360&submit.x=11&submit.y=11&submit=submit, accessed April 20, 2008.

24. Steven Scullen et al., "Forced Distribution Rating Systems and the Improvement of Workforce Potential: A Baseline Simulation," *Personnel Psychology* 58 (2005): 1; Jena McGregor, "The Struggle to Measure Performance," *Business Week* (January 9, 2006): 26. See also D. J Schleicher et al., "Rater Reactions to Forced Distribution Rating Systems," *Journal of Management* 35, no. 4 (August 2009): 899–927.

25. Del Jones, "More Firms Cut Workers Ranked at Bottom to Make Way for Talent," *USA Today* (May 30, 2001): B1; "Straight Talk about Grading on a Curve," *BNA Bulletin to Management* (November 1, 2001): 351; Steve Bates, "Forced Ranking," *HR Magazine* (June 2003): 63–68.

26. Herman Aguinis, *Performance Management* (Upper Saddle River, NJ: Pearson, 2007): 179.

27. "Survey Says Problems with Forced Ranking Include Lower Morale and Costly Turnover," *BNA Bulletin to Management* (September 16, 2004): 297.

28. Steve Bates, "Forced Ranking: Why Grading Employees on a Scale Relative to Each Other Forces a Hard Look at Finding Keepers, Losers May Become Weepers," *HR Magazine* 48, no. 6 (June 2003): 62.

29. "Straight Talk about Grading Employees on a Curve," *BNA Bulletin to Management* (November 1, 2001): 351.

30. www.employeeappraiser.com/index.php, accessed January 10, 2008.

31. Drew Robb, "Appraising Appraisal Software," *HR Magazine* (October 2008): 68.

32. www.halogensoftware.com/products/halogen-eappraisal/, accessed January 10, 2008.

33. Drew Robb, "Building a Better Workforce," *HR Magazine* (October 2004): 87–94.

34. See, for example, Stoney Alder and Maureen Ambrose, "Towards Understanding Fairness Judgments Associated with Computer Performance Monitoring: An Integration of the Feedback, Justice, and Monitoring Research," *Human Resource Management Review* 15, no. 1 (March 2005): 43–67.

35. See, for example, John Aiello and Y. Shao, "Computerized Performance Monitoring," paper presented at the Seventh Conference of the Society for Industrial and Organizational Psychology, Montreal, Quebec, Canada, May 1992.

36. Hsi-An Shih, Yun-Hwa Chiang, and In-Sook Kim, "Expatriate Performance Management from MNEs of Different National Origins," *International Journal of Manpower* 26, no. 2 (February 2005): 157–175.

37. Rasha Madkour, "NASA Shooting Suspect Received Poor Job Review and Feared Being Fired, Police Say," *Associated Press* (April 21, 2007).

38. See, for example, "Communicating Beyond the Ratings Can Be Difficult," *Workforce Management* (April 24, 2006): 35.

39. See, for example, Manuel London, Edward Mone, and John C. Scott, "The Contributions of Psychological Research to HRM: Performance Management and Assessment—Methods for Improved Rater Accuracy and Employee Goal Setting," *Human Resource Management* 43, no. 4 (Winter 2004): 319–336.

40. M. Ronald Buckley et al., "Ethical Issues in Human Resources Systems," *Human Resource Management Review* 11 (2001): 11, 29. See also Ann Pomeroy, "The Ethics Squeeze," *HR Magazine* (March 2006): 48–55.

41. G.R Weaver and L.K Treviño, "The Role of Human Resources in Ethics/Compliance Management: A Fairness Perspective," *Human Resource Management Review,* 11: 113–134. Researchers recently conducted studies of 490 police officers undergoing standardized promotional exams. Among their conclusions was that ". . . Organizations should strive to ensure that candidates perceived justice both in the content of personnel assessments and in the way they are treated during the assessment process." Julie McCarthy et al., "Progression Through the Ranks: Assessing Employee Reactions to High Stakes Employment Testing," *Personnel Psychology* 62 (2009): 826.

42. See, for example, Jochen Reb and Gary Gregures, "Understanding Performance Ratings: Dynamic Performance, Attributions, and Rating Purpose," *Journal of Applied Psychology* 95, no. 1 (2010): 213–220.

43. H. John Bernardin et al., "Conscientiousness and Agreeableness as Predictors of Rating Leniency," *Journal of Applied Psychology* 85, no. 2 (2000): 232–234.

44. Gary Gregures et al., "A Field Study of the Effects of Rating Purpose on the Quality of Multiscore Ratings," *Personnel Psychology* 56 (2003): 1–21.

45. Madeleine Heilman et al., "Penalties for Success: Reactions to Women Who Succeed at Male Gender Type Tasks," *Journal of Applied Psychology* 89, no. 3 (2004): 416–427.

46. Ibid., 426. Another study found that successful female managers didn't usually suffer such a fate when those rating them saw them as supportive, caring, and sensitive to their needs. Madeleine Heilmann and Tyler Okimoto, "Why Are Women Penalized for Success at Male Tasks?: The Implied Communality Deficit," *Journal of Applied Psychology,* 92, no. 1 (2007): 81–92.

47. "Flawed Ranking System Revives Workers Bias Claim," *BNA Bulletin to Management* (June 28, 2005): 206.

48. James Austin, Peter Villanova, and Hugh Hindman, "Legal Requirements and Technical Guidelines Involved in Implementing Performance Appraisal Systems," in Gerald Ferris and M. Ronald Buckley, *Human Resources Management*, 3rd ed. (Upper Saddle River, NJ: Prentice Hall, 1996): 271–288.

49. Ibid., 282.

50. But beware: one problem with training raters to avoid rating errors is that, sometimes, what appears to be an error—such as leniency—isn't an error at all, as when all subordinates really are superior performers. Manuel London, Edward Mone, and John Scott, "Performance Management and Assessment: Methods for Improved Rater Accuracy and Employee Goal Setting," *Human Resource Management* 43, no. 4 (Winter 2004): 319–336.

51. Donald Fedor and Charles Parsons, "What Is Effective Performance Feedback?" in Gerald Ferris and M. Ronald Buckley, *Human Resources Management*, 3rd ed. (Upper Saddle River, NJ: Prentice Hall, 1996): 265–270. See also Herman Aguinis, *Performance Management* (Upper Saddle River, NJ: Pearson, 2007): 196–219.

52. Brian Cawley et al., "Participation in the Performance Appraisal Process and Employee Reactions: A Meta-Analytic Review of Field Investigations," *Journal of Applied Psychology* 83, no. 4 (1998): 615–633.

53. Peter Glendinning, "Performance Management: Pariah or Messiah," *Public Personnel Management* 31, no. 2 (Summer 2002): 161–178. See also Herman Aguinis, *Performance Management* (Upper Saddle River, NJ: Prentice Hall, 2007): 2.

54. Howard Risher, "Getting Serious about Performance Management," *Compensation and Benefits Review* (November/December 2005): 19.

55. Clinton Wingrove, "Developing an Effective Blend of Process and Technology in the New Era of Performance Management," *Compensation and Benefits Review* (January/February 2003): 27.

56. These are quoted or paraphrased from Howard Risher, "Getting Serious about Performance Management," *Compensation and Benefits Review* (November/December 2005): 19.

57. www.activestrategy.com/events_and_news/press_releases/050108.aspx, accessed March 23, 2009.

58. Adapted or quoted from "Next Generation Talent Management," Hewitt.com, accessed June 2010.

59. Ibid.

60. Adapted or quoted from Gunter Stahl et al., "Global Talent Management: How Leading Multinationals Build and Sustain their Talent Pipelines," Faculty & Research Working Paper, INSEAD, 2007.

61. Ibid.

62. Ibid.

8

Compensating Employees

SYNOPSIS

- What Determines How Much You Pay?
- How Employers Establish Pay Rates
- Current Trends in Compensation
- Incentive Plans
- Employee Benefits

Source: Chris Mueller/Redux Pictures.

When you finish studying this chapter, you should be able to:

1. Discuss four basic factors determining pay rates.

2. Explain each of the five basic steps in establishing pay rates.

3. Compare and contrast piecework and team or group incentive plans.

4. List and describe each of the basic benefits most employers might be expected to offer.

employee compensation

All forms of pay or rewards going to employees and arising from their employment.

1 Discuss four basic factors determining pay rates.

Fair Labor Standards Act

Congress passed this act in 1938 to provide for minimum wages, maximum hours, overtime pay, and child labor protection. The law has been amended many times and covers most employees.

INTRODUCTION

Even with tough competition from Walmart and other chains, Wegmans Food Markets chose to pay above-average wages and provide all its full- and part-time employees with free health coverage. Management's assumption, as its human resources head put it, is that "if we take care of our employees, they will take care of our customers."[1] Wegmans' pay strategy seems to be working. Its larger stores each average about $950,000 a week in sales, compared to the national grocery store average of about $361,564. Similarly, Wegmans' employee turnover figures are well below retail store national averages. Wegmans' strategy is to compete with other grocery chains based on productivity and service. Its compensation strategy supports that competitive strategy.

Employee compensation refers to all forms of pay or rewards going to employees and arising from their employment. It has two main components: *direct financial payments* (in the form of wages, salaries, incentives, commissions, and bonuses) and *indirect payments* (in the form of financial benefits like employer-paid insurance and vacations). We'll discuss both in this chapter. ■

WHAT DETERMINES HOW MUCH YOU PAY?

Four basic factors determine what people are paid: legal, union, policy, and equity factors. We'll look at each, starting with legal considerations.

Some Important Compensation Laws

Numerous laws such as the following stipulate what employers can or must pay in terms of minimum wages, overtime rates, and benefits.[2]

1938 FAIR LABOR STANDARDS ACT The **Fair Labor Standards Act** (FLSA), passed in 1938 and since amended many times, contains minimum wage, maximum hours, overtime pay, equal pay, record-keeping, and child labor provisions covering most U.S. workers—virtually anyone engaged in producing or selling goods for interstate and foreign commerce.

One well-known provision governs overtime pay. It states that employers must pay overtime at a rate of at least one and a half times normal pay for any hours worked over 40 in a workweek.[3] The act also sets a minimum wage, which sets a floor for employees covered by the act (and usually bumps up wages for practically all workers when Congress raises the minimum). The minimum wage for the majority of those covered by the act was $7.25 per hour in July 2010.[4] (Several states and about 80 municipalities have their own, higher, minimum wages. For example, in 2010 the state minimum wage in California was $8 per hour.[5])

The act also contains child labor provisions. These provisions prohibit employing minors between 16 and 18 years of age in hazardous occupations (such as mining), and further restrict employment of those under 16.

EXEMPT/NON-EXEMPT Specific categories of employees are *exempt* from the act or certain provisions of the act, and particularly from the act's overtime provisions—they are "exempt employees."

A person's exemption depends on his or her responsibilities, duties, and salary. Bona fide executive, administrative (like office managers), and professional (like architects) employees are generally exempt from the act's minimum wage and overtime requirements.[6] A white-collar worker earning more than $100,000 and performing any one exempt administrative, executive, or professional duty is automatically ineligible for overtime pay. Other employees can generally earn up to $23,660 per year and still automatically get overtime pay. (So, most employees earning less than $455 per week are non-exempt and earn overtime.)[7]

If an employee is exempt from the FLSA's minimum wage provisions, then he or she is also exempt from its overtime pay provisions. However, certain employees are always exempt from overtime pay provisions. They include, among others, agricultural employees, live-in household employees, taxicab drivers, outside sales employees, and motion picture theater employees.[8]

As noted, some jobs—for example, top managers and lawyers—are clearly exempt, while others—such as office workers earning less than $23,660 per year—are non-exempt. Unfortunately, beyond the obvious categorizations, it's generally advisable to do some analyses

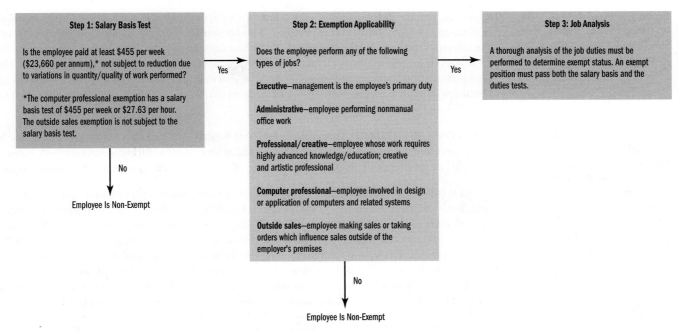

Step 1: Salary Basis Test

Is the employee paid at least $455 per week ($23,660 per annum),* not subject to reduction due to variations in quantity/quality of work performed?

*The computer professional exemption has a salary basis test of $455 per week or $27.63 per hour. The outside sales exemption is not subject to the salary basis test.

Yes →

No ↓

Employee Is Non-Exempt

Step 2: Exemption Applicability

Does the employee perform any of the following types of jobs?

Executive—management is the employee's primary duty

Administrative—employee performing nonmanual office work

Professional/creative—employee whose work requires highly advanced knowledge/education; creative and artistic professional

Computer professional—employee involved in design or application of computers and related systems

Outside sales—employee making sales or taking orders which influence sales outside of the employer's premises

Yes →

No ↓

Employee Is Non-Exempt

Step 3: Job Analysis

A thorough analysis of the job duties must be performed to determine exempt status. An exempt position must pass both the salary basis and the duties tests.

FIGURE 8.1
Who Is Exempt? Who Is Not Exempt?

HR APPs 4 U
Mobile PDA Handheld Timesheet Solutions

Keeping track of employees' hours when they're working out of the office isn't easy. That's why vendors such as Pacific Timesheet (www.pacifictimesheet.com/) provide mobile payroll time sheets. Employees who work outside can access and fill these in via their iPhones or similar devices. This improves attendance and payroll accuracy, reduces the need to adjust payrolls, and helps reduce overtime overpayments.[12]

before classifying a job as exempt or non-exempt. Figure 8.1 presents a procedure for making this decision. Note that in all but the clearest situations, it's advisable to review the person's job description. Make sure, for instance, that the job does in fact require that the person perform, say, a supervisory duty.[9] A study of low-wage workers in Chicago, New York, and Los Angeles found that about one-fourth were paid below the minimum wage in the week prior to the survey. Among the other wage and hour violations the survey found: 76% of the workers had unpaid or underpaid overtime and 56% didn't receive a pay stub as required by law.[10]

Even giant firms make FLSA errors. Walmart recently agreed to pay up to $640 million to settle 63 wage and hour suits alleging infractions such as failing to pay overtime.[11] Other firms assert that employees doing, say, computer programming, are not employees but "independent contractors" (who are more like consultants). For example, FedEx Ground is battling many lawsuits as it defends its right to maintain the status of its roughly 15,000 delivery truck owner-operators as independent contractors (it recently won one such case).[13] Whether the person is an employee or an independent contractor depends on numerous factors such as the amount of control the employer exercises over the person's duties and schedule.[14]

One company, Healthcare Management Group, estimates that "clock creep"—employees regularly clocking in a bit early or late—cost it as much as $250,000 per year in overtime. The company remedied this by installing an automated time and attendance system. These systems help provide real-time labor data to line managers, and automatically update timing systems for changes such as daylight savings time.[15]

1963 EQUAL PAY ACT The **Equal Pay Act**, an amendment to the Fair Labor Standards Act, states that employees of one sex may not be paid wages at a rate lower than that paid to employees of the

Equal Pay Act of 1963
An amendment to the Fair Labor Standards Act designed to require equal pay for women doing the same work as men.

Civil Rights Act of 1964, Title VII
Law that makes it unlawful practice for an employer to discriminate against any individual with respect to hiring, compensation, terms, conditions, or privileges of employment because of race, color, religion, sex, or nation.

opposite sex for doing roughly equivalent work. Specifically, if the work requires equal skills, effort, and responsibility and is performed under similar working conditions, employees of both sexes must receive equal pay unless the differences in pay are based on a seniority system, a merit system, the quantity or quality of production, or any factor other than sex.[16] The act notwithstanding, women still earn about 24% less than men overall. The gender gap was largest between men and women with advanced degrees (31%) and narrowest for those with high school degrees and some college (27%).[17]

1964 CIVIL RIGHTS ACT Title VII of the **Civil Rights Act** makes it an unlawful practice for an employer to discriminate against any individual with respect to hiring, compensation, terms, conditions, or privileges of employment because of race, color, religion, sex, or national origin.

OTHER DISCRIMINATION LAWS Various other laws influence compensation decisions. For example, the Age Discrimination in Employment Act prohibits age discrimination against employees who are 40 years of age and older in all aspects of employment, including compensation. The Americans with Disabilities Act similarly prohibits discrimination against qualified persons with disabilities in all aspects of employment, including compensation. The Family and Medical Leave Act entitles eligible employees, both men and women, to take up to 12 weeks of unpaid, job-protected leave for the birth of a child or for the care of a child, spouse, or parent. Employers that are federal government contractors or subcontractors are required by various executive orders not to discriminate.

How Unions Influence Compensation Decisions

For unionized companies, union-related issues also influence pay plan design. The National Labor Relations Act (NLRA) of 1935 granted employees the right to organize, to bargain collectively, and to engage in concerted activities for the purpose of collective bargaining or other mutual aid or protection. Historically, the wage rate is the main issue in collective bargaining. However, other pay-related issues including time off with pay, income security (for those in industries with periodic layoffs), cost-of-living adjustments, and various benefits such as health care are also important.[18]

Compensation Policies

As at Wegmans, an employer's strategy and compensation policies significantly influence the wages and benefits it pays. For example, a hospital might have a pay policy of starting nurses at a wage 20% above the prevailing market wage. Other important pay policies include the basis for salary increases, foreign pay differentials, and overtime pay.

Distinguishing between high and low performers is another important pay policy. For example, for many years Payless ShoeSource hardly distinguished in pay among high and low performers. However, after seeing its market share drop over several years, management embarked on a turnaround plan. The plan included new compensation policies. It now differentiates more aggressively between top performers and others.[19] (See the accompanying Managing HR in Challenging Times feature.)

The important point is that as at Wegmans, the compensation plan should support the employer's strategic aims—management should produce an *aligned reward strategy*. The basic aim is to create a total reward package, including wages, incentives, and benefits, that aims to elicit the employee behaviors the firm needs to support and achieve its competitive strategy.[20]

MANAGING HR IN CHALLENGING TIMES

Salary and Incentives in Tough Times

Not surprisingly, one way that employers deal with economically challenging times is by instituting policies to reduce salary increases and merit pay. Surveys by human resource management consulting companies such as Hewitt Associates and Mercer showed that as the recent recession deepened, at least half the employers in America (and more abroad) were planning to cut salary increases. On average, the survey suggested that salaried exempt employees' raises would drop from about 3.8% in 2008 to about 2.5% in 2009, while about 10% of U.S. employers surveyed were instituting pay freezes. Interestingly though, many were also establishing special funds to reward high-performing employees with incentives like long-term equity grants and retention bonuses.[21]

TALENT MANAGEMENT: ACTIVELY MANAGING COMPENSATION ALLOCATIONS As we saw in previous chapters, employers are increasingly segmenting their employees and actively assigning more resources to those they deem "mission-critical" in terms of the firm's strategy. Recall, for instance, that Accenture uses a 4x4 matrix to plot employees by Performance (exceptional, high, medium, low) and Value to the Organization (mission-critical, core, necessary, nonessential). It then allocates pay and other resources based on where the employee places in the matrix.[22] The decisions on whether to allocate pay on such a basis, and if so how to do so are therefore important policy matters for employers.

Many employers are taking this more active, segmentation approach. For example, we saw that one telecommunications firm previously spread development money and compensation evenly over its 8,000 employees. When the recession came, it segmented its talent into business impact, high performers, high potentials and critical skills. Then they shifted their dollars away from low performers and those not making an impact to high performers and high potentials.[23]

As another example, the human resources consulting company Hewitt says that,

"In the next generation of talent management, organizations will use consumer-marketing technologies to customize total rewards packages. Through personalized Web portals, organizations will offer rewards menus and associated dollar credits that are tailored to groups of workers and even individual workers. Dollar amounts will be tied to role and performance as opposed to age or seniority. Options offered will go beyond the traditional flexible benefits fare to include choice in work assignments and location, time and money for training, and working time flexibility. For example, AstraZeneca PLC offers workers customized rewards menus, allowing them to design the specifics of their rewards packages."[24]

Equity and Its Impact on Pay Rates

Equity is a key factor in determining pay rates.[25] Externally, pay must compare favorably with rates in other companies, or an employer will find it hard to attract and retain qualified employees. Internally, each employee should view his or her pay as equitable given other employees' pay in the organization. For example, in one study turnover of retail buyers was significantly lower when the buyers perceived fair treatment in the amount of rewards and in the methods employers used to allocate rewards.[26] Somewhat more counterintuitively, *overpaying* people relative to what they think they're worth can backfire too, perhaps "due to feelings of guilt or discomfort."[27] (For an additional perspective on how motivation influences pay and incentive design, please see this chapter's appendix.)

Some firms maintain secrecy over internal pay matters. However, online pay forums on sites like Salary.com, Wageweb.com, and Futurestep.com make it relatively easy today for employees to judge if they're being paid equitably externally.

---

2 Explain each of the five basic steps in establishing pay rates.

HOW EMPLOYERS ESTABLISH PAY RATES

In practice, setting pay rates while ensuring external and internal equity usually entails five steps:

1. Conduct a salary survey of what other employers are paying for comparable jobs (to price benchmark jobs and help ensure external equity).
2. Determine the worth of each job in your organization through job evaluation (to help ensure internal equity). An employee evaluation committee (possibly including an HR specialist) usually does the evaluation.
3. Group similarly paid jobs into pay grades.
4. Price each pay grade by using wage curves.
5. Develop rate ranges.

We explain each of these steps in this section, starting with salary surveys.

salary (or compensation) survey
A survey aimed at determining prevailing pay rates. Provides specific wage rates for specific jobs.

Step 1: Conduct the Salary Survey

Salary (or compensation) surveys—formal or informal surveys of what other employers are paying for similar jobs—play a central role in pricing jobs. Most employers therefore conduct such surveys for pricing one or more jobs.

Sponsor	Internet Address	What It Provides	Downside
Salary.com	Salary.com	Salary by job and zip code, plus job and description, for hundreds of jobs	Adapts national averages by applying local cost-of-living differences
Wageweb	www.wageweb.com	Average salaries for more than 150 clerical, professional, and managerial jobs	Charges for breakdowns by industry, location, etc.
U.S. Office of Personnel Management	www.opm.gov/oca/09Tables/index.asp	Salaries and wages for U.S. government jobs, by location	Limited to U.S. government jobs
Job Smart	http://jobstar.org/tools/salary/sal-prof.php	Profession-specific salary surveys	Necessary to review numerous salary surveys for each profession
cnnmoney.com	cnnmoney.com	Input your current salary and city, and this gives you comparable salary in destination city	Based on national averages adapted to cost-of-living differences

FIGURE 8.2
Some Pay Data Web Sites

Employers use salary surveys in three ways. First, they use them to price *benchmark jobs.* These anchor the employer's pay scale. The manager slots other jobs around them, based on their relative worth to the firm. (*Job evaluation*, explained next, is how you determine the relative worth of each job.) Second, employers usually price 20% or more of their positions directly in the marketplace (rather than relative to the firm's benchmark jobs), based on a formal or informal survey of what comparable firms are paying for comparable jobs. (This is particularly true for pricing fast-changing high-tech jobs, for instance.) Finally, surveys also collect data on benefits such as insurance, sick leave, and vacation time.

Finding salary data is not as mysterious as it used to be, thanks to the Internet. Figure 8.2 summarizes some popular salary Web sites. For example, the U.S. Department of Labor's Bureau of Labor Statistics' (BLS) *National Compensation Survey (NCS)* provides comprehensive reports of occupational earnings, compensation cost trends, and benefits (www.bls.gov/bls/wages.htm). Detailed occupational earnings are available from this survey for over 800 occupations in the United States, regions, states, and many metropolitan areas (http://stats.bls.gov/oes/current/oes_nat.htm). Many private consultants such as Watson Wyatt also supply salary surveys.[28]

Step 2: Determine the Worth of Each Job: Job Evaluation

After conducting a salary survey, the employer turns to job evaluation.

job evaluation
A formal and systematic comparison of jobs to determine the worth of one job relative to another.

PURPOSE OF JOB EVALUATION   **Job evaluation** is a formal and systematic comparison of jobs to determine the worth of one job relative to another. The basic job evaluation procedure is to compare the content of jobs in relation to one another, for example, in terms of their effort, responsibility, and skills. Suppose you know (based on your salary survey and compensation policies) how to price key benchmark jobs, and can use job evaluation to determine the relative worth of all the other jobs in your firm relative to these key jobs. Then you are well on your way to being able to equitably price all the jobs in your organization.

compensable factors
Fundamental, compensable elements of a job, such as skills, effort, responsibility, and working conditions.

COMPENSABLE FACTORS   There are two basic approaches to comparing the worth of several jobs. First, you could take an intuitive approach. You might decide that one job is more important than another is and not dig any deeper into why in terms of specific job-related factors.

As an alternative, you could compare the jobs based on certain basic factors they have in common. In compensation management, these basic factors are called **compensable factors**. They are the factors that determine your definition of job content. They also establish how the jobs compare to each other, and set the compensation paid for each job. For example, the Equal Pay Act focuses on four compensable factors: skills, effort, responsibility, and working conditions. Several years ago, Walmart instituted a new wage structure based on knowledge, problem-solving skills, and accountability requirements.

ranking method
The simplest method of job evaluation that involves ranking each job relative to all other jobs, usually based on a job's overall difficulty.

JOB EVALUATION METHODS The simplest job evaluation method ranks each job relative to all other jobs, usually based on some overall compensable factor such as job difficulty. There are several steps in this *job **ranking method***, as the HR in Practice feature summarizes. *Job classification* is another simple, widely used method. Here the manager categorizes jobs into groups based on their similarity in terms of compensable factors such as skills and responsibility. The groups are called *classes* if they contain similar jobs, or *grades* if they contain jobs that are similar in difficulty but otherwise different. Thus, in the federal government's pay grade system, a press secretary and a fire chief might both be graded GS-10 (GS stands for General Schedule). The *point method* is a quantitative job evaluation technique. It involves identifying several compensable factors, each having several degrees, and then assigning points based on the number of degrees so as to come up with a total number of points for each job.

HR IN PRACTICE

Steps in the Ranking Method of Job Evaluation

1. Obtain job information. Job analysis is the first step in the ranking method. Job descriptions for each job are prepared, and these provide the information (in terms of "overall job difficulty," for instance) on which the rankings are made.
2. Select raters and jobs to be rated. It is often not practical to make a single ranking of all jobs in an organization. The usual procedure is to rank jobs by department or in clusters (such as factory workers and clerical workers).
3. Select compensable factors. In the ranking method, it is common to use just one factor (such as job difficulty) and to rank jobs based on the whole job. Regardless of the number of factors you choose, explain the definition of the factor(s) to the evaluators so that they evaluate the jobs consistently.
4. Rank jobs. Next, the jobs are ranked. The simplest way is to give each rater a set of index cards, each of which contains a brief description of a job. They then rank these cards from lowest to highest on each compensable factor such as overall job difficulty. Some managers use an alternation ranking method for making the procedure more accurate; they use the cards to choose the highest and the lowest, and then the next highest and next lowest, and so forth until all the cards have been ranked. Table 8.1 illustrates a job ranking. Jobs in this hospital are ranked from maid up to office manager. Online programs,

as at www.hr-guide.com/data/G909.htm, can help you rank (and check the rankings of) your positions.
5. Combine ratings. Usually several raters rank the jobs independently. Then the rating committee (or employer) can average the rankings.

TABLE 8.1 Job Ranking at Jackson Hospital

Ranking Order	Annual Pay Scale
1. Office manager	$48,000
2. Chief nurse	47,500
3. Bookkeeper	39,000
4. Nurse	37,500
5. Cook	36,000
6. Nurse's aide	33,500
7. Maid	30,500

Note: After ranking, it becomes possible to slot additional jobs (based on overall job difficulty, for instance) between those already ranked and to assign each an appropriate wage rate.

Step 3: Group Similar Jobs into Pay Grades

Once a job evaluation method has been used to determine the relative worth of each job, the evaluation committee can start assigning pay rates to each job; it usually first groups jobs into pay grades. A *pay grade* comprises jobs of approximately equal difficulty or importance as determined by job evaluation. If the point method were used, the pay grade would consist of jobs falling within a range of points. If the ranking plan were used, the grade would consist of all jobs that fall within two or three ranks. If the classification system were used, then the jobs are already categorized into classes or grades. Ten to 16 grades per job cluster (or logical grouping such as factory jobs, clerical jobs, etc.) are common.

Step 4: Price Each Pay Grade: Wage Curves

wage curve
Shows the relationship between the relative value of the job (in points) and the average wage paid for this job.

The next step is to assign average pay rates to each of the pay grades. (Of course, if you choose not to slot jobs into pay grades, an individual pay rate has to be assigned to each individual job.) Assigning pay rates to each pay grade (or to each job) is usually accomplished with the help of a **wage curve**, which shows the average pay rates currently being paid for jobs in each pay grade, relative to the points or rankings assigned to each job or grade by the job evaluation.

Figure 8.3 illustrates a wage curve. The wage curve shows, for each job or job class, the relationship between (1) the value of the job as determined by one of the job evaluation methods and

FIGURE 8.3
Wage Structure

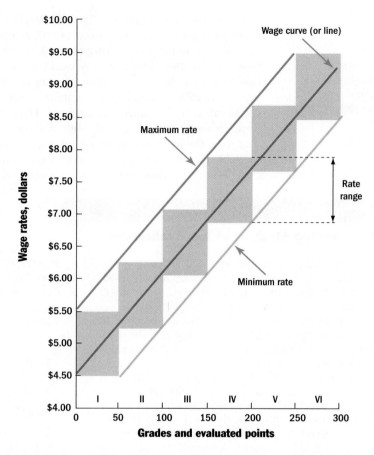

(2) the current average pay rates for the job or grade. Basically, you create a wage curve as you would any graph, in this case, by showing pay rates on the *y* vertical axis and job value or difficulty on the *x* horizontal axis, and then plotting the corresponding points for each job based on what you are paying now for each job or or job grade. The wage curve (or line) then becomes the target for wages or salary rates for all the jobs in each pay grade.

Step 5: Develop Rate Ranges

Finally, most employers do not just pay one rate for all jobs in a particular pay grade. Instead, they develop rate ranges for each grade. Thus, there might be 10 levels or steps within each of the 6 pay grades shown in Figure 8.3, and 10 corresponding pay rates within each pay grade. The employer may then fine-tune pay rates to account for individual circumstances.

Pricing Managerial and Professional Jobs

For managerial and professional jobs, job evaluation provides only a partial answer to the pay question. Managerial and professional jobs tend to emphasize nonquantifiable factors like judgment and problem solving. There is also more of a tendency to pay managers and professionals based on their performance, on what competitors are paying, or on what they can do, rather than on intrinsic job demands such as working conditions.[29]

Studies provide some insights. One concluded that three main factors, *job complexity* (span of control, the number of divisions over which the executive has direct responsibility, and management level), the employer's *ability to pay* (total profit and rate of return), and the executive's *human capital* (educational level, field of study, work experience) accounted for most of executive compensation variance.[30] In another study, of large companies, market factors such as competitors' pay levels and whether the CEO was likely to be "raided" by other firms were as or more important than firm size and annual performance in determining CEO pay.[31]

However, the recent economic downturn exposed the enormous disconnect between what many executives were earning and their performance. President Obama appointed a "pay czar" to oversee executive compensation in the financial institutions in which the United States had taken an equity interest.[32] In general, this person pressed the institution to deemphasize high salaries and big bonuses,

CHAPTER 8 • COMPENSATING EMPLOYEES **221**

substituting instead restricted stock (which the executives couldn't sell for at least two or three years). Now, even many non-bailout firms have moved toward such performance-based pay plans. At Ingersoll-Rand PLC, for instance, the company now grants stock to executives based on the company's performance over a three-year period rather than one year.[33] There is no doubt that most employers, particularly large ones, are now linking executive pay more to financial performance.[34]

RESEARCH NOTE The enormous risks apparently taken by some bonus-oriented employees in the past few years highlight the fact that incentives sometimes work too well. Evidence obtained via magnetic resonance imaging of people's brains suggests that money may have an even bigger impact on behavior than previously thought. As one recent article notes, "in today's cash focused culture, where new research suggests that money may have similar influences on individual actions as drugs or sex, the unexpected impact of plans that reward certain behaviors with cash is perhaps more than first thought."[35]

ELEMENTS For a company's top executives, the compensation plan generally consists of four main components: base salary, short-term incentives, deferred long-term incentives, and executive benefits and perks.[36]

- *Base salary* includes the obvious fixed compensation paid regularly as well as, often, guaranteed bonuses such as "10% of pay at the end of the fourth fiscal quarter, regardless of whether the company makes a profit," and discretionary bonuses.
- *Short-term incentives* are usually paid in cash or stock for achieving short-term goals, such as year-to-year increases in sales revenue. Companies like Nucor Corp. also have annual profit sharing and/or gainsharing plans in which their executives participate.
- *Deferred long-term incentives* include such things as stock options, which generally give the executive the right to purchase stock at a specific price for a specific period of time. These aim at encouraging the executive to take actions that will drive up the value of the company's stock. They are "deferred" insofar as they reflect a contractual agreement between the executive and employer to make payments at a later date. The deferred compensation may also include a "golden parachute" clause, aimed at giving the executive special pay and benefits in the event the firm is sold.
- Finally, *executive benefits and perks* might include supplemental retirement plans, supplemental life insurance, and health insurance without a deductible or coinsurance. Other popular executive perks include leased automobiles, automobile allowance, and free medical examinations.

CURRENT TRENDS IN COMPENSATION

How employers pay employees has been evolving.[37] This section looks at three important trends: competency-based pay, broadbanding, and board oversight of executive pay.[38] We'll discuss a fourth trend, performance-based pay, later in this chapter.

Talent Management: Competency- and Skill-Based Pay

Some question whether job evaluation's tendency to slot jobs into narrow cubbyholes ("Grade II," "Grade III," and so on) might not actually be counterproductive in today's high-performance work systems. Systems like these depend on flexible, multiskilled job assignments and on teamwork. There's thus no place for employees who say, "That's not my job." Yet if you want someone in Grade I to do a Grade II job for a while, that's actually what the response may be. Competency-based pay (and broadbanding, explained later) aims to avoid this problem, by paying people for what they can do, not for what jobs they hold.[39] This helps explain why talent management-oriented firms organize their recruiting, testing, training, appraising, and pay policies around competency models or profiles. Doing so should produce an integrated set of HR decisions based on the employee competencies the company needs to achieve its strategic aims.

In any case, with competency- or skill-based pay, you pay the employee for the skills and knowledge he or she is capable of using rather than for the responsibilities of the job currently held.[40] *Competencies* are demonstrable personal characteristics such as knowledge, skills, and behaviors.

Why pay employees based on the skill levels they achieve, rather than based on the jobs they're assigned to? The answer is to encourage the person to become more multiskilled. With more companies organizing around project teams, employers expect employees to be able to rotate among jobs. Doing so requires having more skills. Note, though, that there is today "a renewed interest in job evaluation and market pricing."[41] In economically challenging times, the efficiencies of job evaluation-based pay plans (paying only for the job being done, not one that might be done) may outweigh the flexibility of other approaches).

ELEMENTS Skill-based pay programs generally contain five main elements. The employer *defines* the specific skills required, and chooses a *method* for tying the person's pay to his or her skill level. A *training* system lets employees seek and acquire skills. There is a formal competency/skill *testing* system. And, the work is *designed* in such a way that employees can easily move among jobs of varying skill levels.

In practice, competency-based pay usually comes down to pay for knowledge or skill-based pay.[42] Pay-for-knowledge rewards employees for learning relevant knowledge—for instance, you might pay a new waiter more once he or she memorizes the menu. With skill-based pay, the employee earns more after developing relevant skills—Microsoft pays programmers more as they master the skill of writing new programs.

Broadbanding

Most firms end up with pay plans that slot jobs into classes or grades, each with its own vertical pay rate range. For example, the U.S. government's pay plan consists of 18 main grades (GS-1 to GS-18), each with its own pay range. For an employee whose job falls in one of these grades, the pay range for that grade dictates his or her minimum and maximum salary.

The question is how wide should the salary grades be, in terms of the number of job evaluation points or rankings they include? There is a downside to having narrow grades. Again, for instance, if you want a grade 2 person to learn about a job that happens to be in grade 3, he or she might object to the reassignment without a corresponding raise to grade 3 pay. Traditional grade pay plans thus breed inflexibility.

That is why some firms broadband their pay plans. Broadbanding means collapsing salary grades and ranges into just a few wide ranges, or bands, each of which contains a relatively wide range of jobs and salary levels. Figure 8.4 illustrates this. In this figure, the company's previous

FIGURE 8.4

Broadbanded Structure and How It Relates to Traditional Pay Grades and Ranges

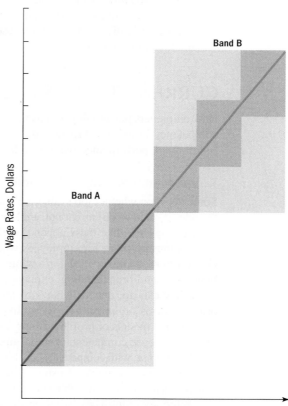

Wage Rates, Dollars

Band A

Band B

Grades and Evaluated Points

six pay grades are consolidated into two broadbands. Thus, for example, instead of having 10 salary grades, each of which contains a salary range of $15,000, the firm might collapse the 10 grades into 3 broadbands, such that the difference between the lowest and highest paid jobs might be $40,000 or more.

The Global Issues in HR feature addresses one global aspect of pay policy.

GLOBAL ISSUES IN HR

Compensating Expatriate Employees

With dramatically different costs of living among countries, compensating managers who are sent to work abroad is never easy. Most North American companies use what experts call the *balance sheet method* to compute the expatriate manager's pay. The aim here is to make sure the person's compensation remains consistent with what it would have been if he or she had stayed home. The person's base salary reflects the salaries in his or her home country. Then the employer layers on additional payments to cover things like housing costs, tax differences, and other living expenses (such as private schools for the person's children).[43] At the other extreme, some employers pay the manager based on what people are earning in the host country. This is known as the "host-country-based" or "going-rate" approach.

Each approach has pros and cons. The balance sheet approach makes it easier to repatriate employees, and generally elicits less resistance from the employees themselves (who might object to having their salaries slashed just because they're moving from high-cost New York to low-cost Bangalore). On the other hand, paying the expatriate more can lead to tensions between the manager and his or her host-country peers. The country-based approach has the advantage of integrating the expatriate better, since he or she is earning what his or her host country peers are earning. But it can mean slashing an employee's salary, hardly a practical option.

Board Oversight of Executive Pay

For 15 years, the board of directors of UnitedHealth Group Inc. supported its CEO with almost $2 billion in compensation. Then the board ousted him, allegedly because, as the *Wall Street Journal* put it, "his explanation for a pattern of unusually well-timed stock option grants didn't add up."[44]

There are various reasons why boards are clamping down on executive pay. The Securities and Exchange Commission (SEC) now requires filing more compensation-related information. The Sarbanes-Oxley Act makes executives personally liable, under certain conditions, for corporate financial oversight lapses.[45] The net result is that lawyers specializing in executive pay suggest that boards of directors ask themselves these questions:

● Has our compensation committee thoroughly identified its duties?
● Is our compensation committee being appropriately advised? (Government regulators and commentators strongly encourage this.)
● Are there particular executive compensation issues that our committee should address?
● Do our procedures demonstrate diligence and independence? (This demands careful deliberations and records.)
● Is our committee appropriately communicating its decisions? How will shareholders react?[46]

3 Compare and contrast piecework and team or group incentive plans.

incentive plan
A compensation plan that ties pay to performance.

INCENTIVE PLANS

Many—perhaps most—employees don't just earn a salary or hourly wage. They also earn some type of incentive. Indeed, "paying for performance" may be the most significant compensation trend today.

This section addresses some popular **incentive plans**. *Individual incentive programs* give performance-based pay to individual employees. *Variable pay* generally refers to group pay plans that tie payments to productivity or to some other measure of the firm's profitability.[47]

Traditionally, all incentive plans are pay-for-performance plans. They pay all employees based on the employee's performance. Several incentive plan examples follow.

Piecework Plans

piecework
A system of incentive pay tying pay to the number of items processed by each individual worker.

Piecework is the oldest incentive plan and still the most commonly used. Pay is tied directly to what the worker produces: The person is paid a "piece rate" for each unit he or she produces. Thus, if Tom Smith gets $0.40 for each address he finds on the Web, then he would make $40 for finding 100 addresses a day and $80 for 200.

Incentives for Salespeople

Most companies pay their salespeople a combination of salary and commissions, usually with a sizable salary component. Typical is a 70% base salary/30% incentive mix. This cushions both the downside risk from the salesperson's point of view and limits the risk that the rewards are too high from the firm's point of view.[48]

Setting effective quotas is an art. Questions to ask include: Are quotas communicated to the sales force within 1 month of the start of the period? Does the sales force know how their quotas are set? Are returns and debookings reasonably low? And, has your firm generally avoided compensation-related lawsuits?[49] One expert suggests the following as a rule of thumb as to whether the sales incentive plan is effective: 75% or more of the sales force achieving quota or better; 10% of the sales force achieving higher performance level (than previously); 5% to 10% of the sales force achieving below-quota performance and receiving performance development coaching.[50]

Some salespeople respond more positively to fixed salary plans while others prefer incentives. As a result, human resource and sales managers need to carefully select salespeople based at least partly on whether the job is commission or salary-based.[51]

AN EXAMPLE: AUTO DEALERS Commission rates vary by industry, but a look at how auto dealers set their salespersons' commission rates provides some insights. Compensation for car salespeople ranges from a high of 100% commission to a small base salary with commission accounting for most of the total compensation. Commission is generally based on the net profit on the car when it's delivered to the buyer. This promotes precisely the sorts of behaviors the car dealers want to encourage. For example, it encourages the salesperson to hold firm on the retail price, and to push after-sale products like floor mats and car alarms. Car dealers also use short-term incentives. For helping sell slow-moving vehicles, the salesperson may be offered a "spiff"—a car dealer term for an extra incentive bonus over commission.[52]

Compensation for car salespeople ranges from a high of 100% commission to a small base salary with commission accounting for most of the total compensation.

Source: Marc Romanelli/Jupiter Images Royalty Free.

Recognition-Based Awards

Recognition is one of several types of nonmonetary incentives. The term *recognition programs* usually refers to formal programs, such as employee-of-the-month programs. *Social recognition programs* refer to more informal manager–employee exchanges such as praise, approval, or expressions of appreciation for a job well-done. *Performance feedback* is similar to social recognition, but means "providing quantitative or qualitative information on task performance for the purpose of changing or maintaining performance and specific ways."[53] The HR in Practice feature explains how supervisors use these methods.

Recognition has a positive impact on performance, either alone or in conjunction with financial rewards.[54] It's therefore not surprising that in one survey, 78% of CEOs and 58% of HR vice presidents said their firms were using performance recognition programs.[55] At American Skandia, which provides insurance and financial planning products and services, customer service reps who exceed standards receive a plaque, a $500 check, their story on the firm's internal Web site, and a dinner for them and their teams.[56] Reward and recognition programs represent about 2.7% of the annual payroll for U.S. employers.[57] One survey of 235 managers found that the most-used rewards to motivate employees (top-down from most used to least) were:[58]

- Employee recognition
- Gift certificates
- Special events
- Cash rewards
- Merchandise incentives
- E-mail/print communications
- Training programs
- Variable pay
- Work-life benefits
- Group travel
- Individual travel
- Sweepstakes

HR IN PRACTICE

Incentives Supervisors Can Use

As you can see, the individual line manager should not rely just on the employer's incentive plans for motivating subordinates. There are simply too many opportunities to motivate employees every day to let those opportunities pass. There are three guides to follow.

First, the best option for motivating employees is also the simplest—*make sure the employee has a doable goal* and that he or she agrees with it. It makes little sense to try to motivate employees with financial incentives if they don't know their goals or don't agree with them. Psychologist Edwin Locke and his colleagues have consistently found that specific, challenging goals lead to higher task performance than do vague goals or no goals.

Second, *recognizing an employee's contribution* is a powerful motivation tool. Studies show that recognition has a positive impact on performance, either alone or in combination with financial rewards. For example, in one study, combining financial rewards with recognition produced a 30% performance improvement in service firms, almost twice the effect of using each reward alone.

Third, there are numerous *positive reinforcement rewards* you can use on a day-to-day basis. A short list includes:[59]

- Challenging work assignments
- Freedom to choose own work activity
- Having fun built into work
- More of preferred task
- Role as boss's stand-in when he or she is away
- Role in presentations to top management
- Job rotation
- Encouragement of learning and continuous improvement
- Being provided with ample encouragement
- Being allowed to set own goals
- Compliments
- Expression of appreciation in front of others
- Note of thanks
- Employee-of-the-month award
- Special commendation
- Bigger desk
- Bigger office or cubicle

Online Award Programs

If there's a downside to financial recognition programs, it's that they're expensive to administer. Many firms—including Levi Strauss & Co. and Barnes & Noble—therefore partner with online incentive firms to expedite the process. Management consultant Hewitt Associates uses www.bravanta.com to help its managers more easily recognize exceptional employee service with special awards. Additional Internet incentive/recognition sites include www.premierchoiceaward.com, www.giveanything.com, and www.incentivecity.com. They and others like them enable client firms' supervisors to make awards easily.

Merit Pay as an Incentive

merit pay (merit raise)
Any salary increase awarded to an employee based on his or her individual performance.

Merit pay, or a **merit raise**, is any salary increase awarded to an employee based on his or her individual performance. It is different from a bonus in that it usually becomes part of the employee's base salary, whereas a bonus is a one-time payment. Although the term *merit pay* can apply to the incentive raises given to any employee, the term is more often used with respect to white-collar employees and particularly professional, office, and clerical employees.

Merit pay has both advocates and detractors. Advocates argue that only rewards like these that are tied directly to performance can motivate improved performance. Detractors say it can undermine teamwork, and that, since the merit pay typically depends on the performance appraisal, unfair appraisals will lead employees to perceive the pay as unfair, too.

Team Incentive Plans

Businesses increasingly organize their efforts around teams, and therefore want to incentivize the team to meet its goals. There are several ways to do this. One company created a pool of money such that if the company reached 100% of its overall goal, the employees would share in about 5% of any savings. That 5% pool was then divided by the number of employees to arrive at the value of a share. Each *work team* then received two goals. If the team achieved both of its goals, each employee would earn one full share (in addition to his or her base pay). Employees on teams that reached only one goal would earn a half-share. Those on teams reaching neither goal earned no shares.[60]

A group incentive plan's main disadvantage is that each worker's rewards are not based just on his or her own efforts. If the person does not see his or her effort translating directly into proportional rewards, a group plan may be less effective than an individual plan.[61] One compensation expert says, "The best advice I can give is to get the [team] set up right; pay comes later, if at all, to reward team members for performance."[62]

NUCOR TEAM INCENTIVE EXAMPLE Nucor Corp. is the largest steel producer in the United States; it also has the highest productivity, highest wages, and lowest labor cost per ton in the American steel industry.[63] Its bonus plans help explain this.

Nucor employees earn bonuses of 100% or more of base salary. All participate in one of four performance-based incentive plans. With the *production incentive plan*, plant operating and maintenance employees and supervisors get weekly bonuses based on their workgroup's productivity. The *department manager incentive plan* pays department managers annual incentive bonuses based mostly on the ratio of net income to dollars of assets employed for their division. With the *professional and clerical bonus plan,* employees who are not in one of the two previous plans get bonuses based on their division's net income return on assets. Finally, under the *senior officers incentive plan*, Nucor senior managers (whose base salaries are lower than those of executives in comparable firms) get bonuses based on Nucor's annual overall percentage of net income to stockholder's equity.[64] Including bonuses, a typical Nucor steel mill worker earns about $72,000 a year, not counting the profit-sharing plan that recently paid out an additional $18,000 per employee.[65]

Incentives for Managers and Executives

Managers play a central role in influencing profitability, and most firms therefore put considerable thought into how to reward them.[66] For CEOs, salary generally accounts for less than 25% of total direct compensation. As you can see in Figure 8.5, bonuses then account for around 24%

FIGURE 8.5

CEO Total Direct Compensation

Source: Robert Grossman, "Executive Pay: Perception and Reality," *HR Magazine,* April 2009, page 29. Reprinted with permission of the Society for Human Resource Management (www.shrm.org), Alexandria, VA, publisher of *HR Magazine.* © SHRM.

Types of CEO pay, By Industry.

Industry Category	Number of Companies in Survey	Salary	Bonus	Long-Term Incentive
Basic materials	25	17	27	56
Consumer goods	56	17	24	59
Consumer services	89	25	21	54
Financials	55	14	29	57
Health care	31	16	24	60
Industrials	71	17	25	58
Oil and gas	23	12	22	66
Technology	29	18	27	55
Telecommunications	6	11	13	76
Utilities	32	17	22	61
All industries	417	18	24	58

of total compensation and long-term incentives about 55%.[67] Employers generally pay out bonus and short-term incentive awards in cash. Long-term incentives more often take the form of company stock, sometimes stock options.

stock option
The right to purchase a stated number of shares of company stock at a set price at some time in the future.

STOCK OPTIONS A **stock option** is the right to purchase a specific number of shares of company stock at a specific price during a period of time. The executive hopes to profit by exercising his or her option to buy the shares in the future, but at today's price. The firm's profitability and growth affects its stock price, and because the executive can affect these factors, the stock option supposedly is an incentive.

The chronic problem with stock options is that they often don't motivate performance. For example, some firms discover that their managers can profit from their options simply because the stock prices of all the firms in the industry rose due to favorable economic trends.

Many also blame stock options for contributing to numerous corporate scandals. For example, some executives allegedly manipulated the dates they received their options to maximize their returns. Furthermore, until recently, most companies did not treat stock options as an expense. This made the firm's expenses look less than they really were. With more companies trying to emphasize accuracy and transparency in financial statements, more are now expensing stock options. This in turn makes options less attractive to employers. As mentioned earlier, incentives may also encourage counterproductive behaviors such as excessive risk, if misdesigned.

In any case, when the market plummets, employers must scramble to sweeten their managers' stock option plans.[68] When stock markets dropped in 2008–2009, Google announced it would allow employees to exchange underwater options for stock, a decision that earned Googlers over $2 billion by year's end.[69]

SARBANES-OXLEY The Sarbanes-Oxley Act of 2002 affects how employers formulate their executive incentive programs. Congress passed Sarbanes-Oxley to inject a higher level of responsibility into both executives' and board members' decisions. It makes them personally liable for violating their fiduciary responsibilities to their shareholders. The act also requires that CEOs and CFOs of a public company repay any bonuses, incentives, or equity-based compensation received from the company during the 12-month period following the issuance of a financial statement that the company must restate due to material noncompliance with a financial reporting requirement as a result of misconduct.[70]

profit-sharing plan
A plan whereby most employees share in the company's profits.

Profit-Sharing Plans

In a **profit-sharing plan**, most employees receive a share of the company's annual profits, usually at the end of the fiscal year. With *current profit-sharing* plans, employees share in a portion of the employer's profits quarterly or annually. With *deferred profit-sharing* plans, the employer puts cash awards into trust accounts for the employees' retirement. In general, employers base the pool of profit-sharing funds on a fixed or graduated percentage of the firm's profits. They then distribute the profit-sharing awards to employees based on a percentage of the employee's salary, or some measure of the employee's contribution to company profits.[71]

Research on the effectiveness of such plans is sketchy. One early study concluded that there was "ample" evidence that profit-sharing plans boost productivity, but that their effect on profits is insignificant, once you factor in the costs of the plans' payouts.[72]

Employee Stock Ownership Plans

employee stock ownership plan (ESOP)
A corporation contributes shares of its own stock to a trust to purchase company stock for employees. The trust distributes the stock to employees upon retirement or separation from service.

Employee stock ownership plans (ESOPs) are company-wide plans in which a corporation contributes shares of its own stock—or cash to be used to purchase such stock—to a trust established to purchase shares of the firm's stock for employees. The firm generally makes these contributions annually in proportion to total employee compensation, with a limit of 15% of compensation. The trust holds the stock in individual employee accounts. It then distributes it to employees upon retirement (or other separation from service), assuming the person has worked long enough to earn ownership of the stock. (Traditional stock options, as discussed elsewhere in this chapter, go directly to the employees individually to use as they see fit, rather than into a retirement trust.) Trustees and possibly top management can and have been held responsible for ESOP trust problems, as when funds are lost.[73]

ESOPs have several advantages. The corporation receives a tax deduction equal to the fair market value of the shares that it transfers to the trustee. It can also claim an income tax deduction for dividends paid on stock the ESOP owns. Employees aren't taxed until they receive a distribution from the trust, usually at retirement when they normally have a reduced tax rate. And the **Employee Retirement Income Security Act (ERISA)** allows a firm to borrow against employee stock held in trust. The employer can then repay the loan in pretax rather than in after-tax dollars, another ESOP tax incentive.

Employee Retirement Income Security Act (ERISA)
Signed into law by President Ford in 1974 to require that pension rights be vested, and protected by a government agency, the Pension Benefits Guarantee Corporation.

gainsharing plan
An incentive plan that engages employees in a common effort to achieve productivity objectives and share the gains.

Scanlon plan
An incentive plan developed in 1937 by Joseph Scanlon and designed to encourage cooperation, involvement, and sharing of benefits.

Gainsharing Plans

The aim of **gainsharing plans** is to encourage improved employee productivity by sharing resulting financial gains with employees. Popular types of gainsharing plans include the Scanlon plan, Rucker plan, and Improshare plan.[74] All are variable pay plans.

FEATURES The **Scanlon plan** is typical, and has five basic features.[75] The first is the *philosophy of cooperation* on which it is based. This philosophy assumes that managers and workers should rid themselves of the "us" and "them" attitudes that normally inhibit employees from developing a sense of ownership in the company. It substitutes instead a climate in which everyone cooperates because he or she understands that economic rewards are contingent on honest cooperation.

A second feature of a Scanlon plan is *identity*. This means that to focus employee efforts, the company's mission or purpose must be clear to employees, and employees must understand how the business operates in terms of customers and costs, for instance. *Competence* is a third basic feature. The plan, say three experts, "explicitly recognizes that a Scanlon plan demands a high level of competence from employees at all levels."[76]

The fourth feature is the *involvement system*.[77] This takes the form of two levels of committees—the departmental level and the executive level. Employees present productivity-improving suggestions to the appropriate departmental-level committees, which transmit the valuable ones to the executive-level committee. The latter then decides whether to implement the suggestions.

The fifth feature of the plan is the *sharing of benefits formula*. The Scanlon plan assumes that employees should share directly in any extra profits resulting from their cost-cutting suggestions. For example, if a suggestion is implemented and successful, all employees might share in 75% of the savings.

Earnings-at-Risk Pay Plans

In an *earnings-at-risk* pay plan, employees agree to put some portion of their normal pay (say, 6%) at risk if they don't meet their goals, in return for the possibility of obtaining a much larger bonus (say, 12%) if they exceed their goals. For example, suppose in one department the employees' base pay will be 94% of their counterparts' salary in other (not-at-risk) departments. If the department

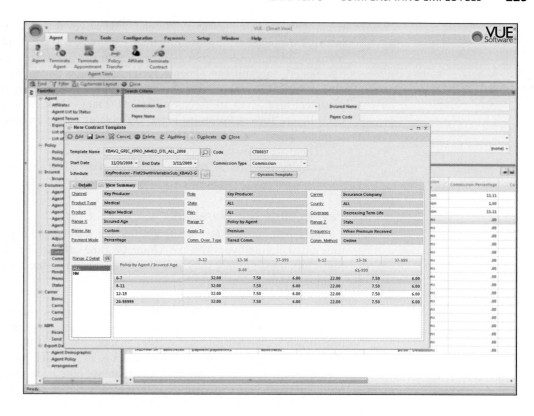

then achieves its goals, the employees get their full pay; if it exceeds its goals, they would receive a 12% bonus.

One study concluded that the employees they studied were dissatisfied with their lower base salary, but that this dissatisfaction seemed to motivate them to work harder to earn the incentive and thereby raise their total pay.[78]

Improving Productivity through HRIS: Incentive Management Systems

Somewhat astonishingly, given the amount of money employers pay out in commissions, most still track sales performance and sales commissions much as they did decades ago, using spreadsheets (although now computerized ones). To maximize performance, the sales manager typically needs evidence, such as, "Do the sales team members understand the compensation plans? Do they know how we measure and reward performance? Are quotas set fairly? Is there a positive correlation between performance and commission earnings? Are commissions more than covering total salespersons expenses? And, does our commission plan maximize sales of our most profitable products?"[79] It is difficult or impossible to gather this evidence or answer these questions because the spreadsheets don't easily support these types of analyses.

Gathering this evidence and conducting these analyses require software programs, namely Enterprise Incentive Management applications.[80] Several vendors supply these systems. One is VUE Software, which supplies VUE Compensation Management.[81] With the aid of charts such as that in the screen grab above, VUE Compensation enables the sales manager to conduct the necessary analyses. For example, he or she can trend and analyze compensation and performance data, conduct "what-if" analyses and reports, do trend analysis for performance data, and model changes to existing compensation plans.[82]

4 List and describe each of the basic benefits most employers might be expected to offer.

benefits
Indirect financial payments given to employees. They may include health and life insurance, vacation, pension, education plans, and discounts on company products, for instance.

EMPLOYEE BENEFITS

Benefits represent an important part of just about every employee's pay.[83] They are "indirect monetary and nonmonetary payments an employee receives for continuing to work for the company." Benefits include such things as time off with pay, health and life insurance, and child care facilities. In one survey, 78% of employees cited health care benefits as most crucial to retaining them; 75% cited compensation. But the same survey found that only 34% are satisfied with their health care benefits.[84] Most full-time employees in the United States do receive benefits. Virtually all employers—99%—offer some health insurance coverage.[85]

Benefits are a major expense for most employers. Employee benefits account for 33% to 40% of wages and salaries (or about 28% of total payrolls); legally required benefits (like unemployment insurance) are the most expensive single benefit cost, followed by health insurance. Consultants Towers Perrin estimates the cost of medical coverage alone to be about $888 per month for family coverage.[86]

There are many benefits and various ways to classify them. In the remainder of this section, we classify benefits as pay for time not worked, insurance benefits, retirement benefits, employee services, and family-friendly benefits.

Pay for Time Not Worked

Supplemental pay benefits, or pay for time not worked, are expensive benefits because of all the time off that employees receive. Common time-off-with-pay benefits include holidays, vacations, jury duty, military duty, sick leave, and unemployment insurance payments for laid-off or terminated employees.

UNEMPLOYMENT INSURANCE   All states have unemployment insurance or compensation acts, which provide for weekly benefits if a person is unable to work through some fault other than his or her own.[87] The benefits derive from an unemployment tax on employers that can range from 0.1% to 5% of taxable payroll in most states. States each have their own unemployment laws, which follow federal guidelines. An organization's unemployment tax reflects its personnel termination rate and experience.

Unemployment benefits aren't for all dismissed employees, only for those terminated through no fault of their own. Thus, strictly speaking, a worker fired for chronic lateness has no legitimate claim to benefits. But in practice, many managers take a lackadaisical attitude toward protecting their employers against unwarranted claims. Therefore, employers spend thousands of dollars more per year on unemployment taxes than would be necessary if they protected themselves—for instance, by keeping careful records of lateness and absences, and by warning employees whose performance is inadequate.[88]

VACATIONS AND HOLIDAYS   Most firms offer vacation leave benefits. Eighty-four percent of human resource professionals said their firms offered paid vacation for employees, and more than half (51%) reported offering paid personal days.[89] On average, American workers get 8.9 days of leave after one year's employment. Days off rises to about 11 after 3 years, 14 after 5 years, and 16 after 10 years.[90] The average number of annual vacation days varies around the world, for example, from 6 days in Mexico to 10 days in Japan, 25 in France, and 33 in Denmark.

More firms are moving to a more flexible vacation leave approach. For example, all of IBM's 350,000 plus employees are eligible for at least 3 weeks vacation. However, IBM doesn't formally track how much vacation each person takes, or when he or she takes it. Instead, employees make informal vacation arrangements with their direct supervisors.[91]

SICK LEAVE   Sick leave provides pay to employees when they are out of work because of illness. Most sick leave policies grant full pay for a specified number of permissible sick days, usually up to about 12 per year. The sick days often accumulate at the rate of approximately 1 day per month of service.

Sick leave pay causes consternation for many employers. The problem is that although many employees use their sick days only when they are legitimately sick, others (in the eyes of some employers) use it as if it's extra vacation time, whether they are sick or not. One survey a few years ago found that the average cost of absenteeism per employee per year was about $789, with personal illness accounting for about a third of the absences.[92]

Employers utilize several tactics to eliminate or reduce this problem:

- Many use *pooled paid leave* plans. About two-thirds of firms surveyed have such plans, which lump together days off for sick leave, vacation, and holidays into a single leave pool (with fewer total days).[93]

- Other firms buy back unused sick leave at the end of the year by paying their employees a daily equivalent pay for each sick leave day not used. The drawback is that this can encourage legitimately sick employees to come to work.
- Others hold monthly lotteries in which only employees with perfect attendance are able to participate; those who participate are eligible to win a cash prize.
- Still others aggressively investigate all unplanned absences, for instance, by calling the absent employees at their homes when they are taking sick days.

FMLA Sick leave policy depends to some extent on the Family and Medical Leave Act of 1993 (FMLA). Among its provisions, the law stipulates that:

1. Private employers of 50 or more employees must provide eligible employees up to 12 weeks of unpaid leave for their own serious illness; the birth or adoption of a child; or the care of a seriously ill child, spouse, or parent.
2. Employers may require employees to take any unused paid sick leave or annual leave as part of the 12-week leave provided in the law.
3. Employees taking leave are entitled to receive health benefits while they are on unpaid leave under the same terms and conditions as when they were on the job.
4. In most cases, employers must guarantee employees the right to return to their previous or equivalent position with no loss of benefits at the end of the leave.[94]

severance pay
A one-time payment employers provide when terminating an employee.

SEVERANCE PAY Many employers provide **severance pay**—a one-time separation payment— when terminating an employee. Other firms provide "bridge" severance pay by keeping employees (especially managers) on the payroll for several months. About half of employers surveyed give white-collar and exempt employees one week of severance pay per year of service, and about one-third do the same for blue-collar workers. It is uncommon to pay severance when employees quit or are fired for cause (though some employers do, to head off lawsuits).[95]

Severance pay makes sense on several grounds. It is a humanitarian gesture as well as good public relations. In addition, most managers expect employees to give them at least 1 or 2 weeks' notice if they plan to quit; it is therefore appropriate (and in some states mandatory) to provide at least one pay period's severance pay if an employee is terminated. Such payments can also reduce the possibility that a terminated employee will litigate.[96]

Things to keep in mind when designing the severance plan include:[96]

- List the situations for which the firm will pay severance, such as layoffs resulting from internal reorganizations. Indicate that management will determine action regarding other situations.
- Require signing of a waiver/general release prior to remittance of any severance pay, absolving the employer from employment-related liability. To be an effective release, the release must be knowing and voluntary, and there are additional legal requirements.
- Reserve the right to terminate or alter the policy.

Plant closings and downsizings have put millions of employees out of work, often with little or no notice or severance pay. *The Worker Adjustment and Retraining Notification ("plant closing") Act* of 1989 requires covered employers to give employees 60 days' written notice (not severance) of plant closures or mass layoffs.

Insurance Benefits

workers' compensation
Provides income and medical benefits to work-related accident victims or their dependents regardless of fault.

WORKERS' COMPENSATION Workers' compensation laws aim to provide sure, prompt income and medical benefits to work-related accident victims or their dependents, regardless of fault. Every state has its own workers' compensation law, and some states offer their own insurance programs. However, most require employers to purchase workers' compensation insurance through private state-approved insurance companies. These firms then charge the employer an annual premium based in part on the employer's accident and claims rates.

Workers' compensation benefits can be either monetary or medical. In the event of a worker's death or disablement, the person or his or her beneficiary gets a cash benefit based on prior earnings— usually one-half to two-thirds of the worker's average weekly wage, per week of employment. In most states, there is a set time limit—such as 500 weeks—for receiving benefits. If the injury causes a specific loss (such as loss of an arm), the employee may receive additional benefits based on a statutory list of losses, even though he or she may return to work. In addition to cash benefits, employers must furnish accident-related medical, surgical, and hospital services needed by the employee.

For an injury or illness to be covered by workers' compensation, the employee need only prove that it arose while he or she was on the job. It does not matter that the employee may have been at fault or disregarded instructions. If he or she was on the job when the injury occurred, he or she is entitled to workers' compensation.

Many, or most, workers' compensation claims are legitimate, but some are not. Supervisors should be aware of typical red flags of fraudulent claims. These include vague accident details and minor accidents resulting in major injuries.

Hospitalization, Medical, and Disability Insurance

Health care benefits top employees' desired benefits. Seventy-five percent of respondents in one survey said they considered health care benefits their most important benefits.[97]

Most employers therefore offer their employees some type of hospitalization, medical, and prescription insurance (see Table 8.2).[98] Many offer membership in a health maintenance organization (HMO) as a hospital/medical option. The HMO is a medical organization consisting of numerous specialists (surgeons, psychiatrists, etc.) operating out of a community-based health care center. Preferred provider organizations (PPOs) let employees select providers (such as participating physicians) who agree to provide price discounts and submit to certain utilization controls, such as the number of diagnostic tests that can be ordered.

THE PREGNANCY DISCRIMINATION ACT The Pregnancy Discrimination Act (PDA) aims to prohibit sex discrimination based on "pregnancy, childbirth, or related medical conditions." The act requires employers to treat women affected by pregnancy, childbirth, or related medical conditions the same as any employee not able to work, with respect to all benefits, including sick leave and disability benefits, and health and medical insurance. For example, if an employer provides up to 26 weeks of temporary disability income to employees for all illnesses, it is also required to provide up to 26 weeks for pregnancy and childbirth or related medical conditions.

Patient Protection and Affordable Care Act (PPACA)
The act contains various provisions, for instance expanding Medicaid eligibility, subsidizing health insurance premiums, and encouraging businesses to provide health care benefits.

THE PATIENT PROTECTION AND AFFORDABLE CARE ACT President Obama signed the **Patient Protection and Affordable Care Act (PPACA)** into law in March 2010. In brief, the act contains various provisions, for instance expanding Medicaid eligibility, subsidizing health insurance premiums, and encouraging businesses to provide health care benefits. Aimed at expanding health care coverage for Americans, some critics argue that the act may actually encourage some employers to reduce their health care insurance costs, by incentivizing them to move employees from a company plan to a government-run insurance plan.

TABLE 8.2 Percentage of Employers Offering Popular Health Benefits—Change Over Time

	Yes (%) 2005	Yes (%) 2009
Prescription drug program coverage	97	96
Dental insurance	95	96
Mail order prescription program	90	91
PPO (preferred provider organization)	87	81
Chiropractic coverage	56	80
Mental health insurance	72	80
Vision insurance	80	76
Employee assistance program	73	75
Medical spending account	80	71
Life insurance for dependents	67	58
HMO (health maintenance organization)	53	35

Source: Adapted from 2009 SHRM Employee Benefits Survey Report, p. 5.

Health care benefits top
employees' desired benefits.

Source: Spencer Platt/Getty Images, Inc.–Liaison.

COBRA REQUIREMENTS The ominously titled COBRA—Consolidated Omnibus Budget Reconciliation Act—requires most private employers to make available to terminated or retired employees and their families continued health benefits for a period of time, generally 18 months. If the former employee chooses to continue these benefits, he or she must pay for them, as well as a small fee for administrative costs.[99]

Take care in administering COBRA, especially when informing employees of their COBRA rights. For example, you do not want a separated uninsured employee to be injured and come back and claim she didn't know that she could have continued her insurance coverage. Therefore, when a new employee first becomes eligible for your company's insurance plan, the employee should receive and acknowledge having received an explanation of COBRA rights. More important, all employees separated from the company should sign a form acknowledging that they have received and understand their COBRA rights.[100]

MENTAL HEALTH PARITY ACT OF 1996 The World Health Organization estimates that more than 34 million people in the United States between the ages of 18 and 64 suffer from mental illness.[101] The Mental Health Parity Act of 1996 (as amended in 2008) sets minimum mental health care benefits; it also prohibits employer group health plans from adopting mental health benefits limitations without comparable limitations on medical and surgical benefits.[102]

COST CONTROL Health care costs are spiraling. Since 2004, health care premiums have risen about 78%, while inflation rose only 17%.[103] Health costs rose an estimated 7% in 2010.[104] Employers are using several tactics to address this problem.

Cost containment specialists Many are using companies that specialize in helping employers reduce their health care costs. For example, health care containment companies can use their network of contacts with PPOs to help employers obtain the best PPO coverage for their needs.

Online administration Other big savings come from automating health care plan administration, for instance, by making online enrollment by employees mandatory.

Defined benefits Other employers are moving toward defined contribution health care plans. Under defined contribution health care plans, each employee has a medical allotment that he or she can use for copayments or discretionary medical costs, rather than a health care benefits package with open-ended costs.

Deductibles Other firms are moving toward offering plans with high deductibles—more than $1,000—for individual coverage.[105]

Outsourcing Outsourcing is another option. For example, 84% of firms in one survey said they were outsourcing employee assistance and counseling, and 53% were outsourcing health care benefits administration.[106]

Wellness programs Medical experts believe that many illnesses are preventable, and studies show that controlling health risks can reduce illnesses and health care costs.[107] Most large employers (and many small ones) therefore offer some form of preventive services or "wellness benefits." *Clinical prevention* programs include things like mammograms, immunizations, and routine checkups. *Health promotion and disease prevention* programs include things like incentives aimed at improving health by modifying lifestyles.[108]

For example, Vaught Aircraft Industries Inc. kicked off its wellness program with health fairs in all its locations. Employees and families could come to the fairs to receive one-on-one health assessments (including blood samples and blood pressure readings). Vaught also offers a 24-hour telephone hotline to answer employees' health and lifestyle questions, as well as workshops on things like stress management.[109]

Claims audits Many employers pay out thousands or millions of dollars in erroneous health claims. The industry standard for percentage of claims dollars actually paid in error is 1%; in two recent years the *actual* percentage of claims dollars paid in error were 3.5% and 3.3%. Setting standards for errors, and then aggressively auditing the claims being paid, may be the most direct way to reduce employer health care expenses.[110] One simple method is to ensure that dependents enrolled are actually eligible for coverage.[111]

Medical tourism "Medical tourism" is another option. Here employers encourage employees to have some non-urgent medical procedures done overseas. Hospitals in Brazil or Malaysia may charge half what a U.S. hospital would for shoulder surgery, for instance. The key question is quality of care, but (while many people have successfully used this option) it's still not entirely clear how to assess overseas medical quality.[112]

Technology Experts hope that the approximately $19 billion in health information technology funding in the federal government's recent stimulus package will help employers reduce health care benefit costs by automating their paper-based systems.[113]

Mini Plans Some employers are offering limited-benefit health care insurance plans. Unlike typical health care plans with lifetime coverage limits of $1 million or more, these new mini plans have annual caps of about $2,000–$10,000 per year. The advantage is that the premiums are correspondingly lower as well.[114]

LONG-TERM CARE There are many types of long-term care—care to support older persons in their old age—for which employers can provide insurance benefits for their employees. For example, adult day-care facilities offer social and recreational activities. Assisted-living facilities offer shared housing and supervision for those who can't function independently. Home care is care received at home from a nurse, an aide, or another specialist.

Retirement Benefits

SOCIAL SECURITY There are three types of Social Security benefits. First are the familiar *retirement benefits*, which provide an income if the employee retires at age 62 or thereafter and is insured under the Social Security Act. Second, survivor's or *death benefits* provide monthly payments to dependents regardless of the employee's age at death, again assuming the employee was insured under the Social Security Act. Finally, *disability payments* provide monthly payments to an employee and his or her dependents if the employee becomes totally disabled for work and meets specified work requirements. The Social Security system also administers the Medicare program, which provides health services to people 65 and over.

"Full retirement age"—the usual age for receiving your full Social Security benefit—used to be 65. However, full retirement age to collect Social Security rose gradually over the years. It's now 67 for those born in 1960 or later. Social Security benefits are funded by a tax on earnings that the employer and employee share. As of 2010, the maximum amount of someone's earnings subject to Social Security tax was $106,800.[115] Employer and employee each paid 7.65%.[116]

PENSION PLANS Pensions provide income to individuals in their retirement, and just over half of full-time workers participate in some type of pension plan at work.

We can classify pension plans in three basic ways: contributory versus noncontributory plans, qualified versus nonqualified plans, and defined contribution versus defined benefit plans.[117] The employee contributes to the contributory pension plan, while the employer makes all contributions to the noncontributory pension plan. Employers derive certain tax benefits (such as tax deductions) for contributing to qualified pension plans (they are "qualified" for preferred tax treatment by the IRS); nonqualified pension plans get less favorable tax treatment.

defined benefit plan
A plan that contains a formula for specifying retirement benefits.

With **defined benefit plans**, the employee's pension is specified or "defined" ahead of time. Here the person knows ahead of time the pension benefits he or she will receive. How is this possible? There is usually a formula that ties the person's pension to (1) a percentage of (2) the person's pre-retirement pay (for instance, to an average of his or her last 5 years of employment), multiplied by (3) the number of years he or she worked for the company. Due to tax law changes and other reasons, defined benefit plans now represent a minority of pension benefit plans.[118]

defined contribution plan
A plan in which the employer's contribution to employees' retirement or savings funds is specified.

Defined contribution plans specify ("define") what contribution the employee and employer will make to the employee's retirement or savings fund. Here the contribution is defined, not the pension. With a *defined benefit* plan, the employee can compute what his or her retirement benefits will be upon retirement. With a *defined contribution* plan, the person only knows for sure what he or she is contributing to the pension plan; the actual pension will depend on the amounts contributed to the fund *and* on the success of the retirement fund's investment earnings. Defined contribution plans are popular among employers today because of their relative ease of administration, favorable tax treatment, and other factors. **Portability**—making it easier for employees who leave the firm prior to retirement to take their accumulated pension funds with them—is easier with defined contribution plans.

portability
Making it easier for employees who leave the firm prior to retirement to take their accumulated pension funds with them.

401(k) Plans The 401(k) plan is one defined contribution plan. Under the 401(k) plan (based on Section 401[k] of the Internal Revenue Code), employees have the employer place a portion of their compensation, which would otherwise be paid in cash, into a company profit-sharing or stock bonus plan, or into investments (such as mutual funds) the employee selects. This results in a pretax reduction in salary, so the employee isn't taxed on those set-aside dollars until after he or she retires (or removes the money from the fund). Some employers also match a portion of what the employee contributes to the 401(k) plan.

The employer has a fiduciary responsibility to its employees, and must monitor the pension fund and its administration.[119] Under the Pension Protection Act of 2006, employers who sponsor plans that facilitate both *automatic enrollment* and *allocation to default investments* (such as age-appropriate "lifestyle funds") reduce their compliance burdens.[120] It's also crucial that employers monitor 401(k) housekeeping issues. For example, the IRS recently reported the top 10 most common violations that 401(k) plans encounter, such as late deposits and incorrect employer matching contributions.[121]

As the downturn intensified in 2008–2009, more employees began making "hardship withdrawals" from their 401(k) plans (on which no taxes are due, for a time).[122] Recent stories, like that of a 47-year-old engineer, suggest caution. His adviser told him that, "if we saved very aggressively, I might be able to retire in my early 70s." Such experiences underscore the need for employee education, or at least automatically directing funds into (relatively) prudent investments.[123] Also, many defined benefit pension plans were underfunded due to falls in market values.[124] The Pension Protection Act of 2006 stipulates that defined benefit plans that have suffered losses must pay extra to compensate for the losses or other shortfalls. This may force employers to pay excise taxes to supplement their plans.

CASH BALANCE PENSION PLANS One problem with *defined benefits* plans is that to get your maximum pension, you generally must stay with your employer until you retire—the formula, recall, takes the number of years you work into consideration. With *defined contribution* plans, your pension is more portable—you can leave with it at any time, perhaps rolling it over into your next employer's pension plan. Without delving into all the details, *cash balance* plans are a hybrid; they have a defined benefit plan's more predictable benefits, but they have the portability advantages of defined contribution plans.[125]

ERISA The Employee Retirement Income Security Act (ERISA) aims to protect the pensions of workers and to stimulate pension plan growth. Before enactment of ERISA, pension plans often failed to deliver expected benefits to employees. Many reasons, such as business failure and inadequate funding, could result in employees losing their expected pensions and being unable to retire.

vested

The proportion of the employee's contribution to the employee's pension plan that is guaranteed to the employee and which the employee can therefore take when he or she leaves.

VESTING Under ERISA, pension rights must be **vested**—guaranteed to the employee—under one of three formulas. With *cliff vesting*, the period for acquiring a nonforfeitable right in employer matching contributions (if any) is 3 years. So, the employee must have nonforfeitable rights to these funds by the end of 3 years. With the second option (*graded vesting*), participants in pension plans must receive nonforfeitable rights to the matching contributions as follows: 20% after 2 years, and then 20% for each succeeding year, with a 100% nonforfeitable right by the end of 6 years. The third option is to allow for faster vesting, such as in one year.

Among other things, the Pension Benefits Guarantee Corporation (PBGC) was established under ERISA to ensure that pensions meet their obligations should a plan fail.[126] However, the PBGC guarantees only defined benefit, not defined contribution plans. Furthermore, it will only pay an individual a pension of up to a maximum of about $54,000 per year for someone 65 years of age with a plan terminating in 2010.[127] So, high-income workers may still end up with reduced pensions if a plan fails.

As with all pay plan components, employers should ensure retirement benefits support their strategic needs by setting guiding principles such as "assist in attracting employees" and "assist in retaining knowledgeable employees."[128]

MANAGING THE NEW WORKFORCE

Domestic Partner Benefits

A survey by the Society for Human Resource Management found that of 578 companies responding, about 23% offer same-sex domestic partner benefits, 31% offer opposite-sex domestic partner benefits, and about 2% plan to do one or both.[129] For example, Northrop Grumman Corp. extends domestic partner benefits to the 9,500 salaried workers at its Newport News shipyard.[130]

When employers provide *domestic partner benefits* to employees, it generally means that employees' same-sex or opposite-sex domestic partners are eligible to receive the same benefits (health care, life insurance, and so forth) as do the husband, wife, or legal dependent of one of the firm's employees.[131] Under the Defense of Marriage Act passed in 1996, no state or political subdivision in the United States *need* treat same-sex domestic partners the same as employees' spouses, and the federal government *may not* do so, for purposes of federal law. There is thus some debate as to whether the benefits extended to domestic partners will be federal tax free, as they generally are for the relatives enumerated above.

Personal Services Benefits

Many employers provide access to the sorts of personal services that employees need at one time or another. These include credit unions, legal services, counseling, and social and recreational opportunities. (Some employers use the term *voluntary benefits* to cover personal services benefits that range from things like pet insurance to automobile insurance.)[132] We'll look at a few of these.

CREDIT UNIONS Credit unions are usually separate businesses run by independent companies to help employees with borrowing and saving needs, but some employers establish their own. Employees usually become members by purchasing a share of the credit union's stock for a small fee—perhaps $5 or $10. Members can then deposit savings that accrue interest at a rate determined by the credit union's directors. Loan eligibility and the loan's rate of interest are usually more favorable than are those of banks and finance companies.

EDUCATIONAL BENEFITS As another service benefit example, employers may also offer employees full or partial college tuition reimbursement. The idea is to help attract upwardly mobile recruits, retain employees who might otherwise leave, and provide promotable employees with the educations they need to move up. However, enhanced mobility is a double-edged sword. An analysis of the U.S. Navy's tuition assistance program found that those who used the assistance were also significantly more likely to leave the Navy.[133]

Employee Assistance Program (EAP)

A formal employer program for providing employees with counseling and/or treatment programs for problems such as alcoholism, gambling, or stress.

EMPLOYEE ASSISTANCE PROGRAMS Employee Assistance Programs (EAPs) are another personal services benefit example. Originally aimed at supporting employees with alcohol and mental health problems, today's EAPs are generally wide ranging, addressing matters such as elder care, domestic violence, and legal problems.[134] EAPs are increasingly popular, with more than 60% of larger firms offering such programs.[135] Most employers contract for the necessary services with vendors such as Magellan Health Services and CIGNA Behavioral Health.[136]

For the employer, programs like these produce advantages as well as costs. For example, sick family members and problems such as depression account for many of the sick-leave days employees take. Employers can reduce these absences with programs that provide advice on issues like elder care referrals and personal counseling.[137]

Work–Life/Family-Friendly Benefits

The term *family-friendly* or work–life benefits refers to benefits like in-house health clubs, the overall aim of which is to make it easier for employees to balance their work life and home life responsibilities. For example, software giant SAS Institute offers preschool child care centers, a gym, a full-time in-house elder care consultant, and a standard 35-hour workweek.

As you can see in Figure 8.6, the list of possible family-friendly benefits is quite long, but three popular benefits deserve special note. More employers are offering *emergency child care benefits*, for instance, for when a young child's regular babysitter is a no-show. For example, Canadian financial services company CIBC is expanding its on-site child care center to handle last-minute emergencies.[138] Similarly, with more older workers in the workforce, about 120 million Americans

(*n* = 90) Companies now offering:	Yes	No	Plan to
Dependent care flexible spending account	76%	22%	2%
Life insurance for dependents	65%	34%	1%
Flextime	58%	40%	3%
Telecommuting on an ad-hoc basis	48%	52%	1%
Compressed workweek	38%	60%	2%
Health care benefits for dependent grandchildren	38%	61%	1%
Domestic partner benefits (same-sex partners)	33%	66%	2%
Domestic partner benefits (opposite-sex partners)	33%	66%	2%
Telecommuting on a part-time basis	33%	66%	1%
Paid family leave	33%	67%	*
Bring child to work in emergency	29%	70%	1%
Health care benefits for foster children	29%	70%	1%
Family leave above and beyond required federal FMLA leave	27%	73%	1%
Lactation program/designated area	26%	72%	2%
Family leave above and beyond required state FMLA leave	24%	76%	1%
Eldercare referral service	22%	77%	1%
Childcare referral service	21%	78%	1%
Telecommuting on a full-time basis	21%	78%	1%
Parental leave above and beyond federal FMLA	21%	79%	1%
Adoption assistance	20%	78%	2%
Job sharing	20%	78%	2%
Parental leave above and beyond state FMLA	20%	80%	1%
Scholarships for members of employees' families	20%	80%	1%

FIGURE 8.6

Popular Family-Friendly Benefits

Source: Adapted from SHRM Foundation 2007 Benefits Survey Report.
Note: Data sorted in descending order by the "Yes" column. Percentages are row percentages and may not total 100% due to rounding.

are now or have in the past cared for an adult relative or friend. Employers therefore increasingly offer *adult care support*, including counseling and adult day care centers.[139] Some employers enrich their *parental leave plans* to make it more attractive for mothers to return from maternity leave, for instance, offering reduced travel and hours.[140]

WORKPLACE FLEXIBILITY Employees are increasingly conducting business from nontraditional office settings using technology like BlackBerry-type devices.[141] As a result, more employers are introducing workplace flexibility programs. **Workplace flexibility** means arming employees with the information technology tools they need to get their jobs done wherever the employees are. For example, Capital One Financial Corp. has its Future of Work program. Certain Capital One employees received mobile technology tools such as wireless access laptops and BlackBerry-type devices. The program seems to have led to about a 41% increase in overall workplace satisfaction, a 31% reduction in time needed to get input from peers, and a 53% increase in those who say their workplace enhances group productivity.[142]

Flexible Benefits

Employees tend to differ in what benefits they want and need. Young workers with families may want more child care. Older workers may want elder care advice and resources.

Flexible benefits plans are also called *cafeteria plans* because employees can spend their benefits allowances on a choice of benefits options. Either way, the idea is to let the employee put together his or her own benefit package, subject to two constraints. First, the employer must carefully limit total cost for each benefit package. Second, each benefit plan must include certain non-optional items, including, for example, Social Security, workers' compensation, and unemployment insurance. About 37% of employers offer a flexible benefits plan (ability to select from a variety of benefits).[143]

Flexible benefits plans are also subject to Internal Revenue Service regulations. For example, new IRS regulations require formal written plans describing the employer's cafeteria plan, including benefits and procedures for choosing them.[144]

Benefits and Employee Leasing

Employee leasing firms (also known as professional employer organizations) arrange to have all the employer's employees transferred to the employee leasing firm's payroll. The employee leasing firm becomes the legal employer and handles the employer's employee-related paperwork. This usually includes recruiting, hiring, paying tax liabilities (Social Security payments, unemployment insurance, etc.), and handling day-to-day details such as performance appraisals (with the assistance of the on-site supervisor). However, it is with respect to benefits management that employee leasing is often most advantageous.

---

workplace flexibility
Arming employees with the information technology tools they need to get their jobs done wherever the employees are.

flexible benefits plan
Individualized plans allowed by employers to accommodate employee preferences for benefits.

Workplace flexibility means arming employees with the information technology tools they need to get their jobs done wherever the employees are.

Source: George Shelley/CORBIS–NY.

Getting insurance is often the most serious personnel problem smaller employers face. Remember that the leasing firm is the legal employer of the other company's employees. Therefore, the employees are absorbed into a much larger insurable group (along with other employers' former employees). The employee leasing company can therefore often offer benefits smaller companies can't obtain at such a low cost.

Benefits Web Sites

To reduce the costs of administering benefits, many employers enable employees to manage much of their own benefits changes (dependents, 401(k), health plan, and so on) themselves, via the employer's (or an outside vendor's) Web site.

Employers are adding new services to their benefits Web sites. In addition to offering things like self enrollment, the insurance company USAA's Web site helps employees achieve better work–life balance. For example, suppose the employee clicks on the "today, I'm feeling . . ." menu. Here employees can respond to a list of words (such as "stressed"), and from there see suggestions for dealing with (in this case) stress.[145] With Boeing's Pay & Benefits Profile site employees can get real-time information about their salary and bonuses, benefits, pension, and even special services such as child care referrals.[146]

REVIEW

SUMMARY

1. Establishing pay rates involves five steps: conduct salary survey, evaluate jobs, develop pay grades, use wage curves, and develop pay ranges.

2. Job evaluation is aimed at determining the relative worth of a job. It compares jobs to one another based on their content, which is usually defined in terms of compensable factors such as skills, effort, responsibility, and working conditions.

3. Most managers group similar jobs into wage or pay grades for pay purposes. These grades are composed of jobs of approximately equal difficulty or importance as determined by job evaluation.

4. Developing a compensation plan for executive, managerial, and professional personnel is complicated by the fact that factors such as performance and creativity must take precedence over static factors such as working conditions. Market rates, performance, and incentives and benefits thus play a much greater role than does job evaluation for these employees.

5. Broadbanding means collapsing salary grades and ranges into just a few wide levels or bands, each of which then contains a relatively wide range of jobs and salary levels.

6. Piecework is the oldest type of incentive plan; a worker is paid a piece rate for each unit he or she produces. Team incentives are another option. With team incentives, the employee's team receives an incentive payment (shared by team members) for achieving a target. Unlike individual incentive plans team-based plans pay incentives on how the team does, so that individual workers who do exemplary work may feel underpaid.

7. Profit sharing and the Scanlon plan are examples of organization-wide incentive plans. The problem with such plans is that the link between a person's efforts and rewards is sometimes unclear. Merit plans are other popular incentive plans.

8. Supplemental pay benefits provide pay for time not worked. They include unemployment insurance, vacation and holiday pay, severance pay, and supplemental unemployment benefits.

9. Insurance benefits are another type of employee benefit. Workers' compensation, for example, is aimed at ensuring prompt income and medical benefits to work accident victims or their dependents, regardless of fault. Most employers also provide group life insurance and group hospitalization, accident, and disability insurance.

10. Two types of retirement benefits are Social Security and pensions. Social Security covers not only retirement benefits but also survivors and disability benefits. One of the critical issues in pension planning is vesting the money that the employer has placed in the latter's pension fund, which cannot be forfeited for any reason. ERISA ensures that pension rights become vested and protected after a reasonable amount of time.

KEY TERMS

DISCUSSION QUESTIONS

1. Discuss four basic factors determining pay rates.
2. Explain each of the five basic steps in establishing pay rates.
3. Compare and contrast piecework and team or group incentive plans.
4. List and describe each of the basic benefits most employers might be expected to offer.
5. What is the difference between exempt and non-exempt jobs?
6. What is the relationship between compensable factors and job specifications?
7. What is merit pay? Do you think it's a good idea to award employees merit raises? Why or why not?

INDIVIDUAL AND GROUP ACTIVITIES

1. Working individually or in groups, conduct salary surveys for the following positions: entry-level accountant and entry-level chemical engineer. What sources did you use, and what conclusions did you reach? If you were the HR manager for a local engineering firm, what would you recommend that you pay for each job?
2. Working individually or in groups, develop compensation policies for the teller position at a local bank. Assume that there are four tellers: two were hired in May and the other two were hired in December. The compensation policies should address the following: appraisals, raises, holidays, vacation pay, overtime pay, method of pay, garnishments, and time cards.
3. Working individually or in groups, access relevant Web sites to determine what equitable pay ranges are for the jobs of chemical engineer, marketing manager, and HR manager, all with a bachelor's degree and five years of experience. Do so for the following cities: New York, New York; San Francisco, California; Houston, Texas; Denver, Colorado; Miami, Florida; Atlanta, Georgia; Chicago, Illinois; Birmingham, Alabama; Detroit, Michigan; and Washington, D.C. For each position in each city, what are the pay ranges and the average pay?

Does geographical location impact the salaries of the different positions? If so, how?
4. Working individually or in groups, use published (Internet or other) wage surveys to determine local area earnings for the following positions: file clerk I, accounting clerk II, and secretary V. How do the published figures compare with comparable jobs listed in your Sunday newspaper? What do you think accounts for any discrepancy?
5. Working individually or in groups, use the ranking method to evaluate the relative worth of the jobs listed in question 4. (You may use the Department of Labor's O*NET as an aid.) To what extent do the local area earnings for these jobs correspond to your evaluations of the jobs?
6. Working individually or in groups, develop an incentive plan for the following positions: chemical engineer, plant manager, and used-car salesperson. What factors did you have to consider in reaching your conclusions?
7. A state university system in the Southeast instituted a Teacher Incentive Program for its faculty. Faculty committees within each of the university's colleges were told to award $5,000 raises (not bonuses) to about 40% of their faculty members based on how good a job they did teaching

undergraduates and how many they taught per year. What are the potential advantages and pitfalls of such an incentive program? How well do you think it was accepted by the faculty? Do you think it had the desired effect?

8. Working individually or in groups, research and compile a list of the perks available to the following individuals: the head of your local airport, the president of your college or university, and the president of a large company in your area. Do they all have certain perks in common? What do you think accounts for any differences?

9. You are the HR consultant to a small business with about 40 employees. At the present time the business offers 5 days of vacation, 5 paid holidays, and legally mandated benefits such as unemployment insurance payments.

Develop a list of other benefits you believe the firm should offer, along with your reasons for suggesting them.

10. Some of America's executives have come under fire recently because their pay seemed to some to be excessive, given their firms' performances. To choose just two of very many: one Citigroup division head was due a $97 million bonus in 2009, and Merrill Lynch paid tens of millions in bonuses soon after Bank of America rescued it. However, big institutional investors are no longer sitting back and not complaining. For example, TV's *Nightly Business Line* says that pension manager TIAA-CREF is talking to 50 companies about executive pay. And the U.S. government's pay czar is looking to roll back some such payouts. Do you think they are right to make a fuss? Why?

WEB-e's (WEB EXERCISES)

1. Based on sites such as www.starbucks.com/career-center/us-careers/partner-experience, what do you think of the benefits that Starbucks offers its employees? Do you think they are better, worse, or about average, and why?

2. Judging from what you can find at www.wegmans.com/webapp/wcs/stores/servlet/CategoryDisplay?identifier=CATEGORY_533&catalogId=10002&storeId=10052&

langId=-1, what sorts of pay policies does Wegmans seem to have, and why do you think they follow such policies?

3. President Obama's "pay czar" tried to reduce the pay of executives at AIG. According to sites such as www.huffingtonpost.com/2009/12/08/pay-czar-caves-on-aig-pay_n_383973.html, how successful was he, and why?

APPLICATION EXERCISES

HR IN ACTION CASE INCIDENT 1
Inserting the Team Concept into Compensation—or Not

One of the first things Sandy Caldwell wanted to do in his new position at Hathaway Manufacturing was improve productivity through teamwork at every level of the firm. As the new human resource manager for the suburban plant, Sandy set out to change the culture to accommodate the team-based approach he had become so enthusiastic about in his most recent position.

Sandy started by installing the concept of team management at the highest level, to oversee the operations of the entire plant. The new management team consisted of manufacturing, distribution, planning, technical, and human resource plant managers. Together they developed a new vision for the 500-employee facility, which they expressed in the simple phrase "Excellence Together." They drafted a new mission statement for the firm that focused on becoming customer driven and team based, and that called upon employees to raise their level of commitment and begin acting as "owners" of the firm.

The next step was to convey the team message to employees throughout the company. The communication process went surprisingly well, and Sandy was happy to see his idea of a "workforce of owners" begin to take shape. Teams trained together, developed production plans together, and embraced the technique of 360-degree feedback, in which an employee's performance evaluation is obtained from supervisors, subordinates, peers, and internal or external customers. Performance and morale improved, and

productivity began to tick upward. The company even sponsored occasional celebrations to reward team achievements, and the team structure seemed firmly in place.

Sandy decided to change one more thing. Hathaway's long-standing policy had been to give all employees the same annual pay increase. But Sandy felt that in the new team environment, outstanding performance should be the criterion for pay raises. After consulting with CEO Regina Cioffi, Sandy sent a memo to all employees announcing the change to team-based pay for performance.

The reaction was immediate and 100% negative. None of the employees were happy with the change, and among their complaints, two stood out. First, because the 360-degree feedback system made everyone responsible in part for someone else's performance evaluation, no one was comfortable with the idea that pay raises might also somehow be linked to peer input. Second, there was a widespread perception that the way the change was decided upon, and the way it was announced, put the firm's commitment to team effort in doubt. Simply put, employees felt left out of the decision process.

Sandy and Regina arranged a meeting for early the next morning. Sitting in Regina's office over their coffee, they began a painful debate. Should the new policy be rescinded as quickly as it was adopted, or should it be allowed to stand?

Questions

1. Does the new pay-for-performance plan seem like a good idea? Why or why not?
2. What advice would you give Regina and Sandy as they consider their decision?
3. What mistakes did they make in adopting and communicating the new salary plan? How might Sandy have approached this major compensation change a little differently?
4. Assuming the new pay plan is eventually accepted, how would you address the fact that in the new performance evaluation system, employees' input affects their peers' pay levels?

Note: The incident in this case is based on an actual event at Frito-Lay's Kirkwood, New York, plant, as reported in C. James Novak, "Proceed with Caution When Paying Teams," *HR Magazine* (April 1997): 73.

HR IN ACTION CASE INCIDENT 2
Carter Cleaning Company: The Incentive Plan

The question of whether to pay Carter Cleaning Centers employees an hourly wage or an incentive of some kind has always intrigued Jack Carter. His basic policy has been to pay employees an hourly wage, except that his managers receive an end-of-year bonus depending, as Jack puts it, "on whether their stores do well or not that year."

He is, however, considering using an incentive plan in one store. Jack knows that a presser should press about 25 "tops" (jackets, dresses, blouses) per hour. Most of his pressers do not attain this ideal standard, though. In one instance, a presser named Walt was paid $8 per hour, and Jack noticed that regardless of the amount of work he had to do, Walt always ended up going home at about 3 P.M., so he earned about $300 at the end of the week. If it was a holiday week, for instance, and there were a lot of clothes to press, he might average 22 to 23 tops per hour (someone else did pants) and so he'd earn perhaps $300 and still finish up each day in time to leave by 3 P.M. so he could pick up his children at school. But when things were very slow in the store, his productivity would drop to perhaps 12 to 15 pieces an hour, so that at the end of the week he'd end up earning perhaps $280, and in fact not go home much earlier than he did when it was busy.

Jack spoke with Walt several times, and while Walt always promised to try to do better, it gradually became apparent to Jack that Walt was simply going to earn his $300 per week no matter what. While Walt never told him so directly, it dawned on Jack that Walt had a family to support and was not about to earn less than his "target" wage regardless of how busy or slow the store was. The problem was that the longer Walt kept pressing each day, the longer the steam boilers and compressors had to be kept on to power his machines, and the fuel charges alone ran close to $6 per hour. Jack clearly needed some way short of firing Walt to solve the problem, since the fuel bills were eating up his profits.

His solution was to tell Walt that instead of an hourly $8 wage he would henceforth pay him $0.33 per item pressed. That way, said Jack to himself, if Walt presses 25 items per hour at $0.33 he will in effect get a small raise. He'll get more items pressed per hour and will therefore be able to shut the machines down earlier.

On the whole, the experiment worked well. Walt generally presses 25 to 35 pieces per hour now. He gets to leave earlier, and with the small increase in pay he generally earns his target wage. Two problems have arisen, though. The quality of Walt's work has dipped a bit, plus, his manager has to spend a minute or two each hour counting the number of pieces Walt pressed that hour. Otherwise Jack is fairly pleased with the results of his incentive plan and he's wondering whether to extend it to other employees and other stores.

Questions

1. Should this plan in its present form be extended to pressers in the other stores? Why?
2. Should other employees (cleaner-spotters, counter people) be put on a similar plan? Why? Why not? If so, how, exactly?
3. Is there another incentive plan you think would work better for the pressers?
4. A store manager's job is to keep total wages to no more than 30% of sales and to maintain the fuel bill and the supply bill at about 9% of sales each. Managers can also directly affect sales by ensuring courteous customer service and by ensuring that the work is done properly. What suggestions would you make to Jennifer and her father for an incentive plan for store managers?

EXPERIENTIAL EXERCISE

Job Evaluation at the University

Purpose: The purpose of this exercise is to give you experience in performing a job evaluation using the ranking method.

Required Understanding: You should be thoroughly familiar with the ranking method of job evaluation and obtain (or write) job descriptions for your college's dean, department chairperson, and your professor.

How to Set Up the Exercise/Instructions: Divide the class into groups of four or five students. The groups will perform a job evaluation of the positions of dean, department chairperson, and professor using the ranking method.

1. Perform a job evaluation by ranking the jobs. You may use one or more compensable factors.

2. If time permits, a spokesperson from each group can put his or her group's ratings on the board. Did the groups end up with about the same results? How did they differ? Why do you think they differed?

BUSINESS IN ACTION EDU-EXERCISE

Building Your *Finance and Budgeting* Knowledge

No manager should formulate pay policies without understanding how total compensation fits within the department's and company's budgets. For example, embarking on a plan to raise wages 5% is probably foolhardy if, given the financial situation, the employer won't be able to afford the extra expenses. Those formulating compensation plans must thus have at least a good working knowledge of budgeting (and of what their company's budget constraints are).

Budgets are formal financial expressions of a manager's plans. They show targets for things like sales, cost of materials, production levels, and profit, expressed in dollars. These planned targets are the standards against which the manager compares and controls the unit's actual performance. Budgets are the most widely used control device. Each manager, from first-line supervisor to company president, usually has an operating budget to use as a standard of comparison.

The first step in budgeting is generally to develop a sales forecast and sales budget. The sales budget shows the planned sales activity for each period (usually in units per month) and the revenue expected from the sales.

The manager can then produce various operating budgets. *Operating budgets* show the expected sales and/or expenses for each of the company's departments for the planning period in question. For example, the *production and materials budget* (or plan) shows what the company will spend for materials, labor, and administration to implement the sales budget. The *personnel budget* shows what executing the plan will cost in terms of employee wages, incentives, and benefits.

The next step is to combine all these departmental budgets into a profit plan for the coming year. This profit plan is the budgeted *income statement* or pro forma income statement. It lists expected sales, then expected expenses, and then expected income or profit (or loss) for the year. In practice, cash from sales usually doesn't flow into the firm so that it coincides precisely with cash disbursements. (Some customers may take 35 days to pay their bills, for instance, but employees expect paychecks every week.) The *cash budget* or plan shows, for each month, the amount of cash the company can expect to receive and the amount it can expect to disperse. The manager can use it to anticipate his or her cash needs, and to arrange for short-term loans, if need be.

The company also has a budgeted *balance sheet*. The budgeted balance sheet shows managers, owners, and creditors what the company's projected financial picture should be at the end of the year. It shows assets (such as cash and equipment), liabilities (such as long-term debt), and net worth (the excess of assets over other liabilities).

The firm's accountants compile the financial information and feed it back to the appropriate managers. A *performance report* shows budgeted or planned targets. Next to these numbers, it shows the department's actual performance numbers. *Variances* show the differences between budgeted and actual amounts. The report may provide a space for the manager to explain any variances. After reviewing the performance report, management can take corrective action.

Questions

1. As the owner of a small business, how would you go about deciding how big a salary increase to award your 25 employees? For example, would you create an operating budget first, or proceed in some other way, and why?

2. If time permits, obtain a copy of some organization's budget. What subsidiary (operating, production, personnel, etc.) budgets does it contain? What share of the total budget do total personnel costs represent? How does that compare with the percentage for other organizations' budgets obtained by other groups? What do you think accounts for the differences?

PERSONAL COMPETENCIES EDU-EXERCISE

Building Your *Team-Building* Skills and Team Incentives

Businesses increasingly organize their efforts around teams. For instance, work teams run the General Mills cereal plant in Lodi, California. At Johnsonville foods, similar self-managing teams recruit, hire, evaluate, and (if necessary) fire on their own. Because teams are so important at work today, all managers need a working knowledge of what teams are, and how to organize and incentivize them. A *team* is "a small number of people with complementary skills who are committed to a common purpose, set of performance goals, and approach for which they hold themselves mutually accountable."[147]

Teams are important at work for several reasons. One reason is that, for better or worse, teams influence their members' behavior. They exert their influence largely through *group norms*. These are informal rules that teams adopt to regulate and regularize their members' behavior. Researchers, during a classic project known as the Hawthorne studies, described, for instance, how production levels that exceeded the group norms triggered a slap on the hand for the team members producing too much. The other side of the coin is that teams with positive attitudes can have a positive effect. In companies like Honda, highly motivated work teams make sure that team members have the training and values necessary to keep production and quality high.

Unfortunately, the evidence regarding work team productivity is mixed. After Kodak's consumer film finishing division instituted a team-based structure, the division's costs declined by 6% per year and productivity rose by over 200% in six years. On the other hand, experts generally blame an ill-conceived team incentive plan instituted at Levi Strauss' American factories with hastening the closure of those factories.

Given results like these, experts argue against assuming that team incentives themselves are a panacea. Motivating the team should start with organizing the team properly—in terms of membership, leadership, and training.

Questions

1. Give two examples of how group norms might influence the effectiveness of a team incentive plan.
2. Use the Internet to research the problem with the Levi Strauss incentive plan. What was the problem, and what would you have done to make the plan more workable?

APPENDIX
MOTIVATION AND INCENTIVES

Several motivation theories have particular relevance to designing incentive plans. We'll look at several.

The Hierarchy of Needs and Abraham Maslow

Abraham Maslow made what may be the most popular observation on what motivates people. He said that people have a hierarchy of five types of needs: *physiological* (food, water, warmth), *security* (a secure income, knowing one has a job), *social* (friendships and camaraderie), *self-esteem* (respect), and *self-actualization* (becoming the person you believe you can become). According to Maslow's *prepotency process principle*, people are motivated first to satisfy each lower-order need and then, in sequence, each of the higher-level needs. For example, if someone is out of work and insecure, getting a job may drive everything he or she does. (So, during periods of high unemployment, one may see even former executives taking low-level jobs to make ends meet.) A secure employee may then turn to being concerned with building friendships, getting respect, and going to school to get the degree required to be a top executive. We usually envision Maslow's hierarchy of needs as a stepladder or pyramid.

Maslow's theory has many practical implications. For example, don't try to motivate someone with more challenging work if he or she doesn't earn enough to pay the bills.

Motivators and Frederick Herzberg

Frederick Herzberg said the best way to motivate someone is to organize the job so that doing it provides the feedback and challenge that helps satisfy the person's higher-level needs for things like accomplishment and recognition. These needs are relatively insatiable, says Herzberg, so recognition and challenging work provide a sort of built-in motivation generator. Satisfying lower-level needs for things like better pay and working conditions just keep the person from becoming dissatisfied.

Herzberg says the factors ("hygienes") that satisfy lower-level needs are different from those ("motivators") that satisfy or partially satisfy higher-level needs. If *hygiene* factors (factors outside the job itself, such as working conditions, salary, and incentive pay) are inadequate, employees become dissatisfied. However, adding more of these hygienes (like incentives) to the job (supplying what Herzberg calls extrinsic motivation) is an inferior way to try to motivate someone, because lower-level needs are quickly satisfied. Soon the person simply says, in effect, "What have you done for me lately? I want another raise."

Instead of relying on hygienes, says Herzberg, the managers interested in creating a self-motivated workforce should emphasize "job content" or *motivator* factors. Managers do this by enriching workers' jobs so that the jobs are more challenging, and by providing feedback and recognition—make doing the job intrinsically motivating, in other words. Here, just doing the job provides the motivation. Among other things, Herzberg's theory makes the point that relying exclusively on financial incentives is risky. The employer should also provide the recognition and challenging work that most people desire.

Expectancy Theory and Victor Vroom

Another important motivational fact is that, in general, people won't pursue rewards they find unattractive, or where the odds of success are very low. Psychologist Victor Vroom's expectancy motivation theory echoes these commonsense observations. He says a person's motivation to exert some level of effort depends on three things: the person's expectancy (in terms of probability) that his or her effort will lead to performance;[148] instrumentality, or the perceived connection (if any) between successful performance and actually obtaining

expectancy
A person's expectation that his or her effort will lead to performance.

instrumentality
The perceived relationship between successful performance and obtaining the reward.

valence

The perceived value a person attaches to the reward.

the rewards; and **valence,** which represents the perceived value the person attaches to the reward.[149] In Vroom's theory, motivation is thus a product of three things: Motivation = (E × I × V), where, of course, E represents expectancy, I is instrumentality, and V is valence. If E, I, or V is zero or inconsequential, there will be no motivation.

Vroom's theory has three implications for how managers design incentive plans.

- First, if employees don't *expect* that effort will produce performance, no motivation will occur. So, managers must ensure that their employees have the skills to do the job, and believe they can do the job. Thus training, job descriptions, and confidence building and support are important in using incentives.
- Second, Vroom's theory suggests that employees must see the *instrumentality* of their efforts—they must believe that successful performance will in fact lead to getting the reward. Managers can accomplish this, for instance, by creating easy to understand incentive plans.

- Third, the reward itself must be of *value* to the employee. So ideally, the manager should take into account individual employee preferences.

Behavior Modification/ Reinforcement and B. F. Skinner

Using incentives also assumes you know something about how consequences affect behavior.[150] Psychologist B. F. Skinner's findings provide the foundation for much of what we know about this. Managers apply Skinner's principles by using *behavior modification*. **Behavior modification** means changing behavior through rewards or punishments that are contingent on performance. For managers, behavior modification boils down to two main principles: (1) That behavior that appears to lead to a positive consequence (reward) tends to be repeated, while behavior that appears to lead to a negative consequence (punishment) tends not to be repeated; and (2) that, therefore, managers can get someone to change his or her behavior by providing the properly scheduled rewards (or punishment).

behavior modification

Using contingent rewards or punishment to change behavior.

ENDNOTES

1. Elayne Robertson Demby, "Two Stores Refused to Join the Race to the Bottom for Benefits and Wages," *Workforce Management* (February 2004): 57; and see www.wegmans.com/webapp/wcs/ stores/servlet/CategoryDisplay?langId=-1&storeId= 10052&catalogId=10002&categoryId=256548, accessed April 21, 2008.
2. Richard Henderson, *Compensation Management* (Reston, VA: Reston 1980); Joseph Martocchio, *Strategic Compensation* (Upper Saddle River, NJ: Prentice Hall, 2006): 67–94.
3. The act exempts certain workers. For example, bus drivers that transport passengers among airports, hotels, and cruise ships in Florida are exempted by the motor carrier exemption to the Fair Labor Standards Act from receiving overtime pay. "American Coastlines Drivers Exempt from Overtime Pay," *BNA Bulletin to Management* (August 18, 2009): 262. Congress periodically changes the Fair Labor Standards Act's rules regarding who is covered. For example, it recently passed an act amending the FLSA that for the first time brought drivers, helpers, and mechanics of smaller trucks under the Fair Labor Standards Act's overtime provisions. "Changes to FLSA Present Opportunities, Challenges," *BNA Bulletin to Management* (December 8, 2009): 391.
4. "Senate Passes Minimum Wage Increase that Includes Small-Business Tax Provisions," *BNA Bulletin to Management* (February 6, 2007): 41; www.dol.gov/esa/whd/flsa/, accessed August 12, 2007.
5. John Kilgour, "Wage and Hour Law in California," *Compensation & Benefits Review* 42, no. 1 (January/February 2010): 17.
6. For a description of exemption requirements see Jeffrey Friedman, "The Fair Labor Standards Act Today: A Primer," *Compensation* (January/February 2002): 51–54.
7. "Employer Ordered to Pay $2 Million in Overtime," *BNA Bulletin to Management* (September 26, 1996): 308–309.

See also "Restaurant Managers Awarded $2.9 Million in Overtime Wages for Nonmanagement Work," *BNA Bulletin to Management* (August 30, 2001): 275.
8. Exactly how to apply these rules is still in a state of flux. If there's doubt about exemption eligibility, it's probably best to check with the local Department of Labor Wage and Hour office. See, for example, "Attorneys Say FLSA Draws a Fine Line Between Exempt/Nonexempt Employees," *BNA Bulletin to Management* (July 5, 2005): 219; "DOL Releases Letters on Administrative Exemption, Overtime," *BNA Bulletin to Management* (October 18, 2005): 335.
9. See, for example, Jeffrey Friedman, "The Fair Labor Standards Act Today: A Primer," *Compensation* (January/February 2002): 53; Andre Honoree, "The New Fair Labor Standards Act Regulations and the Sales Force: Who Is Entitled to Overtime Pay?" *Compensation & Benefits Review* (January/February 2006): 31; www.shrm.org/issues/FLSA, accessed August 12, 2007; www.dol.gov/esa/whd/flsa, accessed August 12, 2007.
10. "Study Finds Widespread Wage Theft," *Workforce Management* (November 16, 2009): 29.
11. "Wal-Mart to Settle 63 Wage and Hour Suits, Paying Up to $640 Million to Resolve Claims," *BNA Bulleting to Management* (January 13, 2009): 11.
12. www.pacifictimesheet.com/timesheet_products/pacific_timesheet_ handheld_pda_field_data_entry_software.htm, accessed March 23, 2009.
13. "FedEx Ground in Reverse on Driver Status," *Workforce Management* (April 21, 2008): 4. In April 2009, one jury in Seattle ruled in favor of FedEx, deeming the drivers to be independent contractors. Another jury in California ruled instead for the drivers in another case. Alex Roth, "Verdict Backs FedEx in Labor Case," *New York Times* (April 2, 2009): B4.

14. Recently, several state legislatures have moved to tighten regulations regarding misclassifying workers as independent contractors, some going so far as adding criminal penalties for violations. "Misclassification Cases Draw More Attention, Attorneys Say," *BNA Bulletin to Management* (December 15, 2009): 399.

15. Jennifer Arnold, "Reining in Overtime Costs," *HR Magazine* (April 2009): 74–76.

16. In January 2009, Congress passed the Lilly Ledbetter Fair Pay Act. This overturns a previous U.S. Supreme Court decision, and basically says that each new paycheck triggers a new potential discrimination claim. See "Ledbetter Law Raises Open Legal Issues, Practical Issues for Covert Employees," *BNA Bulletin to Management* (November 17, 2009): 361.

17. "Women's Wage Gap Ranges from 25% to 31%, Census Bureau Report Finds," *BNA Bulletin to Management* (February 17, 2009): 51.

18. Richard Henderson, *Compensation Management* (Reston, VA: Reston, 1980): 101–127; Arthur Sloane and Fred Witney, *Labor Relations* (Upper Saddle River, NJ: Prentice Hall, 2004): 273–287.

19. Jessica Marquez, "Raising the Performance Bar," *Workforce Management* (April 24, 2006): 31–32.

20. See, for example, Robert Heneman, "Implementing Total Rewards of Strategies," SHRM Foundation, www.shrm.org/foundation, accessed March 2, 2009.

21. http://markets.on.nytimes.com/research/stocks/news/press_release.asp?docKey=600-200902040900BIZWIRE_USPR_____BW5153-7ENARVBIKO0QHDGGFHUTBKEMIS&provider=Businesswire&docDate=February%204%2C%202009&press_symbol=US%3BHEW, accessed March 21, 2009; www.shrm.org/hrdisciplines/benefits/Articles/Pages/AmericanstoSeeLowestPayRaisesinThreeDecades.aspx, accessed March 21, 2009.

22. "The New Talent Equation," http://www.accenture.com/NR/rdonlyres/7438E440-F7D5-4F81-B012-8D3271891D92/0/Accenture_Outlook_The_New_Talent_Equation.pdf, accessed November 9, 2010.

23. "Five Rules for Talent Management in the New Economy," http://www.towerswatson.com/viewpoints/2606, accessed November 9, 2010.

24. "Next Generation Talent Management," http://www.hewitt associates.com/_MetaBasicCMAssetCache_/Assets/Articles/next_generation.pdf, accessed November 9, 2010.

25. As one study recently put it, "Our research suggests that employees who perceived organization as providing competitive pay are likely to hold positive work attitudes and conceivably engage in behaviors leading to high levels of labor productivity and customer satisfaction." Mahdesh Subramony et al., "The Relationship Between Human Resource Investments and Organizational Performance: A Firm Level Examination of Equilibrium Theory," *Journal of Applied Psychology* 93, no. 4 (2008): 786.

26. James DeConick and Dane Bachmann, "An Analysis of Turnover among Retail Buyers," *Journal of Business Research* 58, no. 7 (July 2005): 874–882.

27. Michael Harris et al., "Keeping Up with the Joneses: A Field Study of the Relationships Among Upward, Lateral, and Downward Comparisons and Pay Level Satisfaction," *Journal of Applied Psychology* 93, no. 3 (2008): 665–673.

28. See www.watsonwyatt.com/search/publications.asp?ArticleID=21432, accessed October 29, 2009.

29. A recent analysis of how companies arrive at executive compensation decisions revealed six potential problem areas: Often, the human resource department hires in the executive compensation consultant, who may in turn feel obligated to formulate CEO incentives that favor the CEO; if the board is going to identify a peer group of firms for executive compensation comparison purposes, those firms should be ones that compete for talent and for business; boards of directors and senior executive should have a "clear understanding of the measures that drive shareholder value if they are going to be used for reward or compensation purposes"; using stock options and executive compensation is potentially risky, given the possibility that an executive can indirectly manipulate share prices through misleading disclosure; don't simply adapt another employer's incentive plan—instead, develop one with the company's business strategy and compensation plan objectives in mind; the board should make sure that it fully understands the cost of long-term implications of the executive compensation decisions. Michel Magnan and Imen Tebourbi, "A Critical Analysis of Six Practices Underlying Executive Compensation Practices," *Compensation & Benefits Review* (May/June 2009): 42–54.

30. Syed Tahir Hijazi, "Determinants of Executive Compensation and Its Impact on Organizational Performance," *Compensation & Benefits Review* (March/April 2007): 58–59. See also "Appraising and Rewarding Managerial Performance in Challenging Economic Times: Part 2," *Journal of Compensation & Benefits* 25 no. 4 (July/August 2009): 5–12.

31. Ingrid Fuller, "The Elephant in the Room: Labor Market Influences on CEO Compensation," *Personnel Psychology* 62 (2009): 659–695.

32. In 2008 and 2009, the U.S. government adopted executive compensation restrictions as part of its Troubled Asset Relief Program and American Recovery and Reinvestment Act of 2009 program. The programs themselves were aimed at supporting financial institutions which would otherwise have been in danger of failing in the financial crisis. The executive compensation restrictions were numerous. Severance payments to senior executives were severely restricted. Boards of directors had to adopt company-wide policies on luxury expenditures such as office renovations and aviation services. Laura Thatcher, "Executive Compensation Restrictions Under the American Recovery and Reinvestment Act of 2009," *Compensation & Benefits Review* (May/June 2009): 20–28.

33. "Range of Firms Alter Executive-Pay Policies," *Wall Street Journal* (October 24–25, 2009): 84.

34. "Executive Pay Remains Linked to Performance," *Compensation & Benefits Review* (March/April 2008): 10. See also K. Dillon, "The Coming Battle Over Executive Pay," *Harvard Business Review* 87, no. 9 (September 2009): 96–103.

35. Christine Bevilacqua and Parbudyal Singh, "Pay for Performance—Panacea or Pandora's Box? Revisiting an Old Debate in the Current Economic Environment," *Compensation & Benefits Review* 41 (September/October 2009): 20–26.

36. Mark Meltzer and Howard Goldsmith, "Executive Compensation for Growth Companies," *Compensation & Benefits Review* (November/December 1997): 41–50; Bruce Ellig, "Executive Pay: A Primer," *Compensation & Benefits Review* (January/February 2003): 44–50; Joseph Martocchio, *Strategic Compensation* (Upper Saddle River, NJ: Prentice Hall, 2006): 421–428. See also Martin J. Conyon, "Executive Compensation and Incentives," *The Academy of Management Perspectives* 20, no. 1 (February 2006): 25(20); and "Realities of Executive Compensation—2006/2007 Report on Executive Pay and Stock Options," www.watsonwyatt.com/research/resrender.asp?id=2006-US-0085&page=1, accessed May 20, 2007.

37. See, for example, Patricia Zingheim and Jay Schuster, "The Next Decade for Pay and Rewards," *Compensation & Benefits Review* (January/February 2005): 29; Patricia Zingheim and Jay Schuster, "What Are Key Pay Issues Right Now?" *Compensation & Benefits Review* (May/June 2007): 51–55; and

"A Framework for Understanding New Concepts in Compensation Management," *Benefits & Compensation Digest* 46 no. 9 (September 2009): 13–16.

38. Another dubious trend is that U.S. wage disparities are rising. Those with high salaries have seen their pay rise much faster in the past 20 or so years than have those at the bottom. Increased demand for the skills that come through education (for instance, for more skilled workers as manufacturing facilities became computerized) explains much of this. The wage gap has not grown as much in Europe, in part because "unions in Europe were and are still more powerful and able to keep up [workers'] wages." Thomas Atchison, "Salary Trends in the United States and Europe," *Compensation & Benefits Review* (January/February 2007): 36.

39. See, for example, Hai-Ming Chen et al., "Key Trends of the Total Reward System in the 21st Century," *Compensation & Benefits Review* (November/December 2006): 64–70.

40. See, for example, Robert Heneman and Peter LeBlanc, "Development of an Approach for Valuing Knowledge Work," *Compensation & Benefits Review* (July/August 2002): 47; and B. Lokshin et al., "Crafting Firm Competencies to Improve Innovative Performance," *European Management Journal* 27, no. 3 (June 2009): 187–196.

41. John Kilgour, "Job Evaluation Revisited: The Point Factor Method," *Compensation & Benefits Review* (July/August 2008): 37.

42. Joseph Martocchio, *Strategic Compensation* (Upper Saddle River, NJ: Prentice Hall, 2006): 168. See also B. Lokshin et al., "Crafting Firm Competencies to Improve Innovative Performance," *European Management Journal* 27, no. 3 (June 2009): 187–196.

43. Bobby Watson Jr. and Gangaram Singh, "Global Pay Systems: Compensation in Support of Multinational Strategy," *Compensation & Benefits Review* (January/February 2005): 33–36.

44. Jamison Bandler and Charles Forelle, "How a Giant Insurer Decided to Oust Hugely Successful CEO," *Wall Street Journal* (December 7, 2006): A1.

45. The federal government also recently introduced new compensation disclosure rules, and these are affecting executive compensation. For example, corporations must now list a single dollar figure to represent an executive's total pay, including salary, bonus, prerequisites, long-term incentives, and retirement benefits. They must also be more diligent in listing all executive perquisites. The net effect of this greater transparency will probably be to pressure employers to increasingly link their executives' pay with the company's performance. See Brent Longnecker and James Krueger, "The Next Wave of Compensation Disclosure," *Compensation & Benefits Review* (January/February 2007): 50–54.

46. Ibid.

47. Note that the employer needs to beware of instituting so many incentive plans (cash bonuses, stock options, recognition programs, and so on) tied to so many different behaviors that employees don't have a clear picture of the employer's priorities. Stephen Rubenfeld and Jennifer David, "Multiple Employee Incentive Plans: Too Much of a Good Thing?" *Compensation & Benefits Review* (March/April 2006): 35–43.

48. See, for example, Leslie Stretch, "From Strategy to Profitability: How Sales Compensation Management Drives Business Performance," *Compensation & Benefits Review* (May/June 2008): 32–37; and Pankaj Madhani, "Sales Employees Compensation: An Optimal Balance Between Fixed and Variable Pay," *Compensation & Benefits Review* (July/August 2009): 44–51.

49. S. Scott Sands, "Ineffective Quotas: The Hidden Threat to Sales Compensation Plans," *Compensation & Benefits Review* (March/April 2000): 35–42. See also "Driving Profitable Sales Growth: 2006/2007 Report on Sales Effectiveness," www.watsonwyatt.com/research/resrender.asp?id=2006-US-0060&page=1, accessed May 20, 2007; and C. Albrech, "Moving to a Global Sales Incentive Compensation Plan," *Compensation & Benefits Review* 41, no. 4 (July/August 2009): 52.

50. Peter Gundy, "Sales Compensation Programs: Built to Last," *Compensation & Benefits Review* (September/October 2002): 21–28. See also Tara Burnthorne Lopez, Christopher D. Hopkins, and Mary Anne Raymond, "Reward Preferences of Salespeople: How Do Commissions Rate?" *Journal of Personal Selling & Sales Management* 26, no. 4 (Fall 2006): 381(10); and C. Albrech, "Moving to a Global Sales Incentive Compensation Plan," *Compensation & Benefits Review* 41, no. 4 (July/August 2009): 52.

51. James M. Pappas and Karen E. Flaherty, "The Moderating Role of Individual-Difference Variables in Compensation Research," *Journal of Managerial Psychology* 21, no. 1 (January 2006): 19–35.

52. Peter Glendinning, "Kicking the Tires of Automotive Sales Compensation," *Compensation & Benefits Review* (September/October 2000): 47–53. See also "Driving Profitable Sales Growth: 2006/2007 Report on Sales Effectiveness," www.watsonwyatt.com/research/resrender.asp?id=2006-US-0060&page=1, accessed May 20, 2007.

53. Suzanne Peterson and Fred Luthans, "The Impact of Financial and Nonfinancial Incentives on Business Unit Outcomes over Time," *Journal of Applied Psychology* 91, no. 1 (2006): 158. See also "Delivering Incentive Compensation Plans that Work," *Financial Executive* 25, no. 7 (September 2009): 52–54.

54. See, for example, Suzanne Peterson and Fred Luthans, "The Impact of Financial and Nonfinancial Incentives on Business Unit Outcomes over Time," *Journal of Applied Psychology* 91, no. 1 (2006): 156–165.

55. Leslie Yerkes, "Motivating Workers in Tough Times," *Incentives* 75, no. 10 (October 2001): 120. See also "Incentives, Motivation and Workplace Performance," Incentive Research Foundation, www.incentivescentral.org/employees/whitepapers, accessed May 19, 2007. For some examples of recognition programs in practice, see www.recognition.org, accessed April 21, 2008; and "Employee Recognition," *WorldatWork* (April 2008) available at www.worldatwork.org/waw/adimLink?id=25653, accessed November 3, 2009.

56. Ibid. See also Chris Taylor, "On-the-Spot Incentives," *HR Magazine* (May 2004): 80–85.

57. Michelle Rafter, "Back in a Giving Mood," *Workforce Management* (September 14, 2009): 25.

58. Charlotte Huff, "Recognition that Resonates," *Workforce Management* (September 11, 2006): 25–29. See also Scott Jeffrey and Victoria Schaffer, "The Motivational Properties of Tangible Incentives," *Compensation & Benefits Review* (May/June 2007): 44–50.

59. Bob Nelson, *1001 Ways to Reward Employees* (New York: Workmen Press, 1994): 19. See also Sunny C. L. Fong and Margaret A. Shaffer, "The Dimensionality and Determinants of Pay Satisfaction: A Cross-Cultural Investigation of a Group Incentive Plan," *International Journal of Human Resource Management* 14, no. 4 (June 2003): 559(22).

60. Richard Seaman, "Rejuvenating an Organization with Team Pay," *Compensation & Benefits Review* (September/October

1997): 25–30. See also Sunny C. L. Fong and Margaret A. Shaffer, "The Dimensionality and Determinants of Pay Satisfaction: A Cross-Cultural Investigation of a Group Incentive Plan," *International Journal of Human Resource Management* 14, no. 4 (June 2003): 559(22); and Mark Kroll, Jeffrey A. Krug, Michael Pettus, and Peter Wright, "Influences of Top Management Team Incentives on Firm Risk Taking," *Strategic Management Journal* 28, no. 1 (January 2007): 81–89.

61. See, for example, Kimberly Merriman, "On the Folly of Rewarding Team Performance, While Hoping for Teamwork," *Compensation & Benefits Review* (January/February 2009): 61–66.

62. Matt Bolch, "Rewarding the Team," *HR Magazine* 52, no. 2 (Fall 2007): 91–93.

63. Janet Wiscombe, "Can Pay for Performance Really Work?" *Workforce* (August 2001): 30.

64. Susan Marks, "Incentives That Really Reward and Motivate," *Workforce* (June 2001): 108–114. For other examples, see also "Delivering Incentive Compensation Plans that Work," *Financial Executive* 25, no. 7 (September 2009): 52–54.

65. Matt Bolch, "Rewarding the Team," *HR Magazine* 52, no. 2 (Fall 2007): 91–93. See also Jessica Marquez, "Retooling Pay: Premium on Productivity," *Workforce Management* 84, no. 12 (November 7, 2005): 1, 22–23, 25–26, 28, 30; www.scribd.com/doc/12824332/NUCOR-CORP-8K-Events-or-Changes-Between-Quarterly-Reports-20090224, accessed November 3, 2009; and www.nucor.com/careers/, accessed November 3, 2009.

66. See, for example, Bruce Ellig, "Executive Pay Financial Measurements," *Compensation & Benefits Review* (September/October 2008): 42–49.

67. Robert Grossman, "Executive Pay: Perception and Reality," *HR Magazine* (April 2009): 29.

68. Benjamin Dunford et al., "Underwater Stock Options and Voluntary Executive Turnover: A Multidisciplinary Perspective Integrating Behavioral and Economic Theories," *Personnel Psychology* 61 (2008): 687–726.

69. "Google Announces It Will Allow Employees to Exchange 'Underwater' Options for Stock," *BNA Bulletin to Management* (January 27, 2009): 27. See also Phred Dvorak, "Slump Yields Employee Rewards," *Wall Street Journal* (October 10, 2008): B2; Don Clark and Jerry DiColo, "Intel to Let Workers Exchange Options," *Wall Street Journal* (March 24, 2009): B3.

70. "Impact of Sarbanes-Oxley on Executive Compensation," www.thelenreid.com, accessed December 11, 2003; Thelen, Reid, and Priest, L.L.P. See also Brent Longnecker and James Krueger, "The Next Wave of Compensation Disclosure," *Compensation & Benefits Review* (January/February 2007): 50–54.

71. Joseph Martocchio, *Strategic Compensation* (Upper Saddle River, NJ: Prentice Hall, 2006): 163–165.

72. Seongsu Kim, "Does Profit Sharing Increase Firms' Profits?" *Journal of Labor Research* (Spring 1998): 351–371. See also Jacqueline Coyle-Shapiro et al., "Using Profit-Sharing to Enhance Employee Attitudes: A Longitudinal Examination of the Effects on Trust and Commitment," *Human Resource Management* 41, no. 4 (Winter 2002): 423–449. One recent study, conducted in Spain, concluded that profit-sharing plans can enhance employees' commitment toward the organization. Alberto Bayo-Moriones and Martin Larraza-Kintana, "Profit Sharing Plans and Effective Commitment: Does the Context Matter?" *Human Resource Management* 48, no 2 (March–April 2009): 207–226.

73. For instance, see "ESOP Trustees Breached Their Fiduciary Duties under ERISA by Failing to Make Prudent Investigation into Value of Stock Purchased by ESOP," *Tax Management Compensation Planning Journal* 30, no. 10 (October 4, 2002): 301(1); and Jeffery D. Mamorsky, "Court Approves ERISA Action against ENRON Executives, Trustee, and Plan Auditor for Retirement Plan Losses," *Journal of Compensation & Benefits* 20, no. 1 (January/February 2004): 46(7).

74. Brian Moore and Timothy Ross, *The Scanlon Way to Improved Productivity: A Practical Guide* (New York: Wiley, 1978): 2. For recent research in gainsharing and Scanlon plans, see, for example, James Reynolds and Daniel Roble, "Combining Pay for Performance with Gainsharing," *Healthcare Financial Management* 60, no. 11 (November 2006): 50(6); Max Reynolds and Joane Goodroe, "The Return of Gainsharing: Gainsharing Appears to Be Enjoying a Renaissance," *Healthcare Financial Management* 59, no. 11 (November 2005): 114(6); Dong-One Kim, "The Benefits and Costs of Employee Suggestions under Gainsharing," *Industrial and Labor Relations Review* 58, no. 4 (July 2005): 631(22); Geoffrey B. Sprinkle and Michael G. Williamson, "The Evolution from Taylorism to Employee Gainsharing: A Case Study Examining John Deere's Continuous Improvement Pay Plan," *Issues in Accounting Education* 19, no. 4 (November 2004): 487(17); and Woodruff Imberman, "Are You Ready to Boost Productivity with a Gainsharing Plan? To Survive and Prosper in Our Hyper-Competitive Environment, Board Converters Must Motivate Employees at All Levels," *Official Board Markets* 82, no. 47 (November 25, 2006): 5(2).

75. Based in part on Steven Markham, K. Dow Scott, and Walter Cox Jr., "The Evolutionary Development of a Scanlon Plan," *Compensation & Benefits Review* (March/April 1992): 50–56. See also Geoffrey B. Sprinkle and Michael G. Williamson, "The Evolution from Taylorism to Employee Gainsharing: A Case Study Examining John Deere's Continuous Improvement Pay Plan," *Issues in Accounting Education* 19, no. 4 (November 2004): 487(17).

76. Steven Markham, K. Dow Scott, and Walter Cox Jr., "The Evolutionary Development of a Scanlon Plan," *Compensation & Benefits Review* (March/April 1992): 51.

77. Brian Moore and Timothy Ross, *The Scanlon Way to Improved Productivity: A Practical Guide* (New York: Wiley, 1978): 1–2.

78. Robert Renn et al., "Earnings and Risk Incentive Plans: A Performance, Satisfaction and Turnover Dilemma," *Compensation & Benefits Review* (July/August 2001): 68–72.

79. Bob Conlin, "Best Practices for Designing New Sales Compensation Plans," *Compensation & Benefits Review* (March/April 2008): 51.

80. Ibid, 53.

81. www.vuesoftware.com/Product/Compensation_Management. aspx, accessed March 4, 2009.

82. Ibid.

83. See, for example, Crain's Benefits Outlook 2009, www.Crains benefits.com.

84. "Trouble Ahead? Dissatisfaction with Benefits, Compensation," *HR Trendbook* (2008): 16.

85. "Survey Finds 99 Percent of Employers Providing Health-Care Benefits," *Compensation & Benefits Review* (September/October 2002): 11. See also "National Compensation Survey: Employee Benefits in Private Industry in the United States, March 2006," U.S. Department of Labor, U.S. Bureau of Labor Statistics (August 2006).

86. "Employers Face Fifth Successive Year of Major Heath Cost Increases, Survey Finds," *BNA Human Resources Report* (October 6, 2003): 1050; and "National Compensation Survey: Employee Benefits in Private Industry in the United States, March 2006," U.S. Department of Labor, U.S. Bureau of Labor Statistics (August 2006).

87. As unemployment rose dramatically the past few years, many states responded by increasing significantly the tax they levy on employers to support their state unemployment funds. About 14 states reportedly had to obtain federal unemployment trust fund loans, and the unemployment insurance trust funds in 18 states were reportedly "near insolvency." Susan Wells, "Unemployment Insurance: How Much More Will It Cost?" *HR Magazine* (July 2009): 35–38.

88. See, for example, Laurie Nacht, "Make an Appealing Case: How to Prepare For and Present an Unemployment Insurance Appeal," *Society for Human Resource Management Legal Report* (March/April 2004): 1–8.

89. "2007 Benefits," A Survey Report by the Society for Human Research Management, 2007.

90. "National Compensation Survey: Employee Benefits in Private Industry in the United States, March 2006," U.S. Department of Labor, U.S. Bureau of Labor Statistics (August 2006): 26.

91. Ken Belson, "At IBM, a Vacation Anytime, or Maybe No Vacation at All," *New York Times* (August 31, 2007): A1–A18.

92. "Unscheduled Employee Absences Cost Companies More Than Ever," *Compensation & Benefits Review* (March/April 2003): 19.

93. "SHRM Benefits Survey Finds Growth in Employer Use of Paid Leave Pools," *BNA Bulletin to Management* (March 21, 2002): 89.

94. The Department of Labor updated its revised regulations for administering the Family and Medical Leave Act in November 2008. See "DOL Issues Long-Awaited Rules; Address a Serious Health Condition, Many Other Issues," *BNA Bulletin to Management* (November 18, 2008): 369. In 2008, Congress also amended the Family and Medical Leave Act to include, among other things, leave rights, particularly for military families. See Sarah Martin, "FMLA Protection Recently Expanded to Military Families: Qualifying Exigency and Servicemember Family Leave," *Compensation & Benefits Review* (September/October 2009): 43–51.

95. Terry Baglieri, "Severance Pay," www.SHRM.org, accessed December 23, 2006.

96. Ibid.

97. "Healthcare Tops List of Value Benefits," *BNA Bulletin to Management* (April 24, 2007): 132.

98. As an example of the direction new federal health insurance may take post-2009, see A. Mathews, "Making Sense of the Debate on Health Care," *Wall Street Journal* (Eastern Edition) (September 30, 2009): D1, D5.

99. When unemployment began rising in 2008–2009, Congress passed, and President Obama signed on February 17, 2009, the American Recovery and Reinvestment Act of 2009. This new law had the immediate effect of making it easier for qualified employees who were involuntarily dismissed for any reason (other than gross misconduct) anytime after September 1, 2008 (the act was retroactive), to sign up for COBRA. It makes it easier to utilize COBRA because the new law requires that the employer pay 65% of the premium. (The employer then receives a credit for that full amount back from the U.S. government.) The former employee must pay the remaining 35%. See www.recovery.gov/, accessed March 21, 2009. See also Patrick Muldowney, "COBRA and the Stimulus Act: A Sign of Things to Come?" *Compensation & Benefits Review* 42, no. 1 (January/February 2010): 24–49.

100. Note that the American Recovery and Reinvestment Act of 2009 includes changes to several benefits-related programs including COBRA, the Mental-Health Parity Act, and the Americans with Disabilities Act Amendments Act. Susan Relland, "Compliance Requirements and What More to Expect for Health and Welfare Plan for Sponsors in 2009," *Compensation & Benefits Review* (May/June 2009): 29–41.

101. Society for Human Resource Management, "Mental Health Trends," *Workplace Visions* 2, http://moss07.shrm.org/Research/FutureWorkplaceTrends/Pages/0303.aspx, accessed July 28, 2009.

102. "Mental-Health Parity Measure Enacted as Part of Financial Rescue Signed by Bush," *BNA Bulletin to Management* (October 7, 2008): 321.

103. "Health Coverage Premiums: Upward Bound," *HR Trend Book* (2008): 8. However, in 2009, employee costs rose only 6.4% compared with an average 15% since 2002, largely because of the employer cost-containment efforts we'll discuss shortly. "Health Benefit Costs Expected to Rise 7%," *BNA Bulletin to Management* (October 20, 2009): 332.

104. "Health Benefit Trends: Employer Medical Benefit Costs Will Rise 7% in 2010," *Compensation & Benefits Review* 42, no. 1 (January/February 2010): 9–10.

105. "High Deductible Plans Might Catch On," *BNA Human Resource Report* (September 15, 2003): 967.

106. "HR Outsourcing: Managing Costs and Maximizing Provider Relations," *BNA, Inc* 21, no. 11 (Washington, D.C.: November 2003): 10. Benefits management ranks high on any list of HR activities that employers outsource. For example, in one survey, 94% outsource flexible spending accounts, 89% outsource defined contribution plans, 72% outsource defined benefit plans, and 68% outsource the auditing of dependents. Bill Roberts, "Outsourcing in Turbulent Times," *HR Magazine* (November 2009): 45.

107. Ron Finch, "Preventive Services: Improving the Bottom Line for Employers and Employees," *Compensation & Benefits Review* (March/April 2005): 18.

108. Ibid. See also Josh Cable, "The Road to Wellness," *Occupational Hazards* (April 2007): 23–27.

109. "Employer Partners to Launch a Three-Year Wellness Initiative," *BNA Bulletin to Management* (August 7, 2007): 255.

110. Vanessa Fuhrmanns, "Oops! As Health Plans Become More Complicated, They're Also Subject to a Lot More Costly Mistakes," *Wall Street Journal* (January 24, 2005): R4.

111. "Dependent Eligibility Audits Can Help Rein in Health Care Costs, Analysts Say," *BNA Bulletin to Management* (September 9, 2008): 289.

112. Betty Liddick, "Going the Distance for Health Savings," *HR Magazine* (March 2007): 51–55. J. Wojcik, "Employers Consider Short-Haul Medical Tourism," *Business Insurance* 43, no. 29 (August 24, 2009): 1, 20.

113. Jeremy Smerd, "Digitally Driven," *Workforce Management* (April 6, 2009): 23–26.

114. Martha Frase, "Minimalist Health Coverage," *HR Magazine* (June 2009): 107–112.

115. www.ssa.gov/pressoffice/colafacts.htm, accessed March 6, 2009.

116. The 7.65% tax rate is the combined rate for Social Security and Medicare.

117. Joseph Martocchio, *Strategic Compensation* (Upper Saddle River, NJ: Prentice Hall, 2006): 245–248; and Lin Grensing-Pophal,

"A Pension Formula that Pays Off," *HR Magazine* (February 2003): 58–62.

118. Many employers are considering terminating their plans but most employers are considering instead either ceasing benefits accruals for all participants or just for future participants. Michael Cotter, "The Big Freeze: The Next Phase in the Decline of Defined Benefit Plans," *Compensation & Benefits Review* (March/April 2009): 44–53.

119. Nancy Pridgen, "The Duty to Monitor Appointed Fiduciaries under ERISA," *Compensation & Benefits Review* (September/October 2007): 46–51; "Individual 401(k) Plan Participant Can Sue Plan Fiduciary for Losses, Justices Rule," *BNA Bulletin to Management* (February 26, 2008): 65.

120. Jack VanDerhei, "The Pension Protection Act and 401(k)s," *Wall Street Journal* (April 22, 2008): 12. The Bureau of Labor Statistics reports that about half of companies automatically enrolled employees into defined contribution benefit plans. "Nearly Half of Employers Automatically Enrolled Employees," *BNA Bulletin to Management* (October 6, 2009): 316.

121. For a discussion, see Jewel Esposito, "Avoiding 401(k) ERISA Disasters," *Compensation & Benefits Review* 42, no. 1 (January/February 2010): 39–45.

122. Jessica Marquez, "More Workers Yanking Money Out of 401(k)s," *Workforce Management* (August 11, 2008): 4.

123. Jessica Marquez, "Retirement Out of Reach," *Workforce Management* (November 3, 2008): 1, 24.

124. James Podleski and Nicholas Paleveda, "Small Retirement Plans Face Funding Dilemma," *Journal of Accountancy* 207, no. 5 (May 2009): 26–28, 32.

125. "New Pension Law Plus a Recent Court Ruling Doom Age-Related Suits, Practitioners Say," *BNA Bulletin to Management* 57, no. 36 (September 5, 2006): 281–282; and www.dol.gov/ebsa/FAQs/faq_consumer_cashbalanceplans.html, accessed January 9, 2010.

126. James Benson and Barbara Suzaki, "After Tax Reform, Part III: Planning Executive Benefits," *Compensation & Benefits Review* 20, no. 2 (March/April 1988): 45–57; "Post-Retirement Benefits Impact of FASB New Accounting Rule" (February 23, 1989): 57.

127. www.pbgc.gov/workers-retirees/benefits-information/content/page789.html, accessed March 6, 2009.

128. For one recent example of how to do this, see Gail Nichols, "Reviewing and Redesigning Retirement Plans," *Compensation & Benefits Review* (May/June 2008): 40–47.

129. SHRM/SHRM Foundation, 2003 Benefits Survey: 2.

130. Carolyn Shapiro, "More Companies Cover Benefits for Employee's Domestic Partners," *Knight-Ridder/Tribune Business News* (July 20, 2003).

131. "What You Need to Know to Provide Domestic Partner Benefits," *HR Focus* 80, no. 3 (August 2003): 3.

132. Carolyn Hirschman, "Employees' Choice," *HR Magazine* (February 2006): 95–99.

133. Richard Buddin and Kanika Kapur, "The Effect of Employer-Sponsored Education on Job Mobility: Evidence from the U.S. Navy," *Industrial Relations* 44, no. 2 (April 2005): 341–363. See also Michael Laff, "US Employers Tighten Reins on Tuition Reimbursement," *Training and Development* (July 2006): 18.

134. Donna Owens, "EAPs for a Diverse World," *HR Magazine* 51, no. 10 (October 2006): 91–96.

135. The Mental Health Parity Act of 1996 (as amended in 2008) sets minimum mental health care benefits; it also prohibits employer group health plans from adopting mental health benefits limitations without comparable limitations on medical and surgical benefits. "Mental-Health Parity Measure Enacted as Part of Financial Rescue Signed by Bush," *BNA Bulletin to Management* (October 7, 2008): 321.

136. "EAP Providers," *Workforce Management* (July 14, 2008): 16.

137. "Making Up for Lost Time: How Employers Can Curb Excessive Unscheduled Absences," *BNA Human Resources Report* (October 20, 2003): 1097. Family-friendly benefits may improve a firm's bottom line in some less obvious ways. One study found that when employees experienced work–family conflict, the employees were more likely to exhibit guilt and hostility at work and at home. "Therefore, when work family conflict causes employees to feel guilty and angry, it is likely that the service encounter will be affected negatively." (Timothy Judge et al., "Work Family Conflict and Emotions: Effects at Work and at Home," *Personnel Psychology* 50, no. 9 (2006): 779–814. See also W. H. J. Hassink et al., "Do Financial Bonuses Reduce Employee Absenteeism? Evidence from a Lottery." *Industrial and Labor Relations Review* 62, no. 3 (April 2009): 327–342.

138. Brian O'Connell, "No Baby Sitter? Emergency Child Care to the Rescue" (May 2005), www.SHRM.org/rewards/library, accessed December 23, 2006; Kathy Gurchiek, "Give Us Your Sick," *HR Magazine* (January 2007): 91–93.

139. "Employers Gain from Elder Care Programs by Boosting Workers Morale, Productivity," *BNA Bulletin to Management* 57, no. 10 (March 7, 2006): 73–74.

140. Sue Shellenbarger, "The Mommy Drain: Employers Beef Up Perks to Lure New Mothers Back to Work," *Wall Street Journal* (September 28, 2006): D1.

141. Farrokh Mamaghani, "Impact of Information Technology on the Workforce of the Future: An Analysis," *International Journal of Management* 23, no. 4 (2006): 845–850. Jessica Marquez, "Connecting a Virtual Workforce," *Workforce Management* (September 22, 2008): 1–3.

142. Ann Pomeroy, "The Future Is Now," *HR Magazine* (September 2007): 46–52.

143. "2007 Benefits," A Survey Report by the Society for Human Research Management (2007): 23.

144. "Employers Should Update Cafeteria Plans Now Based on Proposed Regs, Experts Say," *BNA Bulletin to Management* (September 4, 2007): 281–282.

145. Scott Harper, "Online Resources System Boosts Worker Awareness," *BNA Bulletin to Management* (April 10, 2007): 119.

146. Drew Robb, "A Total View of Employee Records," *HR Magazine* (August 2007): 93–96.

147. Jack Orsburn et al., *Self-Directed Work Teams: The New American Challenge* (Homewood, IL: Business One Irwin, 1990): 34.

148. R. Kanfer, "Motivation Theory and Industrial and Organizational Psychology," in M. Dunnette (ed.), *Handbook of Industrial and Organizational Psychology* (Palo Alto, CA: Consulting Psychologists Press, Inc., 1990): 75–170.

149. For a discussion, see John P. Campbell and Robert Prichard, "Motivation Theory in Industrial and Organizational Psychology," in Marvin Dunnette (ed.), *Industrial and Organizational Psychology* (Chicago: Rand McNally, 1976): 74–75; and Kanfer, "Motivation Theory," 115–116.

150. See, for example, Aubrey Daniels et al., "The Leader's Role in Pay Systems and Organizational Performance," *Compensation & Benefits Review* (May/June 2006): 58–60; and Suzanne Peterson and Fred Luthans, "The Impact of Financial and Non-Financial Incentives on Business Unit Outcomes Over Time," *Journal of Applied Psychology* 91, no. 1 (2006): 156–165.

9

Ethics, Employee Rights, and Fair Treatment at Work

Source: Daniel Acker/Getty Images, Inc.–Bloomberg News.

When you finish studying this chapter, you should be able to:

1. Explain what is meant by ethical behavior.
2. Discuss important factors that shape ethical behavior at work.
3. Discuss at least four specific ways in which HR management can influence ethical behavior at work.
4. Exercise fair disciplinary practices.
5. Discuss at least four procedural suggestions for managing dismissals effectively.

INTRODUCTION

The New York Times reported recently that some of the faculty and students at one university don't think their university's president should have been serving on the board of directors of the banking firm Goldman Sachs.[1] Fairly or not, some questioned whether it was appropriate for their president to be so closely identified with a banking firm that some felt had benefited during the recent economic downturn. The university's trustees said they saw no conflict with the president serving on the board and helping Goldman make its executive pay decisions. The university president said a debate like that at a university was understandable. Yet some still questioned the situation's ethics. ■

BASIC CONCEPTS IN ETHICS AND FAIR TREATMENT AT WORK

People face ethical choices every day. For example, is it wrong to use company e-mail for personal reasons? Is a $50 gift to a boss unacceptable? The quiz in Figure 9.1 may provide you with some insights.

Most everyone reading this book rightfully views him or herself as an ethical person, so we should start by asking, "Why include ethics in a human resource management book?" For two reasons. First, ethics is not theoretical. Instead, it greases the wheels that make businesses work.

The spread of technology into the workshop has raised a variety of new ethical questions and many old ones still linger. Compare your answers with those of other Americans surveyed, on page 279.

Office Technology

1. Is it wrong to use company e-mail for personal reasons?
   ☐ Yes   ☐ No

2. Is it wrong to use office equipment to help your children or spouse do schoolwork?
   ☐ Yes   ☐ No

3. Is it wrong to play computer games on office equipment during the workday?
   ☐ Yes   ☐ No

4. Is it wrong to use office equipment to do Internet shopping?
   ☐ Yes   ☐ No

5. Is it unethical to blame an error you made on a technological glitch?
   ☐ Yes   ☐ No

6. Is it unethical to visit pornographic Web sites using office equipment?
   ☐ Yes   ☐ No

Gifts and Entertainment

7. What's the value at which a gift from a supplier or client becomes troubling?
   ☐ $25   ☐ $50   ☐ $100

8. Is a $50 gift to a boss unacceptable?
   ☐ Yes   ☐ No

9. Is a $50 gift *from* the boss unacceptable?
   ☐ Yes   ☐ No

10. Of gifts from suppliers: Is it OK to take a $200 pair of football tickets?
    ☐ Yes   ☐ No

11. Is it OK to take a $120 pair of theater tickets?
    ☐ Yes   ☐ No

12. Is it OK to take a $100 holiday food basket?
    ☐ Yes   ☐ No

13. Is it OK to take a $25 gift certificate?
    ☐ Yes   ☐ No

14. Can you accept a $75 prize won at a raffle at a supplier's conference?
    ☐ Yes   ☐ No

Truth and Lies

15. Due to on-the-job pressure, have you ever abused or lied about sick days?
    ☐ Yes   ☐ No

16. Due to on-the-job pressure, have you ever taken credit for someone else's work or idea?
    ☐ Yes   ☐ No

FIGURE 9.1

The *Wall Street Journal* Workplace Ethics Quiz

Source: Wall Street Journal (October 21, 1999): B1–B4. Ethics Officer Association, Belmont, MA: Ethics Leadership Group.

Managers who promise raises but don't deliver, salespeople who say "the order's coming" when it's not, production managers who take kickbacks from suppliers—they all corrode the trust that day-to-day business transactions depend on, and eventually run the businesses (or at least the managers) into the ground. According to one recent lawsuit, marketers for Pfizer Inc. influenced the company to suppress unfavorable studies about one of its drugs.[2] Plaintiffs are suing for billions.

Second, managers' human resource–type decisions are usually replete with ethical consequences.[3] For example, one survey found that 6 of the 10 most serious ethical work issues—workplace safety, employee records security, employee theft, affirmative action, comparable work, and employee privacy rights—were HR-related.[4] Another survey of human resource professionals found that 54% had observed misconduct ranging from violations of Title VII to violations of the Occupational Safety and Health Act.[5]

Ethical Dilemmas

In fact, ethical dilemmas are a familiar part of human resource management decision making. For example:

- You know that your team shouldn't start work on the new machine until all the safety measures have been checked, but your boss is pressing you to get started: What should you do?
- You dismissed an employee in an angry moment, and now she has applied for unemployment insurance, saying you never warned her. Should you create and place in her file a note of warning, to protect your employer from paying higher unemployment taxes?
- You have an incompetent employee who you would like to get rid of, and someone just called you to get a job reference. How honest should you be?
- You've just taken over as the HR manager of a company in a depressed economic area, only to find that it has been hiring illegal aliens. If you complain, the company will probably close, putting 600 area residents out of work. What should you do?

Of course, the manager's human resource–related decisions need not be a hotbed of ethical misdeeds. Instead, HR activities can play a central role in the company's ethics efforts. Let's look first at what *ethics* means.

The Meaning of Ethics

ethics
The study of standards of conduct and moral judgment; also the standards of right conduct.

Ethics are "the principles of conduct governing an individual or a group"—the principles people use to decide what their conduct should be.[6] However, ethical decisions don't include just any type of conduct. For instance, deciding which car to buy generally wouldn't involve ethics. Instead, ethical decisions are always rooted in morality. *Morality* means society's accepted standards of behavior. Like the Ten Commandments, morality involves basic questions of right and wrong, such as stealing, murder, and how to treat other people. As such, how to treat employees is almost always as much of an ethical question as it is a legal one.[7]

Ethics and the Law

1 Explain what is meant by ethical behavior.

Perhaps surprisingly, the law is a far-from-perfect guide to what is ethical, because something may be legal but not right or right but not legal. Firing a 38-year-old employee with 20 years' tenure without notice may be unethical, but still legal, for instance. The vice president for business practices at United Technologies Corp. (and a former trial lawyer) put it this way: "Don't lie, don't cheat, don't steal. We were all raised with essentially the same values. *Ethics* means making decisions that represent what you stand for, not just what the laws are."[8]

The law may not be a foolproof guide to what's ethical, but some managers use it as if it is. Businesses exist to produce a profit, so economic value tends to be the initial screen when managers make decisions. After profits, "Is it legal?" may be the next screen, because of the consequences of breaking laws. Unfortunately, "Is it ethical" may then arise only as a third afterthought, if at all.

FIGURE 9.2

Partial List of Legal Areas Under Which Workers Have Legal Rights

- Leave of absence and vacation rights
- Injuries and illnesses rights
- Noncompete agreement rights
- Employees' rights on employer policies
- Discipline rights
- Rights on personnel files
- Employee pension rights
- Employee benefits rights
- References rights
- Rights on criminal records
- Employee distress rights
- Defamation rights
- Employees' rights on fraud
- Rights on assault and battery
- Employee negligence rights
- Right on political activity
- Union/group activity rights
- Whistleblower rights
- Workers' compensation rights

Employee Rights and the Law

In fact, few societies rely solely on managers' ethics or sense of fairness to ensure that they do what's right by their employees. They also put in place various laws. Laws like Title VII give employees (or prospective employees, and sometimes past employees) numerous *rights*. For example, under Title VII of the Civil Rights Act, employers can't turn someone down for a job based on his or her color. The Occupational Safety and Health Act gives employees the right to refuse to work under unsafe conditions.[9] Figure 9.2 presents a partial list of legal areas under which workers have rights.[10]

NOTIFICATION Governments like America's also don't generally leave informing employees about their legal rights to chance. Most federal employment laws and regulations require employers to post official notices of employee rights. Many states have similar posting requirements. For example, the required OSHA safety poster lists employees' rights under OSHA, including "the right to request an OSHA inspection if you believe that there are unsafe and unhealthful conditions in your workplace."

EXPANDING EMPLOYEES' RIGHTS The trend is to expand employees' legal rights. Over the past century, we've seen the introduction of union relations laws, civil rights and equal employment laws, and occupational safety laws, for instance. This trend shows no indication of slowing. For example, 11 states, including Connecticut, Hawaii, New Jersey, and New York, were recently debating legislation that would give victims of verbally abusive bosses the right to sue for damages.[11]

EMPLOYEE RIGHTS ABROAD The concept of employee rights is not limited to the United States. In fact, in some places, including Europe, employees' rights are, if anything, broader than in the United States. For example, employees in much of Europe have more job security and require more notice for termination than do U.S. employees.[12]

Workplace Unfairness

One way a company's ethics manifest themselves is in how fairly it treats its employees. Anyone who's suffered unfair treatment at work knows it is demoralizing. Studies confirm this common-sense observation. Unfair treatment reduces morale, increases stress, and has negative effects on performance. Employees of abusive supervisors are more likely to quit, and to report lower job and life satisfaction and higher stress.[13]

Sometimes workplace unfairness is subtle, and sometimes it's blatant. For example, unstated policies that require CPA associates to work and travel 7 days per week to make partner may subtly eliminate working mothers from the partner track. But some unfairness is blatant. For example, some supervisors are workplace bullies. One survey of 1,000 U.S. employees concluded that about 45% said they had worked for abusive bosses. Another researcher concluded that "a surprising 80% had personally been the target of bullies."[14]

The employer should always prohibit such behavior, and many firms do have anti-harassment policies. For example, Walgreens' mission statement says, "We will treat each other with respect and dignity and do the same for all we serve."[15] At work, fair treatment reflects concrete actions such as "employees are trusted," "employees are treated with respect," and "employees are treated fairly" (see Figure 9.3).[16]

What is your organization like most of the time? Circle YES if the item describes your organization, NO if it does not describe your organization, and ? if you cannot decide.

IN THIS ORGANIZATION . . .

1. Employees are praised for good work	Yes	?	No
2. Supervisors yell at employees (R)	Yes	?	No
3. Supervisors play favorites (R)	Yes	?	No
4. Employees are trusted	Yes	?	No
5. Employees' complaints are dealt with effectively	Yes	?	No
6. Employees are treated like children (R)	Yes	?	No
7. Employees are treated with respect	Yes	?	No
8. Employees' questions and problems are responded to quickly	Yes	?	No
9. Employees are lied to (R)	Yes	?	No
10. Employees' suggestions are ignored (R)	Yes	?	No
11. Supervisors swear at employees (R)	Yes	?	No
12. Employees' hard work is appreciated	Yes	?	No
13. Supervisors threaten to fire or lay off employees (R)	Yes	?	No
14. Employees are treated fairly	Yes	?	No
15. Co-workers help each other out	Yes	?	No
16. Co-workers argue with each other (R)	Yes	?	No
17. Co-workers put each other down (R)	Yes	?	No
18. Co-workers treat each other with respect	Yes	?	No

FIGURE 9.3

Perceptions of Fair Interpersonal Treatment Scale

Note: R = the item is reverse scored.
Source: Michelle A. Donovan et al., "The Perceptions of Their Interpersonal Treatment Scale: Development and Validation of a Measure of Interpersonal Treatment in the Workplace," *Journal of Applied Psychology* 83, no. 5 (1998): 692. Copyright © 1997 by Michelle A. Donovan, Fritz Drasgow, and Liberty J. Munson at the University of Illinois at Urbana-Champaign. All rights reserved.

Why Treat Employees Fairly?

There are many reasons that managers should be fair, some more obvious than others. The golden rule is one obvious reason: As management guru Peter Drucker has said, "[T]hey're not employees, they're people," and the manager should treat people with dignity and respect. An increasingly litigious workforce is another reason. The manager wants to be sure to institute disciplinary and discharge procedures that will survive the scrutiny of arbitrators and the courts.

What may not be so obvious is that employees' fairness perceptions also have important organizational outcomes. For example, victims exhibit more workplace deviance, such as theft and sabotage.[17] Perceptions of fairness also relate to enhanced employee commitment; enhanced satisfaction with the organization, jobs, and leaders; and enhanced organizational citizenship behaviors.[18]

EXAMPLE A study illustrates this. College instructors first completed surveys concerning the extent to which they saw their colleges as treating them with *procedural* and *distributive justice*. (Procedural justice refers to fair processes; distributive justice refers to fair outcomes.) The procedural justice items included, for example, "In general, the department/college's procedures allow for requests for clarification or for additional information about a decision." The distributive justice items included, "I am fairly rewarded considering the responsibilities I have." Then the instructors completed organizational commitment questionnaires. These included questions such as "I am proud to tell others that I am part of this department/college." Their students then completed surveys. These contained items such as "The instructor was sympathetic to my needs," and "The instructor treated me fairly."

The results were telling.

- Instructors who perceived high distributive and procedural justice reported higher organizational commitment.
- Furthermore, these instructors' students reported higher levels of instructor effort, prosocial behaviors, and fairness, as well as more positive reactions to their instructors.

"Overall," as the researcher says, "the results imply that fair treatment of employees has important organizational consequences."[19]

WHAT SHAPES ETHICAL BEHAVIOR AT WORK?

Whether a person acts ethically at work is usually not a consequence of any one thing. For example, could it be that everyone running some of the banks that triggered the subprime mortgage mess was simply unethical? Not likely. There must have been more to it.

There's No One Smoking Gun

2 Discuss important factors that shape ethical behavior at work.

A recent review of over 30 years of ethics research concluded that three factors combine to determine the ethical choices a person makes.[20] The authors titled their paper "Bad Apples, Bad Cases, and Bad Barrels." This title highlighted their conclusion that no single "smoking gun" determines ethical behavior. Instead, "bad apples" (people who are inclined to make unethical choices), "bad cases" (ethical situations that are ripe for unethical choices), and "bad barrels" (environments that foster or condone unethical choices) combine to determine what a person's ethical choices will be. The following discussion summarizes their overall findings.

INDIVIDUAL CHARACTERISTICS: WHO ARE THE BAD APPLES? Some people are just more inclined to make unethical choices. Most importantly, people differ in their level of "cognitive moral development." The most principled people, with the highest level of cognitive moral development, think through the implications of their decisions and apply ethical principles.

However, most adults don't operate at this high level. Instead, most base their judgment about what is right on the expectations of their colleagues and other important people with whom they interact, or on company policies and what the law says.

Finally, people at the lowest level make their ethical choices solely based on obeying what they're told and on avoiding punishment.

WHICH ETHICAL SITUATIONS MAKE FOR BAD (ETHICALLY DANGEROUS) SITUATIONS? Similarly, some ethical dilemmas are more likely to prompt unethical choices. Most importantly, apparently "smaller" dilemmas prompt more bad choices. Influential issues here include the total harm that can befall victims of an unethical choice, the likelihood that the action will result in harm, and the number of people potentially affected by the act. In apparently less serious situations, it's more likely that someone might say, in effect, "it's okay to do this, even though I know it's wrong."

WHAT ARE THE "BAD BARRELS"? WHAT OUTSIDE FACTORS MOLD ETHICAL CHOICES? These researchers also concluded that, "our findings suggest that organizations create bad and good social environments ("barrels") that can influence individual level unethical choices." In particular, companies that promote an "everyone for himself" atmosphere are more likely to trigger unethical choices. On the other hand, emphasizing that employees should focus on the well-being of everyone leads to choices that are more ethical. Furthermore, "a strong ethical culture that clearly communicates the range of acceptable and unacceptable behavior [such as through leader role models] is associated with fewer unethical decisions in the workplace." Having a code of conduct, by the way, had "no detectable impact on ethical choices." [21] Instead, it was the sum total of the culture of the employer created. Based on this evidence, we'll look more closely at several of the things that influence ethical behavior at work.

The Person (What Makes Bad Apples?)

Because people bring to their jobs their own ideas of what is morally right and wrong, each person must shoulder much of the credit (or blame) for his or her ethical choices. We just saw that some people are more principled than others. For example, researchers surveyed CEOs to study the CEOs' intentions to engage in two questionable practices: soliciting a competitor's technological secrets, and making illegal payments to foreign officials. The researchers concluded that the CEOs' personal predispositions more strongly affected their decisions than did outside pressures or characteristics of their firms.[22]

TRAITS The problem is it's hard to generalize about what makes the characteristics of ethical or unethical people. Some studies suggest that age is a factor. One study surveyed 421 employees to measure the degree to which various traits influenced responses to ethical decisions. (Decisions included "doing personal business on company time" and "calling in sick to take a day off for personal use.") Older workers generally had stricter interpretations of ethical standards and made more ethical decisions than did younger ones.

Honesty testing (as we discussed in Chapter 5) shows that some people are more inclined to make the wrong ethical choice. How would you rate your own ethics? Figure 9.4 presents a short self-assessment survey for helping you answer that question.

Instrument

Indicate your level of agreement with these 15 statements using the following scale:
1 = Strongly disagree
2 = Disagree
3 = Neither agree nor disagree
4 = Agree
5 = Strongly agree

	1	2	3	4	5
1. The only moral of business is making money.	1	2	3	4	5
2. A person who is doing well in business does not have to worry about moral problems.	1	2	3	4	5
3. Act according to the law, and you can't go wrong morally.	1	2	3	4	5
4. Ethics in business is basically an adjustment between expectations and the ways people behave.	1	2	3	4	5
5. Business decisions involve a realistic economic attitude and not a moral philosophy.	1	2	3	4	5
6. "Business ethics" is a concept for public relations only.	1	2	3	4	5
7. Competitiveness and profitability are important values.	1	2	3	4	5
8. Conditions of a free economy will best serve the needs of society. Limiting competition can only hurt society and actually violates basic natural laws.	1	2	3	4	5
9. As a consumer, when making an auto insurance claim, I try to get as much as possible regardless of the extent of the damage.	1	2	3	4	5
10. While shopping at the supermarket, it is appropriate to switch price tags on packages.	1	2	3	4	5
11. As an employee, I can take home office supplies; it doesn't hurt anyone.	1	2	3	4	5
12. I view sick days as vacation days that I deserve.	1	2	3	4	5
13. Employees' wages should be determined according to the laws of supply and demand.	1	2	3	4	5
14. The business world has its own rules.	1	2	3	4	5
15. A good businessperson is a successful businessperson.	1	2	3	4	5

ANALYSIS AND INTERPRETATION

Rather than specify "right" answers, this instrument works best when you compare your answer to those of others. With that in mind, here are mean responses from a group of 243 management students. How did your responses compare?

1. 3.09	6. 2.88	11. 1.58
2. 1.88	7. 3.62	12. 2.31
3. 2.54	8. 3.79	13. 3.36
4. 3.41	9. 3.44	14. 3.79
5. 3.88	10. 1.33	15. 3.38

FIGURE 9.4

How Do My Ethics Rate?

Source: Adapted from A. Reichel and Y. Neumann, *Journal of Instructional Psychology* (March 1988): 25–53. With permission of the authors.

Outside Forces That Shape Ethical Decisions (Bad Barrels)

COMPANY PRESSURES Outside pressures weaken (or strengthen) one's ethical compass. If people did unethical things at work solely for personal gain, it perhaps would be understandable (though inexcusable). The scary thing about unethical behavior at work is that it's often not driven by personal interests.

Table 9.1 summarizes the results of one ethics survey. In this case, the researchers were studying the principal causes of ethical lapses, as reported by six levels of employees and managers.

As you can see, organizational pressures are a big factor. For example, "meeting schedule pressure" was the number one reported factor in causing ethical lapses. For most of these employees, "meeting overly aggressive financial or business objectives" and "helping the company survive" were the two other top causes. "Advancing my own career or financial interests" ranked toward the bottom of the list. Thus (at least in this case), most ethical lapses occurred because employees were under the gun to do what they thought was best to help their companies.

Several years ago, a judge sentenced a company called WorldCom Corp.'s former chief financial officer to 5 years in jail, allegedly for helping the firm's former chair mask WorldCom's deteriorating financial situation. Among other things, the government accused him of instructing underlings to fraudulently book accounting entries, and of filing false statements with the SEC. Why, as someone trained to protect the interests of his shareholders, would the CFO do such a thing? "I took these actions, knowing they were wrong, in a misguided attempt to preserve the company to allow it to withstand what I believed were temporary financial difficulties."[23]

Just having rules on the books forbidding such behavior does not seem to work. For example, several years ago, New York's attorney general filed charges against Merrill Lynch. He alleged that several of its analysts had issued optimistic ratings on stocks, while privately expressing concerns about those same stocks. The allegation was that they did so to aid and support Merrill Lynch's investment banking relationships with these companies. As one Merrill e-mail said,

> Some of the communication with the go-to people and the bankers prior to the initiation may have been a technical violation of the firm's written policies and procedures (which, I have now learned, say the company's bankers should not be told what the proposed rating is or will be, even if the company isn't currently under coverage), so my guess is the lawyers will want to offer this in detail. From what they've told me, however, even if there was a violation, this is not a big deal.[24]

TABLE 9.1 Principal Causes of Ethical Compromises

	Senior Mgmt.	Middle Mgmt.	Front Line Supv.	Prof. Non-Mgmt.	Admin. Salaried	Hourly
Meeting schedule pressure	1	1	1	1	1	1
Meeting overly aggressive financial or business objectives	3	2	2	2	2	2
Helping the company survive	2	3	4	4	3	4
Advancing the career interests of my boss	5	4	3	3	4	5
Feeling peer pressure	7	7	5	6	5	3
Resisting competitive threats	4	5	6	5	6	7
Saving jobs	9	6	7	7	7	6
Advancing my own career or financial interests	8	9	9	8	9	8
Other	6	8	8	9	8	9

Note: 1 is high; 9 is low.
Source: O. C. Ferrell and John Fraedrich, *Business Ethics,* 3rd ed. (New York: Houghton Mifflin, 1997): 28. Adapted from Rebecca Goodell, *Ethics in American Business: Policies, Programs, and Perceptions* (1994): 54. Permission provided courtesy of the Ethics Resource Center.

Several years ago, a judge sentenced WorldCom's former chief financial officer to 5 years in jail, allegedly for helping the firm's former chair mask WorldCom's deteriorating financial situation.

Source: Rogelio Solis/AP Wide World Photos.

PRESSURE FROM THE BOSS Another "bad barrel" factor is the extent to which supervisors exhibit and encourage ethical behavior. According to one report, for instance, "the level of misconduct at work dropped dramatically when employees said their supervisors exhibited ethical behavior." Only 25% of employees who agreed that their supervisors "set a good example of ethical business behavior" said they had observed misconduct in the last year, compared with 72% of those who did not feel that their supervisors set good ethical examples.[25] Yet, in another poll, only about 27% of employees strongly agreed that their organizations' leadership is ethical.[26]

Examples of how supervisors knowingly (or unknowingly) lead subordinates astray ethically include:

● Tell staffers to do whatever is necessary to achieve results.
● Overload top performers to ensure that work gets done.

Source: http://www.ibm.com/responsibility/policy2.shtml. Accessed September 1, 2010.

- Look the other way when wrongdoing occurs.
- Take credit for others' work or shift blame.[27]

ETHICS POLICIES AND CODES An ethics policy and code is another way to signal that the firm is serious about ethics. For example, IBM's code of ethics (see the accompanying screen grab) this to say about tips, gifts, and entertainment:

> No IBM employee, or any member of his or her immediate family, can accept gratuities or gifts of money from a supplier, customer, or anyone in a business relationship. Nor can they accept a gift or consideration that could be perceived as having been offered because of the business relationship. "Perceived" simply means this: if you read about it in the local newspaper, would you wonder whether the gift just might have had something to do with a business relationship? No IBM employee can give money or a gift of significant value to a customer, supplier, or anyone if it could reasonably be viewed as being done to gain a business advantage.[28]

Sometimes ethics codes don't work. Enron Corp. allegedly collapsed in part due to the ethical misdeeds of some executives. Yet Enron's ethical principles were easily accessible on the firm's Web site. It stated that, "as a partner in the communities in which we operate, Enron believes it has a responsibility to conduct itself according to certain basic principles." Those include "respect, integrity, communication and excellence."[29]

Beyond the code, some firms urge employees to apply a quick "ethics test" to evaluate whether what they're about to do fits the company's code of conduct. For example, Raytheon Co. asks employees who face ethical dilemmas to ask:

Is the action legal?

Is it right?

Who will be affected?

Does it fit Raytheon's values?

How will it "feel" afterwards?

How will it look in the newspaper?

Will it reflect poorly on the company?[30]

However, codifying the rules without enforcing them is futile. As one study of ethics concludes, "strong statements by managers may reduce the risk of legal and ethical violations by their work forces, but enforcement of standards has the greatest impact."[31] More firms, such as Lockheed Martin Corp., therefore appoint chief ethics officers.[32] *Ethics audits* typically address topics like conflicts of interest, giving and receiving gifts, employee discrimination, and access to company information. [33]

More firms, such as Lockheed Martin Corp., appoint chief ethics officers to monitor employees' ethical behavior.

organizational culture

The characteristic values, traditions, and behaviors a company's employees share.

THE ORGANIZATION'S CULTURE These examples illustrate an important feature of the boss's and the company's influence; that influence is often subliminal. The boss sends signals about the appropriate way to behave. Those signals then create the culture to which employees respond. We can define **organizational culture** as the "characteristic values, traditions, and behaviors a company's employees share." A *value* is a basic belief about what is right or wrong, or about what you should or shouldn't do. ("Honesty is the best policy" would be a value.) Values are important because they guide and channel behavior. Managing people and shaping their behavior therefore depends on shaping the values they use as behavioral guides. For example, if management really believes "honesty is the best policy," the written rules they follow and the things they do should reflect this value. With respect to ethics, managers therefore have to think through how to send not just accurate but the right signals to their employees. Doing so includes:

- *Clarifying Expectations.* First, managers should make clear their expectations with respect to the values they want subordinates to follow. For example, the Johnson & Johnson ethics code says "We believe our first responsibility is to the doctors, nurses and patients, to mothers and fathers and all others who use our products and services."
- *Using Signs and Symbols.* *Symbolism*—what the manager actually does—ultimately does the most to create the company's culture. Managers need to "walk the talk." They cannot expect to say, "don't fudge the financials" and then do so themselves.
- *Providing Physical Support.* Does the firm reward ethical behavior or penalize it?[34] The physical manifestations of the manager's values—the firm's incentive plan, appraisal system, and disciplinary procedures, for instance—signal employees regarding what they should and should not do.

In Summary: Some Things to Keep in Mind About Ethical Behavior at Work

Several experts reviewed the research concerning things that influence ethical behavior in organizations. Here's what their findings suggest for managers:[35]

- Ethical behavior starts with *moral awareness*. In other words, does the person even recognize that a moral issue exists in the situation?
- *Managers* can do a lot to influence employee ethics by carefully cultivating the right norms, leadership, reward systems, and culture.
- Ethics slide when people undergo "*moral disengagement.*" Doing so frees them from the guilt that would normally go with violating one's ethical standards. For example, you're more likely to harm others when you view the victims as "outsiders."
- The most powerful morality comes from *within*. In effect, when the moral person asks, "Why be moral?" the answer is, "because that is who I am." Then, failure to act morally creates emotional discomfort.[36]
- Beware the seductive power of an *unmet goal*. Unmet goals pursued blindly can contribute to unethical behavior.[37]
- Offering *rewards* for ethical behavior can backfire. Doing so may actually undermine the intrinsic value of ethical behavior.
- Don't inadvertently reward someone for *bad behavior*. For example, don't promote someone who got a big sale through devious means.[38]
- Employers should *punish unethical behavior*. Employees who observe unethical behavior expect you to discipline the perpetrators.
- The degree to which employees *openly talk about ethics* is a good predictor of ethical conduct. Conversely, organizations characterized by "moral muteness" suffer more ethically problematic behavior.
- People tend to alter their *moral compasses* when they join organizations. They uncritically equate "what's best for this organization (or team, or department)" with "what's the right thing to do?"

HR MANAGEMENT'S ROLE IN ETHICS AND FAIR TREATMENT

Within the human resource system there are many opportunities to mold and foster ethics. We'll address this next.

Staffing and Selection

3 Discuss at least four specific ways in which HR management can influence ethical behavior at work.

"The simplest way to tune up an organization, ethically speaking, is to hire more ethical people," says one writer.[39] "Screening for ethics" should start before applicants even apply, by creating recruitment materials that emphasize the firm's commitment to ethics. (The Microsoft site in Figure 9.5 is an example.) Employers can then use screening tools like honesty tests, background checks, and questions such as "Have you ever observed someone stretching the rules at work? What did you do about it?" to screen out undesirables.[40]

FIGURE 9.5

Using the Company Web Site to Emphasize Ethics

Source: www.microsoft.com/industry/
government/GovGiftingCompliance.
mspx, accessed April 28, 2009.

Furthermore, "If prospective employees perceive that the hiring process does not treat people fairly, they may assume that ethical behavior is not important in the company."[41]

- **Make the screening procedures fair.** Candidates will tend to view the *formal procedure* (such as the selection interview) as fair to the extent that it tests job-related criteria, provides an opportunity to demonstrate competence, provides a way of redressing an error, and is used consistently with all applicants (or employees).[42]
- **Treat applicants fairly.** The person's *interpersonal treatment* reflects such things as the propriety of the questions, the politeness and respect of the person doing the assessing, and the degree to which there was two-way communication.
- **Provide explanations.** Candidates appreciate employers' *providing explanations.* Applicants see a system as fair to the extent that the employer provides useful knowledge about the employer's assessment procedures.[43]
- **Choose tests carefully.** Applicants or employees tend to view some *selection tools* as fairer. For example, they tend to view tools like work sample tests that are clearly job-related as fair.

Training

For all practical purposes, ethics training is mandatory. Since 1991, federal sentencing guidelines have prescribed reduced penalties for employers accused of misconduct who implement codes of conduct and ethics training.[44] The Sarbanes-Oxley Act of 2002 makes ethics training even more important.

Ethics training usually involves showing employees how to recognize ethical dilemmas, how to apply codes of conduct to resolve problems, and how to use personnel activities like disciplinary practices in ethical ways.[45] The training should emphasize the moral underpinnings of the ethical choice and the company's deep commitment to integrity and ethics. Include participation by top managers in the program to underscore that commitment.[46]

Improving Productivity through HRIS:
Web-Based Ethics Training

Ethics training is often Internet-based. In one program, Lockheed Martin had its 160,000 employees take ethics and legal compliance training via the firm's intranet. Lockheed's ethics program software also kept track of how well the company and its employees were doing maintaining high ethical standards. For instance, the program helped top managers see that in one year, 4.8% of the company's ethics allegations involved conflicts of interest, and that it took about 30 days to complete an ethics violation internal investigation.[47] Online ethics training programs vendors include *Business Ethics*, from skillsoft.com, and two online courses, *Ethical Decision Making* and *Managerial Business Ethics*, both from netG.com.[48]

Figure 9.6 summarizes the nuts and bolts of typical ethics training programs. Note that new hire orientation, annual refresher training, and distributing the companies' policies and handbooks are all quite important.

Performance Appraisal

Unfair appraisals tend to suggest that the employer may condone unethical behavior. In fact, some managers do ignore accuracy and honesty in performance appraisals.[49] With a fair appraisal process:

- The employees' standards should be clear.
- Employees should understand the basis on which they're going to be appraised.
- The supervisor should perform the appraisal objectively and fairly.[50]

Reward and Disciplinary Systems

Employees expect their employers to punish unethical conduct.[51] Where it does not, often the ethical employees (not unethical ones) feel punished. Similarly, the employer should discipline executives, not just underlings, who misbehave.[52]

Workplace Aggression and Violence

In February 2010, a professor at the University of Alabama, denied tenure, allegedly shot her department chair and several colleagues. We'll see in Chapter 11 that workplace aggression is a serious problem, as well as one that often stems from real or perceived inequities. Rightly or

FIGURE 9.6

The Role of Training in Ethics

Source: HR Magazine by Susan Wells. Copyright 1999 by Society for Human Resource Management (SHRM). Reprinted with permission of the Society for Human Resource Management (www.shrm.org), Alexandria, VA, publisher of *HR Magazine* © SHRM.

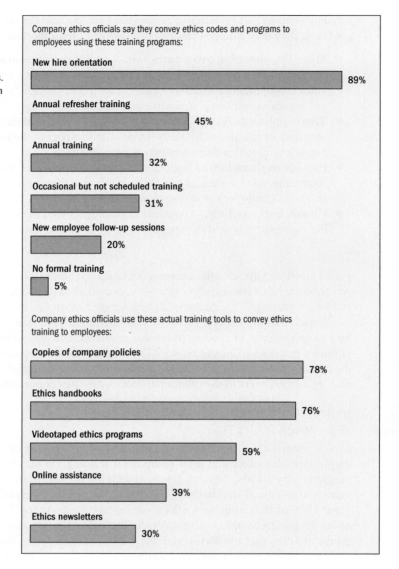

wrongly, the employee concludes that the firm is treating him or her unethically and unfairly. Employees who believe that they're underpaid or unfairly dismissed may retaliate.[53] Possible counterproductive behaviors might include employee theft or destruction of company property. Real or imagined mistreatment also makes it more likely the employee will resign, and will show higher levels of "work withdrawal" (show up for work, but not do his or her best).[54]

Building Two-Way Communication

The opportunity for two-way, interactive communication affects our perceptions of how fairly people are treating us. One study concluded that three actions contributed to perceived fairness in business settings. One was *engagement* (involving individuals in the decisions that affect them by asking for their input and allowing them to refute the merits of one another's ideas and assumptions). A second was *explanation* (ensuring that everyone involved and affected should understand why final decisions are made as they are and of the thinking that underlies the decisions). The third was *expectation clarity* (making sure everyone knows by what standards they will be judged and the penalties for failure).[55]

STEPS TO TAKE Many employers institute systems to facilitate two-way communication. Some administer periodic opinion surveys. Thus, the FedEx Survey Feedback Action (SFA) program includes an anonymous survey. This lets employees express feelings about the company and their managers and to some extent about service, pay, and benefits. Each manager then has an opportunity to discuss the anonymous department results with his or her subordinates, and create an action plan for improving work group commitment. Sample questions include:

"I can tell my manager what I think."

"My manager tells me what is expected."

"My manager listens to my concerns."

"My manager keeps me informed."

WALMART EXAMPLE Some people accused Walmart of unfairness after it instituted a new policy requiring employees to come to work at a moment's notice, depending on their stores' last-minute needs. From Walmart's point of view, the change made strategic sense. Its competitive advantage is low costs. The new employee scheduling policy enabled Walmart to minimize labor costs when stores were slow (by sending employees home). Would you consider Walmart's new store staffing policy to be unethical? Why?

EMPLOYEE DISCIPLINE AND PRIVACY

discipline

A procedure that corrects or punishes a subordinate for violating a rule or procedure.

The purpose of **discipline** is to encourage employees to behave sensibly at work (where *sensible* means adhering to rules and regulations). Discipline is necessary when an employee violates one of the rules.[56]

The Three Pillars

The manager builds a fair discipline process on three pillars: rules and regulations, a system of progressive penalties, and an appeals process.

RULES A set of clear disciplinary rules and regulations is the first pillar. The rules should address issues such as theft, destruction of company property, drinking on the job, and insubordination. Examples of rules include:

> *Poor performance is not acceptable.* Each employee is expected to perform his or her work properly and efficiently and to meet established standards of quality.
> *Alcohol and drugs do not mix with work.* The use of either during working hours and reporting for work under the influence of either are both strictly prohibited.

The purpose of the rules is to inform employees ahead of time what is and is not acceptable behavior. Employees should be told, preferably in writing, what is not permitted. This usually occurs during the employee's orientation. The employee orientation handbook should contain the rules and regulations. The Managing the New Workforce feature provides another perspective.

MANAGING THE NEW WORKFORCE

Comparing Males and Females in a Discipline Situation

Watching a classic movie like *King Arthur* may lead you to conclude that chivalry in general and a protective attitude toward women in particular is a well-established value in many societies, but that may not be the case. Not only is chivalry not necessarily a prevailing value, there is even a competing hypothesis in the research literature.[57] What several researchers unfortunately call the "Evil Woman Thesis" certainly doesn't argue that women are evil. Instead, it "argues that women who commit offenses violate stereotypic assumptions about the proper behavior of women. These women will [then] be penalized for their inappropriate sex role behavior in addition to their other offenses." In other words, it argues that when a woman doesn't act the way other men and women think she should act the men and women tend to overreact and treat her more harshly than they might if a man committed it.

While such a thesis might seem ridiculous on its face, the results of at least one careful study seem to support it. In this study, 360 graduate and undergraduate business school students reviewed a labor arbitration case. The case involved two employees, one male and one female, with similar work records and tenure with their employers. Both were discharged for violation of company rules related to alcohol and drugs. The case portrays one worker's behavior as a more

(continued)

serious breach of company rules: The more culpable worker (a male in half the study and a female in the other half) had brought the intoxicant to work. The students had to express their agreement with two alternative approaches to settling the dispute that arose after the discharge.

In their study, the researchers found bias against the female employee by both the male and female students. The female workers in the case received recommendations for harsher treatment from both the male and female students. As the researchers conclude, " . . . women, as decision makers, appear to be as willing as men to impose harsher discipline on women than upon men."

PENALTIES A system of progressive penalties is the second pillar of effective discipline. The severity of the penalty is usually a function of the offense and the number of times it has occurred. For example, most companies issue warnings for the first unexcused lateness. However, for a fourth offense, discharge is the usual disciplinary action.

APPEALS PROCESS Third, an appeals process should be part of the disciplinary process. The aim here is to ensure that supervisors mete out discipline fairly.

guaranteed fair treatment
Employer programs aimed at ensuring that all employees are treated fairly, generally by providing formalized, well-documented, and highly publicized vehicles through which employees can appeal any eligible issues.

FedEx's **guaranteed fair treatment** multi-step program illustrates this. In *step 1, management review,* the complainant submits a written complaint to a middle manager. The department head(s) review all relevant information; hold a meeting with the complainant; make a decision to either uphold, modify, or overturn management's action; and communicate their decision in writing to the complainant and the department's HR representative.

If not satisfied, then in *step 2, officer complaint,* the complainant submits a written appeal to the vice president or senior vice president of the division.

Finally, in *step 3, executive appeals review,* the complainant may submit a written complaint to the employee relations department. The complaint is then investigated and a case file prepared for the executive review appeals board. The appeals board—the CEO, the COO, the chief HR officer, and three senior vice presidents—then reviews all relevant information and makes a decision to uphold, overturn, or initiate a board of review or to take other appropriate action.

4 Exercise fair disciplinary practices.

Some supervisory behavior may be impossible to overcome. For example, the employer can sometimes mitigate the effects of unfair disciplinary procedures by establishing disciplinary procedures that are transparent and contain appeals processes. However, behaviors that attack the employee's personal and/or social identity are difficult to remedy.[58] The HR in Practice feature summarizes fair discipline guidelines.

HR IN PRACTICE

Fair Discipline Guidelines

Useful discipline guidelines for supervisors to keep in mind include:

- *Make sure the evidence supports the charge of employee wrongdoing.* Arbitrators often cite "The employer's evidence did not support the charge of employee wrongdoing" when reinstating discharged employees.
- *Make sure to protect the employees' due process rights.* Arbitrators normally reverse discharges and suspensions when the process that led to them is obviously unfair or violates due process.[59]
- *Adequately warn the employee of the disciplinary consequences of his or her alleged misconduct.* Have the employee sign a form as in Figure 9.7.
- *The rule that allegedly was violated should be "reasonably related" to the efficient and safe operation of the particular work environment.*
- *Fairly and adequately investigate the matter before administering discipline.*
- *The investigation should produce substantial evidence of misconduct.*

- *Apply applicable rules, orders, or penalties without discrimination.*
- *Maintain the employee's right to counsel.* For example, all union employees generally have the right to bring a representative to an interview that they reasonably believe might lead to disciplinary action.
- *Don't rob your subordinate of his or her dignity.*
- *Remember that the burden of proof is on you.* In U.S. society, a person is considered innocent until proven guilty.
- *Get the facts.* Don't base your decision on hearsay evidence or on your general impression.
- *Don't act while angry.* Very few people can be objective when they are angry.
- *Use ombudsmen.* Some companies establish *ombudsmen,* neutral counselors outside the chain of command to whom employees who believe they were treated unfairly can turn to for advice.[60]

FIGURE 9.7
Report of Employee Discipline

Apex Telecommunications Corporation
Report of Disciplinary Action and Warning

Employee's Name_____
Employee's Department_____
Date of Misconduct_____   Today's Date_____

Description of Incident and misconduct (including witnesses, if any)_____
_____
_____
_____

Witnesses to Incident_____
_____
_____

If the misconduct violated an Apex Co. policy or rule, state the policy or rule_____
_____
_____

Employee's explanation for misconduct, if any_____
_____
_____

Disciplinary action taken, if any_____
_____
_____

The employee was warned today that if misconduct such as this reoccurs at any time during the next_____
weeks, he or she may be subject to the following disciplinary action _____
_____
_____
_____

_____   _____
Supervisor's signature   Employee's signature

_____   _____
Print name   Print name

DISCIPLINE WITHOUT PUNISHMENT Traditional discipline has two main drawbacks. First, no one likes being punished. Second, punishment tends to gain short-term compliance, but not long-term cooperation.

Discipline without punishment (or alternative or nonpunitive discipline) aims to avoid these drawbacks. It does this by gaining employees' acceptance of the rules and by reducing the punitive nature of the discipline itself. Steps include:[61]

1. *Issue an oral reminder.*
2. *Should another incident arise within 6 weeks, issue a formal written reminder, and place a copy in the employee's personnel file.* Also, hold a second private discussion with the employee.
3. *Give a paid, 1-day "decision-making leave."* If another incident occurs in the next 6 weeks or so, tell the employee to take a 1-day leave with pay, and to consider whether he or she wants to abide by the company's rules. When the employee returns to work, he or she meets with you and gives you a decision.
4. *If no further incidents occur in the next year or so, purge the 1-day paid suspension from the person's file.* If the behavior is repeated, the next step is dismissal.

The process would not apply to exceptional circumstances. Criminal behavior or in-plant fighting might be grounds for immediate dismissal, for instance.

Employee Privacy[62]

As heated discussions about airports' full-body scans suggest, many (or most) people view invasions of their privacy as both unethical and unfair. At work, employee privacy violations include *intrusion* (such as locker room and email surveillance), *publication* of private matters, *disclosure* of medical records, and *appropriation* of an employee's name or likeness for commercial purposes.[63] Background checks, monitoring off-duty conduct and lifestyle, drug testing, workplace searches, and workplace activities monitoring trigger most privacy violations.[64] We'll look more closely at monitoring.

EMPLOYEE MONITORING A few years ago, a New Jersey court found an employer liable when one of its employees used his company computer at work to distribute child pornography. (Someone had previously alerted the employer to the suspicious activity and the employer had not taken action.)[65] The increased popularity of tools like blogging and Twitter has further heightened employers' concerns.[66]

Managing and monitoring company e-mail is an urgent problem. About one-third of U.S. companies recently investigated suspected leaks, via e-mail, of confidential or proprietary information. One hospital found that, to facilitate working at home, some medical staff were e-mailing patients' confidential records to themselves, violating federal privacy laws. Other employers face demands to produce employee e-mail as part of litigation, as when one employee sues another for sexual harassment.[67] A recent U.S. Federal Trade Commission decision may even make employers liable for deceptive company endorsements that employees post on their own blogs or on social media sites such as Facebook, even if the employers didn't authorize the statements.[68]

It's therefore not surprising that one survey found that 41% of employers with more than 20,000 employees have someone reading employee e-mails.[69] Ninety-six percent block access to adult Web sites, 61% to game sites.[70] Some check employees' personal blogs or Facebook sites, to see if they're publicizing work-related matters.[71] Even Twitter is becoming a monitoring issue.[72]

Monitoring today goes far beyond listening in on phone lines. New York's Bronx Lebanon Hospital uses biometric scanners to ensure that employees that clock in really are who they say they are.[73] Iris scanning tends to be the most accurate authorization device. Some organizations like the Federal Aviation Authority use it to control employees' access to its network information systems.[74]

Location monitoring is becoming pervasive.[75] Employers ranging from United Parcel Service to the City of Oakland, California, use GPS units to monitor their truckers' and street sweepers' whereabouts. Inexpensive GPS technologies will contribute to wider use of location monitoring.

Employers also routinely use software to monitor (usually secretly) what their employees are doing online. When one employer noticed that employees were piling up overtime claims, they installed new software and discovered many employees were spending hours each day shopping online instead of working. Such monitoring raises privacy issues.

LEGAL ISSUES Electronic eavesdropping is legal—up to a point. For example, federal law and most state laws allow employers to monitor employees' phone calls in the ordinary course of business. However, they must stop listening once it becomes clear that a conversation is personal rather than business related. You can also intercept e-mail to protect the property rights of the e-mail provider.

However, one recent U.S. Court of Appeals case suggests employers may have fewer rights to monitor e-mail than previously assumed.[76] To be safe, employers issue e-mail and online service usage policies. These warn employees that those systems are to be used for business purposes only. Employers also have employees sign e-mail and telephone monitoring acknowledgment statements like that in Figure 9.8. Many employees probably assume that their communications using the corporate e-mail system are open to review, but that e-mails they send via the employer's system but using their personal e-mail accounts (such as Gmail) aren't. Recently, courts in New York and New Jersey have supported this assumption, although on a limited basis. It's still not entirely a clear-cut situation.

An attorney should review the e-mail policy, but at a minimum make it clear that employees should have no expectation of privacy in their e-mail and Internet usage,[77] and that all messages sent and received on the employer's e-mail system are company property and not confidential.[78]

FIGURE 9.8

Sample Telephone Monitoring Acknowledgment Statement

I understand that XYZ Company periodically monitors any e-mail communications created, sent, or retrieved using this company's e-mail system. Therefore I understand that my e-mail communications may be read by individuals other than the intended recipient. I also understand that XYZ Company periodically monitors telephone communications, for example to improve customer service quality.

Signature   Date

Print Name   Department

dismissal
Involuntary termination of an employee's employment with the firm.

terminate at will
The idea, based in law, that the employment relationship can be terminated at will by either the employer or the employee for any reason.

Videotaped workplace monitoring calls for more legal caution. Continuous video surveillance of employees in an office setting may not be a problem. But a Boston employer had to pay over $200,000 to five workers it secretly videotaped in an employee locker room, after they sued.[79] Some employers, such as Eastman Kodak, appoint chief privacy officers to ensure that the human resource and other departments don't endanger the company by conducting inappropriate investigations of applicants or employees.[80]

MANAGING DISMISSALS

Because **dismissal** is the most drastic disciplinary step, the manager should ensure that the dismissal is fair and warranted. On those occasions that require immediate dismissal, the manager still needs to ensure that the action is humane.

The best way to "handle" a dismissal is to avoid it in the first place, when possible. Many dismissals start with bad hiring decisions. Using sound selection practices including assessment tests, reference and background checks, drug testing, and clearly defined jobs can reduce the need for dismissals.[83]

Termination at Will

For more than 100 years, the prevailing rule in the United States has been that without an employment contract, either the employer or the employee can **terminate at will** the employment relationship. In other words, the employee could resign for any reason, at will, and the employer could similarly dismiss an employee for any reason, at will. Today, however, dismissed employees increasingly take their cases to court, and in many cases employers are finding that they no longer have a blanket right to fire.

TERMINATION AT WILL EXCEPTIONS Three main protections against wrongful discharge eroded the termination-at-will doctrine—*statutory exceptions, common law exceptions,* and *public policy exceptions.*

First, in terms of *statutory exceptions,* federal and state equal employment and workplace laws prohibit specific types of dismissals. For example, Title VII of the Civil Rights Act of 1964 prohibits discharging employees based on race, color, religion, sex, or national origin.[84]

Second, numerous *common law exceptions* exist. For example, a court may decide that an employee handbook promising termination only "for just cause" may create an exception to the at-will rule.[85]

HR APPs 4 U

iPods and Ethics at Work

With more employees using their iPod and other MP3 players at work, employers are becoming uneasy. One employer gave employees iPods as a reward, and found the employees were now clogging the firm's servers with illegal music downloads.[81] Security is a problem, too. One "4-gigabyte MP3 player, such as the first generation of iPod Mini . . . can take home a lot of corporate data," said one employer (a process some graphically describe as "podslurping."[82] Allowing iPod use at work thus seems to require some special planning and policies.

Finally, under the *public policy exception,* courts have held a discharge to be wrongful when it was against an explicit, well-established public policy (for instance, the employer fired the employee for refusing to break the law).

Grounds for Dismissal

There are four bases for dismissal: unsatisfactory performance, misconduct, lack of qualifications for the job, and changed requirements of (or elimination of) the job.

Unsatisfactory performance may be defined as a persistent failure to perform assigned duties or to meet prescribed standards on the job.[86] Specific reasons include excessive absenteeism; tardiness; a persistent failure to meet normal job requirements; or an adverse attitude toward the company, supervisor, or fellow employees.

Misconduct is deliberate and willful violation of the employer's rules and may include stealing, rowdy behavior, and insubordination.

Lack of qualifications for the job is an employee's inability to do the assigned work, although he or she is diligent. Because in this case the employee may be trying to do the job, it is reasonable for the employer to try to salvage him or her—perhaps by assigning the employee to another job, or retraining the person.

Changed requirements of the job is an employee's incapability of doing the work assigned after the nature of the job has been changed. Similarly, you may have to dismiss an employee when his or her job is eliminated. Again, the employee may be industrious, so it is reasonable to retrain or transfer this person, if possible.

insubordination
Willful disregard or disobedience of the boss's authority or legitimate orders.

Insubordination, a form of misconduct, is sometimes the grounds for dismissal. Stealing, chronic tardiness, and poor-quality work are concrete grounds for dismissal, but insubordination is sometimes harder to translate into words. Some acts should be deemed insubordinate whenever and wherever they occur. These include:[87]

1. Direct disregard of the boss's authority
2. Direct disobedience of, or refusal to obey, the boss's orders, particularly in front of others
3. Deliberate defiance of clearly stated company policies, rules, regulations, and procedures
4. Public criticism of the boss
5. Blatant disregard of reasonable instructions
6. Contemptuous display of disrespect
7. Disregard for the chain of command
8. Participation in (or leadership of) an effort to undermine and remove the boss from power

FAIRNESS IN DISMISSALS Dismissing employees is never easy, but at least the employer can try to ensure the employee views the process as fair. Communication is important. One study found that "individuals who reported that they were given full explanations of why and how termination decisions were made were more likely to (1) perceive their layoff as fair, (2) endorse the terminating organization, and (3) indicate that they did not wish to take the past employer to court."[88]

Avoiding Wrongful Discharge Suits

In what *BusinessWeek* referred to as a "fear of firing," the magazine described how some employers—even when faced with employee theft—were reluctant to terminate disruptive employees for fear of lawsuits. In practice, plaintiffs (the dismissed employees) only win a tiny fraction of such suits. However, the cost of defending the suits is still huge.[89]

wrongful discharge
An employee dismissal that does not comply with the law or does not comply with the contractual arrangement stated or implied by the firm via its employment application forms, employee manuals, or other promises.

Wrongful discharge occurs when an employee's dismissal does not comply with the law or with the contractual arrangement stated or implied by the firm via its employment application forms, employee manuals, or other promises. (In a *constructive discharge* claim, the plaintiff argues that he or she quit, but had no choice because the employer made the situation so intolerable at work.[90]) The time to protect against such suits is before the manager errs and suits are filed.

PROCEDURAL STEPS Protecting against wrongful discharge suits requires two things: following procedural steps, and fairness safeguards. First lay the groundwork that will help avoid such suits. Procedural steps include:[91]

Is the employee covered by any type of written agreement, including a collective bargaining agreement?_____

Is a defamation claim likely?_____

Is there a possible discrimination allegation?_____

Is there any workers' compensation involvement?_____

Have reasonable rules and regulations been communicated and enforced?_____

Has the employee been given an opportunity to explain any rule violations or to correct poor performance?_____

Have all monies been paid within 24 hours after separation?_____

Has the employee been advised of his or her rights under COBRA?_____

FIGURE 9.9

Questions to Ask Before Making the Dismissal Final

Source: Sovereign, Kenneth L., *Personnel Law,* 4th ed., © 1999. Electronically reproduced by permission of Pearson Education, Inc., Upper Saddle River, New Jersey.

---

5 Discuss at least four procedural suggestions for managing dismissals effectively.

- Have applicants sign the employment application. Make sure it contains a statement that the employer can terminate at any time.
- Review your employee manual to look for and delete statements that could undermine your defense in a wrongful discharge case. For example, delete any reference to "employees can be terminated only for just cause."
- Have written rules listing infractions that may require discipline and discharge.
- If a rule is broken, get the worker's side of the story in front of witnesses, and preferably get it signed. Then check out the story.
- Be sure that employees get a written appraisal at least annually. If an employee shows evidence of incompetence, give that person a warning and provide an opportunity to improve.
- Keep careful confidential records of all actions such as employee appraisals, warnings or notices, and so on.
- Finally, ask the questions in Figure 9.9.

FAIRNESS SAFEGUARDS Terminated employees are less likely to sue if they walk away feeling you treated them fairly. Therefore, employ practices (like those we listed earlier in this chapter) that help ensure the fairness of the dismissal.[92] People who are fired and walk away feeling that they've been embarrassed or treated unfairly financially (for instance, in terms of severance pay) are more likely to seek retribution in the courts. Some employers therefore sometimes use severance pay to blunt a dismissal's sting. Figure 9.10 summarizes typical severance policies in manufacturing and service industries. You can't make a termination pleasant, but at least handle it

---

FIGURE 9.10

Median Weeks of Severance Pay by Job Level

Source: Severance Pay: Current Trends and Practices, July 2007, Table 4, www.culpepper.com/info/CS/default. asp.CulpeppereBulletin, July 2007. Complimentary subscriptions at: www.culpepper.com/eBulletin.

Severance Calculation Method	Median Weeks of Severance		
	Executives	**Managers**	**Professionals**
Fixed	26	6	4
Variable Amount by Employment Tenure			
1 year	4	2	2
3 years	7	5	5
5 years	10	7	7
10 years	20	12	10
15 years	26	16	15
Maximum	39	26	24

with fairness and justice. (As the economy deteriorated in 2009 and layoffs rose, more employers reduced what they awarded for severance pay, for instance, awarding lump sum payments rather than payments tied to years with the company.[93])

Personal Supervisory Liability

Courts sometimes hold managers personally liable for their supervisory actions, particularly those actions covered by the Fair Labor Standards Act and the Family and Medical Leave Act.[94] The Fair Labor Standards Act defines *employer* to include "any person acting directly or indirectly in the interest of an employer in relation to any employee." This can mean the individual supervisor.

STEPS TO TAKE There are several ways to avoid creating situations in which personal liability becomes an issue.

- *Follow company policies and procedures.* An employee may initiate a claim against a supervisor who he or she alleges did not follow policies and procedures.
- Administer the discipline in a manner that does not add to the employee's *emotional hardship* (as would having them publicly collect their belongings and leave the office).
- *Do not act in anger,* since doing so undermines the appearance of objectivity.
- Finally, *utilize the HR department* for advice regarding how to handle difficult disciplinary matters.

The Termination Interview

Dismissing an employee is one of the most difficult tasks you can face at work.[95] The dismissed employee, even if warned many times in the past, may still react with disbelief or even violence. Guidelines for the **termination interview** itself are as follows:

1. *Plan the interview carefully.* According to experts at Hay Associates, this includes:
   - Make sure the employee keeps the appointment time.
   - Never inform an employee over the phone.
   - Allow 10 minutes as sufficient time for the interview.
   - Use a neutral site, not your own office.
   - Have employee agreements, the human resource file, and a release announcement prepared in advance.
   - Be available at a time after the interview in case questions or problems arise.
   - Have phone numbers ready for medical or security emergencies.
2. *Get to the point.* As soon as the employee enters your office, give the person a moment to get comfortable and then inform him or her of your decision.
3. *Describe the situation.* Briefly, in three or four sentences, explain why the person is being let go. For instance, "Production in your area is down 4%, and we are continuing to have quality problems. We have talked about these problems several times in the past 3 months, and the solutions are not being followed through on. We have to make a change."[96] Don't personalize the situation by saying things like "Your production is just not up to par." Also, emphasize that the decision is final and irrevocable.
4. *Listen.* Continue the interview until the person appears to be talking freely and reasonably calmly.
5. *Review the severance package.* Describe severance payments, benefits, access to office support people, and the way references will be handled. However, under no conditions make any promises or benefits beyond those already in the support package.
6. *Identify the next step.* The terminated employee may be disoriented and unsure what to do next. Explain where the employee should go next, upon leaving the interview.

OUTPLACEMENT COUNSELING With **outplacement counseling** the employer arranges for an outside firm to provide terminated employees with career planning and job search skills. *Outplacement firms* usually provide the actual outplacement services. Employees (usually they're managers) who are let go typically have office space and secretarial services they can use at local offices of such firms, in addition to the counseling services. The outplacement counseling is part of the terminated employee's support or severance package.

---

termination interview
The interview in which an employee is informed of the fact that he or she has been dismissed.

outplacement counseling
A systematic process by which a terminated person is trained and counseled in the techniques of self-appraisal and securing a new position.

exit interviews
Interviews conducted by the employer immediately prior to the employee leaving the firm with the aim of better understanding what the employee thinks about the company.

EXIT INTERVIEW Many employers conduct **exit interviews** with employees leaving the firm. These are interviews, usually conducted by a human resource professional just prior to the employee leaving, that elicit information about the job or related matters with the aim of giving employers insights into their companies. Exit interview questions include: How were you recruited? Was the job presented correctly and honestly? What was the workplace environment like? What was your supervisor's management style like? What did you like most/least about the company?[97] Women and minorities are more likely to quit early in their employment, so this is one specific issue for which to watch.[98]

The assumption, of course, is that because the employee is leaving, he or she will be candid. However, the information one gets is likely to be questionable.[99] Researchers found that at the time of separation, 38% of those leaving blamed salary and benefits, and only 4% blamed supervision. Followed up 18 months later, 24% blamed supervision and only 12% blamed salary and benefits.

Getting to the real issues during the exit interview may thus require digging. Yet these interviews can be useful. When Blue Cross of Northeastern Pennsylvania laid off employees, many said, in exit interviews, "This is not a stable place to work." The firm took steps to correct that misperception for those who stayed with Blue Cross.

Layoffs and the Plant Closing Law

Nondisciplinary separations are a fact of life, and may be initiated by either employer or employee. For the *employer,* reduced sales or profits or the desire for more productivity may require layoffs. *Employees* may leave to retire or to seek better jobs. The Worker Adjustment and Retraining Notification Act (WARN Act, or the plant closing law) requires employers of 100 or more employees to give 60 days' notice before closing a facility or starting a layoff of 50 or more people.[100]

layoff
A situation in which employees are told there is no work for them but that management intends to recall them when work is again available.

A **layoff,** in which the employer sends workers home for a time for lack of work, is usually not a permanent dismissal (although it may turn out to be). Rather, it is a temporary one, which the employer expects will be short term. However, some employers use the term *layoff* as a euphemism for discharge or termination. In the recession years of 2008 in 2009 combined, employers carried out a total of about 51,000 mass layoffs, idling over 5 million workers.[101] The Managing HR in Challenging Times feature nearby expands on this.

THE LAYOFF PROCESS A study illustrates one firm's layoff process. In this company, senior management first met to make strategic decisions about the size and timing of the layoffs. These managers also debated the relative importance of the skill sets they thought the firm needed going forward. Front-line supervisors assessed their subordinates, rating their nonunion employees either A, B, or C (union employees were covered by a union agreement making layoffs dependant on seniority). The front-line supervisors then informed each of their subordinates about his or her A, B, or C rating, and told each that those employees with C grades were designated "surplus" and most likely to be laid off.[102]

LAYOFF'S EFFECTS It's not surprising that layoffs "tend to result in deleterious psychological and physical health outcomes for employees who lose their jobs" as well as for the survivors.[103]

Furthermore, not just the "victims" and "survivors" suffer. In one study, researchers "found that the more managers were personally responsible for handing out WARN notices to employees . . . the more likely they were to report physical health problems, to seek treatment for these problems, and to complain of disturbed sleep."[104]

Given this, many employers try to avoid or minimize layoffs during downturns. Reducing everyone's work hours and mandating vacations are two options. Others reduce layoffs by offering financial bonuses for improved productivity.[105]

Ironically, when some employees most need employee assistance programs—after they're laid off—they lose them. More firms are therefore extending these program benefits for a month or two to former employees. For example, Florida's Sarasota County extended employee assistance program benefits for two months after it laid off some employees. Most didn't use the service, but even they viewed it "like having a safety net."[106]

MANAGING HR IN CHALLENGING TIMES

Preparing for Layoffs

As the United States slipped into recession, large layoffs climbed ominously, up by about 9.4% in mid-2009. How do managers prepare for the layoffs that almost invariably result from such challenging times?

Interestingly, the initial focus shouldn't be on the layoffs, but on the employer's appraisal systems. One expert says that in preparing for large scale layoffs, management needs to:[107]

- Make sure appraisals are up-to-date.
- Identify top performers and get them working on the company's future.
- Have leaders committed to the company's turnaround.

Another HR consultant says companies that "don't closely manage their performance appraisal systems suddenly learn during a reduction in force that everyone has been ranked a 'four' out of 'five'; that information is meaningless."[108]

So the essential point about layoffs is to prepare in advance by ensuring you have an effective performance appraisal system in place. If you don't, then when the time comes to lay off significant numbers of employers, you may find yourself with no rational basis on which to decide who stays or leaves.

Adjusting to Downsizings and Mergers

downsizing
Refers to the process of reducing, usually dramatically, the number of people employed by the firm.

Downsizing means reducing, usually dramatically, the number of people employed by a firm. The basic idea is to cut costs and raise profitability. Downsizings (some call them "productivity transformation programs")[109] require careful consideration of several matters.

1. One is to make sure *the right people* are let go; again, this requires having an effective appraisal system in place (see the Managing HR in Challenging Times feature).
2. Second is *compliance with all applicable laws,* including WARN.
3. Third is ensuring that the employer executes the dismissals in a manner that is *just and fair.*
4. Fourth is the practical consideration of *security,* for instance, with respect to retrieving keys and ensuring that those leaving do not take any prohibited items with them.
5. Fifth is to reduce the remaining *employees' uncertainty* and to address their concerns. This typically involves a post-downsizing announcement and program, including meetings where senior managers field questions from the remaining employees.

Downsizings aren't pleasant but needn't be unfair. Information sharing (in terms of providing advanced notice regarding the layoff) and interpersonal sensitivity (in terms of the manager's demeanor during layoffs) can both help cushion the otherwise negative effects.[110] Layoffs can be more difficult abroad, as the Global Issues in HR feature shows.

Workforce reductions can reduce the attractiveness of the firm for prospective job applicants. However, employers who downsize but provide support to those dismissed are nearly as attractive to applicants as employers that don't downsize.[111]

GLOBAL ISSUES IN HR

Employment Contracts

Note that layoffs are often subject to additional constraints abroad. Businesses expanding abroad soon discover that hiring, disciplining, and discharging employees in Europe requires more stringent communication than they do in the United States. For example, the European Union (EU) has a directive (law) that requires employers to provide employees with very explicit contracts of employment, usually within 2 months of their starting work.

How employers comply with this law varies by country. In the United Kingdom, the employee must be given a written contract specifying, among other things, name of employer, grievance procedure, job title, rate of pay, disciplinary rules, pension plan, hours of work, vacation and sick-leave policies, pay periods, and date when employment began. In Germany, the contracts need not be in writing, although they customarily are, given the amount of detail they must cover, including minimum notice prior to layoff, wages, vacations, maternity/paternity rights, equal pay, invention rights, noncompetition clause, and sickness pay. The contract need not be in writing in Italy, but again, it usually is. Items covered include start date, probationary period, working hours, job description, place of work, basic salary, and a noncompetition clause. In France, the contract must be in writing, and specify information such as the identity of the parties, place of work, type of job or job descriptions, notice period, dates of payment, and work hours.

REVIEW

SUMMARY

1. Unfair treatment reduces morale, increases stress, and has negative effects on performance. Managers, and HR management, can take steps to reduce such unfairness.

2. Ethics refers to the principles of conduct governing an individual or a group, and specifically to the standards you use to decide what your conduct should be.

3. Numerous factors shape ethical behavior at work. These include individual factors, organizational factors, the boss's influence, ethics policies and codes, and the organization's culture.

4. Employees have many legal and moral rights. Laws like Title VII don't just list what employers can and can't do in the workplace. They also give employees (or prospective employees, and sometimes past employees) numerous rights. For example, ERISA's so-called retaliation provision gives employees who believe they were denied profit-sharing or pension benefits due to discrimination the right to seek to redress the violations. On a broader level, many societies agree that people (workers included) share certain inalienable or moral rights—rights they have just because they are people living in civil societies. For example, the rights to "life, liberty, and the pursuit of happiness" are ingrained in American culture

5. HR management can influence ethics and fair treatment at work in numerous ways. For example, having a fair and open selection process that emphasizes the company's stress on integrity and ethics, establishing special ethics training programs, measuring employees' adherence to high ethical standards during performance appraisals, and rewarding (or disciplining) ethical (or unethical) work-related behavior are some examples.

6. Firms give employees avenues through which to express opinions and concerns. For example, Toyota's hotline provides employees with an anonymous channel through which they can express concerns to top management. Firms such as FedEx engage in periodic anonymous opinion surveys.

7. Guaranteed fair treatment programs, such as the one at FedEx, help to ensure that grievances are handled fairly and openly. Steps include management review, officer complaint, and executive appeals review.

8. A fair and just discipline process is based on three prerequisites: rules and regulations, a system of progressive penalties, and an appeals process. A number of discipline guidelines are important, including that discipline should be in line with the way management usually responds to similar incidents, that management must adequately investigate the matter before administering discipline, and that managers should not rob a subordinate of his or her dignity.

9. The basic aim of discipline without punishment is to gain an employee's acceptance of the rules by reducing the punitive nature of the discipline itself. In particular, an employee is given a paid day off to consider his or her infraction before more punitive disciplinary steps are taken.

10. Managing dismissals is an important part of any supervisor's job. Among the reasons for dismissal are unsatisfactory performance, misconduct, lack of qualifications, changed job requirements, and insubordination. In dismissing one or more employees, however, remember that termination at will as a policy has been weakened by exceptions in many states. Furthermore, great care should be taken to avoid wrongful discharge suits.

11. Dismissing an employee is always difficult, and the termination interview should be handled properly. Specifically, plan the interview carefully (for instance, early in the week), get to the point, describe the situation, and then listen until the person has expressed his or her feelings. Then discuss the severance package and identify the next step.

12. Nondisciplinary separations such as layoffs and retirement occur all the time. The plant closing law (the Worker Adjustment and Retraining Notification Act) outlines requirements to be followed with regard to official notice before operations with 50 or more people are to be closed down.

13. Disciplinary actions are a big source of grievances. Discipline should be based on rules and adhere to a system of progressive penalties, and it should permit an appeals process.

KEY TERMS

ethics   253
organizational culture   261
discipline   265
guaranteed fair treatment   266
dismissal   269
terminate at will   269
insubordination   270

wrongful discharge   270
termination interview   272
outplacement counseling   272
exit interviews   273
layoff   273
downsizing   274

DISCUSSION QUESTIONS

1. Explain what is meant by ethical behavior.
2. Discuss important factors that shape ethical behavior at work.
3. Discuss at least four specific ways in which HR management can influence ethical behavior at work.
4. Give examples of four fair disciplinary practices.
5. Discuss at least four procedural suggestions for managing dismissals effectively.
6. Describe the similarities and differences between a program such as FedEx's guaranteed fair treatment program and your college or university's student grievance process.

7. Explain how you would ensure fairness in disciplining, discussing particularly the prerequisites to disciplining, disciplining guidelines, and the discipline without punishment approach.
8. Why is it important to manage dismissals properly?
9. What techniques would you use as alternatives to traditional discipline? What do such alternatives have to do with "organizational justice"? Why do you think alternatives like these are important, given industry's current need for highly committed employees?

INDIVIDUAL AND GROUP ACTIVITIES

1. Working individually or in groups, interview managers or administrators at your employer or college in order to determine the extent to which the employer or college endeavors to build two-way communication, and the specific types of programs used. Do the managers think they are effective? What do the employees (or faculty members) think of the programs in use at the employer or college?
2. Working individually or in groups, obtain copies of the student handbook for your college and determine to what extent there is a formal process through which students can air grievances. Based on your contacts with other

students, has it been an effective grievance process? Why or why not?
3. Working individually or in groups, determine the nature of the academic discipline process in your college. Do you think it is effective? Based on what you read in this chapter, would you recommend any modifications?
4. What techniques would you use as alternatives to traditional discipline? What do such alternatives have to do with "organizational justice"? Why do you think alternatives like these are important, given industry's current need for highly committed employees?

WEB-e's (WEB EXERCISES)

1. Recently, several top managers including one from IBM and a consultant for McKinsey & Co. became embroiled in an alleged insider trading scandal. Based on sites such as http://abcnews.go.com/Blotter/rajaratnams-alleged-insider-trading-scheme-big-thought/story?id=9502787, do you think these allegations are fair, and if so what seems to have prompted these people to have become involved?
2. Web sites such as www.bankersacademy.com/codeofconduct.php describe ethics training programs.

What points from this chapter does this particular ethics training program cover, and is it one you would recommend to your employer? Why or why not?
3. In politics, ethics problems are certainly not unique to Democrats or Republicans. Use sites such as www.newsweek.com/id/216687 to list five recent ethics violations allegations made against Democrats and Republicans.

APPLICATION EXERCISES

HR IN ACTION CASE INCIDENT 1
Enron, Ethics, and Organizational Culture

For many people, Enron Corp. still ranks as one of history's classic examples of ethics run amok. Even in 2010—10 years after the fact—courts (including the U.S. Supreme Court) were debating the fates of one of Enron's top executives. During the 1990s and early 2000s, Enron was in the business of wholesaling natural gas and electricity. Rather than actually owning the gas or electric, Enron made its money as the intermediary (wholesaler) between suppliers and customers. Without getting into all the details, the nature of Enron's business, and the fact that Enron didn't actually own the assets, meant that its accounting procedures were unusual. For example, the profit statements and balance sheets listing the firm's assets and liabilities were unusually difficult to understand.

As most people know by now, it turned out that the lack of accounting transparency enabled the company's managers to make Enron's financial performance look much better than it actually was. Outside experts began questioning Enron's financial statements in 2001. In fairly short order Enron's house of cards collapsed, and several of its top executives were convicted of things like manipulating Enron's reported assets and profitability. Many investors (including former Enron employees) lost all or most of their investments in Enron.

It's probably always easier to understand ethical breakdowns like this in retrospect, rather than to predict they are going to happen. However, in Enron's case the breakdown is perhaps more perplexing than usual. As one writer recently said,

> Enron had all the elements usually found in comprehensive ethics and compliance programs: a code of ethics, a reporting system, as well as a training video on vision and values led by [the company's top executives].[112]

Experts subsequently put forth many explanations for how a company that was apparently so ethical on its face could actually have been making so many bad ethical decisions without other managers (and the board of directors) noticing. The explanations ranged from a "deliberate concealment of information by officers" to more psychological explanations such as employees not wanting to contradict their bosses, and the "surprising role of irrationality in decision making."[113]

But perhaps the most persuasive explanation of how an apparently ethical company could go so wrong concerns organizational culture. Basically, the reasoning here is that it's not the rules but what

employees feel they should do that determines ethical behavior. For example (speaking in general, not specifically about Enron), the executive director of the Ethics Officer Association put it this way:

> [W]e're a legalistic society, and we've created a lot of laws. We assume that if you just knew what those laws meant that you would behave properly. Well, guess what? You can't write enough laws to tell us what to do at all times every day of the week in every part of the world. We've got to develop the critical thinking and critical reasoning skills of our people because most of the ethical issues that we deal with are in the ethical gray areas. Virtually every regulatory body in the last year has come out with language that has said in addition to law compliance, businesses are also going to be accountable to ethics standards and a corporate culture that embraces them.[114]

How can one tell or measure when a company has an "ethical culture"? Key attributes of a healthy ethical culture include:

- Employees feel a sense of responsibility and accountability for their actions and for the actions of others.[115]
- Employees freely raise issues and concerns without fear of retaliation.
- Managers model the behaviors they demand of others.
- Managers communicate the importance of integrity when making difficult decisions.

Questions

1. Based on what you read in this chapter, summarize in one page or less how you would explain Enron's ethical meltdown.
2. It is said that when one securities analyst tried to confront Enron's CEO about the firm's unusual accounting statements, the CEO publicly used vulgar language to describe the analyst, and that Enron employees subsequently thought doing so was humorous. If true, what does that say about Enron's ethical culture?
3. This case and this chapter both had something to say about how organizational culture influences ethical behavior. What role do you think culture played at Enron? Give five specific examples of things Enron's CEO could have done to create a healthy ethical culture.

HR IN ACTION CASE INCIDENT 2
Carter Cleaning Company: Guaranteeing Fair Treatment

Being in the laundry and cleaning business, the Carters have always felt strongly about not allowing employees to smoke, eat, or drink in their stores. Jennifer was therefore surprised to walk into a store and find two employees eating lunch at the front counter. There was a large pizza in its box, and the two of them were sipping colas and eating slices of pizza and submarine sandwiches off paper plates. Not only did it look messy, but there were also grease and soda spills on the counter and the store smelled from onions and pepperoni, even with the four-foot-wide exhaust

fan pulling air out through the roof. In addition to being a turnoff to customers, the mess on the counter increased the possibility that a customer's order might actually become soiled in the store.

While this was a serious matter, neither Jennifer nor her father felt that what the counter people were doing was grounds for immediate dismissal, partly because the store manager had apparently condoned their actions. The problem was, they didn't know what to do. It seemed to them that the matter called for more than just a warning but less than dismissal.

Questions

1. What would you do if you were Jennifer, and why?
2. Should a disciplinary system be established at Carter Cleaning Centers?
3. If so, what should it cover, and how would you suggest it deal with a situation such as the one with the errant counter people?
4. How would you deal with the store manager?

EXPERIENTIAL EXERCISE

The Cloning Dilemma

Purpose: The purpose of this exercise is to provide you with some experience in analyzing and handling an ethics-based situation.

Required Understanding: Students should be thoroughly familiar with the information provided in the following case, and with our discussions in this chapter.

You work for a medical genetics research firm as a marketing person. You love the job. The location is great, the hours are good, and the work is challenging and flexible. You receive a much higher salary than you ever anticipated. However, you've just heard via the rumor mill that the company's elite medical team has cloned the first human, the firm's CEO. It was such a total success that you have heard

that they may want to clone every employee so that they can use the clones to harvest body parts as the original people age or become ill. You are not sure you endorse the cloning of humans. You joined the firm for its moral and ethical reputation. You feel that the image presented to you was one of research and development of life-saving drugs and innovative medical procedures. The thought of cloning was never on your mind, but now it must be.

How to Set Up the Exercise/Instructions: Divide the class into groups of four or five students. Each group should answer the following questions:

1. What, if any, is the ethical decision to be made?
2. What would you do? Why?

BUSINESS IN ACTION EDU-EXERCISE

Building Your *Employee Rights and Business Law* Knowledge

Most industrial societies don't rely solely on employers' ethical compasses or sense of fair play when it comes to employees. Instead, they also pass laws to codify employees' rights.

What these "rights" are depends on several things. For example, most societies hold that people (workers included) share certain inalienable rights—rights they have just because they are people living in civil societies. Thus, the rights to "life, liberty, and the pursuit of happiness" are ingrained in American culture. For workers everywhere, the International Labor Organization's *Declaration on Fundamental Principles and Rights at Work* lists these workers' rights:[116]

- The freedom of association and effective recognition of the right to collective bargaining
- The elimination of forced or compulsory labor
- The abolition of child labor

- The elimination of discrimination with respect to employment and occupation

In the United States and England, employees also have certain rights under common law—the law that evolved out of court decisions over time.[117] For example, under common law, an employee may have the right to sue the employer whose supervisor published or promulgated embarrassing private and personal information about the employee.[118]

Questions

1. What, according to this chapter, are the five rights the U.S. government has legislated to provide for its workers?
2. Name several examples of rights embedded in U.S. law that address some of the International Labor Organization's *Declaration on Fundamental Principles and Rights at Work*.

PERSONAL COMPETENCIES EDU-EXERCISE

Building Your *Organizational Culture* Skills

Organizational culture is the characteristic values, traditions, and behaviors a company's employees share. A *value* is a basic belief about what is right or wrong, or about what you should or shouldn't do. ("Honesty is the best policy" would be a value.) Values are important because they guide behavior. Managing people and shaping their behavior therefore depends on shaping

the values they use as behavioral guides. The firm's culture should therefore send unambiguous signals about what is and is not acceptable behavior.

To an outside observer, a company's culture reveals itself in several ways. You can see it in employees' *patterns of behavior*, such as ceremonial events and written and spoken commands. For example, managers and employees may engage in behaviors such as hiding information, politicking, or (more positively) expressing concern when a colleague bends ethical rules. You also can see it in the *physical manifestations* of a company's behavior, such as written rules, office layout, organizational structure, and ethics codes.

In turn, these cultural symbols and behaviors reflect the firm's shared *values*, such as "the customer is always right" or "be honest." If management and employees really believe "honesty is the best policy," the written rules they follow and the things they do should reflect this value. JetBlue Airlines' founder, David Neeleman, wanted all employees to get the

message that "we're all in this together." You'd therefore often find him helping out at the gate, or handing luggage up into the plane.

Questions

1. How would you describe the organizational culture of a company in which you've worked, based on the discussion in this exercise?
2. How would you describe the organizational culture of the college you attend, based on the discussion in this exercise?

ETHICS QUIZ ANSWERS

Quiz is on page 252.

1. 34% said personal e-mail on company computers is wrong.
2. 37% said using office equipment for schoolwork is wrong.
3. 49% said playing computer games at work is wrong.
4. 54% said Internet shopping at work is wrong.
5. 61% said it's unethical to blame your error on technology.
6. 87% said it's unethical to visit pornographic sites at work.
7. 33% said $25 is the amount at which a gift from a supplier or client becomes troubling, while 33% said $50, and 33% said $100.

8. 35% said a $50 gift to the boss is unacceptable.
9. 12% said a $50 gift from the boss is unacceptable.
10. 70% said it's unacceptable to take the $200 football tickets.
11. 70% said it's unacceptable to take the $120 theater tickets.
12. 35% said it's unacceptable to take the $100 food basket.
13. 45% said it's unacceptable to take the $25 gift certificate.
14. 40% said it's unacceptable to take the $75 raffle prize.
15. 11% reported they lie about sick days.
16. 4% reported they take credit for the work or ideas of others.

ENDNOTES

1. Graham Bowley, "At Brown, Spotlight on the President's Role at a Bank," *New York Times* (March 2, 2010).
2. Keith Winstein, "Suit Alleges Pfizer Spun Unfavorable Drug Studies," *Wall Street Journal* (October 8, 2008): B1.
3. "What Role Should HR Play in Corporate Ethics?" *HR Focus* 81, no. 1 (January 2004): 3. See also Dennis Moberg, "Ethics Blind Spots in Organizations: How Systematic Errors in Person Perception Undermine Moral Agency," *Organization Studies* 27, no. 3 (2006): 413–428.
4. Kevin Wooten, "Ethical Dilemmas in Human Resource Management: An Application of a Multidimensional Framework, A Unifying Taxonomy, and Applicable Codes," *Human Resource Management Review* 11 (2001): 161. See also Sean Valentine et al., "Employee Job Response As a Function of Ethical Context and Perceived Organization Support," *Journal of Business Research* 59, no. 5 (2006): 582–588.
5. Paul Schumann, "A Moral Principles Framework for Human Resource Management Ethics," *Human Resource Management Review* 11 (2004): 94.
6. Manuel Velasquez, *Business Ethics: Concepts and Cases* (Upper Saddle River, NJ: Prentice Hall, 1992): 9. See also O. C. Ferrell, John Fraedrich, and Linda Ferrell, *Business Ethics* (Boston: Houghton Mifflin, 2008).
7. For further discussion of ethics and morality, see Tom Beauchamp and Norman Bowie, *Ethical Theory and Business* (Upper Saddle River, NJ: Prentice Hall, 2001): 1–19.
8. Richard Osborne, "A Matter of Ethics," *Industry Week* 49, no. 14 (September 4, 2000): 41–42.
9. Ibid., 236.
10. This list is from http://legaltarget.com/employee_rights.htm, accessed April 24, 2008.
11. *Miami Daily Business Review* (April 20, 2007).
12. Hugh Williamson, "Allianz Deal Set to Boost Employee Rights," *The Financial Times* (September 22, 2006): 24.
13. Bennett Tepper, "Consequences of Abusive Supervision," *Academy of Management Journal* 43, no. 2 (2000): 178–190. See also Samuel Aryee et al., "Antecedents and Outcomes of Abusive Supervision: A Test of a Trickle-Down Model," *Journal of Applied Psychology* 92, no. 1 (2007): 191–201.
14. Teresa Daniel, "Tough Boss or Workplace Bully?" *HR Magazine* (June 2009): 83–86.
15. http://diversity.walgreens.com/ourcommitment/ missionstatement.html, accessed July 2010.
16. Michelle Donovan et al., "The Perceptions of Fair Interpersonal Treatment Scale: Development and Validation of a Measure of Interpersonal Treatment in the Workplace," *Journal of Applied Psychology* 83, no. 5 (1998): 683–692.
17. Bennett Tepper et al., "Abusive Supervision and Subordinates Organization Deviance," *Journal of Applied Psychology* 93, no. 4 (2008): 721–732.
18. Gary Weaver and Linda Treviño, "The Role of Human Resources in Ethics/Compliance Management: A Fairness Perspective," *Human Resource Management Review* 11 (2001): 117.
19. Suzanne Masterson, "A Trickle-Down Model of Organizational Justice: Relating Employees' and Customers' Perceptions of and Reactions to Fairness," *Journal of Applied Psychology* 86, no. 4 (2001): 594–601.

20. Jennifer Kish-Gephart, David Harrison, and Linda Treviño, "Bad Apples, Bad Cases, and Bad Barrels: Meta-Analytic Evidence About Sources of Unethical Decisions That Work," *Journal of Applied Psychology* 95, no. 1 (2010): 1–31.

21. Ibid., 21.

22. Sara Morris et al., "A Test of Environmental, Situational, and Personal Influences on the Ethical Intentions of CEOs," *Business and Society* (August 1995): 119–147. See also Dennis Moberg, "Ethics Blind Spots in Organizations: How Systematic Errors in Person's Perception Undermine Moral Agency," *Organization Studies* 27, no. 3 (2006): 413–428. Recently, the U.S. Department of Justice has been more aggressive in investigating and prosecuting bribery related cases under the Foreign Corrupt Practices Act. "Beef Up Compliance Programs and Codes of Conduct to Avoid Corruption, Lawyers Say," *BNA Bulletin to Management* (February 9, 2010): 41–42.

23. "Former CEO Joins WorldCom's Indicted," *Miami Herald* (March 3, 2004): 4C.

24. Gretchen Morgenson, "Requiem for an Honorable Profession," *New York Times* (May 5, 2002): B1.

25. "Ethics Policies Are Big with Employers, but Workers See Small Impact on the Workplace," *BNA Bulletin to Management* (June 29, 2000): 201.

26. Jennifer Schramm, "Perceptions on Ethics," *HR Magazine* (November 2004): 176.

27. From Guy Brumback, "Managing Above the Bottom Line of Ethics," *Supervisory Management* (December 1993): 12. See also E. E. Umphress et al., "The Influence of Distributive Justice on Lying for and Stealing from a Supervisor," *Journal of Business Ethics* 86, no. 4 (June 2009): 507–518.

28. Quoted in Tom Beauchamp and Norman Bowie, *Ethical Theory and Business* (Upper Saddle River, NJ: Prentice Hall, 2001): 109.

29. James Kunen, "Enron Division (and Values) Thing," *New York Times* (January 19, 2002): A19. For another example, see Heather Tesoriero and Avery Johnson, "Suit Details How J&J Pushed Sales of Procrit," *Wall Street Journal Eastern Edition* (April 10, 2007): B1(1).

30. Dayton Fandray, "The Ethical Company," *Workforce* 79, no. 12 (December 2000): 74–77.

31. Richard Beatty et al., "HR's Role in Corporate Governance: Present and Prospective," *Human Resource Management 42,* no. 3 (Fall 2003): 268.

32. Dale Buss, "Corporate Compasses," *HR Magazine* (June 2004): 127–132.

33. Eric Krell, "How to Conduct an Ethics Audit," *HR Magazine* (April 2010): 48–51.

34. Sometimes the most straightforward way of changing a company's culture is to move fast to change its top management. For example, some observers believe that GM's board fired CEO Fritz Henderson in part because he hadn't moved fast enough to telegraph the need for change in the company by changing the company's top management. Jeremy Smerd, "A Stalled Culture Change?" *Workforce Management* (December 14, 2009): 1, 3.

35. This list based on Linda K. Treviño, Gary R. Weaver, and Scott J. Reynolds, "Behavioral Ethics in Organizations: A Review," *Journal of Management* 32, no. 6 (2006): 951–990.

36. R. Bergman, "Identity as Motivation: Toward a Theory of the Moral Self." In D. K. Lapsley and D. Narvaez (Eds.), *Moral Development, Self and Identity* (Mahwah, NJ: Lawrence Erlbaum, 2004): 21–46.

37. M. E. Schweitzer, L. Ordonez, and B. Douma, "Goal Setting as a Motivator of Unethical Behavior," *Academy of Management Journal* 47, no. 3 (2004): 422–432.

38. N. M. Ashkanasy, C. A. Windsor, and L. K. Treviño, "Bad Apples in Bad Barrels Revisited: Cognitive Moral Development, Just World Beliefs, Rewards, and Ethical Decision Making," *Business Ethics Quarterly* 16 (2006): 449–474.

39. J. Krohe Jr., "The Big Business of Business Ethics," *Across the Board* 34 (May 1997): 23–29; Deborah Wells and Marshall Schminke, "Ethical Development and Human Resources Training: An Integrator Framework," *Human Resource Management Review* 11 (2001): 135–158.

40. "Ethical Issues in the Management of Human Resources," *Human Resource Management Review* 11 (2001): 6. Joel Lefkowitz, "The Constancy of Ethics Amidst the Changing World of Work," *Human Resource Management Review* 16 (2006): 245–268; William Byham, "Can You Interview for Integrity?" *Across the Board* 41, no. 2 (March/April 2004): 34–38. For a description of how the United States Military Academy uses its student admission and socialization processes to promote character development, see Evan Offstein and Ronald Dufresne, "Building Strong Ethics and Promoting Positive Character Development: The Influence of HRM at the United States Military Academy at West Point," *Human Resource Management* 46, no. 1 (Spring 2007): 95–114.

41. Gary Weaver and Linda Treviño, "The Role of Human Resources in Ethics/Compliance Management: A Fairness Perspective," *Human Resource Management Review* 11 (2001): 123. See also Linda Andrews, "The Nexus of Ethics," *HR Magazine* (August 2005): 53–58.

42. Weaver and Treviño, op. cit. In a similar study, researchers conducted studies of 490 police officers undergoing standardized promotional exams. Among their conclusions was that "Organizations should strive to ensure that candidates perceived justice both in the content of personnel assessments and in the way they are treated during the assessment process." Julie McCarthy et al., "Progression Through the Ranks: Assessing Employee Reactions to High Stakes Employment Testing," *Personnel Psychology* 62 (2009): 793–832.

43. Russell Cropanzano and Thomas Wright, "Procedural Justice and Organizational Staffing: A Tale of Two Paradigms," *Human Resource Management Review* 13, no. 1 (2003): 7–40.

44. Kathryn Tyler, "Do the Right Thing: Ethics Training Programs Help Employees Deal with Ethical Dilemmas," *HR Magazine* (February 2005): 99–102.

45. "Ethical Issues in the Management of Human Resources," *Human Resource Management Review* 11 (2001): 6.

46. Gary Weaver and Linda Treviño, "The Role of Human Resources in Ethics/Compliance Management: A Fairness Perspective," *Human Resource Management Review* 11 (2001): 123.

47. M. Ronald Buckley et al., "Ethical Issues in Human Resources Systems," *Human Resource Management Review* 11, nos. 1, 2 (2001): 11, 29. See also Ann Pomeroy, "The Ethics Squeeze," *HR Magazine* (March 2006): 48–55.

48. Tom Asacker, "Ethics in the Workplace," *Training and Development* (August 2004): 44.

49. M. Ronald Buckley et al., "Ethical Issues in Human Resources Systems," *Human Resource Management Review* 11, nos. 1, 2 (2001): 11, 29.

50. Gary Weaver and Linda Treviño, "The Role of Human Resources in Ethics/Compliance Management: A Fairness Perspective," *Human Resource Management Review* 11 (2001): 113–134.

51. Ibid., 125.

52. Robert Grossman, "Executive Discipline," *HR Magazine* 50, no. 8 (August 2005): 46–51. See also Jean Thilmany, "Supporting Ethical Employees," *HR Magazine* 52, no. 9 (September 2007): 105–106, 108, 110, 112.

53. M. Ronald Buckley et al., "Ethical Issues in Human Resources Systems," *Human Resource Management Review* 11, nos. 1, 2 (2001): 11, 29. See also Helge Hoel and David Beale, "Workplace Bullying, Psychological Perspectives and Industrial Relations: Towards a Contextualized and Interdisciplinary Approach," *British Journal of Industrial Relations* 44, no. 2 (June 2006): 239–262.

54. Wendy Boswell and Julie Olson-Buchanan, "Experiencing Mistreatment at Work: The Role of Grievance Filing, Nature of Mistreatment, and Employee Withdrawal," *Academy of Management Journal* 47, no. 1 (2004): 129–139. See also Helge Hoel and David Beale, "Workplace Bullying, Psychological Perspectives and Industrial Relations: Towards a Contextualized and Interdisciplinary Approach," *British Journal of Industrial Relations* 44, no. 2 (June 2006): 239–262; and Samuel Aryee et al., "Antecedents and Outcomes of Abusive Supervision: A Test of a Trickle-Down Model," *Journal of Applied Psychology* (2007): 191–201.

55. W. Chan Kim and Rene Mauborgne, "Fair Process: Managing in the Knowledge Economy," *Harvard Business Review,* (July/August 1997): 65–75.

56. Lester Bittel, *What Every Supervisor Should Know* (New York: McGraw-Hill, 1974): 308; Paul Falcone, "Fundamentals of Progressive Discipline," *HR Magazine* (February 1997): 90–92; and Thomas Salvo, "Practical Tips for Successful Progressive Discipline," SHRM White Paper (July 2004), www.shrm.org/hrresources/whitepapers_published/CMS_009030.asp, accessed January 5, 2008.

57. Robert Grossman, "Executive Discipline," *HR Magazine* 50, no. 8 (August 2005): 46–51. "The Evil Women Theses," based on Sandra Hartman et al., "Males and Females in a Discipline Situation Exploratory Research on Competing Hypotheses," *Journal of Managerial Issues* 6, no. 1 (Spring 1994): 57, 64–68; "A Woman's Place," *The Economist* 356, no. 8184 (August 19, 2000): 56.

58. David Mayer et al., "When Do Fair Procedures Not Matter? A Test of the Identity Violation Effect," *Journal of Applied Psychology* 94, no. 1 (2009): 142–161.

59. George Bohlander, "Why Arbitrators Overturn Managers in Employee Suspension and Discharge Cases," *Journal of Collective Negotiations* 23, no. 1 (1994): 76–77.

60. "Employers Turn to Corporate Ombuds to Defuse Internal Ticking Time Bombs," *BNA Bulletin to Management* (August 9, 2005): 249.

61. Dick Grote, "Discipline without Punishment," *Across the Board* 38, no. 5 (September 2001): 52–57.

62. Milton Zall, "Employee Privacy," *Journal of Property Management* 66, no. 3 (May 2001): 16.

63. Morris Attaway, "Privacy in the Workplace on the Web," *Internal Auditor* 58, no. 1 (February 2001): 30.

64. Declam Leonard and Angela France, "Workplace Monitoring: Balancing Business Interests with Employee Privacy Rights," *Society for Human Resource Management Legal Report* (May–June 2003): 3–6.

65. "After Employer Found Liable for Worker's Child Porn, Policies May Need to Be Revisited," *BNA Bulletin to Management* (March 21, 2006): 89.

66. "Twitter Is Latest Electronic Tool to Pose Challenges and Opportunities for Employers," *BNA Bulletin to Management,* (June 16, 2009): 185; See also Sean Valentine et al., "Exploring the

Ethicality of Firing Employees Who Blog," *Human Resource Management* 49, no. 1 (January/February 2010): 87–108.

67. Rita Zeidner, "Keeping E-Mail in Check," *HR Magazine* (June 2007): 70–74.

68. "FTC Rules May Make Employers Liable for Worker Web Conduct," *BNA Bulletin to Management* (January 19, 2010): 23.

69. Fredric Leffler and Lauren Palais, "Filter Out Perilous Company E-Mails," *Society for Human Resource Management Legal Report* (August 2008): 3. A recent survey of 220 large U.S. firms suggests that about 38% of them have people reading or otherwise analyzing employees' outgoing e-mail. Dionne Searcey, "Some Courts Raise the Bar on Reading Employee E-Mail," *Wall Street Journal* (November 19, 2009): 817.

70. Bill Roberts, "Stay Ahead of the Technology Use Curve," *HR Magazine* (October 2008): 57–61.

71. One attorney notes that problems can arise with the Federal Stored Communications Act if the employer uses illicit or coercive means to access the employee's private social media accounts. *BNA Bulletin to Management* (July 21, 2009): 225.

72. See also "Twitter Is Latest Electronic Tool to Pose Challenges and Opportunities for Employers," *BNA Bulletin to Management* (June 16, 2009): 185.

73. "Time Clocks Go High Touch, High Tech to Keep Workers From Gaming the System," *BNA Bulletin to Management* (March 25, 2004): 97.

74. Andrea Poe, "Make Foresight 20/20," *HR Magazine* (February 2000): 74–80.

75. Gundars Kaupin et al., "Recommended Employee Location Monitoring Policies," www.shrm.org, accessed January 2, 2007.

76. *Quon v Arch Wireless Operating Co.* (529f.3d 892 ninth circuit 2008), "Employers Should Re-Examine Policies in Light of Ruling," *BNA Bulletin to Management* (August 12, 2008): 263.

77. Dionne Searcey, "Some Courts Raise the Bar on Reading Employee E-Mail," *Wall Street Journal* (November 19, 2009): 817.

78. "When Can an Employer Access Private E-Mail on Its System?" *BNA Bulletin to Management* (July 14, 2009): 224. One employment lawyer says that courts look to whether the employer's process is reasonable when determining if the employer's monitoring practices are acceptable. Electronic monitoring is generally reasonable "where there is a legitimate business purpose, where policies exist to set the privacy expectations of employees, and where employees are informed of the rules and understand the methods used to monitor the workplace." Nicole Kamm, "I Got Electronic Information," *HR Magazine* (January 2010): 57–58.

79. Bill Roberts, "Are You Ready for Biometrics?" *HR Magazine* (March 2003): 95–96.

80. Rita Zeidner, "New Face in the C-Suite," *HR Magazine* (January 2010): 39.

81. Kathy Gurchiek, "iPods Can Hit Sour Note in the Office," *HR Magazine* (April 2006).

82. Ibid.

83. Andrea Poe, "Make Foresight 20/20," *HR Magazine* (February 20, 2000): 74–80. See also Nancy Hatch Woodward, "Smoother Separations," *HR Magazine* (June 2007): 94–97.

84. Robert Lanza and Morton Warren, "United States: Employment at Will Prevails Despite Exceptions to the Rule," *Society for Human Resource Management Legal Report* (October–November 2005): 1–8.

85. Ibid.

86. Joseph Famularo, *Handbook of Modern Personnel Administration* (New York: McGraw Hill, 1982): 65.3–65.5. See also Carolyn Hirschman, "Off Duty, Out of Work," *HR Magazine,* www.shrm.org/hrmagazine/articles/0203/0203hirschman.asp, accessed January 10, 2008.

87. Kenneth Sovereign, *Personnel Law* (Upper Saddle River, NJ: Prentice Hall, 1999): 148.

88. Connie Wanderg et al., "Perceived Fairness of Layoffs Among Individuals Who Have Been Laid Off: A Longitudinal Study," *Personnel Psychology* 52 (1999): 59–84. See also Nancy Hatch Woodward, "Smoother Separations," *HR Magazine* (June 2007): 94–97. Upon termination, there are several legal requirements regarding the former employee's final paycheck. Most state laws give employers more time to issue final paychecks when employees voluntarily resign, but in many cases, final pay is due almost immediately where someone is terminated involuntarily. Some states also have statutes requiring employers paid vacation or sick pay upon termination. See Jessica Roe and S. Chad Cardon, "Legal Requirements upon Termination," *Compensation & Benefits Review* (May/June 2009): 61–67.

89. Michael Orey, "Fear of Firing," *Business Week* (April 23, 2007): 52–54.

90. Paul Falcon, "Give Employees the (Gentle) Hook," *HR Magazine* (April 2001): 121–128.

91. James Coil III and Charles Rice, "Three Steps to Creating Effective Employee Releases," *Employment Relations Today*, Spring 1994, 91–94; "Fairness to Employees Can Stave Off Litigation," *BNA Bulletin to Management* (November 27, 1999): 377; Richard Bayer, "Termination with Dignity," *Business Horizons* 43, no. 5 (September 2000), 4–10; Betty Sosnin, "Orderly Departures," *HR Magazine* 50, no. 11 (November 2005): 74–78; "Severance Pay: Not Always the Norm," *HR Magazine* (May 2008): 28.

92. "Fairness to Employees Can Stave Off Litigation," *BNA Bulletin to Management* (November 27, 1997): 377.

93. "Severance Decisions Swayed by Cost, Legal, Morale Concerns," *BNA Bulletin to Management* (May 12, 2009): 151.

94. Edward Isler et al., "Personal Liability and Employee Discipline," *Society for Human Resource Management Legal Report* (September–October 2000): 1–4.

95. Based on James Coil III and Charles Rice, "Three Steps to Creating Effective Employee Releases," *Employment Relations Today* (Spring 1994): 91–94. See also Martha Frase-Blunt, "Making Exit Interviews Work," *HR Magazine* (August 2004): 9–11.

96. William J. Morin and Lyle York, *Outplacement Techniques* (New York: AMACOM, 1982): 101–131; F. Leigh Branham, "How to Evaluate Executive Outplacement Services," *Personnel Journal* 62 (April 1983): 323–326; Sylvia Milne, "The Termination Interview," *Canadian Manager* (Spring 1994): 15–16. There is debate regarding what is the best day of the week on which to terminate an employee. Some say Friday to give the employee a few days to "cool off"; others suggest mid-week, in order to allow employees "who remain in the department or in the immediate work group some time to process the change and to talk with each other to sort it out." See Jeffrey Connor, "Disarming Terminated Employees," *HR Magazine* (January 2000): 113–114.

97. Marlene Piturro, "Alternatives to Downsizing," *Management Review* (October 1999): 37–42; "How Safe Is Your Job?" *Money* (December 1, 2001): 130.

98. Peter Hom et al., "Challenging Conventional Wisdom about Who Quits: Revelations from Corporate America," *Journal of Applied Psychology* 93, no. 1 (2008): 1–34.

99. Joseph Zarandona and Michael Camuso, "A Study of Exit Interviews: Does the Last Word Count," *Personnel* 62, no. 3 (March 1981): 47–48. For another point of view, see "Firms Can Profit from Data Obtained from Exit Interviews," *Knight-Ridder/Tribune Business News* (February 13, 2001): Item 0104 4446.

100. See Rodney Sorensen and Stephen Robinson, "What Employers Can Do to Stay Out of Legal Trouble When Forced to Implement Layoffs," *Compensation & Benefits Review* (January/February 2009): 25–32.

101. "Mass Layoffs at Lowest Level Since July 2008, BLS Says," *BNA Bulletin to Management* (January 12, 2010): 13.

102. Leon Grunberg, Sarah Moore, and Edward Greenberg, "Managers' Reactions to Implementing Layoffs: Relationship to Health Problems and Withdrawal Behaviors," *Human Resource Management* 45, no. 2 (Summer 2006): 159–178.

103. Ibid.

104. Ibid.

105. "Adopting Laid-Off Alternatives Could Help Employers Survive, Even Thrive, Analysts Say," *BNA Bulletin to Management* (February 24, 2009): 57.

106. Joann Lublin, "Employers See Value in Helping Those Laid Off," *Wall Street Journal* (September 24, 2007): B3.

107. Adrienne Fox, "Prune Employees Carefully," *HR Magazine* (April 1, 2008).

108. Ibid.

109. "Calling a Layoff a Layoff," *Workforce Management* (April 21, 2008): 41.

110. "Communication Can Reduce Problems, Litigation After Layoffs, Attorneys Say," *BNA Bulletin to Management* (April 14, 2003): 129.

111. John Krammeyer and Hui Liao, "Workforce Reduction and Jobseeker Attraction: Examining Jobseekers' Reactions to Firm Workforce-Reduction Strategies," *Human Resource Management,* 45, no. 4 (Winter 2006): 585–603.

112. David Gebler, "Is Your Culture a Risk Factor?" *Business and Society Review* 111, no. 3 (Fall 2006): 337–362.

113. John Cohan, "'I Didn't Know' and 'I Was Only Doing My Job': Has Corporate Governance Careened Out of Control? A Case Study of Enron's Information Myopia," *Journal of Business Ethics* 40, no. 3 (October 2002): 275–299.

114. David Gebler, "Is Your Culture a Risk Factor?" *Business and Society Review* 111, no. 3 (Fall 2006): 337–362.

115. Ibid.

116. Garrett Brown, "Corporate Social Responsibility Brings Limited Progress on Workplace Safety in Global Supply Chains," *Occupational Hazards* (August 2007): 16.

117. Basically, *common law* refers to legal precedents. Judges' rulings set precedents, which then generally guide future judicial decisions.

118. Kenneth Sovereign, *Personnel Law* (Upper Saddle River, NJ: Prentice Hall, 1999): 192.

10 Working with Unions and Resolving Disputes

SYNOPSIS

- The Labor Movement
- Unions and the Law
- The Union Drive and Election
- The Collective Bargaining Process
- What's Next for Unions?

Source: Stephen Chernin/Getty Images, Inc.—Liaison.

When you finish studying this chapter, you should be able to:

1. Briefly describe the history and structure of the U.S. union movement.

2. Discuss the nature of the major federal labor relations laws.

3. Describe the process of a union drive and election.

4. Discuss the main steps in the collective bargaining process.

5. Explain why union membership dropped, and what the prospects are for the union movement.

INTRODUCTION

The U.S. Department of Labor's National Labor Relations Board (NLRB) accused Starbucks of breaking the law by trying to prevent workers in some of its New York shops from unionizing. Among other things, the NLRB accused managers in those stores of retaliating against workers who wanted to unionize, by interrogating them about their union inclinations. A Starbucks spokesperson said the company believes the allegations are baseless, and that the firm will vigorously defend itself.[1] ■

THE LABOR MOVEMENT

1 Briefly describe the history and structure of the U.S. union movement.

Don't underestimate unions. Just over 17.7 million U.S. workers belong to unions—around 12.4% of the total number of men and women working in this country.[2] Many are still blue-collar workers. But workers including doctors, psychologists, graduate teaching assistants, government office workers, and even fashion models are forming or joining unions.[3] Over 40% of America's 20 million federal, state, and municipal public employees belong to unions.[4] In 2009, for the first time, just over half of all union members were from the public sector.[5] And in some industries—including transportation and public utilities, where over 26% of employees are union members—it's hard to get a job without joining a union.[6] Union membership in other countries is declining, but still very high (over 35% of employed workers in Canada, Mexico, Brazil, and Italy, for instance). Union membership also ranges widely by state, from over 20% in Michigan and New York, down to about 4% in North Carolina. Seven big unions recently formed their own federation, with the aim of aggressively organizing workers (more on this below). U.S. union membership peaked at about 34% in 1955. It has consistently fallen since then due to factors such as the shift from manufacturing to service jobs, and new worker protection legislation (such as occupational safety laws). But for the first time in many years, union membership in America actually rose a bit in 2008–2009.[7]

Furthermore, don't assume that unions are bad for employers. For example, perhaps by professionalizing the staff and/or systematizing company practices, unionization may actually improve performance. In one study, researchers found that heart attack mortality among patients in hospitals with unionized registered nurses were 5% to 9% lower than in nonunion hospitals.[8] Another study found a negative relationship between union membership and employees' intent to quit.[9]

Why Do Workers Organize?

People have spent much time analyzing why workers unionize, and they've proposed many theories. Yet there is no simple answer.

It's clear that workers don't unionize just to get more pay, although the pay issue is important. In fact, union members' weekly earnings are higher than nonunion workers'. For example, the recent median weekly wage for union workers was $781, while for nonunion workers it was $612.[10]

But pay isn't always the issue. Often, the urge to unionize seems to boil down to the workers' belief that it's only through unity that they can protect themselves from arbitrary managerial whims. For example, a butcher hired by Walmart said his new supervisor told him he'd be able to start management training and possibly move up to supervisor. The butcher started work, and bought a car for the commute. However, after the butcher hurt his back at work his supervisor never mentioned the promotion again. Faced with high car payments and feeling cheated, the butcher went to the Grocery Workers Union, which sent an organizer. The store's meat cutters voted to unionize. A week later Walmart announced it would switch to prepackaged meats, and that its stores no longer required butchers.[11]

RESEARCH FINDINGS A study of an Australian banking firm found that employer unfairness does play a big role: "Individuals who believe that the company rules or policies were administered unfairly or to their detriment were more likely to turn to unions as a source of assistance."[12]

In this case, unfairness alone was not enough to prompt a pro-union vote in this bank. Employees were more likely to join where they also "perceived that the union was effective in the area of wages and benefits and protection against unfair dismissals."[13]

In sum, employees turn to unions at least partly because they seek protection against the employer's whims. One labor relations lawyer put it this way, "The one major thing unions offer is making you a 'for cause' instead of an 'at will' employee, which guarantees a hearing and arbitration if you're fired."[14] Several years ago, Kaiser Permanente's San Francisco Medical Center cut back on vacation and sick leave. The pharmacists' union won back the lost vacation days. As one staff pharmacist said, "Kaiser is a pretty benevolent employer, but there's always the pressure to squeeze a little."[15]

What Do Unions Want? What Are Their Aims?

We can generalize by saying that unions have two sets of aims, one for union security and one for improved wages, hours, working conditions, and benefits for their members.

UNION SECURITY First and probably foremost, unions seek to establish security for themselves. They fight hard for the right to represent a firm's workers and to be the *exclusive* bargaining agent for all employees in the unit. (As such, they negotiate contracts for all employees, including those who are not members of the union.) Five types of union security are possible:

1. *Closed shop.*[16] The company can hire only current union members. Congress outlawed closed shops in interstate commerce in 1947, but they still exist in some states for particular industries (such as printing). They account for less than 5% of union contracts.
2. *Union shop.* The company can hire nonunion people, but they must join the union after a prescribed period and pay dues. (If not, they can be fired.) This category accounts for about 73% of union contracts. Unions and employers also tend to negotiate versions of the union shop, for instance, letting older workers quit the union when the contract ends.
3. *Agency shop.* Employees who do not belong to the union still must pay the union an amount equal to union dues (on the assumption that the union's efforts benefit *all* the workers).
4. *Preferential shop.* Union members get preference in hiring, but the employer can still hire nonunion members.
5. *Maintenance of membership arrangement.* Employees do not have to belong to the union. However, union members employed by the firm must maintain membership in the union for the contract period. These account for about 4% of union agreements.

Not all states give unions the right to require union membership as a condition of employment. **Right to work** "is a term used to describe state statutory or constitutional provisions banning the requirement of union membership as a condition of employment."[17] Section 14(b) of the Taft-Hartley Act (an early labor relations act that we'll discuss later in more detail) permits states to forbid the negotiation of compulsory union membership provisions, not just for firms engaged in interstate commerce but also for those in intrastate commerce. Right-to-work laws don't outlaw unions. They do outlaw (within those states) any form of union security. This understandably inhibits union formation in those states. Recently, there were 23 right-to-work states.[18] After Oklahoma became the 22nd state to pass right-to-work legislation Oklahoma's union membership dropped dramatically in the next 3 years.[19]

IMPROVED WAGES, HOURS, WORKING CONDITIONS, AND BENEFITS FOR MEMBERS Once their security is assured, unions fight to better the lot of their members—to improve their wages, hours, and working conditions, for example. The typical labor agreement also gives the union a role in other HR activities, including recruiting, selecting, compensating, promoting, training, and discharging employees.

The AFL-CIO

The American Federation of Labor and Congress of Industrial Organizations (AFL-CIO) is a voluntary federation of about 56 national and international labor unions in the United States. It resulted from the merger of the AFL and CIO in 1955.

For many people, the AFL-CIO is still synonymous with the word *union*, but union federation membership is in flux. Several years ago, six big unions—the Service Employees' International Union (SEIU), the International Brotherhood of Teamsters, the United Food and Commercial Workers, the United Farm Workers, the Laborers International Union, and UNITE

---

closed shop
A form of union security in which the company can hire only union members. This was outlawed in 1947 for interstate commerce, but still exists in some industries (such as printing).

union shop
A form of union security in which the company can hire nonunion people but they must join the union after a prescribed period of time and pay dues. (If they do not, they can be fired.)

agency shop
A form of union security in which employees who do not belong to the union must still pay union dues on the assumption that union efforts benefit all workers.

preferential shop
Union members get preference in hiring, but the employer can still hire nonunion members.

right to work
The public policy in a number of states that prohibits union security of any kind.

HERE (which represents garment and service workers) left the AFL-CIO and established their own federation, called the Change to Win Coalition. Together, the departing unions represented over one-fourth of the AFL-CIO's membership and budget. Change to Win plans to be more aggressive about organizing workers than they say the AFL-CIO was. Then in 2009, UNITE HERE rejoined the AFL-CIO, possibly slowing Change to Win's momentum.[20] About 7 million workers belong to unions not affiliated with the AFL-CIO.

UNIONS AND THE LAW

2 Discuss the nature of the major federal labor relations laws.

Until about 1930, there were no special labor laws. Employers didn't have to engage in collective bargaining with employees and were virtually unrestrained in their behavior toward unions. The use of spies and the firing of agitators was widespread. "Yellow dog" contracts, whereby management could require nonunion membership as a condition for employment, were widely enforced. Most union weapons—even strikes—were illegal.

This one-sided situation lasted in the United States from the Revolution to the Great Depression (around 1930). Since then, in response to changing public attitudes, values, and economic conditions, labor law has gone through three clear changes: from "strong encouragement" of unions, to "modified encouragement coupled with regulation," to "detailed regulation of internal union affairs."[21]

Period of Strong Encouragement: The Norris-LaGuardia Act (1932) and the National Labor Relations Act (1935)

Norris-LaGuardia Act

This law marked the beginning of the era of strong encouragement of unions and guaranteed to each employee the right to bargain collectively "free from interference, restraint, or coercion."

Wagner Act

A law that banned certain types of unfair labor practices and provided for secret-ballot elections and majority rule for determining whether or not a firm's employees want to unionize.

National Labor Relations Board (NLRB)

The agency created by the Wagner Act to investigate unfair labor practice charges and to provide for secret-ballot elections and majority rule in determining whether or not a firm's employees want a union.

The **Norris-LaGuardia Act** set the stage for an era in which government encouraged union activity. The act guaranteed to each employee the right to bargain collectively "free from interference, restraint, or coercion." It declared yellow dog contracts unenforceable. It limited the courts' abilities to issue injunctions for activities such as peaceful picketing and payment of strike benefits.[22]

Yet this act did little to restrain employers from fighting labor organizations by whatever means they could muster. Therefore, the National Labor Relations (or **Wagner**) Act was passed in 1935 to add teeth to the Norris-LaGuardia Act. It did this by banning certain unfair labor practices, providing for secret-ballot elections and majority rule for determining whether a firm's employees were to unionize, and creating the **National Labor Relations Board (NLRB)** for enforcing these two provisions.

In addition to activities like overseeing union elections, the NLRB periodically issues interpretive rulings. For example, about 6 million employees fall under the "contingent" or "alternative" employee umbrella today. The NLRB therefore ruled that temporary employees could join the unions of permanent employees in the companies where their employment agencies assign them to work.[23]

UNFAIR EMPLOYER LABOR PRACTICES The Wagner Act deemed as "statutory wrongs" (but not crimes) five unfair labor practices used by employers:

1. It is unfair for employers to "interfere with, restrain, or coerce employees" in exercising their legally sanctioned right of self-organization.
2. It is an unfair practice for company representatives to dominate or interfere with either the formation or the administration of labor unions. Among other management actions found to be unfair under practices 1 and 2 are bribing employees, using company spy systems, moving a business to avoid unionization, and blacklisting union sympathizers.
3. Employers are prohibited from discriminating in any way against employees for their legal union activities.
4. Employers are forbidden to discharge or discriminate against employees simply because the latter file unfair practice charges against the company.
5. Finally, it is an unfair labor practice for employers to refuse to bargain collectively with their employees' duly chosen representatives.[24]

An unfair labor practice charge may be filed (see Figure 10.1) with the NLRB. The board then investigates the charge. Possible actions include dismissal of the complaint, request for an injunction against the employer, and an order that the employer cease and desist.

FIGURE 10.1

NLRB Form 501: Filing an Unfair Labor Practice

Source: www.nlrb.gov/nlrb/shared_files/forms/nlrbform501.pdf, accessed April 28, 2009.

FORM NLRB 501
(2 81)

FORM EXEMPT UNDER
44 U.S.C. 3512

UNITED STATES OF AMERICA
NATIONAL LABOR RELATIONS BOARD
CHARGE AGAINST EMPLOYER

INSTRUCTIONS: File an original and 4 copies of this charge with NLRB Regional Director for the region in which the alleged unfair labor practice occurred or is occurring.

DO NOT WRITE IN THIS SPACE

CASE NO.

DATE FILE

1. EMPLOYER AGAINST WHOM CHARGE IS BROUGHT

a. NAME OF EMPLOYER

b. NUMBER OF WORKERS EMPLOYED

c. ADDRESS OF ESTABLISHMENT (*street and number, city, State, and ZIP code*)

d. EMPLOYER REPRESENTATIVE TO CONTACT

e. PHONE NO.

f. TYPE OF ESTABLISHMENT (*factory, mine, wholesaler, etc.*)

g. IDENTIFY PRINCIPAL PRODUCT OR SERVICE

h. THE ABOVE-NAMED EMPLOYER HAS ENGAGED IN AND IS ENGAGING IN UNFAIR LABOR PRACTICES WITHIN THE MEANING OF SECTION 8(a), SUBSECTIONS (1) AND _____ OF THE NATIONAL
(*list subsections*)
LABOR RELATIONS ACT, AND THESE UNFAIR LABOR PRACTICES ARE UNFAIR LABOR PRACTICES AFFECTING COMMERCE WITHIN THE MEANING OF THE ACT.

2. BASIS OF THE CHARGE (*be specific as to facts, names, addresses, plants involved, dates, places, etc.*)

BY THE ABOVE AND OTHER ACTS, THE ABOVE-NAMED EMPLOYER HAS INTERFERED WITH, RESTRAINED, AND COERCED EMPLOYEES IN THE EXERCISE OF THE RIGHTS GUARANTEED IN SECTION 7 OF THE ACT.

3. FULL NAME OF PARTY FILING CHARGE (*if labor organization, give full name, including local name and number*)

4a. ADDRESS (*street and number, city, State, and ZIP code*)

4b. TELEPHONE NO.

5. FULL NAME OF NATIONAL OR INTERNATIONAL LABOR ORGANIZATION OF WHICH IT IS AN AFFILIATE OR CONSTITUENT UNIT (*to be filled in when charge is filed by a labor organization*)

6. DECLARATION

I declare that I have read the above charge and that the statements therein are true to the best of my knowledge and belief.

By _____
(signature of representative or person filing charge)

(title, if any)

Address _____

(telephone number)

(date)

WILLFULLY FALSE STATEMENTS ON THIS CHARGE CAN BE PUNISHED BY FINE AND IMPRISONMENT
(*U.S. CODE, TITLE 18, SECTION 1001*)

FROM 1935 TO 1947 Union membership increased quickly after passage of the Wagner Act in 1935. Other factors such as an improving economy and aggressive union leadership contributed to this as well. But by the mid-1940s, the tide had begun to turn. Largely because of a series of massive postwar strikes, public policy began to shift against what many viewed as the union excesses of the times.

Taft-Hartley Act

A law prohibiting union unfair labor practices and enumerating the rights of employees as union members. It also enumerates the rights of employers.

Period of Modified Encouragement Coupled with Regulation: The Taft-Hartley Act (1947)

The **Taft-Hartley Act** (or Labor Management Relations Act) reflected the public's less enthusiastic attitudes toward unions. It amended the Wagner Act with provisions aimed at limiting unions in four ways: by prohibiting unfair union labor practices, by enumerating the rights of employees as union members, by enumerating the rights of employers, and by allowing the president of the United States to temporarily bar national emergency strikes.

UNFAIR UNION LABOR PRACTICES The Taft-Hartley Act enumerated several labor practices that unions were prohibited from engaging in:

1. Unions were banned from restraining or coercing employees from exercising their guaranteed bargaining rights.
2. It is an unfair labor practice for a union to cause an employer to discriminate in any way against an employee in order to encourage or discourage his or her membership in a union.
3. It is an unfair labor practice for a union to refuse to bargain in good faith with the employer about wages, hours, and other employment conditions.

RIGHTS OF EMPLOYEES The Taft-Hartley Act also protected the rights of employees against their unions. For example, many people felt that compulsory unionism violated the basic U.S. right of freedom of association. The new *right-to-work laws* sprang up in 19 states (mainly in the South and Southwest); as noted, these outlawed labor contracts that made union membership a condition for keeping one's job.

In general, the National Labor Relations Act does not restrain unions from unfair labor practices to the extent that it does employers. Unions may not restrain or coerce employees. However, "violent or otherwise threatening behavior or clearly coercive or intimidating union activities are necessary before the NLRB will find an unfair labor practice."[25] Examples here would include physical assaults or threats of violence, economic reprisals, and mass picketing that restrains the lawful entry or leaving of a work site. In one typical case, *Pattern Makers* v. *National Labor Relations Board,* the U.S. Supreme Court found the union guilty of an unfair labor practice when it tried to fine some members for resigning from the union and returning to work during a strike.[26]

RIGHTS OF EMPLOYERS The Taft-Hartley Act also explicitly gave employers certain rights. For example, it gave them full freedom to express their views concerning union organization. Thus, a manager can tell his or her employees that in his or her opinion unions are worthless, dangerous to the economy, and immoral. A manager can even hint, generally speaking, that unionization and subsequent high-wage demands *might* result in the permanent closing of the plant (but not in its relocation). Employers can set forth the union's record concerning violence and corruption, if appropriate, and can play on the racial prejudices of workers by describing the union's philosophy toward integration. The only major restraint is that there can be no threat of reprisal or force or promise of benefit.[27]

The employer also cannot meet with employees on company time within 24 hours of an election or suggest to employees that they vote against the union while they are at home or in the employer's office, although he or she can do so while in their work area or where they normally gather.

national emergency strikes
Strikes that might "imperil the national health and safety."

NATIONAL EMERGENCY STRIKES The Taft-Hartley Act also allows the U.S. president to intervene in **national emergency strikes**, which are strikes (for example, on the part of steel firm employees) that might imperil national health and safety. The president may appoint a board of inquiry and, based on its report, apply for an injunction restraining the strike for 60 days. If no settlement is reached during that time, the injunction can be extended for another 20 days. During this period, employees are polled in a secret ballot to ascertain their willingness to accept the employer's last offer.

Period of Detailed Regulation of Internal Union Affairs: The Landrum-Griffin Act (1959)

Landrum-Griffin Act
A law aimed at protecting union members from possible wrongdoing on the part of their unions.

In the 1950s, senate investigations revealed unsavory practices on the part of some unions, and the result was the **Landrum-Griffin Act** (officially, the Labor Management Reporting and Disclosure Act). An overriding aim was to protect union members from possible wrongdoing on the part of their unions. It was also an amendment to the Wagner Act.

The Landrum-Griffin Act contains a bill of rights for union members. Among other things, this provides for certain rights in the nomination of candidates for union office. It also affirms a member's right to sue his or her union. And, it ensures that no member can be fined or suspended without due process (including a list of charges, and a fair hearing).

The act also laid out rules regarding union elections. For example, national and international unions must elect officers at least once every 5 years, using some type of secret-ballot mechanism.

The senate investigators also discovered flagrant examples of employer wrongdoing. The Landrum-Griffin Act therefore also greatly expanded the list of unlawful employer actions. For example, companies can no longer pay their own employees to entice them not to join the union. The pendulum therefore again shifted a bit back towards strengthening unions.

THE UNION DRIVE AND ELECTION

It is through the union drive and election that a union tries to be recognized to represent employees. This process has five basic steps: initial contact, authorization cards, hearing, campaign, and election.

Step 1: Initial Contact

3 Describe the process of a union drive and election.

During the initial contact stage, the union determines the employees' interest in organizing, and establishes an organizing committee.

The initiative for the first contact between the employees and the union may come from the employees, from a union already representing other employees of the firm, or from a union representing workers elsewhere. Sometimes a union effort starts with a disgruntled employee contacting the local union to learn how to organize his or her place of work (as at Walmart). Sometimes, though, the campaign starts when a union decides it wants to expand to representing other employees in the firm or industry, or when the company looks like an easy one to organize. (For instance, the Teamsters Union, which was already firmly in place at UPS, began an intensive organizing campaign at FedEx.) In any case, there is an initial contact between a union representative and a few employees.

THE UNION REP When an employer becomes a target, a union official usually assigns a representative to assess employee interest. The representative visits the firm to determine whether enough employees are interested to make a union campaign worthwhile. He or she also identifies employees who would make good leaders in the organizing campaign and calls them

The Teamsters Union—already firmly in place at UPS—began an intensive organizing campaign at FedEx.

Source: Paul Sakuma/AP Wide World Photos.

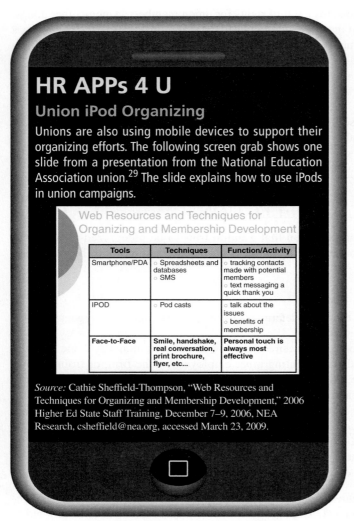

HR APPs 4 U
Union iPod Organizing

Unions are also using mobile devices to support their organizing efforts. The following screen grab shows one slide from a presentation from the National Education Association union.[29] The slide explains how to use iPods in union campaigns.

Web Resources and Techniques for Organizing and Membership Development

Tools	Techniques	Function/Activity
Smartphone/PDA	○ Spreadsheets and databases ○ SMS	○ tracking contacts made with potential members ○ text messaging a quick thank you
IPOD	○ Pod casts	○ talk about the issues ○ benefits of membership
Face-to-Face	Smile, handshake, real conversation, print brochure, flyer, etc...	Personal touch is always most effective

Source: Cathie Sheffield-Thompson, "Web Resources and Techniques for Organizing and Membership Development," 2006 Higher Ed State Staff Training, December 7–9, 2006, NEA Research, csheffield@nea.org, accessed March 23, 2009.

together to create an organizing committee. The objective is to "educate the committee about the benefits of forming a union, the law and procedures involved in forming a local union, and the issues management is likely to raise during a campaign."[28]

CONTACT PROCEDURES The union must follow certain procedures when it starts contacting employees. The law allows union organizers to solicit employees for membership as long as it doesn't endanger the performance or safety of the employees. Therefore, much of the contact takes place off the job. Organizers can also safely contact employees on company grounds during off hours (such as break time). Under some conditions, union representatives may solicit employees at their workstations, but this is rare. In practice, there will be much informal organizing at the workplace as employees debate organizing. In any case, this initial contact stage may be deceptively quiet. In some instances the first inkling management has of a union campaign is the distribution of a handbill soliciting union membership.[30]

LABOR RELATIONS CONSULTANTS Both management and unions may use outside advisors. The use by management of consultants (who unions often disparagingly refer to as *union busters*) has grown considerably. This so-called "union avoidance industry" includes the consultants, law firms, industry psychologists, and strike management firms that employers often turn to when the union comes to call.[31] One study found management consultants involved in 75% of the elections they surveyed.[32]

One expert says an employer's main goal shouldn't be to win representation elections, but to avoid them altogether. He says doing so means taking fast action when the first signs of union activity appear. His advice in a nutshell: Don't just ignore the union's efforts while it spreads pro-union rumors, such as "If we had a union, we wouldn't have to work so much overtime." Retain an attorney and react at once.[33]

union salting

A union organizing tactic by which workers who are employed by a union as undercover union organizers are hired by unwitting employers.

UNION SALTING Unions are also not without creative ways to win elections, one of which is union salting. The National Labor Relations Board defines **union salting** as "placing of union members on nonunion job sites for the purpose of organizing." Critics claim that "salts" also often interfere with business operations and harass employees.[34] A U.S. Supreme Court decision, *NLRB* v. *Town and Country Electric,* held the tactic to be legal.

Improving Productivity through HRIS:
Unions Go Online

As one expert asked, "If faster and more powerful ways of communicating enable companies to compete in a quickly changing and challenging environment, shouldn't they also make unions stronger and more efficient as organizations and workplace representatives?"[35]

In fact, e-mail and the Internet have supercharged many union campaigns. Unions now can publicize their efforts and gather donations online, as well as put membership and union authorization forms online. Of course, they also mass e-mail announcements to collective bargaining unit members, and use mass e-mail to reach supporters and government officials.

For example, the group trying to organize Starbucks workers (the Starbucks Workers' Union) set up their own Web site (www.starbucksunion.org). It includes notes like, "Starbucks managers monitored internet chatrooms and eavesdropped on party conversations in a covert campaign to identify employees agitating for union representation at the coffee chain, internal emails reveal."[36]

Step 2: Authorization Cards

authorization cards

In order to petition for a union election, the union must show that at least 30% of employees may be interested in being unionized. Employees indicate this interest by signing authorization cards.

For the union to petition the NLRB for the right to hold an election, it must show that a sizable number of employees may be interested in being organized. The next step is thus for union organizers to try to get the employees to sign **authorization cards** (Figure 10-2). Among other things, these usually authorize the union to seek a representation election and state that the employee has applied to join the union. Before the union can petition an election, 30% of the eligible employees in an appropriate bargaining unit must sign.

During this stage, both union and management typically use propaganda. The union claims it can improve working conditions, raise wages, increase benefits, and generally get the workers better deals. Management need not be silent; it can attack the union on ethical and moral grounds and cite the cost of union membership, for example. Management can also explain its record, express facts and opinions, and explain to its employees the law applicable to organizing campaigns and the meaning of the duty to bargain in good faith (if the union should win the election).

However, neither side can threaten, bribe, or coerce employees. Further, an employer may not make promises of benefits to employees or make unilateral changes in terms and conditions of employment that were not planned to be implemented prior to the onset of union organizing activity. Managers also should not look through signed authorization cards if confronted with them by union representatives. Doing so could be construed as spying on those who signed, which is an unfair labor practice.

During this stage, unions can picket the company, subject to three constraints: The union must file a petition for an election within 30 days after the start of picketing, the firm cannot already be lawfully recognizing another union, and there cannot have been a valid NLRB election during the past 12 months. The union would file a petition using NLRB Form 502.

FIGURE 10.2

Sample Authorization Card

SAMPLES UNIONS of AMERICA
Authorization for Representation

I hereby authorize Local 409 of the SAMPLES union to be my exclusive representative for the purposes of collective bargaining with my employer. I understand that my signature on this card may be used to obtain certification of Local 409 as our exclusive bargaining representative without an election.

This card will verify that I have applied for union membership and that effective
_____I hereby authorize you to deduct each pay period from my earnings an amount equal to the regular current rate of monthly union dues and initiation fee.

Employer _____ Worksite _____

Date: _____ Name: _____

Street address: _____ City:_____ Zip Code:_____

Home Phone: _____Cell Phone: _____ Home E-mail: _____

Department: _____

Job Title/Classification _____

Signature _____

You must print and mail in this authorization card for it to be recognized. Only original cards are valid and should be submitted. Mail to:

SAMPLES Unions of America, Local 409

301 Samples Way

Miami, FL 33101

Step 3: The Hearing

After the authorization cards are collected, one of three things can occur. The employer may choose not to contest union recognition, in which case no hearing is needed and a *consent election* is held immediately. The employer may choose not to contest the union's *right to an election* (and/or the scope of the bargaining unit, or which employees are eligible to vote in the election), in which case no hearing is needed and the parties can stipulate an election. Or, the employer may contest the union's right, in which case it can insist on a *hearing* to determine those issues. An employer's decision about whether to insist on a hearing is a strategic one based on the facts of each case, and whether it feels it needs more time to try to persuade a majority of its employees not to elect a union to represent them.

Most companies contest the union's right to represent their employees, and thus decline to voluntarily recognize the union: They claim that a significant number of their employees do not really want the union. It is at this point that the U.S. Labor Department's NLRB gets involved. The NLRB is usually contacted by the union, which requests a hearing. Based on this, the regional director of the NLRB sends a hearing officer to investigate. (For example, did 30% or more of the employees in an appropriate bargaining unit sign the authorization cards?) The examiner sends both management and the union a notice of representation hearing that states the time and place of the hearing.

bargaining unit
The group of employees the union will be authorized to represent.

The **bargaining unit** is one decision to come out of the hearing; it is the group of employees that the union will be authorized to represent and bargain for collectively.

Finally, if the results of the hearing are favorable for the union, the NLRB directs that an election be held. It issues a Decision and Direction of Election notice to that effect and sends NLRB Form 666 ("Notice to Employees") to the employer to post, notifying employees of their rights under federal labor relations law.

Step 4: The Campaign

During the campaign that precedes the election, the union and employer appeal to employees for their votes. The union emphasizes that it will prevent unfairness, set up a grievance/seniority system, and improve unsatisfactory wages. Union strength, they'll say, will give employees a voice in determining wages and working conditions. Management emphasizes that improvements such as those the union promises don't require unionization, and that wages are equal to or better than they would be with a union contract. Management also emphasizes the financial cost of union dues; the fact that the union is an "outsider"; and that if the union wins, a strike may follow.[37] It can even attack the union on ethical and moral grounds, while insisting that employees will not be as well off and may lose freedom. But neither side can threaten, bribe, or coerce employees.

THE SUPERVISOR'S ROLE Supervisors must know (see the HR in Practice feature) what they can and can't do to hamper organizing activities legally, lest they commit unfair labor practices. Such practices could cause a new election to be held after the company won a previous election. In one case, a plant superintendent prohibited distribution of union literature in the lunchroom. Because solicitation of off-duty workers in nonwork areas is generally legal, the company subsequently allowed the union to post and distribute union literature in the plant's nonworking areas. However, the NLRB still ruled that the initial act of prohibiting distribution of the literature was an unfair labor practice. The NLRB used the superintendent's action as one reason to invalidate an election that the company won.[38]

HR IN PRACTICE

The Supervisor's Role in the Unionizing Effort

One company helps its supervisors remember what they may and may not do with respect to unionization with the acronyms TIPS and FORE.[39]

Use TIPS to remember what *not* to do:

T—Threaten. Do not threaten or imply the company will take adverse action of any kind for supporting the union.[40] Do not

threaten to terminate employees because of their union activities, and don't threaten to close the facility if the union wins the election.

I—Interrogate. Don't interrogate or ask employees their position concerning unions, or how they are going to vote in an election.

P—Promise. Don't promise employees a pay increase, special favors, better benefits, or promotions.

S—Spy. Don't spy at any union activities or attend a union meeting, even if invited.

Use FORE to remember what the supervisor *may do* to discourage unionization.

F—Facts. Do tell employees that by signing the authorization card the union may become their legal representative in matters regarding wages and hours, and do tell them that by signing a union authorization card it does not mean they must vote for the union.

O—Opinion. You may tell employees that management doesn't believe in third-party representation, and that

management believes in having an open-door policy to air grievances.

R—Rules. Provide factually correct advice such as telling employees that the law permits the company to permanently replace them if there's a strike, and that the union can't make the company agree to anything it does not want to during negotiations.

E—Experience. The supervisor may share personal experiences he or she may have had with a union.[41]

RULES REGARDING LITERATURE AND SOLICITATION To avoid problems, employers should have rules governing distribution of literature and solicitation of workers and train supervisors in how to apply them.[42] For example:

- Nonemployees can always be barred from soliciting employees during their work time—that is, when the employee is on duty and not on a break.
- Employers can usually stop employees from soliciting other employees for any purpose if one or both employees are on paid-duty time and not on a break.
- Most employers (not including retail stores, shopping centers, and certain other employers) can bar nonemployees from the building's interiors and work areas as a right of private property owners.

Such restrictions are valid only if the employer does not impose them in a discriminatory manner. For example, if company policy permits employees to collect money for baby gifts or to engage in other solicitation during their working time, the employer will not be able to prohibit them from union soliciting during work time.

Finally, remember that there are more ways to commit unfair labor practices than just keeping union organizers off your private property. For example, one employer decided to have a cookout and paid day off 2 days before a union representation election. The NLRB held that this was too much of a coincidence and represented coercive conduct; it called a second election. The union had lost the first vote but won the second.[43]

Figure 10.3 illustrates what the employer and union generally cannot do during campaigns.

STARBUCKS' EXAMPLE It's not easy for Starbucks managers at Seattle headquarters to monitor what employees are doing in its far-flung stores. The company therefore works hard to encourage employees to control themselves—by making them "partners" and by providing excellent benefits and stock options. As a company that provides excellent benefits and working conditions, Starbucks executives were surprised that some employees expressed a desire to unionize. Nevertheless, the allegations that some local managers may have tried to retaliate against employees who favored the union underscore why all employers must carefully train supervisors in how to react when the union comes to call.

Step 5: The Election

Finally, the election can be held within 30 to 60 days after the NLRB issues its Decision and Direction of Election. The election is by secret ballot. The NLRB provides the ballots (see Figure 10.4), as well as the voting booth and ballot box. It also counts the votes and certifies the results of the election. Historically, the more workers who vote, the less likely the union is to win. This is probably because more workers who are not strong union supporters end up voting. Which union is important, too. For example, the Teamsters union is somewhat less likely than other unions to win a representation election.[44]

The union becomes the employees' representative if it wins the election, and winning means getting a majority of the votes cast, not a majority of the workers in the bargaining unit. The

FIGURE 10.3

NLRA Union Campaign Violations

Source: Adapted from www.nlrb.gov/workplace_rights/ nlra_violations.aspx, accessed January 14, 2008.

Examples of Employer Conduct Which Violate the NLRA:
- Threatening employees with loss of jobs or benefits if they join or vote for a union or engage in protected concerted activity (such as two or more employees together asking their employer to improve working conditions and pay).
- Threatening to close the plant if employees unionize.
- Promising benefits to employees to discourage their union support.
- Transferring, laying off, terminating, assigning employees more difficult work tasks, or otherwise punishing employees because they engaged in union or protected concerted activity.
- Transferring, laying off, terminating, assigning employees more difficult work tasks, or otherwise punishing employees because they filed unfair labor practice charges or participated in an investigation by NLRB.

Examples of Labor Organization Conduct Which Violate the NLRA:
- Threats to employees that they will lose their jobs unless they support the union.
- Seeking the suspension, discharge, or other punishment of an employee for not being a union member even if the employee has paid or offered to pay a lawful initiation fee and periodic fees thereafter.
- Refusing to process a grievance because an employee has criticized union officials or because an employee is not a member of the union in states where union security clauses are not permitted.
- Fining employees who have validly resigned from the union for engaging in protected concerted activities following their resignation or for crossing an unlawful picket line.
- Engaging in picket line misconduct, such as threatening, assaulting, or barring non-strikers from the employer's premises.
- Striking over issues unrelated to employment terms and conditions or coercively enmeshing neutrals into a labor dispute.

FIGURE 10.4

Sample NLRB Ballot

UNITED STATES OF AMERICA

National Labor Relations Board

OFFICIAL SECRET BALLOT

FOR CERTAIN EMPLOYEES OF

_____

Do you wish to be represented for purposes of collective bargaining by —

_____

MARK AN "S" IN THE SQUARE OF YOUR CHOICE

YES   NO

□   □

DO NOT SIGN THIS BALLOT. Fold and drop in ballot box.
If you spoil this ballot return it to the Board Agent for a new one.

union typically wins just over half of such elections. In one recent year, the union win rate rose to 66.8%, higher than it had been for decades.[45]

Decertification Elections: When Employees Want to Oust Their Union

Winning an election and signing an agreement do not necessarily mean that the union is in the company to stay. The same law that grants employees the right to unionize also gives them a way to terminate legally the union's right to represent them. The process is *decertification*. There are around 450 to 500 decertification elections each year, of which unions usually win around 30%.[46] That's actually a more favorable rate for management than the rate for the original representation elections.

Decertification campaigns don't differ much from certification campaigns.[47] The union organizes membership meetings and house-to-house visits, mails literature to homes, and uses phone calls, NLRB appeals, and (sometimes) threats and harassment to win the election. Managers use meetings—including one-on-one meetings, small-group meetings, and meetings with entire units—as well as legal or expert assistance, letters, improved working conditions, and subtle or not-so-subtle threats in its attempts to win a decertification vote.

THE COLLECTIVE BARGAINING PROCESS

What Is Collective Bargaining?

When and if the union is recognized as a company's employees' representative, a day is set for meeting at the bargaining table. Representatives of management and the union meet to negotiate a labor contract that contains agreements on specific provisions covering wages, hours, and working conditions.

collective bargaining
The process through which representatives of management and the union meet to negotiate a labor agreement.

What exactly is **collective bargaining**? According to the Wagner Act:

> For the purpose of (this act) to bargain collectively is the performance of the mutual obligation of the employer and the representative of the employees to meet at reasonable times and confer in good faith with respect to wages, hours, and terms and conditions of employment, or the negotiation of an agreement, or any question arising thereunder, and the execution of a written contract incorporating any agreement reached if requested by either party, but such obligation does not compel either party to agree to a proposal or require the making of a concession.

In plain language, this means that both management and labor are required by law to negotiate wages, hours, and terms and conditions of employment "in good faith." We'll see that court decisions have clarified the specific provisions that are negotiable.

What Is Good-Faith Bargaining?

good-faith bargaining
A term that means both parties are communicating and negotiating and that proposals are being matched with counterproposals, with both parties making every reasonable effort to arrive at agreements. It does not mean that either party is compelled to agree to a proposal.

Good-faith bargaining means that proposals are matched with counterproposals and that both parties make every reasonable effort to arrive at an agreement. It does not mean that either party is compelled to agree to a proposal. Nor does it require that either party make any specific concessions (although in practice, some may be necessary). In practice, good-faith bargaining includes things like the duty to meet and confer with the representative of the employees (or employer); the duty to supply, on request, information that is "relevant and necessary" to allow the employees' representative to bargain intelligently; and the duty to deal with whoever the employees' representative designates to carry on negotiations.[48]

WHEN IS BARGAINING NOT IN GOOD FAITH? In assessing whether the party has violated its good-faith obligations, it is the *totality of conduct* by each of the parties that is of prime importance to the NLRB and the courts.[49] As interpreted by the NLRB and the courts, examples of a violation of the requirements for good-faith bargaining may include:

1. *Surface bargaining.* This involves going through the motions of bargaining without any real intention of completing a formal agreement.
2. *Proposals and demands.* The NLRB considers the advancement of proposals as a positive factor in determining overall good faith.
3. *Withholding information.* The NLRB and courts expect management to furnish information on matters such as wages, hours, and other terms of employment that union negotiators request and legitimately require.[50]
4. *Dilatory tactics.* The law requires that the parties meet and "confer at reasonable times and intervals." It does not require management to meet at the time and place dictated just by the union.[51] However, inordinately delaying the meeting or refusing to meet with the other party may reflect bad-faith bargaining.
5. *Concessions.* The law does not require either party to make concessions. However, being willing to compromise during negotiations is a crucial ingredient of good-faith bargaining.
6. *Unilateral changes in conditions.* This is a strong indication that the employer is not bargaining with the required intent of reaching an agreement.

The Negotiating Team

Both union and management send a negotiating team to the bargaining table, and both teams usually go into the bargaining sessions having done their research. Union representatives have sounded out union members on their desires and conferred with union representatives of related unions.

Similarly, management does several things to prepare for bargaining. For example, it compiles pay and benefit data, including comparisons to local pay rates and rates paid for similar jobs in the industry. Management also carefully "costs" the current labor contract and determines the increased cost—total, per employee, and per hour—of the union's demands. It also tries to identify probable union demands and to size up the ones more important to the union. It uses information from grievances and feedback from supervisors to determine ahead of time what the union's demands might be and thus prepare counteroffers and arguments ahead of time.

One collective bargaining expert says, "The mistake I see most often is [HR professionals who] enter the negotiations without understanding the financial impact of things they put on the table. The thing you give up can make or break your employer. . . . For example, the union wants 3 extra vacation days. That doesn't sound like a lot, except that in some states, if an employee leaves, you have to pay them for unused vacation time. Now [therefore] your employer has to carry that liability on their books at all times."[52]

Bargaining Items

voluntary (permissible) bargaining items
Items in collective bargaining for which bargaining is neither illegal nor mandatory—neither party can be compelled to negotiate over those items.

illegal bargaining items
Items in collective bargaining that are forbidden by law; for example, the clause agreeing to hire "union members exclusively" would be illegal in a right-to-work state.

mandatory bargaining items
Items in collective bargaining that a party must bargain over if they are introduced by the other party—for example, pay.

Labor law sets out *voluntary, illegal,* and *mandatory* items that are subject to collective bargaining.

Voluntary (or permissible) bargaining items are neither mandatory nor illegal; they become a part of negotiations only through the joint agreement of both management and union. Neither party can be compelled against its wishes to negotiate over voluntary items. An employee cannot hold up signing a contract because the other party refuses to bargain on a voluntary item.

Illegal bargaining items are forbidden by law. The clause agreeing to hire "union members exclusively" would be illegal in a right-to-work state, for example.

About 70 **mandatory bargaining items** exist, some of which we present in Figure 10.5. These include wages, hours, rest periods, layoffs, transfers, benefits, and severance pay. Others are added as the law evolves. For instance, drug testing evolved into a mandatory item as a result of NLRB decisions.

MANDATORY	PERMISSIBLE	ILLEGAL
Rates of pay	Indemnity bonds	Closed shop
Wages	Management rights as	Separation of employees
Hours of employment	to union affairs	based on race
Overtime pay	Pension benefits of	Discriminatory
Shift differentials	retired employees	treatment
Holidays	Scope of the bargaining unit	
Vacations	Including supervisors	
Severance pay	in the contract	
Pensions	Additional parties to	
Insurance benefits	the contract such as	
Profit-sharing plans	the international	
Christmas bonuses	union	
Company housing,	Use of union label	
meals, and discounts	Settlement of unfair	
Employee security	labor charges	
Job performance	Prices in cafeteria	
Union security	Continuance of past	
Management–union	contract	
relationship	Membership of bargaining	
Drug testing	team	
of employees	Employment of strikebreakers	

FIGURE 10.5

Bargaining Items

Bargaining Stages[53]

4 Discuss the main steps in the collective bargaining process

Bargaining typically goes through several stages.[54] First, each side presents its demands. At this stage, both parties are usually quite far apart on some issues. Indeed, labor negotiators use the term *blue-skying* to refer to demands (such as swimming pools and 17 paid holidays, including Valentine's Day) that negotiators have been known to propose. Second, there is a reduction of demands. At this stage, each side trades off some of its demands to gain others, a process called *trading points*. Third are the subcommittee studies: The parties form joint subcommittees or study groups to try to work out reasonable alternatives. Fourth, the parties reach an informal settlement, and each group goes back to its sponsor. Union representatives check informally with their superiors and the union members; management representatives check with top management. Finally, when everything is in order, the parties fine-tune, proofread, and sign a formal agreement. The HR in Practice feature presents some negotiating guidelines.

Impasses, Mediation, and Strikes

IMPASSES Signing the agreement assumes everything is in order, and that there are no insurmountable disagreements. If there are, the parties may instead declare an impasse. For example, a few years ago the National Hockey League informed the NLRB that it had reached an impasse in its negotiations with the National Hockey League Players' Association. The parties must get past the impasse for the contract to be agreed on and signed.

An impasse usually occurs because one party demands more than the other offers. Sometimes an impasse can be resolved through a *third party*, a disinterested person such as a mediator or arbitrator. If the impasse is not resolved in this way, the union might call a work stoppage, or *strike*, to pressure management.

HR IN PRACTICE

Negotiating Guidelines[55]

1. *Set clear objectives* for every bargaining item and understand on what grounds the objectives are established.
2. *Do not hurry.*
3. When in doubt, *caucus* with your associates.
4. Be *well prepared* with firm data supporting your position.
5. Always strive to keep some *flexibility* in your position.
6. Don't just concern yourself with what the other party says and does; *find out why*.
7. Respect the importance of *face saving* for the other party.
8. Constantly be alert to the *real intentions* of the other party.
9. Be a good *listener.*
10. Build a reputation for *being fair but firm.*
11. Learn to *control your emotions;* don't panic.
12. Be sure as you make each bargaining move that you know its *relationship* to all other moves.
13. Measure each move against your *objectives*.
14. Pay close attention to the *wording* of every clause renegotiated; words and phrases are often sources of grievances.
15. Remember that collective bargaining negotiations are, by nature, part of a *compromise* process.
16. Consider the impact of present negotiations on those in *future years*.
17. Don't be so open, honest, and straightforward that you start making excessive concessions.[56]

---

mediation

Labor relations intervention in which a neutral third party tries to assist the principals in reaching agreement.

fact-finder

In labor relations, a neutral party who studies the issues in a dispute and makes a public recommendation for a reasonable settlement.

arbitration

The most definitive type of third-party intervention, in which the arbitrator often has the power to determine and dictate the settlement terms.

THIRD-PARTY INVOLVEMENT Opposing parties use three types of third-party interventions to overcome an impasse: mediation, fact-finding, and arbitration. With **mediation,** a neutral third party tries to assist the principals in reaching agreement. The mediator usually holds meetings with each party to determine where each stands regarding its position. He or she then uses this information to find common ground for further bargaining. For example, in 2009, the union representing U.S. Airways pilots, which had been seeking a new contract since U.S. Air merged with America West Holdings Corp. in 2005, applied for federal mediation.[57]

The mediator communicates assessments of the likelihood of a strike, the possible settlement packages available, and the like. The mediator does not have the authority to insist on a position or make a concession. However, he or she may—and probably will—provide leadership by making his or her position on some issue clear.

In certain situations (as in a national emergency dispute in which the president of the United States determines that a strike would be a national emergency), a fact-finder may be appointed. A **fact-finder** is a neutral party. He or she studies the issues and makes a public recommendation of what a reasonable settlement ought to be.

Arbitration is the most definitive type of third-party intervention because the arbitrator may have the power to decide and dictate settlement terms. Unlike mediation and fact-finding, arbitration can guarantee a solution to an impasse. With *binding arbitration,* both parties are

Even professional hockey, baseball, basketball, and football players, all relatively well-paid, have gone on strike for better wages and benefits.

Source: Manuel Balce Ceneta/AP Wide World Photos.

committed to accepting the arbitrator's award. With *nonbinding arbitration,* they are not. Arbitration may also be voluntary or compulsory (in other words, imposed by a government agency). In the United States, voluntary binding arbitration is the most prevalent.

Arbitration may not always be as impartial as it's thought to be. Researchers studied 391 arbitrated cases in baseball over about 20 years. Arbitrator awards favored teams 61% of the time. They concluded that (at least in baseball) "self-interested behavior by arbitrators" might lead to bias against players, and particularly against players of African-American and Latin ancestry.[58]

SOURCES OF THIRD-PARTY ASSISTANCE Various public and professional agencies make arbitrators and mediators available. For example, the American Arbitration Association (AAA) represents and provides the services of thousands of arbitrators and mediators to employers and unions requesting their services. The U.S. Office of Arbitration Services, part of the U.S. Office of Mediation & Conciliation Service (www.fmcs.gov/internet/), maintains a roster of arbitrators qualified to hear and decide disputes. Figure 10.6 shows the form employers or unions use to request arbitrator or mediator services from the U.S. government's Federal Mediation and Conciliation Service (FMCS).

FIGURE 10.6
Form to Request Mediation Services

FMCS Form F-53
Revised 5-92

Form Approved
OMB No. 3076-0005

FEDERAL SECTOR LABOR RELATIONS
NOTICE TO FEDERAL MEDIATION AND CONCILIATION SERVICE

Mail To:
Notice Processing Unit
FEDERAL MEDIATION AND CONCILIATION SERVICE
2100 K Street, N.W.
Washington, D.C. 20427

THIS NOTICE IS IN REGARD TO: (MARK "X")

(1)
☐ AN INITIAL CONTRACT (INCLUDED FLRA CERTIFICATION NUMBER) # ________
☐ A CONTRACT REOPENER REOPENER DATE ________
☐ THE EXPIRATION OF AN EXISTING AGREEMENT EXPIRATION DATE: ________

(2) ☐ ***OTHER REQUESTS FOR THE ASSISTANCE OF FMCS IN BARGAINING*** ***(MARK "X")***
SPECIFY TYPE OF ISSUE(S)

(3) ☐ ***REQUEST FOR GRIEVANCE MEDIATION (SEE ITEM #10)*** ***(MARK "X")***
ISSUE(S)

(4) NAME OF FEDERAL AGENCY | NAME OF SUBDIVISION OR COMPONENT, IF ANY
STREET ADDRESS OF AGENCY | CITY | STATE | ZIP
AGENCY OFFICIAL TO BE CONTACTED | AREA CODE & PHONE NUMBER

(5) NAME OF NATIONAL UNION OR PARENT BODY | NAME AND/OR LOCAL NUMBER
STREET ADDRESS | CITY | STATE | ZIP
UNION OFFICIAL TO BE CONTACTED | AREA CODE & PHONE NUMBER

LOCATION OF NEGOTIATIONS OR WHERE MEDIATION WILL BE HELD
(6) STREET ADDRESS | CITY | STATE | ZIP

(7) APPROX. # OF EMPLOYEES IN BARGAINING UNIT(S) >> | IN ESTABLISHMENT>>

(8) THIS NOTICE OR REQUEST IS FILED ON BEHALF OF ***(MARK "X")*** ☐ UNION ☐ AGENCY

(9) NAME AND TITLE OF OFFICIAL(S) SUBMITTING THIS NOTICE OR REQUEST | AREA CODE AND PHONE NUMBER
STREET ADDRESS | CITY | STATE | ZIP

FOR GRIEVANCE MEDIATION, THE SIGNATURES OF BOTH PARTIES ARE REQUIRED:*

(10) SIGNATURE (AGENCY) | DATE | SIGNATURE (UNION) | DATE

*Receipt of this form does not commit FMCS to offer its services. Receipt of this form will not be acknowledged in writing by FMCS. While use of this form is voluntary, its use will facilitate FMCS service to respondents. Public reporting burden for this collection of information is estimated to average 10 minutes per response, including time for reviewing the collection of information. Send comments regarding this burden estimate or any other aspect of this collection of information, including suggestions for reducing this burden, to FMCS Division of Administrative Services, Washington, D.C. 20427, and to the Office of Management and Budget, Paperwork Reduction Project. Washington, D.C. 20603

For Instructions, See Back

An economic strike results from a failure to agree on the terms of a contract—from an impasse, in other words.

Source: Paul Sakuma/AP Wide World Photos.

economic strike
A strike that results from a failure to agree on the terms of a contract that involve wages, benefits, and other conditions of employment.

unfair labor practice strike
A strike aimed at protesting illegal conduct by the employer.

wildcat strike
An unauthorized strike occurring during the term of a contract.

sympathy strike
A strike that takes place when one union strikes in support of another's strike.

boycott
The combined refusal by employees and other interested parties to buy or use the employer's products.

STRIKES A strike is a withdrawal of labor. There are four main types of strikes. An **economic strike** results from a failure to agree on the terms of a contract—from an impasse, in other words. An **unfair labor practice strike** protests illegal conduct by the employer. A **wildcat strike** is an unauthorized strike occurring during the term of a contract. A **sympathy strike** occurs when one union strikes in support of the strike of another.

Strikes needn't be an inevitable result of the bargaining process. Instead, studies show that they are often avoidable, but occur because of mistakes during the bargaining process. Mistakes include discrepancies between union leaders' and rank-and-file members' expectations, and misperceptions regarding each side's bargaining goals.[59]

Picketing is one of the first activities occurring during a strike. The purpose of picketing is to inform the public about the existence of the labor dispute and often to encourage others to refrain from doing business with the employer against whom the employees are striking.

DEALING WITH A STRIKE Employers can make several responses when they become the object of a strike. One is to halt their operations until the strike is over. A second alternative is to contract out work during the duration of the strike in order to blunt the effects of the strike on the employer. A third alternative is for the employer to continue operations, perhaps using supervisors and other nonstriking workers to fill in for the striking workers. A fourth alternative is the hiring of replacements for the strikers. In an economic strike, such replacements can be deemed permanent and would not have to be let go to make room for strikers who decided to return to work. If the strike were an unfair labor practice strike, the strikers would be entitled to return to their jobs if the employer makes an unconditional offer for them to do so. When Northwest Airlines began giving permanent jobs to 1,500 substitute workers it hired to replace striking mechanics, the strike by the Aircraft Mechanics Fraternal Association basically fell apart.[60]

OTHER RESPONSES Management and labor both use other methods to try to break an impasse. The union, for example, may resort to a *corporate campaign.* This is an organized effort by the union that exerts pressure on the employer by pressuring the company's other unions, shareholders, directors, customers, creditors, and government agencies, often directly. For example, a member of the company's board of directors might find that the union has organized its members to **boycott**—stop doing business with—the director's own business.

Unions use corporate campaigns to good effect. Sometimes also called *advocacy* or *comprehensive campaigns,* they helped unions organize several health care firms, including Sutter Health in California, for instance.[61]

Inside games are union efforts to convince employees to impede or to disrupt production. They might do this, for example, by slowing the work pace, refusing to work overtime, holding sickouts, filing mass charges with governmental agencies, or refusing to do work without receiving detailed instructions from supervisors (even though such instruction has not previously been required).

lockout
A refusal by the employer to provide opportunities to work.

LOCKOUTS Employers can try to break an impasse with lockouts. A **lockout** is a refusal by the employer to provide opportunities to work. The company (often literally) locks out employees and prohibits them from doing their jobs (and thus from being paid).

The NLRB does not generally view a lockout as an unfair labor practice. For example, if your product is perishable (such as vegetables), then a lockout may legitimately serve to neutralize union power. The NLRB views a lockout as an unfair labor practice only when the employer acts for a prohibited purpose. It is not a prohibited purpose to try to bring about a settlement of negotiations on terms favorable to the employer. However, employers are usually reluctant to cease operations when employees are willing to continue working (even though there may be an impasse at the bargaining table).

INJUNCTIONS During the impasse, both employers and unions can seek injunctive relief if they believe the other side is taking actions that could irreparably harm the other party. To obtain such relief, the NLRB must show the district court that an unfair labor practice—such as interfering with the union organizing campaign—if left unremedied, will irreparably harm the other party's statutory rights. (For example, if the employer is unfairly interfering with the union's organization campaign, or if the union is retaliating against employees for trying to gain access to the NLRB, the other side might press the NLRB for 10[j] injunctive relief.) Such relief is requested after the NLRB issues an unfair labor practices complaint. The *injunctive relief* is a judicial order calling for a cessation of certain actions deemed injurious.[62]

The Contract Agreement

The contract agreement itself may be 20 or 30 pages long or longer. The main sections of a typical contract cover subjects such as:

1. Management rights
2. Union security and automatic payroll dues deduction
3. Grievance procedures
4. Arbitration of grievances
5. Disciplinary procedures
6. Compensation rates
7. Hours of work and overtime
8. Benefits such as vacation, holidays, insurance, and pension
9. Health and safety provisions
10. Employee security seniority provisions
11. Contract expiration date

Handling Grievances

Signing the labor agreement is not the end of the process, because questions will always arise about what various clauses really mean. The *grievance process* addresses these issues. It is the process or steps that the employer and union have agreed to follow to ascertain whether some action violated the agreement. The grievance process is not supposed to renegotiate contract points. Instead, the aim is to clarify what those points really mean, in the context of addressing grievances regarding things like time off, disciplinary action, and pay. Recently, the Cleveland Browns' head coach fined one of his players $1,701 for not paying the hotel's bill for a $3 bottle of water. Some of the other players quickly filed several grievances with the NFL.[63]

CONTRACT ADMINISTRATION In unionized companies, grievance handling is often called *contract administration,* because no labor contract can ever be so complete that it covers all contingencies and answers all questions. For example, suppose the contract says you can discharge an employee only for "just cause." You subsequently discharge someone for speaking back to you in harsh terms. Was speaking back to you harshly "just cause"? The grievance procedure would handle and settle disagreements like these. It involves interpretation only, and generally would not involve renegotiating all or parts of the agreement.

SOURCES OF GRIEVANCES Employees will use just about any issue involving wages, hours, or conditions of employment as the basis of a grievance. Discipline cases and seniority problems (including promotions, transfers, and layoffs) would probably top the list. Others would include grievances growing out of job evaluations and work assignments, overtime, vacations, incentive plans, and holidays.

Sometimes the grievance process gets out of hand. For example, members of American Postal Workers Union, Local 482, filed 1,800 grievances at the Postal Service's Roanoke, Virginia, mail processing facility (the usual rate is about 800 grievances per year). The employees apparently were responding to job changes, including transfers triggered by the Postal Service's efforts to further automate its processes.[64]

THE GRIEVANCE PROCEDURE Whatever the source of the grievances, many firms today (and virtually all unionized ones) do (or should) give employees some means through which to air and settle their grievances. Grievance procedures are invariably a part of the labor agreement. But, even in nonunion firms, such procedures can help ensure that labor–management peace prevails.

Grievance procedures are typically multistep processes. For example, step one might be to file a form like that in Figure 10-7. Step two might require the grievant to try to work out an agreement with his or her supervisor, perhaps with a union officer or colleague present. Appeals may then go to the supervisor's boss, then that person's boss, and perhaps finally to an arbitrator.

GUIDELINES FOR HANDLING GRIEVANCES It is generally best, but not always possible, to develop a work environment in which grievances don't occur in the first place. Doing so depends on being able to recognize, diagnose, and correct the underlying causes of potential employee dissatisfaction before they become grievances. Typical causes include unfair appraisals, inequitable wages, or poor communications. Yet, in practice, grievances can be minimized, but not eradicated. There will probably always be a need to interpret what some clause in the agreement means. The HR in Practice feature presents important guidelines.

Effective Dispute Resolution Practices

Disputes often arise as part of the bargaining process, and as part of managing personnel. Strikes trigger corporate campaigns and negotiations; negotiations break down and require mediators; and disciplinary actions lead to grievances, for instance. Mediators, arbitrators, grievance processes, and negotiating are all important dispute resolution mechanisms—ways to manage and resolve disputes.[65]

HR IN PRACTICE

Guidelines for How to Handle a Grievance[66]

Do

- Investigate and handle every case as though it may eventually result in an arbitration hearing.
- Talk with the employee about his or her grievance; give the person a full hearing.
- Require the union to identify specific contractual provisions allegedly violated.
- Comply with the contractual time limits for handling the grievance.
- Visit the work area of the grievance.
- Determine whether there were any witnesses.
- Examine the grievant's personnel record.
- Fully examine prior grievance records.
- Treat the union representative as your equal.
- Hold your grievance discussion privately.
- Fully inform your own supervisor of grievance matters.

Don't

- Discuss the case with the union steward alone—the grievant should be there.

- Make arrangements with individual employees that are inconsistent with the labor agreement.
- Hold back the remedy if the company is wrong.
- Admit to the binding effect of a past practice.
- Relinquish to the union your rights as a manager.
- Settle grievances on the basis of what is "fair." Instead, stick to the labor agreement.
- Bargain over items not covered by the contract.
- Treat as subject to arbitration claims demanding the discipline or discharge of managers.
- Give long written grievance answers.
- Trade a grievance settlement for a grievance withdrawal (or try to make up for a bad decision in one grievance by bending over backward in another).
- Deny grievances on the premise that your "hands have been tied by management."
- Agree to informal amendments in the contract.

FIGURE 10.7

Sample Online Grievance Form

Click to Fill in Text or Check a Box
Tab to Next Field

Date Received at Step B *(MM/DD/YYYY)*

UNITED STATES POSTAL SERVICE

USPS-NALC Joint Step A Grievance Form

INFORMAL STEP A — NALC Shop Steward Completes This Section

1. Grievant's Name *(Last, first, middle initial)* | 2. Home Telephone No.

3. Seniority Date *(MM/DD/YYYY)* | 4. Status *(Check one)* ☐ FT ☐ FTF ☐ PTR ☐ PTF ☐ TE | 5. Grievant's SSN

6. Installation/Work Unit | 7. Finance Number

8. NALC Branch No. | 9. NALC Grievance No. | 10. Incident Date *(MM/DD/YYYY)* | 11. Date Discussed with Supervisor *(Filing Date)*

12a. Companion MSPB Appeal? ☐ Yes ☐ No | 12b. Companion EEO Appeal? ☐ Yes ☐ No

13a. Supervisor's Printed Name and Initials *(Completed by Supervisor)* | 13b. Steward's Printed Name and Initials *(Completed by Steward)*

FORMAL STEP A — Formal Step A Parties Complete This Section

14. USPS Grievance No.

15. Issue Statement/Provide Contract Provision(s) and Frame the Issue(s)

16. Undisputed Facts *(List and Attach All Supporting Documents)* — Attachments? ☐ No ☐ Yes Number____

17. UNION'S full, detailed statement of disputed facts and contentions *(List and Attach All Supporting Documents)* — Attachments? ☐ No ☐ Yes Number____

18. MANAGEMENT'S full, detailed statement of disputed facts and contentions *(List and Attach All Supporting Documents)* — Attachments? ☐ No ☐ Yes Number____

19. Remedy Requested/Offered

20. Disposition and Date *(Check one)* ☐ Resolved ☐ Withdrawn ☐ Not Resolved | Date of Formal Step A Meeting *(MM/DD/YYYY)*

21a. USPS Representative Name | 21b. Telephone No. *(Include Area Code)*

21c. USPS Representative Signature | 21d. Date *(MM/DD/YYYY)*

22a. NALC Representative Name | 22b. Telephone No. *(Include Area Code)*

22c. NALC Representative Signature | 22d. Date *(MM/DD/YYYY)*

PS Form 8190, August 2002 *(Page 1 of 2)*

While union–management relations trigger many or most of the obvious employment disputes, other personnel actions cause their share of disagreements. For example, an applicant believes the employer discriminated against him due to age; or an employee feels she would have been promoted had her boss not wanted to promote a man. Potential disputes like these are the reason why, as we saw in Chapter 4, more employers are requiring applicants to sign mandatory alternative dispute resolution forms as part of their applications.

Most firms, though, don't seem to be doing a very good job of managing disputes. For example, one recent survey in the United Kingdom found that:[67]

- 79% of respondents said disputes were not handled very well in most organizations,
- 65% agreed that emotions and personal pride affected their chances of reaching a solution, and
- 47% agreed that a personal dislike of the other side led them to expensive litigation.

Given the influence of personal emotions in resolving disputes, it's apparent that employers can't rely solely on traditional dispute resolution mechanisms like grievance procedures. Instead, it's preferable that disputes don't take root. Employers can do at least three things to help achieve this.

EMPHASIZE FAIRNESS First, as we discussed in Chapter 9, employers need policies that encourage employees to treat each other with *fairness and respect*. For example, many grievances stem from disciplinary matters. So, prior to disciplining someone, make sure the evidence supports the charge, protect the employees' due process rights, and warn the employee of the disciplinary consequences of his or her alleged misconduct.

CULTIVATE TRUST Second, whether dealing with disciplinary matters, grievances, or union negotiations, behave in a way that *fosters trust*. Behaviors that signal trustworthiness include:

- *Integrity*—honestly and truthfulness[68]
- *Competence*—technical and interpersonal knowledge and skills
- *Consistency*—reliability, predictability, and good judgment in handling situations
- *Loyalty*—willingness to protect and save face for a person
- *Openness*—willingness to share ideas and information freely[69]
- *Community*—willingly offer materials and resources to help the team move ahead
- *Respect*—recognize the strengths and abilities of others[70]
- *Cooperation*—behave cooperatively, and put oneself in the other person's position
- *Dependability*—partners "promise cautiously, and then keep their promises"

MANAGE INTERPERSONAL CONFLICT Third, when disagreements do arise, some *interpersonal conflict resolution approaches* are better than others. For example, having the parties meet to confront the facts and hammer out a solution is usually better than pushing problems under a rug. Yet there are times when letting things cool down is advisable.

In practice, people usually don't rely on a single conflict-resolution style; they use several simultaneously. A study of police sergeants and subordinates illustrates this. At least for these police sergeants, using three conflict resolution styles together—*problem solving* while being moderately *accommodating* and still maintaining a strong hand in *controlling* the conflict-resolution process—was an especially effective combination.

WHAT'S NEXT FOR UNIONS?

For years, construction trade unions in western New York State placed a huge inflatable rat balloon in front of construction sites that they were protesting. However, they recently gave up the rat and are now taking a more "business friendly approach." As the business manager for the local plumbers and steamfitters union put it, "our philosophy for the past 15 years hasn't created any more market share for us. We have been viewed as troublemakers. . . . Now we are going to use [public relations] to dispel those perceptions."[71]

Why the Union Decline?

5 Explain why union membership dropped, and what the prospects are for the union movement.

We saw early in this chapter that several factors contributed to the decline in union membership over the past 60 or so years. Unions traditionally appealed mostly to blue-collar workers, and the proportion of blue-collar jobs has been decreasing as service-sector and white-collar service jobs have increased. Furthermore, several economic factors, including intense international competition, have put unions under further pressure. Globalization increases competition, and competition increases pressures on employers to cut costs and boost productivity. This in turn puts unions in a squeeze. Other factors pressuring employers and unions include the deregulation of trucking, airlines, and communications; outdated equipment and factories; mismanagement; new technology; and laws (such as Title VII) that somewhat reduced the need for unions.

The effect of all this has been the permanent layoff of hundreds of thousands of union members, the permanent closing of company plants, the relocation of companies to nonunion settings (either in the United States or abroad), and mergers and acquisitions that eliminated union jobs and affected collective bargaining agreements. Union membership as a percent of people working has dropped by about two-thirds over 50 years. (Although the news is not all bleak. For one thing, union membership recently bumped up a bit.[72])

Card Check and Other New Union Tactics

Of course, unions are not sitting idly by and just watching their numbers dwindle, and the recent uptick may reflect their new tactics.[73] The priorities of the Change to Win Coalition (whose members broke off from the AFL-CIO) illustrate the new union strategies. They,

> Make it our first priority to help millions more workers form unions so we can build a strong movement for rewarding work in America [and] unite the strength of everyone who works in the same industry so we can negotiate with today's huge global corporations for everyone's benefit.[74]

In practice, this means several things. Change to Win will be very aggressive about trying to organize workers, will focus on organizing women and minority workers, will focus more on organizing temporary or contingent workers, and will target specific multinational companies for international campaigns.[75]

MORE AGGRESSIVE Unions are in fact becoming more aggressive. Unions are pushing Congress to pass the *Employee Free Choice Act*. This would make it easier for employees to unionize. Instead of secret-ballot elections, the act would institute a "card check" system. Here the union would win recognition when a majority of workers signed authorization cards saying they want the union. Several large companies, including Cingular Wireless, have already agreed to the card check process.[76] The act would also require binding arbitration to set a first contract's terms if the company and union can't negotiate an agreement within 120 days.[77] Unions are also using *class action lawsuits* to support employees in non-unionized companies, to pressure employers. For example, unions recently used class action lawsuits to support workers' claims under the Fair Labor Standards Act, and the Equal Pay Act.[78]

EXAMPLE The steps UNITE took against Cintas Corp. illustrate some unions' new tactics. In their effort against Cintas, UNITE (which later merged with another union to form UNITE HERE) didn't petition for an NLRB election. Instead, UNITE proposed using the card check process. They also filed a $100 million class action suit against the company. Then, Cintas workers in California filed a lawsuit claiming that the company was violating a nearby municipality's "living wage" law. UNITE then joined forces with the Teamsters union, which in turn began targeting Cintas' delivery people.[79]

COORDINATION Unions are becoming more proactive in terms of coordinating their efforts.[80] For example, consider what UNITE (the Union of Needletrades, Industrial and Textile Employees, now part of UNITE HERE) did. They used their "Voice at Work" campaign to coordinate 800 workers at one employer's distribution center with others at the employer's New York City headquarters and with local activists and international unions throughout Europe. This forced the employer's parent company, a French conglomerate, to cease resisting the union's organizing efforts. In its "Union Cities" campaigns, AFL-CIO planners work with local labor councils and individual unions to gain the support of a target city's elected officials. In Los Angeles, this helped the service workers' union organize janitors in that city.

COOPERATIVE ARRANGEMENTS Another, somewhat more risky (for the unions) approach is to agree to enter into more cooperative pacts with employers—for instance, working with them in developing team-based employee participation programs. About half of all collective bargaining agreements encourage cooperative labor–management relationships. *Cooperative clauses* cover things like joint committees to review drug problem, health care, and safety issues.[81]

A recent review of union research and literature provides some insight. The author says that unions "that have a cooperative relationship with management can play an important role in overcoming barriers to the effective adoption of practices that have been linked to organizational competitiveness."[82] However, she concludes that employers who want to capitalize on that potential need to change their way of thinking, avoiding adversarial industrial relations and emphasizing a cooperative partnership with their unions.

GLOBAL CAMPAIGNS Unions are also forcefully extending their reach overseas, as the Global Issues in HR feature illustrates.

GLOBAL ISSUES IN HR

Unions Go Global

Walmart, a company that traditionally works hard to prevent its stores from going union, recently had to agree to let the workers in its stores in China join unions. Walmart's China experience stems in part from efforts of global union campaigns by the Service Employees' International Union (SEIU). These campaigns reflect the belief, as SEIU puts it, that "huge global service sector companies routinely cross national borders and industry lines as they search for places where they can shift operations to exploit workers with the lowest possible pay and benefits . . . " SEIU is therefore strengthening its alliances with unions in other nations, with the goal of uniting workers in specific multinational companies and industries around the globe.[83] For example, SEIU recently worked with China's All China Federation of Trade Unions (ACFTU) to help the latter organize China's Walmart stores.[84] And recently, the United Steelworkers merged with the largest labor union in Britain to create "Workers Uniting" to better help the new union deal with multinational employers.[85] So, any company that thinks it can avoid unionization by sending jobs abroad may be in for a surprise.

REVIEW

SUMMARY

1. In addition to improved wages and working conditions, unions seek security when organizing. There are five possible arrangements, including the closed shop, the union shop, the agency shop, the preferential shop, and maintenance of membership.

2. The AFL-CIO is a national federation comprising about 100 national and international unions. It can exercise only the power it is allowed to exercise by its constituent national unions.

3. During the period of strong encouragement of unions, the Norris-LaGuardia Act and the Wagner Act were passed; these marked a shift in labor law from repression to strong encouragement of union activity. They did this by banning certain types of unfair labor practices, by providing for secret-ballot elections, and by creating the NLRB.

4. The Taft-Hartley Act reflected the period of modified encouragement coupled with regulation. It enumerated the rights of employees with respect to their unions, enumerated the rights of employers, and allowed the U.S. president to temporarily bar national emergency strikes. Among other things, it also enumerated certain union unfair labor practices. For example, it banned unions from restraining or coercing employees from exercising their guaranteed bargaining rights. And employers were explicitly given the right to express their views concerning union organization.

5. The Landrum-Griffin Act reflected the period of detailed regulation of internal union affairs. It grew out of discoveries of wrongdoing on the part of both management and union leadership and contained a bill of rights for union members. (For example, it affirms a member's right to sue his or her union.)

6. There are five steps in a union drive and election: the initial contact, obtaining authorization cards, holding a hearing with the NLRB, the campaign, and the election itself. Remember that the union need only win a majority of the votes cast, *not* a majority of the workers in the bargaining unit.

7. Bargaining collectively in good faith is the next step if and when the union wins the election. Good faith means that both parties communicate and negotiate, and that proposals are matched with counterproposals. Some hints on bargaining include do not hurry, be prepared, find out why, and be a good listener.

8. An impasse occurs when the parties aren't able to move further toward settlement. Third-party involvement—namely, arbitration, fact-finding, or mediation—is one alternative. Sometimes, though, a strike occurs. Responding to the strike involves such steps as shutting the facility, contracting out work, or possibly replacing the workers. Boycotts and lockouts are two other anti-impasse weapons sometimes used by labor and management.

9. Disputes are part of the bargaining process. Mediators, arbitrators, grievance processes, and negotiating are all important ways to manage and resolve disputes. Most firms, though, don't seem to be doing a very good job of managing disputes. Employers can do at least three other things to help reduce disputes. Employers need policies and practices that encourage employees to treat each other with fairness and respect, behave in a way that fosters trust, and, when disagreements do arise, some *interpersonal conflict resolution approaches* are better than others.

10. Unions are not sitting idly by watching their numbers dwindle. For example, *Change to Win* will be very aggressive about trying to organize workers. Unions are pushing Congress to pass the *Employee Free Choice Act.* This would, among other things, make it more difficult for employers to inhibit workers from trying to form a union. Unions are also using *class action lawsuits* to support employees in nonunionized companies, so as to pressure employers. And unions are becoming more proactive in terms of *coordinating their efforts.*

KEY TERMS

closed shop   285
union shop   285
agency shop   285
preferential shop   285
right to work   285
Norris-LaGuardia Act   286
Wagner Act   286
National Labor Relations Board (NLRB)   286
Taft-Hartley Act   287
national emergency strikes   288
Landrum-Griffin Act   288
union salting   290
authorization cards   291
bargaining unit   292

collective bargaining   295
good-faith bargaining   295
voluntary (permissible) bargaining items   296
illegal bargaining items   296
mandatory bargaining items   296
mediation   298
fact-finder   298
arbitration   298
economic strike   300
unfair labor practice strike   300
wildcat strike   300
sympathy strike   300
boycott   300
lockout   301

DISCUSSION QUESTIONS

1. Briefly describe the history and structure of the U.S. union movement.
2. Discuss the nature of the major federal labor relations laws.
3. Explain in detail each step in a union drive and election.
4. Discuss the main steps in the collective bargaining process.
5. Explain why union membership dropped, and what the prospects are for the union movement.
6. Why do employees join unions? What are the advantages and disadvantages of being a union member?
7. What actions might make employers lose elections?
8. Describe important tactics you would expect the union to use during the union drive and election.
9. Briefly illustrate how labor law has gone through a cycle of repression and encouragement.
10. What is meant by good-faith bargaining? Using examples, explain when bargaining is not in good faith.
11. Define impasse, mediation, and strike, and explain the techniques that are used to overcome an impasse.

INDIVIDUAL AND GROUP ACTIVITIES

1. You are the manager of a small manufacturing plant. The union contract covering most of your employees is about to expire. Working individually or in groups, discuss how to prepare for union contract negotiations.
2. Working individually or in groups, use Internet resources to find situations where company management and the union reached an impasse at some point during their negotiation process, but eventually resolved the impasse. Describe the issues on both sides that led to the impasse. How did they move past the impasse? What were the final outcomes?
3. Several years ago, 8,000 Amtrak workers agreed not to disrupt service by walking out, at least not until a court hearing was held. Amtrak had asked the courts for a temporary restraining order, and the Transport Workers Union of America was actually pleased to postpone its walkout. The workers were apparently not upset at Amtrak, but at Congress, for failing to provide enough funding for Amtrak. What, if anything, can an employer do when employees threaten to go on strike, not because of what the employer did, but because of what a third party—in this case, Congress—has done or not done? What laws would prevent the union from going on strike in this case?

WEB-e's (WEB EXERCISES)

1. We saw that the U.S. Department of Labor's National Labor Relations Board (NLRB) accused Starbucks of breaking the law in trying to prevent workers in some of its New York shops from unionizing. Use sites such as www.nlrb.gov/shared_files/Board%20Decisions/354/v354 99.pdf to explain how the suit finally ended up.

2. The Kaiser Permanente Health System is often held out as an employer with very good labor relations. What can you discern from Web sites such as www.kaiserpermanent ejobs.org/jobs.aspx that might explain such a reputation?

3. What does www.seiu.org/ tell you about this union's aims and how they intend to achieve them?

APPLICATION EXERCISES

HR IN ACTION CASE INCIDENT 1

Negotiating with the Writers Guild of America

The talks between the Writers Guild of America (WGA) and the Alliance of Motion Picture & Television Producers (producers) started off tense in 2007, and then got tenser. In their first meeting, the two sides got nothing done. As *Law & Order* producer Dick Wolf said, "everyone in the room is concerned about this."[86]

The two sides were far apart on just about all the issues. However, the biggest issue was how to split revenue from new media, such as when television shows move on to CDs or the Internet. The producers said they wanted a profit-splitting system rather than the current residual system. Under the residual system, writers continue to receive "residuals," or income from shows they write, every time they're shown (such as when *Seinfeld* appears in reruns, years after the last original show was shot). Writers Guild executives did their homework. They argued, for instance, that the projections showed producers' revenues from advertising and subscription fees jumped by about 40% between 2002 and 2006.[87] Writers wanted part of that.

The situation grew more tense. After the first few meetings, one producers' representative said, "We can see after the dogfight whose position will win out. The open question there, of course, is whether each of us take several lumps at the table, reaches an agreement then licks their wounds later—none the worse for wear—or whether we inflict more lasting damage through work stoppages that benefit no one before we come to an agreement."[88] Even after meeting six times, it seemed that, "the parties' only apparent area of agreement is that no real bargaining has yet to occur."[89]

In October 2007, the Writers Guild asked its members for strike authorization, and the producers were claiming that the Guild was just trying to delay negotiations until the current contract expired (at the end of October). As the president of the television producers association said, "We have had six across the table sessions and there was only silence and stonewalling from the WGA leadership. . . . We have attempted to engage on major issues, but no dialogue has been forthcoming from the WGA leadership. . . . The WGA leadership apparently has no intention to bargain in good faith."[90] As evidence, the producers claimed that the WGA negotiating committee left one meeting after less than an hour at the bargaining table.

Both sides knew timing in these negotiations was very important. During the fall and spring, television series production is in full swing. So, a strike now by the writers would have a bigger impact than waiting until, say, the summer to strike. Perhaps not surprisingly, by January 2008 some movement was discernible. In a separate set of negotiations, the Directors Guild of America reached an agreement with the producers that addressed many of the issues that the writers were focusing on, such as how to divide up the new media income.[91] In February 2008, the WGA and producers finally reached agreement. The new contract was "the direct result of renewed negotiations between the two sides, which culminated Friday with a marathon session including top WGA officials and the heads of the Walt Disney Co. and News Corp."[92]

Questions

1. The producers said the WGA was not bargaining in good faith. What did they mean by that, and do you think the evidence is sufficient to support the claim?

2. The WGA did eventually strike. What tactics could the producers have used to fight back once the strike began? What tactics do you think the WGA used?

3. This was basically a conflict between professional and creative people (the WGA) and TV and movie producers. Do you think the conflict was therefore different in any way than are the conflicts between, say, the auto workers or teamsters unions against auto and trucking companies? Why?

4. What role did negotiating skills seem to play in the WGA–producers negotiations? Provide examples.

HR IN ACTION CASE INCIDENT 2
Carter Cleaning Company: The Grievance

On visiting one of Carter Cleaning Company's stores, Jennifer was surprised to be taken aside by a long-term Carter employee, who met her as she was parking her car. "Murray (the store manager) told me I was suspended for two days without pay because I came in late last Thursday," said George. "I'm really upset, but around here the store manager's word seems to be law, and it sometimes seems like the only way anyone can file a grievance is by meeting you or your father like this in the parking lot." Jennifer was very disturbed by this revelation and promised the employee she would look into it and discuss the situation with her father. In the car heading back to headquarters she began mulling over what Carter Cleaning Company's alternatives might be.

Questions

1. Do you think it is important for Carter Cleaning Company to have a formal grievance process? Why or why not?
2. Based on what you know about the Carter Cleaning Company, outline the steps in what you think would be the ideal grievance process for this company.
3. In addition to the grievance process, can you think of anything else that Carter Cleaning Company might do to make sure that grievances and gripes like this one get expressed and also get heard by top management?

EXPERIENTIAL EXERCISE

An Organizing Question on Campus[93]

Purpose: The purpose of this exercise is to give you practice in dealing with some of the elements of a union organizing campaign.

Required Understanding: You should be familiar with the material covered in this chapter, as well as the following incident.

Art Tipton is a human resources director of Pierce University, a private university located in a large urban city. Ruth Ann Zimmer, a supervisor in the maintenance and housekeeping services division of the university, has just come into his office to discuss her situation. Zimmer's division of the university is responsible for maintaining and cleaning physical facilities of the university. Zimmer is one of the department supervisors who supervise employees who maintain and clean on-campus dormitories.

In the next several minutes, Zimmer proceeds to express her concerns about a union-organizing campaign that has begun among her employees. According to Zimmer, a representative of the Service Workers Union has met with a number of the employees, urging them to sign union authorization cards. She has observed several of her employees "cornering" other employees to talk to them about joining the union and urge them to sign union authorization (or representation) cards. Zimmer even observed this during the working hours as employees were going about their normal duties in the dormitories. Zimmer says a number of employees have asked her for her opinions about the union. They reported to her that several other supervisors in the department had told their employees

not to sign any union authorization cards and not to talk about the union at any time while they were on campus. Zimmer also reports that one of her fellow supervisors told his employees in a meeting that anyone who was caught talking about the union or signing a union authorization card would be disciplined and perhaps terminated.

Zimmer says that the employees are very dissatisfied with their wages and many of the conditions that they have endured from students, supervisors, and other staff people. She says that several employees told her that they had signed union cards because they believed that the only way university administration would pay attention to their concerns was if the employees had a union to represent them. Zimmer says that she made a list of employees whom she felt had joined or were interested in the union, and she could share these with Tipton if he wanted to deal with them personally. Zimmer closes with the comment that she and other department supervisors need to know what they should do in order to stomp out the threat of unionization in their department.

How to Set Up the Exercise/Instructions: Divide the class into groups of four or five students. Assume that you are labor relations consultants retained by the college to identify the problems and issues involved and to advise Art Tipton about what to do next. Each group will spend about 45 minutes discussing the issues and outlining those issues as well as an action plan for Tipton. What should he do now?

If time permits, a spokesperson from each group should list on the board the issues involved and the group's recommendations.

BUSINESS IN ACTION EDU-EXERCISE

Building Your *Social Responsibility* Knowledge

To some degree, the issue of how influential unions should be boils down to what you believe about corporate social responsibility. *Corporate social responsibility* refers to the extent to which companies should and do take steps to improve members of society other than the firm's owners.

Corporate social responsibility advocates say there must be a balance between what a business takes from society and what it gives back. Socially responsible behavior might include creating jobs for minorities, paying a "fair day's wage," controlling pollution, or taking employees' needs into account when contemplating closing a plant. In deciding whether to close the plant, for instance, do you just do what's best for the owners (cut costs)? Or do you try to help your employees keep their jobs? Unions, as we've seen, emerged at least in part to provide a way to ensure that managers didn't just consider the owners' needs.

The topic of social responsibility provokes lively debate. Many perfectly ethical people believe that a company's only social responsibility is to its stockholders. Others disagree.

The classical view is that a corporation's main purpose is to maximize profits for stockholders. This view is most notably associated with economist Milton Friedman. Basically, he said that the only social responsibility of a business is to increase its profits, so long as it stays within the rules of the game (in terms of complying with the law, for instance). He argued that all society would gain if businesspeople made their companies as competitive as possible. (For example, how long could employees expect to keep their jobs if a company was less competitive than the one down the road?)

An opposing view is that business has a social responsibility to serve all the corporate stakeholders affected by its business decisions. A corporate stakeholder is anyone who is vital to a business' success. Experts in this area traditionally identify six stakeholder groups: stockholders (owners), employees, customers, suppliers, managers, and the local community. Stakeholder advocates would say top managers can't just close a plant because it's good for the owners; they must take the employees' (and community's) welfare into account (even if it means higher production costs).

So, to some extent, the whole history of labor legislation in the United States reflects (to oversimplify things) pressures from managerial capitalism advocates versus stakeholder advocates. Undoubtedly, even many managerial capitalists looked at the maltreatment some employees were suffering and willingly backed pro-union legislation. But, as we said, unions (and pro-labor laws) emerged at least in part to provide a way to ensure that managers didn't just consider the owners' needs.

Questions

1. Use the Internet to find evidence in union Web sites of the social responsibility aspects of their efforts to unionize employees.
2. Make the case (whether you agree or not) that managerial capitalism is such a powerful notion that unions should in fact be marginalized. Then make the opposite case—that even if managerial capitalism should prevail, society needs unions.

PERSONAL COMPETENCIES EDU-EXERCISE

Building Your *Negotiating* Skills

Hammering out a satisfactory labor agreement requires negotiating skills. Experienced negotiators use *leverage, desire, time, competition, information, credibility,* and *judgment* to improve their bargaining positions. *Leverage* means using factors that help or hinder the negotiator, usually by putting the other side under pressure.[94] Things you can leverage include *necessity, desire, competition,* and *time.* For example, the union knows that an employer who needs to fill a big order fast (time) is at a disadvantage. Being able to walk away (or to look like you can) wins the best terms.

Similarly, some contract terms (such as reduced pension benefits) may be crucial. However, the employer who makes its *desires* too obvious undercuts his or her position. *Competition* is important too. There is no more convincing ploy than subtly hinting you've got an alternative (like shifting services abroad). *Time* (and particularly your deadlines) can also tilt things for or against you.

Also, as we said, "knowledge is power" when you're negotiating. Having information about the other side and about the situation puts you at an advantage. And, the other side will be trying to decide if you're bluffing, so *credibility* is important. Finally, good negotiators need *judgment:* the ability to "strike the right balance between gaining advantages and reaching compromises, in the substance as well as in the style of [their] negotiating technique."[95]

One expert says that negotiators typically make several big mistakes. Here's what he suggests to avoid them:[96]

- *Neglecting the other side's problems* As in all communication, negotiations usually go best when they produce a common basis of understanding—each party is "on the same page" in terms of understanding each others' point of view. Good negotiators therefore strive to understand the other person's concerns and point of view.

- *Letting price overwhelm other issues* Most of the labor agreement's elements probably come down to price, but don't neglect nonfinancial issues. Things like working conditions and disciplinary procedures may be as important as purely financial issues.

- *Neglecting BANTRA* Robert Fisher, Billy Urey, and Bruce Patton stress the importance of knowing your "best alternative to a negotiated agreement" (BANTRA). For example, the best alternative may be *not* getting an agreement now, but walking away and letting the other side face its constituents' pressures.

Questions

1. Explain with specifics how you would use these negotiating techniques to get a better price when buying a used car.
2. Use the Internet to find out more about an actual union–management bargaining situation (such as the Writers' Guild we present in the case on page 308). Then list specific negotiating strategies each side seems to have taken.

ENDNOTES

1. Steven Greenhouse, "Board Accuses Starbucks of Trying to Block Union," *New York Times* (April 3, 2007): B2; www.starbucksunion.org/, accessed March 25, 2009.
2. www.bls.gov/news.release/union2.nr0.htm, accessed April 2, 2009.
3. Ibid.; "Union Membership Rises," *Compensation & Benefits Review* (May/June 2008): 9 .
4. Joseph Adler, "The Past as Prologue? A Brief History of the Labor Movement in the United States," *International Personnel Management Association for HR* 35, no. 4 (Winter 2006): 311–329.
5. Stephen Greenhouse, "Most US Union Members Are Working for the Government, New Data Shows," *New York Times* (January 23, 2010): B1–B5.
6. Ibid.
7. www.bls.gov/news.release/union2.nr0.htm, accessed April 2, 2009.
8. Michael Ash and Jean Seago, "The Effect of Registered Nurses' Unions on Heart Attack Mortality," *Industrial and Labor Relations Review* 57, no. 3 (April 2004): 422–442.
9. Steven Abraham et al., "The Impact of Union Membership on Intent to Leave," *Employee Responsibilities and Rights* 17, no. 4 (2005): 21–23.
10. Paul Monies, "Unions Hit Hard by Job Losses, Right to Work," *The Daily Oklahoman* (via Knight Ridder/Tribune Business News) (February 1, 2005), www.accessmylibrary.com/article-1G1-127994772/unions-hithard-job.html, accessed August 11, 2009.
11. Ann Zimmerman, "Pro-Union Butchers at Wal-Mart Win a Union Battle but Lose War," *Wall Street Journal* (April 11, 2000): A14. See also Steven Greenhouse, "Report Assails Wal-Mart Over Unions," *The New York Times* (May 1, 2007): C3.
12. Donna Buttigieg et al., "An Event History Analysis of Union Joining and Leaving," *Journal of Applied Psychology* 92, no. 3 (2007): 829–839.
13. Ibid., 836. See also Lois Tetrick et al., "A Model of Union Participation: The Impact of Perceived Union Support, Union Instrumentality, and Union Loyalty," *Journal of Applied Psychology* 92, no. 3 (2007): 820–828.
14. Robert Grossman, "Unions Follow Suit," *HR Magazine* (May 2005): 49.
15. Kris Maher, "The New Union Worker," *Wall Street Journal* (September 27, 2005): B1, B11.
16. Arthur Sloane and Fred Witney, *Labor Relations* (Upper Saddle River, NJ: Prentice Hall, 2007): 335–336.
17. Benjamin Taylor and Fred Witney, *Labor Relations Law* (Upper Saddle River, NJ: Prentice Hall, 1992): 170–171.
18. www.dol.gov/whd/state/righttowork.htm, accessed February 13, 2010. Indiana's law applies only to school teachers; without Indiana there are 22 right-to-work states.
19. "Unions Hit Hard by Job Losses, Right to Work," *The Daily Oklahoman* (via Knight Ridder/Tribune Business News) (February 1, 2005). See also www.dol.gov/esa/programs/whd/ state/righttowork.htm, accessed January 13, 2008.
20. Steven Greenhouse, "Union Rejoining AFL-CIO," *New York Times* (September 18, 2009): A18.
21. The following material is based on Arthur Sloane and Fred Witney, *Labor Relations* (Upper Saddle River, NJ: Prentice Hall, 2007): 83–132. See also http://history.eserver.org/us-labor-law.txt, accessed April 26, 2008.
22. Sloane and Witney, op. cit., 106.
23. Karen Robinson, "Temp Workers Gain Union Access," *HR News, Society for Human Resource Management* 19, no. 10 (October 2000): 1.
24. See www.nlrb.gov/workplace_rights/nlra_violations.aspx, accessed January 14, 2008.
25. Michael Carrell and Christina Heavrin, *Labor Relations and Collective Bargaining* (Upper Saddle River, NJ: Pearson, 2004): 180.
26. Ibid., 179.
27. Arthur Sloane and Fred Witney, *Labor Relations* (Upper Saddle River, NJ: Prentice Hall, 2007): 102–106.
28. William Fulmer, "Step by Step Through a Union Election," *Harvard Business Review* 60 (July/August 1981): 94–102. For an example of what to expect, see Edward Young and William Levy, "Responding to a Union-Organizing Campaign: Do You and Your Supervisors Know the Legal Boundaries in a Union Campaign?" *Franchising World* 39, no. 3 (March 2007): 45–49.
29. Cathie Sheffield-Thompson, "Web Resources and Techniques for Organizing and Membership Development," 2006 Higher Ed State Staff Training, December 7–9, 2006. NEA Research, csheffield@nea.org.
30. Ibid.
31. John Logan, "The Union Avoidance Industry in the United States," *British Journal of Industrial Relations* 44, no. 4 (December 2006): 651–675.
32. Arthur Sloane and Fred Witney, *Labor Relations* (Upper Saddle River, NJ: Prentice Hall, 2007): 28.

33. Jonathan Segal, "Expose the Union's Underbelly," *HR Magazine* (June 1999): 166–176.

34. "Some Say Salting Leaves Bitter Taste for Employers," *BNA Bulletin to Management* (March 4, 2004): 79; www.nlrb.gov/global/search/index.aspx?mode=s&qt=salting&col=nlrb&gb=y, accessed January 14, 2008.

35. Gary Chaison, "Information Technology: The Threat to Unions," *Journal of Labor Research* 23, no. 2 (Spring 2002): 249–260.

36. www.starbucksunion.org, accessed January 14, 2008.

37. William Fulmer, "Step by Step Through a Union Election," *Harvard Business Review* 60 (July/August 1981): 94.

38. Frederick Sullivan, "Limiting Union Organizing Activity Through Supervisors," *Personnel* 55 (July/August 1978): 55–65. Richard Peterson, Thomas Lee, and Barbara Finnegan, "Strategies and Tactics in Union Organizing Campaigns," *Industrial Relations* 31, no. 2 (Spring 1992): 370–381. See also Edward Young and William Levy, "Responding to a Union-Organizing Campaign: Do You and Your Supervisors Know the Legal Boundaries in a Union Campaign?" *Franchising World* 39, no. 3 (March 2007): 45–49. Some labor lawyers report an increase in the use by unions of corporate campaigns. Janet Walthall, "Unions Increasingly Using Corporate Campaigns," *BNA Bulletin to Management* (February 16, 2010): 55.

39. Michael Carrell and Christina Heavrin, *Labor Relations and Collective Bargaining* (Upper Saddle River, NJ: Pearson, 2004): 166.

40. Ibid., 167–168.

41. Doug Cahn, "Reebok Takes the Sweat Out of Sweatshops," *Business Ethics* 14, no. 1 (January 2000): 9; Mei Fong and Kris Maher, "U.S. Labor Chief Moves into China," *Wall Street Journal Asia* (June 22–24, 2007): 1.

42. Jonathon Segal, "Unshackle Your Supervisors to Stay Union Free," *HR Magazine*, June 1998, pp. 62–65. See also www.nlrb.gov/workplace_rights/nlra_violations.aspx, accessed January 14, 2008.

43. B&D Plastics, Inc. 302 NLRB No. 33, 1971, 137 LRRM 1039; discussed in "No Such Thing as a Free Lunch," *BNA Bulletin to Management* (May 23, 1991): 153–154.

44. Edwin Arnold et al., "Determinants of Certification Election Outcomes in the Service Sector," *Labor Studies Journal* 25, no. 3 (Fall 2000): 51.

45. "2008 Union Win Rate Rose to 66.8%; Number of Elections Increased, Data Show," *BNA Bulletin to Management* (May 12, 2009): 145–152.

46. Clyde Scott and Edwin Arnold, "Deauthorization and Decertification Elections: An Analysis and Comparison of Results," *Working USA* 7, no. 3 (Winter 2003): 6–20; www.nlrb.gov/nlrb/shared_files/brochures/rpt_september2002.pdf, accessed January 14, 2008.

47. Michael Carrell and Christina Heavrin, *Labor Relations and Collective Bargaining* (Upper Saddle River, NJ: Pearson, 2004): 120–121.

48. www.nlrb.gov/nlrb/shared_files/brochures/basicguide.pdf, accessed January 14, 2008.

49. Terry Leap, *Collective Bargaining and Labor Relations* (Upper Saddle River, NJ: Prentice Hall, 1995). See also www.nlrb.gov/nlrb/shared_files/brochures/basicguide.pdf, accessed January 14, 2008.

50. Leap, op. cit., 307–309.

51. Ibid., 308.

52. Kathryn Tyler, "Good-Faith Bargaining," *HR Magazine* (January 2005): 52.

53. Bargaining items based on Reed Richardson, *Collective Bargaining by Objectives* (Upper Saddle River, NJ: Prentice Hall, 1997): 113–115; see also Arthur Sloane and Fred Witney, *Labor Relations* (Upper Saddle River, NJ: Prentice Hall, 2007): 180–217.

54. Sloane and Witney, *Labor Relations*, 192–220.

55. From Reed Richardson, *Collective Bargaining by Objectives* (Upper Saddle River, NJ: Prentice Hall, 1977): 150.

56. D. Scott DeRue et al., "When Is Straightforwardness a Liability in Negotiations? The Role of Integrative Potential and Structural Power," *Journal of Applied Psychology* 94, no. 4 (2009): 1032–1047.

57. www.thedeal.com/corporatedealmaker/2009/11/us_airways_pilots_seek_federal.php, accessed November 17, 2009.

58. John Burger and Steven Walters, "Arbitrator Bias and Self-Interest: Lessons from the Baseball Labor Market," *Journal of Labor Research* 26, no. 2 (Spring 2005): 267–280.

59. Jonathan Kramer and Thomas Hyclak, "Why Strikes Occur: Evidence from the Capital Markets," *Industrial Relations* 41, no. 1 (January 2002): 80–93.

60. Micheline Maynard and Jeremey Peters, "Northwest Airlines Threatens to Replace Strikers Permanently," *New York Times* (August 26, 2005): C3.

61. Melanie Evans, "Labor Pains: As Membership Slides, Unions Have Turned to Provocative Corporate Campaigns," *Modern Health Care* 34, no. 26 (December 6, 2004): 26.

62. Arthur Sloane and Fred Witney, *Labor Relations* (Upper Saddle River, NJ: Prentice Hall, 2007): 84.

63. http://sports.espn.go.com/nfl/news/story?id=4508545, accessed November 17, 2009.

64. Duncan Adams, "Worker Grievances Consume Roanoke, VA, Mail Distribution Center," Knight-Ridder/Tribune Business News (March 27, 2001), item 1086009.

65. See, for example, "Top Ten Practical Tips to Achieving the Best Result through Timely Dispute Resolution," *Mondaq Business Briefing* (October 15, 2007).

66. Walter Baer, *Grievance Handling: 101 Guides for Supervisors* (New York: American Management Association, 1970).

67. "Ongoing Problem of Dispute Resolution," 117 *Personnel Today* (November 13, 2007).

68. Steven Robbins, *Organizational Behavior* (Upper Saddle River, NJ: Prentice Hall, 1998).

69. Ibid., 294.

70. The following is adapted from Eileen Aranda et al., *Teams: Structure, Process, Culture, and Politics* (Upper Saddle River, NJ: Prentice Hall, 1998): 116–117.

71. Jessica Marquez, "NY Unions Cage Inflatable Rat, Try Teamwork," *Workforce Management* (November 3, 2008): 10.

72. www.bls.gov/news.release/union2.nr0.htm, accessed April 2, 2009.

73. See, for example, Jo Blandon et al., "Have Unions Turned the Corner? New Evidence on Recent Trends in Union Recognition in UK Firms," *British Journal of Industrial Relations* 44, no. 2 (June 2006): 169–190.

74. Jennifer Schramm, "The Future of Unions," *Society for Human Resource Management, Workplace Visions* 4 (2005): 1–8.

75. Ibid. See also www.changetowin.org/about-us.html, accessed February 13, 2010.

76. "The Limits of Solidarity," *The Economist* (September 23, 2006): 34.

77. Chris Maher, "Specter Won't Support Union-Backed Bill," *Wall Street Journal* (March 25, 2009): A3.

78. "Unions Using Class Actions to Pressure Nonunion Companies," *BNA Bulletin to Management* (August 22, 2006): 271. Some believe that today, "long-term observers see more bark than bite in organized labors efforts to revitalize." See, for example, Robert Grossman, "We Organized Labor and Code," *HR Magazine* (January 2008): 37–40.

79. Andy Meisler, "Who Will Fold First?" *Workforce Management,* January 2004, 28–38.

80. Dean Scott, "Unions Still a Potent Force," *Kiplinger Business Forecasts* (March 26, 2003).

81. "Contracts Call for Greater Labor Management Teamwork," *BNA Bulletin to Management* (April 29, 1999): 133. See also Mark Schoeff Jr., "Labor on the March," *Workforce Management* (February 2010): 1, 18–19.

82. Carol Gill, "Union Impact on the Effective Adoption of High Performance Work Practices," *Human Resource Management Review* 19 (2009): 39–50.

83. Jennifer Schramm, "The Future of Unions," *Society for Human Resource Management, Workplace Visions*, no. 4 (2005): 6.

84. Mei Fong and Kris Maher, "US Labor Chief Moves into China," *Wall Street Journal Asia* (June 22–24, 2007): 1.

85. Steven Greenhouse, "Steelworkers Merge with British Union," *New York Times* (July 3, 2008): C4.

86. Chris Purcell, "Rhetoric Flying in WGA Talks," *Television Week* 26, no. 30 (July 23–30, 2007): 3, 35.

87. Ibid.

88. Ibid.

89. James Hibberd, "Guild Talks Break with No Progress," *Television Week* 26, no. 38 (October 8–15, 2007): 1, 30.

90. Ibid.

91. "DGA Deal Sets the Stage for Writers," *Television Week* 27, no. 3 (Jan 21, 2008): 3, 33.

92. "WGA, Studios Reach Tentative Agreement," *UPI News Track* (February 3, 2008).

93. Raymond L. Hilgert and Cyril C. Ling, *Cases and Experiential Exercises in Human Resource Management* (Upper Saddle River, NJ: Prentice Hall, 1996): 291–292.

94. These are based on James C Freund, *Smart Negotiating* (New York: Simon & Schuster, 1992): 42–46.

95. Ibid., 33.

96. James Sebenius, "Six Habits of Merely Effective Negotiators," *Harvard Business Review* (April 2001): 87–95.

11 Improving Occupational Safety, Health, and Security

Source: Phil Masturzo/AP Wide World Photos.

When you finish studying this chapter, you should be able to:

1. Discuss OSHA and how it operates.
2. Explain in detail three basic causes of accidents.
3. Explain how to prevent accidents at work.
4. Discuss major health problems at work and how to remedy them.

INTRODUCTION

It must have been a frightening way to die. The worker, 30 years old, "suffocated when the tumbling dirt and debris rose to his chest, creating pressure so great that he could not breathe, even though his head remained uncovered." Other workers had warned the owner of the Brooklyn construction site that the trench was an accident waiting to happen. He allegedly did nothing about it. The prosecutor subsequently charged the owner with manslaughter.[1] ■

EMPLOYEE SAFETY AND HEALTH: AN INTRODUCTION

Why Employee Safety and Health Are Important

Ten men died when BP's Deepwater Horizon rig exploded in April 2010.

Providing a safe work environment is important for several reasons, one of which is the staggering number of work-related accidents. For example, in one recent year, about 5,000 U.S. workers died in workplace incidents. The U.S. Department of Labor reports that over 3.8 million occupational injuries and illnesses result from accidents at work—that's roughly 4.4 cases per 100 full-time U.S. workers per year.[2] And these figures may underestimate the actual numbers by two or three times (due to underreporting employers).[3]

Accidents are also expensive. For example, the health care costs of a forklift accident might be $4,500. However, the indirect costs for things like forklift damage and lost production time could raise the bill to $18,000 or more.[4] And the cost to the worker and his or her family in psychological terms may be many times greater.

Dangerous workplaces aren't limited to manufacturing. For example, knives, hot surfaces, and slippery floors bedevil commercial kitchens. In restaurants, slips and falls account for about a third of all worker injury cases. Employers could eliminate most of these by requiring slip-resistant shoes.[5]

A Manager's Briefing on Occupational Law

Congress passed the **Occupational Safety and Health Act of 1970**[6] "to assure so far as possible every working man and woman in the nation safe and healthful working conditions and to preserve our human resources." The act covers most employers. The main employers it doesn't cover are self-employed persons, farms employing only the employer's immediate family members, and certain workplaces protected by other federal agencies or statutes. The act covers federal agencies. It usually doesn't apply to state and local governments in their role as employers.

The act created the **Occupational Safety and Health Administration (OSHA)** within the Department of Labor. OSHA's basic purpose is to administer the act and to set and enforce the safety and health standards that apply to almost all workers in the United States. Recently, OSHA had about 2,150 employees, including 1,100 inspectors working from branch offices throughout the country.[7] With a limited number of inspectors, OSHA recently has focused on fair and effective enforcement, combined with outreach, education, and compliance assistance, and various OSHA-employer cooperative programs.[8]

OSHA STANDARDS OSHA operates under the "general duty clause," that each employer:

> shall furnish to each of his [or her] employees employment and a place of employment which are free from recognized hazards that are causing or are likely to cause death or serious physical harm to his [or her] employees.

To carry out this basic mission, OSHA is responsible for promulgating legally enforceable standards. The standards are very complete and cover just about every conceivable hazard, in detail. Figure 11.1 shows a small part of the standard governing handrails for scaffolds.

OSHA RECORD-KEEPING PROCEDURES Under OSHA, employers with 11 or more employees must maintain a record of, and report, occupational injuries and occupational illnesses.

Occupational Safety and Health Act of 1970
The law passed by Congress in 1970 "to assure so far as possible every working man and woman in the nation safe and healthful working conditions and to preserve our human resources."

Occupational Safety and Health Administration (OSHA)
The agency created within the Department of Labor to set safety and health standards for almost all workers in the United States.

---

1 Discuss OSHA and how it operates.

FIGURE 11.1

OSHA Standards Example

Source: www.osha.gov/pls/oshaweb/owadisp.show_document?p_id=9720&p_table=STANDARDS, accessed May 25, 2007.

Guardrails not less than 2" × 4" or the equivalent and not less than 36" or more than 42" high, with a midrail, when required, of a 1" × 4" lumber or equivalent, and toeboards, shall be installed at all open sides on all scaffolds more than 10 feet above the ground or floor. Toeboards shall be a minimum of 4" in height. Wire mesh shall be installed in accordance with paragraph [a] [17] of this section.

An *occupational illness* is any abnormal condition or disorder caused by exposure to environmental factors associated with employment. This includes acute and chronic illnesses caused by inhalation, absorption, ingestion, or direct contact with toxic substances or harmful agents.

As summarized in Figure 11.2, employers must report all occupational illnesses.[9] They must also report most occupational injuries, specifically those that result in medical treatment (other than first aid), loss of consciousness, restriction of work (1 or more lost workdays), restriction of motion, or transfer to another job.[10] If an on-the-job accident results in the death of an employee or in the hospitalization of five or more employees, all employers, regardless of size, must report the accident to the nearest OSHA office.

OSHA's latest record-keeping rules streamline the job of reporting occupational injuries or illnesses. The rules continue to presume that an injury or work illness that resulted from an event in or exposure to the work environment is work related. However, it allows the employer to conclude that the event was not job related (and needn't be reported) if the facts so warrant— such as if a worker breaks a wrist after catching his leg on his car's bumper when parked on the company lot.

Inspections and Citations

OSHA enforces its standards through inspections and (if necessary) citations. The inspection is usually unannounced. OSHA may not conduct warrantless inspections without an employer's consent. However, it may inspect after acquiring an authorized search warrant or its equivalent.[11] With a limited number of inspectors, OSHA recently has focused on "fair and effective enforcement," combined with outreach, education and compliance assistance,

FIGURE 11.2

What Accidents Must Be Reported under the Occupational Safety and Health Act (OSHA)?

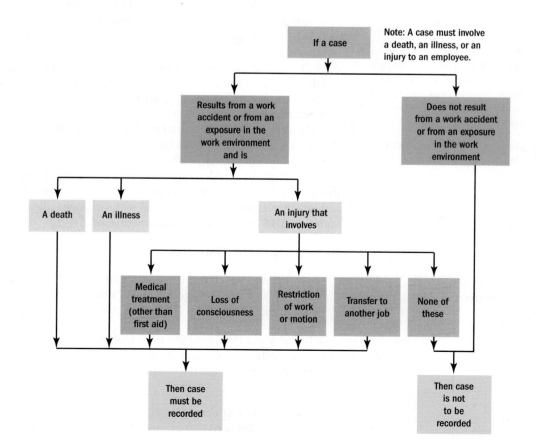

and various OSHA-employer cooperative programs (such as its "Voluntary Protection Programs").[12]

VOLUNTARY CONSULTATION With only about 1,000 inspectors, OSHA has tried to encourage cooperative safety programs rather than rely just on inspections and citations.[13] So, for example, OSHA provides free on-site safety and health services for small businesses. This service uses safety experts from state governments to provide safety consultations, usually at the employer's workplace. According to OSHA, this consultation program is separate from the OSHA inspection effort, and no citations are issued or penalties proposed.

The employer triggers this process by contacting the nearest OSHA Area Office to speak to the compliance assistance specialist about a voluntary consultation. When the president of one steel installation company in Colorado realized her workers' compensation costs were higher than her payroll, she joined with similar Colorado firms for help. At the group's request, OSHA helped draft new safety systems, created educational materials, and provided inspections that were more cooperative than adversarial. Accidents and workers' compensation costs subsequently dropped markedly.[14]

INSPECTION PRIORITIES However, OSHA still makes extensive use of inspections, taking a "worst-first" approach to setting priorities. Priorities include, from highest to lowest, imminent dangers, catastrophes and fatal accidents, employee complaints, high-hazard industries inspections, and follow-up inspections.[15] In one recent year, OSHA conducted just over 39,000 inspections. Of these, complaints or accidents prompted 9,176, about 21,500 were high-hazard targeted, and follow-ups and referrals prompted 8,415.[16]

THE INSPECTION OSHA inspectors look for violations of all types, but some potential problem areas—such as scaffolding, fall protection, and inadequate hazard communications— grab more of their attention. Figure 11.3 summarizes the most frequent OSHA serious violation areas.[17]

After the inspector submits the report to the local OSHA office, the area director determines what citations, if any, to issue. The **citations** inform the employer and employees of the regulations and standards that have been violated and of the time set for rectifying the problem.

citations
Summons informing employers and employees of the regulations and standards that have been violated in the workplace.

PENALTIES OSHA can also impose penalties. In general, OSHA calculates these based on the violation's gravity, but it also usually considers factors like the size of the business, the firm's compliance history, and the employer's good faith. Penalties generally range from $5,000 up to $70,000 for willful or repeat serious violations, although they can be far higher (occasionally, in

FIGURE 11.3

Safety Standards OSHA Cited for Penalties Most Frequently

Source: www.osha.gov/pls/imis/ citedstandard.sic?p_esize=&p_state=F EFederal&p_sic=all, accessed May 26, 2007.

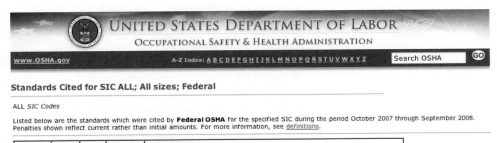

Standard	#Cited	#Insp	$Penalty	Description
Total	115044	29042	105224214	
19260451	10223	3962	9497057	General requirements.
19260501	7081	6422	9664000	Duty to have fall protection.
19101200	7061	3712	1808357	Hazard Communication.
19100147	4271	2262	4201860	The control of hazardous energy (lockout/tagout).
19100134	4187	1811	1662891	Respiratory Protection.
19100305	3484	2144	2050473	Wiring methods, components, and equipment for general use.
19100178	3427	2286	2826717	Powered industrial trucks.
19261053	3061	2270	1863798	Ladders.
19100212	2937	2414	3558430	General requirements for all machines.

Standards Cited for SIC ALL; All sizes; Federal

ALL *SIC Codes*

Listed below are the standards which were cited by **Federal OSHA** for the specified SIC during the period October 2007 through September 2008. Penalties shown reflect current rather than initial amounts. For more information, see definitions.

the millions). The OSHA Area Director may enter into settlement agreements that revise citations and penalties to avoid prolonged legal disputes. Therefore, many cases are settled before litigation. OSHA then issues the citation and agreed-on penalties simultaneously, after the employers initiate negotiation settlements.[18]

In practice, OSHA must have a final order from the independent Occupational Safety and Health Review Commission (OSHRC) to enforce a penalty. Although that appeals process is quicker now than in the past, an employer who files a notice of contest can still drag out an appeal for years.

Inspectors and their superiors don't look just for specific hazards but also for a comprehensive safety approach. For example, factors contributing to a firm's OSHA liability include lack of a systematic safety approach; sporadic or irregular safety meetings; a lack of responsiveness to safety audit recommendations; and failure to inspect the workplace regularly.[19]

Some employers understandably view OSHA inspections with some trepidation. However, the inspection tips in Figure 11.4—such as "check the inspector's credentials" and "accompany the inspector and take detailed notes"—can help ensure a smooth inspection.[20]

Responsibilities and Rights of Employers and Employees

Both employers and employees have responsibilities and rights under the Occupational Safety and Health Act. For example, employers are responsible for providing "a workplace free from recognized hazards," for being familiar with mandatory OSHA standards, and for examining workplace conditions to make sure they conform to applicable standards (see poster on page 319).

Employees also have rights and responsibilities, but OSHA can't cite them for violations of their responsibilities. They are responsible, for example, for complying with all applicable OSHA standards, for following all employer safety and health rules and regulations, and for reporting hazardous conditions to the supervisor. Employees have a right to demand safety and health on the job without fear of punishment. Employers are forbidden to punish or discriminate against workers who complain to OSHA about job safety and health hazards. However, employers must make "a diligent effort to discourage, by discipline if necessary, violations of safety rules by employees."[21]

FIGURE 11.4

OSHA Inspection Tips

Initial Contact

- Refer the inspector to your OSHA coordinator.
- Check the inspector's credentials.
- Ask the inspector why he or she is inspecting your workplace. Is it a complaint? Programmed visit? Fatality or accident follow-up? Imminent danger investigation?
- If the inspection is the result of a complaint, the inspector won't identify the complainant, but you are entitled to know whether the person is a current employee.
- Notify your OSHA counsel, who should review all requests from the inspector for documents and information. Your counsel also should review the documents and information you provide to the inspector.

Opening Conference

- Establish the focus and scope of the planned inspection: Does the inspector want to inspect the premises or simply study your records?
- Discuss the procedures for protecting trade-secret areas, conducting employee interviews, and producing documents.
- Show the inspector that you have safety programs in place. He or she may not go to the work floor if paperwork is complete and up-to-date.

Walk-Around Inspection

- Accompany the inspector and take detailed notes.
- If the inspector takes a photo or video, you should too.
- Ask the inspector for duplicates of all physical samples and copies of all test results.
- Be helpful and cooperative, but don't volunteer information.
- To the extent possible, immediately correct any violation the inspector identifies.

WHAT CAUSES ACCIDENTS?

2 Explain in detail three basic causes of accidents

Accidents occur for three main reasons: chance occurrences, unsafe working conditions, and unsafe acts by employees. Chance occurrences (such as walking in a park just as a tree branch falls) contribute to accidents but are more or less beyond management's control; we will therefore focus on unsafe conditions and unsafe acts.

Unsafe Working Conditions

Unsafe conditions are one main cause of accidents. These include obvious factors such as:

- Faulty scaffolds
- Improperly guarded equipment
- Frayed wiring
- Unsafe storage, such as overloading
- Improper illumination
- Improper ventilation

The basic remedy here is to eliminate or minimize the unsafe conditions. OSHA standards address potentially accident-causing mechanical and physical working conditions like these. The manager can also use a checklist of unsafe conditions, as in the HR in Practice feature that follows. The Environmental Health and Safety (EHS) magazine Web site (www.ehs.com) is another good source for safety, health, and industrial hygiene information.

Although accidents can occur anywhere, there are some high-danger zones. Many industrial accidents occur around forklift trucks, wheelbarrows, and other handling and lifting areas. The most serious accidents usually occur near metal and woodworking machines and saws, or around transmission machinery such as gears, pulleys, and flywheels.

HR IN PRACTICE

Checklist of Mechanical or Physical Accident-Causing Conditions[22]

I. GENERAL HOUSEKEEPING

- ☐ Adequate and wide aisles—no materials protruding into aisles
- ☐ Parts and tools stored safely after use—not left in hazardous positions that could cause them to fall
- ☐ Even and solid flooring—no defective floors or ramps that could cause falling or tripping accidents
- ☐ Waste and trash cans—safely located and not overfilled
- ☐ Material piled in safe manner—not too high or too close to sprinkler heads
- ☐ All work areas clean and dry
- ☐ All exit doors and aisles clean of obstructions
- ☐ Aisles kept clear and properly marked; no air lines or electric cords across aisles

II. MATERIAL HANDLING EQUIPMENT AND CONVEYANCES

On all conveyances, electric or hand, check to see that the following items are all in sound working condition:
- ☐ Brakes—properly adjusted
- ☐ Not too much play in steering wheel
- ☐ Warning device—in place and working
- ☐ Wheels—securely in place; properly inflated
- ☐ Fuel and oil—enough and right kind
- ☐ No loose parts

Cables, hooks, or chains—not worn or otherwise defective
Suspended chains or hooks
- ☐ Safety loaded
- ☐ Properly stored

III. LADDERS, SCAFFOLDS, BENCHES, STAIRWAYS, ETC.

The following items of major interest to be checked:
- ☐ Safety feet on straight ladders
- ☐ Guardrails or handrails
- ☐ Treads, not slippery
- ☐ No splintered, cracked, or rickety stairs
- ☐ Ladders properly stored

- ☐ Extension ladder ropes in good condition
- ☐ Toeboards

IV. POWER TOOLS (STATIONARY)

- ☐ Point of operation guarded
- ☐ Guards in proper adjustment
- ☐ Gears, belts, shafting, counterweights guarded
- ☐ Foot pedals guarded
- ☐ Brushes provided for cleaning machines
- ☐ Adequate lighting
- ☐ Properly grounded
- ☐ Tool or material rests properly adjusted
- ☐ Adequate work space around machines
- ☐ Control switch easily accessible
- ☐ Safety glasses worn
- ☐ Gloves worn by persons handling rough or sharp materials
- ☐ No gloves or loose clothing worn by persons operating machines

V. HAND TOOLS AND MISCELLANEOUS

- ☐ In good condition—not cracked, worn, or otherwise defective
- ☐ Properly stored
- ☐ Correct for job
- ☐ Goggles, respirators, and other personal protective equipment worn where necessary

VI. SPRAY PAINTING

- ☐ Explosion-proof electrical equipment
- ☐ Proper storage of paints and thinners in approved metal cabinets
- ☐ Fire extinguishers adequate and suitable; readily accessible
- ☐ Minimum storage in work area

VII. FIRE EXTINGUISHERS

- ☐ Properly serviced and tagged
- ☐ Readily accessible
- ☐ Adequate and suitable for operations involved

SAFETY CLIMATE After BP's Gulf of Mexico Deepwater Horizon rig exploded and collapsed in 2010, critics alleged that rig managers had ignored numerous warning signs and taken a lax approach to safety.

In fact, not all working condition–related causes of accidents are as obvious as broken scaffolds. Sometimes the workplace suffers from a toxic "safety climate," in other words, from a set of mostly psychological factors that set the stage for employees to act unsafely.

One early study focused on the fatal accidents suffered by offshore British oil workers in the North Sea.[23] Employees who are under stress, a strong pressure to quickly complete the work, and, generally, a poor safety climate—for instance, supervisors who never mention safety—were some of the not-so-obvious working conditions that set the stage for oil rig accidents.

The participants in another safety climate study were nurses working in 42 large U.S. hospitals. The researchers measured safety climate with items like "the nurse manager on this unit emphasizes safety." The results revealed that "safety climate predicted medication errors, nurse back injuries, urinary tract infections, [and] patient satisfaction."[24]

OTHER WORKING CONDITION FACTORS Work schedules and fatigue also affect accident rates. Accident rates usually don't increase too noticeably during the first 5 or 6 hours of the workday, but after 6 hours, the accident rate accelerates. This is due partly to fatigue and partly to the fact that accidents occur more often during night shifts.

Accidents also occur more frequently in plants with a high seasonal layoff rate, hostility among employees, and blighted living conditions. Temporary stress factors such as high workplace temperature, poor illumination, and a congested workplace also relate to accident rates.

Unsafe Acts

In practice, it's impossible to eliminate accidents just by reducing unsafe conditions. People usually cause accidents, and no one has a surefire way to eliminate *unsafe acts* such as:

- Throwing materials
- Operating or working at unsafe speeds
- Making safety devices inoperative by removing, adjusting, or disconnecting them
- Lifting improperly

There is no one explanation for why an employee may behave in an unsafe manner. Sometimes, as noted, the working conditions may set the stage for unsafe acts. For instance, stressed-out oil rig employees may behave unsafely even if they know better. Sometimes, employees aren't trained adequately in safe work methods; some companies don't supply employees with the right safe procedures, and employees may simply develop their own (often bad) work habits.

Thus in one accident, a maintenance worker followed the plant's lockout/tagout procedure (for ascertaining that a powered device is disconnected) by calling the control room to have them shut off the roof exhaust fan he was about to work on. When he arrived on the roof, he noticed the fan was still turning, and assumed that the wind was turning the blades. After waiting several minutes, he wrapped a rag around his hand and tried to stop the blade with his hand, causing serious injury. He had followed the procedure by calling the control room to shut the fan. But the employer should have emphasized in its training that the point of the procedure was not just to tell the control room to disconnect the power, but "to make sure that the fan is not turning before you touch it."[25]

WHAT TRAITS CHARACTERIZE "ACCIDENT-PRONE" PEOPLE? Unsafe acts like these can undo even the best attempts to reduce unsafe conditions. The problem is that there are no easy answers to the question of what causes people to act recklessly.

It may seem intuitively obvious that some people are simply accident prone, but the research is mixed.[26] On closer inspection, some apparently accident-prone people were just unlucky, or may have been more meticulous about reporting their accidents.[27] However, there is evidence that people with specific traits may indeed be accident prone. For example, people who are impulsive, sensation seeking, extremely extroverted, and less conscientious (in terms of being less fastidious and dependable) are more likely to have accidents.[28]

Furthermore, the person who is accident prone on one job may not be so on a different job. Driving is one familiar example. Personality traits that correlate with filing vehicular insurance claims include *entitlement* ("bad drivers think there's no reason they should not speed or run lights");

People usually cause accidents, and no one has a surefire way to eliminate an unsafe act.

Source: Steven Puetzer/Getty Images, Inc.–Liaison.

impatience ("drivers with high claim frequency were 'always in a hurry'"); *aggressiveness* ("always the first to want to move when the red light turns green"); and *distractibility* ("easily and frequently distracted by cell phones, eating, drinking, and so on"). A study in Thailand similarly found that drivers who are naturally *competitive* and prone to *anger* are particularly risky drivers.[29]

HOW TO PREVENT ACCIDENTS

3 Explain how to prevent accidents at work.

Following an accident in which four workers lost their lives, managers at the Golden Eagle refinery east of San Francisco Bay shut down the facility for 4 months and retrained all employees in safety methods. Then they turned to other remedies.[30] In practice, we've seen that accident causes tend to be multifaceted, so employers must take a multifaceted approach to preventing them.

Reduce Unsafe Conditions

You're repairing a lamp that you think is unplugged and then learn, with a shock, that it is plugged in. Lockout/tagout aims to avoid such situations. *Lockout/tagout* is a formal procedure to disable equipment, to avoid unexpected releases of electrical or other energy. It involves disarming the device and affixing a "disabled" tag to the equipment.[31]

Reducing unsafe conditions is always an employer's first line of defense in accident prevention. Safety engineers should design jobs to remove or reduce physical hazards. Sometimes (as with the lamp) the solution is clear. For example, slippery floors in commercial kitchens often cause slips and falls. Employers work with safety engineers to "engineer out" potentially hazardous conditions like these, for instance, by placing non-slip mats in kitchens, or guardrails around moving machines. For machinery, for example, employees can use emergency stop devices like the one shown in the photo below to cut power to hazardous machines.[32] OSHA standards list the guidelines here (you can use a checklist as in Figure 11.5).

Personal Protective Equipment

Once this is done, management can make available personal protective equipment (PPE). For example, Prevent Blindness America estimates that each year, more than 700,000 Americans injure their eyes at work, and that employers could avoid 90% of these injuries with safety eyewear.[33]

Getting employees to wear personal protective equipment is famously difficult. Wearability is important.[34] In addition to providing reliable protection, protective gear should fit properly; be easy to care for, maintain, and repair; be flexible and lightweight; provide comfort and reduce heat stress; have rugged construction; and be relatively easy to put on and remove.[35] Of course, it makes sense to require wearing the personal protective equipment before the accident, rather than after it. For example, a combustible dust explosion at a sugar refinery recently killed 14 employees and burned many others. The employer subsequently required that all employees wear fire resistant clothing, unfortunately too late for the victims.[36]

Note, though, that reducing unsafe conditions (such as enclosing noisy equipment) is always the first line of defense. Then use administrative controls (such as job rotation to reduce long-term exposure to the hazard). Only then turn to PPE.[37]

The accompanying Managing the New Workforce feature (page 325) expands on this.

FIGURE 11.5

Supervisor's Safety Checklist

Source: http://ocio.os.doc.gov/s/ groups/public/@doc/@os/@ocio/@oit pp/documents/content/dev01_002574. pdf, accessed April 28, 2009.

FORM **CD-574**
(9/02)

U.S. Department of Commerce
Office Safety Inspection Checklist for
Supervisors and Program Managers

Name:	Division:
Location:	Date:
Signature:	

This checklist is intended as a guide to assist supervisors and program managers in conducting safety and health inspections of their work areas. It includes questions relating to general office safety, ergonomics, fire prevention, and electrical safety. Questions which receive a "**NO**" answer require corrective action. If you have questions or need assistance with resolving any problems, please contact your safety office. More information on office safety is available through the Department of Commerce Safety Office website at http://ohrm.doc.gov/safetyprogram/safety.htm.

Work Environment

Yes	No	N/A	
O	O	⊙	Are all work areas clean, sanitary, and orderly?
O	O	⊙	Is there adequate lighting?
O	O	⊙	Do noise levels appear high?
O	O	⊙	Is ventilation adequate?

Walking / Working Surfaces

Yes	No	N/A	
O	O	⊙	Are aisles and passages free of stored material that may present trip hazards?
O	O	⊙	Are tile floors in places like kitchens and bathrooms free of water and slippery substances?
O	O	⊙	Are carpet and throw rugs free of tears or trip hazards?
O	O	⊙	Are hand rails provided on all fixed stairways?
O	O	⊙	Are treads provided with anti-slip surfaces?
O	O	⊙	Are step ladders provided for reaching overhead storage areas and are materials stored safely?
O	O	⊙	Are file drawers kept closed when not in use?
O	O	⊙	Are passenger and freight elevators inspected annually and are the inspection certificates available for review on-site?
O	O	⊙	Are pits and floor openings covered or otherwise guarded?
O	O	⊙	Are standard guardrails provided wherever aisle or walkway surfaces are elevated more than 48 inches above any adjacent floor or the ground?
O	O	⊙	Is any furniture unsafe or defective?
O	O	⊙	Are objects covering heating and air conditioning vents?

Ergonomics

Yes	No	N/A	
O	O	⊙	Are employees advised of proper lifting techniques?
O	O	⊙	Are workstations configured to prevent common ergonomic problems? (Chair height allows employees' feet to rest flat on the ground with thighs parallel to the floor, top of computer screen is at or slightly below eye level, keyboard is at elbow height. Additional information on proper configuration of workstations is available through the Commerce Safety website at http://ohrm.doc.gov/safetyprogram/safety.htm)
O	O	⊙	Are mechanical aids and equipment, such as; lifting devices, carts, dollies provided where needed?
O	O	⊙	Are employees surveyed annually on their ergonomic concerns?

(*continued*)

FIGURE 11.5
(Continued)

FORM **CD-574**
(9/02)

Emergency Information (Postings)

Yes	No	N/A	
○	○	⊙	Are established emergency phone numbers posted where they can be readily found in case of an emergency?
○	○	⊙	Are employees trained on emergency procedures?
○	○	⊙	Are fire evacuation procedures/diagrams posted?
○	○	⊙	Is emergency information posted in every area where you store hazardous waste?
○	○	⊙	Is established facility emergency information posted near a telephone?
○	○	⊙	Are the OSHA poster, and other required posters displayed conspicuously?
○	○	⊙	Are adequate first aid supplies available and properly maintained?
○	○	⊙	Are an adequate number of first aid trained personnel available to respond to injuries and illnesses until medical assistance arrives?
○	○	⊙	Is a copy of the facility fire prevention and emergency action plan available on site?
○	○	⊙	Are safety hazard warning signs/caution signs provided to warn employees of pertinent hazards?

Fire Prevention

Yes	No	N/A	
○	○	⊙	Are flammable liquids, such as gasoline, kept in approved safety cans and stored in flammable cabinets?
○	○	⊙	Are portable fire extinguishers distributed properly (less than 75 feet travel distance for combustibles and 50 feet for flammables)?
○	○	⊙	Are employees trained on the use of portable fire extinguishers?
○	○	⊙	Are portable fire extinguishers visually inspected monthly and serviced annually?
○	○	⊙	Is the area around portable fire extinguishers free of obstructions and properly labeled ?
○	○	⊙	Is heat-producing equipment used in a well ventilated area?
○	○	⊙	Are fire alarm pull stations clearly marked and unobstructed?
○	○	⊙	Is proper clearance maintained below sprinkler heads (i.e., 18" clear)?

Emergency Exits

Yes	No	N/A	
○	○	⊙	Are doors, passageways or stairways that are neither exits nor access to exits and which could be mistaken for exits, appropriately marked "NOT AN EXIT," "TO BASEMENT," "STOREROOM," etc.?
○	○	⊙	Are a sufficient number of exits provided?
○	○	⊙	Are exits kept free of obstructions or locking devices which could impede immediate escape?
○	○	⊙	Are exits properly marked and illuminated?
○	○	⊙	Are the directions to exits, when not immediately apparent, marked with visible signs?
○	○	⊙	Can emergency exit doors be opened from the direction of exit travel without the use of a key or any special knowledge or effort when the building is occupied?
○	○	⊙	Are exits arranged such that it is not possible to travel toward a fire hazard when exiting the facility?

FIGURE 11.5

(Continued)

FORM **CD-574**
(9/02)

Electrical Systems
(Please have your facility maintenance person or electrician accompany you during this part of the inspection)

Yes	No	N/A	
○	○	⊙	Are all cord and cable connections intact and secure?
○	○	⊙	Are electrical outlets free of overloads?
○	○	⊙	Is fixed wiring used instead of flexible/extension cords?
○	○	⊙	Is the area around electrical panels and breakers free of obstructions?
○	○	⊙	Are high-voltage electrical service rooms kept locked?
○	○	⊙	Are electrical cords routed such that they are free of sharp objects and clearly visible?
○	○	⊙	Are all electrical cords grounded?
○	○	⊙	Are electrical cords in good condition (free of splices, frays, etc.)?
○	○	⊙	Are electrical appliances approved (Underwriters Laboratory, Inc. (UL), etc)?
○	○	⊙	Are electric fans provided with guards of not over one-half inch, preventing finger exposures?
○	○	⊙	Are space heaters UL listed and equipped with shutoffs that activate if the heater tips over?
○	○	⊙	Are space heaters located away from combustibles and properly ventilated?
○	○	⊙	In your electrical rooms are all electrical raceways and enclosures securely fastened in place?
○	○	⊙	Are clamps or other securing means provided on flexible cords or cables at plugs, receptacles, tools, equipment, etc., and is the cord jacket securely held in place?
○	○	⊙	Is sufficient access and working space provided and maintained about all electrical equipment to permit ready and safe operations and maintenance? (This space is 3 feet for less than 600 volts, 4 feet for more than 600 volts)

FORM **CD-574**
(9/02)

Material Storage

Yes	No	N/A	
○	○	⊙	Are storage racks and shelves capable of supporting the intended load and materials stored safely?
○	○	⊙	Are storage racks secured from falling?
○	○	⊙	Are office equipment stored in a stable manner, not capable of falling?

MANAGING THE NEW WORKFORCE

Protecting Vulnerable Workers

Employers need to pay special attention to vulnerable workers, those who are "unprepared to deal with hazards in the workplace," either due to lack of education, ill-fitting personal protective equipment, physical limitations, or cultural reasons. Among others, these may include young workers, immigrant workers, aging workers, and women workers.[38]

For example, although about half of all workers today are women, most machinery and PPE (like gloves) are designed for men.[39] (Hand injuries account for about one million emergency department visits annually by U.S. workers.[40]) Women may thus have to use makeshift platforms or stools to reach machinery controls, or wear safety goggles that don't really fit. The solution is to make sure the equipment and machines women use are appropriate for their size.[41]

Similarly, with more workers postponing retirement, older workers are doing more manufacturing jobs.[42] For example, at one Allegany Ludlam Stainless Steel Corp. facility, about two-thirds of the workers are within 10 years of retirement.[43] They can do these jobs very effectively. However, there are potential physical changes associated with aging, including loss of strength, loss of muscular flexibility, and reduced reaction time.[44] This means that employers should make special provisions, such as designing jobs to reduce heavy lifting.[45] The fatality rate for older workers is about three times that of younger workers.[46]

Reducing Unsafe Acts

While reducing unsafe conditions is the first line of defense, human misbehavior can short-circuit even the best safety efforts. Sometimes the misbehavior, like disconnecting a safety switch, is intentional, but often it's not. For example, distractions—whether from cell phones or glancing back to check on a child—contribute to at least half of all car accidents. At work, not noticing moving or stationary objects or that a floor is wet often causes accidents.[47] And, ironically, "making a job safer with machine guards or PPE lowers people's risk perceptions and thus can lead to an increase in at-risk behavior."[48]

Unfortunately, just telling employees to "pay attention" is usually not enough. Instead, it requires a process. First, identify and try to eliminate potential risks, such as unguarded equipment. Next, reduce potential distractions, such as noise, heat, and stress. Then, carefully screen and train employees, as we explain next.

Use Screening to Reduce Unsafe Acts

Accidents are similar to other types of poor performance, and psychologists have had success in screening out individuals who might be accident prone for some specific job. The basic technique is to identify the human trait (such as visual skill) that might relate to accidents on the specific job. Then determine whether scores on this trait predict accidents on the job.

Again, driving is an example. Thus, screening prospective delivery drivers for traits like impatience and aggressiveness might be sensible.[49]

Use Posters and Other Propaganda

Propaganda such as safety posters can also help reduce unsafe acts. In an early study, their use apparently increased safe behavior by more than 20% (see poster on page 327).[50] However, employers should combine the safety poster with other techniques, such as screening and training, to reduce unsafe conditions and acts.

Provide Safety Training

Safety training can reduce accidents.[51] It is especially important to instruct new employees in safe practices and procedures, warn them of potential hazards, and work on developing their predisposition toward safety. Delta Air Lines tells supervisors to use personal anecdotes to motivate employees to wear hearing protection. For example, "a lot of the old-timers have terrible stories and terrible hearing, because whatever they did in their past jobs—whether they worked here or somewhere else—they didn't wear hearing protection."[52]

Improving Productivity through HRIS:
Internet-Based Safety Improvement Solutions

Employers also use the Web to support their safety training. For example, PureSafety (www.puresafety.com) enables firms to create their own training Web sites, complete with a "message from the safety director." Once an employer installs the PureSafety Web site, it can populate the site with courses from companies that supply health and safety courses via PureSafety.com. PureSafety.com also develops or modifies existing courses for employers. OSHA, NIOSH, and numerous private vendors also provide online safety training solutions.[53]

Sites like PureSafety.com make it easy for employers to launch a health and safety program for their employees, and to deliver individual courses efficiently. For example, go to www.puresafety.com/public/foodservice.asp. This site describes, among others, a safety course for drivers. The online course covers topics like Pre-trip Inspections, and Unloading products at customer locations.

SAFETY TRAINING FOR HISPANIC WORKERS With increasing numbers of Spanish-speaking workers in the United States, many employers offer special training for Hispanic workers.[54] One example was a 40-hour training course for construction workers at the Dallas/Fort Worth airport expansion project. Based on this program's apparent success, there are several useful conclusions one can draw about what a program like this should look like.

1. *Teach the program in Spanish.* OSHA requirements already demand this.
2. Recruit instructors who are from the *ethnic groups* they are training, and preferably from (in this case) construction.

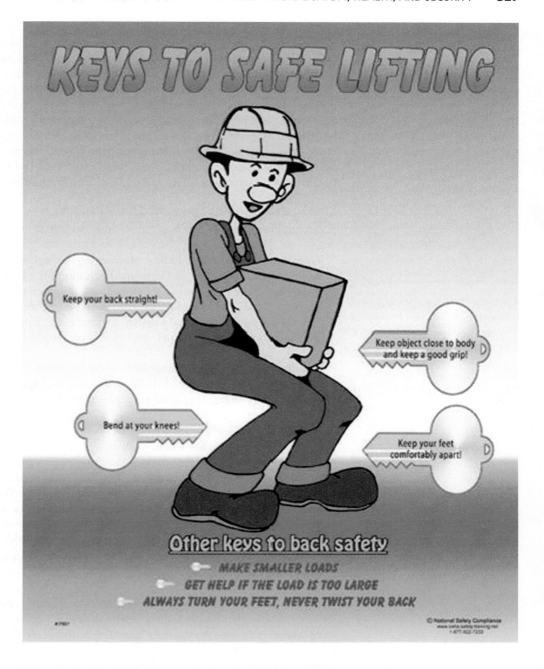

3. Provide for some *multilingual cross-training* for specific phrases. For example, the course teaches non-Hispanic trainees to say "peligro" (danger) or "cuidado" (be careful).[55]
4. Address *cultural differences.* For example, the Dallas program found that some workers usually want to be greeted first, instead of just told, "you are doing something wrong."
5. *Don't skimp on training.* Because of the multilingual aspects, the 40-hour course at Dallas/Fort Worth cost about $500 tuition per student (not counting the worker's wages).

Use Incentives and Positive Reinforcement

Some firms award employees incentives like cash bonuses if they meet safety goals. Safety incentives needn't be complicated. One organization uses a suggestion box. Employees make suggestions for improvements regarding unsafe acts or conditions. The employer follows up on all suggestions, the best of which result in gift certificates.[56] Management at San Francisco's Golden Eagle refinery instituted a safety incentive plan. Employees earn "WINGS" points for engaging in one or more of 28 safety activities, such as conducting safety meetings and taking emergency response training. Employees can earn up to $20 per month per person by accumulating points.[57]

THREE CAVEATS Some contend that safety incentive programs may do more harm than good. With respect to safety incentives, keep three potential drawbacks in mind.

First, such programs can't replace comprehensive safety programs: "All other pieces/parts of a comprehensive safety program need to be in place," says one expert.[58]

Second, OSHA argues that such plans may not actually cut down on injuries or illnesses but only on injury and illness *reporting*.[59]

Third, such programs aim to produce, through positive reinforcement, habitual safe behavior. But safety experts caution against this. Habitual behavior occurs without thinking. When it comes to safety, employers want employees paying attention to what they're doing.[60] One option is to emphasize nontraditional reinforcement.[61] For example, give employees recognition awards for attending safety meetings, or for demonstrating their safety proficiency.[62]

Emphasize Top-Management Commitment

Safety programs require a strong and obvious management commitment to safety. For example:

> One of the best examples I know of in setting the highest possible priority for safety takes place at a DuPont Plant in Germany. Each morning at the DuPont Polyester and Nylon Plant, the director and his assistants meet at 8:45 to review the past 24 hours. The first matter they discuss is not production, but safety. Only after they have examined reports of accidents and near misses and satisfied themselves that corrective action has been taken do they move on to look at output, quality, and cost matters.[63]

As another example of top management safety commitment, Weyerhaeuser discharged the plant manager and safety manager at its West Virginia facility. Weyerhaeuser alleged they failed to report numerous injuries and illnesses at the plant.[64]

The Supervisor's Role in Safety

After inspecting a work site where workers were installing pipes in a trench, an OSHA inspector cited an employer for violating the rule requiring employers to have a "stairway, ladder, ramp, or other safe means of egress" in deep trenches.[65] Workers needed a quick way out. As in most such cases, the employer had the primary responsibility for safety. The local supervisor was responsible for day-to-day inspections. Here, the supervisor did not properly do his inspection. The trench collapsed, and several employees were severely injured. The point is that for a supervisor, "a daily [safety] walk-through of your workplace—whether you are working in outdoor construction, indoor manufacturing, or any place that poses safety challenges—is an essential part of your work."[66]

Foster a Culture of Safety

Employers and supervisors should create a safety-conscious culture by showing that they take safety seriously. One study measured safety culture in terms of questions like "my supervisor says a good word whenever he sees the job done according to the safety rules" and "my supervisor approaches workers during work to discuss safety issues." The workers here developed consistent perceptions concerning their supervisors' safety commitment. In turn, these workers' perceptions of the plant's safety culture apparently influenced the workers' safety behavior in the months following the survey.[67]

According to one safety expert, a workplace with a safety-oriented culture exhibits:

1. *Teamwork*, in the form of management and employees both involved in safety;
2. Highly visible and interactive *communication and collaboration* on safety matters;
3. A *shared vision* of safety excellence (specifically, an overriding attitude that all accidents and injuries are preventable);
4. *Assignment* of critical safety functions to specific individuals or teams; and,
5. A *continuous effort* toward identifying and correcting workplace safety problems and hazards.[68]

Establish a Safety Policy

The company's written safety policy should emphasize that accident prevention is of the utmost importance at your firm, and that the firm will do everything practical to eliminate or reduce accidents and injuries. Figure 11.6 shows a sample policy.

FIGURE 11.6

Sample Safety Policy

Source: Employment Law Information
Network, www.elinfonet.com/
pickedpol/139.html, accessed
January 20, 2008.

The safety of our employees is very important. We expect all employees to be safety-conscious, follow safety rules, and to immediately alert management to any conditions in the workplace that are believed to be unsafe or unhealthy. Accident prevention is important to the well being of our employees and visitors and also a factor in our costs and profits. When an accident does occur, ask yourself how it could have been prevented and take the necessary steps to prevent a similar accident in the future. Violation of safety and security rules is a serious offense warranting disciplinary action, including termination.

As you go through the training program for your specific job position, additional safety procedures will be explained to you. However, every employee must be familiar with the six major causes and results of accidents in most workplaces—customers, collisions, slips and falls, cuts, lifting, and burns. The following basic safety rules have been developed to protect you and others from injury while on the job. Accidents can happen—but remember, safety is everyone's responsibility.

Set Specific Loss Control Goals

Set specific safety goals to achieve. For example, set safety goals in terms of frequency of lost-time injuries per number of full-time employees.

Conduct Regular Safety and Health Inspections

Routinely inspect all premises for possible safety and health problems using checklists such as those in the HR in Practice feature on page 320 and in Figure 11.5 as aids. Similarly, investigate all accidents and "near misses" and have a system in place for letting employees notify management about hazardous conditions.[69] The term *safety audit* means two things. It refers to the actual safety inspection using a checklist as in Figure 11.5. *Safety audit* also refers to the employer's review and analysis of its safety-related data, for instance, regarding accidents, workers' compensation claims, and days lost due to injuries. Metrics might include the percent conformance to safety-critical behaviors and processes, and the rate of adverse outcomes, such as injury rates.[70]

Beyond Zero Accidents

The trend is away from making safety something "employees are supposed to do," to making it part of how they live. To paraphrase the safety director of one company, "we made the transition to the belief that safety is each employee's moral obligation. It is now something that is integral to how everyone thinks and lives." This company calls its safety program "Zero 4 life." "Zero" means zero injuries, hazards, and near misses. The "4" means the program's four principles of accountability, behavior, communication, and dedication. "Life" means living safely all the time and sharing this value with family and friends.[73]

Organize a Safety Committee

Employee safety committees can improve workplace safety. For example, when airborne sawdust became a problem at a Boise Cascade facility, plant management appointed an employee safety committee. The committee took on the role of safety watchdog, and trained its members in hazard identification. After talking to employees who worked with the woodchips where the sawdust originated, the committee members discovered the sawdust became airborne as the workers transferred the woodchips from one belt to another. They were able to correct the problem quickly.[74]

Figure 11.7 summarizes these and other safety steps.

HR APPs 4 U

PDA Safety Audits

Managers expedite safety audits by using personal digital assistants.[71] For example, Process and Performance Measurement (PPM) is a Windows application for designing and completing safety audit questionnaires. To use this application, the manager gives the safety audit a name, enters the audit questions, and lists possible answers. A typical question for a fire extinguisher audit might include, "Are fire extinguishers clearly identified and accessible?"[72] The supervisor or employee then uses his or her PDA to record the audit and transmit it to the firm's safety office.

FIGURE 11.7

Steps to Take to Reduce Workplace Accidents

- Reduce unsafe conditions.
- Reduce unsafe acts.
- Use posters and other propaganda.
- Provide safety training.
- Use positive reinforcement.
- Emphasize top-management commitment.
- Emphasize safety.
- Establish a safety policy.
- Set specific loss control goals.
- Conduct safety and health inspections regularly.
- Monitor work overload and stress.

MANAGING HR IN CHALLENGING TIMES

Cutting Safety Costs Without Cutting Costs

When economic times turn challenging, it's hard to think of a more dubious way to cut costs than by cutting safety and health spending. Reducing expenditures on activities like safety training or safety incentives may reduce short term expenses. But they may well drive up accident-related costs, including workers' compensation, almost as quickly. The solution isn't to cut safety costs across the board, but to cut them selectively and intelligently. For example, employers are migrating from more expensive classroom training to less expensive online training. And within online safety training, many in these challenging times are migrating from paid programs to free online programs, like those offered by NIOSH or at Web sites such as www.freetraining.com.

They are also applying practices such as more diligently reviewing workers' compensation claims and reducing accidents before they occur, for instance, with more diligent safety checks and audits and more careful employee background checks. This is also a good time to review how you actually administer your safety programs (OSHA data collection, for instance), with an eye toward reducing costs there. For example, there are online safety management Web sites (which charge a monthly fee) as well as PC-based packages that reside on your company's server. ZeraWare (www.zeraware.com) is an example of the latter.[75]

WORKPLACE HEALTH HAZARDS: PROBLEMS AND REMEDIES

4 Discuss major health problems at work and how to remedy them.

Most workplace hazards aren't obvious ones like unguarded equipment or slippery floors. Many are unseen hazards (like chemicals) that the company produces as part of its production processes. Other problems, like drug abuse, the employees may create for themselves. In either case, these hazards are often more dangerous to workers' health and safety than are obvious hazards like slippery floors. Typical workplace exposure hazards include chemicals and other hazardous materials such as asbestos, as well as alcohol abuse, stressful jobs, ergonomic hazards (such as uncomfortable equipment), infectious diseases, smoking, and biohazards (such as mold and anthrax).[76] We will look at several of these.

Chemicals and Industrial Hygiene

OSHA standards list exposure limits for about 600 chemicals. Hazardous substances like these require air sampling and other precautionary measures. They are also more widespread than most managers realize. For example, manufacturers use ethyl alcohol as a solvent in industrial processes.[77]

Managing such exposure hazards comes under the area of *industrial hygiene,* and involves recognition, evaluation, and control. First, the facility's health and safety officers must *recognize* possible exposure hazards. This typically involves activities like conducting plant/facility walk-around surveys.

Having identified a possible hazard, the *evaluation* phase involves determining how severe the hazard is. This requires measuring the exposure, comparing the measured exposure to some benchmark, and determining whether the risk is within tolerances.[78]

Finally, the hazard *control* phase involves eliminating or reducing the hazard. Personal protective gear (such as face masks) is generally the *last* option. Before relying on these, the employer must install engineering controls (such as ventilation) and administrative controls (including training); this is mandatory under OSHA.[79]

Alcoholism and Substance Abuse

Workplace substance abuse is a serious problem at work. About two-thirds of people with an alcohol disorder work full-time.[80] About 15% of the U.S. workforce (just over 19 million workers) "has either been hung over at work, been drinking shortly before showing up for work, or been drinking or impaired while on the job at least once during the previous year."[81]

Recognizing the alcoholic on the job isn't easy. Early symptoms such as tardiness are similar to those of other problems. The supervisor is not a psychiatrist, and without specialized training, identifying and dealing with the alcoholic is difficult.

Whether the alcohol abuse reflects a "disability" under the ADA depends on several things including whether the person is alcohol dependant.[82] In general, employers can hold alcohol dependent employees to the same performance standards as they hold non-alcoholics. Employers often make available employee assistance programs (EAPs) to provide the counselling necessary to support employees with alcohol or drug abuse problems.

Increasingly, it's not just intoxicated employees but "intexicated" ones causing problems. Studies indicate that cell phone activity probably contributes to over 636,000 motor vehicle crashes per year. Many businesses are therefore banning cell phone use and texting activities among their drivers.[83] In 2009, President Obama signed an executive order prohibiting most federal employees from text messaging while driving on official business using government equipment.[84]

TESTING For many employers, dealing with substance abuse begins with substance abuse testing.[85] It's unusual to find employers who don't at least test job candidates for substance abuse before formally hiring them. And many states are instituting mandatory random drug testing for high-hazard workers. For example, New Jersey now requires random drug testing of electrical workers.[86]

There is some debate about whether drug tests reduce workplace accidents. The answer seems to be that pre-employment tests pick up only about half the workplace drug users, so ongoing random testing is advisable. One study, conducted in three hotels, concluded that pre-employment drug testing seemed to have little effect on workplace accidents. However, a combination of pre-employment and random ongoing testing was associated with a significant reduction in workplace accidents.[87]

DEALING WITH SUBSTANCE ABUSE Ideally, a drug-free workplace program includes five components:

1. A drug-free workplace policy
2. Supervisor training
3. Employee education
4. Employee assistance
5. Drug testing

The policy should state, at a minimum, "The use, possession, transfer, or sale of illegal drugs by employees is prohibited." It should also explain the employer's rationale for the policy, and the consequences for violating it (including discipline up to and including dismissal). Supervisors should be trained to monitor employees' performance, and to stay alert to drug-related performance problems.

TOOLS Several tools are available to screen for alcohol or drug abuse. The most widely used self-reporting screening instruments for alcoholism are the 4-item CAGE and the 25-item Michigan Alcoholism Screening Test (MAST). The former asks questions like these: Have you ever (1) attempted to Cut back on alcohol, (2) been Annoyed by comments about your drinking, (3) felt Guilty about drinking, (4) had an Eye-opener first thing in the morning to steady your nerves?[88]

Table 11.1 shows observable behavior patterns that indicate alcohol-related problems. As you can see, alcohol-related problems range from tardiness in the earliest stages of alcohol abuse to prolonged, unpredictable absences in its later stages.[89]

TABLE 11.1 Observable Behavior Patterns Indicating Possible Alcohol-Related Problems

Alcoholism Stage	Some Possible Signs of Alcoholism Problems	Some Possible Alcoholism Performance Issues
Early	Arrives at work late	Reduced job efficiency
	Untrue statements	Misses deadlines
	Leaves work early	
Middle	Frequent absences, especially Mondays	Accidents
	Colleagues mentioning erratic behavior	Warnings from boss
	Mood swings	Noticeably reduced performance
	Anxiety	
	Late returning from lunch	
	Frequent multi-day absences	
Advanced	Personal neglect	Frequent falls, accidents
	Unsteady gait	Strong disciplinary actions
	Violent outbursts	Basically incompetent
	Blackouts and frequent forgetfulness	Performance
	Possible drinking on job	

Sources: Gopal Patel and John Adkins, Jr., "The Employer's Role in Alcoholism Assistance," *Personnel Journal* 62, no. 7 (July 1983): 570; Mary-Anne Enoch and David Goldman, "Problem Drinking and Alcoholism: Diagnosis and Treatment," *American Family Physician* (February 1, 2002), www.aafp.org/afp/20020201/441.html, accessed July 20, 2008; and Ken Pidd, et al., "Alcohol and Work: Patterns of Use, Workplace Culture, and Safety," www.nisu.flinders.edu.au/pubs/reports/2006/injcat82.pdf, accessed July 20, 2008.

A combination of pre-employment and ongoing random testing is most effective. Pre-employment drug testing discourages those on drugs from applying for or coming to work for employers who do testing. (One study found that over 30% of regular drug users employed full-time said they were less likely to work for a company that conducted pre-employment screening.[90]) Some applicants or employees may try to evade the test, for instance, by purchasing "clean" specimens. Several states, including New Jersey, North Carolina, Virginia, Oregon, South Carolina, Pennsylvania, Louisiana, Texas, and Nebraska have laws making drug-test fraud a crime.[91] The newer oral fluid drug test eliminates the "clean specimen" problem and is much less expensive to administer.[92]

The Problems of Job Stress and Burnout

Problems like alcoholism and drug abuse sometimes stem from *job stress.*[93] Northwestern National Mutual Life found that one-fourth of all employees it surveyed viewed their jobs as the number one stressor in their lives.[94] Even employees with technologically advanced jobs, like computer workers, suffer high levels of job stress.[95]

A variety of external factors can trigger stress. These include work schedule, pace of work, job security, route to and from work, workplace noise, and the number and nature of customers.[96] However, no two people react the same because personal factors also influence stress.[97] For example, those with Type A personalities—people who are **workaholics** and who feel driven to always be on time and meet deadlines—normally place themselves under greater stress than do others.

workaholic

People who feel driven to always be on time and meet deadlines and so normally place themselves under greater stress than do others.

CONSEQUENCES Job stress has serious consequences for employer and employer. The human consequences of job stress include anxiety, depression, anger, and various physical consequences, such as cardiovascular disease, headaches, accidents, and possibly even early-onset Alzheimer's disease.[98] Stress also has serious consequences for the employer. These include diminished performance, and increased absenteeism, turnover, grievances, and health care costs. A study of 46,000 employees concluded that health care costs of high-stress workers were 46% higher than those of their less-stressed coworkers.[99] Yet not all stress is dysfunctional. Some people, for example, are more productive as a deadline approaches.

REDUCING YOUR OWN JOB STRESS A person can do several things to alleviate stress. These include commonsense remedies like getting more sleep, eating better, finding a more suitable

Source: Peter Griffith.

To reduce stress, choose a quiet place with soft light, sit comfortably, and then meditate by focusing your thoughts, for instance, by counting breaths.

job, getting counseling, and planning each day's activities. In his book *Stress and the Manager,* Dr. Karl Albrecht suggests the following to reduce job stress:[100]

- Build rewarding, pleasant, cooperative relationships with as many of your colleagues and employees as you can.
- Don't bite off more than you can chew.
- Build an especially effective and supportive relationship with your boss.
- Understand the boss's problems and help him or her to understand yours.
- Negotiate with your boss for realistic deadlines on important projects.
- Find time every day for detachment and relaxation.
- Get away from your office from time to time for a change of scene and a change of mind.
- Don't put off dealing with distasteful problems.
- Write down the problems that concern you, and beside each write down what you're going to do about it.

Meditation works for some. Choose a quiet place with soft light, sit comfortably, and then meditate by focusing your thoughts, for instance, by counting breaths or by visualizing a calming location such as a beach. When your mind wanders, just bring it back to focusing on your breathing, or the beach.[101]

WHAT THE EMPLOYER CAN DO The employer can also help reduce job stress. Indeed, one's relationship with his or her immediate supervisor is an important factor in one's peace of mind at work.

One British firm follows a three-tiered approach to managing workplace stress.[102] First is *primary prevention,* which focuses on ensuring that things like job designs are correct. Second involves *intervention,* including individual employee assessment, attitude surveys to find sources of stress such as personal conflicts on the job, and supervisory intervention. Third is *rehabilitation* through employee assistance programs and counseling. Huntington Hospital in Pasadena, California, introduced an on-site concierge service to help its employees. It takes care of tasks like mailing bills and making vacation plans for them.[103] Several years ago, World Bank employees were experiencing high stress levels. Several times a week trainers from a Buddhist meditation instruction company ran meditation classes at the bank. Employees generally felt the classes were useful.[104] Employers recognize that employee wellness programs can reduce such problems. For example, rather than focusing just on programs like weight management and smoking cessation, they're broadening their efforts to include high stress and depression.[105]

burnout
The total depletion of physical and mental resources caused by excessive striving to reach an unrealistic work-related goal.

BURNOUT **Burnout** is closely associated with job stress. Experts define *burnout* as the total depletion of physical and mental resources caused by excessive striving to reach an unrealistic work-related goal. Burnout doesn't just spontaneously appear. Instead, it builds gradually, manifesting itself in irritability, discouragement, entrapment, and resentment.[106]

What can a burnout candidate do? In his book *How to Beat the High Cost of Success,* Dr. Herbert Freudenberger suggests:

- *Break your patterns.* Survey how you spend your time. The more well-rounded your life, the better protected you are against burnout.
- *Get away from it all periodically.* Schedule occasional periods of introspection during which you escape your usual routine, perhaps alone, to seek a perspective on where you are and where you are going.
- *Reassess your goals in terms of their intrinsic worth.* Are the goals you've set for yourself attainable? Are they really worth the sacrifices you'll have to make?
- *Think about your work.* Could you do as good a job without being so intense or also by pursuing outside interests?

DEPRESSION Stress and burnout aren't the only psychological health problems at work.[107] For example, one *Journal of the American Medical Association* study calculated that depressed workers cost their employers $44 billion per year in absenteeism or in reduced performance at work.[108]

Employers apparently need to work harder to ensure that depressed employees utilize support services. Depression is an illness, and it makes no more sense to tell a depressed person to "snap out of it" than it does to tell a heart patient to "stop acting tired." One survey found that while about two-thirds of large firms offered employee assistance programs covering depression, only about 14% of employees with depression said they ever used one.[109] Training managers to recognize signs of depression—persistent sad moods, sleeping too little, reduced appetite, difficulty in concentrating, and loss of interest in activities once enjoyed, for instance—and then making assistance more readily available can help.

Asbestos Exposure at Work

There are four major sources of occupational respiratory diseases: asbestos, silica, lead, and carbon dioxide. Of these, asbestos has become a major concern, in part because of publicity surrounding numerous huge lawsuits alleging asbestos-related diseases.

OSHA standards require several actions with respect to asbestos. They require that companies monitor the air whenever an employer expects the level of asbestos to rise to one-half the allowable limit (0.1 fibers per cubic centimeters). Engineering controls—walls, special filters, and so forth—are required to maintain an asbestos level that complies with OSHA standards. Respirators can only be used if they are then still required to achieve compliance.

Computer Monitor Health Problems and How to Avoid Them

Even with advances in computer screen technology, there's still a risk of monitor-related health problems. Problems include short-term eye burning, itching, and tearing, as well as eyestrain and eye soreness. Backaches and neck aches are also widespread. These occur when employees try to compensate for monitor problems by maneuvering into awkward positions. Computer users may also suffer from carpal tunnel syndrome, caused by repetitive use of the hands and arms at uncomfortable angles.[110] OSHA has no specific standards for computer workstations. It does have general standards that might apply, regarding, for instance, radiation, noise, and electrical hazards.[111]

NIOSH (the National Institute of Occupational Safety and Health) provides general recommendations regarding the use of computer screens. These include:

1. Employees should take a 3–5 minute break from working at the computer every 20–40 minutes, and use the time for other tasks, like making copies.
2. Design maximum flexibility into the workstation so it can be adapted to the individual operator. Don't stay in one position for long.
3. Reduce glare with devices such as recessed or indirect lighting.[112]
4. Give workers a preplacement vision exam to ensure properly corrected vision.
5. Allow the user to position his or her wrists at the same level as the elbow.
6. Put the screen at or just below eye level, at a distance of 18 to 30 inches from the eyes.
7. Let the wrists rest lightly on a pad for support.
8. Put the feet flat on the floor, or on a footrest.[113]

Repetitive Motion Disorders

According to the U.S. National Institutes of Health, repetitive motion disorders include disorders such as carpal tunnel syndrome, bursitis, and tendonitis, and result from too many uninterrupted repetitions of an activity or motion, or from unnatural motions such as twisting the arm or wrist, or incorrect posture. It usually affects people who perform repetitive tasks such as assembly line work or computer work. Employers can reduce the problem, for instance, with programs to help workers adjust their pace of work.[114]

Infectious Diseases

With many employees travelling to and from international destinations, monitoring and controlling infectious diseases has become an important safety issue.[115]

Employers can take steps to prevent the entry or spread of infectious diseases. These steps include:

1. Closely monitor the Centers for Disease Control and Prevention (CDC) travel alerts. Access this information at www.cdc.gov.
2. Provide daily medical screenings for employees returning from infected areas.
3. Deny access for 10 days to employees or visitors who have had contact with suspected infected individuals.
4. Tell employees to stay home if they have a fever or respiratory system symptoms.
5. Clean work areas and surfaces regularly. Make sanitizers containing alcohol easily available.
6. Stagger breaks. Offer several lunch periods to reduce overcrowding.

Special situations prompt special requirements. For example, in 2009 the CDC advised employers that health care workers working with H1N1 patients should use special respirators to reduce virus inhalation risks.[116]

Workplace Smoking

To some extent, the problem of workplace smoking is becoming moot. For example, states including Delaware, Connecticut, California, and New York have barred smoking in most workplaces.[117] Yet smoking continues to be a problem for employees and employers. Costs derive from higher health and fire insurance, as well as increased absenteeism and reduced productivity (which occurs when, for instance, a smoker takes a 10-minute break to smoke a cigarette outside).

WHAT YOU CAN AND CANNOT DO Many states and municipalities now ban indoor smoking in public areas (see www.smokefreeworld.com/usa.shtml for a list). Beyond that, can employers institute smoking bans? That depends on several things. For example, instituting a smoking ban in a unionized facility, which formerly allowed employees to smoke, may be subject to collective bargaining.[118]

In general, you can deny a job to a smoker as long as you don't use smoking as a surrogate for some other discrimination. A "no-smokers-hired" policy generally does not violate the Americans with Disabilities Act (smoking is not considered a disability), nor, in general, other federal law. About 67% of human resources professionals responding to a SHRM online survey said their companies have established smoke-free workplace policies.[119] Yet about 78% of smoker-employees in these firms said the smoke-free policies did *not* motivate them to quit. Therefore, also offering smoke-cessation benefits is important. The Centers for Disease Control ranks smoke cessation policies (along with aspirin therapy and childhood vaccinations) as the number one cost effective benefit employers can provide.[120] WEYCO Inc. first gave employees 15 months warning and offered smoking secession assistance. Then they began firing or forcing out all its workers who smoke, including those who do so in the privacy of their homes.[121]

Smoking cessation programs can more than pay for themselves. A smoking cessation program that includes therapy and selected pharmaceuticals costs about $0.45 per health plan member per month. However, it can produce annual savings of about $210 per year per smoker who quits (by reducing costs like smoking-related heart disease).[122]

Dealing with Violence at Work

A disgruntled long-term employee walked into Chrysler's Ohio Jeep assembly plant and fatally shot one worker, after reportedly being involved in an argument with a supervisor.[123]

Violence against employees is a huge problem at work.[124] On average, 20 workers are murdered and 18,000 assaulted each week at work. Customers are more often the perpetrators than are coworkers or supervisors.[125] By one early estimate, workplace violence costs employers about $4 billion a year.[126] One report called bullying the "silent epidemic" of the workplace, "where abusive behavior, threats, and intimidation often go unreported."[127] Sadly, much of this violence involves acts by one intimate partner against another. For example, the Centers for Disease Control reported almost 5 million such attacks against women (and 3 million against men) recently (not all at work).[128] And workplace violence isn't aimed just at people. It also manifests itself in sabotaging the firm's property.

Reducing Workplace Violence

Workplace violence incidents by employees are predictable and avoidable. *Risk Management Magazine* estimates that about 86% of past workplace violence incidents were anticipated by coworkers, who had brought them to management's attention prior to the incidents actually occurring. Yet management usually did little or nothing.[129] Human resource managers can take several steps to reduce the incidence of workplace violence. They include the following.

HEIGHTEN SECURITY MEASURES Heightened security measures are the first line of defense, whether the violence derives from coworkers, customers, or outsiders. According to OSHA, measures should include those in Figure 11.8.

IMPROVE EMPLOYEE SCREENING With about 30% of workplace attacks committed by coworkers, screening out potentially violent applicants is the employer's next line of defense.

Personal and situational factors correlate with workplace aggression. Men, and individuals scoring higher on "trait anger" (the predisposition to respond to situations with hostility), are more likely to exhibit workplace aggression. In terms of the situation, interpersonal injustice and poor leadership predict aggression against supervisors.[130]

STEPS TO TAKE Employers can screen out potentially violent workers before they're hired. Obtain an employment application, and check the applicant's employment history, education, and references.[131] Sample interview questions include "What frustrates you?" and "Who was your worst supervisor and why?"[132] Certain background circumstances, such as the following, may indicate the need for a more in-depth background investigation of an applicant:[133]

- An unexplained gap in employment
- Incomplete or false information on the résumé or application
- A negative, unfavorable, or false reference
- Prior insubordinate or violent behavior on the job[134]
- A criminal history involving harassing or violent behavior
- A prior termination for cause with a suspicious (or no) explanation
- History of drug or alcohol abuse
- Strong indications of instability in the individual's work or personal life as indicated, for example, by frequent job changes or geographic moves
- Lost licenses or accreditations[135]

USE WORKPLACE VIOLENCE TRAINING You can also train supervisors to identify the clues that typify potentially violent current employees. Common clues include:[136]

- An act of violence on or off the job
- Erratic behavior evidencing a loss of perception or awareness of actions

FIGURE 11.8

How to Heighten Security in Your Workplace

- Improve external lighting.
- Use drop safes to minimize cash on hand.
- Post signs noting that only a limited amount of cash is on hand.
- Install silent alarms and surveillance cameras.
- Increase the number of staff on duty.
- Provide staff training in conflict resolution and nonviolent response.
- Close establishments during high-risk hours late at night and early in the morning.
- Issue a weapons policy, for instance, "firearms or other dangerous or deadly weapons cannot be brought onto the facility either openly or concealed."[137]

- Overly confrontational or antisocial behavior
- Sexually aggressive behavior
- Isolationist or loner tendencies
- Insubordinate behavior with a threat of violence
- Tendency to overreact to criticism
- Exaggerated interest in war, guns, violence, mass murders, catastrophes, and so on
- Commission of a serious breach of security
- Possession of weapons, guns, knives, or like items in the workplace
- Violation of privacy rights of others, such as searching desks or stalking
- Chronic complaining and the raising of frequent, unreasonable grievances
- A retributory or get-even attitude

The U.S. Postal Service took steps to reduce workplace assaults. The steps include more background checks, drug testing, a 90-day probationary period for new hires, more stringent security (including a hotline that lets employees report threats), and training managers to create a healthier culture.[138] The HR in Practice feature lists useful guidelines for firing high-risk employees.

HR IN PRACTICE

Guidelines for Firing a High-Risk Employee

When firing a high-risk employee:

- plan all aspects of the meeting, including its time, location, the people to be present, and agenda;
- involve security enforcement personnel;
- advise the employee that he or she is no longer permitted onto the employer's property;
- conduct the meeting in a room with a door leading to the outside of the building;
- keep the termination brief and to the point;

- make sure he or she returns all company-owned property at the meeting;
- don't let the person return to his or her workstation;
- conduct the meeting early in the week and early in the morning so he or she has time to meet with employment counselors or support groups;
- offer as generous a severance package as possible; and
- protect the employee's dignity by not advertising the event.[139]

VIOLENCE TOWARD WOMEN AT WORK Men have more fatal occupational injuries than do women, but the proportion of women who are victims of assault is much higher. The Gender-Motivated Violence Act (part of the comprehensive Violence Against Women Act expanded by Congress in 2006) imposes significant liabilities on employers whose women employees become violence victims.[140]

Fatal workplace violence against women has several sources. Of all females murdered at work, more than three-fourths are victims of random criminal violence carried out by an assailant unknown to the victim, as during a robbery. Family members, coworkers, or previous friends or acquaintances commit the remaining criminal acts. Tangible security improvements including better lighting, cash-drop boxes, and similar steps are especially pertinent in reducing such violent acts against women. Women (and men) should have access to domestic crisis hotlines, such as www.ndvh.org, and to the employer's employee assistance programs.

Enterprise Risk Management

Many of these anti-violence actions stem from employers' heightened focus on risk management. Identifying security and other corporate risks falls within the domain of *enterprise risk management,* which means identifying risks, and planning to and actually mitigating these risks. Thus, as part of its risk management, Walmart asks questions such as, "What are the risks? And what are we going to do about these risks?"[141] Reducing crime (as discussed earlier) and enhancing facility security are two important issues here.

SETTING UP A BASIC SECURITY PROGRAM In simplest terms, instituting a basic security program requires analyzing the current level of risk, and then installing mechanical, natural, and organizational security systems.[142]

Security programs often start with an analysis of the facility's *current level of risk.* The employer, preferably with the aid of security experts, should assess the company's exposure. Start with the obvious. For example, what is the neighborhood like? Is your facility close to major highways or railroad tracks (where, for instance, toxic fumes from the trains could present a problem)?

Having assessed the potential current level of risk, the employer then turns its attention to assessing and improving *three basic sources of facility security:* natural security, mechanical security, and organizational security.[143]

Natural security means taking advantage of the facility's natural or architectural features to minimize security problems. For example, do stacks of boxes in front of your windows prevent police officers from observing what's happening in your facility at night?

Mechanical security is the utilization of security systems such as locks, intrusion alarms, access control systems, and surveillance systems in a cost-effective manner that will reduce the need for continuous human surveillance.[144] Thus, for access security, biometric scanners that read thumb or palm prints or retina patterns make it easier to enforce plant security.[145]

Finally, *organizational security* means using good management to improve security. For example, it means properly training and motivating security staff and lobby attendants.[146] Similarly, a SHRM survey found that about 85% of responding organizations now have a formal disaster plan.[147]

Many employers establish cross-functional threat assessment teams to continually monitor and address potential threats. At one university, for instance, "The Team meets regularly to discuss issues relating to violence, security and potential threats directed at students, faculty and staff at the Metropolitan Campus."[148]

Terrorism

The employer can take several steps to protect its employees and physical assets from terrorist attack. These steps, now familiar at many workplaces, include:

- Screen the identities of everyone entering the premises.
- Check mail carefully.
- Identify ahead of time a lean "crisis organization" that can run the company on an interim basis after a terrorist threat.
- Identify in advance under what conditions you will close the company down, as well as what the shutdown process will be.
- Institute a process to put the crisis management team together.
- Prepare evacuation plans and make sure exits are well marked and unblocked.
- Designate an employee who will communicate with families and off-site employees.
- Identify an upwind, off-site location near your facility to use as a staging area for all evacuated personnel.
- Designate in advance several employees who will do headcounts at the evacuation staging area.
- Establish an emergency text-messaging policy and procedure to notify affected individuals that an emergency may exist.[149]

Employers don't just need emergency plans for terrorist attacks; it's also important to have emergency plans in place for dealing with health issues such as swine flu epidemics, for instance, in terms of how the employer will communicate with employees and deal with extraordinary sick leave issues.[150]

It is not just a case of minimizing safety and health problems but being prepared in case an emergency arises. For example, in the case of the cardiac arrest emergency, early access, early CPR, and the use of an automated external defibrillator are all essential. These devices should be available and one or more local employees trained in emergency procedures and their use.[151] The Global Issues in HR feature provides another perspective.

GLOBAL ISSUES IN HR

Crime and Punishment Abroad

Particularly when traveling in areas where medical facilities may not meet developed-country standards, dramatic events—sudden illnesses or serious accidents, for instance—can be very serious abroad. Language difficulties, cultural misunderstandings, lack of normal support and infrastructure systems (such as telephones) can all combine to make an accident or illness that may be manageable in one country a disaster in another.

Cultural differences can cause surprises. In one hospital abroad, for instance, the doctor would not perform a heart surgery until receiving $40,000 in cash. As a result, many multinationals brief their business travelers and expatriates about what to expect and how to react when confronted with a health or safety problem abroad. Many employers therefore contract with international security firms. For example, International SOS has over 1,300 medical professionals staffing its regional centers and clinics.[152]

One security expert says that the terrorist attacks on a Mumbai, India, hotel in 2008 show why employers need a way to track global employees, as well as methods for assessing overseas risks and a response plan should a crisis occur.[153]

REVIEW

SUMMARY

1. The area of safety and accident prevention is of concern to managers partly because of the staggering number of deaths and accidents occurring at work.

2. The purpose of OSHA is to ensure every working person a safe and healthful workplace. OSHA standards are complete and detailed, and are enforced through a system of workplace inspections. OSHA inspectors can issue citations and recommend penalties to their area directors.

3. There are three basic causes of accidents: chance occurrences, unsafe conditions, and unsafe acts on the part of employees. In addition, three other work-related factors—the job itself, the work schedule, and the psychological climate—also contribute to accidents.

4. Unsafe acts on the part of employees are a main cause of accidents. Such acts are to some extent the result of certain behavior tendencies on the part of employees, and these tendencies are possibly the result of certain personal characteristics.

5. Experts differ on whether there are accident-prone people who have accidents regardless of the job. Some traits do predict accidents, but the person who is accident prone in one job may not be on a different job. For example, vision is related to accident frequency for drivers and machine operators, but might not be for other workers, such as accountants.

6. There are several approaches to preventing accidents. One is to reduce unsafe conditions. The other approach is to reduce unsafe acts—for example, through selection and placement, training, positive reinforcement, propaganda, and top-management commitment.

7. Alcoholism, drug addiction, stress, and emotional illness are four important and growing health problems among employees. Alcoholism is a particularly serious problem that can drastically lower the effectiveness of your organization. Techniques including disciplining, discharge, in-house counseling, and referrals to an outside agency are used to deal with these problems.

8. Stress and burnout are other potential health problems at work. An employee can reduce job stress by getting away from work for a while each day, not putting off dealing with distasteful problems, and writing down the problems that concern you, and what you're going to do about it.

9. Violence against employees is an enormous problem at work. Steps that can reduce workplace violence include improved security arrangements, better employee screening, and violence-reduction training.

10. Basic facility security relies on natural security, mechanical security, and organizational security.

KEY TERMS

Occupational Safety and Health Act of 1970   315
Occupational Safety and Health Administration (OSHA)   315
citations   317

workaholic   332
burnout   333

DISCUSSION QUESTIONS

1. Discuss OSHA and how it operates.
2. Explain in detail three basic causes of accidents.
3. Explain how to prevent accidents at work.
4. Discuss major health problems at work and how to remedy them.
5. How would you go about providing a safer work environment for your employees?
6. Discuss the basic facts about OSHA—its purpose, standards, inspection, and rights and responsibilities.
7. Explain the supervisor's role in safety.
8. Explain what causes unsafe acts.
9. Explain how an employee could reduce stress at work.

INDIVIDUAL AND GROUP ACTIVITIES

1. Working individually or in groups, answer the question, "Is there such a thing as an accident-prone person?" Develop your answer using examples of actual people you know who seemed to be accident prone on some endeavor.
2. Working individually or in groups, compile a list of the factors at work or in school that create dysfunctional stress for you. What methods do you use for dealing with the stress?
3. An issue of the journal *Occupational Hazards* presented some information about what happens when OSHA refers criminal complaints about willful violations of OSHA standards to the U.S. Department of Justice (DOJ). Between 1982 and 2002, OSHA referred 119 fatal cases allegedly involving willful violations of OSHA to the DOJ for criminal prosecution. The DOJ declined to pursue 57% of them, and some were dropped for other reasons. Of the remaining 51 cases, the DOJ settled 63% with pretrial settlements involving no prison time. So, counting acquittals, of the 119 cases OSHA referred to the DOJ, only nine resulted in prison time for at least one of the defendants. "The Department of Justice is a disgrace," charged the founder of an organization for family members of workers killed on the job. One possible explanation for this low conviction rate is that the crime in cases like these is generally a misdemeanor, not a felony, and the DOJ generally tries to focus its attention on felony cases. Given this information, what implications do you think this has for how employers and their managers should manage their safety programs, and why do you take that position?
4. Recently, a 315-foot-tall, 2-million-pound crane collapsed on a construction site in East Toledo, Ohio, killing four ironworkers. Do you think catastrophic failures like this are avoidable? If so, what steps would you suggest the general contractor take to avoid a disaster like this?
5. In groups of three or four students, spend 15 minutes walking around the building in which your class is held or where you are now, listing possible natural, mechanical, and organizational security measures you'd suggest to the building's owner.

WEB-e's (WEB EXERCISES)

1. Based on sites such as www.nytimes.com/2008/06/12/nyregion/12indict.html, what events led up to the trench collapse accident discussed in the opening scenario, and how do you think it might have been avoided?
2. Use sites such as www.osha.gov/pls/oshaweb/owadisp.show_document?p_table=NEWS_RELEASES&p_id=16029 to explain the sorts of violations OSHA has levied large penalties for in the past few years, and what you think the employers could have done to avoid the violations.
3. Con Edison supplies power to the New York metropolitan area. Using sites such as http://www.conedison.com/ehs/, what specifically are they doing to reduce employee accidents and improve employee safety?

APPLICATION EXERCISES

HR IN ACTION CASE INCIDENT 1
The Office Safety and Health Program

LearnInMotion is a dot-com firm that delivers employee training, both online and via delivery of CD/DVDs. At first glance, a dot-com is probably one of the last places you'd expect to find potential safety and health hazards—or so the owners, Jennifer and Mel, thought. There's no danger of moving machinery, no high-pressure lines, no cutting or heavy lifting, and certainly no forklift trucks. However, there are safety and health problems.

In terms of accident-causing conditions, for instance, the one thing dot-com companies have is lots of cables and wires. There are cables connecting the computers to each other and to the servers, and in many cases separate cables running from some computers to separate printers. There are 10 wireless telephones in the office, the bases of which are connected to 15-foot phone lines that always seem to be snaking around chairs and tables. There is, in fact, an astonishing amount of cable considering this is an office with less than 10 employees.

When the installation specialists wired the office (for electricity, high-speed cable, phone lines, burglar alarms, and computers), they estimated they used well over 5 miles of cables of one sort or another. Most of these are hidden in the walls or ceilings, but many of them snake their way from desk to desk, and under and over doorways. Several employees have tried to reduce the nuisance of having to trip over wires whenever they get up by putting their plastic chair pads over the wires closest to them. However, that still leaves many wires unprotected. In other cases, they brought in their own packing tape and tried to tape down the wires in those spaces where they're particularly troublesome, such as across doorways.

The cables and wires are only one of the more obvious potential accident-causing conditions. The firm's programmer, before he left the firm, had tried to repair the main server while the unit was still electrically alive. To this day, they're not sure exactly where he stuck the screwdriver, but the result was that he was "blown across the room," as Mel puts it. He was all right, but it was still a scare. And while they haven't yet received any claims, every employee spends hours at his or her computer, so carpal tunnel syndrome is a risk, as are a variety of other problems such as eyestrain and strained backs.

One recent accident particularly scared them. The firm uses independent contractors to deliver the firm's book- and CD/DVD–based courses in New York and two other cities. A delivery person was riding his bike at the intersection of Second Avenue and East 64th Street in New York when he was struck by a car. Luckily, he was not hurt, but the bike's front wheel was wrecked, and the close call got Mel and Jennifer thinking about their lack of a safety program.

And it's not just the physical conditions. They also have some concerns about potential health problems such as job stress and burnout. While the business may be (relatively) safe with respect to physical conditions, it is also relatively stressful in terms of the demands it makes in hours and deadlines. It is not at all unusual for employees to get to work by 7:30 or 8:00 in the morning and to work through until 11:00 or 12:00 at night, at least 5 and sometimes 6 or 7 days per week. Just getting the company's new service operational required five of LearnInMotion's employees to work 70-hour workweeks for 3 weeks.

The bottom line is that both Jennifer and Mel feel they need to do something about implementing a health and safety plan. Now they want you, their management consultants, to help them actually do it. Here's what they want you to do for them.

Questions

1. Based on your knowledge of health and safety matters and your actual observations of operations that are similar to ours, make a list of the potential hazardous conditions employees and others face at LearnInMotion. What should we do to reduce the potential severity of the top five hazards?
2. Would it be advisable for us to set up a procedure for screening out stress-prone or accident-prone individuals? Why or why not? If so, how should we screen them?
3. Write a short position paper on what we should do to get all our employees to behave more safely at work.
4. Based on what you know and on what other dot-coms are doing, write a short position paper on what we can do to reduce the potential problems of stress and burnout in our company.

HR IN ACTION CASE INCIDENT 2
Carter Cleaning Company: Motivating Safe Behavior

Employees' safety and health are very important in the laundry and cleaning business. Each facility is a small production plant in which machines, powered by high-pressure steam and compressed air, work at high temperatures washing, cleaning, and pressing garments, often under very hot, slippery conditions. Chemical vapors are continually produced, and caustic chemicals are used in the cleaning process. High-temperature stills are almost continually "cooking down" cleaning solvents in order to remove impurities so that the solvents can be reused. If a mistake is made in this process—like injecting too much steam into the

still—a boil over occurs, in which boiling chemical solvent erupts out of the still and over the floor, and on anyone who happens to be standing in its way.

As a result of these hazards and the fact that these stores continually produce chemically hazardous waste, several government agencies (including OSHA and the EPA) have strict guidelines regarding management of these plants. For example, posters must be placed in each store notifying employees of their right to be told what hazardous chemicals they are dealing with and what the proper method for handling each chemical is. Special waste-management firms must be used to pick up and properly dispose of the hazardous waste.

A chronic problem the Carters (and most other laundry owners) have is the unwillingness on the part of the cleaning-spotting workers to wear safety goggles. Not all the chemicals they use require safety goggles, but some—like the hydrofluorous acid used to remove rust stains from garments—are very dangerous. The latter is kept in special plastic containers, since it dissolves glass. The problem is safety goggles are somewhat uncomfortable, and they become smudged easily and thus reduce visibility. As a result, Jack has found it almost impossible to get these employees to wear their goggles.

Questions

1. How should the firm go about identifying hazardous conditions that should be rectified? Use data and checklists such as in Figure 11.5 and the HR in Practice feature on pages 320 and 323, to list at least 10 possible dry cleaning store hazardous conditions.
2. Would it be advisable for the firm to set up a procedure for screening out accident-prone individuals? How should it do so?
3. In general, how would you suggest the Carters get all employees to behave more safely at work?
4. Describe in detail how you would use motivation to get those who should be wearing goggles to do so.

EXPERIENTIAL EXERCISE

How Safe Is My University?

Purpose: The purpose of this exercise is to give you practice in identifying unsafe conditions.

Required Understanding: You should be familiar with material covered in this chapter, particularly that on unsafe conditions and that in Figure 11.5.

How to Set Up the Exercise/Instructions: Divide the class into groups of four. Assume that each group is a safety committee retained by your college or university's safety engineer to identify and report on any possible unsafe conditions in and around the school building. Each group will spend about 45 minutes in and around the building you are now in for the purpose of identifying and listing possible unsafe conditions. (Make use of Figure 11.5, and the HR in Practice feature on pages 320 and 323.)

Return to the class in about 45 minutes. A spokesperson for each group should list on the board the unsafe conditions you think you have identified. How many were there? Do you think these also violate OSHA standards? How would you go about checking?

BUSINESS IN ACTION EDU-EXERCISE

Building Your *General Management* Knowledge

It's traditional to distinguish between two types of managers, *general managers* and *departmental or functional managers*. Plant managers, safety managers, sales managers, and human resource managers are departmental or functional managers—they focus on relatively specialized tasks and activities.

General managers are a different breed. Whether they're army "general officers," university presidents, or Toyota's CEO, the general manager is always the person with overall responsibility for the entire organization (including all those departmental/functional managers).

When safety experts say that employee safety requires "top management" commitment, you might assume they mean the plant manager or department manager. But in fact, safety experts are very explicit: it's the company's *top manager*—usually, the CEO or president—that they mean. He or she must ensure that the whole company and chain of command commits to safety. The subordinate departmental managers then just follow the top manager's lead.

An explosion several years ago at British Petroleum's (BP) Texas City, Texas, refinery shows why safety must start with the CEO (general manager). The explosion and fire killed 15 people and injured 500. It was the worst U.S. industrial accident in more than 10 years. The disaster triggered three investigations. As one example of the investigators' conclusions, the Chemical Safety Board found that "BP's global management was aware of problems with maintenance, spending, and infrastructure well before March 2005." Apparently, faced with numerous earlier accidents, BP did make some safety improvements. However, it focused mostly on emphasizing personal employee safety behaviors and procedural compliance. The problem was that plantwide safety problems like "unsafe and antiquated equipment designs" remained.

To put the results of the three investigations into context, under its then-current top management BP seems to have been, for at least 10 years, more obviously committed to cost cutting and profits than to safety. The basic conclusion of the investigations was that cost-cutting helped compromise safety at Texas City. For several reasons, possibly including the Texas City explosion, BP's CEO stepped down soon after the investigators submitted their conclusions.

Questions

1. In BP's case, who was the general officer who was ultimately responsible for BP's safety policies, and why?

2. What relationship if any do you see between BP's competitive strategy and its problems at Texas City?

3. If you were BP's CEO, what would you do to try to ensure an accident like Texas City did not reoccur?

PERSONAL COMPETENCIES EDU-EXERCISE

Applying Your *Motivational Skills* to Boost Employee Safety

As we explained in Chapter 7, goal-setting is a powerful motivation technique. People are generally highly motivated to pursue goals that they deem reasonable and acceptable. Briefly, that means:

1. Employees who get *specific goals* usually perform better than those who do not.
2. Put goals in *quantitative terms and include target dates* or deadlines.
3. Goals should be *challenging*, but not so difficult that they appear impossible or unrealistic.

At work, many employers successfully apply these concepts with *positive reinforcement programs*. For example, provide workers with safety goals, and with positive feedback on how they're doing. The feedback is usually in the form of graphical performance reports and supervisory support.

Researchers introduced one such program in a wholesale bakery.[154] The researchers set and communicated a reasonable safety goal (in terms of observed incidents performed safely). Next, employees participated in a 30-minute training session by viewing pairs of slides depicting scenes that the researchers staged in the plant. One slide showed the supervisor climbing over a conveyor; the parallel slide showed him walking around the conveyor. After viewing an unsafe act, employees had to describe, "What's unsafe here?" Then, the researchers demonstrated the same incident again but performed in a safe manner, and explicitly stated the safe-conduct rule ("go around, not over or under, conveyors").

At the conclusion of training, supervisors showed employees a graph with their pretraining safety record (in terms of observed incidents performed safely) plotted. Supervisors then encouraged workers to consider increasing their performance to the new safety goal for their own protection, to decrease costs, and to help the plant get out of its last place in safety ranking. Then the researchers posted the graph and a list of safety rules.

Whenever observers walked through the plant collecting safety data, they posted on the graph the percentage of incidents they had seen the group as a whole perform safely. Workers could compare their current safety performance with both their previous performance and their assigned goal. This gave the workers positive feedback. In addition, supervisors praised workers when they performed safely. Safety in the plant subsequently improved markedly.

Question

1. Spend some time in your school cafeteria, observing the employees. Identify a safe practice you think is worthwhile emphasizing. Then use the example in this exercise to develop a program the cafeteria manager could use for improving that safe practice.

ENDNOTES

1. Michael Wilson, "Manslaughter Charge in Trench Collapse," *New York Times* (June 12, 2008): B1.
2. All data refer to 2006. See www.bls.gov/iif/oshwc/osh/os/ostb1757.txt, accessed January 19, 2008.
3. "BLS Likely Underestimating Injury and Illness Estimates," *Occupational Hazards* (May 2006): 16. The U.S. government accounting office recently conducted a survey in which it concluded that OSHA overlooks certain worker injuries and illnesses. "OSHA: GAO Findings on Injury and Illness Reporting Are Alarming," *EHS Today* (December 2009): 12.
4. David Ayers, "Mapping Support for an E. H. S. Management System," *Occupational Hazards* (June 2006): 53–54.
5. Katherine Torres, "Stepping into the Kitchen: Food Protection for Food Workers," *Occupational Hazards* (January 2007): 29–30.
6. Based on *All About OSHA*, rev. ed. (Washington, DC: U.S. Department of Labor, 1980); www.OSHA.gov, accessed January 19, 2008.
7. http://osha.gov/as/opa/oshafacts.html, accessed January 19, 2008.
8. Ibid.

9. "OSHA Hazard Communication Standard Enforcement," *BNA Bulletin to Management* (February 23, 1980): 13. See also William Kincaid, "OSHA vs. Excellence in Safety Management," *Occupational Hazards* (December 2002): 34–36.

10. "What Every Employer Needs to Know About OSHA Record Keeping," U.S. Department of Labor, Bureau of Labor Statistics (Washington, DC), report 412–3, p. 3; and http://osha.gov/ recordkeeping/index.html, accessed January 19, 2008.

11. "Supreme Court Says OSHA Inspectors Need Warrants," *Engineering News Record* (June 1, 1978): 9–10; W. Scott Railton, "OSHA Gets Tough on Business," *Management Review* 80, no. 12 (December 1991): 28–29. Steve Hollingsworth, "How to Survive an OSHA Inspection," *Occupational Hazards* (March 2004): 31–33.

12. http://osha.gov/as/opa/oshafacts.html, accessed January 19, 2008; Edwin Foulke Jr., "OSHA's Evolving Role in Promoting Occupational Safety and Health," *EHS Today* (November 2008): 44–49. Some believe that under the new Democratic administration of President Obama, OSHA may move from voluntary programs back to increased attention on inspections. See, for example, Laura Walter, "Safety Roundtable: The View from the End of an Era," *EHS Today* (December 2008): 30–31

13. www.osha.gov/dcsp/smallbusiness/consult.html, accessed February 16, 2010.

14. Lisa Finnegan, "Industry Partners with OSHA," *Occupational Hazards* (February 1999): 43–45. OSHA recently instituted a pilot Voluntary Protection Program (VPP) for companies with exemplary safety practices. On-site VPP evaluation teams evaluate such things as supervisory safety training and safety and health communications programs. VPP certification removes a facility from OSHA's routine inspection list. Sara Escborn and Mary Giddings, "The Ripple Effect of Fluor's Corporate VPP Status," *EHS Today* (February 2009): 44–45.

15. www.osha.gov/Publications/osha2098.pdf+OSHA+inspection+priorities&hl=en&ct=clnk&cd=1&gl=us, accessed January 19, 2008.

16. www.OSHA.gov, accessed May 28, 2005; and http://osha.gov/pls/oshaweb/owadisp.show_document?p_table=NEWS_RELEASES&p_id=14883, accessed January 19, 2008.

17. www.osha.gov, accessed May 26, 2007.

18. www.osha.gov/Publications/osha2098.pdf, accessed April 27, 2008.

19. Jim Lastowka, "Ten Keys to Avoiding OSHA Liability," *Occupational Hazards* (October 1999): 163–170. See also "Half of All Working Americans Feel Immune to Workplace Injuries," www.mem-ins.com/newsroom/pr072803.htm, accessed August 11, 2009.

20. Robert Grossman, "Handling Inspections: Tips from Insiders," *HR Magazine* (October 1999): 41–50.

21. Arthur Sapper, "The Oft-Missed Step: Documentation of Safety Discipline," *Occupational Hazards* (January 2006): 59.

22. Courtesy of the Insurance Services Office, Inc., from "A Safety Committee Man's Guide" (1977): 1–64.

23. For a discussion of this, see David Hofmann and Adam Stetzer, "A Cross-Level Investigation of Factors Influencing Unsafe Behaviors and Accidents," *Personnel Psychology* 49 (1996): 307–308.

24. David Hofman and Barbara Mark, "An Investigation of the Relationship between Safety Climate and Medication Errors as Well as Other Nurse and Patient Outcomes," *Personnel Psychology* 50, no. 9 (2006): 847–869.

25. Jimi Michalscheck, "The Basics of Lock Out/Tag Out Compliance: Creating an Effective Program," *EHS Today* (January 2010): 35–37.

26. Duane Schultz and Sydney Schultz, *Psychology and Work Today* (Upper Saddle River, NJ: Prentice Hall, 1998): 351.

27. Robert Pater and Robert Russel, "Drop That Accident Prone Tag: Look for Causes Beyond Personal Issues," *Industrial Safety and Hygiene News* 38, no. 1 (January 2004): 50, http://findarticles.com/p/articles/mi_hb5992/is_200401/ai_n24195869/, accessed August 11, 2009.

28. Discussed in Douglas Haaland, "Who Is the Safest Bet for the Job? Find Out Why the Guy in the Next Cubicle May Be the Next Accident Waiting to Happen," *Security Management* 49, no. 2 (February 2005): 51–57.

29. "Thai Research Points to Role of Personality in Road Accidents" (February 2, 2005), www.driveandstayalive.com/info%20section/news/individual%20news%20articles/x_050204_personality-in-crash-causation_thailand.htm, accessed August 11, 2009; Donald Bashline et al., "Bad Behavior: Personality Tests Can Help Underwriters Identify High-Risk Drivers," *Best's Review* 105, no. 12 (April 2005): 63–64.

30. Don Williamson and Jon Kauffman, "From Tragedy to Triumph: Safety Grows Wings at Golden Eagle," *Occupational Hazards* (February 2006): 17–25.

31. Benjamin Mangan, "Lockout/Tagout Prevents Workplace Injuries and Save Lives," *Occupational Hazards* (March 2007): 59–60.

32. Mike Carlson, "Machine Safety Solutions for Protecting Employees and Safeguarding Against Machine Hazards," *EHS Today* (July 2009): 24.

33. James Nash, "Beware the Hidden Eye Hazards," *Occupational Hazards* (February 2005): 48–51.

34. You can find videos about new personal protective products at "SafetyLive TV" at www.occupationalhazards.com, accessed March 14, 2009.

35. James Zeigler, "Protective Clothing: Exploring the Wearability Issue," *Occupational Hazards* (September 2000): 81–82; Sandy Smith, "Protective Clothing and the Quest for Improved Performance," *Occupational Hazards* (February 2008): 63–66.

36. Laura Walter, "FR Clothing: Leaving Hazards in the Dust." *EHS Today* (January 2010): 20–22.

37. "The Complete Guide to Personal Protective Equipment," *Occupational Hazards* (January 1999): 49–60. See also Edwin Zalewski, "Noise Control: It's More than Just Earplugs: OSHA Requires Employers to Evaluate Engineering and Administrative Controls Before Using Personal Protective Equipment," *Occupational Hazards* 68, no. 9 (September 2006): 48(3). You can find videos about new personal protective products at "SafetyLive TV" at www.occupationalhazards.com, accessed March 14, 2009.

38. Sandy Smith, "Protecting Vulnerable Workers," *Occupational Hazards* (April 2004): 25–28. In addition to millions of women in factory jobs, about 10% of the construction industry workforce is female, and there are almost 200,000 women in the US military. Women also represent almost 80% of health care workers, where puncture- and chemical-resistant gloves are

particularly important. David Shutt, "Protecting the Hands of Working Women," *EHS Today* (October 2009): 29–32.

39. See, for example, Laura Walter, "What's in a Glove?" *Occupational Hazards* (May 2008): 35–36.

40. Donald Groce, "Keep the Gloves On!" *Occupational Hazards* (June 2008): 45–47.

41. Linda Tapp, "We Can Do It: Protecting Women Workers," *Occupational Hazards* (October 2003): 26–28.

42. Katherine Torres, "Don't Lose Sight of the Older Workforce," *Occupational Hazards* (June 2008): 55–59.

43. Ibid.

44. Robert Pater, "Boosting Safety with an Aging Workforce," *Occupational Hazards* (March 2006): 24.

45. Michael Silverstein, M.D., "Designing the Age Friendly Workplace," *Occupational Hazards* (December 2007): 29–31.

46. Elizabeth Rogers and William Wiatrowski, "Injuries, Illnesses, and Fatalities among Older Workers," *Monthly Labor Review* 128, no. 10 (October 2005): 24–30.

47. Robert Pater and Ron Bowles, "Directing Attention to Boost Safety Performance," *Occupational Hazards* (March 2007): 46–48.

48. E. Scott Geller, "The Thinking and Seeing Components of People-Based Safety," *Occupational Hazards* (December 2006): 38–40.

49. *Asia and Africa Intelligence Wire;* Bashline et al., op. cit.

50. S. Laner and R. J. Sell, "An Experiment on the Effect of Specially Designed Safety Posters," *Occupational Psychology* 34 (1960): 153–169; Ernest McCormick and Joseph Tiffin, *Industrial Psychology* (Upper Saddle River, NJ: Prentice Hall, 1974): 536.

51. See, for example, Laura Walter, "10 Tips for More Effective EHS Training," *EHS Today* (February 2009): 35–37.

52. See also Josh Cable, "Erring on the Side of Caution," *Occupational Hazards* (February 2007): 21–22.

53. Laura Walter, "Surfing for Safety," *Occupational Hazards* (July 2008): 23–29.

54. Hispanic worker safety is a concern. See, for example, "Hispanic Workers' Deaths Rise, Fatal Occupational Injuries Down," *BNA Bulletin to Management* (August 21, 2007): 271.

55. Quoted in Josh Cable, "Seven Suggestions for a Successful Safety Incentives Program," *Occupational Hazards* 67, no. 3 (March 2005): 39–43.

56. J. Nigel Ellis and Susan Warner, "Using Safety Awards to Promote Fall Prevention," *Occupational Hazards* (June 1999): 59–62. See also William Atkinson, "Safety Incentive Programs: What Works?" *Occupational Hazards* (August 2004): 35–39.

57. Don Williamson and Jon Kauffman, "From Tragedy to Triumph: Safety Grows Wings at Golden Eagle," *Occupational Hazards* (February 2006): 17–25.

58. Quoted in Josh Cable, "Seven Suggestions for a Successful Safety Incentives Program," *Occupational Hazards* 67, no. 3 (March 2005): 39–43. See also J. M. Saddler, "Gift Cards Make Safety Motivation Simple," *Occupational Health & Safety* 78, no. 1 (January 2009): 39–40.

59. John Dominic, "Improve Safety Performance and Avoid False Reporting," *HR Magazine* 49, no. 9 (September 2004): 110–119; See also Josh Cable, "Safety Incentives Strategies," *Occupational Hazards* 67, no. 4 (April 2005): 37.

60. See Kelly Rowe, "OSHA and Small Businesses: A Winning Combination," *Occupational Hazards* (March 2007): 33–38.

61. See, for example, Deb Carl, "The Truth about Safety Incentives," *Occupational Hazards* 69, no. 9 (September 2007): 52, 54.

62. James Nash, "Rewarding the Safety Process," *Occupational Hazards* (March 2000): 29–34; Shel Siegel, "Incentives: Small Investments Equal Big Rewards," *Occupational Hazards* (August 2007): 42–44.

63. Willie Hammer, *Occupational Safety Management and Engineering* (Upper Saddle River, NJ: Prentice Hall, 1985): 62–63. See also "DuPont's 'STOP' Helps Prevent Workplace Injuries and Incidents," *Asia Africa Intelligence Wire* (May 17, 2004).

64. James Nash, "Weyerhaeuser Fires Plant, Safety Managers for Record-Keeping Abuses," *Occupational Hazards* (November 2004): 27–28.

65. In a similar case, the owner of a Brooklyn New York construction site was arrested for manslaughter when a worker died in a collapsed trench. Michael Wilson, "Manslaughter Charge in Trench Collapse," *New York Times* (June 12, 2008): B1.

66. "A Safety Committee Man's Guide," 17–21.

67. Dov Zohar, "A Group Level Model of Safety Climate: Testing the Effect of a Group Climate on Students in Manufacturing Jobs," *Journal of Applied Psychology* 85, no. 4 (2000): 587–596. See also Steven Yule, Rhona Flin, and Andy Murdy, "The Role of Management and Safety Climate in Preventing Risk-Taking at Work," *International Journal of Risk Assessment and Management* 7, no. 2 (December 20, 2006): 137.

68. Quoted from Sandy Smith, "Breakthrough Safety Management," *Occupational Hazards* (June 2004): 43. For a discussion of developing a safety climate survey, see also Sara Singer et al., "Workforce Perceptions of Hospital Safety Culture: Development and Validation of the Patient Safety Climate in Healthcare Organizations Survey," *Health Services Research* 42, no. 5 (October 2007): 19–23.

69. "Workplace Safety: Improving Management Practices," *BNA Bulletin to Management* (February 9, 1989): 42, 47. See also Linda Johnson, "Preventing Injuries: The Big Payoff," *Personnel Journal* (April 1994): 61–64; David Webb, "The Bathtub Effect: Why Safety Programs Fail," *Management Review* (February 1994): 51–54.

70. Thomas Krause, "Steps in Safety Strategy: Executive Decision-Making & Metrics," *EHS Today* (September 2009): 24.

71. www.aihaaps.ca/palm/occhazards.html, accessed April 26, 2009.

72. Michael Blotzer, "PDA Software Offers Auditing Advances," *Occupational Hazards* (December 2001): 11.

73. Sandy Smith, "Zero Isn't Good Enough at Amec Earth & Environmental," *EHS Today* (November 2009): 26; Laura Walter, "Safety Evolves at the Concrete Pipe Division of Cemex US Operations," *EHS Today* (November 2009): 27.

74. Katherine Torres, "Making a Safety Committee Work for You," *Occupational Hazards* 68, no. 10 (Oct 2006): 51(6).

75. www.zeraware.com, accessed March 22, 2009.

76. This is based on Paul Puncochar, "The Science and Art to Identifying Workplace Hazards," *Occupational Hazards* (September 2003): 50–54.

77. Recently, the United States has been moving toward adopting the United Nations' globally harmonized system of classification and labeling of chemicals. See Jytte Syska, "GHS: What You Need to Know," *EHS Today* (November 2009): 43.

78. Ibid., 52.

79. Where employees may encounter chemical spills, OSHA standards require that emergency eye washers and showers be available for employees to use. Michael Bolden, "Choosing and Maintaining Emergency Eye Washers/Showers," *EHS Today* (January 2010): 39–41.

80. "Intervention: What Employers Can and Should Do About Excessive Alcohol Use," www.ensuringsolutions.org/resources/resources_show.htm?doc_id=673239, accessed August 11, 2009.

81. "15% of Workers Drinking, Drunk, or Hung Over While at Work, According to New University Study," *BNA Bulletin to Management* (January 24, 2006): 27.

82. Beth Andrus, "Accommodating the Alcoholic Executive," Society for Human Resource Management legal report (January 2008): 1, 4.

83. Teresa Long, "Intexicated Drivers and Employer Liability," *EHS Today* (September 2009): 22–23.

84. "Feds Ordered, Contractors Urged, Not to Text While Driving," *BNA Bulletin to Management* (October 6, 2009): 314.

85. See, for example, L. Claussen, "Can You Spot the Meth Addict?" *Safety & Health* 179, no. 4 (April 2009): 48–52.

86. "New Jersey Union Takes on Mandatory Random Drug Tests," *Record* (Hackensack, NJ, January 2, 2008).

87. Frank Lockwood et al., "Drug Testing Programs and Their Impact on Workplace Accidents: A Time Series Analysis," *Journal of Individual Employment Rights* 8, no. 4 (2000): 295–306; Sally Roberts, "Random Drug Testing Can Help Reduce Accidents for Construction Companies; Drug Abuse Blamed for Heightened Risk in the Workplace," *Business Insurance* 40 (October 23, 2006): 6.

88. www.dol.gov/asp/programs/drugs/workingpartners/sab/screen.asp, accessed April 27, 2008.

89. Gopal Pati and John Adkins Jr., "The Employer's Role in Alcoholism Assistance," *Personnel Journal* 62, no. 7 (July 1983): 570. See also Commerce Clearing House, "How Should Employers Respond to Indications an Employee May Have an Alcohol or Drug Problem?" *Ideas and Trends* (April 6, 1989): 53–57; "The Employer's Role in Alcoholism Assistance," *Personnel Journal* 62, no. 7 (July 1983): 568–572.

90. William Current, "Pre-Employment Drug Testing," *Occupational Hazards* (July 2002): 56. See also William Current, "Improving Your Drug Testing ROI," *Occupational Health & Safety* 73, no. 4 (April 2004): 40, 42, 44.

91. Diane Cadrain, "Are Your Employees' Drug Tests Accurate?" *HR Magazine* (January 2003): 41–45.

92. Sally Roberts, "Random Drug Testing Can Help Reduce Accidents for Construction Companies; Drug Abuse Blamed for Heightened Risk in the Workplace," *Business Insurance* 40 (October 23, 2006): 6.

93. The research is quite clear that work stress increases alcohol use among normal drinkers and this has several implications for employers. Employers and supervisors should take steps to reduce stressful daily work experiences such as interpersonal conflicts at work, role ambiguity, and excessive workloads as way to reduce stress. Songqi Liu et al., "Daily Work Stress and Alcohol Use: Testing the Cross Level Moderation Effects of Neuroticism and Job Involvement," *Personnel Psychology* 60, no. 2 (2009): 575–597.

94. www.OSHA.gov, accessed May 28, 2005.

95. Patrick Thibodeau, "Stress Causes Strains in IT Shops: Job Demands Overtax Some Workers, Data Center Pros Say," *Computerworld* 40, no. 34 (August 21, 2006): 1(2).

96. Eric Sundstrom et al., "Office Noise, Satisfaction, and Performance," *Environment and Behavior*, no. 2 (March 1994): 195–222; "Stress: How to Cope with Life's Challenges," *American Family Physician* 74, no. 8 (October 15, 2006).

97. A. S. Antoniou, F. Polychroni, A. N. Vlachakis, "Gender and Age Differences in Occupational Stress and Professional Burnout between Primary and High-School Teachers in Greece," *Journal of Managerial Psychology* 21, no. 7 (September 2006): 682–690.

98. "Failing to Tackle Stress Could Cost You Dearly," *Personnel Today* (September 12, 2006); www.sciencedaily.com/releases/2007/06/070604170722.htm, accessed November 3, 2009: "Research Brief: Stress May Accelerate Alzheimer's," *GP* (September 8, 2006): 2.

99. "Stress, Depression Cost Employers," *Occupational Hazards* (December 1998): 24; Patricia B. Gray, "Hidden Costs of Stress," *Money* 36, no. 12 (Dec 2007): 44.

100. Karl Albrecht, *Stress and the Manager* (Upper Saddle River, NJ: Prentice Hall, 1979): 253–255. Reprinted by permission. See also "Stress: How to Cope with Life's Challenges," *American Family Physician* 74, no. 8 (October 15, 2006).

101. Catalina Dolar, "Meditation Gives Your Mind Permanent Working Holiday; Relaxation Can Improve Your Business Decisions and Your Overall Health," *Investors Business Daily* (March 24, 2004): 89.

102. "Going Head to Head with Stress," *Personnel Today* (April 26, 2005): 1.

103. Kathryn Tyler, "Stress Management," *HR Magazine* (September 2006): 79–82.

104. "Meditation Helps Employees Focus, Relieve Stress," *BNA Bulletin to Management* (February 20, 2007): 63. See also "Workplace Yoga, Meditation Can Reduce Stress," *EHS Today* (September 2009): 21.

105. George DeVries III, "Innovations in Workplace Wellness: Six New Tools to Enhance Programs and Maximize Employee Health and Productivity," *Compensation & Benefits Review* 42, no. 1 (January/February 2010): 46–51.

106. Madan Mohan Tripathy, "Burnout Stress Syndrome in Managers," *Management and Labor Studies* 27, no. 2 (April 2002): 89–111. See also Jonathon R. B. Halbesleben and Cheryl Rathert, "Linking Physician Burnout and Patient Outcomes: Exploring the Dyadic Relationship Between Physicians and Patients," *Health Care Management Review* 33, no. 1 (January–March 2008): 29(11).

107. See, for example, Michael Christian et al., "Workplace Safety: A Meta-Analysis of the Roles of Person and Situation Factors," *Journal of Applied Psychology* 94, no. 5 (2009): 1103–1127.

108. Andy Meisler, "Mind Field," *Workforce Management* (September 2003): 58.

109. "Employers Must Move From Awareness to Action in Dealing with Worker Depression," *BNA Bulletin to Management* (April 29, 2004): 137.

110. "Risk of Carpal Tunnel Syndrome Not Linked to Heavy Computer Work, Study Says," *BNA Bulletin to Management* (June 28, 2001): 203.

111. www.OSHA.gov, accessed May 28, 2005.

112. Anne Chambers, "Computer Vision Syndrome: Relief Is in Sight," *Occupational Hazards* (October 1999): 179–184; www.OSHA.gov/ETOOLS/computerworkstations/index.html, accessed May 28, 2005.

113. Sandra Lotz Fisher, "Are Your Employees Working Ergosmart?" *Personnel Journal* (December 1996): 91–92. See also www.cdc.gov/od/ohs/Ergonomics/compergo.htm, accessed May 26, 2007.

114. ww.ninds.nih.gov/disorders/repetitive_motion/repetitive_ motion.htm, accessed February 28, 2010.

115. Sandy Smith, "SARS: What Employers Need to Know," *Occupational Hazards* (July 2003): 33–35.

116. "CDC Recommends Respirators in Revised H1N1 Flu Guidance for Healthcare Workers," *BNA Bulletin to Management* (October 20, 2009): 329–336; and Pamela Ferrante, "H1N1: Spreading The Message," *EHS Today* (January 2010): 25–27.

117. Diane Cadrain, "Smoking and Workplace Laws Ensnaring HR," *HR Magazine* 49, no. 6 (June 2004): 38–39.

118. Kenneth Sovereign, *Personnel Law* (Upper Saddle River, NJ: Prentice Hall, 1999): 76–79.

119. Stephen Miller, "Employers Want to Help Employees QuitSmoking, But How?" (January 2007), www.shrm.org/rewards/library_published/benefits/nonIC/CMS_ 019756.asp, accessed April 27, 2008.

120. Ibid. See also "Workplace Smoking: How Far Should You Go?" *Managing Benefits Plans* 5–6 (June 2005): 2(2).

121. Stephen Bates, "Where There Is Smoke, There Are Terminations: Smokers Fired to Save Health Costs," *HR Magazine* 50, no. 3 (March 2005): 28–29.

122. Pamela Babcock, "Helping Workers Kick the Habit," *HR Magazine* (September 2007): 120.

123. "Worker Opens Fire at Ohio Jeep Plant," *Occupational Hazards* (March 2005): 16.

124. "Workplace Violence Takes a Deadly Toll," *EHS Today* (December 2009): 17.

125. Jerry Hoobler and Jennifer Swanberg, "The Enemy Is Not Us," *International Personnel Management Association for HR* 35, no. 3 (Fall 2006): 229–246.

126. "Violence in Workplace Soaring, New Study Says," *Baltimore Business Journal* 18, no. 34 (January 5, 2001): 24.

127. "Bullies Trigger 'Silent Epidemic' at Work, but Legal Cures Remain Hard to Come By," *BNA Bulletin to Management* (February 24, 2000): 57.

128. www.cdc.gov/ncipc/dvp/ipv_factsheet.pdf, accessed February 28, 2010.

129. Paul Viollis and Doug Kane, "At-Risk Terminations: Protecting Employees, Preventing Disaster," *Risk Management Magazine* 52, no. 5 (May 2005): 28–33.

130. M. Sandy Hershcovis et al., "Predicting Workplace Aggression: A Meta-Analysis," *Journal of Applied Psychology* 92, no. 1 (2007): 228–238.

131. Alfred Feliu, "Workplace Violence and the Duty of Care: The Scope of an Employer's Obligation to Protect Against the Violent Employee," *Employee Relations Law Journal* 20, no. 3 (Winter 1994/95): 395.

132. Dawn Anfuso, "Deflecting Workplace Violence," *Personnel Journal* (October 1994): 66–77.

133. Alfred Feliu, "Workplace Violence and the Duty of Care: The Scope of an Employer's Obligation to Protect Against the Violent Employee," *Employee Relations Law Journal* 20, no. 3 (Winter 1994/95): 395.

134. See, for example, James Thelan, "Is That a Threat?" *HR Magazine* (December 2009): 61–63.

135. Feliu, op cit.

136. Ibid., 401–402.

137. See "Creating a Safer Workplace: Simple Steps Bring Results," *Safety Now* (September 2002): 1–2. See also L. Claussen, "Disgruntled and Dangerous," *Safety & Health* v. 180, no. 1 (July 2009): 44-47

138. "Employers Battling Workplace Violence Might Consider Postal Service Plan," *BNA Bulletin to Management* (August 5, 1999): 241.

139. Paul Viollis and Doug Kane, "At-Risk Terminations: Protecting Employees, Preventing Disaster," *Risk Management* 52, no. 15 (May 2005): 28–33.

140. Kenneth Diamond, "The Gender-Motivated Violence Act: What Employers Should Know," *Employee Relations Law Journal* 25, no. 4 (Spring 2000): 29–41; "Bush Signs 'Violence Against Women Act'; Funding Badly Needed Initiatives to Prevent Domestic & Sexual Violence, Help Victims," *The America's Intelligence Wire* (January 5, 2006).

141. Sources of *external* risk include legal/regulatory, political and business environment (economy, e-business, etc.). *Internal* risks sources include financial, strategic, operational [including safety and security] and integrity (embezzlement, theft, fraud, etc.). William Atkinson, "Enterprise Risk Management at Wal-Mart," www.rmmag.com/MGTemplate.cfm?Section= RMMagazine&NavMenuID=128&template=/Magazine/ DisplayMagazines.cfm&MGPreview=1&Volume=50& IssueID=205&AID=2209&ShowArticle=1, accessed April 1, 2009.

142. Unless otherwise noted, the following is based on Richard Maurer, "Keeping Your Security Program Active," *Occupational Hazards* (March 2003): 49–52.

143. Ibid., 50.

144. Ibid., 50.

145. Della Roberts, "Are You Ready for Biometrics?" *HR Magazine* (March 2003): 95–99.

146. Richard Maurer, "Keeping Your Security Program Active," *Occupational Hazards* (March 2003): 52.

147. "Survey Finds Reaction to September 11 Attacks Spurred Companies to Prepare for Disasters," *BNA Bulletin to Management* (November 29, 2005): 377.

148. http://view.fdu.edu/default.aspx?id=3705, accessed February 28, 2010.

149. Lloyd Newman, "Terrorism: Is Your Company Prepared?" *Business and Economic Review* 48, no. 2 (February 2002): 7–10; Li Yuan et al., "Texting When There's Trouble," *Wall Street Journal* (April 18, 2007): B1.

150. "Swine Flu Tests Employer Emergency Plan; Experts Urge Communicating Best Practices," *BNA Bulletin to Management* (May 5, 2009): 137–144.

151. Sandy Devine, "Are You Ready for a Sudden Cardiac Arrest Emergency?" *EHS Today* (April 2009): 26–29.

152. Cynthia Roth, "How to Protect the Aging Workforce," *Occupational Hazards* 67 no. 1 (2005), http://ehstoday.com/ health/ergonomics/ehs_imp_37390/index.html, accessed July, 2010.

153. "Importance of Taking Precautions for Overseas Operations Underscored by Mumbai Attacks," *BNA Bulletin to Management* (January 6, 2009): 1–8.

154. Judi Komaki, Kenneth Barwick, and Lawrence Scott, "A Behavioral Approach to Occupational Safety: Pinpointing and Reinforcing Safe Performance in a Food Manufacturing Plant," *Journal of Applied Psychology* 63 (August 1978): 434–445. See also Anat Arkin, "Incentives to Work Safely," *Personnel Management* 26, no. 9 (September 1994): 48–52; Peter Making and Valerie Sutherland, "Reducing Accidents Using a Behavioral Approach," *Leadership and Organizational Development Journal* 15, no. 5 (1994): 5–10; Sandy Smith, "Why Cash Isn't King," *Occupational Hazards* (March 2004): 37–38.

12 Managing Human Resources in Entrepreneurial Firms

SYNOPSIS

- The Small Business Challenge
- Using Internet and Government Tools to Support the HR Effort
- Leveraging Small Size: Familiarity, Flexibility, Fairness, Informality, and HRM
- Using Professional Employer Organizations
- Managing HR Systems, Procedures, and Paperwork

Source: Jeff Greenberg/Alamy Images.

When you finish studying this chapter, you should be able to:

1. Explain why HRM is important to small businesses and how small business HRM is different.

2. Give four examples of how entrepreneurs can use Internet and government tools to support the HR effort.

3. List five ways entrepreneurs can use their small size to improve their HR processes.

4. Discuss how you would choose and deal with a professional employee organization.

5. Describe how you would create a start-up human resource system for a new small business.

INTRODUCTION

It's not easy running a restaurant. Customers are notoriously fickle, food hygiene is always a concern, and (perhaps most unnerving to many restaurant owners) it's exceedingly difficult to hire and keep good employees. Half of all restaurant employees are under 30 years old, and turnover of more than 100% per year is the norm.[1] So, when the owner of 11 IHOP restaurants around Atlanta looked at the industry's turnover statistics, he knew he and his partner needed to do something. The question was what to do?[2] ■

THE SMALL BUSINESS CHALLENGE

Why Entrepreneurship Is Important

In terms of the U.S. economy, the phrase *small business* is a misnomer. More than half the people working in the United States—about 68 million out of 118 million—work for small firms.[3] Small businesses as a group also account for most of the 600,000 or so new businesses created every year, as well as for most of business growth (small firms grow faster than big ones). And small firms account for about three-quarters of the employment growth in the U.S. economy—in other words, they create most of the new jobs in the United States.[4]

Statistically speaking, therefore, most people graduating from colleges in the next few years either do or will work for small businesses—those with less than 200 or so employees. Anyone interested in human resource management thus needs to understand how managing human resources in small firms is different from doing so in huge multinationals.

How Small Business Human Resource Management Is Different

Managing human resources in small firms is different for four main reasons: *size, priorities, informality*, and the nature of the *entrepreneur*.

SIZE For one thing, it would be very unusual to find a very small business—say, under 90 or so employees—with a dedicated human resource management professional.[5] The rule of thumb is that it's not until a company reaches the 100-employee milestone that it can afford an HR specialist. That's not to say that small businesses don't have human resource tasks. Even five- to six-person retail shops must recruit, select, train, and compensate employees, for instance. It's just that in such situations, it's usually the owner and (sometimes) his or her assistant that does all the HR paperwork and tasks. SHRM's *Human Capital Benchmarking Study* found, for instance, that even firms with under 100 employees often spend the equivalent of two-or-so people's time each year addressing human resource management issues.[6] But, that time is usually just coming out of the owner's very long workday.

PRIORITIES It's not just size but the realities of the situation that drive many entrepreneurs to expend more time and resources on non-HR issues. After studying small e-commerce firms in the United Kingdom, one researcher concluded that, as important as human resource management is, it simply wasn't a high priority for these firms:

> Given their shortage of resources in terms of time, money, people and expertise, a typical SME [small and medium size enterprise] manager's organizational imperatives are perceived elsewhere, in finance, production and marketing, with HR of diminished relative importance.[7]

INFORMALITY One effect of this is that human resource management activities tend to be less formalized (more informal) in smaller firms. For example, one study analyzed training practices in about 900 family and non-family small companies.[8] Training tended to be informal, with an emphasis, for instance, on methods like coworker and supervisory on-the-job training.

Such informality isn't just due to a lack of expertise and resources (although that's part of it); it's also partly a "matter of survival." Entrepreneurs must be able to react quickly to changes in competitive conditions. Given that, there's some logic in keeping things like compensation policies flexible. As one researcher says, the need for small businesses to adapt quickly to competitive challenges often means handling matters like raises, appraisals, and time off "on an informal, reactive basis with a short time horizon."[9]

THE ENTREPRENEUR *Entrepreneurs* are people who create businesses under risky conditions, and starting new businesses from scratch is always risky. Entrepreneurs therefore need to be dedicated and visionary. Researchers therefore believe that small firms' relative informality partly stems from entrepreneurs' unique personalities. Entrepreneurs tend (among other things) to be somewhat controlling: "Owners tend to want to impose their stamp and personal management style on internal matters, including the primary goal and orientation of the firm, its working conditions and policies, and the style of internal and external communication and how this is communicated to the staff."[10]

IMPLICATIONS These four differences have several human resource management–related implications for small businesses.

- First, small business owners run the risk that their relatively rudimentary human resource practices will put them at a *competitive disadvantage*. A small business owner not using tools like Web-based recruiting is accumulating unnecessary costs, and probably deriving inferior results than (larger) competitors.
- Second, there is a *lack of specialized HR expertise*.[11] In most (larger) small businesses, there is at most one or two dedicated human resource management people responsible for the full range of HR functions. This makes it more likely that entrepreneurs may miss problems in specific areas, such as equal employment law, or occupational safety. This may produce legal or other problems.
- Third, the smaller firm is probably not adequately addressing potential *workplace litigation*. The firm often hasn't the time or specialized expertise to really understand the *legal implications*—for instance, of innocently (but inappropriately) asking a female job candidate if she's thinking of "starting a family."
- Fourth, the small business owner may not be fully complying with *compensation regulations and laws*. These include (as examples) how to pay compensatory time for overtime hours worked, and distinguishing between employees and independent contractors.
- Fifth, paperwork duplication leads to inefficiencies and *data entry errors*. For small businesses, many of which don't use human resource information systems, employee data (name, address, marital status, and so on) often appears on multiple human resource management forms (medical enrollment forms, W-4 forms, and so on). Any change requires manually changing all forms. This is time-consuming and inefficient, and can precipitate errors.

---

1 Explain why HRM is important to small businesses and how small business HRM is different.

Why HRM Is Important to Small Businesses

Entrepreneurs need to take these implications to heart. Small firms need all the advantages they can get, and for them effective human resource management is a competitive necessity. Small firms that have effective HR practices do better than those that do not.[12] For example, researchers studied 168 family-owned fast growth small and medium size enterprises (SMEs). They concluded that successful high-growth SMEs placed greater importance on training and development, performance appraisals, recruitment packages, maintaining morale, and setting competitive compensation levels than did low-performing firms: "These findings suggest that these human resource activities do in fact have a positive impact on performance [in smaller businesses]."[13]

For many small firms, effective human resource management is also mandatory for getting and keeping big customers. Most suppliers (and therefore *their* suppliers) must comply with international quality standards. Thus, to comply with ISO-9000 requirements, large customers "either directly checked for the presence of certain HR policies, or, satisfying their service demands indirectly necessitated changes in, for example, [the small vendor's] training and job design."[14]

We turn in this chapter to methods entrepreneurs can use to improve their human resource management practices, starting with Internet and government tools.

USING INTERNET AND GOVERNMENT TOOLS TO SUPPORT THE HR EFFORT

City Garage's managers knew they would never implement their firm's growth strategy without changing how they tested and hired employees.[15] At this fast-growing chain of repair shops, the old hiring process consisted of a paper-and-pencil application and one interview, followed by a hire/don't hire decision. The process ate up valuable management time, and was not particularly effective. City Garage's solution was to purchase the Personality Profile Analysis (PPA) online test from Thomas International USA. Now, after a quick application and background check, likely candidates take the 10-minute, 24-question PPA. City Garage staff then enter the answers into the PPA Software system, and receive test results in less than 2 minutes. These show whether the applicant is high or low in four personality characteristics.

Like City Garage, no small business owner needs to cede the advantage to big competitors when it comes to human resource management. One way to level the terrain is to use Internet-based HR resources, including the free resources of the U.S. government. We'll look at how small firms do this, for things such as legal compliance and employee selection and training, next.

Complying with Employment Laws

Complying with federal (and state and local) employment law is a thorny issue for entrepreneurs. For example, under the law, the entrepreneur needs to know, "What can I ask a job candidate?" "Must I pay this person overtime?" and, "Must I report this injury?"

2 Give four examples of how entrepreneurs can use Internet and government tools to support the HR effort.

Addressing such issues starts with deciding which federal employment laws apply to the company. For example, Title VII of the Civil Rights Act of 1964 applies to employers with 15 or more employees, while the Age Discrimination in Employment Act of 1967 applies to those with 20 or more.[16] Small business owners will find the legal answers they need online at federal agencies' Web sites like the following.

THE DOL The U.S. Department of Labor's "*FirstStep* Employment Law Advisor" (see www.DOL.gov/elaws/firststep/) helps small businesses determine which laws apply to their business. First, the elaws wizard takes the owner through questions such as "What is the maximum number of employees your business or organization employs or will employ during the calendar year?" (See Figure 12.1).

Proceeding through the wizard, the small business owner arrives at a "results" page. This says, "Based on the information you provided in response to the questions in the Advisor, the following employment laws administered by the Department of Labor (DOL) may apply to your business or organization."[17] For a typical small firm, these laws might include the Consumer

City Garage's managers knew they would never implement their firm's growth strategy without changing how they tested and hired employees.

FIGURE 12.1

FirstStep **Employment Law Advisor**

Source: www.dol.gov/elaws/firststep, accessed June 2008.

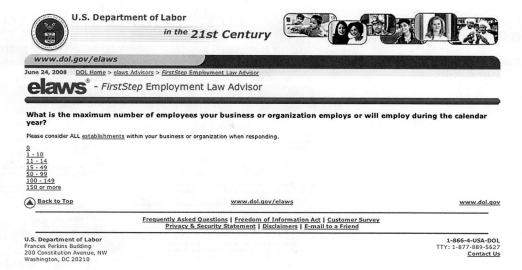

Credit Protection Act, Employee Polygraph Protection Act, Fair Labor Standards Act, Immigration and Nationality Act, Occupational Safety and Health Act, Uniformed Services Employment and Reemployment Rights Act, and Whistleblower Act.

A linked DOL site (www.dol.gov/whd/flsa/index.htm) provides information on the Fair Labor Standards Act (FLSA). It contains several specific "elaws Advisors." Each provides practical guidance on questions such as when to pay overtime. Figure 12.2 presents, from this Web site, a list of elaws Advisors.

THE EEOC The U.S. Equal Employment Opportunity Commission (EEOC) administers Title VII of the Civil Rights Act of 1964 (Title VII), the Age Discrimination in Employment Act of 1967 (ADEA), Title I of the Americans with Disabilities Act of 1990 (ADA), and the Equal Pay Act of 1963 (EPA). Its Web site (www.EEOC.gov/employers/) contains important information regarding matters such as:

- How do I determine if my business is covered by EEOC laws?
- Who may file a charge of discrimination with the EEOC?
- Can a small business resolve a charge without undergoing an investigation or facing a lawsuit?

As the EEOC says, "While the information in this section of our website applies to all employers, it has been specifically designed for small businesses which may not have a human resources department or a specialized EEO staff." (http://www.eeoc.gov/employers/index.cfm) The site provides small business owners with practical advice. For example, "What should I do when someone files a charge against my company?"

FIGURE 12.2

Sample DOL Elaws Advisors

Note: These are from www.dol.gov/whd/flsa/index.htm, accessed May 28, 2010.

- The *Coverage and Employment Status Advisor* helps identify which workers are employees covered by the FLSA.
- The *Hours Worked Advisor* provides information to help determine which hours spent in work-related activities are considered FLSA "hours worked" and, therefore, must be paid.
- The *Overtime Security Advisor* helps determine which employees are exempt from the FLSA minimum wage and overtime pay requirements under the Part 541 overtime regulations.
- The *Overtime Calculator Advisor* computes the amount of overtime pay due in a sample pay period based on information from the user.
- The *Child Labor Rules Advisor* answers questions about the FLSA's youth employment provisions, including at what age young people can work and the jobs they can perform.
- The *Section 14(c) Advisor* helps users understand the special minimum wage requirements for workers with disabilities.

FIGURE 12.3

OSHA Web Site

Source: www.osha.gov/dcsp/ smallbusiness/index.html.

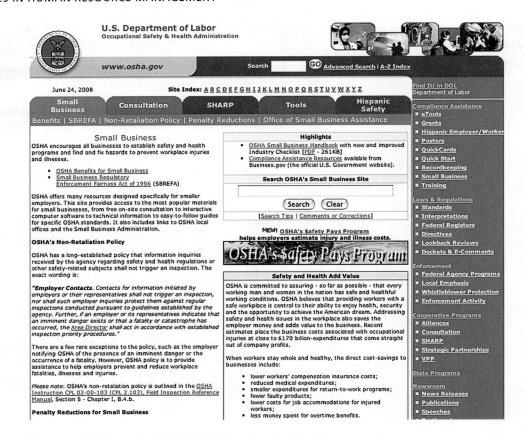

OSHA The DOL's Occupational Safety and Health Administration site (www.OSHA.gov/) similarly supplies small business guidance. (See Figure 12.3.) OSHA's site provides, among other things, easy access to the *OSHA Small Business Handbook.* This contains practical information, including industry-specific safety and accident checklists.

Employment Planning and Recruiting

Internet resources can make small business owners as effective as their large competitors at writing job descriptions and building applicant pools. As we saw in Chapter 4 (page 116), the Department of Labor's O*NET (http://online.onetcenter.org) illustrates this. Its online wizard enables business owners to create accurate and professional job descriptions and job specifications quickly.

WEB-BASED RECRUITING Similarly, small business owners can use the online recruiting tools we discussed in Chapter 4. For example, it's easy to post positions on Internet job boards such as Careerbuilder.com, on the sites of professional associations, or on the sites of local newspapers.

Employment Selection

For the small business, one or two hiring mistakes could wreak havoc. A formal testing program, preferably one that's Web-based like that at City Garage, is advisable.

Some tests are so easy to use they are particularly good for smaller firms. One is the *Wonderlic Personnel Test,* which measures general mental ability. With questions somewhat similar to the SAT, it takes less than 15 minutes to administer the four-page booklet. The tester reads the instructions, and then keeps time as the candidate works through the 50 problems. The tester scores the test by totaling the number of correct answers. Comparing the person's score with the minimum scores recommended for various occupations shows whether the person achieved the minimally acceptable score for the job in question.

The *Predictive Index* is another example. It measures work-related personality traits, drives, and behaviors—in particular dominance, extroversion, patience, and blame avoidance. A template makes scoring simple. The Predictive Index program includes 15 standard benchmark personality patterns. For example, there is the "social interest" pattern, for a person who is generally unselfish, congenial, persuasive, patient, and unassuming. This person would be good with people and a good personnel interviewer, for instance.

Many vendors, including Wonderlic and the Predictive Index, offer online applicant compilation and screening services. Wonderlic's service (which costs about $8,500 per year for a firm with, say, 35 employees) first provides job analyses for the employer's jobs. Wonderlic then provides a Web site the small businesses' applicants can log into to take one or several selection tests (including the Wonderlic Personnel Test). Figure 12.4 shows a partial report for a sample applicant. Here are suggestions from *Inc.* magazine for supercharging a small business's recruiting and screening processes:

- **Keep It in the Industry** Use online job boards that target a particular industry or city to minimize irrelevant applicants.[18] For example, Jobing.com maintains 41 city-specific job sites in 19 states. Beyond.com hosts more than 15,000 industry-specific communities.
- **Automate the Process** Automated applicant processing systems are inexpensive enough for small employers. For example, systems from Taleo, NuView Systems, and Accolo accept résumés and help automate the screening process. NuView, which costs about $6 to $15 per month per user, can instantly ask applicants questions, and bump out those without, for instance, the required education.[19]
- **Test Online** Use online tests, for instance, to test an applicant's typing speed, proficiency at QuickBooks, or even ability to sell over the phone. For example, PreVisor and Kenexa offer close to 1,000 online assessments, charging from several dollars to $50 a test.[20]
- **Poll Your Inner Circle** Tap friends and employees for recommendations and use social networking sites such as LinkedIn, Facebook, and MySpace. Many employers announce job openings through LinkedIn. One says, "I get people vouching for each applicant, so I don't have to spend hours sorting through résumés," he says.[21]
- **Send a Recording** InterviewStream, in Bethlehem, Pennsylvania, records online video interviews, for about $30 to $60. InterviewStream sends the candidate an e-mail invitation with a link. When he or she clicks the link, a video interviewer asks the company's prerecorded questions. A Webcam captures the candidate's answers. Employers can let candidates rerecord their answers. Hiring managers can review the videos at their leisure.[22]

FIGURE 12.4

Wonderlic Personnel Test: Part of a Sample Report

Source: Wonderlic (www.wonderlic.com).

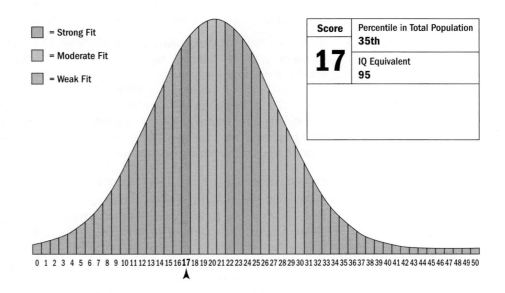

Score Interpretation

Job Fit: Test takers who score in this range do not meet the cognitive ability requirements identified for this job. The complexity present within this position may make it difficult for these individuals to meet minimum standards for job performance.

Training Potential: This test taker is likely to receive maximum benefit from training that follows a programmed or mastery approach to learning. Given enough time, this individual may have the ability to learn a limited number of lengthy, routine procedures. Allow for sufficient time with hands-on-training before requiring this individual to work independently.

COMPLYING WITH THE LAW Particularly when using personality and ability tests at work, the caveat, of course, is to comply with equal employment laws. Unfortunately, given the time pressures facing most small business owners, confirming the validity of those tests one buys online or through office supply stores is probably the exception, not the rule. As Chapter 2 explained, there is no rational or legal basis upon which to expose applicants to tests or devices, the validity of which are unknown. Many test providers will actually assist the employer in setting up a testing procedure. For example, as we noted, Wonderlic will review your job descriptions as part of its process. The only surefire way to ascertain that, say, a test of sales potential really makes sense for your firm is to make sure the test is valid.

Employment Training

Small companies can't compete with the training resources of giants like General Electric. However, Internet training can provide, at a relatively low cost, employee training that used to be beyond most small employers' reach.

PRIVATE VENDORS The small business owner can tap hundreds of suppliers of prepackaged training solutions. These range from self-study programs from the American Management Association (www.amanet.org) and SHRM (www.shrm.org), to specialized programs. For example, the employer might arrange with PureSafety to have its employees take occupational safety courses from www.puresafety.com.

SkillSoft is another example (http://skillsoft.com/catalog/default.asp). Its courses include software development, business strategy and operations, professional effectiveness, and desktop computer skills. As an example, the course "interviewing effectively" targets managers, team leaders, and human resource professionals. About 2 1/2 hours long, it shows trainees how to use behavioral questioning to interview candidates.[23]

The buyer's guide from the American Society of Training and Development (http://www.astd.org/) is a good place to start to find a vendor (check under Resources).

THE SBA The federal government's Small Business Administration (www.SBA.gov/training/) provides a virtual campus that offers online courses, workshops, publications, and learning tools aimed toward supporting entrepreneurs.[24] For example, the small business owner can link under "Small Business Planner" to "Writing Effective Job Descriptions," "Employees versus Contractors: What's the Difference?" and "The Interview Process: How to Select the Right Person" (see Figure 12.5).

NAM The National Association of Manufacturers (NAM) is the largest industrial trade organization in the United States. It represents about 14,000 member manufacturers, including 10,000 small and midsized companies.

NAM's Virtual University (www.namvu.com) helps employees maintain and upgrade their work skills and continue their professional development. It offers almost 650 courses.[25] There are no long-term contracts to sign. Employers simply pay about $10–$30 per course taken by each employee. The catalog includes OSHA, quality, and technical training as well as courses in areas like business and finance, personal development, and customer service.

Employment Appraisal and Compensation

Small employers have easy access to computerized and online appraisal and compensation services. For example, Employee Appraiser (www.employeeappraiser.com/index.php) presents a menu of more than a dozen evaluation dimensions, including dependability, initiative, communication, decision making, leadership, judgment, and planning and productivity.[26] Within each dimension are various performance factors, again in menu form. The eAppraisal system from Halogen Software is another example.[27]

Similarly, lack of easy access to salary surveys once made it difficult and time-consuming for smaller businesses to fine-tune their pay scales. Today, sites like www.salary.com make it easy to determine local pay rates.

Employment Safety and Health

Safety is an important issue for small employers. One European study found that the majority of all the workplace accidents and serious workplace accidents occur in firms with less than 50 employees.[28] OHSA provides several free services for small employers.

FIGURE 12.5

Some Online Courses Offered by the Small Business Administration's Virtual Campus for Small Business Training

Source: www.sba.gov/ smallbusinessplanner/manage/ manageemployees/index.html, accessed April 28, 2009.

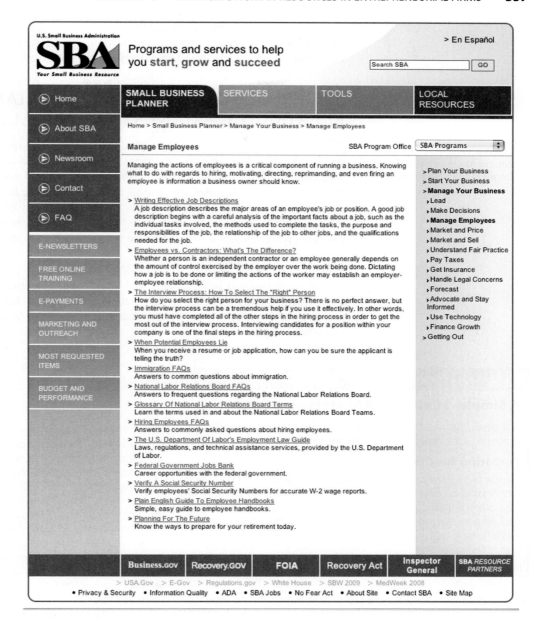

OSHA CONSULTATION Without human resource managers or safety departments, small businesses often don't know where to turn for advice on promoting employee safety.[29] OSHA provides free on-site safety and health services for small businesses. OSHA uses safety experts from state governments who provide consultations, usually at the employer's workplace. Employers can contact their nearest OSHA area office to speak to the compliance assistance specialist. (Employers can also check out the OSHA Training Institute training available in Chicago or in one of about 20 education centers located at U.S. colleges and universities.)

The employer triggers the process by requesting a voluntary consultation. There is then an opening conference with a safety expert, a walk-through, and a closing conference at which the employer and safety expert discuss the latter's observations. The consultant then sends you a detailed report explaining the findings. The employer's only obligation is to commit to correcting serious job safety and health hazards in a timely manner.

OSHA SHARP The OSHA Sharp program is a certification process through which OSHA certifies that small employers have achieved commendable levels of safety awareness.[30] Employers request a consultation and visit, and undergo a complete hazard identification survey. The employer agrees to correct all hazards identified, and to implement and maintain a safety and health management system that, at a minimum, addresses OSHA's safety and health program management guidelines. In addition to producing a certifiably safe workplace, OSHA's on-site project manager may recommend that OSHA exempt the Sharp employer for 2 years from scheduled inspections.

LEVERAGING SMALL SIZE: FAMILIARITY, FLEXIBILITY, FAIRNESS, INFORMALITY, AND HRM

3 List five ways entrepreneurs can use their small size to improve their HR processes.

Because small businesses need to capitalize on their strengths, they should capitalize on their smallness when dealing with employees. Smallness should translate into personal *familiarity* with each employee's strengths, needs, and family situation. And it should translate into the luxury of being able to be relatively *flexible* and *informal* in the human resource management policies and practices the company follows. Smaller businesses must quickly adapt to competitive challenges. This often means that raises, appraisals, and time off tend to be conducted "on an informal, reactive basis with a short time horizon."[31] Flexibility is often key.

Simple, Informal Employee Selection Procedures

Just as small business managers can use Internet-based recruitment and selection tools to help even the recruitment/selection terrain,[32] there are also many low-tech things he or she can do to improve employee selection. We'll look at two streamlined interviews (see the HR in Practice), and work-sampling tests.

HR IN PRACTICE

A Simple, Streamlined Interviewing Process

The small business owner, pressed for time, may use the following practical, streamlined employment interview process:[33]

Preparing for the Interview

Even a busy entrepreneur can quickly specify the kind of person who would be best for the job. One way to do so is to focus on four basic required factors—knowledge and experience, motivation, intellectual capacity, and personality. To proceed this way, ask the following questions:

- *Knowledge and experience:* What must the candidate know to perform the job? What experience is necessary to perform the job?
- *Motivation:* What should the person like doing to enjoy this job? Is there anything the person should not dislike? Are there any essential goals or aspirations the person should have?
- *Intellectual capacity:* Are there any specific intellectual aptitudes required (mathematical, mechanical, and so on)? How complex are the problems the person must solve? What must a person be able to demonstrate he or she can do intellectually?
- *Personality factor:* What are the critical personality qualities needed for success on the job (ability to withstand boredom, decisiveness, stability, and so on)? How must the job incumbent handle stress, pressure, and criticism? What kind of interpersonal behavior is required in the job?

Specific Factors to Probe in the Interview

Next, ask a combination of situational questions plus open-ended questions to probe the candidate's suitability for the job. For example:

- *Knowledge and experience factor:* Here, probe with situational questions such as "How would you organize such a sales effort?" or "How would you design that kind of Web site?"

- *Motivation factor:* Probe such areas as the person's likes and dislikes (for each thing done, what he or she liked or disliked about it), aspirations (including the validity of each goal in terms of the person's reasoning about why he or she chose it), and energy level, perhaps by asking what he or she does on, say, a "typical Tuesday."
- *Intellectual factor:* Here, ask questions that judge such things as complexity of tasks the person has performed, grades in school, test results (including scholastic aptitude tests, and so on), and how the person organizes his or her thoughts and communicates.
- *Personality factor:* Here, probe by looking for self-defeating behaviors (aggressiveness, compulsive fidgeting, and so on) and by exploring the person's past interpersonal relationships. Ask questions about the person's past interactions (working in a group at school, working with fraternity brothers or sorority sisters, leading the work team on the last job, and so on). Also, try to judge the person's behavior in the interview itself—Is the candidate personable? Shy? Outgoing?

Conducting the Interview

- *Have a Plan.* Devise and use a plan to guide the interview. According to interviewing expert John Drake, significant areas to touch on include the candidate's:
  - College experiences
  - Work experiences—summer, part-time
  - Work experience—full-time (one by one)
  - Goals and ambitions
  - Reactions to the job you are interviewing for
  - Self-assessments (by the candidate of his or her strengths and weaknesses)
  - Military experiences
  - Present outside activities[34]

● *Follow Your Plan.* Perhaps start with an open-ended question for each topic, such as "Could you tell me about what you did when you were in high school?" Keep in mind that you are trying to elicit information about four main traits—knowledge and experience, motivation, intelligence, and personality. You can then accumulate the information in each of these four areas as the person answers. Follow up by asking questions like "Could you elaborate on that, please?"

Match the Candidate to the Job

You should now be able to draw conclusions about the person's knowledge and experience, motivation, intellectual capacity, and personality, and to summarize the candidate's strengths and limits. Next, compare your conclusions to the job description and the list of requirements you developed when preparing for the interview. This should provide a rational basis for matching the candidate to the job—one based on an analysis of the traits and aptitudes the job actually requires.

WORK-SAMPLING TESTS What should you do if you are trying to hire, say, a marketing manager, and want a simple way to screen your job applicants? Devising a *work-sampling test* is one simple solution. A work-sampling test means having the candidates perform actual samples of the job in question. Such tests have obvious face validity (they should clearly measure actual job duties) and are easy to devise.

The process is simple. Break down the job's main duties into component tasks. Then have the candidate complete a sample task. For example, for the marketing manager position, ask the candidate to spend an hour designing an ad, and also to spend a half hour writing out a marketing research program for a hypothetical product.

Flexibility in Training

Small companies also typically take a more informal approach to training and development. For example, one study of 191 small and 201 large firms in Europe found that smaller firms were much more informal in their approaches to training and development.[35] Many of the small firms didn't systematically monitor their managers' skill needs, and fewer than 50% (as opposed to 70% of large firms) had career development programs. The smaller firms also tended to focus any management development training on learning specific firm-related competencies (such as how to sell the firm's products).[36] They did so due to resource constraints and a reluctance to invest too much in managers who may then leave.

FOUR-STEP TRAINING PROCESS Limited resources or not, small businesses must have training procedures. A simple but still effective four-step training process follows.

Step 1: **Write a Job Description** A detailed job description is the heart of a training program. List the tasks of each job, along with a summary of the steps in each task.

Step 2: **Develop a Task Analysis Record Form** The small business owner can use an abbreviated *Task Analysis Record Form* (Table 12.1) containing four columns to guide the required coaching.

TABLE 12.1 Sample Summary Task Analysis Record Form

Task List	Performance Standards	Trainable Skills Required	Aptitudes Required
1. Operate paper cutter			
1.1 Start motor	Start by push-button on first try	To start machine without accidentally attempting re-start while machine is running	Ability to understand written and spoken instructions
1.2 Set cutting distance	Maximum +/– tolerance of 0.007 inches	Read gauge	Able to read tolerances on numerical scale
1.3 Place paper on cutting table	Must be completely even to prevent uneven edges	Lift paper correctly	At least average manual dexterity
1.4 Push paper up to paper cutter blade		Must be even with blade	At least average manual dexterity
1.5 Grasp safety release with left hand	100% of the time, for safety	Must keep both hands on releases to prevent hand contact with cutting blade	Ability to understand written and spoken warnings

Note: This shows the first five steps in one of the tasks (operate paper cutter) for which a printing factory owner would train the person doing the cutting of the paper before placing the paper on the printing presses.

- In the first column, list *specific tasks*. Include what is to be performed in terms of each of the main tasks, and the steps involved in each task.
- In the second column, list *performance standards* (in terms of quantity, quality, accuracy, and so on).
- In the third column, list *trainable skills* required—things the employee must know or do to perform the task. Include skills (such as "Keep both hands on the wheel") that you want to emphasize in training.
- In the fourth column, list *aptitudes required*. These are the human aptitudes (such as mechanical comprehension) the employee must have to be trainable, and for which he or she should be screened.

Step 3: Develop a Job Instruction Sheet Next, develop a Job Instruction Sheet for the job. As in Table 12.2, a Job Instruction Sheet shows the steps in each task as well as key points for each.

Step 4: Prepare Training Program for the Job At a minimum, the job's training manual should include the job description, Task Analysis Record Form, and Job Instruction Sheet, all compiled in a training manual. Perhaps also include a brief overview/introduction to the job, and a graphical and/or written explanation of how the job fits with other jobs in the plant or office.

You also have to decide what training media to use. A simple but effective on-the-job training program using current employees or supervisors as trainers requires only the written materials we just listed. However, the nature of the job or the number of trainees may require producing or purchasing special training media. For many jobs such as supervisor or bookkeeper, vendors like those we discussed in Chapter 6 provide packaged multi-media training programs.

INFORMAL TRAINING METHODS Training expert Stephen Covey says small businesses can do many things to provide job-related training without actually establishing expensive formal training programs. His suggestions include:[37]

- Offer to cover the tuition for special classes
- Identify online training opportunities
- Provide a library of tapes and DVDs for systematic, disciplined learning during commute times
- Encourage the sharing of best practices among associates
- When possible, send people to special seminars and association meetings for learning and networking
- Create a learning ethic by having everyone teach each other what they are learning

Flexibility in Benefits and Rewards

The Family and Work Institute surveyed the benefits practices of about 1,000 small and large companies. They examined benefits such as flexible work, child care assistance, and health

---

TABLE 12.2 Sample Job Instruction Sheet

Steps in Task	Key Points to Keep in Mind
1. Start motor	None
2. Set cutting distance	Carefully read scale—to prevent wrong-sized cut
3. Place paper on cutting table	Make sure paper is even—to prevent uneven cut
4. Push paper up to cutter	Make sure paper is tight—to prevent uneven cut
5. Grasp safety release with left hand	Do not release left hand—to prevent hand from being caught in cutter
6. Grasp cutter release with right hand	Do not release right hand—to prevent hand from being caught in cutter
7. Simultaneously pull cutter and safety releases	Keep both hands on corresponding releases—avoid hands being on cutting table
8. Wait for cutter to retract	Keep both hands on releases—to avoid having hands on cutting table
9. Retract paper	Make sure cutter is retracted; keep both hands away from releases
10. Shut off motor	None

At Wards Furniture, workers can share job responsibilities, and work part-time from home.

care.[38] Not surprisingly, they found that large firms offer more *extensive* benefits packages than do smaller ones. However, many small firms overcame their bigger competitors by offering more flexibility. "They've discovered how to turn tiny into tight-knit, earning employees' trust by keeping them in the loop on company news and financials, and their loyalty by providing frequent feedback on performance."[39] At ID Media, with 90 employees, CEO Lynn Fantom gives all new employees a welcome breakfast on their first day. "It shows she wanted to meet us and get our opinions," says one. Internet startup appssavvy Inc.'s CEO foregoes PowerPoint presentations in favor of humorous YouTube videos.[40]

A CULTURE OF FLEXIBILITY Basically, the study found that small companies, because of the relative intimacy that comes from the owners personally interacting with all employees each day, did a better job of fostering a "culture of flexibility." Most importantly, this meant "that supervisors are more supportive and understanding when work/life issues emerge."[41] Wards Furniture in Long Beach, California, exemplifies this. Many of Wards' 17 employees have been with the firm for 10 to 20 years. Brad Ward, an owner, attributes this in part to his firm's willingness to adapt to its workers' needs. For example, workers can share job responsibilities, and work part-time from home.

WORK–LIFE BENEFITS The point is that even without the deep pockets of larger firms, small firms can offer employees work–life benefits that large employers usually can't easily match. Here are some examples:[42]

- *Extra time off* For example, Friday afternoons off in the summer.
- *Compressed workweeks* For example, in the summer, offer compressed workweeks that let them take longer weekends.
- *Bonuses at critical times* Small business owners are more likely to know what's happening in the lives of their employees. Use this knowledge to provide special bonuses, for instance, if an employee has a new baby.
- *Flexibility* For example "if an employee is having a personal problem, help him or her create a work schedule that allows the person to solve problems without feeling like they're going to be in trouble."[43]
- *Sensitivity to employees' strengths and weaknesses* The intimacy of the small business should enable the owner to be better attuned to his or her employees' strengths, weaknesses, and aspirations. Therefore, be more attentive with each of your employees, ask them which jobs they feel most comfortable doing, and give them an opportunity to train for and move into the jobs they desire.
- *Help them better themselves* For example, pay employees to take a class to help them develop their job skills.
- *Feed them* Particularly after a difficult workweek or when, say, a big sale occurs, provide free meals every now and then, perhaps by taking your employees to lunch.
- *Make them feel like owners* For example, endeavor to give your employees input into major decisions, let them work directly with clients, get them client feedback, share company performance data with them, and give them an opportunity to share in the company's financial success.
- *Make sure they have what they need to do their jobs* Performance = Ability × Motivation. Having highly motivated employees is only half the challenge. Also ensure they have the tools they need to do their jobs—for instance, the necessary training, procedures, computers, and so on.
- *Constantly recognize a job well done* Capitalize on your day-to-day interactions with employees to "never miss an opportunity to give your employees the recognition they deserve."[44]

RECOGNITION Everyone likes recognition for a job well done. Studies show that recognition can often be as powerful as financial rewards. The personal nature of small business interactions makes it easier to recognize employees. There are numerous *positive reinforcement rewards* you can use on a day-to-day basis. A short list would include:[45]

- Challenging work assignments
- Freedom to choose own work activity
- Having fun built into work
- More of preferred task
- Role as boss's stand-in when he or she is away
- Role in presentations to top management
- Job rotation
- Encouragement of learning and continuous improvement
- Being provided with ample encouragement
- Being allowed to set own goals
- Compliments
- Expression of appreciation in front of others
- Note of thanks
- Employee-of-the-month award
- Special commendation
- Bigger desk
- Bigger office or cubicle

MANAGING HR IN CHALLENGING TIMES: BENEFITS FOR BAD TIMES

The recession hit smaller businesses' benefits particularly hard. For example, smaller firms' lack of negotiating leverage meant they faced increases in health care premiums of 15% or more, compared with national averages closer to 9%. Many are therefore moving to cheaper policies and having workers pay more.[46] Thus, when the monthly cost of a family policy for Brennan's Prime Meats, a meat wholesaler and retailer with six employees in Marine Park in Brooklyn, jumped almost 30%, to $1,780, its owner, Glenn Izzo, switched to a less expensive plan. His new plan costs $1,137 a month per family. Participating employees will have to absorb new co-payments and possibly pick up half of the premium cost.

A recent survey of 480 U.S. companies found that with the recession, more firms were focusing their retention efforts on job security and "anything they can do to get high performers to feel appreciated."[47] For many employers, this means bulking up their recognition programs. For example, Baudville, a workplace recognition vendor, unveiled an e-card service called ePraise. Employers use this to remind employees of how much they're appreciated. Intuit shifted its employee recognition, years of service, patent awards, and wellness awards programs from several vendors to Globoforce several years ago. The move "allowed us to build efficiencies and improved effectiveness" into the programs' management, says Intuit's vice president of performance, rewards, and workplace.[48]

SIMPLE RETIREMENT BENEFITS Access to retirement benefits is more prevalent in large firms than small ones. About 75% of large firms offer them, while about 35% of small ones do.[49]

There are several straightforward ways for small firms to provide retirement plans for their employees. The *Pension Protection Act of 2006* provides for a new type of retirement benefit that combines traditional defined benefit and 401(k) (defined contribution) plans.[50] Only available to employers with less than 500 employees, it exempts employers from the complex pension rules to which large employers must adhere. With this new benefit, the employees get a retirement plan that blends a defined pension set by the plan, plus returns on the part of the investment that plan participants contributed.[51]

Probably the easiest way for small businesses to provide retirement benefits is through a *SIMPLE IRA plan*. With the *SIMPLE* (for *Savings Incentive Match Plan for Employees*) *IRA*, employers must (and employees may) make contributions to traditional employee IRAs. These plans are for employers or small businesses with 100 or fewer employees and no other type of retirement plan.

SIMPLE IRAs have many advantages—starting with simplicity. Basically, the owner just contacts an eligible financial institution and fills out several IRS forms. The IRS needs to have previously approved the financial institution. However, banks, mutual funds, and insurance companies that issue annuity contracts are generally eligible.[52] The plan has very low administrative costs. Employer contributions are tax-deductible. With a SIMPLE IRA, each employee is always 100% vested.[53]

Under these plans, the employer *must* contribute and employees *may* contribute. A typical employer contribution might match employee contributions dollar for dollar up to 3% of pay. The financial institution usually handles the IRS paperwork and reporting.

Improved Communications

Seeking to shield their 11 IHOP restaurants from the industry's sky-high turnover rates, the owners from the opening scenario hit on a solution. They dramatically reduced turnover with a new online system. It lets new employees anonymously report their opinions about the hiring process.[54] Feedback from that simple communication tool enabled them to recalibrate their firm's training and orientation methods, and reduce turnover by about a third.

Effective communications are especially important for those managing small businesses. With a thousand or more employees, one or two disgruntled employees may get lost in the shuffle. But in a small shop with 5 or 10 employees, one or two disgruntled employees can destroy the business's service. That's why simple programs, like the one at IHOP or the following ones, are important.

NEWSLETTER In Bonita Springs, Florida, Mel's Gourmet Diner keeps employees informed with a quarterly newsletter. It distributes copies at the chain's 10 locations, but also posts it on the company Web site, and plans to translate it into Spanish. "It sounds like a cliché, but our people are the keys to our success," says the owner. "We want to make sure we give them all the information and tools they need."[55]

ONLINE Each time employees of Tampa, Florida-based Let's Eat! go to one of the firm's computers to input a guest's order, they can quickly review the chain's menu changes, special promotions, and mandatory employee meetings.[56]

THE HUDDLE Sea Island Shrimp House in San Antonio, Texas, keeps employees in its seven restaurants communicating with what it calls "cascading huddles." As in football parlance, the huddles are very quick meetings. At 9 A.M. top management meets in the first of the day's "huddles." The next huddle is a conference call with store managers. Then, store managers meet with hourly employees at each location before the restaurants open, to make sure the news of the day gets communicated. "It's all about alignment and good, timely communications," says the company. "Any issues on that day that needed to be communicated would happen in that huddles sequence."[57]

Fairness and the Family Business

Most small businesses are "family businesses," since the owner (and, often, one or more managers and employees) are family members.

Being a non-family employee here isn't easy. Feeling like outsiders can be bad enough. In addition the tendency to treat family and non-family employees differently can undermine perceptions of fairness and morale. If so, as one writer puts it, "It's a sure bet that their lower morale and simmering resentments are having a negative effect on your operations and sapping your profits."[58] Reducing such "fairness" problems involves several steps, including:[59]

- *Set the ground rules.* One family business consultant says,

    During the hiring process the applicant should be informed as to whether he or she will be essentially a placeholder, or whether there will be potential for promotion. At a minimum, make the expectations clear, regarding matters such as the level of authority and decision-making the person can expect to attain.[60]

- *Treat people fairly.* Most employees in a family business understand that they won't be treated exactly the same as family members. However, they do expect to be treated fairly. This means working hard to avoid "any appearance that family members are benefiting unfairly from the sacrifice of others."[61] For that reason, family members in many family businesses avoid ostentatious purchases like expensive cars. (Several years ago, a book titled *The Millionaire Next Door* explained that some small business owners were so frugal that their neighbors didn't realize they were millionaires.)

● *Confront family issues.* Discord and tension among family members distracts and demoralizes other employees. Family members must confront and work out their differences.
● *Erase privilege.* Family members "should avoid any behavior that would lead people to the conclusion that they are demanding special treatment in terms of assignments or responsibilities."[62] Family employees should come in earlier, work harder, and stay later than other employees stay. Endeavor to show that family members earned their promotions.

USING PROFESSIONAL EMPLOYER ORGANIZATIONS

The 40 employees at First Weigh Manufacturing in Sanford, Florida, don't work for a giant company, but they get benefits as if they do. That's because Tom Strasse, First Weigh's owner, signed with ADP Total Source, a *professional employer organization.* It now handles all First Weigh's HR processes. "I didn't have the time or the personnel to deal with the human resources, safety, and OSHA regulations," Strasse says.[63]

At the end of the day, many small business owners, like Tom Strasse, look at the issues involved with managing personnel, and decide to outsource most of their human resource functions to outside vendors. These vendors go by the names *professional employer organizations* (PEOs), *human resource outsourcers* (HROs), or sometimes *employee* or *staff leasing firms.*

4 Discuss how you would choose and deal with a professional employee organization.

How Do PEOs Work?

These vendors range from specialized payroll companies to those that handle all an employer's human resource management requirements.[64] At a minimum, these firms take over the employer's payroll tasks.[65] Usually, however, PEOs assume most of the employer's human resources chores.

PEOs have several characteristics. By transferring the client firm's employees to the PEO's payroll, PEOs become co-employers of record for the employer's employees. That enables the PEO to fold the client's employees into the PEO's insurance and benefits program, usually at a lower cost. The PEO usually handles employee-related activities such as recruiting, hiring (with client firms' supervisors' approvals), and payroll and taxes (Social Security payments, unemployment insurance, and so on). Most PEOs focus on employers with under 100 employees, and charge fees of 2% to 4% of a company's payroll. HROs usually handle these functions on an "administrative services only"—they're basically your "HR office," but your employees still work for you.[66]

Why Use a PEO?

Employers turn to PEOs for several reasons:

LACK OF SPECIALIZED HR SUPPORT Small firms with fewer than 100 or so employees typically have no dedicated HR managers, and even larger ones may have few specialists. That means the owner has most of the human resource management burden on his or her shoulders.

PAPERWORK The Small Business Administration estimates that small business owners spend up to 25% of their time on personnel-related paperwork, such as background checks and benefits sign-ups.[67] The association that represents employee leasing firms estimates that the average cost of regulations, paperwork, and tax compliance for smaller firms is about $5,000 per employee per year.[68] Because the PEO takes over most of this, many small businesses conclude that it's cheaper for them just to pay the employee leasing firm's fees. For instance, when First Weigh's Strasse has a question about employee legal issues, he just calls his ADP representative.

LIABILITY Staying in compliance with pension plan rules, Title VII, OSHA, COBRA, the Fair Labor Standards Act, and other such laws can be perilous. Legally, PEOs generally "contractually share liability with clients and have a vested interest in preventing workplace injuries and employee lawsuits."[69] The PEO should thus help ensure the small business fulfills all its personnel-related legal responsibilities. The issues that Peter McCann and his embroidery company Ideal Images faced help illustrate the liability issue. His 27-employee firm was studiously nondiscriminatory. However, a former employee still filed a discrimination charge against Ideal. The investigation absorbed several tense weeks of McCann's time. Between that, and the fact that he was starting to find his chores "nearly all-consuming," he turned to Alliance Group, a PEO.[70]

BENEFITS Insurance and benefits are often the big PEO attraction. Getting health and other insurance is a problem for smaller firms. Even group rates for life or health insurance can be high when only 20 or 30 employees are involved. First Weigh Manufacturing's health insurance carrier dropped the firm after its first two years, and Strasse had to scramble to find a new carrier. He did, with premiums that were 30% higher.

That's where the leasing firm comes in. Remember that the leasing firm is the legal employer of your employees. The employees therefore are absorbed into a much larger insurable group, along with other employers' former employees. As a result, a small business owner may be able to get insurance (as well as benefits like 401(k)s for its people that it couldn't otherwise.[71]

PERFORMANCE Finally, the professionalism that the PEO brings to recruiting, screening, training, compensating, and maintaining employee safety and welfare will hopefully translate into improved employee and business results.

Caveats

Using vendors like these may sound too good to be true and it often is. "If your PEO is poorly managed, or goes bankrupt, you could find yourself with an office full of uninsured workers."[72] Many employers view their human resource management processes (training and rewarding new engineers, for instance) as a strategic advantage, and aren't inclined to turn over strategy-sensitive tasks like screening and training to outside firms. There are also more concrete risks to consider. Several years ago, the employee leasing industry tarnished itself when one or two firms manipulated the pension benefits offered to higher-paid employees.[73]

Using vendors like these can also raise its own liability concerns. The question is, Who's responsible if things go wrong? For example, some states have not universally upheld workers' compensation as the sole remedy for injuries at work. Who is responsible if an employee here gets hurt, the PEO or the employer? The contract should address this.[74]

WARNING SIGNS Several things may signal problems with the prospective PEO. One is *lax due diligence*. Because they share liability with the employer, they should question you extensively about your firm's workplace safety and human resource policies and practices.[75] Another is a *recent name change*. Search the Internet and Better Business Bureaus to see if there's been a recent name change. Finally, it's unlikely that the employer will gain more than a modest savings (if any) by partnering with a PEO (relative to overseeing its own HR). Therefore, be suspect of anyone *promising substantial savings*. Figure 12.6 summarizes guidelines for finding and working with PEOs.

FIGURE 12.6

Guidelines for Finding and Working with PEOs

Sources: Based on Robert Beck and J. Starkman, "How to Find a PEO that Will Get the Job Done," *National Underwriter* 110, no. 39 (October 16, 2006): 39, 45. Lyle DeWitt, "Advantages of Human Resource Outsourcing," *The CPA Journal* 75, no. 6 (June 2005): 13, and www.peo.com/dnn/, accessed April 28, 2008. Layne Davlin, "Human Resource Solutions for the Franchisee," *Franchising World* 39, no. 10 (October 2007): 27.

Employers should choose and manage the PEO relationship carefully. Guidelines for doing so include:

- *Conduct a needs analysis.* Know ahead of time exactly what human resource concerns your company wants to address.
- *Review the services* of all PEO firms you're considering. Determine which can meet all your requirements.
- *Determine if the PEO is accredited.* There is no rating system. However, the Employer Services Assurance Corporation of Little Rock, Arkansas (www.Esacorp.org), imposes higher financial, auditing, and operating standards on its members. Also check the National Association of Professional Employer Organizations (www.NAPEO.org), and www.PEO.com.
- *Check* the provider's bank, credit, insurance, and professional *references*.
- Understand how the *employee benefits will be funded*. Is it fully insured or partially self-funded? Who is the carrier? Confirm that employers will receive first-day coverage.
- See if the contract assumes the *compliance liabilities in the applicable states*.
- *Review the service agreement* carefully. Are the respective parties' responsibilities and liabilities clear?
- Investigate *how long the PEO has been in business*.
- *Check out the prospective PEO's staff.* Do they seem to have the expertise to deliver on its promises?
- Ask, *how will the firm deliver its services?* In person? By phone? Via the Web?
- Ask about *upfront fees* and how these are determined.
- *Periodically get proof that payroll taxes and insurance premiums are being paid properly* and that any legal issues are handled correctly.

MANAGING HR SYSTEMS, PROCEDURES, AND PAPERWORK

Introduction

Consider the paperwork required to run a five-person retail shop. Just to start with, recruiting and hiring an employee might require a help wanted advertising listing, an employment application, an interviewing checklist, various verifications—of education and immigration status, for instance—and a telephone reference checklist. You then might need an employment agreement, confidentiality and noncompetition agreements, and an employer indemnity agreement. To process that new employee you might need a background verification, a new employee checklist, and forms for withholding tax and to obtain new employee data. And to keep track of the employee once on board, you'd need—just to start—a personnel data sheet, daily and weekly time records, an hourly employee's weekly time sheet, and an expense report. Then come all the performance appraisal forms, a disciplinary notice, an employee orientation record, separation notice, and employment reference response.

In fact, the preceding list barely scratches the surface of the policies, procedures, and paperwork you'll need to run the human resource management part of your business. Perhaps with just one or two employees you could keep track of everything in your head, or just write a separate memo for each HR action, and place it in a manila folder for each worker. But with more than a few employees, you'll need to create a human resource system comprised of standardized forms. As the company grows, you'll then have to computerize various parts of the HR system—payroll, or appraising, for instance.

Basic Components of Manual HR Systems

5 Describe how you would create a start-up human resource system for a new small business.

Very small employers (say, with 10 employees or less) will probably start with a manual human resource management system. From a practical point of view, this generally means obtaining and organizing a set of standardized personnel forms covering each important aspect of the HR—recruitment, selection, training, appraisal, compensation, safety—process, as well as some means for organizing all this information for each of your employees.

BASIC FORMS   The number of forms you would conceivably need even for a small firm is quite large, as the illustrative list in Table 12.3 shows.[76] One simple way to obtain the basic component forms of a manual HR system is to start with one of the books or CDs that provide compilations

TABLE 12.3 Some Important Employment Forms

New Employee Forms	Current Employee Forms	Employee Separation Forms
Application	Employee Status	Retirement Checklist
New Employee Checklist	Change Request	Termination Checklist
Employment Interview	Employee Record	COBRA Acknowledgment
Reference Check	Performance Evaluation	Unemployment Claim
Telephone Reference Report	Warning Notice	Employee Exit Interview
Employee Manual Acknowledgment	Vacation Request	
Employment Agreement	Probation Notice	
Employment Application Disclaimer	Job Description	
Employee Secrecy Agreement	Probationary Evaluation	
	Direct Deposit Acknowledgment	
	Absence Report	
	Disciplinary Notice	
	Grievance Form	
	Expense Report	
	401(k) Choices Acknowledgment	
	Injury Report	

Source: Jeff Greenberg/PhotoEdit Inc.

Office Depot sells packages of individual personnel forms.

of HR forms. The forms you want can then be adapted from these sources for your particular situation. Office supply stores (such as Office Depot and Office Max) also sell packages of personnel forms. For example, Office Depot sells packages of individual personnel forms as well as a "Human Resource Kit" containing 10 copies of each of the following: Application, Employment Interview, Reference Check, Employee Record, Performance Evaluation, Warning Notice, Exit Interview, and Vacation Request, plus a Lawsuit-Prevention Guide.[77] Also available (and highly recommended) is a package of Employee Record Folders. Use the folders to maintain a file on each individual employee; on the outside of the pocket is printed a form for recording information such as name, start date, company benefits, and so on.

OTHER SOURCES Several direct-mail catalog companies similarly offer a variety of HR materials. For example, HRdirect (www.hrdirect.com) offers packages of personnel forms. These include, for instance, Short- and Long-Form Employee Applications, Applicant Interviews, Employee Performance Reviews, Job Descriptions, Exit Interviews, and Absentee Calendars and Reports. There are also various legal-compliance forms, including standardized Harassment Policy and FMLA Notice forms, as well as posters (for instance, covering legally required postings for matters such as the Americans with Disabilities Act and Occupational Safety and Health Act) available.

G. Neil Company, of Sunrise, Florida (www.gneil.com), is another direct-mail personnel materials source. In addition to a complete line of personnel forms, documents, and posters, it also carries manual systems for matters like attendance history, job analyses, and for tracking vacation requests and safety records. It has a complete HR "start-up" kit containing 25 copies of each of the basic components of a manual HR system. These include Long Form Application for Employment, Attendance History, Performance Appraisal, Payroll/Status Change Notice, Absence Report, and Vacation Request & Approval, all organized in a file box.

Automating Individual HR Tasks

As the small business grows, it becomes increasingly unwieldy to rely on manual HR systems. For a company with 40 or 50 employees or more, the amount of management time devoted to things like attendance history and performance appraisals can swell into weeks. It is therefore at about this point that most small- to medium-sized firms begin computerizing individual human resource management tasks.

PACKAGED SYSTEMS Here again there are a variety of resources available. For example, at the Web site for the International Association for Human Resource Information Management (www.ihrim.org) you'll find, within the Buyers Guide tab, a categorical list of HR software vendors.[78] These firms provide software solutions for virtually all personnel tasks, ranging from benefits management to compensation, compliance, employee relations, outsourcing, payroll, and time and attendance systems.

The G. Neil Company sells software packages for monitoring attendance, employee record keeping, writing employee policy handbooks, and conducting computerized employee appraisals. HRdirect offers software for writing employee policy manuals, writing performance reviews, creating job descriptions, tracking attendance and hours worked for each employee, employee scheduling, writing organizational charts, managing payroll, conducting employee surveys, scheduling and tracking employee training activities, and managing OSHA compliance. *People Manager®* (see for example, www.hrtools.com/products/PeopleManager.aspx) maintains employee records (including name, address, marital status, number of dependents, emergency contact and phone numbers, hire date, and job history). It also enables management to produce 30 standard reports on matters such as attendance, benefits, and ethnic information quickly.

Then, as the company grows, the owner will probably decide to transition to an integrated human resource management system; we discuss the basics of this in the Business in Action Edu-Exercise at the end of this chapter.

REVIEW

SUMMARY

1. Managing human resources in small firms is different for four main reasons: *size, priorities, informality,* and the nature of the *entrepreneur.* These have several implications. First, small business owners run the risk that their relatively rudimentary human resource practices will put them at a *competitive disadvantage.* Second, there is a *lack of specialized HR expertise.* Third, the smaller firm is probably not adequately addressing potential *workplace litigation.* Fourth, the small business owner may not be fully complying with *compensation regulations and laws.* Fifth, duplication and paperwork lead to inefficiencies and *data entry errors.*

2. The U.S. Department of Labor's "*FirstStep* Employment Law Advisor" helps employers (and particularly small businesses) determine which laws apply to their business. The DOL's site also provides information on the Fair Labor Standards Act (FLSA). It contains several "elaws Advisors." The U.S. Equal Employment Opportunity Commission's (EEOC) Web site provides important information regarding EEOC matters, such as Title VII. The DOL's Occupational Safety and Health Administration site similarly presents a wealth of information for small business owners. OSHA's site provides, among other things, easy access to things like the *OSHA Handbook for Small Businesses.*

3. Internet resources can make small business owners more effective in HRM. For example, the Department of Labor's O*NET is effective for creating job descriptions. Small businesses can use the online recruiting tools we discussed in Chapter 4. Wonderlic's applicant tracking service also provides job analyses for the employer's jobs. There are many suppliers of prepackaged training solutions. These range from self-study programs from the American Management Association (www.amanet.org/) and SHRM (www.shrm.org), to specialized programs. The federal government's Small Business Administration (www.SBA.gov/training/) offers online courses. Small employers can also do performance appraisals online. OSHA provides free on-site safety and health services for small businesses.

4. Small businesses need to capitalize on their strengths, and in dealing with employees they should capitalize on their smallness. Smallness should translate into personal *familiarity* with each employee's strengths, needs, and family situation. And it should translate into the luxury of being able to be relatively *flexible* and *informal* in the human resource management policies and practices the company follows. Even without the deep pockets of larger firms, small firms can offer employees work-life benefits that large employers usually can't match.

5. Access to retirement benefits is more prevalent in large firms than small ones. Roughly 75% of large firms offer such benefits, while about 35% of small ones do. There are several straightforward ways that small firms can provide retirement plans for their employees. For example, the *Pension Protection Act of 2006* contains a provision for a new type of retirement benefit that combines traditional defined benefit and 401(k) plans.

6. Small firms rely on more informal employee selection, recruitment, and training practices. Devising a *work sampling test* is one simple solution. Limited resources or not, small businesses must have training procedures. Training is a hallmark of good management. Having high-potential employees doesn't guarantee they'll succeed. Instead, they must know what you want them to do and how you want them to do it. We discussed a less complex but still effective job-instruction training process.

7. Most small businesses are family businesses. Inequitable treatment of family and non-family employees can undermine perceptions of fairness, as well as morale. We discussed methods for reducing problems.

8. Effective communications are important for any manager, but especially for those managing small businesses. We discussed simple programs, including newsletters and "huddles" for improving communications.

9. Many small business owners look at all the issues involved with managing personnel, and decide to outsource all or most of their human resource functions to outside vendors (generally called *professional employer organizations* or PEOs, *human resource outsourcers,* or sometimes *employee* or *staff leasing firms*). At a minimum these take over the employer's payroll tasks. Usually, PEOs assume most of the employer's human resources chores. The PEO usually handles employee-related activities such as recruiting, hiring (with client firms' supervisors' approvals), and payroll and taxes.

10. Even small businesses use extensive HR-related paperwork. Very small employers start with a manual human resource management system. This generally means obtaining and organizing a set of standardized personnel forms covering each aspect of HR—recruitment, selection, training, appraisal, compensation, and safety—as well as some means for organizing all this information. Office Depot, Staples, and several direct-mail catalog companies similarly offer a variety of HR materials. As the company grows, most small- to medium-sized firms begin computerizing individual HR tasks. For example, the G. Neil Company sells off-the-shelf software packages for monitoring attendance, employee record keeping, writing job descriptions, writing employee policy handbooks, and conducting computerized employee appraisals.

DISCUSSION QUESTIONS

1. How and why is HR in small businesses different than in large firms?
2. Explain why HRM is important to small businesses.
3. Explain and give at least four examples of how entrepreneurs can use Internet and government tools to support the HR effort.
4. Explain and give at least five examples of ways entrepreneurs can use small size—familiarity, flexibility, and informality—to improve their HR processes.

5. Discuss what you would do to find, retain, and deal with on an ongoing basis a professional employee organization.
6. Describe with examples how you would create a startup paper-based human resource system for a new small business.

INDIVIDUAL AND GROUP ACTIVITIES

1. Individually or as a group of 3–5 people, visit a small local retail business, and spend several minutes observing the activities of the owner or manager, and the employees. Based on your observations, what is your impression of whether or not this is a well-managed business? List and discuss three human resource tools that you believe would help the owner do a better job of managing the retail business.

2. Individually or in groups of 3–5 students, discuss in detail your experience working in a small family-owned business. To what extent did you experience any of the negative aspects of working for a small family business that we addressed in this chapter? Did the owner seem to use any of the tools (such as simple testing techniques, and informality) that this chapter discussed? What small business type human resource tools from this chapter would you suggest the owner use, and why?

WEB-e's (WEB EXERCISES)

1. ADP is one of the largest providers of HR services to businesses. Go to their site (http://www.adp.com/) and write a short outline addressing the subject: "How I Could Use ADP to Help Me Manage the HR Aspects of My Small Business."

2. Go to the Web site of a firm that supplies human resource management forms and systems, such as Staples or http://www.gneil.com. Assume you are thinking of starting a small business. What startup HR packages would you obtain from this vendor, and why?

APPLICATION EXERCISES

HR IN ACTION CASE INCIDENT 1
The Liquidity Crisis and the New Hedge Fund[79]

After 12 years working for various hedge funds, Emily Thomas was laid off as a managing director with one of the midsize funds in January 2009. As the subprime and liquidity crises worsened, the fund she managed, in the media industry, was actually doing fairly well. Unfortunately, several of her colleagues in the hedge fund's other industry sectors had taken huge gambles, which did not pan out. As a result, the hedge fund's investors were clamoring to redeem their investments, and Emily was let go as part of a consolidation. Sitting in a small restaurant just off Water Street in lower Manhattan with two friends, Guy and Bill, the three decided that if they were ever going to start their own hedge fund, now was the time. "The time to start something like this is at the bottom, not at the top," as Guy put it, so the three of them began making plans. They pooled their savings and incorporated EGB Funds.

Because of regulatory and tax issues, there is much more to starting a hedge fund than just hanging a sign on the door.[80] The fund must have local accounting and valuations expertise. For example, U.S. investors expect accounting reports to follow America's "generally accepted accounting procedures," or GAAP. Many hedge funds establish a "master-feeder structure" to attract investors' capital in a tax-efficient way. This involves establishing on- and offshore feeder funds, which in turn invest directly into the master fund, where all trading activity takes place. In the past, most funds performed everything from trading to back office support in-house. The rationale was that with such specialized work to do, the hedge fund operators want total control of all the operations. Increasingly, however, fund managers have been outsourcing some activities to cut costs. But like all funds, EGB will have to appoint an internal fund manager. That person will in turn essentially be the operational head of the firm. He or she will work with lawyers to establish the fund's corporate legal structure. He or she will have to make sure that all of the necessary policies and procedures are clearly documented and in place; for a financial institution such as this, these necessarily include not just the usual office administrative types of matters but also, for instance, anti-money laundering procedures for investors. In addition, the fund manager (in this case working with Emily, Guy, and Bill) will find and rent office space and determine staffing requirements.

Given all of the legal, compliance, and accounting issues they face, the minutiae of staffing the company and instituting human resource policies and procedures frankly seemed secondary. On the other hand, they weren't foolish, and they understood that at its heart, their hedge fund was going to be no better than the people that they hired. They planned to hire about seven people, including a fund manager, chief financial officer, four analysts, and a secretary/receptionist. Knowing that you are a human resource management expert, they've come to you for advice. Here's what they want to know.

Questions

1. In terms of staffing or human resource management, where should we start? Do we put in the HR system first? Or hire the people first?
2. Should we hire the fund manager first, and let him or her do all the necessary staffing/human resource management? Or should we have some HR processes in place first, so that we do a better job of hiring the fund manager?
3. If you are going to institute an HR system first, what's the best way to go about doing that? What would you suggest in terms of the sorts of HR policies, procedures, and practices we will need, and where should we get them?
4. We know there are professional employment organizations that will essentially handle most of the personnel-related matters for our fund. In our brief case synopsis, we've told you something about starting a hedge fund and the sorts of employees we need. Based on that, would you suggest we use a PEO? Why?

HR IN ACTION CASE INCIDENT 2
Carter Cleaning Company: The New Pay Plan

Carter Cleaning does not have a formal wage structure nor does it have rate ranges or use compensable factors. Wage rates are based mostly on those prevailing in the surrounding community and are tempered with an attempt on the part of Jack Carter to maintain some semblance of equity between what workers with different responsibilities in the stores are paid.

Needless to say, Carter does not make any formal surveys when determining what his company should pay. He peruses the want ads almost every day and conducts informal surveys among his friends in the local chapter of the laundry and cleaners trade association. While Jack has taken a "seat-of-the-pants" approach to paying employees, his salary schedule has been guided by several basic pay policies. While many of his dry cleaner colleagues adhere to a policy of paying absolutely minimum rates, Jack has always followed a policy of paying his employees about 10% above what he feels are the prevailing rates, a policy that he believes reduces turnover while fostering employee loyalty. Of somewhat more concern to Jennifer is her

father's informal policy of paying men about 20% more than women for the same job. Her father's explanation is, "They're stronger and can work harder for longer hours, and besides they all have families to support."

Questions

1. Is the company at the point where it should be setting up a formal salary structure based on a complete job evaluation? Why?
2. How exactly could Carter use free online sources like O*NET to help create the necessary salary structure?
3. Do you think paying 10% more than the prevailing rates is a sound idea, and how would Jack determine that?
4. How could Jack Carter use online government sources to determine if his policy of a male–female differential pay rate is wise and if not, why not?
5. Specifically, what would you suggest Jennifer do now with respect to her company's pay plan?

EXPERIENTIAL EXERCISE

Building an HRIS

Purpose: The purpose of this exercise is to give you practice in creating a human resource information system (HRIS).

Required Understanding: You should be fully acquainted with the material in this chapter.

How to Set Up the Exercise/Instructions: Divide the class into teams of five or six students. Each team will need access to the Internet.

Assume that the owners of a small business (perhaps like the Carters, or Emily, Guy, and Bill in Case 1) come to you with the following problem. They have a company with less than 40 employees, and have been doing their HR paperwork informally, mostly on little slips of paper, and with memos. They want you to build them a human resource management information system—how computerized it is will be up to you, but they can only afford a budget of $5,000 upfront

(not counting your consulting), and then about $500 per year for maintenance. You know from your HR training that there are various sources of paper-based and online systems. Write a two-page proposal telling them exactly what your team would suggest, based on its accumulated existing knowledge, and from online research.

BUSINESS IN ACTION EDU-EXERCISE

Building Your *Human Resource Information System (HRIS)* Knowledge

Companies need information systems to get their work done. For example, the sales team needs some way to tell accounting to bill a customer, and to tell production to fill the order. The term information system refers to the interrelated people, data, technology, and organizational procedures a company uses to collect, process, store, and disseminate information. Information systems may or may not be computerized. All the HR paperwork systems we described—for collecting information on new employees, and for keeping track of their appraisals, benefits, and training, for instance—are information systems, although they're not computerized. Of course, as the company grows, it makes sense to computerize its information systems.

Levels of Information Systems

Companies tend to install information systems from the bottom up, level by organizational level. *Transaction-processing systems* often come first; they provide the company's managers and accountants with detailed information about short-term, daily activities, such as accounts payables, tax liabilities, and order status.

Management information systems *(MIS)* are a level up; they help managers make better decisions by producing standardized, summarized reports on a regular basis. For example, an MIS may take raw data (say, on sales by location) and show the sales manager the trend of sales for the past two weeks; or show the production manager a graph of weekly inventory levels; or show the CEO a report summarizing the company's revenues, expenses, and profits for the quarter.

One more level up, *executive support systems* provide top managers with information for making decisions on matters such as 5-year plans. For example, the CEO of Chrysler might use his executive support system to put the sales of each of Chrysler's various cars last month into context, by comparing them with sales of competing brands.

As companies grow, they also often turn to integrated human resource information systems (HRIS). We can define an *HRIS* as interrelated components working together to collect, process, store, and disseminate information to support decision making, coordination, control, analysis, and visualization of an organization's human resource management activities.[81] There are several reasons for installing an HRIS. The first is improved transaction processing.

Improved Transaction Processing

The day-to-day minutiae of maintaining and updating employee records takes an enormous amount of time. One study found that 71% of HR employees' time was devoted to transactional tasks like checking leave balances, maintaining address records, and monitoring employee benefits distributions.[82] HRIS packages substitute powerful computerized processing for a wide range of the firm's HR transactions.

Online Self-Processing

HR information systems also make it possible (or easier) to make the company's employees part of the HRIS. For example, at Provident Bank, an HR compensation system called Benelogic lets the bank's employees self-enroll in all their desired benefits programs over the Internet at a secure site. It also "support[s] employees' quest for 'what if' information relating to, for example, the impact on their take-home pay of various benefits options, W-4 changes, insurance coverage, retirement planning and more."[83] That's all work that HR employees would previously have had to do for Provident's employees.

Improved Reporting Capability

Because the HRIS integrates numerous individual HR tasks (training records, appraisals, employee personal data, and so on), installing an HRIS boosts HR's reporting capabilities. In practice, the variety of reports possible is limited only by the manager's imagination. For a start, for instance, reports might be available (company-wide and by department) for health care cost per employee, pay and benefits as a percent of operating expense, cost per hire, report on training, volunteer turnover rates, turnover costs, time to fill jobs, and return on human capital invested (in terms of training and education fees, for instance).

HR System Integration

Because the HRIS's software components (record keeping, payroll, appraisal, and so forth) are integrated, the employer can dramatically reengineer its HR function. The system PeopleSoft (now part of Oracle Corporation) installed in its own offices provides an illustration. For example, its HRIS electronically routes salary increases, transfers, and other e-forms through the organization to the proper managers for approval. As one person signs off, it's routed to the next.

If anyone forgets to process a document, a smart agent issues reminders until the task is completed.

HRIS Vendors

Many firms today offer HRIS packages. The Web site for the International Association for Human Resource Information Management (www.ihrim.org/), for instance, lists Automatic Data Processing, Inc., Business Information Technology, Inc., Human Resource Microsystems, Lawson Software, Oracle Corporation, SAP America, Inc., and about 25 other firms as HRIS vendors.

HR and Intranets

Employers are increasingly creating intranet-based HR information systems. For example, LG&E Energy Corporation uses its intranet for benefits communication. Employees can access the benefits homepage and (among other things) review the company's 401(k) plan investment options, get answers to frequently asked questions about the company's medical and dental plans, and report changes in family status. Other uses for human resource intranets include, for instance: automate job postings and applicant tracking, set up training registration, provide electronic pay stubs, publish an electronic employee handbook, and let employees update their personal profiles and access their accounts, such as 401(k)s.

Questions

1. Use the Internet to find two HRIS systems. What do their vendors say the systems do? What are their advantages for the small business owner?
2. Using the Internet, find company-wide "enterprise systems" that include an integrated HRIS along with integrated systems for other functions such as production, accounting, and sales. What would be the advantages of using enterprise systems like these, rather than stand-alone HRIS systems?

ENDNOTES

1. Dina Berta, "Job Trekker's Odyssey Offers HR Insights," *Nations Restaurant News* 42, no. 6 (February 11, 2008): 1, 12.
2. Dina Berta, "IHOP Franchise Employs Post-hiring Surveys to Get Off Turnover 'Treadmill,'" *Nation's Restaurant News* 41, no 39 (October 1, 2007): 6.
3. "Statistics of U.S. Businesses and Non-Employer Status," www.sba.gov/advo/research/data.html, accessed November 5, 2009.
4. "Small Business Economic Indicators 2000," Office of Advocacy, U.S. Small Business Administration (Washington, D.C., 2001): 5. See also "Small Business Laid Foundation for Job Gains," www.sba.gov/advo, accessed March 9, 2006.
5. Studies show that the size of the business impacts human resource activities such as executive compensation, training, staffing, and HR outsourcing. Peter Hausdorf and Dale Duncan, "Firm Size and Internet Recruiting in Canada: A Preliminary Investigation," *Journal of Small-Business Management* 42, no. 3 (July 2004): 325–334.
6. *SHRM Human Capital Benchmarking Study 2007*, Society for Human Resource Management, p. 12.
7. Graham Dietz et al., "HRM Inside UK E-commerce Firms," *International Small Business Journal* 24, no. 5 (October 2006): 443–470.
8. Bernice Kotey and Cathleen Folker, "Employee Training in SMEs: Effect of Size and Firm Type—Family and Nonfamily," *Journal of Small-Business Management* 45, no. 2 (April 2007): 14–39.
9. Graham Dietz et al., "HRM Inside UK E-commerce Firms," *International Small Business Journal* 24, no. 5 (October 2006): 443–470.
10. Ibid. See also N. Wasserman, "Planning a Start-Up? Seize the Day . . . Then Expect to Work All Night," *Harvard Business Review* 87, no. 1 (January 2009): 27.
11. The following four points based on Kathy Williams, "Top HR Compliance Issues or Small Businesses," *Strategic Finance* (February 2005): 21–23.
12. However, one study concluded that the increased labor costs associated with high-performance work practices offset the productivity increases associated with high-performance work practices. Luc Sels et al., "Unraveling the HRM–Performance Link: Value Creating and Cost Increasing Effects of Small-Business HRM," *Journal of Management Studies* 43, no. 2 (March 2006): 319–342. For supporting evidence of HR's positive effects on small companies, see also Andrea Rauch et al., "Effects of Human Capital and Long-Term Human Resources Development and Utilization on Employment Growth of Small-Scale Businesses: A Causal Analysis," *Entrepreneurship Theory and Practice* 29, no. 6 (November 2005): 681–698; Andre Grip and Inge Sieben, "The Effects of Human Resource Management on Small Firms' Productivity and Employee's Wages," *Applied Economics* 37, no. 9 (May 20, 2005): 1047–1054.
13. Dawn Carlson et al., "The Impact of Human Resource Practices and Compensation Design on Performance: An Analysis of Family-owned SMEs," *Journal of Small Business Management* 44, no. 4 (October 2006): 531–543. See also, Jake Messersmith and James Guthrie, "High Performance Work Systems in Emergent Organizations: Implications for Firm Performance," *Human Resource Management* 49, no. 2 (March–April 2010): 241–264.
14. Graham Dietz et al., "HRM Inside UK E-Commerce Firms," *International Small Business Journal* 24, no. 5 (October 2006): 443–470.
15. Gilbert Nicholson, "Automated Assessments for Better Hires," *Workforce* (December 2000): 102–107.
16. www.EEOC.gov/employers/overview.html, accessed February 10, 2008.
17. www.DOL.gov/elaws, accessed February 10, 2008.
18. Daren Dahl, "Recruiting: Tapping the Talent Pool . . . without Drowning in Resumes," *Inc.* 31, no. 3 (April 2009): 121–122.
19. Ibid.
20. Ibid.
21. Ibid.
22. Ibid.

23. Paul Harris, "Small Businesses Bask in Training's Spotlight," *T + D* 59, no. 2 (Fall 2005): 46–52.
24. Ibid.
25. Ibid.
26. www.employeeappraiser.com/index.php, accessed January 10, 2008.
27. www.halogensoftware.com/products/halogen-eappraisal, accessed January 10, 2008.
28. Jan de Kok, "Precautionary Actions within Small- and Medium-Sized Enterprises," *Journal of Small Business Management* 43, no. 4 (October 2005): 498–516.
29. Sean Smith, "OSHA Resources Can Help Small Businesses Spot Hazards," *Westchester County Business Journal* (August 4, 2003): 4. See also www.osha.gov/as/opa/osha-faq.html, accessed May 26, 2007.
30. www.osha.gov/dcsp/smallbusiness/sharp.html, accessed February 17, 2010.
31. Graham Dietz et al., "HRM Inside UK E-Commerce Firms," *International Small Business Journal* 24, no. 5 (October 2006): 443–470.
32. Adrienne Fox, "McMurray Scouts Top Talent to Produce Winning Results," *HR Magazine* 51, no. 7 (July 2006): 57.
33. This is based on John Drake, *Interviewing for Managers: A Complete Guide to Employment Interviewing* (New York, AMACOM, 1982).
34. Ibid.
35. Colin Gray and Christopher Mabey, "Management Development: Key Differences Between Small and Large Businesses in Europe," *International Small Business Journal* 23, no. 5 (October 2005): 467–485.
36. Ibid. See also Essi Saru, "Organizational Learning and HRD: How Appropriate Are They for Small Firms?" *Journal of European Industrial Training* 31, no. 1 (January 2007): 36–52.
37. From Stephen Covey, "Small Business, Big Opportunity," *Training* 43, no. 11 (November 2006): 40.
38. Gina Ruiz, "Smaller Firms in Vanguard of Flex Practices," *Workforce Management* 84, no. 13 (November 21, 2005): 10.
39. Kira Bindrum, "Little Firms Redefine Culture of Work," *Crain's New York Business* 25, no. 49 (December 7–13, 2009): 20.
40. Kira Bindrum, "Little Firms Redefine Culture of Work," *Crain's New York Business* 25, no. 49 (December 2009): 7–13.
41. Ruiz, op. cit.
42. These are from Ty Freyvogel, "Operation Employee Loyalty," *Training Media Review* (September–October 2007).
43. Ibid.
44. Ibid.
45. Based on Bob Nelson, *1001 Ways to Reward Employees* (New York: Workmen Publishing, 1994): 19. See also Sunny C. L. Fong and Margaret A. Shaffer, "The Dimensionality and Determinants of Pay Satisfaction: A Cross-Cultural Investigation of a Group Incentive Plan," *International Journal of Human Resource Management* 14, no. 4 (June 2003): 559(22).
46. Judith Medina, "No Help in Sight for Soaring Costs," *Crain's New York Business* 26, no. 2 (January 11–17, 2010): 10, 13.
47. Michelle V. Rafter, "Back in a Giving Mood," *Workforce Management* 88, no. 10 (September 14, 2009): 25–29.
48. Ibid.
49. Jeffrey Marshall and Ellen Heffes, "Benefits: Smaller Firm Workers Often Getting Less," *Financial Executive* 21, no. 9 (November 1, 2005): 10.
50. www.dol.gov/ebsa/pdf/ppa2006.pdf, accessed February 18, 2008.
51. Bill Leonard, "New Retirement Plans for Small Employers," *HR Magazine* 51, no. 12 (December 2006): 30.
52. Kristen Falk, "The Easy Retirement Plan for Small Business Clients," *National Underwriter* 111, no. 45 (December 3, 2007): 12–13.
53. Ibid.
54. Dina Berta, "IHOP Franchisee Employs Post-Hiring Surveys to Get Off Turnover 'Treadmill,'" *Nation's Restaurant News* 41, no. 39 (October 1, 2007): 6.
55. Kate Leahy, "The 10 Minute Manager's Guide to . . . Communicating with Employees," *Restaurants & Institutions* 116, no. 11 (June 1, 2006): 22–23.
56. Ibid.
57. Ibid.
58. Phillip Perry, "Welcome to the Family," *Restaurant Hospitality* 90, no. 5 (May 2006): 73, 74, 76, 78.
59. Ibid.
60. Ibid.
61. Ibid.
62. Ibid.
63. Jane Applegate, "Employee Leasing Can Be a Savior for Small Firms," *Business Courier Serving Cincinnati–Northern Kentucky* (January 28, 2000): 23.
64. Robert Beck and Jay Starkman, "How to Find a PEO that Will Get the Job Done," *National Underwriter* 110, no. 39 (October 16, 2006): 39, 45.
65. Layne Davlin, "Human Resource Solutions for the Franchisee," *Franchising World* 39, no. 10 (October 2007): 27–28.
66. Robert Beck and J. Starkman, "How to Find a PEO That Will Get the Job Done," *National Underwriter* 110, no. 39 (October 16, 2006): 39, 45.
67. Lyle DeWitt, "Advantages of Human Resources Outsourcing," *The CPA Journal* 75, no. 6 (June 2005): 13.
68. Harriet Tramer, "Employee Leasing Agreement Can Ease Personnel Concerns," *Cranes Cleveland Business* (July 24, 2000): 24.
69. Max Chafkin, "Fed Up with HR?" *Inc.* 28, no. 5 (May 2006): 50–52.
70. Ibid.
71. Ibid.
72. Ibid.
73. Jane Applegate, "Employee Leasing Can Be a Savior for Small Firms," *Business Courier Serving Cincinnati–Northern Kentucky* (January 28, 2000): 23.
74. Diana Reitz, "Employee Leasing Breeds Liability Questions," *National Underwriter Property and Casualty Risk and Benefits Management* 104, no. 18 (May 2000): 12.
75. Max Chafkin, "Fed Up with HR?" *Inc.* 28, no. 5 (May 2006): 50–52.
76. For a more complete list, see, for example, Sondra Servais, *Personnel Director* (Deerfield Beach, FL: Made E-Z Products, 1994); and www.hoovers.com/business-forms/—pageid_16436—/global-mktg-index.xhtml?cm_ven=PAID&cm_cat=GGL&cm_pla=FRM&cm_ite=employment_contract_forms, accessed July 20, 2008.
77. Office Depot, Winter 2003 Catalog (Delray Beach, FL: Office Depot, 2003).
78. www.ihrim.org, accessed April 28, 2008.
79. © Gary Dessler PhD.

80. Portions based on Gustavo Rodriguez, "Starting a Hedge Fund," *LatinFinance* 201, no. 47 (2008), http://vnweb.hwwilsonweb. com.ezproxy.fiu.edu/hww/results/results_single_fulltext.jhtml;h wwilsonid=VIMPEAQW53NMFQA3DIKSFGOADUNGIIV0, accessed March 26, 2009.

81. Adapted from Kenneth Laudon and Jane Laudon, *Management Information Systems: New Approaches to Organization and Technology* (Upper Saddle River, NJ: Prentice Hall, 1998): G7. See also Michael Barrett and Randolph Kahn, "The Governance of Records Management," *Directors and Boards* 26, no. 3 (Spring 2002): 45–48; Anthony Hendrickson, "Human Resource Information Systems: Backbone Technology of Contemporary Human Resources," *Journal of Labor Research* 24, no. 3 (Summer 2003): 381–395.

82. "HR Execs Trade Notes on Human Resource Information Systems," *BNA Bulletin to Management* (December 3, 1998): 1. See also Brian Walter, "But They Said Their Payroll Program Complied with the FLSA," *Public Personnel Management* 31, no. 1 (Spring 2002): 79–94.

83. "HR Execs Trade Notes on Human Resource Information Systems," *BNA Bulletin to Management* (December 3, 1998): 2. See also Ali Velshi, "Human Resources Information," *The Americas Intelligence Wire* (February 11, 2004).

13 Managing HR Globally

SYNOPSIS

- HR and the Internationalization of Business
- Improving International Assignments through Selection

- Training and Maintaining International Employees
- How to Implement a Global HR System

Source: Liu Xingliang/Newscom.

When you finish studying this chapter, you should be able to:

1. List the HR challenges of international business.
2. Illustrate how intercountry differences affect HRM.
3. Explain why foreign assignments fail and what to do to minimize the problems.
4. List and describe the basic steps in training employees who the employer is about to transfer abroad.
5. Explain the main things to keep in mind when designing and implementing a global HR system.

INTRODUCTION

Walmart, a company famously resistant to unions in America, recently had a surprise. Opening stores in China at a fast clip, it attempted to dissuade local unions there from organizing Walmart's employees. However, the All China Federation of Trade Unions (ACFTU), with strong government backing, quickly established itself in several Walmart stores. At first, it seemed likely that the union would succeed in unionizing many Walmart China workers. But Walmart was vigorously resisting.[1] ■

HR AND THE INTERNATIONALIZATION OF BUSINESS

Companies are increasingly doing business abroad. Multinationals like IBM and Sony have long done business abroad, of course. But with the growth of demand in Asia, Africa, and other parts of the world, even small firms' success depends on marketing and managing overseas.

This confronts employers with some interesting management challenges. For one thing, managers now must formulate and execute their market, product, and production plans on a worldwide basis. Ford Motor, for instance, recently implemented a new "One Ford" strategy aimed at offering similar Ford cars like the Fusion internationally.

Going abroad also means employers must address international human resource management issues. For example, "Should we staff our local offices in Europe with local or U.S. managers?" "How should we appraise and pay our Asia employees?" "How should we deal with the unions in our offices in Dubai?"[2]

Furthermore, globalization means that even employees who never leave the home office may need to be "internationalized." As one article put it, "Cultural diversity isn't just for expatriates or frequent flying executives. Cube dwellers increasingly need to work, often virtually, across borders with people whose first language is not English, who don't have the same cultural touch points as U.S. employees do, and who don't approach business in the same way that Americans do."[3] In this chapter, we'll look at how global issues like cultural differences influence human resource management practices.

The Human Resource Challenges of International Business

1 List the HR challenges of international business.

Dealing with global human resource challenges isn't easy. The employer faces an array of political, social, legal, and cultural differences among countries abroad. What works in one country may not work in another: An incentive plan may work in the United States, but backfire in some Eastern Europe countries, where workers need a predictable weekly wage to buy necessities. But in spite of these intercountry differences, the employer needs to create, for each country's local facility and for the company as a whole, effective human resource practices. These include methods for things like candidate selection, cultural and language orientation and training, and compensation administration.[4] The vast geographic distances add to the challenge. For example, how should Starbucks' chief HR officer, based in Seattle, keep track of Starbucks' top managers' performers overseas? Some other global HR challenges include:[5]

- *Deployment.* Getting the right people skills to where we need them, regardless of geographic location.
- *Knowledge and innovation dissemination.* Spreading state-of-the-art knowledge and practices throughout the company, regardless of where they originate.
- *Identifying and developing talent on a global basis.* Identifying the firm's top talent, and developing their abilities.[6]

What Is International Human Resource Management?

international human resource management

The human resource management concepts and techniques employers use to manage the human resource challenges of their international operations.

Employers rely on **international human resource management** (IHRM) to deal with global HR challenges like these. We can define IHRM as the human resource management concepts and techniques employers use to manage the human resource challenges of their international operations. The subject matter of international human resource management generally focuses on three main topics:[7]

1. Managing human resources in global companies (for example *selecting, training, and compensating employees who work or are assigned abroad*);
2. *Managing expatriate employees* (those the employer posts abroad); and,
3. *Comparing human resource management practices* in a variety of different countries.

Underlying these three topics is the idea that intercountry differences in things like culture and legal systems affect how employers manage human resources from country to country. Let's look at this first.

How Intercountry Differences Affect Human Resource Management

As we said, the challenges of managing human resource activities abroad don't just stem from the distances involved (though this is important). The bigger issue is dealing with the cultural, political, legal, and economic differences among countries and their people. The result is that what works in one country might fail in another.

THE ISSUE Companies operating just within the United States generally have the luxury of dealing with a relatively limited set of economic, cultural, and legal variables. It's true that the U.S. workforce reflects a multitude of cultural and ethnic backgrounds. However, the United States is a capitalist society, and its citizens share values (such as appreciation for democracy) that help to blur cultural differences. Different states and municipalities do have their own laws affecting HR. However, a basic federal framework helps produce a fairly predictable set of legal guidelines regarding matters such as employment discrimination, labor relations, and safety and health. Similarly, political risks within the United States are minimal. *Political risks* "are any governmental action or politically motivated event that could adversely affect the long-run profitability or value of the firm."[8] For example, Venezuela's president recently moved to nationalize the country's oil industries.

A company operating multiple units abroad isn't blessed with such homogeneity. For example, even with the European Union's increasing standardization, minimum mandated holidays range from none in the United Kingdom to 5 weeks per year in Luxembourg. And while Italy has no formal requirements for employee representatives on boards of directors, they're required in Denmark. The point is that the need to adapt personnel policies and procedures to the differences among countries complicates human resource management in multinational companies.

CULTURAL FACTORS For one thing, countries differ widely in their cultures—in the basic values that their citizens share, and in how these values manifest themselves in the nation's arts, social programs, and ways of doing things. A few years ago, Britain's government asked its citizens to submit a motto that most characterized their country. The winner was "No mottos please, we're British."

Cultural differences mean people abroad react differently to the same or similar situations. For example, in one study of managers from Hong Kong, mainland China, and the United States, U.S. managers tended to be most concerned with getting the job done. Chinese managers were most concerned with maintaining a harmonious environment. Hong Kong managers fell between these extremes.[9]

Several years ago, researchers surveyed the cultural values of managers in 62 countries. They concluded that the countries differed along four cultural dimensions:[10]

- *Assertiveness*—how much people in a society are expected to be tough, confrontational, and competitive. The most assertive countries in the survey included Germany, Greece, and the United States; the least assertive were Sweden, New Zealand, and Switzerland.
- *Future orientation*—the level of importance the society attaches to future-oriented behaviors such as planning and investing in the future. The most future-oriented cultures were Switzerland and Singapore; the least were Russia, Argentina, and Poland.
- *Performance orientation*—the importance of performance improvement and excellence in the society. The most performance-oriented cultures included Singapore, Hong Kong, New Zealand, and the United States. The least performance-oriented were Russia, Argentina, and Greece.
- *Humane orientation*—the extent to which a society encourages and rewards people for being fair, altruistic, and kind. Malaysia, Ireland, and the Philippines scored highest on humane orientation. Germany, Spain, and France scored lowest.

2 Illustrate how intercountry differences affect HRM.

A classic study by Professor Geert Hofstede identified other international cultural differences. For example, Hofstede says societies differ in *power distance*—in other words, the extent to which the less powerful members of institutions accept and expect an unequal distribution of power.[11] He concluded that acceptance of such inequality was higher in some countries (such as Mexico) than in others (such as Sweden).

Cultural differences such as these help shape a firm's human resource policies, in part by molding public policy and laws. For example, Americans' emphasis on individualism—on "standing on one's own feet"—may help explain why American human resource managers face fewer legal constraints on actions such as firing employees.[12] Conversely, European HR managers are much more restricted, for instance, with respect to the notice they must give workers before firing them, in how much severance pay employees get, and in the complexity of the legal process involved in dismissing workers. As another example, differences in cultural values may influence the effectiveness of various recruitment techniques. For example, emphasizing individual benefits like promotional opportunities and bonuses may actually backfire among prospective recruits in collectivist cultures.[13]

LEGAL AND POLITICAL FACTORS *Legal differences* blindside even sophisticated companies. After spending billions expanding into Germany, Walmart discovered that Germany's commercial laws discourage ads based on price comparisons. It soon left Germany.

As other examples, the U.S. practice of employment at will does not exist in Europe, where firing or laying off workers is usually expensive. And in many European countries, *works councils* replace the worker–management mediations typical in U.S. firms. **Works councils** are formal, employee-elected groups of worker representatives that meet monthly with managers to discuss topics ranging from no-smoking policies to layoffs.[14]

Co-determination is the rule in Germany and several other countries. **Co-determination** means employees have the legal right to a voice in setting company policies. Workers elect their own representatives to the supervisory board of the employer.[15] In the U.S., by comparison, HR policies on most matters (such as wages and benefits) are set by the employer, or in negotiations with its labor unions.

Managing globally also requires monitoring political risks. As noted earlier, political risks "are any governmental actions or politically motivated events that could adversely affect the long run profitability or value of the firm."[16]

ECONOMIC SYSTEMS Similarly, differences in *economic systems* translate into differences in intercountry HR practices. For instance, France—though a capitalist society—imposed restrictions on the rights of employers to discharge workers several years ago, and limited to 35 the number of hours an employee could legally work each week. (It began lifting some of those limitations in 2008.)

---

works councils
Formal, employee-elected groups of worker representatives that meet monthly with managers to discuss topics ranging, for instance, from no-smoking policies to layoffs.

co-determination
The right to a voice in setting company policies; workers generally elect representatives to the supervisory board.

According to news reports Walmart suffered losses totaling hundreds of millions of Euros for its German operations.

Source: Sean Gallup/Getty Images, Inc.—Liaison.

Labor costs also vary widely. For example, hourly compensation costs (in U.S. dollars) for production workers range from $2.92 in Mexico, to $6.58 in Taiwan, $24.59 in the United States, $29.73 in the United Kingdom, and $37.66 in Germany.[17]

There are other labor costs to consider. For example, compared to the usual 2 or 3 weeks of U.S. vacation, workers in France can expect $2\frac{1}{2}$ days of paid holiday per full month of service per year, and Germans get 18 working days per year after 6 months of service.

EXAMPLE 1: EUROPE To appreciate the employment effects of cultural, economic, and legal differences like these, consider Europe. Over the past two decades, the separate countries of the former European Community (EC) unified into a common market for goods, services, capital, and even labor called the European Union (EU). Generally speaking, products and even labor can move from country to country with few impediments. The employment situation in the EU helps illustrate the legal, cultural, and industrial relations aspects of globalization.

Companies doing business in Europe (including U.S.-based companies like Ford) must adjust their human resource policies and practices to both European Union (EU) directives and to country-specific employment laws. The "directives" are basically EU laws. The directives' objectives are binding on all member countries (although each member country can implement the directives as it so chooses). For example, consider the EU directive on *confirmation of employment*. It requires employers to provide employees with written terms and conditions of their employment. However, these terms vary from country to country.[18] In England, a detailed written statement is required, including things like rate of pay, date employment began, and hours of work. Germany doesn't require a written contract. However, it's still customary to have one.

The interplay of directives and country laws means that human resource practices vary from country to country in the EU. For example:[19]

- Most EU countries have *minimum wage systems* in place. Some set national limits. Others allow employers and unions to work out their own minimum wages.
- The EU sets the *workweek* at 48 hours, but most countries set it at 40 hours a week, and France implemented a 35-hour workweek.
- Europe has many levels of *employee representation*. In France, for instance, employers with 50 or more employees must consult with their employees' representatives on matters including working conditions, training, and profit-sharing plans and layoffs. Most EU companies must "inform and consult" employees about employee-related actions, even if the firms don't operate outside their own countries' borders.[20]
- We saw that in many European countries, works councils replace the informal or union-based worker-to-management mediations typical in U.S. firms. Similarly, co-determination is the rule in Germany and several other countries. In the United States, wages and benefits are set by the employer, or by the employer in negotiations with its labor unions. The co-determination laws, including the Works Constitution Act, largely determine the nature of HR policies in many German firms.
- The U.S. practice of *employment at will* does not exist in Europe, where firing and laying off workers is usually time-consuming and expensive.

EXAMPLE 2: CHINA For many years, Walmart and other employers inside and outside China have relied on that country's huge workforce to provide products and services at very low cost. Part of the reason for the low labor cost was the relative lack of labor laws governing things like severance pay, minimum wages, and benefits.

Now that is changing. Several years ago, the People's Republic of China implemented its new labor contract law. Overall, this law adds numerous new employment protections for employees, and makes it correspondingly more expensive for employers in China to implement personnel actions such as layoffs. For example, multinational companies doing business in China said the new law would reduce employment flexibility, raise labor costs, and make it difficult to lay off employees by instituting new large severance package requirements.[21]

IMPROVING INTERNATIONAL ASSIGNMENTS THROUGH SELECTION

Filling your company's jobs abroad has traditionally been the heart of international human resource management. The process involves identifying and selecting the people who will fill the positions abroad, and then placing them in those positions.

International Staffing: Home or Local?

In general, we can classify an international company's employees as *expatriates, home country nationals, locals,* or *third-country nationals.*[22] **Expatriates** are noncitizens of the countries in which they are working. **Host country nationals** are citizens of the country in which the multinational company has its headquarters (thus, the *parent country*); these employees may also thus be expatriates when posted abroad. **Locals** (also know as *host country nationals*) work for the company abroad and are citizens of the countries where they are working. **Third-country nationals** are citizens of a country other than the parent or the host country—for example, a French executive working in the Shanghai branch of a U.S. multinational bank.[23]

expatriates
Employees a company posts abroad, and who are non-citizens of the country in which they are working.

host country nationals
Citizens of the country in which the multinational company has its headquarters.

locals
Employees that work for the company abroad and are citizens of the countries where they are working, also known as host country nationals.

third-country nationals
Citizens of a country other than the parent or host country.

WHY LOCAL? Most of the employees in a multinational company's office abroad will be "locals," for good reason. Within the United States, it's not easy bringing workers in from abroad, so using U.S. "locals" may be a necessity. (Under existing rules, U.S. employers must try to recruit U.S. workers before filing foreign labor certification requests with the Department of Labor. They must post open positions in the Department of Labor's job bank, and run two Sunday newspaper advertisements before filing such requests.[24])

Cost is a very big consideration in "hiring local." Some companies don't realize what it costs to send expatriates abroad. Agilent Technologies estimated that it cost about three times the expatriate's annual salary to keep the person abroad for 1 year. But when Agilent hired an outside firm to handle its expatriate program, it discovered that the costs were much higher. Agilent then dramatically reduced the number of expats it sent abroad, from about 1,000 to 300 per year.[25] Yet cost may also work in the opposite direction. For example, difficulties attracting management trainees to work in relatively low-wage hospitality jobs in the United States prompts some hotel chains to hire in people from abroad to fill these jobs.

Finally, politics may be a consideration. The host country's government and citizens may view the multinational as a "better citizen" if it uses local management talent.

WHY EXPATS? There are also good reasons to use expatriates—either home country or third-country nationals—for staffing subsidiaries. The main reason is that employers often can't find local candidates with the required technical qualifications. As noted earlier, companies also view a successful stint abroad as a required step in developing top managers. (For instance, the expat head of General Electric's Asia-Pacific region transferred back to a top position as vice chairman at GE.) Control is also important. The assumption is that home country managers are already steeped in the firm's policies and culture, and thus more likely to implement headquarters' instructions and ways of doing things.

In any case, for the past 10 years or so the trend seems to have been toward using locals or toward other solutions. Posting expatriates abroad is expensive, security problems give potential expats pause, returning expats often leave for other employers, colleges are producing top quality candidates abroad, and the recent recession made the cost of posting employees abroad even more unattractive. One survey found that new expatriate postings are not only down, but many employers are bringing them home early.[26] Another survey found that about 47% of U.S. multinationals are maintaining the size of their expat workforces; 18% were increasing it, and 35% were decreasing the number of expatriates.[27]

A HYBRID SOLUTION Today, the choice is not just between expatriate versus local employees; there's a hybrid solution. One survey found that about 78% of employers had some form of "localization" policy. This is a policy of transferring a home country national employee to a foreign subsidiary as a "permanent transferee." The employer here does not treat the employee (who assumedly wants to move abroad) as an expatriate, but instead as, say, a French local hire.[28] For example, U.S. IBM employees originally from India eventually filled many of the 5,000 jobs that

IBM recently shifted from the United States to India. These employees elected to move back to India, albeit at local, India pay rates.

OFFSHORING *Offshoring*—moving business processes such as manufacturing or call center operations abroad, and thus having local employees abroad do jobs that the firm's domestic employees previously did in-house—is growing rapidly. About 3 million jobs will move offshore between 2000 and 2015.[29] (*Outsourcing* means moving a firm's business processes to an external company. *Offshoring* therefore means outsourcing business processes abroad.) For example, American Express and Dell transferred some customer service call center jobs from the United States to India. Merrill Lynch similarly transferred certain security analysis operations abroad. The need to reduce costs (by transferring jobs from high- to low-wage countries) is driving this trend. Reduced telecommunications costs and improved information technology are facilitating it.

Offshoring is controversial. In the 1990s, employers mostly moved manufacturing jobs overseas. Between 2000 and 2015, the U.S. Labor Department and Forrester Research estimate that about 288,000 management jobs will go offshore, 472,000 computer jobs, 184,000 architecture jobs, and almost 75,000 legal jobs and about 1.7 million office jobs. Offshoring's opponents say this job drain will mean millions of fewer white-collar jobs for American workers. Proponents say employers must offshore to remain competitive, and that the money employers save boosts research and development and, eventually, creates jobs for U.S. workers. IBM recently announced that it was shifting about 5,000 U.S. software and sales jobs to India.[30]

Offshoring jobs from the United States to lower wage countries entangles the employer's human resource team in the economic, political, and cultural issues we discussed earlier. The HR in Practice feature illustrates how human resource managers actually deal with some of these issues.

HR IN PRACTICE

What Human Resource Management Can Do to Facilitate Offshoring Operations

Human resource managers play a central role in offshoring decisions. IBM Business Consulting Services surveyed employers to see exactly what roles HR was actually playing in these decisions. Here's a sampling of what they found.[31]

HR's Role in Choosing the Site

It's impossible (or, at least, quite unwise) for employers to choose an offshoring location without input from the human resource team. For example, HR provides that information top management needs:[32]

- To determine *total labor costs*. These include direct wages and benefits, as well as the potential costs of exiting a market (such as costs associated with retraining and severance payments).
- To understand the *composition of local labor markets*, for example, in terms of their size, education levels, and the availability of language skills.
- To understand better how the firm's current *employment-related reputation* in the locale may affect any outsourcing to this locale.
- Regarding the locale's current *business environment*, for instance, in terms of tax incentives and local unions.
- Regarding how much the firm should *integrate the local workforce* into the parent firm's corporate organization. For example, employees performing strategic customer related tasks (such as engineering) might best become employees. Those performing less strategic tasks (call centers) might best remain independent contractors or employees of vendor firms.

HR's Role in Recruitment and Selection

In IBMs' discussions with offshoring employers, the latter emphasized three critical recruitment issues:

- **Skill shortages.** The survey team found that "Despite large candidate pools for entry-level workers, there is an ongoing "war for talent" in many of these [low wage] labor markets."[33] This often requires hiring employees from other local firms, using signing bonuses, higher wages, and improved employee retention policies (for instance, improved promotion opportunities).
- **Hiring in bulk.** The need to hire hundreds or thousands of employees at once complicates the hiring process. Employers are increasingly turning to employment agencies, employee referrals, and other means, including college recruiting.
- **Evaluation hurdle.** "Many respondents indicated that the sheer number of potential candidates often dwarfed the firms' capacity to screen and evaluate these individuals."[34] However, the employer still must take the steps required to hire the right employees.

HR's Role in Employee Retention

IBM found that "Perhaps the greatest HR challenge facing globally distributed back-office and customer care centers is the retention of talented employees."[35] The high-pressure nature of these jobs combines with skill shortages to produce high attrition rates. To reduce high attrition, employers are taking steps such as:

- Deciding what is an acceptable *target attrition rate*, to measure the employer's retention performance.
- Identifying what *"levers"* reduce attrition. These levers include more training and development, improved job design and work environment, better compensation and benefits, and improved career opportunities.

Values and International Staffing Policy

It's not just facts such as technical skills or attrition rates that influence whether employers use expats, locals, or offshore solutions. In addition, the top executives' values also play a role. Some executives are just more "expat-oriented."

Experts sometimes classify people's values as **ethnocentric**, **polycentric**, or **geocentric**, and these values translate into corresponding corporate behaviors and policies.[36] In a firm whose top managers tend to be *ethnocentric*, "the prevailing attitude is that home country attitudes, management style, knowledge, evaluation criteria, and managers are superior to anything the host country might have to offer."[37] In the *polycentric* corporation, "there is a conscious belief that only host country managers can ever really understand the culture and behavior of the host country market; therefore, the foreign subsidiary should be managed by local people."[38] *Geocentric* executives believe they must scour the firm's whole management staff on a global basis, on the assumption that the best manager for a specific position anywhere may be found in any of the countries in which the firm operates.

STAFFING POLICIES These values translate into three broad international staffing policies. With an *ethnocentric* staffing policy, the firm tends to fill key management jobs with home (parent-country) nationals. At Royal Dutch Shell, for instance, financial officers around the world tend to be Dutch nationals. A *polycentric*-oriented firm would staff its foreign subsidiaries with host country nationals, and its home office with parent-country nationals. A *geocentric* staffing policy guides the firm to choose the best people for key jobs regardless of nationality. For example, Sony appointed as CEO a Welshman with dual USA and UK citizenship who'd run the firm's U.S. operations.

Ethics and Codes of Conduct

In terms of values, employers also need to ensure that their employees abroad are adhering to their firm's ethics codes. Doing so is not easy. For example, exporting a firm's ethics rules requires more than having employees abroad use versions of its U.S. employee handbook. For instance, few countries adhere to "employment at will," so even handbooks with at-will disclaimers "can become binding contracts."[39] Furthermore, employees in many countries have extensive rights to consultation on working conditions under their labor laws. Here, U.S.-style handbooks may "breach an employer's information, consultation, and participation duty."[40]

Instead, one international employment lawyer recommends focusing on creating and distributing worldwide a global code of conduct. Sometimes, the employer's main concern is establishing global standards for adhering to U.S. laws that have cross-border impacts. They should set policies on things like discrimination, harassment, bribery, and Sarbanes-Oxley. For other firms, like Nike and Mattel, the main concern may be with enforcing codes of conduct for avoiding, for instance, sweatshop conditions.

In any event, local cultural norms can undermine employers' attempts to institute uniform codes of conduct. Bribery, abhorrent in most counties, is ignored in others. As another example, people in countries with a history of fascist rule still remember how their governments expected them to divulge information about their coworkers. In places like this, employees often frown on U.S.-type rules encouraging whistle-blowing.[41]

Selecting International Managers

In most respects, screening managers for jobs abroad is similar to screening them for domestic jobs. Both types of candidates need the technical knowledge and skills to do the job, and the required intelligence and people skills.

However, foreign assignments are different. The expatriate (and his or her family) will have to cope with colleagues whose culture may be drastically different from one's own. And, there's the stress of being in a foreign land.

In spite of this, many employers don't pay much attention to expatriate screening. Researchers several years ago found that selection for a posting abroad is often so informal they called it "the coffee machine system": Two colleagues meet at the office coffee machine, strike up a conversation about the possibility of a position abroad, and based on that and little more a selection decision is made.[42] As one recent study concluded, "[t]raditionally, most selection of expatriates appears to be done solely on the basis of successful records of job performance in the home country."[43] Whether the candidate could adapt to a new culture was often secondary. Conversely, best practices in international assignee selection include providing *realistic previews* to prospective international assignees, facilitating *self-selection* to enable expatriate candidates to decide for themselves if the assignments are right for them, and using *traditional selection procedures* focusing on traits such as openness.[44] We'll look at each.

TESTING Employers can take steps to improve the expat selection process, and testing is an obvious tool. For example, Performance Programs, Inc. (PPI) has used its Overseas Assignment Inventory (OAI) for over 30 years to help employers do a better job of selecting candidates for assignments abroad. According to PPI, "The OAI is an online assessment that measures nine attributes and six context factors crucial for successful adaptation to another culture. It is provided for both the expatriate job candidate and his or her spouse or partner. PPI establishes local norms, and conducts ongoing validation studies of the OAI."[45] Figure 13.1 illustrates the OAI.

REALISTIC PREVIEWS Even in highly industrialized postings (say, to France) there will be language barriers, bouts of homesickness and loneliness, and the need for any children to adapt to new friends.

Realistic previews about the problems to expect in the new job as well as about the cultural benefits, problems, and idiosyncrasies of the country are thus another important part of the screening process. The rule should always be to "spell it all out" ahead of time, as many multinationals do for their international transferees.[46] That way the candidate and his or her spouse can make an informed decision about whether to take the job.

ADAPTABILITY SCREENING With flexibility and adaptability high on the list of what makes expats succeed, *adaptability screening* should be part of the screening process. Employers often use specially trained psychologists for this. Adaptability screening aims to assess the assignee's (and spouse's) probable success in handling the foreign transfer, and to alert them to issues (such as the impact on children) the move may involve.

Here, experience is often the best predictor of future success. Companies look for overseas candidates whose work and nonwork experience, education, and language skills already demonstrate a commitment to and facility for living and working with different cultures. Even several successful summers spent traveling overseas or in foreign student programs might provide some basis to believe the potential transferee can adjust when he or she arrives abroad.

SELECTION TRENDS The expat selection situation seems to be improving. First, over the past two decades *there's been an increase in the number of selection criteria* companies in Germany, Japan, the United States, and the United Kingdom use to select expatriates. Employers now regularly use selection criteria such as technical/professional skills, expatriates' willingness to go, experience in the country, personality factors (including flexibility), leadership skills, the ability to work with teams, and previous performance appraisals in the selection process. Second, there's been a *big decline in U.S. companies' premature return rates*. This suggests that U.S. employers are becoming more successful at sending expatriates abroad.[47] The Managing the New Workforce feature (page 385) expands on this.

Making Expatriate Assignments Successful

Sending managers abroad to test and to improve their global management skills is common. Almost 80% of *Financial Times'* top 100 company CEOs recently had overseas assignments, up dramatically from 10 years ago.[48] (See the Managing the New Workforce feature on page 385 for a related discussion.)

It's therefore disconcerting to see how often such assignments fail. In one survey, employers reported a 21% attrition rate for *expatriate* employees (those the employer posted abroad), compared with an average of 10% for their general employee populations.[49] Others stay, but are unproductive.[50] Experts attribute much of this turnover to poor expatriate selection, training, and reentry preparations.[51] Yet for some employers, the expat failure rate may be declining. This seems to be because more employers are taking steps to reduce typical expat problems. For example, they're selecting expats more carefully, helping spouses get jobs abroad, and providing ongoing support to the expat and his or her family.[52]

3 Explain why foreign assignments fail and what to do to minimize the problems.

Sample excerpt from the
OVERSEAS ASSIGNMENT INVENTORY

Welcome!

Enter the login information you were provided in the box on the left. This will direct you to a registration page before proceeding to your survey.

This site contains:

Overseas Assignment Inventory—A tool designed to assess cultural adaptability for employees and spouses going on international expatriate assignments.

Global Assessment Inventory—A development tool designed to assess factors related to success in multicultural interactions.

Demographics

Please complete the demographic information requested. Note, your answers will not impact the survey results. Upon completion, you will be directed to the survey.

Background Information

Employee or Spouse/Partner:	☐ Employee	☐ Spouse/Partner
Gender:	☐ Male	☐ Female
Nationality:	_____	
Age:	_____	
Number of Children:	_____	
Have Traveled Outside of Country of Citizenship:	☐ Yes	☐ No
Have Lived Outside of Country of Citizenship:	☐ Yes	☐ No

Employment

Destination Country:	_____
Current Country Location:	_____

Submit

Survey Questions *(page 1 of 6)*

Read each survey question carefully and select the bubble that corresponds to your choice. When answering the questions, keep in mind that there are no "right" or "wrong" answers. Choose the response that is reflective of what you think and do most of the time. Some of the questions appear similar; actually no two are exactly alike. Please answer each one without regard to the others.

	Strongly Agree 1	Agree 2	Uncertain 3	Disagree 4	Strongly Disagree 5

1. I do not want to compromise my present standard of living.   ☐1 ☐2 ☐3 ☐4 ☐5

2. The environment I am comfortable with is similar to that in my destination country.   ☐1 ☐2 ☐3 ☐4 ☐5

3. Generally, my spouse/partner and I understand each other.   ☐1 ☐2 ☐3 ☐4 ☐5

4. I am generally one of the first to speak and take charge in a group.   ☐1 ☐2 ☐3 ☐4 ☐5

5. It is very clear to me how my work on this assignment will be evaluated.   ☐1 ☐2 ☐3 ☐4 ☐5

6. I am fluent in the language spoken in my destination country.   ☐1 ☐2 ☐3 ☐4 ☐5

FIGURE 13.1

Overseas Assignment Inventory

Source: Copyright © 2008. Prudential Relocation. Reprinted with permission of Prudential Relocation. All rights reserved. May not be further copied, reproduced or republished in any medium without the express written permission of Prudential Relocation.

MANAGING THE NEW WORKFORCE

Sending Women Managers Abroad

Recently, 56% of the overseas workforce was under 40, single (43%), and female (21%). So while women represent about 50% of the middle management talent in U.S. companies, they represent only 21% of managers sent abroad. That's up from about 3% in the 1980s and 15% in 2005, but still low.[53] What accounts for this?

Actually, many of the misperceptions that impeded women's progress over the years still exist.[54] Line managers make these assignments, and many assume that women don't want to work abroad, are reluctant to move their families abroad, or can't get their spouses to move.[55] In fact, this survey found, women do want international assignments, they are not less inclined to move their families, and their male spouses are not necessarily reluctant.

Safety is another issue. Employers tend to assume that women abroad are more likely to become crime victims. However, most surveyed women expats said that safety was no more an issue with women than it was with men. As one said, "It doesn't matter if you're a man or woman. If it's a dangerous city, it's dangerous for whomever."[56]

Fear of cultural prejudices against women is another common issue. In some cultures, women do have to follow different rules than do men, for instance, in terms of attire. But as one expat said, "Even in the more harsh cultures, once they recognize that the women can do the job, once your competence has been demonstrated, it becomes less of a problem."[57]

Employers take several steps to short-circuit misperceptions like these, and to identify more women to assign abroad. For example, *formalize a process* for identifying employees who are willing to take assignments abroad. (At Gillette, for instance, supervisors use the performance review to identify the subordinate's career interests, including for assignments abroad.) *Train managers* to understand how employees really feel about going abroad, and what the real safety and cultural issues are. Let successful female expats *help recruit* prospective female expats, and discuss with them the pros and cons of assignments abroad. Provide the expat's spouse with employment assistance.[58]

How to Avoid Having International Assignments Fail

Determining why foreign assignments fail is a cottage industry itself. A study of 750 U.S., European, and Japanese companies provides some clues. The employers that did best in terms of sending people abroad did three things when making international assignments:[59]

- They focus their assignments on knowledge creation and global *leadership development*;
- They assign people overseas whose technical skills are matched or exceeded by their *cross-cultural abilities*; and
- Their expatriate assignments include a deliberate *repatriation* process.

Let's look at some steps employees can take to reduce the chances that an assignment abroad will fail.

Most surveyed women expats said that safety was no more an issue with them than it was with men.

Source: Fuse/Getty Images, Inc.–Liaison.

PERSONALITY Choosing the right person is essential. Expats are increasingly younger, and single. Studies show that 56% of the overseas workforce is under 40, single (43%), and female (21%). That female percentage was up from about 15% in 2004.[60]

In terms of personality, successful expatriate employees tend to be extroverted, agreeable, and emotionally stable individuals.[61] One study found three characteristics—extroversion, agreeableness, and emotional stability—were inversely related to the expatriate's desire to terminate the assignment; conscientiousness was positively related to the expatriate's performance. Another study found a positive relationship between sociability and cross-cultural adjustment.[62] So, not surprisingly, sociable, outgoing, conscientious people seem more likely to fit into new cultural settings.

Intentions are important too: For example, people who want expatriate careers try harder to adjust to such a life.[63] Similarly, expatriates who are more satisfied with their jobs abroad are more likely to adapt to the foreign assignment.[64]

Studies also suggest that it's not how different culturally the host country is from the person's home country that causes problems; it's the person's ability to adapt. *Cultural empathy* is "a working knowledge of the cultural variables affecting management decisions."[65] Some people are so culturally at ease that they do fine transferred anywhere; others will fail anywhere.[66]

STABLE AND DYNAMIC TRAITS Some of the characteristics required for success abroad may be baked into the person's personality, while others are more easily learned. For example, one study concluded that what it called "stable" characteristics are basically part of one's personality and so are relatively fixed. These include tolerance for ambiguity, openness, flexibility, self-confidence, and a sense of humor. Stable characteristics also include abilities and interests. These researchers say that individuals who possess stable characteristics like these make better expatriates, particularly for CEO-type jobs. For example, they are likely to adjust more readily to their assignments. They are also better equipped to detect and respond to cultural nuances abroad.

On the other hand, characteristics like language proficiency, market knowledge, and technical expertise are "dynamic." The person acquires these through training. Here's how the researchers sum it up:

> [Stable traits] are the traits that expatriates not only should have but must have, and if these are lacking, the candidates should either be eliminated or should self-eliminate from consideration early in the selection process. However, if they cross this hurdle, candidates should then be evaluated for the technical expertise, functional competence, and other skills that would be necessary to perform that particular job in that particular location. With the assumption that the baseline criteria have been met, these dynamic skills can be learned.[67]

FAMILY PRESSURES Family pressures loom large in expatriate failures. In one early study, U.S. managers listed the following reasons for leaving early, from high to low in importance: inability of spouse to adjust, managers' inability to adjust, other family problems, managers' personal or emotional immaturity, and inability to cope with larger overseas responsibility.[68] Managers of European firms emphasized only the inability of the manager's spouse to adjust as an explanation for the expatriate's failed assignment. Other studies similarly emphasize dissatisfied spouses' effects on the international assignment.[69]

THE PROBLEM These findings underscore this fact: it's usually not technical or cultural factors but family and personal ones that undermine international assignees. Yet employers still tend to select expatriates based on technical competence rather than interpersonal skills or domestic situations:[70]

> The selection process is fundamentally flawed. . . . Expatriate assignments rarely fail because the person cannot accommodate to the technical demands of the job. . . . They fail because of family and personal issues and lack of cultural skills that haven't been part of the process.[71] (The HR in Practice shows how to avoid this.)

HR IN PRACTICE

Some Practical Solutions to the Expatriate Challenge

Although non-work factors like the adjustment of the spouse can prompt assignees to leave early, that's not inevitable. Managers can take several practical steps to improve the expat's success abroad.

- First, *provide realistic previews of what to expect abroad, careful screening (of both the prospective expat and his or her spouse), improved orientation,* and *improved benefits* packages.
- Simply *shorten the length* of the assignment.
- Use "short-term," "commuter," or "frequent-flier" assignments. These involve much travel but no formal relocation.[72] Such employees are essentially international commuters.[73]

This can be effective, particularly where the commutes are relatively short and inexpensive, as between Europe and the United States.

- Use Internet-based *video technologies* and group decision-making software to enable global virtual teams to conduct business without relocation.[74]
- Form *"global buddy"* programs. Here local managers assist new expatriates with advice on things such as office politics, norms of behavior, and where to receive emergency medical assistance.[75]
- Use executive coaches to mentor and work with expatriate managers.[76]

TRAINING AND MAINTAINING INTERNATIONAL EMPLOYEES

Careful screening is just the first step in ensuring the foreign assignee's success. The employee will then require special training. The firm must also address international human resource policies for appraising and compensating the firm's overseas employees, and for maintaining healthy labor relations.

Orienting and Training Employees on International Assignment

When it comes to supplying the orientation and training required for success overseas, the practices of most U.S. firms reflect more talk than substance. In one survey 56% of employers admitted that the people they sent abroad weren't sufficiently knowledgeable about the host country, but only 20% of them offered the necessary country training.[77]

4 List and describe the basic steps in training employees who the employer is about to transfer abroad.

CROSS-CULTURAL TRAINING *Cross-cultural training* is the most important issue in training expatriates. Cross-cultural training "should result in the expatriate learning both content and skills that will improve interactions with host country individuals by reducing misunderstandings and inappropriate behaviors."[78] One training vendor prescribes a four-step cultural training approach.[79]

- Level 1 training focuses on the *impact of cultural differences* (such as the importance of saving "face" in Asia), and on raising trainees' awareness of such differences and their impact on business outcomes.
- Level 2 aims at getting participants to understand how *attitudes* form and influence behavior. (For example, unfavorable stereotypes may subconsciously influence how a new manager treats his or her new foreign subordinates.)
- Level 3 training provides *factual knowledge* about the target country.
- Level 4 provides skill building in areas like *language* and adjustment and adaptation skills.

As Figure 13.2 illustrates, the actual cross-cultural training methods typically include things like cultural briefings and field experiences.

OTHER EXPATRIATE TRAINING Beyond cross-cultural training, employers use various other methods to train prospective expats. These include *programs* about the country's geography and socioeconomic and political history, *cultural assimilation* to show trainees the sorts of social and interpersonal situations they're likely to encounter, *language training, sensitivity training,* and actual *interactions* with people from other cultures within the trainee's own country.[80] For example, Procter & Gamble sends employees and their spouses destined for China to Beijing for 2 months of language and cultural training.[81]

FIGURE 13.2

Typical Cross-Cultural Training Methods

Source: Francesco, Anne Marie; Gold, Barry A., *International Organizational Behavior*, 2nd, © 2005. Electronically reproduced by permission of Pearson Education, Inc., Upper Saddle River, New Jersey.

● Cultural Briefings	Explain the major aspects of the host country culture, including customs, traditions, and everyday behaviors.	
● Area Briefings	Explain the history, geography, economy, politics, and other general information about the host country and region.	
● Cases	Portray a real-life situation in business or personal life to illustrate some aspect of living or working in the host culture.	
● Role Playing	Allows the trainee to act out a situation that he or she might face living or working in the host country.	
● Culture Assimilator	Provides a written set of situations that the trainee might encounter living or working in the host country. Trainee selects one from a set of responses to the situation and is given feedback on if it is appropriate and why.	
● Field Experiences	Provide an opportunity for the trainee to go to the host country or another unfamiliar culture to experience living and working there for a short time.	

TRAINING EMPLOYEES ABROAD Extending the parent company's training to its local employees abroad is increasingly important. For Kimberly-Clark, for instance, average training per employee abroad has quickly risen from almost none to about 38 hours per year.[82] Starbucks (pronounced "Starbuck-zu" in Japan) brings new management trainees from abroad to its Seattle, Washington, headquarters. This gives them "a taste of the west coast lifestyle and the company's informal culture," as well as the technical knowledge required to manage their local stores.[83]

Managers abroad continue to need traditional training and development. At IBM, for instance, such development includes rotating assignments that enable overseas managers to grow professionally. IBM and other firms also have management development centers around the world where executives hone their skills. And classroom programs (such as those at the London Business School, or at INSEAD in France) provide overseas executives the sorts of educational opportunities (to acquire MBAs, for instance) that similar stateside programs do for their U.S.-based colleagues. Figure 13.3 illustrates some corporate programs to develop global managers.

TRENDS There are several trends in expatriate training and development.

- First, rather than providing only pre-departure cross-cultural training, more firms are providing continuing, in-country cross-cultural training during the early stages of the overseas assignment.
- Second, employers are using returning managers as resources. For example, Bosch holds regular seminars. Here, newly arrived returnees pass on their knowledge and experience to relocating managers and their families.
- Third, employers increasingly use the Internet for cross-cultural training. For example, *Bridging Cultures* is "a specially designed training program geared to developing essential knowledge, awareness and skills for working cooperatively and productively in a multicultural

FIGURE 13.3

Corporate Programs to Develop Global Managers

Source: Francesco, Anne Marie; Gold, Barry A., *International Organizational Behavior*, 2nd, © 2005. Used by permission of Anne-Marie Francesco.

- ABB (Asea Brown Boveri) rotates about 500 managers around the world to different countries every two to three years in order to develop a management cadre of transpatriates to support their global strategy.
- PepsiCo has an orientation program for its foreign managers, which brings them to the United States for one-year assignments in bottling division plants.
- British Telecom uses informal mentoring techniques to induct employees into the ways of their assigned country; existing expatriate workers talk to prospective assignees about the cultural factors to expect.
- Honda of America Manufacturing gives its U.S. supervisors and managers extensive preparation in Japanese language, culture, and lifestyle and then sends them to the parent company in Tokyo for up to three years.
- General Electric likes its engineers and managers to have a global perspective whether or not they are slated to go abroad. The company gives regular language and cross-cultural training for them so that they are equipped to conduct business with people around the world.

and multilingual workplace" (www.prismdiversity.com/products/bridging_cultures. html). It uses short video clips to introduce case study intercultural problems, and then guides users to selecting the strategy to best handle the situation. Other sources of cross-cultural training include www.livingabroad.com, www.globaldynamics.com, www. culturalsavvy.com, and www.peoplegoingglobal.com.[84]

International Compensation

The whole area of international compensation presents some tricky problems. On the one hand, there is some logic in having company-wide pay scales. Here, for instance, the firm pays divisional marketing directors throughout the world within the same pay range. But this is usually not practical, given the large differences in cost of living among countries.

THE BALANCE SHEET APPROACH The most common approach to formulating expatriate pay is therefore to *equalize purchasing power* across countries, a technique known as the *balance sheet* approach.[85]

The basic idea is that each expatriate should enjoy the same standard of living he or she would have at home. With the balance sheet approach, the employer focuses on four main home country groups of expenses—*income taxes, housing, goods and services,* and *discretionary expenses* (child support, car payments, and the like). The employer estimates what each of these four expenses would be in the expatriate's home country, and what each will be in the host country. The employer then pays any differences—such as additional income taxes or housing expenses.

In practice, this usually boils down to building the expatriate's total compensation around five or six separate components. For example, base salary will normally be in the same range as the manager's home country salary. In addition, however, there might be an overseas or foreign service premium. The executive receives this as a percentage of his or her base salary, to compensate for the required cultural and physical adjustments.[86] There may also be several allowances, including a housing allowance, and an education allowance for the expatriate's children. Income taxes represent another area of concern. A U.S. manager posted abroad must often pay not just U.S. taxes but also income taxes in the host country.

Table 13.1 illustrates the balance sheet approach. In this case, the manager's annual earnings are $80,000, and she faces a U.S. income tax rate of 28% and a Belgium income tax rate of 70%. (The other costs are based on the index of living costs abroad published in the "U.S. Department of State Indexes of Living Costs Abroad, Quarters Allowances, and Hardship Differentials," available at http://aoprals.state.gov/content.asp?content_id=186&menu_id=81.)

To help the expatriate manage his or her home and foreign financial obligations, most employers use a *split pay* approach; they pay, say, half a person's actual pay in home country currency and half in the local currency.[87]

INTERCOUNTRY COST DIFFERENCES Once location-specific cash premium allowances, relocation assistance, taxation, and itemized reimbursements (for things like children's schooling) are factored in, the total 3-year cost of sending the same employee abroad would vary widely by country. For example, recently it ranged from about $432,000 for a posting to London, to $990,000 in Tokyo.[88] Figure 13.4 summarizes typical expatriate pay premiums and benefits.

TABLE 13.1 The Balance Sheet Approach (Assumes Base Salary of $80,000)

Annual Expense	Chicago, U.S.	Brussels, Belgium (U.S.$ Equivalent)	Extra Allowance
Housing & utilities	$35,000	$67,600	$32,600
Goods & services	6,000	9,500	3,500
Taxes	22,400	56,000	33,600
Discretionary income	10,000	10,000	0
Total	$73,400	$143,100	$69,700

Source: Joseph Martocchio, *Strategic Compensation: A Human Resource Management Approach,* 2nd edition (Upper Saddle River, NJ: Prentice Hall, 2001), Table 12–15, p. 294.

FIGURE 13.4

Typical Expatriate Pay Premiums and Benefits

Source: Francesco, Anne Marie; Gold, Barry A., *International Organizational Behavior*, 2nd, © 2005. Electronically reproduced by permission of Pearson Education, Inc., Upper Saddle River, New Jersey.

● Overseas Premium	Additional percentage of base salary (usually 10 percent) paid to compensate for inconvenience of living abroad
● Housing Allowance	Provision of comfortable housing for free or at a rate similar to what the expatriate would incur at home
● Cost of Living Allowance (COLA)	Payment of additional amount to cover extra costs to allow expatriate to live in the same manner as they did at home
● Moving Expenses	Expatriate and family transportation and goods shipment to and from assignment location
● Tuition for Dependent Education	Reimbursement for expatriate's children to receive a home country education, for example, private school in the assignment location or boarding school back home
● Home Leave	Expatriate and family transportation and time off to return home
● Tax Reimbursement Payments	Reimbursement for any additional taxes payable by expatriate as a result of living abroad

INCENTIVES While the situation is changing, performance-based incentives are still somewhat less prevalent abroad. In Europe, firms still tend to emphasize a guaranteed annual salary and company-wide bonus. European compensation directors do want to see more performance-based pay. However, they first have to overcome several problems—including selling the idea of more emphasis on performance-based pay.

The employer also needs to tie the incentives to local realities. In Eastern Europe, workers generally spend 35% to 40% of their disposable income on basics like food and utilities. They therefore require a higher proportion of more predictable base salary than do workers in, say, the United States.[89]

However, incentives are popular in other countries. In Japan, a worker might expect to receive perhaps half (or more) of his or her total annual compensation near year end, as a sort of profit-sharing bonus. In Asia, including the People's Republic of China, incentives, even for production workers, are popular. However many employers in Asia, to preserve group harmony, make incentive pay a small part of the pay package, and team incentives are advisable.[90]

ESTABLISHING A GLOBAL PAY SYSTEM The aim of the employer's global rewards program is to ensure three things: (1) that the pay policies in each geographic location contribute to motivating the employee behaviors the company needs in order to achieve its strategic plan. And that (2) the separate geographic area compensation plans are consistent with each other, while (3) responsive to local conditions.[91] The accompanying Managing HR in Challenging Times feature expands on this.

Designing a global pay plan requires stepping back and deciding first, what employee behaviors you want the pay plan to encourage, given the firm's strategic aims. Then, systematize job descriptions, appraisal processes, and pay policies among company facilities around the world. Figure 13.5 summarizes the steps or phases in designing a global pay plan.

Managing HR in Challenging Times

Getting a Handle on Global Compensation

A recent report on global pay from Hewitt Associates highlights the challenge facing many managers with operations abroad. As the report says, "[W]ith exponential growth in the past years, many U.S. multinational organizations have not given prudent consideration to their compensation cost structures outside the U.S."

Therefore, economic challenges now are forcing many employers to refocus on the effectiveness of their global compensation pay practices. For one thing, they're looking more carefully at who exactly is making the global compensation pay decisions, and how they're making them. Are managers abroad involved? Is it the home-office human resources team? Is it clear who is responsible for what and that the people making these decisions are doing so within the framework of the company's overall pay practices? The aim here is to "ensure that overall compensation spending is managed effectively . . . ." Employers are also focusing more diligently on the details of their overseas pay decisions. For example, is how we're paying our employees abroad competitive? And are we basing our overseas pay decisions by referencing "credible and defendable market data"?[92] Effective pay practices are always important, but particularly so in economically changing times.

Performance Appraisal of International Managers

At factories in Toyota City, Japan, bar charts map individual workers' progress toward meeting their personal work targets. Toyota doesn't intend this public display of performance to humiliate their workers. Instead, it is to "alert [the worker's] coworkers and enlist their help in finding solutions."[93]

Several things complicate the task of appraising an expatriate's performance. Cultural differences are one. For example, an open exchange of views including criticism is often the norm in the United States, but is frowned upon in China, where "face" is a major concern.

Another complication is, Who does the appraisals? Obviously, local management must have some input, but, again, cultural differences may distort the appraisals. (Thus, host country bosses in Peru might evaluate a U.S. expatriate manager there somewhat negatively if they find his or her use of participative decision making culturally inappropriate.) On the other hand, home-office managers, not fully aware of the situation the manager faces locally, may be so out of touch that they can't provide valid appraisals.

In fact, when it comes to appraising expatriates abroad, managers don't always do what they know they should. In one study, the surveyed managers knew that having appraisers from both the host and home countries, and more frequent appraisals, produced the best appraisals. But, in practice, most did not do this. Instead, they conducted appraisals less frequently, and had raters from the host or the home countries do the appraisals.[94]

Suggestions for improving the expatriate appraisal process include:

1. Adapt the performance criteria to the local job and situation.
2. Weigh the evaluation more toward the on-site manager's appraisal than toward the home-site manager's.
3. If the home-office manager does the actual written appraisal, have him or her use a former expatriate from the same overseas location for advice.

FIGURE 13.5

Steps in Designing a Global Pay Plan

Source: Bradley Kirkman et al., "Five Challenges to Virtual Team Success: Lessons from Sabre, Inc.," *Academy of Management Executive* 16, no. 3 (2002): 23–40; M. Schoeff, "Adopting an HR Worldview," *Workforce Management* 87, no. 19 (November 17, 2008): 8.

- **Phase I: Formulate a global compensation framework.** This means:
  1. define your firm's global rewards philosophy (in terms how rewards will help the company achieve its strategic goals),
  2. review your current rewards programs around the world,
  3. assess the extent to which each of these country programs are set up to help the company achieve its strategic goals, and
  4. create a preliminary compensation plan for each location.
- **Phase II: Organize jobs and appraisals.** Next, systematize job descriptions and performance expectations around the world. For example, create more consistent performance assessment practices, establish consistent job descriptions and performance expectations for similar worldwide jobs, and start planning requirements and recruitment worldwide.
- **Phase III: Create detailed pay policies.** Here, devise specific pay policies for each location that make sense in terms of the firm's global compensation philosophy. Among other things, this will require surveys to assess local pay practices.
- **Phase IV: Institute a talent management framework.** Next, institute career development practices, in recognition of the fact that promotional opportunities and career programs are necessary supplements to the company's compensation programs.
- **Phase V: Reevaluate program.** Periodically reevaluate the global pay policies, given the fact that strategic needs and competitors' pay practices may change.

Safety and Fair Treatment Abroad

Employee safety abroad is an important issue for global employers, for several reasons. For one thing, the need to ensure safety and fair treatment doesn't stop at a country's borders. The United States has often taken the lead in occupational safety. However, other countries are quickly adopting such laws, with which anyone doing business in these countries must then comply. And, in any case, it's hard to make a legitimate case for being less safety conscious or fair with workers abroad than you are with those at home. High-profile companies including Nike, Inc. have received bad publicity for—and taken steps to improve—the working conditions, long hours, and low pay rates for factory workers in countries such as Indonesia.

TERRORISM The increased threat of terrorism is also affecting human resource activities abroad. Even stationing employees in assumedly safe countries is no guarantee there won't be problems. In 2009, for instance, workers (but certainly not terrorists) in French factories of Sony Corp., Caterpillar Inc., and 3M Co. took their managers hostage in order to negotiate better benefits for laid off employees.[95] Developments like these had already prompted employers to take steps to protect their expat and foreign employees better. Thus, employers have had to institute more comprehensive safety plans abroad, including, for instance, evacuation plans to get employees to safety, if that becomes necessary. Many employers purchase intelligence services for monitoring potential terrorist threats abroad. The head of one intelligence firm estimates such services at costing $6,000–$10,000 per year.[96]

BUSINESS TRAVEL Keeping business travelers out of crime's way is a specialty all its own, but suggestions here include:[97]

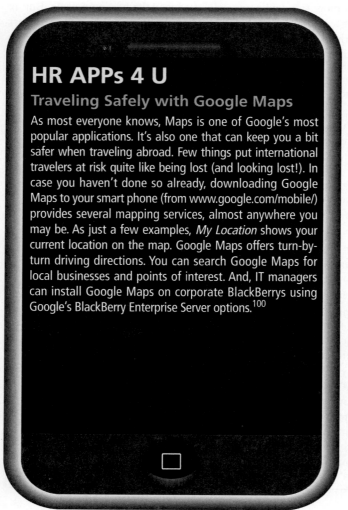

HR APPs 4 U

Traveling Safely with Google Maps

As most everyone knows, Maps is one of Google's most popular applications. It's also one that can keep you a bit safer when traveling abroad. Few things put international travelers at risk quite like being lost (and looking lost!). In case you haven't done so already, downloading Google Maps to your smart phone (from www.google.com/mobile/) provides several mapping services, almost anywhere you may be. As just a few examples, *My Location* shows your current location on the map. Google Maps offers turn-by-turn driving directions. You can search Google Maps for local businesses and points of interest. And, IT managers can install Google Maps on corporate BlackBerrys using Google's BlackBerry Enterprise Server options.[100]

- Provide expatriates with training about traveling, living abroad, and the place they're going to, so they're more oriented.
- Tell them not to draw attention to the fact they're Americans—by wearing T-shirts with American names, for instance.
- Have travelers arrive at airports as close to departure time as possible and wait in areas away from the main flow of traffic.
- Equip the expatriate's car and home with adequate security systems.
- Tell employees to vary their departure and arrival times and take different routes.
- Keep employees current on crime and other problems by regularly checking, for example, the State Department's travel advisories and warnings at http://travel.state.gov/.[98] Click on travel alerts and country information.
- Advise employees to act confident at all times. Body language can attract perpetrators, and those who look like victims often become victimized.[99]

Repatriation: Problems and Solutions

One of the most unfortunate facts about sending employees abroad is that 40% to 60% of them will probably quit within 3 years of returning home. A 3-year assignment abroad for one employee with a base salary of about $100,000 may cost the employer $1 million, once extra living costs, transportation, and family benefits are included.[101] Given the investment the employer makes in sending these high-potential people abroad, it obviously makes sense to do everything possible to keep them with the firm.

For many returnees, coming home is a shock. Dual-career couples listed "the perceived impact of the international assignments upon returning to the U.S." as one of the most important issues in their willingness to relocate.[102] Yet one survey found that only about 31% of employers surveyed had formal repatriation programs for executives.[103] Formal repatriation programs are useful. For instance, one study found that about 5% of returning employees resigned if their firms had formal repatriation programs, while about 22% of those left if their firms had no such programs.[104]

STEPS IN REPATRIATION   The heart and guiding principle of any repatriation program is this: Make sure that the expatriate and his or her family don't feel that the company has left them adrift. For example, one firm has a three-part repatriation program, one that starts before the employee leaves for the assignment abroad.[105]

First, the firm matches the expat and his or her family with a psychologist trained in repatriation issues. The psychologist meets with the family before they go abroad. The psychologist discusses the challenges they will face abroad, assesses with them how well they think they will adapt to their new culture, and stays in touch with them throughout their assignment.

Second, the program makes sure that the employee always feels that he or she is still "in the loop" with what's happening back at the home office. For example, the expat gets a mentor, and travels back to the home office periodically for meetings.

Third, once it's time for the expat employee and his or her family to return home, there's a formal repatriation service. About 6 months before the overseas assignment ends, the psychologist and an HR representative meet with the expat and the family to start preparing them for return. For example, they help plan the employee's next career move, help the person update his or her résumé, and begin putting the person in contact with supervisors back home.[106]

But, in the final analysis, probably the simplest thing the employer can do to improve repatriates' retention is to value their experience more highly. As one returnee put it: "My company was, in my view, somewhat indifferent to my experience in China as evidenced by a lack of monetary reward, positive increase, or leverage to my career in any way." Such feelings then prompt the former expat to look elsewhere for opportunities.[107]

HOW TO IMPLEMENT A GLOBAL HR SYSTEM

With employers increasingly relying on local rather than expatriate employees, transferring one's selection, training, appraisal, pay, and other human resource practices abroad is a top priority. But, given the cross-cultural and other differences, one could reasonably ask, "Is it realistic for a company to try to institute a standardized human resource management system in its facilities around the world?"

A study suggests that the answer is "yes." In brief, the study's results show that employers may have to defer to local managers on some specific human resource management policy issues. However, the findings also suggest that big intercountry HR practice differences are often not necessary or even advisable. The important thing is how you implement the global human resource management system.

In this study, the researchers interviewed human resource personnel from six global companies—Agilent, Dow, IBM, Motorola, Procter & Gamble, and Shell Oil Co.—as well as international human resources consultants.[108] The study's overall conclusion was that employers who successfully implement global HR systems do so by applying several best practices. The basic idea is to *develop* systems that are *acceptable* to employees in units around the world, and ones that the employers can *implement* more effectively. We'll look at each of these three requirements' best practices.

Developing a More Effective Global HR System

5 Explain the main things to keep in mind when designing and implementing a global HR system.

First, these employers engage in two best practices in developing their worldwide human resource policies and practices.

Form global HR networks.   To head off resistance, human resource managers around the world should feel that they're part of the firm's global human resource management team. The researchers found that in developing global HR systems, the most critical factor is "creating an infrastructure of partners around the world that you use for support, for buy-in, for organization of local activities, and to help you better understand their own systems and their own challenges."[109] Treat the local human resource managers as equal partners. For instance, best practice firms formed global teams, to help develop the new human resources systems.

Remember that it's more important to standardize ends and competencies than specific methods. For example, IBM uses a more or less standardized recruitment and selection process worldwide. However, "details such as who conducts the interview (hiring manager vs. recruiter) or whether the prescreen is by phone or in person, differ by country."[110]

Making the Global HR System More *Acceptable*

Next, employers engage in three best practices so that the global human resource systems they develop will be *acceptable* to local managers around the world. These practices include:

Remember that truly global organizations find it easier to install global systems. For example, truly global companies require their managers to work on global teams, and identify and recruit and place the employees they hire globally. As one Shell manager put it, "If you're truly global, then you are hiring here [the United States] people who are going to immediately go and work in the Hague, and vice versa."[111] This global mindset makes it easier for managers everywhere to accept the wisdom of having a standardized human resource management system.

Investigate pressures to differentiate and determine their legitimacy. Local managers will insist, "You can't do that here, because we are different culturally." These researchers found that these "differences" are usually not persuasive. For example, when Dow wanted to implement an online recruitment and selection tool abroad, the local hiring managers said that their managers would not use it. After investigating the supposed cultural roadblocks, Dow successfully implemented the new system.[112]

The operative word here is "investigate." Carefully assess whether the local culture or other differences might in fact undermine the new system. Be knowledgeable about local legal issues, and be willing to differentiate where necessary.

Try to work within the context of a strong corporate culture. Companies that create a strong corporate culture find it easier to obtain agreement among far-flung employees. For example, because of how P&G recruits, selects, trains, and rewards them, its managers have a strong sense of shared values. For instance, new recruits quickly learn to think in terms of "we" instead of "I." They learn to value thoroughness, consistency, self-discipline, and a methodical approach. Because all P&G managers worldwide tend to share these values, they are in a sense more similar to each other than they are geographically different. Having such global unanimity in values makes it easier to implement standardized human resource practices worldwide.

Implementing the Global HR System

Finally, two best practices helped ensure success in actually *implementing* the globally consistent human resource policies and practices.

"You can't communicate enough." "There's a need for constant contact [by HR] with the decision makers in each country, as well as the people who will be implementing and using the system."[113]

Dedicate adequate resources. For example, don't require the local human resource management offices to implement new job analysis procedures unless the head office provides adequate resources for these additional activities.

Improving Productivity through HRIS: Taking the HRIS Global

For global firms, it makes particular sense to expand the firm's human resource information systems to include the firm's operations abroad. For example, electrical components manufacturer Thomas & Betts once needed 83 faxes to get a head count of its 26,000 employees in 24 countries; it can now do so with the push of a button, thanks to its global HRIS system.[114] Such systems automate the collection and integration of HR-related information on matters from employee test results to appraisal ratings, training, and benefits. Most global HRIS do more. For example, without a database of a firm's worldwide management talent, selecting employees for assignments abroad and keeping track of each unit's compensation plans, benefits, and personnel practices and policies can be overwhelming.

When Buildnet, Inc., decided to automate and integrate its separate systems for things like applicant tracking, training, and compensation, it chose a Web-based software package called MyHRIS, from NuView, Inc. (www.nuviewinc.com). This is an Internet-based system that includes human resource and benefits administration, applicant tracking and résumé scanning, training administration, and succession planning and development.[115] With MyHRIS, managers at any of the firm's locations around the world can access and update more than 200 built-in reports such as "termination summary" or "open positions."[116] And the firm's home-office managers can access data and monitor global human resource activities on a real-time basis.

Employers are also increasingly taking their employee self-service HR portals international. For example, Time Warner's "Employee Connection" portal lets its 80,000 worldwide employees self-manage much of their benefits, compensation planning, merit review, and personal information updating online.[117]

REVIEW

SUMMARY

1. International business is important to almost every business today, and so firms must increasingly be managed globally. This confronts managers with many new challenges, including coordinating production, sales, and financial operations on a worldwide basis. As a result, companies today have pressing international HR needs with respect to selecting, training, paying, and repatriating global employees.

2. Intercountry differences affect a company's HR management processes. Cultural factors such as assertiveness and humane orientation suggest differences in values, attitudes, and therefore behaviors and reactions of people from country to country. Economic and labor cost factors help determine whether HR's emphasis should be on efficiency, or some other approach. Industrial relations and specifically the relationship among the workers, the union, and the employer influence the nature of a company's specific HR policies from country to country.

3. A large percentage of expatriate assignments fail, but the batting average can be improved through careful selection. There are various sources HR can use to staff domestic and foreign subsidiaries. Often managerial positions are filled by locals rather than by expatriates, but this is not always the case.

4. Selecting managers for expatriate assignments means screening them for traits that predict success in adapting to dramatically new environments. Such traits include both "stable" and "dynamic" traits, such as adaptability and flexibility, self-orientation, job knowledge and motivation, relational skills, extracultural openness, and family situation. Adaptability screening focusing on the family's probable success in handling the foreign assignment can be an especially important step in the selection process.

5. Training for overseas managers typically focuses on cultural differences, on how attitudes influence behavior, and on factual knowledge about the target country. The most common approach to formulating expatriate pay is to equalize purchasing power across countries, a technique known as the balance sheet approach. The employer estimates expenses for income taxes, housing, goods and services, and discretionary costs, and pays supplements to the expatriate in such a way as to maintain the same standard of living he or she would have had at home.

6. The expatriate appraisal process can be complicated by the need to have both local and home-office supervisors provide input into the performance review. Suggestions for improving the process include stipulating difficulty level, weighing the on-site manager's appraisal more heavily, and having the home-site manager get background advice from managers familiar with the location abroad before completing the expatriate's appraisal.

7. Repatriation problems are common, but you can minimize them. They include the often well-founded fear that the expatriate is "out of sight, out of mind" and difficulties in re-assimilating the expatriate's family back into the home country culture. Suggestions for avoiding these problems include using repatriation agreements, assigning a sponsor, offering career counseling, and keeping the expatriate plugged in to home-office business.

KEY TERMS

international human resource management   376
works councils   378
co-determination   378
expatriates   380
host country nationals   380

locals   380
third-country nationals   380
ethnocentric   382
polycentric   382
geocentric   382

DISCUSSION QUESTIONS

1. List the HR challenges of international business.
2. Illustrate how intercountry differences affect HRM.
3. Explain why foreign assignments fail and what to do to minimize the problems.
4. List and describe the basic steps in training employees who the employer is about to transfer abroad.
5. Explain the main things to keep in mind when designing and implementing a global HR system.
6. Give several examples of how each intercountry difference that affects HR managers may specifically affect an HR manager.
7. What special training do overseas candidates need? In what ways is such training similar to and different from traditional diversity training?
8. How does appraising an expatriate's performance differ from appraising that of a home-office manager? How would you avoid some of the unique problems of appraising the expatriate's performance?

INDIVIDUAL AND GROUP ACTIVITIES

1. Working individually or in groups, write an expatriation and repatriation plan for your professor, whom your school is sending to Bulgaria to teach HR for the next 3 years.
2. Give three specific examples of multinational corporations in your area. Check in the library or Internet or with each firm to determine in what countries these firms have operations, and explain the nature of some of their operations, and whatever you can find out about their international HR policies.
3. Choose three traits useful for selecting international assignees, and create a straightforward test to screen candidates for these traits.
4. Use a library or Internet source to determine the relative cost of living in five countries as of this year, and explain the implications of such differences for drafting a pay plan for managers being sent to each country.

WEB-e's (WEB EXERCISES)

1. Look at the careers sections of Web sites for several companies abroad, such as for Walmart China (www.wal-martchina.com/english/career/career.htm). What differences possibly caused by cultural differences do you see from what you might expect in the U.S. units of these companies?
2. Go to Web sites of vendors such as Kwintessential (www.kwintessential.co.uk/cultural-services/articles/expat-cultural-training.html) who offer cross cultural training to expatriates going abroad. What sorts of issues do they discuss that expats should be prepared for? Do the vendors differ in how they prepare train expats? If so, how?

APPLICATION EXERCISES

HR IN ACTION CASE INCIDENT 1
"Boss, I Think We Have a Problem"

Central Steel Door Corporation has been in business for about 20 years, successfully selling a line of steel industrial-grade doors, as well as the hardware and fittings required for them. Focusing mostly in the United States and Canada, the company had gradually increased its presence from the New York City area, first into New England and then down the Atlantic Coast, then through the Midwest and West, and finally into Canada. The company's basic expansion strategy was always the same: Choose an area, open a distribution center, hire a regional sales manager, then let that regional sales manager help staff the distribution center and hire local sales reps.

Unfortunately, the company's traditional success in finding sales help has not extended to its overseas operations. With the expansion of the European Union, Mel Fisher, president of Central Steel Door, decided to expand his company abroad, into Europe. However, the expansion has not gone smoothly at all. He tried for 3 weeks to find a sales manager by advertising in the *International Herald Tribune*, which is read by businesspeople in Europe and by American expatriates living and working in Europe. Although the ads placed in the *Tribune* also run for about a month in the *Tribune's* Internet Web site, Mr. Fisher so far has received only five applications. One came from a possibly viable candidate, whereas four came from candidates whom Mr. Fisher refers to as "lost souls"—people who seem to have spent most of their time traveling restlessly from country to country sipping espresso in sidewalk cafés. When asked what he had done for the last 3 years, one told Mr. Fisher he'd been on a "walkabout."

Other aspects of his international HR activities have been equally problematic. Fisher alienated two of his U.S. sales managers by sending them to Europe to temporarily run the European operations, but neglected to work out a compensation package that would cover their relatively high living expenses in Germany and Belgium. One ended up staying the better part of the year, and Mr. Fisher was rudely surprised to be informed by the Belgian government that his sales manager owed thousands of dollars in local taxes. The managers had hired about 10 local people to staff each of the two distribution centers. However, without full-time local European sales managers, the level of sales was disappointing, so Fisher decided to fire about half the distribution center employees. That's when he got an emergency phone call from his temporary sales manager in Germany: "I've just been told that all these employees should have had written employment agreements and that in any case we can't fire anyone without at least 1 year's notice, and the local authorities here are really up in arms. Boss, I think we have a problem."

Questions

1. Based on the chapter and the case incident, compile a list of 10 international HR mistakes Mr. Fisher has made so far.
2. How would you have gone about hiring a European sales manager? Why?
3. What would you do now if you were Mr. Fisher?

HR IN ACTION CASE INCIDENT 2
Carter Cleaning Company: Going Abroad

With Jennifer gradually taking the reins of Carter Cleaning Company, Jack decided to take his first long vacation in years and go to Mexico for a month in January 2009. What he found surprised him: While he spent much of the time basking in the sun, he also spent considerable time in Mexico City and was surprised at the dearth of cleaning stores, particularly considering the amount of air pollution in the area. Traveling north he passed through Juarez, Mexico, and was similarly surprised at the relatively few cleaning stores he found there. As he drove back into Texas, and back toward home, he began to think about whether it is advisable to consider expanding his chain of stores into Mexico.

Aside from the possible economic benefits, he had liked what he saw in the lifestyle in Mexico and was also attracted by the idea of possibly facing the sort of exciting challenge he faced 20 years ago when he started Carter Cleaning in the United States: "I guess entrepreneurship is in my blood," is the way he put it.

As he drove home to have dinner with Jennifer, he began to formulate the questions he would have to ask before deciding whether or not to expand abroad.

Questions

1. Assuming they began by opening just one or two stores in Mexico, what do you see as the main HR-related challenges he and Jennifer would have to address? What political, economic, or other local issues should Carter be aware of?
2. How would you go about choosing a manager for a new Mexican store if you were Jack or Jennifer? For instance, would you hire someone locally or send someone from one of your existing stores? Why?
3. The cost of living in Mexico is substantially below that of where Carter is now located: How would you go about developing a pay plan for your new manager if you decided to send an expatriate to Mexico?
4. Present a detailed explanation of the factors you would look for in your candidate for expatriate manager to run the stores in Mexico.

EXPERIENTIAL EXERCISE

Financial Skills in Global HRM: A Taxing Problem for Expatriate Employees

Purpose: The purpose of this exercise is to give you practice identifying and analyzing some of the factors that influence expatriates' pay.

Required Understanding: You should be thoroughly familiar with this chapter and with the Web site www.irs.gov.

How to Set Up the Exercise/Instructions: Divide the class into teams of four or five students. Each team member should read the following:

One of the trickiest aspects of calculating expatriates' pay relates to the question of the expatriate's U.S. federal income tax liabilities. Go to the Internal Revenue Service's Web site, www.irs.gov. Click on Individuals, and then on International Taxpayers. Your team is the expatriate-employee compensation task force for your company, and your firm is about to send several managers and engineers to Japan, England, and Hong Kong. What information did you find on this site that will help your team formulate expat tax and compensation policies? Based on that, what are the three most important things your firm should keep in mind in formulating a compensation policy for the employees you're about to send to Japan, England, and Hong Kong?

BUSINESS IN ACTION EDU-EXERCISE

Building Your *International Business Law* Knowledge

U.S. equal employment opportunity laws, including Title VII, the ADEA, and the ADA, impact U.S. employers doing business abroad, and foreign firms doing business in the United States or its territories.[118] For example, *foreign multinational employers* that operate in the United States or its territories (American Samoa, Guam, Puerto Rico, the U.S. Virgin Islands, and the Commonwealth of the Northern Mariana Islands) generally must abide by EEO laws to the same extent as U.S. employers. Similarly, *U.S. employers*—those incorporated or based in the United States or controlled by U.S. companies—that employ U.S. citizens outside the United States or its territories are subject to Title VII, the ADEA, and the ADA with respect to those U.S. citizen employees. U.S. EEO laws do not apply to *non*-U.S. citizens working for U.S. (or foreign) firms *outside* the United States or its territories.

If equal employment opportunity laws conflict with the laws of the country in which the U.S. employer is operating, the laws of the local country generally take precedence. In particular, U.S. employers are not required to comply with requirements of Title VII, the ADEA, or the ADA if adherence to that law would violate the law of the country where the workplace is located. For example, an employer would have a "Foreign Laws Defense" for a mandatory retirement policy if the law in the country in which the company is located requires mandatory retirement.

Questions

1. From what you can find at www.eeoc.gov, what does the EEOC have to say about foreign employers' EEO obligations within the United States? Do they mention any foreign employers who the EEOC has charged with discrimination?
2. What were these companies, and what were the issues?

PERSONAL COMPETENCIES EDU-EXERCISE

Building Your *Global Management Team* Skills

Multinational enterprises increasingly rely on global management teams to oversee their operations. For example, a Swede and a six-person management team from Sweden, Italy, Holland, the United States, Belgium, and Germany manage Whirlpool International's business.[119] Globally disbursed teams like these need effective ways to foster team member trust, communication, and coordination.

Modern communications tools facilitate this. Teleconferencing, videoconferencing, and information technology devices like BlackBerry smart phones obviously make it easier to stay in touch. Group decision software enables globally disbursed team members to work on projects and then hand their work-in-process on to team members in the next time zone.

Devices like these enable companies to create virtual global teams. These are teams whose members meet in person only occasionally (if at all), "with people around the world conducting meetings and exchanging information via the Internet, enabling the organization to capitalize on 24-hour productivity."[120]

Virtual teams present their own challenges. When most communications take place remotely and (often) asynchronously, the employer should make extra efforts to cultivate trust among team members. Suggestions here include:

1. Establish trust based on *performance consistency* (in other words, by doing what you are supposed to do, when you are supposed to do it), rather than based solely on social bonds;
2. Remember that *rapid responses* to virtual teammates foster trust;
3. Establish norms for *acceptable communication patterns*. For instance, each party should know how to contact each other, when to expect a response, and so on.
4. Team leaders should play important roles in reinforcing timeliness and consistency.[121]

Questions

1. Toward the end of this chapter we discussed what employers can do to develop, gain acceptance for, and implement a global human resources system. Use specific examples to illustrate how an employer could use the sorts of virtual team tools mentioned in this exercise to develop, gain acceptance for, and implement a global HR system.
2. Discuss three other global international human resource management tasks that an employer might use a virtual team to carry out.

ENDNOTES

1. http://talkingunion.wordpress.com/2008/09/27/is-union-reform-possible-in-china/, accessed March 25, 2009.

2. See, for example, Helen Deresky, *International Management* (Upper Saddle River, NJ: Pearson, 2008); and Anne Marie Francesco and Barry Allen Gold, *International Organizational Behavior* (Upper Saddle River, NJ: Pearson, 2005).

3. Martha Frase, "Show All Employees a Wider World," *HR Magazine* (June 2007): 99–102. According to one report, a business can lose millions of dollars due to language or cultural misunderstandings. See, "US Multinationals Hampered by Lack of Foreign Language Skills, Report Says, "*BNA Bulletin to Management* (March 30, 2010): 99.

4. Nancy Wong, "Mark Your Calendar! Important Task for International HR," *Workforce* (April 2000): 72–74.

5. Karen Roberts, Ellen Kossek, and Cynthia Ozeki, "Managing the Global Workforce: Challenges and Strategies," *Academy of Management Executive* 12, no. 4 (1998): 93–106. See also Chris Rowley and Malcolm Warner, "Introduction: Globalizing International Human Resource Management," *International Journal of Human Resource Management* 18, no. 5 (May 2007): 703(14).

6. Roberts et al., op. cit., 94.

7. Anne Marie Francesco and Barry Allen Gold, *International Organizational Behavior* (Upper Saddle River, NJ: Pearson, 2005): 145.

8. Helen Deresky, *International Management* (Upper Saddle River, NJ: Pearson, 2008): 17.

9. David Ralston et al., "Eastern Values: A Comparison of Managers in the United States, Hong Kong, and the People's Republic of China," *Journal of Applied Psychology* 71, no. 5 (1992): 664–671. See also P. Christopher Earley and Elaine Mosakowski, "Cultural Intelligence," *Harvard Business Review* (October 2004): 139–146.

10. Helen Deresky, *International Management* (Upper Saddle River, NJ: Pearson, 2008): 98–99.

11. Geert Hofstede, "Cultural Dimensions in People Management," in Vladimir Pucik, Noel Tishy, and Carole Barnett (eds.), *Globalizing Management* (New York: John Wiley & Sons, 1992): 143; and www.geert-hofstede.com/, accessed February 28, 2010.

12. Chris Brewster, "European Perspectives on Human Resource Management," *Human Resource Management Review* 14 (2004): 365–382.

13. Rong Ma and David Allen, "Recruiting Across Cultures: A Value-Based Model of Recruitment," *Human Resource Management Review* 19 (2009): 334–346.

14. See for example, www.fedee.com/ewc1.html, accessed November 4, 2009.

15. This is discussed in Eduard Gaugler, "HR Management: An International Comparison," *Personnel* (1988): 28. See also E. Poutsma et al., "The Diffusion of Calculative and Collaborative HRM Practices in European Firms," *Industrial Relations* 45, no. 4 (October 2006): 513–546.

16. Helen Deresky, *International Management* (Upper Saddle River, NJ: Pearson, 2008): 17.

17. Annual 2007 figures, www.bls.gov/news.release/pdf/ichcc.pdf, accessed February 19, 2010.

18. Phillips Taft and Cliff Powell, "The European Pensions and Benefits Environment: A Complex Ecology," *Compensation & Benefits Review* (January/February 2005): 37–50.

19. Ibid.

20. "Inform, Consult, Impose: Workers' Rights in the EU," *Economist* (June 16, 2001): 3. See also J. Banyuls et al., "European Works Council at General Motors Europe: Bargaining Efficiency in Regime Competition?" *Industrial Relations Journal* 39, no. 6 (November 2008): 532–547.

21. Lisbeth Clause, "What You Need to Know about the New Labor Contract Law of China," SHRM Global Law Special Report, October to November 2008.

22. Anne Marie Francesco and Barry Allen Gold, *International Organizational Behavior* (Upper Saddle River, NJ: Pearson, 2005): 145.

23. Ibid., 106.

24. "DOL Releases Final Rule Amending Filing, Processing of Foreign Labor Certifications," *BNA Bulletin to Management* (January 11, 2005): 11.

25. Leslie Klass, "Fed Up with High Costs, Companies Winnow the Ranks of Career Expats," *Workforce Management* (October 2004): 84–88.

26. Michelle Rafter, "Return Trip for Ex-Pats," *Workforce Magazine* (March 16, 2009): 1, 3.

27. See "Workforce Trends: Companies Continue to Deploy Ex-Pats," *Compensation & Benefits Review* 42, no. 1 (January/February 2010): 6.

28. Timothy Dwyer, "Localization's Hidden Costs," *HR Magazine* (June 2004): 135–144.

29. Based on Pamela Babcock, "America's Newest Export: White Collar Jobs," *HR Magazine* (April 2004): 50–57.

30. William Bulkeley, "IBM to Cut US Jobs, Expand in India," *Wall Street Journal* (March 26, 2009): B1.

31. The following is based on "Back-Office and Customer Care Centers in Emerging Economies: A Human Capital Perspective," IBM Business Consulting Services, www-05.ibm.com/nl/topmanagement/pdfs/back_office_and_customer_care.pdf, accessed April 29, 2008.

32. Ibid., 3, 4.

33. Ibid., 5, 6.

34. Ibid., 5, 6.

35. Ibid., 10.

36. Helen Deresky, *International Management* (Upper Saddle River, NJ: Pearson, 2008): 36.

37. Arvind Phatak, *International Dimensions of Management* (Boston: PWS Kebt, 1989): 129.

38. Ibid.

39. Donald Dowling Jr., "Export Codes of Conduct, Not Employee Handbooks," *The Society for Human Resource Management Legal Report* (January/February 2007): 1–4.

40. Ibid.

41. "SOX Compliance, Corporate Codes of Conduct Can Create Challenges for US Multinationals," *BNA Bulletin to Management* (March 28, 2006): 97.

42. Hilary Harris and Chris Brewster, "The Coffee Machine System: How International Selection Really Works," *International Journal of Human Resource Management* 10, no. 3 (June 1999): 488–500.

43. Mary G. Tye and Peter Y. Chen, "Selection of Expatriates: Decision-Making Models Used by HR Professionals," *Human Resource Planning* 28, no. 4 (December 2005): 15(6).

44. Paula Caligiuri et al., "Selection for International Assignments," *Human Resource Management Review* 19 (2009): 251–262.

45. www.performanceprograms.com/Surveys/Overseas.shtm, accessed January 31, 2008.

46. P. Blocklyn, "Developing the International Executive," *Personnel* (March 1989): 45. See also Paula M. Caligiuri and Jean M. Phillips, "An Application of Self-Assessment Realistic Job Previews to Expatriate Assignments," *International Journal of Human Resource Management* 14, no. 7 (November 2003): 1102(15).

47. Zsuzsanna Tungli and Maury Peiperl, "Expatriate Practices in German, Japanese, UK and US Multinational Companies: A Comparative Survey of Changes," *Human Resource Management* 48, no. 1 (January/February 2009), 153–171.

48. Helen Deresky, *International Management* (Upper Saddle River, NJ: Pearson, 2008): 369.

49. "Survey Says Expatriates Twice as Likely to Leave Employer as Home-Based Workers," *BNA Bulletin to Management* (May 9, 2006): 147.

50. Margaret Shaffer and David Harrison, "Expatriates' Psychological Withdrawal from International Assignments: Work, Nonwork, and Family Influences," *Personnel Psychology* 51 (1998): 88. See also Jan Selmer, "Psychological Barriers to Adjustment of Western Business Expatriates in China: Newcomers vs. Long Stayers," *International Journal of Human Resource Management* 15, no. 4–5 (June–August 2004): 794–815; and Margaret A. Shaffer and David Harrison, "Forgotten Partners of International Assignments: Development and Test of a Model of Spouse Adjustment," *Journal of Applied Psychology* 86, no. 2 (April 2001): 238.

51. Helen Deresky, *International Management* (Upper Saddle River, NJ: Pearson, 2008): 348.

52. Gary Insch and John Daniels, "Causes and Consequences of Declining Early Departures from Foreign Assignments," *Business Horizons* 46, no. 6 (November–December 2002): 39–48.

53. "More Women, Young Workers on the Move," *Workforce Management* (August 20, 2007): 9.

54. For a good discussion of this see Yochanan Altman and Susan Shortland, "Women and International Assignments: Taking Stock—A 25 Year Review," *Human Resource Management* 47, no. 2 (Summer 2008): 199–216.

55. Kathryn Tyler, "Don't Fence Her In," *HR Magazine* 46, no. 3 (March 2001), pp. 69–77.

56. Ibid.

57. Ibid.

58. See Nancy Napier and Sully Taylor, "Experiences of Women Professionals Abroad," *International Journal of Human Resource Management* 13, no. 5 (August 2002): 837–851; Iris Fischlmayr, "Female Self-Perception as a Barrier to International Careers?" *International Journal of Human Resource Management* 13, no. 5 (August 2002): 773–783; Wolfgang Mayrhofer and Hugh Scullion, "Female Expatriates in International Business: Evidence from the German Clothing Industry," *International Journal of Human Resource Management* 13, no. 5 (August 2002): 815–836; and Yochanan Altman and Susan Shortland, "Women and International Assignments: Taking Stock—A 25 Year Review," *Human Resource Management* 47, no. 2 (Summer 2008): 199–216.

59. Helen Deresky, *International Management* (Upper Saddle River, NJ: Pearson, 2008): 373.

60. "More Women, Young Workers on the Move," *Workforce Management* (August 20, 2007): 9.

61. P. Caligiuri, "The Big Five Personality Characteristics as Predictors of Expatriates' Desire to Terminate the Assignment and Supervisor-Rated Performance," *Personnel Psychology* 53, no. 1 (Spring 2000): 67–88. See also Margaret A. Shaffer et al., "You Can Take It with You: Individual Differences and Expatriate Effectiveness," *Journal of Applied Psychology* 91, no. 1 (January 2006): 109(17).

62. Quoted in Meredith Downes, Iris I. Varner, and Luke Musinski, "Personality Traits as Predictors of Expatriate Effectiveness: A Synthesis and Reconceptualization," *Review of Business* 27, no. 3 (Spring–Summer 2007): 16(8).

63. Jan Selmer, "Expatriation: Corporate Policy, Personal Intentions and International Adjustment," *International Journal of Human Resource Management* 9, no. 6 (December 1998): 997–1007. See also Barbara Myers and Judith K. Pringle, "Self-Initiated Foreign Experience as Accelerated Development: Influences of Gender," *Journal of World Business* 40, no. 4 (November 2005): 421(11).

64. Hung-Wen Lee and Ching-Hsing, "Determinants of the Adjustment of Expatriate Managers to Foreign Countries: An Empirical Study," *International Journal of Management* 23, no. 2 (2006): 302–311.

65. Helen Deresky, *International Management* (Upper Saddle River, NJ: Pearson, 2008): 90.

66. Sunkyu Jun and James Gentry, "An Exploratory Investigation of the Relative Importance of Cultural Similarity and Personal Fit in the Selection and Performance of Expatriates," *Journal of World Business* 40, no. 1 (February 2005): 1–8. See also Jan Selmer, "Cultural Novelty and Adjustment: Western Business Expatriates in China," *International Journal of Human Resource Management* 17, no. 7 (2006): 1211–1222.

67. Ibid.

68. Discussed in Charles Hill, *International Business* (Burr Ridge, IL: Irwin, 1994): 511–515. See also Julia Richardson, "Self-Directed Expatriation: Family Matters," *Personnel Review* 35, no. 4 (July 2006): 469–486.

69. Charlene Solomon, "One Assignment, Two Lives," *Personnel Journal* (May 1996): 36–47; See also Riki Takeuchi, Seokhwa Yun, and Paul E. Tesluk, "An Examination of Crossover and Spillover Effects of Spousal and Expatriate Cross-Cultural Adjustment on Expatriate Outcomes," *Journal of Applied Psychology* 87, no. 4 (August 2002): 655(12); and Julia Richardson, "Self-Directed Expatriation: Family Matters," *Personnel Review* 35, no. 4 (July 2006): 469–486.

70. Barbara Anderson, "Expatriate Selection: Good Management or Good Luck?" *International Journal of Human Resource Management* 16, no. 4 (April 2005): 567–583.

71. Michael Schell, quoted in Charlene Marmer Solomon, "Success Abroad Depends on More Than Job Skills," *Personnel Journal*, v. 73, April 1994, 52.

72. Helene Mayerhofer et al., "Flexpatriate Assignments: A Neglected Issue in Global Staffing," *International Journal of Human Resource Management* 15, no. 8 (December 2004): 1371–1389.

73. Martha Frase, "International Commuters," *HR Magazine* (March 2007): 91–96.

74. M. Harvey et al., "Global Virtual Teams: A Human Resource Capital Architecture," *International Journal of Human Resource Management* 16, no. 9 (September 2005): 1583–1599.

75. Eric Krell, "Budding Relationships," *HR Magazine* 50, no. 6 (June 2005): 114–118. See also Jill Elswick, "Worldly Wisdom: Companies Refine Their Approach to Overseas Assignments,

Emphasizing Cost-Cutting and Work-Life Support for Expatriates," *Employee Benefit News* (June 15, 2004), Item 0416600B.

76. Geoffrey Abbott et al., "Coaching Expatriate Managers for Success: Adding Value Beyond Training and Mentoring," *Asia-Pacific Journal of Human Resources* 44, no. 3 (December 2006): 295–317.

77. Ann Pace, "Training for the League Overseas," *Training & Development* (August 2009): 18.

78. Helen Deresky, *International Management* (Upper Saddle River, NJ: Pearson, 2008): 351–352. See also Julia Brandl and Anne-Katrin Neyer, "Applying Cognitive Adjustment Theory to Cross-Cultural Training for Global Virtual Teams," *Human Resource Management* 48, no. 3 (May–June 2009): 341–353.

79. Valerie Frazee, "Expats Are Expected to Dive Right In," *Personnel Journal* (December 1996): 31; See also Rita Bennett et al., "Cross-Cultural Training: A Critical Step in Ensuring the Success of National Assignments," *Human Resource Management* 39, no. 2–3 (Summer–Fall 2000): 239–250.

80. Helen Deresky, *International Management* (Upper Saddle River, NJ: Pearson, 2008): 353.

81. Ibid., 371.

82. Ibid., 358.

83. Ibid., 359. Some suggest adapting the training program to the cultures and values of the trainees. For example, ask whether the trainees come from a more individualistic or collectivist society, since this may affect the degree to which you want training to be participatory versus non-participatory. Baiyin Yang et al., "Does It Matter Where to Conduct Training? Accounting for Cultural Factors," *Human Resource Management Review* 19 (2009): 324–333.

84. Mark Mendenhall and Gunther Stahl, "Expatriate Training and Development: Where Do We Go from Here?" *Human Resource Management* 39, no. 2–3 (Summer–Fall 2000): 251–265. See also Geoffrey Abbott et al., "Coaching Expatriate Managers for Success: Adding Value Beyond Training and Mentoring," *Asia-Pacific Journal of Human Resources* 44, no. 3 (December 2006): 295–317.

85. Charles Hill, *International Business* (Burr Ridge, IL: Irwin, 1994): 519–520; Joseph Martocchio, *Strategic Compensation* (Upper Saddle River, NJ: Pearson, 2006): 402–403.

86. Martocchio, op. cit.

87. Thomas Shelton, "Global Compensation Strategies: Managing and Administering Split Pay for an Expatriate Workforce," *Compensation & Benefits Review* (January/February 2008): 56–59.

88. Anne Marie Francesco and Barry Allen Gold, *International Organizational Behavior* (Upper Saddle River, NJ: Pearson, 2005): 164.

89. Helen Deresky, *International Management* (Upper Saddle River, NJ: Pearson, 2008): 361.

90. Gary Dessler, "Expanding into China? What Foreign Employers Entering China Should Know About Human Resource Management Today," *SAM Advanced Management Journal* 71, no. 4 (2006): 11–23. See also Joseph Gamble, "Introducing Western-Style HRM Practices to China: Shop Floor Perceptions in a British Multinational," *Journal of World Business* 41, no. 4 (December 2006): 328–340; and Adrienne Fox, "China: Land of Opportunity and Challenge," *HR Magazine* (September 2007): 38–44.

91. Robin White, "A Strategic Approach to Building a Consistent Global Rewards Program," *Compensation & Benefits Review* (July/August 2005): 25.

92. "Recommendations for Managing Global Compensation Costs in a Changing Economy," Hewitt Associates, http://www.hewitt associates.com/_MetaBasicCMAssetCache_/Assets/Articles/2009/hewitt_pov_globalcomp_0109.pdf, accessed July 2010.

93. Helen Deresky, *International Management* (Upper Saddle River, NJ: Pearson, 2008): 339.

94. Hal Gregersen et al., "Expatriate Performance Appraisal in U.S. Multinational Firms," *Journal of International Business Studies* 27, no. 4 (Winter 1996): 711–739. See also Hsi-An Shih, Yun-Hwa Chiang, and In-Sook Kim, "Expatriate Performance Management from MNEs of Different National Origins," *International Journal of Manpower* 26, no. 2 (February 2005): 157–175; and Anne Francesco and Barry Gold, *International Organizational Behavior* (Upper Saddle River, NJ: Pearson, 2005): 152–153.

95. Jessica Marquez, "Hostage-Taking in France Has US Observers on Their Guard," *Workforce Management* (April 20, 2009): 10.

96. Fay Hansen, "Skirting Danger," *Workforce Management* (January 19, 2009): 1, 3.

97. These are based on or quoted from Samuel Greengard, "Mission Possible: Protecting Employees Abroad," *Workforce* (August 1997): 30–32. See also Z. Phillips, "Global Firms Consider Additional Cover for Overseas Execs," *Business Insurance* 43, no. 23 (June 15–22, 2009): 4, 22.

98. http://travel.state.gov/travel/cis_pa_tw/tw/tw_1764.html, accessed April 29, 2008.

99. Greengard, op. cit., 32.

100. www.google.com/mobile/default/maps.html, accessed March 24, 2009.

101. Carla Joinson, "Save Thousands Per Expatriate," *HR Magazine* (July 2002): 77. For a discussion of some personality aspects of the issue, see, for example, Jeffrey Herman and Lois Tetrick, "Problem Focused Versus Emotion Focused Coping Strategies and Repatriation Adjustment," *Human Resource Management* 48, no. 1 (January–February 2009): 69–88.

102. Helen Deresky, *International Management* (Upper Saddle River, NJ: Pearson, 2008): 370.

103. Ibid.

104. Quoted in Leslie Klaff, "The Right Way to Bring Expats Home," *Workforce* (July 2002): 43.

105. Ibid.

106. Ibid.

107. Maria Kraimer, et al., "The Influence of Expatriate and Repatriate Experiences on Career Advancement and Repatriate Retention," *Human Resource Management* 48, no. 1 (January–February 2009): 27–47.

108. Ann Marie Ryan et al., "Designing and Implementing Global Staffing Systems: Part 2—Best Practices," *Human Resource Management* 42, no. 1 (Spring 2003), pp. 85–94.

109. Ibid., p. 89.

110. Ibid., p. 90.

111. Ibid., p. 86. See also M. Schoeff, "Adopting an HR Worldview," *Workforce Management* 87, no. 19 (November 17, 2008): 8.

112. Ryan et al., op. cit., 87.

113. Ibid., p. 92.

114. Bill Roberts, "Going Global," *HR Magazine* (August 2000): 123–128.

115. Diane Turner, "NuView Brings Web-Based HRIS to Buildnet," *Workforce* (December 2000): 90.

116. Jim Meade, "Web-Based HRIS Meets Multiple Needs," *HR Magazine* (August 2000): 129–133. See also "Dynamic HR: Global Applications from IBM," *Human Resource Management* 48, no. 4 (July/August 2009): 641–648.

117. Drew Robb, "Unifying Your Enterprise with a Global HR Portal," *HR Magazine* (March 2006): 119–120.

118. The following is adapted from "The Equal Employment Opportunity Responsibilities of Multinational Employers," The U.S. Equal Employment Opportunity Commission: www.EEOC.gov/facts/multi-employers.html, accessed February 9, 2004.

119. Helen Deresky, *International Management* (Upper Saddle River, NJ: Pearson, 2008): 374. See also James H. Wall and Lynda

Spielman, "Global Team-Building: Developing, Deploying and Connecting: Global Teams Are Quickly Becoming the Standard for Worldwide Organizations," *China Staff* 12, no. 3 (March 2006): 8(3).

120. Helen Deresky, *International Management* (Upper Saddle River, NJ: Pearson, 2008): 375–376.

121. Bradley Kirkman et al., "Five Challenges to Virtual Team Success: Lessons from Sabre, Inc.," *Academy of Management Executive* 16, no. 3 (2002): 71.

14 Building High-Performance Work Systems and Improving Strategic Results

SYNOPSIS

- Building High-Performance Work Systems
- Conducting the Human Resource Management Audit
- HR Metrics and Benchmarking
- Outsourcing Human Resource Management Activities

Source: James Crisp/AP Wide World Photos.

When you finish studying this chapter, you should be able to:

1. Define high-performance work system.
2. List four characteristics of high-performance work systems.
3. Give an example of using evidence-based management.
4. Discuss with examples how to conduct an HR audit.
5. List and explain at least five HR metrics.
6. Explain the process you would use to select an outsourcing vendor.

INTRODUCTION

Until recently, management gurus generally called Toyota Motor Corp.'s human resource management systems both "high performance" and effective. Toyota famously organized plant employees into self-managing teams that continuously improved their production procedures. Toyota also used careful screening and training to hire the best candidates, as well as performance management systems to help employees appraise themselves. The problems that surfaced with sticky Toyota Camry accelerators in 2010 therefore gave many management experts pause. Fairly or not, some questioned how a company with high-performance work systems could have such problems. Others, including the firm's president Akio Toyoda, argued that it wasn't the plant's high performance work systems, but management's misguided focus on cost-cutting that caused the accelerator issue. ■

BUILDING HIGH-PERFORMANCE WORK SYSTEMS

As Mr. Toyoda well knows, these are particularly challenging times for managing companies. Globalization means more competition, and more competition means more pressure to lower costs and to make employees more productive and quality conscious. Technology requires more employees to be technologically well informed, and requires that employers improve their HR processes through technology. In turn, with more employees performing technologically challenging jobs, managers have had to shift their performance focus to building "human capital"—the knowledge, education, training, and skills of their employees.

Economic challenges are intensifying the pressures. We saw in Chapter 1 that Gross National Product (GNP) boomed between 2001 and 2007. Home prices leaped as much as 20% per year. Unemployment remained docile. Then, around 2007/2008, all these measures seemingly fell off a cliff. GNP fell. Home prices dropped by 10% or more. By 2010, unemployment nationwide was still over 9%.

The bottom line is that all managers today need new ways to boost productivity and performance through employees. For human resource managers, this increasingly means building high-performance work systems.

What Are High-Performance Work Systems?

A **high-performance work system** is a set of human resource management policies and practices that together produce superior employee performance. As we saw in Chapter 1, one illustrative study focused on 17 manufacturing plants, some of which adopted high-performance work system practices. For example, the high-performance plants paid more (median wages of $16 per hour compared with $13 per hour for all plants), trained more, used more sophisticated recruitment and hiring practices (tests and validated interviews, for instance), and used more self-managing work teams. These plants also had the best overall performance.[2] Thus, when it comes to managing the people side of the business, one way to improve performance is to design recruiting, selection, training, and other HR practices so that they produce superior employee performance—a high-performance work system.

When Did High-Performance Work Systems Get Their Start?

High-performance work systems became popular in the 1990s. Faced with global competition from the Hondas of the world, U.S. companies needed ways to improve quality, productivity, and responsiveness. The U.S. Department of Labor listed several characteristics of high-performance work organizations.[3] These include multi-skilled work teams, empowered front-line workers, extensive training, labor management cooperation, commitment to quality, and customer satisfaction.[4]

High-Performance Human Resource Policies and Practices

Studies show that in terms of policies and practices, high-performance work systems do differ from less productive ones. Table 14.1 illustrates this. For example, high-performing companies recruit more job candidates, use more selection tests, and spend many more hours training employees. This table illustrates four things about how high-performing firms organize their HR practices.

---

1 Define high-performance work system.

high-performance work system
An integrated set of human resources policies and practices that together produce superior employee performance.

2 List four characteristics of high-performance work systems.

TABLE 14.1 Comparison of HR Practices in High-Performance and Low-Performance Companies

	Low-Performance Company HR System Averages (Bottom 10%, 42 Firms)	High-Performance Company HR System Averages (Top 10%, 43 Firms)
Sample HR Practices		
Number of qualified applicants per position (*Recruiting*)	8.24	36.55
Percentage hired based on a validated *selection* test	4.26	29.67
Percentage of jobs *filled from within*	34.90	61.46
Number of hours of *training* for new employees (less than 1 year)	35.02	116.87
Number of hours of *training* for experienced employees	13.40	72.00
Percentage of employees receiving a regular *performance appraisal*	41.31	95.17
Percentage of workforce whose *merit increase* or *incentive pay* is tied to performance	23.36	87.27
Percentage of workforce who received *performance feedback* from multiple sources (360)	3.90	51.67
Target percentile for total compensation (market rate = 50%)	43.03	58.67
Percentage of the workforce eligible for *incentive pay*	27.83	83.56
Percentage of the workforce routinely working in a self-managed, *cross-functional,* or *project team*	10.64	42.28
Percentage of HR budget spent on *outsourced activities* (e.g., recruiting, benefits, payroll)	13.46	26.24
Number of employees per HR professional	253.88	139.51
Percentage of the eligible workforce covered by a union contract	30.00	8.98
Firm Performance		
Employee turnover	34.09	20.87
Sales per employee	$158,101	$617,576
Market value to book value	3.64	11.06

Source: Based on B. E. Becker, M. A. Huselid, and D. Ulrich, "The HR Scorecard: Linking People, Strategy and Performance," Boston: Harvard Business School Press (2001): pp. 16–17.

human resource metric
The quantitative measure of some human resource management yardstick such as employee turnover, hours of training per employee, or qualified applicants per position.

First, it helps to show why *metrics* are important. A **human resource metric** is the quantitative measure of some human resource management yardstick such as employee turnover, hours of training per employee, or qualified applicants per position. (In Table 14.1, the metric for "Number of qualified applicants per position" is 36.55 in the high-performing companies). You can use such metrics to assess your own company's HR performance, and to compare one company's with another's. Using quantifiable evidence like this is the heart of evidence-based management—using data, facts, and critically evaluated research to support human resource management decisions.[5]

Second, it illustrates *the things human resource systems must do* to be high-performance systems. For example, they hire based on validated selection tests. They fill more jobs from within. They organize work around self-managing teams. They extensively train employees.

Third, the table shows that high-performance work practices usually *aspire to help workers to manage themselves.* In other words, the point of the recruiting, screening, training, and other human resources practices in companies like these is to foster an empowered, self-motivated, and flexible workforce.[6]

Fourth, Table 14.1 highlights *the measurable differences* between the human resource management systems in high-performance and low-performance companies. For example, high-performing companies have more than four times the number of qualified applicants per job than do low performers.

The idea that "better" companies' human resource practices are measurably different from low performers' inspired the human resource management benchmarking movement. *Benchmarking* means comparing the practices of high-performing companies to your own, in order to understand what they do that makes them better.[7]

Evidence-Based Human Resource Management

3 Give an example of using evidence-based management.

Saying you have a high-performance organization assumes that you can measure how you're doing.[8] In today's challenging environment, employers naturally expect their human resource management teams to be able to do this. For example, "How much will that new testing program save us in reduced employee turnover?" "How much more productive will our employees be if we institute that new training program?" And, "How productive is our human resource team, in terms of HR staff per employee, compared to our competitors?"

Providing evidence such as this is the heart of *evidence-based human resource management.* This is the use of data, facts, analytics, scientific rigor, critical evaluation, and critically evaluated research/case studies to support human resource management proposals, decisions, practices, and conclusions.[9] Put simply, evidence-based human resource management is the deliberate use of the best-available evidence in making decisions about the human resource management practices you are focusing on.[10] The evidence may come from *actual measurements* you make (such as, how did the trainees like this program?). It may come from *existing data* (such as, what happened to company profits after we installed this training program?). Or, it may come from published critically evaluated *research studies* (such as, what does the research literature conclude about the best way to ensure that trainees remember what they learn?).

HIGH PERFORMANCE SYSTEM EVIDENCE The research evidence does seem to demonstrate that companies with high-performance policies and practices like those in Table 14.1 do perform significantly better. For example, based on studies of more than 2,800 companies, one researcher concludes, "high-performance HR practices, [particularly] combined with new technology, produce better productivity, quality, sales, and financial performance."[11] Another team of researchers, studying the productivity of 308 companies over 22 years, concluded that empowerment, teamwork, and extensive training—outcomes that high-performance work practices usually aspire to achieve—produced significant performance benefits.[12]

The Manager's Role in Building a High-Performance Work System

That a human resource manager can influence things like "number of qualified applicants per position" and "percentage of jobs filled from within" is apparent. After all, those are the activities that human resource managers oversee.

Not so apparent is that *every* department manager and supervisor can play an important role in activities like these and thus build, within his or her own departmental domain, a higher performing organization.

Table 14.1 again supplies a roadmap for doing so. This shows, for instance that more applicants, more testing, more formal appraisals, better training, and more incentive plans usually correlate with higher performance. You don't have to be a human resource manager to influence activities like these. Every sales manager, production manager, and accounting manager can influence the number of job applicants they get, the testing they do, the quality training they provide, and the sorts of incentives they offer to their employees. The whole point of this book was to show you how to do this. For instance, we saw how to boost the chances that you'll have more applicants, improve your batting average in interviewing candidates, spot applicant dishonesty, avoid mistakes in appraising performance, and use incentives (aside from the company's formal pay plan).

CONDUCTING THE HUMAN RESOURCE MANAGEMENT AUDIT

Benchmarking and evidence-based management require good information. Most CEOs won't accept subjective, off-the-cuff explanations for the worth of projects you ask them to implement. That is why quantitative, data-based analysis is a hallmark of successful management.

What Are HR Audits?

HR audit

An analysis by which an organization measures where it currently stands and determines what it has to accomplish to improve its HR function.

Within the human resource management arena, such data-based analyses often start with HR managers conducting *human resource audits*. One practitioner calls an **HR audit** "an analysis by which an organization measures where it currently stands and determines what it has to accomplish to improve its HR function."[13] Another calls it "a process of examining policies, procedures, documentation, systems, and practices with respect to an organization's HR functions."[14] In sum, the HR audit generally involves reviewing the functioning of most aspects of the company's human resource function (recruiting, testing, training, and so on), usually using a checklist, as well as ensuring that the employer is adhering to government regulations and company policies. Let's look at what to audit in more detail.

What Areas Should the HR Audit Cover?

4 Discuss with examples how to conduct an HR audit.

HR audits vary in scope and focus. As an example, typical broad topic areas to cover with the HR audit include:[15]

1. Roles and head count (including job descriptions, and employees by exempt/nonexempt and full/part-time status)
2. Legal issues (compliance with federal, state, local employment–related legislation)
3. Recruitment and selection (including selection tools, background checks, and so on)
4. Compensation (policies, incentives, survey procedures, and so on)
5. Employee relations (union agreements, performance management, disciplinary procedures, employee recognition)
6. Mandated benefits (social security, unemployment insurance, workers' compensation, and so on)
7. Group benefits (insurance, time off, flexible benefits, and so on)
8. Payroll (internal versus external payroll options, FLSA compliance)
9. Documentation and record keeping (HR information systems, personnel files, I-9 and other forms, and so on)
10. Training and development (new employee orientation, workforce development, technical and safety, career planning, and so on)
11. Employee communications (employee handbook, newsletter, recognition programs)
12. Internal communications (policies and procedures, and so on)
13. Termination and transition policies and practices

Types of Audits

Beyond this, there are different types of audits, such as:[16]

1. *Compliance audits*—in particular, how well is our company complying with current federal, state, and local laws and regulations?
2. *Best practices audits*—in particular, are our recruitment practices, hiring practices, performance evaluation practices, and so on comparable to those of companies with exceptional practices?
3. *Strategic audits*—in particular, are our human resource management practices helping our company achieve its strategic goals, by fostering the required employee behaviors and organizational outcomes (such as in terms of customer service, and productivity)?
4. *Function-specific audits*—in particular, audits of one or more specific human resource management areas, such as compensation, or training and development.

Some Issues Prompting HR Audits

Some employers routinely conduct human resource audits every 2 years or so. More often, pressing issues arise that prompt employers to conduct HR audits. Typical pressing issues include:

- Are we in legal compliance? We've seen that employers need to comply with hundreds of employment laws and regulations. Typical questions here would include: Are our employment interviewers asking any inadvisable questions? Does our application form contain the candidate's certification that all information he or she is providing is true and accurate?[17] Figure 14.1 summarizes some important legal issues to focus on.
- Are our human resource department's practices supporting our company's strategy? For example, are our screening and training practices producing the customer service our strategy requires?
- Are we administering our human resource management function as productively as we might be? For example, are best practice companies employing best HR testing and other practices we might benefit from?
- Did our key human resource projects or initiatives last year produce the results we intended? For example, did the training program produce improved organizational results?
- Are there issues such as low morale or poor performance that might respond to improved HR practices? For example, would incentive plans improve employee performance?
- What improvements can we institute within HR to reduce costs? For example, are there human resource management activities such as benefits enrollment that we could put online so that employees can self-service themselves?
- How can HR improve the company's performance management process? For example, how effective are our current processes for aligning employees' performance with company goals?

FIGURE 14.1

Sample Legal Issues to Audit

Source: See, for example, Dana R. Scott, "Conducting a Human Resources Audit," *New Hampshire Business Review* (August 2007).

It is advisable for employers to audit how well they're complying with the various federal, state, and local laws and regulations, using checklist topics and questions like the following:

- The Fair Labor Standards Act, including minimum wage and overtime and child labor provisions. For example, *do the people we now classify as independent contractors qualify as independent contractors under the FLSA?*
- Occupational Health and Safety Act. For example, *are all machines in our plant properly guarded?*
- Consolidated Omnibus Budget Reconciliation Act (corporate). For example, *do we have new employees certify they've received notice that they can continue COBRA coverage in event of separation from the company?*
- Americans with Disabilities Act. For example, *do we postpone the medical exam until after we've made a formal job offer?*
- Age Discrimination in Employment Act. For example, *do we disregard age when making downsizing decisions?*
- Title VII of the Civil Rights Act. For example, *do we train our supervisors to avoid inadvisable age, race, gender, and national origin–related selection interview questions such as, "Are you thinking of becoming pregnant"?*
- Equal Pay Act. For example, *do we pay women who are doing the same jobs as men at the same performance levels the same as we pay the men?*
- Pregnancy Discrimination Act. For example, *do we award the same time off and other benefits for pregnancy that we do for other types of health-related absence?*
- Immigration Reform and Control Act. For example, *do we require the necessary proof of identification and eligibility to work from everyone we hire?*
- Worker Readjustment and Retraining Notification Act. For example, *do we give the necessary written notice of layoff in event of plant closings?*
- Workers' compensation laws. For example, *do we avoid asking job candidates about their workers' compensation histories?*

- Have we instituted policies and practices that ensure fair treatment of all employees? For example, is there a disciplinary appeals process in place?
- Are there any persistent safety and health issues we should address? For example, are our workers' compensation costs rising too fast?

HIGH-RISK COMPLIANCE AREAS TO AUDIT With respect to employment law compliance, most problem areas (also known as lawsuits) stem from a relative handful of activities. These are:[18]

- Hiring (including job descriptions, application forms, employment contracts, reference procedures)
- Employee evaluations (in particular performance appraisals and promotions)
- Employee discipline (evidence, rules, procedures)
- Terminations (proper warnings, adherence to complaint procedures, and so on)
- Miscalculation of exempt and nonexempt jobs
- Inadequate personnel files, including performance documentation
- Prohibited absentee policies (for instance, related to the family and medical leave)
- Inadequate or inaccurate time records (for instance, plant personnel improperly checking in early)
- Insufficient documentation (for instance, missing or incomplete I-9 forms)

When to Audit?

As noted, most employers conduct HR audits no more than once every 2 years or so. However, several events may signal the need for an HR audit. These include:[19]

- Audit when a business reaches various milestones such as 15 employees, 20 employees, 50 employees, and 100 employees. These are threshold employee numbers at which point various federal, state, and local regulations and laws become applicable.
- Audit when the business grows to the point where line managers can no longer make their own hiring, discipline, promotion, and other decisions without HR management's assistance.
- Audit when the employer creates or modifies an employee handbook, since doing so often means changing and/or memorializing company policies.
- Audit when a new head of human resource management arrives.
- Audit when employee morale, turnover, attendance, or excessive discipline problems seem to signal the need to evaluate HR practices.
- Audit when the company becomes a government contractor or a subcontractor (and therefore becomes subject to new federal regulations).

The HR Audit Process

In conducting an HR audit, the basic approach is to use a checklist-type questionnaire. The audit team may also interview selected HR employees, and managers in non-HR areas, to better assess the human resource function's effectiveness.

We can summarize the basic audit process as follows:[20]

1. *Decide on the scope of the audit.* For example, will we focus on all HR functions, or just on one or two, or perhaps just on legal compliance issues?
2. *Draft an audit team.* Identify the members of the HR audit team, who the leaders are, who the team reports to, and how the team will work.
3. *Compile the checklists and other tools that are available.* For example, what do we now have in terms of internal checklists or other materials, and checklists from corporate counsel? What packaged software HR audit checklist programs are available? (See, for example, sites such as http://catalog.blr.com/product.cfm/product/30519900 for examples of packaged HR audits.)
4. *Know your budget.* Familiarize yourself with the audit's likely costs, and ascertain the budget before moving too far ahead.
5. *Consider the legalities.* Understand that what you unearth during the HR audit may be discoverable by opposing counsel in the event of a lawsuit. At a minimum, discuss the proposed audit with your attorney.

6. *Get top management support.* Top management needs to be committed to the audit and to taking the steps required to remedy any problems.

7. *Develop the audit checklist.* From your various sources, including internal company checklists, packaged software programs, and reviews of other firms' best practices, have the audit team create an audit questionnaire. This is usually a series of checklists. The team will use these to guide them in actually auditing the areas they're about to audit. (For example, one checklist may cover what items should and should not be in the personnel file.) SHRM (www.shrm.org) is an excellent source of audit tools.[21]

8. Use the checklist questionnaire to *collect the data* about the company and its HR practices.

9. *Benchmark the findings*, by comparing them with human resource benchmark standards (more on this below).

10. *Provide feedback* about the results to your firm's HR professionals and senior management team.

11. *Create action plans* aimed at improving areas the audit singles out.

SAMPLE HR AUDIT CHECKLIST ITEMS Here are three illustrative HR audit checklist areas and the sorts of checklist items they would include:

Personnel Files Do our files contain information including résumés and applications, offer letters, job descriptions, performance evaluations, benefit enrollment forms, payroll change notices and/or documentation related to personnel actions, documents regarding performance issues, employee handbook acknowledgments, I-9 Form, medical information (related to a medical leave of absence or FMLA leave), and Workers' Compensation information?[22]

Wage and Hour Compliance Is our time record-keeping process in compliance with state and with federal law (for instance check-in/check-out no more than 3 minutes before starting/stopping work)? Do we conduct a random audit of timecards to ensure that practices are as they should be?[23]

Headcount How many employees are currently on staff? How many employees of these are:
- Regular
- Probationary
- Temporary
- Full Time
- Part Time
- Exempt
- Non-Exempt[24]

HR METRICS AND BENCHMARKING

In conducting the HR audit, most employers will want to benchmark—compare their results to those of comparable companies. Many private human resource management consulting firms (such as Mercer, www.mercer.com) compile and offer such comparable data on a wide range of HR activities. These activities include, for instance, what other employers are paying, and the ratio of HR professionals per company employee. The Society of Human Resource Management provides extensive benchmarking services.

Types of Metrics

5 List and explain at least five HR metrics.

Personnel-related metrics range from broad organizational measures down to measures that focus narrowly on specific human resource management and activities.[25]

Figure 14.2 presents examples of broad measures. This figure gives an overall sense of how efficient an employer's human resource unit is. For example, a company with about 300 employees should have (at the median) just under 1 (0.94) HR employee per company employee.

Figure 14.3 illustrates more focused human resource management metrics. These include absence rate, cost per hire, and health care costs per employee.[26] Again, the basic questions would be, how does our company compare to others?

FIGURE 14.2

HR-to-Employee Ratios (by Organizational Size)

Source: SHRM Human Capital Benchmarking Study: 2007 Executive Summary.

Organizational Size	n	25th Percentile	Median	75th Percentile
Total	751	0.73	1.12	1.88
Fewer than 100	209	1.52	2.41	3.45
100 to 249	230	0.74	1.00	1.65
250 to 499	100	0.67	0.94	1.32
500 to 999	55	0.60	0.83	1.27
1,000 to 2,499	76	0.50	0.79	1.04
2,500 to 7,499	57	0.40	0.72	1.19
7,500 or more	24	0.36	0.72	1.06

FIGURE 14.3

Sample Metrics from SHRM Measurements Library

Source: SHRM, http://shrm.org.

	HR Metrics	
Absence Rate	[(# days absent in month) ÷ (Avg. # of employees during mo.) × (# of work-days)] × 100	Measures absenteeism. Determine if your company has an absenteeism problem. Analyze why and how to address issue. Analyze further for effectiveness of attendance policy and effectiveness of management in applying policy.
Cost per Hire	(Advertising + Agency fees + Employee referrals + Travel cost of applicants and staff + Relocation costs + Recruiter pay and benefits) ÷ Number of Hires	Costs involved with a new hire. For instance use *a Cost per Hire Staffing Metrics Survey* as a benchmark for your organization. Can be used as a measurement to show any substantial improvements to savings in recruitment/retention costs. Determine what your recruiting function can do to increase savings/reduce costs, etc.
Health Care Costs per Employee	Total cost of health care ÷ Total employees	Per capita cost of employee benefits. Indicates cost of health care per employee. See sources such as the U.S. Department of Labor's publication *Employer Costs for Employee Compensation* and *Measuring Trends in the Structure and Levels of Employer Costs for Employee Compensation* for additional information on this topic.
HR Expense Factor	HR expense ÷ Total operating expense	HR expenses in relation to the total operating expenses of organization. In addition, determine if expenditures exceeded, met, or fell below budget. Analyze HR practices that contributed to savings, if any.
Human Capital ROI	Revenue − (Operating expense − [Compensation cost + Benefit cost]) ÷ (Compensation cost + Benefit cost)	Return on investment ratio for employees. Did organization get a return on its investment? Analyze causes of positive/negative ROI metric. Use analysis as opportunity to optimize investment with HR practices such as recruitment, motivation, training, and development. Evaluate if HR practices are having a causal relationship in positive changes to improving metric.

Benchmarking in Action

Metrics are rarely useful by themselves. Instead, you'll usually want to know "How are we doing?" in relation to something. That "something" may be historical company figures (for example, Are our accident rates going up or down?). Or, you will want to *benchmark* your results—in other words, compare them to the figures from other companies.[27]

SHRM provides a customized benchmarking service. This enables employers to compare their own HR-related metric results with other companies'. SHRM's service provides benchmark figures for many industries including construction and mining, educational services, finance, manufacturing, and others. The employer can also request the comparable (benchmark) figures not just by industry, but broken down by employer size, company revenue, and geographic region. (See http://shrm.org/research/benchmarks/.)

Figure 14.4 illustrates one of the many sets of comparable benchmark measures you could obtain from SHRM's benchmark service. Figure 14.4 shows HR expense data—in this case, HR expenses, HR expenses to operating expenses, and HR expenses per full-time employee for firms comparable to this client.

Strategy and Strategy-Based Metrics

Benchmarking (comparing one firm's HR metrics with another's) only provides a partial picture of how your company's human resource management system is performing.[28] It shows how your human resource management system's performance compares to the competition. It may *not* show the extent to which your firm's HR practices are helping your company to achieve its strategic goals. For example, if our strategy calls for doubling profits by improving customer service, to what extent are our new selection and training practices helping to improve customer service?

strategy-based metrics
Metrics that specifically focus on measuring the activities that contribute to achieving a company's strategic aims.

Managers need *strategy-based metrics* to answer that question. **Strategy-based metrics** are metrics that specifically focus on measuring the activities that contribute to achieving a company's strategic aims.[29] Chapter 3 addressed this. In brief, the manager uses SWOT analysis and other planning tools to create a strategic direction for the company. The *strategy map* then outlines the causal flow of activities that contribute to achieving the company's strategy. It shows how various employee competencies, skills, and behaviors contribute to important organizational outcomes like better service, and how outcomes like better service in turn affect organizational success.

As an example:

● Let's say the owners of the "Paris International Hotel" decide to make their hotel one of the 10 top hotels in France.
● They believe doing so will translate into revenues and profits 50% higher than now.
● They decide that achieving those strategic aims requires dramatically improving customer service. They will measure customer service in terms of measures like *guest returns*, and *guest compliments* of employees.

FIGURE 14.4

SHRM Customized Human Capital Benchmarking Report for [Your Organization's Name Here]

Source: SHRM Human Capital Benchmarking Study 2007.

	HR Expense Data		
	2006 HR Expenses	2006 HR Expense to Operating Expenses	2006 HR Expense per FTE
n	12	11	12
25th percentile	$320,000	5.15%	$1,358
Median	$548,215	12.86%	$2,044
75th percentile	$700,000	16.67%	$3,550
Average	$533,421	12.66%	$2,341

- What can the hotel's human resource managers do to help achieve this improved customer service? They can take measurable steps to improve certain targeted HR practices, such as *increase training per year per employee* from 10 hours to 25, *boost incentive pay* (tied to guest service ratings) from zero now to 10% of total salaries, and move from no job candidates tested before hiring to *100% testing* prior to hiring.
- So for the Paris Hotel, the strategic HR metrics would include (among others) 100% employee testing, 80% guest returns, incentive pay as a percent of total salaries, and sales up 50%. If targeted changes in HR practices such as increased training and better incentives have their intended effects, then metrics like guest returns and guest compliments should also rise. And if so, the Paris Hotel should hopefully also achieve its strategic goal of being one of the 10 top hotels in France.

Improving Productivity through HRIS: Tracking Applicant Metrics for Improved Talent Management

Recruiting will be a problem in the years ahead. Baby boomers will be retiring, while employers will face a diminishing pool of younger applicants.

It's therefore ironic that most employers spend thousands of dollars (or more) each year recruiting employees without measuring which hiring source produces the best candidates. The logical solution is to collect and assess recruitment metrics, such as on "quality of new hires" and on "which recruitment sources produce the most new hires."[30]

With respect to recruiting, perhaps the best way to actively track and analyze such data is by using an applicant tracking system (ATS). Many vendors provide ATSs. These include specialized ATS vendors like Authoria, PeopleFilter, Wonderlic, eContinuum, and PeopleClick, as well as outsourcers such as Accenture and IBM.

Regardless of the vendor, the recruitment effectiveness measurement process involves two basic steps.

- First, the employer (and vendor) decides how to measure the performance of new hires. For example, with Authoria's system, hiring managers input their evaluations of each new hire at the end of the employee's first 90 days, using a 1–5 scale. Dell uses employee performance and retention metrics.[31]
- Second, the ATS enables the employer to track the recruitment sources that correlate with superior hires. (It may show, for instance, that new employees hired through "employee referrals" stay longer and work better than those from newspaper ads do.) Most ATSs enable hiring managers to track such hiring metrics on desktop dashboards.

Applicant tracking systems also support the employer's talent management efforts, by helping management to actively manage its staffing by using numbers and evidence. Thus installing an Authoria ATS enabled the global news firm Reuters to *identify the sources, candidate traits, and best practices that work best* in each geographic area where they do business.[32] This in turn enabled them to *reduce recruiting costs,* for instance, by shifting recruitment dollars from less effective sources to more effective ones. Similarly, the ATS should also produce *better employees,* for instance, by helping the employer see which employee competencies correlate with superior performance.

OUTSOURCING HUMAN RESOURCE MANAGEMENT ACTIVITIES

We've seen in this book that employers expect their human resource managers to spend more time on strategic, big picture issues. They want them to spend less time on traditional HR transactional/operational activities (such as maintaining and updating employee records, and enrolling employees in benefits plans). They want them to spend more time as internal consultants, helping top management to put in place HR practices, such as high performance systems, that help the company achieve its strategic goals.

Two Ways to Reduce the Emphasis on Day-to-Day Operational HR Activities

For human resource managers to devote more time to strategic matters like these, they must reduce the time they put into day-to-day operational services. One way to do this is to *use more technology*. For example, we've seen that employers use applicant tracking systems to automate the process of acquiring, compiling, prescreening, and scheduling interviews for applicants. A second way to reduce the transactional/operational workload is to *outsource* one or more specific services such as background checking and benefits administration to specialist outside vendors. We'll focus on outsourcing in this final section.

Outsourcing Doesn't Always Succeed

We saw in Chapter 12 that many employers do outsource their human resource functions to outside vendors. Depending on the range of their services, these vendors include professional employer organizations (PEOs), human resource outsourcers, and employee or staff leasing firms. Employers typically pay the outsourcing vendor about $400–$500 per employee per year, and sign multi-year contracts.

Although such relationships are often productive, others are quickly unwound. For example, a few years ago Starbucks outsourced many of its human resource activities to Cincinnati-based Convergys.[33] For about a year, Convergys managed Starbucks' payroll and HR administration in the United States and Canada, as well as Starbucks' benefits administration for Canadian employees. But Starbucks, facing the need to rev up its in-store performance, soon decided to bring its HR activities back in-house. Now Starbucks' own human resource management team can focus on improving Starbucks employees' morale and performance. The bottom line is that outsourcing isn't always appropriate, and requires special skills. We'll look at these special skills next.

Outsourcing in Practice

SHRM surveys provide an overview of HR outsourcing.[34]

Employers expect their human resource managers to spend more time as internal consultants, helping top management to put in place HR practices that help the company achieve its strategic goals.

Source: Getty Images, Inc.–Liaison.

Source: Ted S. Warren/AP Wide World Photos.

Starbucks briefly outsourced its HR function.

WHO OUTSOURCES WHAT? About 58% of surveyed employers outsource at least some HR functions, 38% do not and have no plans to, and about 4% plan to outsource one or more HR functions in the next several years. Table 14.2 shows HR functions outsourced completely or partially. For example, about 49% of employers completely outsource background and criminal background checks, and 47% outsource their employee assistance/counseling activities. Interestingly, relatively few employers outsource core transactional HR activities such as recruitment and payroll administration.

WHY OUTSOURCE? For most employers, outsourcing seems to be more a cost-cutting tactic, rather than one to free up HR time for more strategizing. In the SHRM survey, the main reasons for outsourcing were to save money/reduce operating costs (cited by 56%), to control legal risks and improve compliance (55%), to gain access to vendor talent (47%), and to streamline human resource management operations (45%).

OUTSOURCING'S ADVANTAGES An SHRM survey summarizes what respondents see as outsourcing's benefits.[35] Seventy-five percent cited "HR is able to focus on core business functions," and 66% said, "It allows HR to spend more time on strategy development and execution." Other reported benefits included, "improves HR metrics/measurement," and "HR had a better reputation among senior management."

TABLE 14.2 **Percent of Surveyed Employers That Outsource HR Functions Completely or Partially**

Function	Outsource Completely	Outsource Partially
Background/criminal background checks	49%	24%
Employee assistance/counseling	47%	19%
Consolidated Omnibus Budget Reconciliation Act (COBRA)	38%	17%
Health care benefits administration	24%	36%
Temporary staffing	21%	33%
Pension benefits administration	19%	36%
Retirement benefits administration	17%	30%
Payroll administration	13%	35%
Work/life balance benefits administration	6%	5%
Compensation and/or incentive plans administration	4%	15%
Executive development and coaching	4%	16%
Human Resource Information Systems (HRIS) development	4%	11%
Recruitment/staffing of employees (nonexecutives)	4%	26%
Recruitment/staffing of executives only	4%	24%
Risk management	4%	8%
Performance management	1%	2%
Training and development programs	1%	20%
Policy development and/or implementation	0%	4%
Strategic business planning	0%	4%

Note: Data based on organizations that currently outsource one or more HR functions. The percentages are not adjusted to reflect cases in which an organization may not perform a particular HR function.

Source: Adapted from SHRM® Human Resource Outsourcing Survey Report (July 2004), http://shrm.org, accessed February 2, 2006.

OUTSOURCING PROBLEMS On the whole, only about 35% of those in the SHRM survey said they were "very satisfied" with their outsourcing vendor services and relationships, about 53% were "somewhat satisfied," and the remainder ranged from indifferent to dissatisfied. The main problem cited was lack of face-to-face contact with employees when a vendor is carrying out one or more HR functions.

Overall, the results suggest that employers must be careful to whom they outsource, and how they outsource. Let's look first at to whom employers can outsource.

To Whom Do Employers Outsource HR Functions?

There are hundreds—probably thousands—of vendors who will manage some or all of an employer's human resource management activities, for a fee. Figure 14.5 shows some top HR outsourcing providers. Most of these are very large, and they generally accept clients with large numbers (at least 15,000) of employees. They include well-known human resource consulting and outsourcing firms like Hewitt Associates, IBM Global Services, and ADP employer services. (For a directory of HR vendors, see Web site www.hr-guide.com.)

Making the Decision to Outsource

The decision to outsource should not be taken lightly. With less than half of the SHRM survey respondents saying that outsourcing had fully met their expectations, managers need to take care

FIGURE 14.5

Some Top HR Outsourcing Vendors

Sources: "Ranking the Top Enterprise HRO Providers," *HRO Today,* www.hrotoday.com/magazine.asp?artID=2074, accessed July 20, 2008; The International Association of Outsourcing Professionals, http://outsourcingprofessional.com/content/23/152/117, accessed July 20, 2008; "2008 Large Market End to End HR Outsourcing Providers," *Workforce Management,* www.workforce.com/section/09/feature/25/56/46/index.html, accessed July 20, 2008.

Supplier	Sample Services	Sample Clients
Accenture	Talent management services; recruitment; performance and progression; learning; compensation	Best Buy, U.S. Transportation Security Administration, Unilever
IBM	Payroll, benefits; talent management (includes recruiting, learning, performance management, compensation, and succession management)	P&G, American Airlines
ADP	Payroll and benefits administration	Carmax, IKEA
Ceridian	Payroll and benefits administration; talent acquisition; regulatory compliance/administration	Comerica, FMC Corp.
Hewitt Associates	Benefits, payroll, performance management; training administration	Air Canada, Marriott
ExcellerateHRO	Compensation management; payroll, recruiting and staffing	Cardinal Health, BP Canada
Fidelity HR Services	Talent management (includes recruiting and staffing, training and development, and performance and rewards)	ABB Inc.; The Hartford
Convergys	Recruiting; compensation; HR administration; payroll, benefits	Fifth Third Bancorp., DuPont
Affiliated Computer Services, Inc	HRIS technology deployment and support; payroll, performance management, recruiting and staffing	Motorola, Delta Airlines
Northgate Arinso	Data input, time management (includes absences/presences, overtime management); payroll management	Cadbury Schweppes, Scotiabank

in deciding whether and what to outsource, and then in managing the vendor relationship. The decisions regarding whether to outsource and what to outsource depend on three things, *employer size, financial pros and cons,* and *strategic issues.*

EMPLOYER SIZE In terms of *size,* many employers have little choice but to outsource some of their HR activities. At an employer with, say, 50 employees, it's unlikely that an in-house payroll management group, background checking capabilities, or perhaps even formal employee screening capabilities will be available. Smaller firms, especially, have therefore tended to rely on vendors like employment agencies (although it wasn't called "outsourcing" in the 1990s).

FINANCIAL PROS AND CONS You will also want to review the *financial pros and cons* of outsourcing specific human resource management functions. For example, calculate the current payroll, benefits, and overhead (office space, and so on) costs of the HR function under review (such as benefits administration), so as to compare these costs with the prospective vendor's costs.[36] The costs of outsourcing then need to be compared to other, internal options, such as creating a central human resources call center to handle employee inquiries, or letting employees self-service routine HR tasks (as for benefits changes) online.

STRATEGIC ISSUES You do not want to discover, as Starbucks apparently did, that maintaining employee morale is so important that HR shouldn't be outsourced. The SHRM survey highlighted some of the *strategic issues* involved in making the decision on whether to outsource. For example, about 75% of respondents said outsourcing enabled them to "focus on core business functions," and 66% said it "allows HR to spend more time on strategy development and execution."

6 Explain the process you would use to select an outsourcing vendor.

But the survey also suggests that employers are much less likely to outsource high-impact strategic activities such as training and development, executive staffing and development, and policy development. As an example, Joseph Slawek, CEO of a small firm that manufactures flavors for foods and beverages, has two full-time and two part-time employees in his firm's HR department. With a total of 135 employees, "that costs us more than if we outsource the function," he says. However, with a unique team of scientists and others, he feels that "HR is part of our competitive advantage." An in-house human resource management team gives his firm the ability to offer the personalized career counseling and other services he feels his employees need.[37] The HR in Practice feature provides a checklist for choosing and managing the vendor relationship.

HR IN PRACTICE

Outsourcing Checklist

In choosing and dealing with a vendor, suggestions include:[38]

1. Decide *which services* to outsource.
2. Agree with vendor on exactly *what HR activities will be outsourced* and what will be retained internally.
3. *Review multiple providers* and decide on one partner.
4. Clarify exactly *what services* the vendor will provide.
5. Make sure to have *metrics* to measure and hold accountable the vendor.
6. Look for *financial stability* in the prospective vendor.
7. Check the prospective vendor's *service record* with other clients.

8. Consider the *costs,* but balance short-term savings with the ability to provide long-term service to employees.
9. Look at the prospective vendor's *technology capabilities* in terms of accommodating your growth plans.
10. Ensure the prospective vendor has an adequate *disaster recovery* plan, because it is managing crucial employee data for you.
11. Make sure the vendor will provide your in-house people with adequate *training* regarding procedures, and so on.

For example, as companies expand globally, more are outsourcing their worldwide recruitment to vendors. Consultants call this "recruitment process outsourcing." The Global Issues in HR feature addresses this.

GLOBAL ISSUES IN HR

Outsourcing the Global Recruitment Function

Here's how Robert McNabb, CEO of the global recruiter firm Futurestep, explains the trend to *recruitment process outsourcing*. "Multinational companies may receive 1,000 resumes a day, and they also need to tap good passive candidates who may be entertaining four or five offers. . . . Companies with big world-class brands have discovered that the perception in the marketplace is that their recruiting process is broken."[39]

That's where vendors such as Futurestep come in. Futurestep (www.futurestep.com/) handles global recruiting for (as an example) a large Madrid-based energy company. The employer recruits in both Europe and Latin America, and wanted a single recruiting source for all its locations.[40] (Futurestep is part of the global human resource outsourcing/executive search firm Korn/Ferry International.)

Recruitment process outsourcing (RPO) does not necessarily mean that the global vendor (such as Futurestep) does all the recruiting itself—placing ads, and so on. It may retain others to do this. The heart of RPO involves outsourcing the entire recruitment *process*, including deciding which sources to use and then managing them. So, for example, Futurestep might be responsible for managing the employer's entire "end-to-end" recruitment activities. This would include managing all the recruiting and staffing-related vendors such as employment agencies.[41]

REVIEW

SUMMARY

1. A *high-performance work system* is a set of human resource management policies and practices that together produce superior employee performance. For example, high-performance systems pay more, train more, use more sophisticated recruitment and hiring practices, and use more self-managing work teams. The point is that when it comes to managing the people side of the business, the way to improve performance is to design its recruiting, selection, training, and other HR practices so that together they produce superior employee performance—a high-performance work system.

2. Evidence-based human resource management is the deliberate use of the best-available evidence in making decisions about the human resource management practices you are focusing on. The evidence may come from *actual measurements* you make (such as, how did the trainees like this program?). It may come from *existing data* (such as, what happened to company profits after we installed this training program?). Or, it may come from published critically evaluated *research studies* (such as, what does the research literature conclude about the best way to ensure that trainees remember what they learn?).

3. Most CEOs won't accept subjective explanations for projects they are asked to implement. Quantitative, data-based analysis is the hallmark of successful organizational consulting. Such analyses often start with human resource managers conducting *human resource audits* of all or part of their operations. One HR practitioner describes an HR audit as "an analysis by which an organization measures where it currently stands and determines what it has to accomplish to improve its HR function."

4. HR audits vary in scope and focus. As an overview, one practitioner suggests 10 possible areas of focus for HR audits: recruitment and selection, compensation, employee relations, mandated (required) benefits, group benefits, payroll, record keeping, training and development, employee communications, and internal communications. Beyond this, we identified four broad types of audits: *compliance audit, best practices, strategic,* and *function specific.* In conducting an HR audit, the basic approach is to use a checklist-type questionnaire.

5. In conducting the HR audit, most employers will want to compare their results to those of comparable companies. Many private human resource management consulting

firms (such as Hewitt Associates) compile and offer such data, as does the Society of Human Resource Management.

6. Human resource–related metrics range from broad organizational measures to measures that focus narrowly on specific human resource management functions and activities. For example, HR-to-employee ratios give an overall feel for how efficient an employer's human resource unit is. The ratio *sales per employee* provides a rough but useful first approximation for how the company is doing. Other typical HR metrics include absence rate, cost per hire, and health care costs per employee. Metrics are rarely useful by themselves. SHRM provides a customized benchmarking service; this enables employers to compare their HR-related metric results with other companies.

7. Benchmarking shows you how you're doing relative to the competition. It may not show you how your human resource management system is helping your company achieve its strategic goals. A strategy map outlines the causal flow of activities that contribute to achieving the company's strategy. It shows how various employee competencies, skills, and behaviors contribute to important organizational outcomes like better service, and how outcomes like better service affect organizational success.

8. For human resource managers to devote more time to strategic matters, they have to reduce the effort they put into day-to-day operational services. For more firms today, the answer is to outsource one or more services such as background checking and benefits administration to specialist outside vendors. The decisions on if (and what) to outsource depend on several things: employer size, financials and costs, and strategic issues. Employers are less likely to outsource high-impact strategic activities such as training and development, executive staffing and development, and policy development.

KEY TERMS

high-performance work system   404
human resource metric   405

HR audit   407
strategy-based metrics   412

DISCUSSION QUESTIONS

1. Define "high-performance work system."
2. List four characteristics of high-performance work systems.
3. Give an example of using evidence-based management.

4. Discuss with examples how to conduct an HR audit.
5. List and explain at least five HR metrics.
6. Explain the process you would use to select an outsourcing vendor.

INDIVIDUAL AND GROUP ACTIVITIES

1. Interview professors at your college and others familiar with how the college operates, and answer this question: To what extent does our college or school use high-performance work practices?
2. As noted in the chapter's opening scenario, many experts lost faith in the famous "Toyota Way" to build cars after the acceleration problem surfaced in 2010. Use Web sites such as http://online.wsj.com/article/SB10001424052748 703510204575084840073648572.html to learn what is meant by the Toyota Way. What aspects of the Toyota Way are based on human resource management activities? What does the Toyota Way prescribe for these activities?

WEB-e's (WEB EXERCISES)

1. According to information at www.shrm.org/Research/ benchmarks/Pages/default.aspx, what sorts of benchmarking information can an employer request from SHRM?

2. Assume you are an HR manager and want to compile a list of what to check in your HR audit. Use sites such as www.hraudit.com/ to compile your list.

APPLICATION EXERCISES

HR IN ACTION CASE INCIDENT 1
Marks & Spencer

The British department store chain Marks & Spencer was long synonymous with retail department and food stores in England and Europe. With increasing economic integration in Europe (as symbolized by the addition of more countries to the European Union, and the adoption by most EU countries outside England of the Euro currency), competition within the EU area became more intense. While Marks & Spencer's many stores continued to be crowded with shoppers, problems had been brewing for many years. In 2001 a Marks & Spencer report referred to rising costs, falling profit margins, and "rock bottom" employee morale.[42]

When Marks & Spencer's HR head left a few years later, experts told the chain's top management "to take HR seriously if it is to have any chance of regaining former glories." One consultant who had worked with Marks & Spencer said, "I have never seen the HR team get to grips with the issues that are affecting the company. HR has never been seen as a contributor for change." Concerning Marks & Spencer's new chief executive, this consultant said, "[he] is a classic example of a chief executive who has no understanding about strategic HR. You can turn a business around by cutting costs, but the likes of Marks & Spencer needs HR-driven change." Anthony Thompson, a former Marks & Spencer manager returning to the company after 8 years, found some HR-related changes that surprised him. For one thing, he saw "very few customer assistants smiling." More than 2,000 people who Marks & Spencer had hired as temporary Christmas employees failed to come to work, apparently because they were offered better jobs elsewhere.

Not surprisingly, one of the first areas the new management addressed was human resource issues, starting with pay. When the new HR manager took over, there were 429 different pay rates for the customer assistants (the retail clerks who assist customers). These rates (converted from British pounds to dollars) ranged from about $10 an hour up to $20 an hour for long-term employees. That

meant newly hired customer assistants earned a bit above the minimum wage. Management changed the customer assistant pay range, so it now ranged from about $11 an hour to about $14.50. That meant long-serving customer assistants would have their pay frozen, and would receive basically no pay raises for several years. On the other hand, newly hired customer assistants could now be paid a higher rate. Long-term employees were somewhat upset that inexperienced new hires were earning close to what those with years of experience were earning. However, the new rate range would also enable Marks & Spencer to hire better entry-level employees, and hopefully give all customers consistently good service.

The company implemented several other HR changes. For example, Marks & Spencer traditionally trained customer assistants through classroom-type training. To speed the process and keep more customer assistants on the floor, Marks & Spencer now trained 8,000 coaches. Their job was to go back and train customer assistants on the floor, while they were helping customers. They also streamlined the performance review process, so that identifying and (if necessary) dismissing low-performing employees was easier.

Questions

1. To what extent does management now seem to be taking a strategic HR approach to the company's problems? What do you base that on?
2. If you were an HR consultant called in by top Marks & Spencer management, what would you have done if you read the confidential Marks & Spencer memo, and heard the experts' comments?
3. As an HR consultant to a CEO who was not too familiar with strategic HR, what would you have done to elicit confidence in you?
4. What, as their consultant, would you do now?

HR IN ACTION CASE INCIDENT 2
Carter Cleaning Company: The High-Performance Work System

On the whole, Jennifer and her father were pleased with the human resource management changes they'd implemented in the past few years. Among other things, they had new EEO compliance, selection, training, appraisal, incentive, discipline, and safety procedures. Jennifer was therefore somewhat surprised and, perhaps, disappointed when her father told her he thought they should consider outsourcing their HR activities to a professional employee organization. "We invested all this time in improving our HR practices; why outsource all this to a stranger now?" she said. "You're probably right, Jen," her father said. "But on the other hand, we may be spending way too much time and money on managing these HR tasks, and the PEO suggested they'd save us money. Really, we don't know how effective all these changes have been. I think we need to really look at the numbers."

Questions

1. Create a strategy map for a typical Carter Cleaning store.
2. List 15 HR metrics you would suggest Carter use in measuring its HR effectiveness.
3. Based on what you learned about Carter Cleaning in the previous 13 chapters and anything else you may know about the cleaning business, write a one-page outline of what you would cover in an HR audit of Carter Cleaning.
4. If the Carters asked you for a summary of why they should *not* outsource their HR activities, what would you tell them?

EXPERIENTIAL EXERCISE

Benchmarking Pay and Benefits

Purpose: The purpose of this exercise is to give you experience in HR benchmarking.

Required Understanding: You should be thoroughly familiar with the material in this chapter, and have access to online HR benchmarking sources.

How to Set Up the Exercise/Instructions: Set up groups of three or four students for this exercise. Then read the following:

By February 2004, the strike by Southern California grocery workers against the state's major supermarket chains was almost 5 months old. Because so many workers were striking (70,000), and because of the issues involved, unions and employers across the country were closely following the negotiations. Indeed, grocery union contracts were set to expire in several cities later in 2004, and many believed the California settlement—assuming one was reached—would set a pattern.

The main issue was employee pay and benefits, including how much (if any) of the employees' health care costs the employees should pay themselves. Based on their existing contract, Southern California grocery workers had unusually good health benefits. For example, they paid nothing toward their health insurance premiums, and paid only $10 copayments for doctor visits. However, supporting these excellent health benefits cost the big Southern California grocery chains over $4.00 per hour per worker.

The big grocery chains were not proposing cutting health care insurance benefits for their existing employees. Instead, they proposed putting any new employees hired after the new contract went into effect into a separate insurance pool, and contributing $1.35 per hour for their health insurance coverage. That meant new employees' health insurance would cost each new employee perhaps $10 per week. And, if that $10 per week wasn't enough to cover the cost of health care, then the employees would have to pay more, or do without some of their benefits.

It was a difficult situation for all the parties involved. For the grocery chain employers, skyrocketing health care costs were undermining their competitiveness, and the current employees feared any step down the slippery slope that might eventually mean cutting their own health benefits. The unions didn't welcome a situation in which they'd end up representing two classes of employees, one (the existing employees) who had excellent health insurance benefits, and another (newly hired employees) whose benefits were relatively meager, and who might therefore be unhappy from the moment they took their jobs and joined the union.[43] Adding to the difficulty was the fact that several new competitors, including Walmart and foreign firms like Tesco, were either in or planning to be in competition with the existing stores very soon. Each side—the retailers and the unions—decided independently that they should better understand the pay and benefits situation by seeking out benchmark figures for their industry and related industries. They want your team to use any on- or offline sources available to get them the figures they need.

1. Explain how and why the HR manager's job has changed, and what HR managers should focus on now.
2. Give examples of what human resource managers can do to move from a provider of operational services to the firm's chief "people" advisor/consultant.

BUSINESS IN ACTION EDU-EXERCISE

Building Your *Supply Chain* Knowledge

Managers can apply principles of *supply chain management* when dealing with vendors such as PEOs, recruiters like Futurestep, or the various application tracking services. Whichever suppliers they use, companies work hard to squeeze out the wastes of unnecessary activities from everything they do. *Supply chain management* supports these aims. The term *supply chain* refers to all of a company's suppliers, manufacturers, distributors, and customers, and to the interactions among them. *Supply chain management* "is the integration of the activities that procure materials, transform them into intermediate goods and final product, and deliver them to customers."[46] The idea is to get all the vendors, truckers, and so on "onto the same page" so they work together to cut waste and get the product or service to the customers as efficiently as possible.

Four main principles underlie successful supply chain management. They are *supplier partnering, transparency, Internet-based purchasing, and channel assembly.*[47]

1. *Supplier partnering* means having a limited number of suppliers, so as to build relationships that improve quality and reliability, rather than just to improve costs.
2. Supply chains also function better with *transparency*. *Transparency* means giving supply chain partners easy access to information about details such as your sales, inventory levels, and status of inbound and outbound shipments, usually through a Web-based portal. This lets supply partners (like suppliers and truckers) accurately predict the customer's needs.
3. *Internet-based purchasing* (also called e-procurement) usually means more than just getting orders via the Web. In today's supply chains, supplier partnering and transparency usually mean that favored suppliers (like Levi's) can monitor the real-time sales of customers (like Walmart). They can thus automatically supply orders to fulfill the customer's needs. Therefore, *Internet-based purchasing* automatically

monitors the customer's needs online and produces the necessary products, shipping documents, and bills.

4. Some companies also make their suppliers or distributors part of their manufacturing processes. *Channel assembly* means having a supplier or distributor perform some of the steps required to create the company's product or service. For example, Hewlett Packard (HP) doesn't send finished printers to its distributors; it sends components and modules.

Companies usually build their supply chains' interconnectedness using special supply chain management software from companies like SAP and Oracle. This links each element in the supply chain. For example, when someone orders a new Dell PC, Dell's software posts the order in its records. It also signals the plant to produce the PC, and signals suppliers (like the one producing the monitor) to prepare to have one picked up. It also notifies UPS to pick up your PC from Dell (and the monitor from the supplier) on a particular day and to deliver it all to you, as ordered. And all this happens automatically.

Questions

1. Assume you are the human resource manager for a large retailer with department stores in 25 cities. You are planning to outsource many of your company's HR activities including recruitment management, testing, and payroll and benefits administration, to outside vendors. Based on what you read in this chapter, what specific issues would you pay attention to before choosing a vendor?

2. Explain with examples how you would use supply chain management concepts to help to ensure a more effective partnership between your company and the HR vendors you choose.

PERSONAL COMPETENCIES EDU-EXERCISE

The Human Resource Manager as an *Internal Consultant* [44]

Any human resource manager who wants to move from being mostly a provider of operational services to being the firm's chief advisor on how to leverage its human resources to add value to the company starts with four basic steps:

1. First, *know what you want to do.* This means having a plan for what transactional services you should reorganize or redeploy, and how to reorganize or redeploy them. For example, "doubling profits" may mean reducing recruitment costs by 40%, which may mean outsourcing the recruitment function.

2. Second, execute the plan to *reduce the assets and efforts* devoted to delivering transactional HR services. This may include using more technology such as applicant tracking systems or call centers, and outsourcing.

3. Third, *develop the skills* required to be an effective internal HR consultant. These include mastering the latest basic human resource management functional skills (in areas like recruiting and interviewing) and the *business knowledge* (in areas such as finance) and strategic skills you'll need to analyze and advise how to best align employees' competencies with the firm's strategic needs.

4. Fourth, *build your credibility.* [45] Credibility starts with accomplishing what your colleagues expect of you. Beyond this, establishing credibility as an expert requires having, among other things:
   - An excellent command of and understanding of the industry, organization, and competition
   - Persuasive, high-quality suggestions
   - A proven ability to solve business problems
   - Effective interpersonal relationships and skills
   - Excellent communication skills
   - A reputation for creating workable solutions

Questions

1. Go to the Web sites of several human resources consulting firms such as Hewitt (www.hewittassociates.com/Intl/NA/en-US/Consulting/ServiceLine.aspx?sln=HR+Consulting), Mercer (www.mercer.com/home.htm), and Futurestep (www.kornferry.com/Futurestep?ckx=1). Judging from these consulting firms' sites, what are the big skills and benefits they offer to their consulting clients?

2. Have you ever been in a situation that required credibility on your part? What did you do to exhibit that credibility?

ENDNOTES

1. www.bls.gov/opub/ted/2006/may/wk2/art01.htm, accessed April 18, 2009.

2. "Super Human Resources Practices Result in Better Overall Performance, Report Says," *BNA Bulletin to Management* (August 26, 2004): 273–274. See also Wendy Boswell, "Aligning Employees with the Organization's Strategic Objectives: Out of Line of Sight, Out of Mind." *International Journal of Human Resource Management* 17, no. 9 (September 2006): 1014–1041. A recent study found that some employers, which the researchers called cost minimizers, intentionally took a lower cost approach to human resource practices, with mixed results. See Soo Min Toh et al., "Human Resource Configurations: Investigating Fit with the Organizational Context," *Journal of Applied Psychology* 93, no. 4 (2008): 864–882.

3. www.bls.gov/mlr/1995/05/art3full.pdf, accessed March 3, 2010.

4. "With High-Performance Work Organizations, Adversaries No More," *Work & Family Newsbrief* (August 2003): 5. See also Karen Kroll, "Repurposing Metrics for HR," *HR Magazine* 51, no. 7 (July 2006), www.SHRM.org/HR magazine/articles, accessed February 4, 2008.

5. See, for example, www.personneltoday.com/blogs/hcglobal-human-capital-management/2009/02/theres-no-such-thing-as-eviden.html, accessed April 18, 2009.

6. Robert McNabb and Keith Whitfield, "Job Evaluation and High-Performance Work Practices: Compatible or Conflictual?" *Journal of Management Studies* 38, no. 2 (March 2001): 294.

7. See, for example, John Sullivan, "The Last Word," *Workforce Management* (November 19, 2007): 42.

8. As one expert puts it, "A great deal of what passes as "best practice" in HRM most likely is not. In some cases, there is simply no evidence that validates what are thought to be best practices, while in other cases there is evidence to suggest that what are thought to be best practices are inferior practices." Edward Lawler III, "Why HR Practices Are Not Evidence-Based," *Academy of Management Journal* 50, no. 5 (2007): 1033.

9. See, for example, www.personneltoday.com/blogs/hcglobal-human-capital-management/2009/02/theres-no-such-thing-as-eviden.html, accessed April 18, 2009.

10. The evidence-based movement began in medicine. In 1996, in an editorial published by the *British Medical Journal*, David Sackett, MD, defined "evidence based medicine" as "use of the best-available evidence in making decisions about patient care," and urged his colleagues to adopt its tenets. "Evidence-Based Training™: Turning Research Into Results for Pharmaceutical Sales Training," An AXIOM White Paper © 2006 AXIOM Professional Health Learning LLC. All rights reserved.

11. Alexander Colvin et al., "How High-Performance Human Resource Practices and Workforce Unionization Affect Managerial Pay," *Personnel Psychology* 54 (2001): 903–934.

12. Kamal Birdi et al., "The Impact of Human Resource and Operational Management Practices on Company Productivity Call Them a Longitudinal Study," *Personnel Psychology* 61 (2008): 467–501. In fact, these researchers concluded that worker empowerment, teamwork, and training had much greater effects on employee and company performance than did the sorts of manufacturing initiatives such as quality management, just-in-time, supply chain partnering, and advanced manufacturing technology that companies often Institute in efforts to improve productivity and performance.

13. Lin Grensing-Pophal, "HR Audits: Know the Market, Land Assignments," SHRM consultants form (December 2004), http://www.shrm.org/hrdisciplines/consultants/Articles/Pages/CMS_010705.aspx, accessed July, 2010.

14. Bill Coy, "Introduction to The Human Resources Audit," La Piana Associates, Inc., www.lapiana.org/consulting, accessed May 1, 2008.

15. Lin Grensing-Pophal, "HR Audits: Know the Market, Land Assignments," SHRM Consultants' Forum (December 2004), op cit.; and Bill Coy, "Introduction to The Human Resources Audit," La Piana Associates, Inc., www.lapiana.org/consulting, accessed May 1, 2008.

16. Based on Teresa Daniel, "HR Compliance Audits: 'Just Nice' or Really Necessary?" SHRM white paper (November 2004), http://www.shrm.org/Research/Articles/Articles/Pages/CMS_010198.aspx accessed July 2010.

17. See, for example, Dana R. Scott, "Conducting a Human Resources Audit," *New Hampshire Business Review* (August 2007).

18. Teresa Daniel, "HR Compliance Audits: 'Just Nice' or Really Necessary?" SHRM white paper (November 2004), op cit. See also Dana R. Scott, "Conducting a Human Resources Audit," *New Hampshire Business Review* (August 2007).

19. From Teresa Daniel, op. cit.

20. See Teresa Daniel, op. cit.; Dana Scott, op. cit.; "Start Your HR Audit with This Checklist," *HR Focus* 84, no. 6 (June 2007): 1, 11, 13–15; and Bill Coy, "Introduction to The Human Resources Audit," La Piana Associates, Inc., www.lapiana.org/consulting, accessed May 1, 2008.

21. For additional detailed information on conducting HR audits see, for example, http://SHRM.org/HRtools/toolkits_published, accessed February 2, 2008.

22. Dana R. Scott, "Conducting a Human Resources Audit," *New Hampshire Business Review* (August 2007).

23. Ibid.

24. Bill Coy, "Introduction to The Human Resources Audit," La Piana Associates, Inc., www.lapiana.org/consulting, accessed May 1, 2008.

25. See, for example, "Using HR Performance Metrics to Optimize Operations and Profits," *PR Newswire* (February 27, 2008); and "How to 'Make Over' Your HR Metrics," *HR Focus* 84, no. 9 (September 2007): 3.

26. For additional information on HR metrics see, for example, Karen M. Kroll, "Repurposing Metrics for HR: HR Professionals Are Looking Through a People-Focused Lens at the CFO's Metrics on Revenue and Income per FTE," *HR Magazine* 51, no. 7 (July 2006): 64(6); and http://shrm.org/metrics/library_publishedover/measurementsystemsTOC.asp, accessed February 2, 2008.

27. See, for example, "Benchmarking for Functional HR Metrics," *HR Focus* 83, no. 11 (November 2006): 1.

28. See Brian Becker and Mark Huselid, "Measuring HR? Benchmarking Is Not the Answer!" *HR Magazine* 8, no. 12 (December 2003), www.charmed.org, accessed February 2, 2008.

29. Ibid.

30. Connie Winkler, "Quality Check: Better Metrics Improve HR's Ability to Measure—and Manage—the Quality of Hires," *HR Magazine* 52, no. 5 (May 2007): 93(4).

31. Ibid.

32. Ibid.

33. "Jessica Marquez, "HRO Deal Bulk of Industry," *Workforce Management* (July 23, 2007): 1, 3.

34. The following is based on a SHRM human resource outsourcing survey report (July 2004), http://shrm.org, accessed February 2, 2006.

35. SHRM® Human Resource Outsourcing Survey Report (July 2004), http://shrm.org, accessed February 2, 2006.

36. Mikio Manuel, "How to Calculate and Maximize Outsourcing ROI," www.shrm.org/RT export/library_published, accessed February 2, 2008.

37. "HR: Outsource or In-house?" *Crain's Chicago Business* 30, no. 41 (September 8, 2007): 38.

38. The following are based on Richard Vosburgh, "The Evolution of HR: Developing HR as an Internal Consulting Organization," *Human Resource Planning* 30, no. 3 (September 2007): 11–12; and Stephen Miller, "Collaboration Is Key to Effective Outsourcing," *HR Magazine* (2008 supp Trendbook): 58, 60–61.

39. Fay Hansen, "Taking on the World with Recruitment Outsourcing; The Demand for Global End-to-End Recruitment Process Outsourcing, or RPO, Is Growing as Multinationals Strengthen Their Presence in a Range of Markets and Accelerate Hiring," *Workforce Management* 85, no. 20 (October 23, 2006): 34.

40. Ibid.

41. Ibid.

42. This case is based on Julia Finch, "Leaked Papers Reveal the Devastating Decline of M&S: Staff Morale Hits Rock Bottom in UK as French Take to the Streets," *The Guardian* (April 7, 2001): 26; Daniel Thomas, "Experts Warn Retailer Over Disregard of HR," *Personnel Today* (November 16, 2004): 1; "Talks Reopen in Bid to Save M&S Deal," *Grocer* (October 14, 2006): 14; Claire Warren, "This Is Not Just HR. . . ," *People Management* 13, no. 1 (January 11, 2007): 26–30.

43. Based on "Settlement Nears for Southern California Grocery Strike," *Knight-Ridder/Tribune Business News* (February 26, 2004): item 04057052.

44. Based on Richard Vosburgh, "The Evolution of HR: Developing HR as an Internal Consulting Organization," *Human Resource Planning* 30, no. 3 (September 2007).

45. Ibid.

46. Jay Heizer and Bernard Render, *Operations Management*, 6th ed. (Upper Saddle River, NJ: Prentice Hall, 2001): 434.

47. Kasra Ferdows et al., "Rapid-Fire Fulfillment," *Harvard Business Review* (November 2004): 104–110.

Employee Retention and Career Management Module

Employers are sailing into uncertain waters as far as the availability of good employees is concerned. With unemployment still high in 2010 due to the recession, recruiting for now is not the big problem. But as demand picks up in the next few years, the twin challenges of retiring baby boomers and fewer younger workers will make getting and keeping good employees a significant challenge. Add to this the fact that employers don't want to lose the "human capital" in which they've invested so much, and it's understandable why effective employee retention programs are essential. We've already discussed involuntary dismissals in Chapter 9. In this module we'll look at why employees leave voluntarily ("quit") and what employers can do to improve their employee retention rates.

WHY DO EMPLOYEES LEAVE?

Most people have thought about quitting at one time or another. As a result, most people understand that most employees don't quit just for more pay. Pay is certainly important. As three authors recently summed up, "given that low pay satisfaction may lead to absenteeism, lack of commitment, lower productivity and increased turnover, pay satisfaction should be an issue of concern to employers and human resource professionals."[1]

Yet other factors invariably loom large, not just in the U.S. but internationally. For example, a survey of Chinese employees found that the primary stated reasons for leaving a job included lack of growth/development opportunities, better career opportunity elsewhere, insufficient compensation, uninteresting work, insufficient awards/recognition, insufficient benefits, did not feel efforts were appreciated, and job was not as expected. Secondary stated reasons included poor relationship with one's manager, poor relationship with coworkers, and felt unfairly treated.[2] A survey by the accountants PriceWaterhouseCoopers found that pay and benefits were not usually the main reason why employees leave. Instead, the quality of the relationship with the supervisor and opportunities for career development and for personal growth were the main reasons employees left their jobs.[3]

In fact, "relationship with supervisor" has long been seen as an important factor in employee satisfaction and performance. Professor Rensis Likert conducted a classic series of studies here. He concluded that "the leadership and other processes of the organization must be such as to ensure a maximum probability that in all interactions and all relationships with the organization each member will, in the light of his background, values, and expectations, view the experience as supportive and one which builds and maintains his sense of personal worth and importance."[4]

WHY DO EMPLOYEES STAY?

Of course, employers don't want employees to leave, but to stay.

Several surveys address the question of what makes employees want to stay. For example, in a survey of about 25,000 employees in the leisure and hospitality industry, the main reasons cited for staying were job satisfaction, extrinsic rewards, attachment to coworkers, organizational commitment, and organizational prestige.[5] In another illustrative survey, coworkers' "job embeddedness"—the tendency of one's coworkers to feel attached to their jobs and not want to leave—had an important influence on whether their coworkers decided to stay or leave.[6]

The reasons people stay thus range from pay to supervision to career development to job satisfaction. Of course, job satisfaction is not monolithic. For example, in his famous studies of job satisfaction (discussed in Chapter 8), Frederick Herzberg listed numerous sources of job satisfaction. These included working conditions, pay, relationships with supervisor, job status, security, relationship with subordinates, and job design—specifically whether the job offered opportunities for achievement, recognition, and responsibility.

HOW EMPLOYERS RETAIN EMPLOYEES

Since there are so many reasons why employees stay or leave, the implication is that there's no one silver bullet for retaining good employees. A variety of factors influence whether an employee decides to stay or leave. Employers thus need to have in place a multifaceted program for retaining employees.

A Comprehensive Approach to Retaining Employees

Experts from the consulting company Development Dimensions International (DDI) and from the employment firm Robert Half International suggest building comprehensive retention programs around the following actions.

Fine-tune selection. "Retention starts up front, in the selection and hiring of the right employees."[7] Selection refers not just to the worker but to choosing the right supervisors as well. For example, FedEx conducts periodic attitude surveys to assess how supervisors are "coming across" to their employees.

Offer professional growth. Inadequate career and professional development prospects prompt many employees to leave. Conversely, a well-thought-out training and career development program can provide a strong incentive for staying with the company. As one expert says, "professionals who feel their company cares about their development and progress are much more likely to stay."[8] We'll address this in more detail later in this module.

Provide career direction. Periodically discuss with employees their career preferences and prospects at your firm, and help them outline potential career plans. Furthermore, "don't wait until performance reviews to remind top employees how valuable they are to your company."[9]

Provide meaningful work and direction. People can't do their jobs if they don't know what to do or what their goals are. Therefore, an important part of retaining employees is to make it clear what your expectations are regarding their performance and what their responsibilities are.

Combine recognition and rewards. Pay that is equitable internally and externally is important. We've also seen that in addition to pay and benefits, employees need and appreciate recognition for a job well done.

Synchronize culture and environment. For example, companies that are very tense and "political" may prompt employees to leave, while companies that make them feel comfortable encourage them to stay.

Promote work/life balance. In one survey conducted by Robert Half and CareerBuilder.com, workers identified "flexible work arrangements" and "telecommuting" as the two top benefits that would encourage them to choose one job or another.

Acknowledge achievements. When employees feel underappreciated, they're more likely to leave. Surveys suggest that frequent recognition of accomplishments is an effective nonmonetary reward. The accompanying Managing the New Workforce feature presents practices for retaining top female employees.

MANAGING THE NEW WORKFORCE

Practices for Retaining Top Female Employees

There are a handful of female CEOs at top companies, such as PepsiCo's CEO Indra Nooyi, but their numbers don't come close to being proportionate to the number of women in the workplace. As one expert on this issue points out, "professional women are entering the workforce at the same rates as men, yet something happens along the way resulting in disproportionate losses of women in managerial positions."[10]

What accounts for this? In part, it's because in many firms, employment practices are still mostly geared to a time when most managerial and professional employees were men. The male bread-winner focused on advancing his career, and the female caregiver stayed home with the children. Today, less than 20% of households reflect this model, so employment and promotion practices that worked 30 or 40 years ago won't work today. Yet, women managers and professionals still often carry a disproportionate share of the caregiver responsibilities at home. Therefore the only way employers can "stop the leak" of competent females leaving is by changing the firm's work practices. Doing so involves five sets of activities:

Flexibility

This expert says, "the number one change that women seek is increased flexibility."[11]

Flexibility covers a variety of issues. For example, on a week-to-week basis, women may need to leave early to get children to an appointment or to pick them up at school. One way to provide this flexibility is by organizing work in teams, so that the team members can organize things themselves to make sure the job gets done. Another tactic is encouraging telecommuting, so employees can do more work while out of the office. In many cases, women must temporarily scale back their efforts at some point in their careers, perhaps by leaving their jobs temporarily or by working part-time at reduced hours. Some companies are therefore dividing work into "chunks" of significant work, for instance, by enabling a female employee to work with fewer clients or to focus on at-home legal research for a period of time. Ideally, women who need to reduce their hours or scale back should still be eligible for career advancement. For example, the accounting firm Ernst and Young lets selected part-time employees be promoted to partner.

Caregiver Support

Employers also need to rethink their maternity leave, child care support, and elder care support policies. For example, the 12 weeks of maternity leave mandated by the Family Medical Leave Act isn't sufficient for many working mothers, particularly because the act does not require companies to pay employees during their leaves. Employers who want to retain female employees need to revisit their maternity leave policies, as well as provide the child care support and elder care support that make it easier for women to stay in their jobs.

Maintaining Contact

As this expert says, "if women do decide to leave, organizations should do all they can to keep the doors open for them when they are ready to return."[12] For example, create alumni networks to keep these former employees in the loop, and provide project work that enables them to tackle contract work or on special projects while they're away.

Welcome Reentries

Many employers are not as receptive to hiring "reentry women" as they should be. The company's policies and practices should encourage competent former employees to reapply and rejoin the company.

Supportive Organizational Culture

Policies regarding flexibility, caregiver support, and reentries are useless without a correspondingly supportive organizational culture. For example, the employer needs to encourage, train, and reward managers and supervisors to behave supportively when women (and men) need to leave early to attend to an emergency caregiver task.

Foster Employee Engagement and Commitment

Sometimes employees don't physically leave, but instead "check out" mentally. For example, the Institute for Corporate Productivity defines engaged employees "as those who are mentally and emotionally invested in their work and in contributing to an employer's success." Unfortunately, studies suggest that less than one-third of the U.S. workforce is engaged.[13] One Gallup study estimated that $350 billion is lost annually in the United States alone due to disengaged workers.[14] And disengaged employees are often the first to leave. As one observer says, "What happens if you lose 20 percent of your top performers when things get better?"[15]

One way to foster employee engagement is to show that the employer is committed to the employees' development and welfare. For example, a survey by the American Society for Training and Development concluded that employers' "investments in training and development always rank at the top of what makes [employees] engaged."[16]

In brief, evidence suggests that fostering employee engagement and commitment requires an integrated series of concrete managerial actions. Employers can take steps like the following.[17]

FOSTER PEOPLE-FIRST VALUES High-commitment companies tend to emphasize "People-first values." Their managers trust their employees, believe in respecting their employees as individuals and in treating them fairly, and are committed to employee welfare. Values like these tend to pervade the whole chain of command. Here's how one United Auto Workers officer at GM's former Saturn plant in Spring Hill, Tennessee put it:

> Our philosophy is, we care about people—and it shows. We involve people in decisions that affect them. . . . Saturn's commitment really comes down to how you feel about people—your attitudes—more than anything, because all the other Saturn programs—the work teases the extensive training the way people are paid—all stem from these people attitudes.[18]

COMMUNICATE YOUR VISION Committed employees need a vision to which to be committed, preferably one that they feel "is bigger than we are." Employees at organizations like Google, the Salvation Army, Facebook, and Ben & Jerry's become, to a certain extent, soldiers in a crusade. Through their employment, they redefine themselves and their goals in terms of the company's mission.

ENCOURAGE EMPLOYEE DEVELOPMENT AND SELF-ACTUALIZATION Even with mergers and layoffs, employers can demonstrate their commitment to employees by showing that they're committed to employees' personal development. Development can provide important job security, whether or not the person stays with the firm.

Firms do this in many ways. For example, train employees to expand their skills and to solve problems. Enrich their jobs. Provide career-oriented interviews.

The results can be dramatic. At FedEx, one manager described his experience as follows: "At Federal Express, the best I can be is what I can be here. I have been allowed to grow with Federal Express. For the people at Federal Express, it's not the money that draws us to the firm. The biggest benefit is that Federal Express made me a man. It gave me the confidence and self-esteem to become the person I had the potential to become."[19]

Talent Management and Employee Retention

All employees are important, but as we explained earlier in this book, talent management–oriented employers emphasize developing and retaining mission-critical employees. For example, we saw that Accenture uses a 4×4 strategic role assessment matrix. It plots employees by performance and by value to the organization. Accenture then ties pay, development, dismissal, and other personnel decisions to each employee's position in the matrix. Compass Group identifies top performers, and then assesses them for promotability and leadership potential. Shell China appoints career stewards to meet regularly with "emerging leaders." Novartis China uses a checklist to assess the attitudes of its most mission-critical employees. The point is that taking a talent management approach to retaining employees suggests focusing extra retention efforts on the company's mission-critical employees.

CAREERS AND CAREER MANAGEMENT

Career development plays an important role in retaining employees. For example, a survey by the human resource management consulting firm Mercer found that as of 2010, employers planned to focus both on money and on career development to retain and engage the right talent.[20] One observer similarly says that "rather than focusing on incentives and perks to entice and retain employees, organizations . . . will hold onto the most talented workers . . . by offering them a range of professional experiences, broad functional and geographic exposure within the organization, and more targeted leadership opportunities."[21] We'll look more closely at career management issues next.

We may define *career* as the occupational positions a person holds over the years. *Career management* is a process for enabling employees to better understand and develop their career skills and interests and to use these skills and interests most effectively both within the company and after they leave the firm. *Career development* is the lifelong series of activities (such as workshops) that contribute to a person's career exploration, establishment, success, and fulfillment. *Career planning* is the deliberate process through which someone becomes aware of his or her personal skills, interests, knowledge, motivations, and other characteristics; acquires information about opportunities and choices; identifies career-related goals; and establishes action plans to attain specific goals.

We'll see that the employee's supervisor and employer both play roles in guiding and developing the employee's career. However, the employee must always accept full responsibility for his or her own career development and career success.

The Employee's Role

For the employee, career planning means matching individual strengths and weaknesses with occupational opportunities and threats. The person wants to pursue occupations, jobs, and a career that capitalizes on his or her interests, aptitudes, values, and skills. He or she also wants to choose occupations, jobs, and a career that makes sense in terms of projected future demand for various types of occupations. There is a wealth of sources to turn to.

SKILLS AND APTITUDES The process logically starts with identifying one's occupational strengths, weaknesses, preferences, aptitudes, and skills. Some people are simply ill-suited for particular jobs, while others flourish in them. The performance appraisal is a good opportunity to address such issues, and the person's employer and manager obviously have an interest in ensuring that there is a good match.

As an example, career-counseling expert John Holland says that personality (including values, motives, and needs) is one career choice determinant. For example, a person with a strong social orientation might be attracted to careers that entail interpersonal rather than intellectual or physical activities and to occupations such as social work. Holland found six such personality types or orientations (he called these Realistic, Investigative, Artistic, Social, Enterprising, and Conventional). Individuals can use his Self-Directed Search (SDS) test (available online at www.self-directed-search.com) to assess their occupational orientations and preferred occupations.

The SDS has an excellent reputation, but the career seeker needs to be wary of some of the other online career assessment sites. One study of 24 no-cost online career assessment Web sites concluded that they were easy to use, but suffered from insufficient validation and confidentiality. However, a number of online career assessment instruments such as Career Key (www.careerkey.org) do reportedly provide validated and useful information.[22]

AN EXERCISE One useful exercise for identifying occupational skills is to take a blank piece of paper and head it "The School or Occupational Tasks I Was Best At." Then write a short essay that describes the tasks. Make sure to go into as much detail as you can about your duties and responsibilities and what you found enjoyable about each task. (In writing your essay, by the way, notice that it's not necessarily the most enjoyable *job* you've had, but the most enjoyable *task* you've had to perform; you may have had jobs that you really didn't like except for one of the specific duties or tasks in the job, which you really enjoyed.) Next, on other sheets of paper, do the same thing for two other tasks you have had. Now go through your three essays and underline the skills that you mentioned the most often. For example, did you especially enjoy the hours you spent in the library doing research for your boss when you worked as an office clerk?[23]

APTITUDES AND SPECIAL TALENTS For career planning purposes, a person's aptitudes are usually measured with a test battery such as the general aptitude test battery (GATB), which most state one-stop career ("unemployment") centers make available. This instrument measures various aptitudes including intelligence and mathematical ability. You can also use specialized tests, such as for mechanical comprehension. However, even Holland's Self-Directed Search will provide some insights into your aptitudes.[24]

IDENTIFY YOUR CAREER ANCHORS Edgar Schein says that career planning is a continuing process of discovery—one in which a person slowly develops a clearer occupational self-concept in terms of what his or her talents, abilities, motives, needs, attitudes, and values are. Schein also says that as you learn more about yourself, it becomes apparent that you have a dominant *career anchor*, a concern or value that you will not give up if a [career] choice has to be made.

Career anchors, as their name implies, are the pivots around which a person's career swings; a person becomes conscious of them by learning, through experience, about his or her talents and abilities, motives and needs, and attitudes and values. Based on his research at the Massachusetts Institute of Technology, Schein believes that career anchors are difficult to predict because they are evolutionary and a product of a process of discovery. Some people may never find out what their career anchors are until they have to make a major choice—such as whether to take the promotion to the headquarters staff or strike out on their own by starting a business. It is at this point that all the person's past work experiences, interests, aptitudes, and orientations converge into a meaningful pattern that helps the person to discover what career anchor is the most important one in driving the person's career choices.

Based on his study of MIT graduates, Schein identified the following five career anchors.[25]

Technical/Functional Competence People who had a strong technical/functional career anchor tended to avoid decisions that would drive them toward general management. Instead, they made decisions that would enable them to remain and grow in their chosen technical or functional fields.

Managerial Competence Other people show a strong motivation to become top managers and their career experience enabled them to believe they had the skills and values required. When pressed to explain why they believed they had the skills necessary to gain such positions, many in Schein's research sample answered that they were qualified because of what they saw as their competencies in a combination of three areas. These were:

1. *Analytical competence*—the ability to identify, analyze, and solve problems under conditions of incomplete information and uncertainty
2. *Interpersonal competence*—the ability to influence, supervise, lead, manipulate, and control people at all levels
3. *Emotional competence*—the capacity to be stimulated by emotional and interpersonal crises rather than exhausted or debilitated by them, and the capacity to bear high levels of responsibility without becoming paralyzed

Creativity Some of the graduates had gone on to become successful entrepreneurs. To Schein these people seemed to have a need "to build or create something that was entirely their own product—a product or process that bears their name, a company of their own, or a personal fortune that reflects their accomplishments." For example, one graduate had become a successful purchaser, restorer, and renter of townhouses in a large city; another had built a successful consulting firm.

Autonomy and Independence Some seemed driven by the need to be on their own, free of the dependence that can arise when a person elects to work in a large organization where promotions, transfers, and salary decisions make them subordinate to others. Many of these graduates also had a strong technical/functional orientation. Instead of pursuing this orientation in an organization, they had decided to become consultants, working either alone or as part of a relatively small firm. Others had become professors of business, freelance writers, and proprietors of a small retail business.

Security A few of the graduates were mostly concerned with long-run career stability and job security. They seemed willing to do what was required to maintain job security, a decent income, and a stable future in the form of a good retirement program and benefits. For those interested in *geographic security*, maintaining a stable, secure career in familiar surroundings was generally more important than pursuing superior career choices, if choosing the latter meant injecting instability or insecurity into their lives by forcing them to pull up roots and move to another city. For others, security meant *organizational security*. They might today opt for government jobs, where tenure still tends to be a way of life. They were much more willing to let their employers decide what their careers should be.

ASSESSING CAREER ANCHORS To help you identify career anchors, says Professor Schein, take a few sheets of blank paper and write your answers to the following questions:[26]

1. What was your major area of concentration (if any) in high school? Why did you choose that area? How did you feel about it?
2. What is (or was) your major area of concentration in college? Why did you choose that area? How did you feel about it?
3. What was your first job after school? (Include military if relevant.) What were you looking for in your first job?
4. What were your ambitions or long-range goals when you started your career? Have they changed? When? Why?
5. What was your first major change of job or company? What were you looking for in your next job?
6. What was your next major change of job, company, or career? Why did you initiate or accept it? What were you looking for? (Do this for each of your major changes of job, company, or career.)
7. As you look back over your career, identify some times you have especially enjoyed. What was it about those times that you enjoyed?
8. As you look back, identify some times you have not especially enjoyed. What was it about those times you did not enjoy?
9. Have you ever refused a job move or promotion? Why?
10. Now review all your answers carefully, as well as the descriptions for the five career anchors (managerial competence, technical/functional, security, creativity, autonomy). Based on your answers to the questions, rate, for yourself, each of the anchors from 1 to 5; 1 equals low importance, 5 equals high importance.

      Managerial competence _____

      Technical/functional competence _____

      Security _____

      Creativity _____

      Autonomy _____

WHAT DO YOU WANT TO DO? We have explained occupational skills, orientations, and career anchors and the role these play in choosing a career. Now, another exercise can prove enlightening. On a sheet of paper, answer the question: "If you could have any kind of job, what would it be?" Invent your own job if need be, and don't worry about what you can do—just what you want to do.[27]

MENTORING Having a mentor—a senior person who is a sounding board for career questions and concerns, and who provides career-related guidance and support—can significantly enhance career satisfaction and success.[28] Realistically, most employees probably don't plan whom they're going to use as a mentor, or how to approach him or her. Instead, they develop a relationship through which they start broaching career issues with someone with whom they work. Some suggestions for finding and using a mentor include:

- Choose an appropriate potential mentor. The mentor should be in a position to offer experienced and objective career advice.
- If you're going to make a formal request that someone mentor you, make it easier for the person to agree to your request by clarifying what you expect in terms of time and advice.
- Have an agenda. Bring an agenda to your first mentoring session that lays out key issues and topics for discussion.
- Respect the mentor's time. Be selective about the work-related issues that you bring to the table. Try to focus on significant career issues.
- Mandatory mentoring is OK. Some employers match mentors with protégés. Studies suggest that mandatory participation is no less effective than voluntary participation in a mentoring program.[29] However, both the mentor and a protégé should have some say about the match.[30]

Many employers, like Charles Schwab and Bank of America, offer formal mentoring programs.[31] The accounting firm KPMG made an online mentoring program part of its "employer of choice" initiative. This initiative also includes flexible work schedules, and community volunteer opportunities with pay and benefits.[32] Dow Chemical Co. has a Web-based mentor technology similar to a Google search. It enables Dow employees who are seeking mentors to screen lists of potential Dow mentors online.[33]

The Employer's Role in Career Management

The roles of the employer and supervisor depend partly on how long the employee has been with the firm. *Before hiring*, realistic job interviews can help prospective employees more accurately gauge whether the job is a good fit with a candidate's skills and interests.

Especially for recent college graduates, *the first job* can be crucial for building confidence and a more realistic picture of what he or she can and cannot do: Providing challenging first jobs (rather than relegating new employees to "jobs where they can't do any harm") and having an experienced mentor who can help the person learn the ropes are important. Some refer to this as preventing reality shock, a phenomenon that occurs when a new employee's high expectations and enthusiasm confront the reality of a boring, unchallenging job.

After the person has been *on the job* for a while, new employer career-management roles arise. Career-oriented appraisals—in which the supervisor is trained not just to appraise the employee but also to match the person's strengths and weaknesses with a feasible career path and required development work—is one important step. Similarly, providing periodic job rotation can help the employee develop a more realistic picture of what he or she is (and is not) good at, and thus the sort of future career moves that might be best. Employers' corporate career development initiatives may also include innovative programs like the following:[34]

1. *Provide each employee with an individual career development budget.* He or she can use this budget for learning about career options and personal development.[35]
2. *Offer on-site or online career centers.* These might include an on- or off-line library of career development tools and materials, and career workshops.
3. *Encourage role reversal.* Have employees temporarily work in different jobs in order to develop a better appreciation of their occupational strengths and weaknesses.
4. *Provide career coaches.* For example, Allmerica Financial Corp. hired 20 career development coaches to assist its 850-person information technology staff. The coaches help individual employees identify their development needs and obtain the training, professional development, and networking opportunities that they need.[36]
5. *Provide career-planning workshops.* A career-planning workshop is a "planned learning event in which participants are expected to be actively involved, completing career planning exercises and inventories and participating in career skills practice sessions."[37]
6. *Use computerized on- and off-line programs for improving the organizational career planning process.* For example, employees can use the Self-Directed Search (www. self-directed-search.com) to identify career preferences.

Gender Issues in Career Development

Women and men face different challenges as they advance through their careers. In one study, promoted women had to receive higher performance ratings than promoted men to get promoted, "suggesting that women were held to stricter standards for promotion."[38] Women report greater barriers (such as being excluded from informal networks) than do men, and more difficulty getting developmental assignments and assignments abroad. Women have to be more proactive than men just to be considered for such assignments. The point is that employers need to focus on breaking down the barriers that impede women's career progress. One study concluded that three corporate career development activities—fast-track programs, individual career counseling, and career planning workshops—were less available to women than to men.[39] Many call this combination of subtle and not-so-subtle barriers to women's progress the *glass ceiling*. Because developmental experiences like these are so important, "organizations that are interested in helping female managers advance should focus on breaking down barriers that interfere with women's access to developmental experiences."[40]

MINORITY WOMEN In these matters, minority women may be particularly at risk. Women of color hold only a small percentage of professional and managerial private-sector positions. (Examples such as Indra Nooyi, PepsiCo's CEO, are exceptions to the rule.) The minority women in one survey several years ago reported that the main barriers to advancement included not having an influential mentor (47%), lack of informal networking with influential colleagues (40%), lack of company role models for members of the same racial or ethnic group (29%), and a lack of high-visibility assignments (28%).[41]

MANAGING PROMOTIONS AND TRANSFERS

Promotions are one of the more significant career-related decisions. In developing promotion policies, employers need to address several issues.

Issues in Promotion Decisions

A main issue concerns seniority versus competence. Competence is normally the basis for promotions. However, in many organizations civil service or union requirements and similar constraints still give an edge to applicants that are more senior.

Furthermore, if competence is to be the basis for promotion, how should we measure it? Defining past performance is usually straightforward. Managers use performance appraisals for this. However, sizing up how even a high-performing employee will do in a new, more challenging job is not so easy. Innumerable great salespeople turn out to be dreadful managers, for instance. Many employers therefore use formal selection devices like tests and (particularly) assessment centers to supplement performance appraisals.

With firms downsizing and flattening their organizations, "promotions" today often mean lateral moves or transfers. In such situations, the promotional aspect is not so much a higher level job or more pay. Instead, it's the opportunity to assume new, same-level responsibilities (such as a salesperson moving into HR) or increased, enriched decision-making responsibilities within the same job.

A transfer is a move from one job to another, usually with no change in salary or grade. Employees may seek transfers not just for advancement but also for noncareer reasons, such as better hours, location of work, and so on.

Finally, in an environment of economic turmoil, not everyone wants (or can have) a "traditional" career moving up the corporate ladder. Some writers urge employees to "pack your own parachutes" by reducing their loyalty to employers and instead moving from employer to employer every few years. Others build careers as independent contractors, using their wits to create a client base as consultants. Some refer to the Protean career. This is a career the person (not the employer) builds and manages, and for which the criterion of success is psychological, rather than purely remunerative.

Retirement Counseling

For many employees, years of career planning end with retirement. Retirement planning is a significant issue for employers. In the United States, the number of 25- to 34-year-olds is growing relatively slowly, and the number of 35- to 44-year-olds is declining. Furthermore, "In the past few years, companies have been so focused on downsizing to contain costs that they largely neglected a looming threat to their competitiveness—a severe shortage of talented workers."[42]

So, with many older employees moving towards traditional retirement age, employers face a longer-term labor shortage. Many have wisely chosen to fill their staffing needs in part with current or soon-to-be retirees. A *New York Times* article explains how "Shorter hours, lighter duties and other perks entice older workers to stay on the job."[43]

Therefore, "retirement planning" is no longer just for helping current employees slip into retirement.[44] It can also enable the employer to retain, in some capacity, the skills and brain power of those who would normally retire and leave the firm. Fortuitously, 78% of employees in one survey said they expect to continue working in some capacity after normal retirement age (64% said they want to do so part-time). Only about a third said they plan to continue work for financial reasons; about 43% said they just wanted to remain active.[45]

The bottom line is that employers should conduct the necessary numerical analyses of pending retirements. This should include a demographic analysis (including a census of the company's employees), a determination of the average retirement age for the company's employees, and a review of how retirement is going to impact the employer's health care and pension benefits. The employer can then determine the extent of the "retirement problem" and take fact-based steps to address it.[46]

DISCUSSION QUESTIONS

1. What is a career anchor? What career anchors (if any) would be predominant for a medical doctor? An accountant? A salesperson? Can you think back to a time when your career anchors influenced you to make a career decision (about, for instance, your choice of major)?

2. If you think it may be worthwhile, go to www.self-directed-search.com (or to a similar Web site) and take the test. What insights did it provide to you? Would you recommend it to a friend?

3. The CEO of a fast food chain tells you her company has employee turnover of more than 100% per year. Write a one-page outline laying out what you think she should do to improve the situation.

ENDNOTES

1. Millicent Nelson et al., "Pay Me More: What Companies Need to Know About Employee Pay Satisfaction," *Compensation & Benefits Review* 40, no. 2 (March/April 2008): 35–42.

2. "Turnover and Retention," *China Business Review* 35, no. 4 (July/August 2008): 28–29.

3. Robert Tate, "Retaining Skilled, Trained Workers," *Financial Executive* 23, no. 5 (June 2007): 16.

4. Rensis Likert, *New Patterns of Management* (New York: McGraw-Hill, 1961): 103.

5. John Hausknecht et al., "Targeted Employee Retention: Performance Based and Job Related Differences in Reported Reasons for Staying," *Human Resource Management* 48, no. 2 (March/April 2009): 69–88.

6. Will Felps et al., "Turnover Contagion: How Coworker's Job Embeddedness and Job Search Behaviors Influence Quitting," *Academy of Management Journal* 52, no. 3 (June 2009): 545–610.

7. Max Messmer, "Employee Retention: Why It Matters Now," *CPA Magazine* (June/July 2009): 28; and "The Employee Retention Challenge," Development Dimensions International, 2009.

8. Messmer, op. cit.

9. Messmer, op. cit.

10. Gary Dessler, "How to Earn Your Employees' Commitment," *Academy of Management Executive* 13, no. 2 (1999): 58–67.

11. Ibid.

12. Ibid.

13. Dean Smith, "Engagement Matters," *T+D* 63, no. 10 (October 14, 2009).

14. Quoted in Smith, op. cit.

15. Ibid.

16. Ibid.

17. The following is based on Gary Dessler, "How to Earn Your Employees' Commitment," *Academy of Management Executive* 13, no. 2 (1999): 58–67. For recent reviews see James McElroy, "Managing Workplace Commitment by Putting People First," *Human Resource Management Review* 11 (2001): 329–334; and Rene Schalk and Wim Van Dijk, "Quality Management and Employee Commitment Illustrated with Examples from Dutch Healthcare," *International Journal of Healthcare Quality Assurance* 18, nos. 2–3 (2005): 170–178.

18. Dessler, op. cit.

19. Gary Dessler, "How to Earn Your Employees' Commitment," *Academy of Management Executive* 13, no. 2 (1999): 58–67.

20. "Organizations Focus on Employee Engagement to Attract and Retain Top Talent," www.Mercer.com, accessed July 24, 2010.

21. Robert Siegfried Jr., "Mapping a Career Path for Attracting & Retaining Talent," *Financial Executive* (November 2008): 52–55.

22. Edward Levinson et al., "A Critical Evaluation of the Web-Based Version of the Career Key," *Career Development Quarterly* 50, no. 1 (September 1, 2002): 26–36.

23. Richard Bolles, *What Color Is Your Parachute?* (Berkeley, CA: Ten Speed Press, 2003): 5–6.

24. Ibid., p. 5. Researchers and career specialists are working with the U.S. government's O*NET to devise a methodology that will enable individuals to make better use of O*NET in identifying and choosing career paths. See, for example, Patrick Converse et al., "Matching Individuals to Occupations Using Abilities and the O*NET: Issues and an Application in Career Guidance," *Personnel Psychology* 57 (2004), www.allbusiness.com/labor-employment/human-resources-personnel/11452396-1.html, accessed August 2010.

25. Edgar Schein, *Career Dynamics* (Reading, MA; Addison Wesley, 1978): 128–129; and Edgar Schein, "Career Anchors Revisited: Implications for Career Development in the 21st Century," *Academy of Management Executive* 10, no. 4 (1996): 80–88.

26. Ibid., 257–262. For a recent test of Schein's career anchors concept, see Yvon Martineau et al., "Multiple Career Anchors of Québec Engineers: Impact on Career Path and Success," *Relations Industrielles/Industrial Relations* 60, no. 3 (Summer 2005): 455–482.

27. This example is based on Richard Bolles, *The Three Boxes of Life* (Berkeley, CA: Ten Speed Press, 1976). See also Richard Bolles, *What Color Is Your Parachute?*

28. Michael Doody, "A Mentor Is a Key to Career Success," *Health-Care Financial Management* 57, no. 2 (February 2003): 92–94.

29. Tammy Allen et al., "The Relationship Between Formal Mentoring Program Characteristics and Perceived Program Effectiveness," *Personnel Psychology* 59 (2006): 125–153.

30. Ibid.

31. Ibid.

32. Donna Owens, "Virtual Mentoring," *HR Magazine* (March 2006): 15–17.

33. Eve Tahmincioglu, "Looking for a Mentor? Technology Can Help Make the Right Match," *Workforce Management* (December 2004): 863–865.

34. See also Yehuda Baruch, "Career Development in Organizations and Beyond: Balancing Traditional and Contemporary Viewpoints," *Human Resource Management Review* 16 (2006): 131.

35. Barbara Greene and Liana Knudsen, "Competitive Employers Make Career Development Programs a Priority," *San Antonio Business Journal* 15, no. 6 (July 20, 2001): 27.

36. Julekha Dash, "Coaching to Aid IT Careers, Retention," *Computerworld* (March 20, 2000): 52.

37. Fred Otte and Peggy Hutcheson, *Helping Employees Manage Careers* (Upper Saddle River, NJ: Prentice Hall, 1992): 143.

38. Karen Lyness and Madeline Heilman, "When Fit Is Fundamental: Performance Evaluations and Promotions of Upper-Level Female and Male Managers," *Journal of Applied Psychology* 91, no. 4 (2006): 777(9).

39. Jan Selmer and Alicia Leung, "Are Corporate Career Development Activities Less Available to Female than to Male Expatriates?" *Journal of Business Ethics* (March 2003): 125–137.

40. Karen Lyness and Donna Thompson, "Climbing the Corporate Ladder: Do Female and Male Executives Follow the Same Route?" *Journal of Applied Psychology* 85, no. 1 (2000): 86–101.

41. "Minority Women Surveyed on Career Growth Factors," *Community Banker* 9, no. 3 (March 2000): 44.

42. Ken Dychtwald et al., "It's Time to Retire Retirement," *Harvard Business Review* (March 2004): 49.

43. Claudia Deutsch, "A Longer Goodbye," *New York Times* (April 21, 2008): H1, 10.

44. See, for example, Matt Bolch, "Bidding Adieu," *HR Magazine* (June 2006): 123–127.

45. "Employees Plan to Work Past Retirement, but Not Necessarily for Financial Reasons," *BNA Bulletin to Management* (February 19, 2004): 57–58. See also Mo Wang, "Profiling Retirees in the Retirement Transition and Adjustment Process: Examining the Longitudinal Change Patterns of Retirees' Psychological Well-Being," *Journal of Applied Psychology* 92, no. 2 (2007): 455–474.

46. Luis Fleites and Lou Valentino, "The Case for Phased Retirement," *Compensation & Benefits Review* (March/April 2007): 42–46.

Appendix

COMPREHENSIVE CASES

BANDAG AUTOMOTIVE

Jim Bandag took over his family's auto supply business in 2009, after helping his father, who founded the business, run it for about 10 years. Based in Illinois, Bandag employs about 300 people, and distributes auto supplies (replacement mufflers, bulbs, engine parts, and so on) through two divisions, one that supplies service stations and repair shops, and a second that sells retail auto supplies through five "Bandag Automotive" auto supply stores.

Jim's father, and now Jim, have always endeavored to keep Bandag's organization chart as simple as possible. The company has a full-time controller, managers for each of the five stores, a manager that oversees the distribution division, and Jim Bandag's executive assistant. Jim (and his father, working part-time) handles marketing and sales.

Jim's executive assistant administers the firm's day-to-day human resource management tasks, but Bandag outsources most HR activities to others, including an employment agency that does its recruiting and screening, a benefits firm that administers its 401(k) plan, and a payroll service that handles its paychecks. Bandag's human resource management systems consist almost entirely of standardized HR forms purchased from an HR supplies company. These include application forms, performance appraisal forms, and an "honesty" test Bandag uses to screen the staff that works in the five stores. The company performs informal salary surveys to see what other companies in the area are paying for similar positions, and uses these results for awarding annual merit increases (which, in fact, are more accurately cost-of-living adjustments).

Jim's father took a fairly paternal approach to the business. He often walked around speaking with his employees, finding out what their problems were, and even helping them out with an occasional loan—for instance, when he discovered that one of their children was sick, or for part of a new home down payment. Jim, on the other hand, tends to be more abrupt, and does not enjoy the same warm relationship with the employees as did his father. Jim is not unfair or dictatorial. He's just very focused on improving Bandag's financial performance, and so all his decisions, including his HR-related decisions, generally come down to cutting costs. For example, his knee-jerk reaction is usually to offer fewer days off rather than more, fewer benefits rather than more, and to be less flexible when an employee needs, for instance, a few extra days off because a child is sick.

It's therefore perhaps not surprising that, while over the past few years Bandag's sales and profits have increased markedly, the firm has found itself increasingly enmeshed in HR/equal employment–type issues. Indeed, Jim now finds himself spending a day or two a week addressing HR problems. For example, Henry Jaques, an employee of one of the stores, came to Jim's executive assistant and told her he was "irate" about his recent firing and was probably going to sue. On Henry's last performance appraisal, his store manager had said Henry did the technical aspects of his job well, but that he had "serious problems interacting with his coworkers." He was continually arguing with them, and complaining to the store manager about working conditions. The store manager had told Jim that he had to fire Henry because he was making "the whole place poisonous," and that (although he felt sorry because he'd heard rumors that Henry suffered from some mental illness) he felt he had to go. Jim approved the dismissal.

Gavin was another problem. Gavin worked for Bandag for 10 years, the last 2 as manager of one of the company's five stores. Right after Jim Bandag took over, Gavin told him he had to take a Family and Medical Leave Act medical leave to have hip surgery, and Jim approved the leave. So far so good, but when Gavin returned from leave, Jim told him that his position had been eliminated. They had decided to close his store and open a new, larger store across from a shopping center about a mile away, and appointed a new manager in Gavin's absence. However, the company gave Gavin a (nonmanagerial) position in the new store as a counter salesperson, at the same salary and with the same benefits as he had before. Even so, "this job is not similar to my old one," Gavin insisted. "It doesn't have nearly as much prestige." His contention is that FMLA requires that the company bring him back in the same or equivalent position, and that this means a supervisory position, similar to what he had before he went on leave. Jim said no, and they seem to be heading toward litigation.

In another sign of the times at Bandag, the company's controller, Miriam, who had been with the company for about 6 years, went on pregnancy leave for 12 weeks in 2009 (also under the FMLA), and then received an additional 3 weeks' leave under Bandag's extended illness days program. Four weeks after she came back, she asked Jim Bandag if she could arrange to work fewer hours per week, and spend about a day per week working out of her home. He refused, and about 2 months later fired her. Jim Bandag said, "I'm sorry, it's not anything to do with your pregnancy-related requests, but we've got ample reasons to discharge you—your monthly budgets have been several days late, and we've got proof you may have forged documents." She replied, "I don't care what you say your reasons are, you're really firing me because of my pregnancy, and that's illegal."

Jim felt he was on safe ground as far as defending the company for these actions, although he didn't look forward to spending the time and money that he knew it would take to fight each. However, what he learned over lunch from a colleague undermined his confidence about another case that Jim had been sure would be a "slam dunk" for his company. Jim was explaining to his friend that one of Bandag's truck maintenance service people had applied for a job driving one of Bandag's distribution department trucks, and that Jim had turned him down because the worker was deaf. Jim (whose wife has occasionally said of him, "No one has ever accused Jim of being politically correct") was mentioning to his friend the apparent absurdity of a deaf person asking to be a truck delivery person. His friend, who happens to work for UPS, pointed out that the U.S. Court of Appeals for the Ninth Circuit had recently decided that UPS violated the Americans with Disabilities Act by refusing to consider deaf workers for jobs driving the company's smaller vehicles.

Although Jim's father is semi-retired, the sudden uptick in the frequency of such EEO-type issues troubled him, particularly after so many years of labor peace. However, he's not sure what to do about it. Having handed over the reins of the company to his son Jim, he was loath to inject himself back into the company's operational decision making. On the other hand, he was afraid that in the short run, these issues were going to drain a great deal of Jim's time and resources, and that in the long run they might be a sign of things to come, with problems like these eventually overwhelming Bandag Auto. He comes to you, who he knows consults in human resource management, and asks you the following questions.

Questions

1. Given Bandag Auto's size, and anything else you know about it, should we reorganize the human resource management function, and if so why and how?
2. What, if anything, would you do to change and/or improve upon the current HR systems, forms, and practices that we now use?
3. Do you think that the employee that Jim fired for creating what the manager called a poisonous relationship has a legitimate claim against us, and if so why and what should we do about it?
4. Is it true that we really had to put Gavin back into an equivalent position, or was it adequate to just bring him back into a job at the same salary, bonuses, and benefits as he had before his leave?
5. Miriam, the controller, is basically claiming that the company is retaliating against her for being pregnant, and that the fact that we raised performance issues was just a smokescreen. Do you think the EEOC and/or courts would agree with her, and, in any case, what should we do now?
6. An employee who is deaf has asked us to be one of our delivery people and we turned him down. He's now threatening to sue. What should we do, and why?
7. In the previous 10 years we had only one equal employment complaint, and now in the last few years we have had four or five. What should I do about it? Why?
8. ***Change Management Question:*** Assuming Jim Bandag's father decides to step back in and implement the required changes, what issues might he encounter, and how exactly would you suggest he plan and execute the changes (using guidelines like those in Chapter 6)?

Based generally on actual facts, but Bandag is a fictitious company. Bandag source notes: "The Problem Employee: Discipline or Accommodation?" *Monday Business Briefing* (March 8, 2005); "Employee Says Change in Duties after Leave Violates FMLA," *BNA Bulletin to Management* (January 16, 2007): 24; "Manager Fired Days After Announcing Pregnancy," *BNA Bulletin to Management* (January 2, 2007): 8; "Ninth Circuit Rules UPS Violated ADA by Barring Deaf Workers from Driving Jobs," *BNA Bulletin to Management* (October 17, 2006): 329.

ANGELO'S PIZZA[*]

Angelo Camero was brought up in the Bronx, New York, and basically always wanted to be in the pizza store business. As a youngster, he would sometimes spend hours at the local pizza store, watching the owner knead the pizza dough, flatten it into a large circular crust, fling it up, and then spread on tomato sauce in larger and larger loops. After graduating from college as a marketing major, he made a beeline back to the Bronx, where he opened his first Angelo's Pizza store, emphasizing its clean, bright interior; its crisp green, red, and white sign; and his all-natural, fresh ingredients. Within 5 years, Angelo's store was a success, and he had opened three other stores and was considering franchising his concept.

Anxious as he was to expand, his 4 years in business school had taught him the difference between being an entrepreneur and being a manager. As an entrepreneur/small-business owner, he knew he had the distinct advantage of being able to personally run the whole operation himself. With just one store and a handful of employees, he could make every decision and watch the cash register, check in the new supplies, oversee the takeout, and personally supervise the service.

When he expanded to three stores, things started getting challenging. He hired managers for the two new stores (both of whom had worked for him at his first store for several years) and gave them only minimal "how to run a store" training, on the assumption that, having worked with him for several years, they already knew pretty much everything they needed to know about running a store. However, he was already experiencing human resource management problems, and he knew there was no way he could expand the number of stores he owned, or (certainly) contemplate franchising his idea, unless he had a system in place that he could clone in each new store to provide the manager (or the franchisee) with the necessary management knowledge and expertise to run their stores. Angelo had no training program in place for teaching his store managers how to run their stores. He simply (erroneously, as it turned out) assumed that by working with him they would learn how to do things on the job. Since Angelo really had no system in place, the new managers were, in a way, starting off below zero when it came to how to manage a store.

There were several issues that particularly concerned Angelo. Finding and hiring good employees was number one. He'd read the new National Small Business Poll from the National Federation of Independent Business Education Foundation. It found that 71% of small-business owners believed that finding qualified employees was "hard." Furthermore, "the search for qualified employees will grow more difficult as demographic and education factors" continue to make it more difficult to find employees. Similarly, reading the *Kiplinger Letter* one day, he noticed that just about every type of business couldn't find enough good employees to hire. Small firms were particularly in jeopardy; the *Letter* said: Giant firms can outsource many (particularly entry-level) jobs abroad, and larger companies can also afford to pay better benefits and to train their employees. Small firms rarely have the resources or the economies of scale to allow outsourcing or to install the big training programs that would enable them to take untrained new employees and turn them into skilled ones.

While finding enough employees was his biggest problem, finding enough honest ones scared him even more. Angelo recalled from one of his business school courses that companies in the United States are losing a total of well over $400 billion annually in employee theft. As a rough approximation, that works out to about $9 per employee per day and about $12,000 a year lost for a typical company. Furthermore, it was small companies like Angelo's that were particularly in the crosshairs, because companies with fewer than 100 employees are particularly prone to employee theft. Why are small firms particularly vulnerable? Perhaps they lack experience dealing with the problem. More importantly: Small firms are more likely to have a single person doing several jobs, such as ordering supplies and paying the delivery person. This undercuts the checks and balances managers often strive for to control theft. Furthermore, the risk of stealing goes up dramatically when the business is largely based on cash. In a pizza store, many people come in and just buy one or two slices and a cola for lunch, and almost all pay with cash, not credit cards.

---

[*]© Gary Dessler, Ph.D.

And, Angelo was not just worried about employees stealing cash. They can steal your whole business idea, something he learned from painful experience. He had been planning to open a store in what he thought would be a particularly good location, and was thinking of having one of his current employees manage the store. Instead, it turned out that this employee was, in a matter of speaking, stealing Angelo's brain—what Angelo knew about customers and suppliers, where to buy pizza dough, where to buy tomato sauce, how much everything should cost, how to furnish the store, where to buy ovens, store layout—everything. This employee soon quit and opened up his own pizza store, not far from where Angelo had planned to open his new store.

That he was having trouble hiring good employees, there was no doubt. The restaurant business is particularly brutal when it comes to turnover. Many restaurants turn over their employees at a rate of 200% to 300% per year—so every year, each position might have a series of two to three employees filling it. As Angelo said, "I was losing two to three employees a month." He also said, "We're a high-volume store, and while we should have [to fill all the hours in a week] about six employees per store, we were down to only three or four, so my managers and I were really under the gun."

The problem was bad at the hourly employee level: "We were churning a lot at the hourly level," said Angelo. "Applicants would come in, my managers or I would hire them and not spend much time training them, and the good ones would leave in frustration after a few weeks, while often it was the bad ones who'd stay behind." But in the last 2 years, Angelo's three company-owned stores also went through a total of three store managers—"They were just blowing through the door," as Angelo put it, in part because, without good employees, their workday was brutal. As a rule, when a small-business owner or manager can't find enough employees (or an employee doesn't show up for work), about 80% of the time the owner or manager does the job him or herself. So, these managers often ended up working 7 days a week, 10 to 12 hours a day, and many just burned out in the end. One night, working three jobs himself with customers leaving in anger, Angelo decided he'd never just hire someone because he was desperate again, but would start doing his hiring more rationally.

Angelo knew he should have a more formal screening process. As he said, "If there's been a lesson learned, it's much better to spend time up-front screening out candidates that don't fit than to hire them and have to put up with their ineffectiveness." He also knew that he could identify many of the traits that his employees needed. For example, he knew that not everyone has the temperament to be a server (he has a small pizza/Italian restaurant in the back of his main store). As Angelo said, "I've seen personalities that were off the charts in assertiveness or overly introverted, traits that obviously don't make a good fit for a waiter or waitress."

As a local business, Angelo recruits by placing help-wanted ads in two local newspapers, and he's been "shocked" at some of the responses and experiences he's had in response to his help-wanted ads. Many of the applicants left voice mail messages (Angelo or the other workers in the store were too busy to answer), and some applicants Angelo "just axed" on the assumption that people without good telephone manners wouldn't have very good manners in the store, either. He also quickly learned that he had to throw out a very wide net, even if only hiring one or two people. Many people, as noted, he just deleted because of the messages they left, and about half the people he scheduled to come in for interviews didn't show up. He'd taken courses in human resource management, so (as he said) "I should know better," but he hired people based almost exclusively on a single interview (he occasionally made a feeble attempt to check references). In total, his HR approach was obviously not working. It wasn't producing enough good recruits, and the people he did hire were often problematical.

What was he looking for? Service-oriented courteous people, for one. For example, he'd hired one employee who used profanity several times, including once in front of a customer. On that employee's third day, Angelo had to tell her, "I think Angelo's isn't the right place for you," and he fired her. As Angelo said, "I felt bad, but also knew that everything I have is on the line for this business, so I wasn't going to let anyone run this business down." Angelo wants reliable people (who'll show up on time), honest people, and people who are flexible about switching jobs and hours as required.

Angelo's Pizza business has only the most rudimentary human resource management system. Angelo bought several application forms at a local Office Depot, and rarely uses other forms of any sort. He uses his personal accountant for reviewing the company's books, and Angelo himself computes each employee's paycheck at the end of the week and writes the checks. Training is entirely on-the-job. Angelo personally trained each of his employees. For those employees who go on to be store managers, he assumes that they are training their own employees the way Angelo trained them (for better or worse, as it turns out). Angelo pays "a bit above" prevailing wage rates (judging by other help-wanted ads), but probably not enough to make a significant difference in the quality of employees that he attracts. If you asked Angelo what his reputation is as an employer, Angelo, being a candid and forthright person, would probably tell you that he is a supportive but hard-nosed employer who treats people fairly, but whose business reputation may suffer from disorganization stemming from inadequate organization and training. He approaches you to ask you several questions.

Questions

1. My strategy is to (hopefully) expand the number of stores and eventually franchise, while focusing on serving only high-quality fresh ingredients. What are three specific human resource management implications of my strategy (including specific policies and practices)?
2. Identify and briefly discuss five specific human resource management errors that I'm currently making.
3. Develop a structured interview form that we can use for hiring (1) store managers, (2) wait staff, and (3) counter people/pizza makers.
4. Based on what you know about Angelo's, and what you know from Chapter 12 and from having visited pizza restaurants, write a one-page outline showing specifically how you think Angelo's should go about selecting employees.
5. *Teambuilding Question:* If Angelo wants to open more stores, he will have to take steps to make sure that teamwork prevails in each store—that employees in each store work together collaboratively, supportively, and in support of each store's goals. What concrete steps can Angelo take to make sure that teamwork prevails in each store?

Based generally on actual facts, but Angelo's Pizza is a fictitious company. Angelo's Pizza source notes: Dino Berta, "People Problems: Keep Hiring from Becoming a Crying Game," *Nation's Business News* 36, no. 20 (May 20, 2002): 72–74; Ellen Lyon, "Hiring, Personnel Problems Can Challenge Entrepreneurs," *Patriot-News* (October 12, 2004); Rose Robin Pedone, "Businesses' $400 Billion Theft Problem," *Long Island Business News* 27 (July 6, 1998): 1B–2B; "Survey Shows Small-Business Problems with Hiring, Internet," *Providence Business News* 16 (September 10, 2001): 1B; "Finding Good Workers Is Posing a Big Problem as Hiring Picks Up," *The Kiplinger Letter* 81 (February 13, 2004).

GOOGLE[*]

Fortune magazine recently named Google the best of the 100 best companies to work for, and there is little doubt why. Among the benefits it offers are free shuttles equipped with Wi-Fi to pick up and drop off employees from San Francisco Bay area locations, unlimited sick days, annual all-expense-paid ski trips, free gourmet meals, five on-site free doctors, $2,000 bonuses for referring a new hire, free flu shots, a giant lap pool, on-site oil changes, on-site car washes, volleyball courts, TGIF parties, free on-site washers and dryers (with free detergent), Ping-Pong and foosball tables, and free famous people lectures. For many people, it's the gourmet meals and snacks that make Google stand out. For example, human resources director Stacey Sullivan loves the Irish oatmeal with fresh berries at the company's Plymouth Rock Cafe, near Google's "people operations" group. "I sometimes dream about it," she says. Engineer Jan Fitzpatrick loves the raw bar at Google's Tapis restaurant, down the road on the Google campus. Then, of course, there are the stock options—each new employee gets about 1,200 options to buy Google shares (recently worth about $480 per share). In fact, dozens of early Google employees ("Googlers") are already multimillionaires thanks to Google stock.

For their part, Googlers share certain traits. They tend to be brilliant, team oriented (teamwork is the norm, especially for big projects), and driven. *Fortune* describes them as people who "almost universally" see themselves as the most interesting people on the planet, and who are happy-go-lucky on the outside, but type A—highly intense and goal directed—on the inside. They're also super hardworking (which makes sense, since it's not unusual for engineers to be in

[*]© Gary Dessler, Ph.D.

the hallways at 3 A.M. debating some new mathematical solution to a Google search problem). They're so team oriented that when working on projects, it's not unusual for a Google team to give up its larger, more spacious offices and to crowd into a small conference room, where they can "get things done." Historically, Googlers generally graduate with great grades from the best universities, including Stanford, Harvard, and MIT. For many years, Google wouldn't even consider hiring someone with less than a 3.7 average—while also probing deeply into the why behind any B grades. Google also doesn't hire lone wolves, but wants people who work together and who have diverse interests (narrow interests or skills are a turnoff at Google). Google also wants people with growth potential. The company is expanding so fast that they need to hire people who are capable of being promoted five or six times—it's only, they say, by hiring such overqualified people that they can be sure that the employees will be able to keep up as Google and their own departments expand.

The starting salaries are highly competitive. Experienced engineers start at about $130,000 a year (plus about 1,200 shares of stock options, as noted), and new MBAs can expect between $80,000 and $120,000 per year (with smaller option grants). Most recently, Google had about 10,000 staff members, up from its start a few years ago with just three employees in a rented garage.

Of course, in a company that's grown from 3 employees to 10,000 and from zero value to hundreds of billions of dollars in about 5 years, it may be quibbling to talk about "problems," but there's no doubt that such rapid growth confronts Google's management, and particularly its "people operations" group, with some big challenges. Let's look at these.

For one, Google, as previously noted, is a 24-hour operation, and with engineers and others frequently pulling all-nighters to complete their projects the company needs to provide a package of services and financial benefits that supports that kind of lifestyle, and that helps its employees maintain an acceptable work–life balance.

As another challenge, Google's enormous financial success is a two-edged sword. While Google usually wins the recruitment race when it comes to competing for new employees against competitors like Microsoft or Yahoo!, Google does need some way to stem a rising tide of retirements. Most Googlers are still in their late twenties and early thirties, but many have become so wealthy from their Google stock options that they can afford to retire. One 27-year-old engineer received a million-dollar founder's award for her work on the program for searching desktop computers, and wouldn't think of leaving "except to start her own company." Similarly, a former engineering vice president retired (with his Google stock profits) to pursue his love of astronomy. The engineer who dreamed up Gmail recently retired (at the age of 30).

Another challenge is that the work not only involves long hours but can also be very tense. Google is a very numbers-oriented environment. For example, consider a typical weekly Google user interface design meeting. Marisa Meyer, the company's vice president of search products and user experience, runs the meeting, where her employees work out the look and feel of Google's products. Seated around a conference table are about a dozen Googlers, tapping on laptops. During the 2-hour meeting, Meyer needs to evaluate various design proposals, ranging from minor tweaks to a new product's entire layout. She's previously given each presentation an allotted amount of time, and a large digital clock on the wall ticks off the seconds. The presenters must quickly present their ideas, but also handle questions such as "What do users do if the tab is moved from the side of the page to the top?" Furthermore, it's all about the numbers—no one at Google would ever say, for instance "the tab looks better in red"—you need to prove your point. Presenters must come armed with usability experiment results, showing, for instance, that a certain percent preferred red or some other color. While the presenters are answering these questions as quickly as possible, the digital clock is ticking, and when it hits the allotted time, the presentation must end, and the next team steps up to present. It is a tough and tense environment, and Googlers must have done their homework.

Growth can also undermine the "outlaw band that's changing the world" culture that fostered the services that made Google famous. Even cofounder Sergi Brin agrees that Google risks becoming less "zany" as it grows. To paraphrase one of its top managers, the hard part of any business is keeping that original innovative, small-business feel even as the company grows.

Creating the right culture is especially challenging now that Google is truly global. For example, Google works hard to provide the same financial and service benefits in every place it does business around the world, but it can't exactly match its benefits in every country because of international laws and international taxation issues. Offering the same benefits everywhere is more important than it might initially appear. All those benefits make life easier for Google staff, and help them achieve a work–life balance. Achieving the right work–life balance is the center-piece of Google's culture, but also becomes more challenging as the company grows. On the one hand, Google expects all of its employees to work super hard; on the other hand, it realizes that it needs to help them maintain some sort of balance. As one manager says, Google acknowledges "that we work hard but that work is not everything."

Recruitment is another challenge. While Google certainly doesn't lack applicants, attracting the right applicants is crucial if Google is to continue to grow successfully. Working at Google requires a special set of traits, and screening employees is easier if the company recruits the right people to begin with. For instance, it needs to attract people who are super-bright, love to work, have fun, can handle the stress, and who also have outside interests and flexibility.

As the company grows internationally, it also faces the considerable challenge of recruiting and building staff overseas. For example, Google now is introducing a new vertical market-based structure across Europe, to attract more business advertisers to its search engine. (By vertical market-based structure, Google means focusing on key vertical industry sectors such as travel, retail, automotive, and technology.) To build these industry groupings abroad from scratch, Google promoted its former head of its U.S. financial services group to be the vertical markets director for Europe; he moved there recently. Google is thus looking for heads for each of its vertical industry groups for all of its key European territories. Each of these vertical market heads will have to educate their market sectors (retailing, travel, and so on) so Google can attract new advertisers. Most recently, Google already had about 12 offices across Europe, and its London office had tripled in size to 100 staff in just 2 years.

However, probably the biggest challenge Google faces is gearing up its employee selection system, now that the company must hire thousands of people per year. When Google first started in business, job candidates typically suffered through a dozen or more in-person interviews, and the standards were so high that even applicants with years of great work experience often got turned down if they had just average college grades. But recently, even Google's cofounders have acknowledged to security analysts that setting such an extraordinarily high bar for hiring was holding back Google's expansion. For Google's first few years, one of the company's cofounders interviewed nearly every job candidate before he or she was hired, and even today one of them still reviews the qualifications of everyone before he or she gets a final offer.

The experience of one candidate illustrates what Google is up against. The company interviewed a 24-year-old for a corporate communications job at Google. Google first made contact with the candidate in May, and then, after two phone interviews, invited him to headquarters. There he had separate interviews with about six people and was treated to lunch in a Google cafeteria. The company also had him turn in several "homework" assignments, including a personal statement and a marketing plan. In August, Google invited the candidate back for a second round, which it said would involve another four or five interviews. In the meantime, he decided he'd rather work at a start-up, and accepted another job at a new Web-based instant messaging provider.

Google's new head of human resources, a former GE executive, says that Google is trying to strike the right balance between letting Google and the candidate get to know each other while also moving quickly. To that end, Google recently administered a survey to all of Google's current employees, in an effort to identify the traits that correlate with success at Google. In the survey, employees had to respond to questions relating to about 300 variables, including their performance on standardized tests, how old they were when they first used a computer, and how many foreign languages they speak. The Google survey team then compared the answers against the 30 or 40 job performance factors kept for each employee. They thereby identified clusters of traits that Google might better focus on during the hiring process. Google is also trying to move from the free-form interviews it has had in the past to a more structured process.

Questions

1. What do you think of the idea of Google correlating personal traits from the employee's answers on the survey to their performance, and then using that as the basis for screening job candidates? In other words, is it or is it not a good idea? Explain your answer.

2. The benefits that Google pays obviously represent an enormous expense. Based on what you know about Google and on what you read in this book, how would you defend all these benefits if you're making a presentation to the security analysts who were analyzing Google's performance?

3. If you wanted to hire the brightest people around, how would you go about recruiting and selecting them?

4. To support its growth and expansion strategy, Google wants (among other traits) people who are super-bright, who work hard (often round-the-clock), and who are flexible and maintain a decent work–life balance. List five specific HR policies or practices that you think Google has implemented or should implement to support its strategy, and explain your answer.

5. What sorts of factors do you think Google will have to take into consideration as it tries transferring its culture and reward systems and way of doing business to its operations abroad?

6. Given the sorts of values and culture Google cherishes, briefly describe four specific activities you suggest it pursue during new-employee orientation.

7. *Cross-Cultural Effectiveness Question:* What sorts of factors will Google have to take into consideration as it tries transferring its culture and reward systems and way of doing business to its operations abroad?

Source notes for Google: "Google Brings Vertical Structure to Europe," *New Media Age* (August 4, 2005): 2; Debbie Lovewell, "Employer Profile—Google: Searching for Talent," *Employee Benefits* (October 10, 2005): 66; "Google Looking for Gourmet Chefs," *Internet Week* (August 4, 2005); Douglas Merrill, "Google's 'Googley' Culture Kept Alive by Tech," *eWeek* (April 11, 2006); Robert Hof, "Google Gives Employees Another Option," *BusinessWeek Online* (December 13, 2005); Kevin Delaney, "Google Adjusts Hiring Process as Needs Grow," *Wall Street Journal* (October 23, 2006): B1, B8; Adam Lishinsky, "Search and Enjoy," *Fortune* (January 22, 2007): 70–82.

MUFFLER MAGIC*

Muffler Magic is a fast-growing chain of 25 automobile service centers in Nevada. Originally started 20 years ago as a muffler repair shop by Ronald Brown, the chain expanded rapidly to new locations, and as it did so Muffler Magic also expanded the services it provided, from muffler replacement to oil changes, brake jobs, and engine repair. Today, one can bring an automobile to a Muffler Magic shop for basically any type of service, from tires to mufflers to engine repair.

Auto service is a tough business. The shop owner is basically dependent upon the quality of the service people he or she hires and retains, and the most qualified mechanics find it easy to pick up and leave for a job paying a bit more at a competitor down the road. It's also a business in which productivity is very important. The single largest expense is usually the cost of labor. Auto service dealers generally don't just make up the prices that they charge customers for various repairs; instead, they charge based on standardized industry rates for jobs like changing spark plugs, or repairing a leaky radiator. For instance, if someone brings a car in for a new alternator and the standard number of hours for changing the alternator is 1 hour, but it takes the mechanic 2 hours, the service center's owner may end up making less profit on the transaction.

Quality is a persistent problem as well. For example, "rework" has recently been a problem at Muffler Magic. A customer recently brought her car to a Muffler Magic to have the car's brake pads replaced, which the store did for her. Unfortunately, when she drove off, she only got about two blocks before she discovered that she had no brake power at all. It was simply fortuitous that she was going so slowly she was able to stop her car by slowly rolling up against a parking bumper. It subsequently turned out that the mechanic who replaced the brake pads had failed to properly tighten a fitting on the hydraulic brake tubes, and the brake fluid had run out, leaving the car with no braking power. In a similar problem the month before, a (different) mechanic replaced a fan belt but forgot to refill the radiator with fluid; that customer's car overheated before he got four blocks away, and Muffler Magic had to replace the

---

*© Gary Dessler, Ph.D.

whole engine. Of course problems like these not only diminish the profitability of the company's profits but, repeated many times over, have the potential for ruining Muffler Magic's word-of-mouth reputation.

Organizationally, Muffler Magic employs about 300 people total, and Ron runs his company with eight managers, including Mr. Brown as president, a controller, a purchasing director, a marketing director, and the human resource manager. He also has three regional managers to whom the eight or nine service center managers in each area of Nevada report. Over the past 2 years, as the company has opened new service centers, company-wide profits have diminished rather than gone up. In part, these diminishing profits reflect the fact that Ron Brown has found it increasingly difficult to manage his growing operation. ("Your reach is exceeding your grasp" is how Ron's wife puts it.)

The company has only the most basic HR systems in place. It uses an application form that the human resource manager modified from one that she downloaded from the Web, and it uses standard employee status change request forms, sign-on forms, I-9 forms, and so on that it purchased from a human resource management supply house. Training is entirely on-the-job. It expects the experienced technicians that it hires to come to the job fully trained; to that end, the service center managers generally ask candidates for these jobs basic behavioral questions that hopefully provide a window into these applicants' skills. However, most of the other technicians hired to do jobs like rotating tires, fixing brake pads, and replacing mufflers are untrained and inexperienced. They are to be trained by either the service center manager or by more experienced technicians, on-the-job.

Ron Brown faces several HR-type problems. One, as he says, is that he faces the "tyranny of the immediate" when it comes to hiring employees. While it's fine to say that he should be carefully screening each employee and checking references and work ethic, from a practical point of view, with 25 centers to run, the centers' managers usually just hire anyone who seems to be breathing, as long as they can answer some basic interview questions about auto repair, such as "What do you think the problem is if a 2006 Camry is overheating, and what would you do about it?"

Employee safety is also a problem. An automobile service center may not be the most dangerous type of workplace, but it is potentially dangerous. Employees are dealing with sharp tools, greasy floors, greasy tools, extremely hot temperatures (for instance, on mufflers and engines), and fast-moving engine parts including fan blades. There are some basic things that a service manager can do to ensure more safety, such as insisting that all oil spills be cleaned up immediately. However, from a practical point of view, there are a few ways to get around many of the problems—such as when the technician must check out an engine while it is running.

With Muffler Magic's profits going down instead of up, Brown's human resource manager has taken the position that the main problem is financial. As he says, "You get what you pay for" when it comes to employees, and if you compensate technicians better than your competitors then you get better technicians, ones who do their jobs better and stay longer with the company—and then profits will rise. So, the HR manager scheduled a meeting between himself, Ron Brown, and a professor of business who teaches compensation management at a local university. The HR manager has asked this professor to spend about a week looking at each of the service centers, analyzing the situation, and coming up with a compensation plan that will address Muffler Magic's quality and productivity problems. At this meeting, the professor makes three basic recommendations for changing the company's compensation policies.

Number one, she says that she has found that Muffler Magic suffers from what she calls "presenteeism"—in other words, employees drag themselves into work even when they're sick, because the company does not pay them if they are out; there are no sick days. In just a few days the professor couldn't properly quantify how much Muffler Magic is losing to presenteeism. However, from what she could see at each shop, there are typically one or two technicians working with various maladies like the cold or flu, and it seemed to her that each of these people was probably really only working about half of the time (although they were getting paid for the whole day). So, for 25 service centers per week, Muffler Magic could well be losing 125 or 130 personnel days per week of work. The professor suggests that Muffler Magic start allowing everyone to take three paid sick days per year, a reasonable suggestion. However, as Ron Brown points out, "Right now, we're only losing about half a day's pay for each employee who comes in and who works unproductively; with your suggestion, won't we lose the whole day?" The professor says she'll ponder that one.

Second, the professor also recommends putting the technicians on a skill-for-pay plan. Basically, here's what she suggests. Give each technician a letter grade (A through E) based upon that technician's particular skill level and abilities. An "A" technician is a team leader and needs to show that he or she has excellent diagnostic troubleshooting skills, and the ability to supervise and direct other technicians. At the other extreme, an "E" technician would be a new apprentice with little technical training. The other technicians fall in between those two levels, based on their individual skills and abilities.

In the professor's system, the "A" technician or team leader would assign and supervise all work done within his or her area but generally not do any mechanical repairs him or herself. The team leader does the diagnostic troubleshooting, supervises and trains the other technicians, and test drives the car before it goes back to the customer. Under this plan, every technician receives a guaranteed hourly wage within a certain range, for instance:

A tech = $25–$30 an hour

B tech = $20–$25 an hour

C tech = $15–$20 an hour

D tech = $10–$15 an hour

E tech = $8–$10 an hour

Third, to directly address the productivity issue, the professor recommends that at the end of each day, each service manager calculate each technician-team's productivity for the day and then at the end of each week. She suggests posting the running productivity total conspicuously for daily viewing. Then, the technicians as a group get weekly cash bonuses based upon their productivity. To calculate productivity, the professor recommends dividing the total labor hours billed by the total labor hours paid to technicians, or total labor hours billed, *divided by* total hours paid to technicians.

Having done some homework, the professor says that the national average for labor productivity is currently about 60%, and that only the best-run service centers achieve 85% or greater. By her rough calculations, Muffler Magic was attaining about industry average (about 60%—in other words, it was billing for only about 60 hours for each 100 hours that it actually had to pay technicians to do the jobs). (Of course, this was not entirely the technicians' fault. Technicians get time off for breaks, and for lunch, and if a particular service center simply didn't have enough business on a particular day or during a particular week, then several technicians may well sit around idly waiting for the next car to come in.) The professor recommends setting a labor efficiency goal of 80% and posting each team's daily productivity results in the workplace to provide them with additional feedback. She recommends that if at the end of a week the team is able to boost its productivity ratio from the current 60% to 80%, then that team would get an additional 10% weekly pay bonus. After that, for every 5% boost of increased productivity above 80%, technicians would receive an additional 5% weekly bonus. (So, if a technician's normal weekly pay is $400, that employee would receive an extra $40 at the end of the week when his team moves from 60% productivity to 80% productivity.)

After the meeting, Ron Brown thanked the professor for her recommendations and told her he would think about it and get back to her. After the meeting, on the drive home, Ron was pondering what to do. He had to decide whether to institute the professor's sick leave policy, and whether to implement the professor's incentive and compensation plan. Before implementing anything, however, he wanted to make sure he understood the context in which he was making his decision. For example, did Muffler Magic really have an incentive pay problem, or were the problems more broad? Furthermore, how, if at all, would the professor's incentive plan impact the quality of the work that the teams were doing? And should Muffler Magic really start paying for sick days? Ron Brown had a lot to think about.

Questions

1. Write a one-page summary outline listing three or four recommendations you would make with respect to each HR function (recruiting, selection, training, and so on) that you think Ron Brown should be addressing with his HR manager now.

2. Develop a 10-question structured interview form Ron Brown's service center managers can use to interview experienced technicians.
3. If you were Ron Brown, would you implement the professor's recommendation addressing the presenteeism problem, in other words, start paying for sick days? Why or why not?
4. If you were advising Ron Brown, would you recommend that he implement the professor's skill-based pay and incentive pay plans as is? Why? Would you implement it with modifications? If you would modify it, be specific about what you think those modifications should be, and why.
5. *Quantitative Analysis Question:* Create a spreadsheet showing the titles of the main measurable factors owner Ron Brown should take into consideration in analyzing whether to take the professor's pay plan advice.

Based generally on actual facts, but Muffler Magic is a fictitious company. This case is based largely on information in Drew Paras, "The Pay Factor: Technicians' Salaries Can Be the Largest Expense in a Server Shop, as Well as the Biggest Headache. Here's How One Shop Owner Tackled the Problem," *Motor Age* (November 2003): 76–79; see also Jennifer Pellet, "Health Care Crisis," *Chief Executive* (June 2004): 56–61; "Firms Press to Quantify, Control Presenteeism," *Employee Benefits* (December 1, 2002).

BP TEXAS CITY[*]

In March 2005, an explosion and fire at British Petroleum's (BP) Texas City, Texas, refinery killed 15 people and injured 500 people in the worst U.S. industrial accident in more than 10 years. The disaster triggered three investigations, one internal investigation by BP, one by the U.S. Chemical Safety Board, and an independent investigation chaired by former U.S. Secretary of State James Baker and an 11-member panel, organized at BP's request.

To put the results of these three investigations into context, it's useful to understand that under its current management, BP has pursued, for the past 10 or so years, a strategy emphasizing cost-cutting and profitability. The basic conclusion of the investigations was that cost-cutting helped compromise safety at the Texas City refinery. It's useful to consider each investigation's findings.

The Chemical Safety Board's (CSB) investigation, according to Carol Merritt, the board's chairwoman, showed that "BP's global management was aware of problems with maintenance, spending, and infrastructure well before March 2005." Apparently, faced with numerous earlier accidents, BP did make some safety improvements. However, it focused primarily on emphasizing personal employee safety behaviors and procedural compliance, thereby reducing safety accident rates. The problem (according to the CSB) was that "catastrophic safety risks remained." For example, according to the CSB, "unsafe and antiquated equipment designs were left in place, and unacceptable deficiencies in preventive maintenance were tolerated." Basically, the CSB found that BP's budget cuts led to a progressive deterioration of safety at the Texas City refinery. Said Ms. Merritt, "In an aging facility like Texas City, it is not responsible to cut budgets related to safety and maintenance without thoroughly examining the impact on the risk of a catastrophic accident."

Looking at specifics, the CSB said that a 2004 internal audit of 35 BP business units, including Texas City (BP's largest refinery), found significant safety gaps they all had in common, including a lack of leadership competence and "systemic underlying issues" such as a widespread tolerance of noncompliance with basic safety rules and poor monitoring of safety management systems and processes. Ironically, the CSB found that BP's accident prevention effort at Texas City had achieved a 70% reduction in worker injuries in the year before the explosion. Unfortunately, this simply meant that individual employees were having fewer accidents. The larger, more fundamental problem was that the potentially explosive situation inherent in the depreciating machinery remained.

The CSB found that the Texas City explosion followed a pattern of years of major accidents at the facility. In fact, there had apparently been an average of one employee death every 16 months at the plant for the last 30 years. The CSB found that the equipment directly involved in

[*]© Gary Dessler, Ph.D.

the most recent explosion was an obsolete design already phased out in most refineries and chemical plants, and that key pieces of its instrumentation were not working. There had also been previous instances where flammable vapors were released from the same unit in the 10 years prior to the explosion. In 2003, an external audit had referred to the Texas City refinery's infrastructure and assets as "poor" and found what it referred to as a "checkbook mentality," one in which budgets were not sufficient to manage all the risks. In particular, the CSB found that BP had implemented a 25% cut on fixed costs between 1998 and 2000 and that this adversely impacted maintenance expenditures and net expenditures, and refinery infrastructure. Going on, the CSB found that, in 2004, there were three major accidents at the refinery that killed three workers.

BP's own internal report concluded that the problems at Texas City were not of recent origin, and instead were years in the making. It said BP was taking steps to address them. Its investigation found "no evidence of anyone consciously or intentionally taking actions or making decisions that put others at risk." Said BP's report, "The underlying reasons for the behaviors and actions displayed during the incident are complex, and the team has spent much time trying to understand them—it is evident that they were many years in the making and will require concerted and committed actions to address." BP's report concluded that there were five underlying causes for the massive explosion:

- The working environment had eroded to one characterized by resistance to change, and a lack of trust.
- Safety, performance, and risk reduction priorities had not been set and consistently reinforced by management.
- Changes in the "complex organization" led to a lack of clear accountabilities and poor communication.
- A poor level of hazard awareness and understanding of safety resulted in workers accepting levels of risk that were considerably higher than at comparable installations.
- A lack of adequate early warning systems for problems, and no independent means of understanding the deteriorating standards at the plant.

The report from the BP-initiated but independent 11-person panel chaired by former U.S. Secretary of State James Baker contained specific conclusions and recommendations. The Baker panel looked at BP's corporate safety oversight, the corporate safety culture, and the process safety management systems at BP at the Texas City plant as well as at BP's other refineries.

Basically, the Baker panel concluded that BP had not provided effective safety process leadership and had not established safety as a core value at the five refineries it looked at (including Texas City).

Like the CSB, the Baker panel found that BP had emphasized personal safety in recent years and had in fact improved personal safety performance, but had not emphasized the overall safety process, thereby mistakenly interpreting "improving personal injury rates as an indication of acceptable process safety performance at its U.S. refineries." In fact, the Baker panel went on, by focusing on these somewhat misleading improving personal injury rates, BP created a false sense of confidence that it was properly addressing process safety risks. It also found that the safety culture at Texas City did not have the positive, trusting, open environment that a proper safety culture required. The Baker panel's other findings included:

- BP did not always ensure that adequate resources were effectively allocated to support or sustain a high level of process safety performance.
- BP's refinery personnel are "overloaded" by corporate initiatives.
- Operators and maintenance personnel work high rates of overtime.
- BP tended to have a short-term focus and its decentralized management system and entrepreneurial culture delegated substantial discretion to refinery plant managers "without clearly defining process safety expectations, responsibilities, or accountabilities."
- There was no common, unifying process safety culture among the five refineries.
- The company's corporate safety management system did not make sure there was timely compliance with internal process safety standards and programs.

- BP's executive management either did not receive refinery specific information that showed that process safety deficiencies existed at some of the plants, or did not effectively respond to any information it did receive.[1]

The Baker panel made several safety recommendations for BP, including these:

1. The company's corporate management must provide leadership on process safety.
2. The company should establish a process safety management system that identifies, reduces, and manages the process safety risks of the refineries.
3. The company should make sure its employees have an appropriate level of process safety knowledge and expertise.
4. The company should involve "relevant stakeholders" in developing a positive, trusting, and open process safety culture at each refinery.
5. BP should clearly define expectations and strengthen accountability for process safety performance.
6. BP should better coordinate its process safety support for the refining line organization.
7. BP should develop an integrated set of leading and lagging performance indicators for effectively monitoring process safety performance.
8. BP should establish and implement an effective system to audit process safety performance.
9. The company's board should monitor the implementation of the panel's recommendations and the ongoing process safety performance of the refineries.
10. BP should transform into a recognized industry leader in process safety management.

In making its recommendations, the panel singled out the company's chief executive at the time, Lord Browne, by saying, "In hindsight, the panel believes if Browne had demonstrated comparable leadership on and commitment to process safety [as he did for responding to climate change] that would have resulted in a higher level of safety at refineries."

Overall, the Baker panel found that BP's top management had not provided "effective leadership" on safety. It found that the failings went to the very top of the organization, to the company's chief executive, and to several of his top lieutenants. The Baker panel emphasized the importance of top management commitment, saying, for instance, that "it is imperative that BP leadership set the process safety tone at the top of the organization and establish appropriate expectations regarding process safety performance." It also said BP "has not provided effective leadership in making certain its management and U.S. refining workforce understand what is expected of them regarding process safety performance."

Lord Browne, the chief executive, stepped down about a year after the explosion. About the same time, some BP shareholders were calling for the company's executives and board of directors to have their bonuses more closely tied to the company's safety and environmental performance in the wake of Texas City. And all this was transpiring several years before BP's Deepwater Horizon rig exploded and burned in the Gulf of Mexico in 2010.

Questions

1. The textbook defines ethics as "the principles of conduct governing an individual or a group," and specifically as the standards one uses to decide what their conduct should be. To what extent do you believe that what happened at BP is as much a breakdown in the company's ethical systems as it is in its safety systems, and how would you defend your conclusion?
2. Are the Occupational Safety and Health Administration's standards, policies, and rules aimed at addressing problems like the ones that apparently existed at the Texas City plant? If so, how would you explain the fact that problems like these could have continued for so many years?
3. Since there were apparently at least three deaths in the year prior to the major explosion, and an average of about one employee death per 16 months for the previous 10 years, how

---

[1]These findings and the following suggestions are based on "BP Safety Report Finds Company's Process Safety Culture Ineffective," *Global Refining & Fuels Report* (January 17, 2007).

would you account for the fact that mandatory OSHA inspections missed these glaring sources of potential catastrophic events?

4. The textbook lists numerous suggestions for "how to prevent accidents." Based on what you know about the Texas City explosion, what do you say Texas City tells you about the most important three steps an employer can take to prevent accidents?

5. Based on what you learned in this text, would you make any additional recommendations to BP over and above those recommendations made by the Baker panel and the CSB? If so, what would those recommendations be?

6. Explain specifically how strategic human resource management at BP seems to have supported the company's broader strategic aims. What does this say about the advisability of always linking human resource strategy to a company's strategic aims?

7. *Change Management Question:* In 2007 Lord Browne stepped down as BP's CEO, and the firm's president took charge. Based on the case, what organizational changes should BP make now and how would you suggest the new CEO go about executing them?

8. *Ethical Decision-Making Question:* The textbook defines ethics as "the principles of conduct governing an individual or a group," and specifically as the standards one uses to decide what their conduct should be. To what extent do you believe that what happened at BP is as much a breakdown in the company's ethical systems as it is in its safety systems, and how would you defend your conclusion? What would you have done differently, ethically? What should the new CEO do now?

9. *Managing Organizational Culture Question:* Based on the case, how would you character-ize the organizational culture at BP company-wide and at its refineries, and what exactly would you do to change that culture (assuming it needs changing)?

10. If you had been CEO of BP between 2005 and 2010, what safety related steps would you have taken to make sure that a disaster (such as 2010's Gulf of Mexico explosion) did not take place? Why, do you think, that after the Texas City disaster such steps were not taken?

Source notes for BP Texas City: Sheila McNulty, "BP Knew of Safety Problems, Says Report," *The Financial Times* (October 31, 2006): 1; "CBS: Documents Show BP Was Aware of Texas City Safety Problems," *World Refining & Fuels Today* (October 30, 2006); "BP Safety Report Finds Company's Process Safety Culture Ineffective," *Global Refining & Fuels Report* (January 17, 2007); "BP Safety Record under Attack," *Europe Intelligence Wire* (January 17, 2007); Mark Hofmann, "BP Slammed for Poor Leadership on Safety, Oil Firm Agrees to Act on Review Panel's Recommendations," *Business Intelligence* (January 22, 2007): 3; "Call for Bonuses to Include Link with Safety Performance," *The Guardian* (January 18, 2007): 24.

Glossary

action learning A training technique by which management trainees are allowed to work full time analyzing and solving problems in other departments.

adverse impact The overall impact of employer practices that result in significantly higher percentages of members of minorities and other protected groups being rejected for employment, placement, or promotion.

affirmative action Steps that are taken for the purpose of eliminating the present effects of past discrimination.

Age Discrimination in Employment Act of 1967 The act prohibiting age discrimination and specifically protecting individuals over 40 years old.

agency shop A form of union security in which employees who do not belong to the union must still pay union dues on the assumption that union efforts benefit all workers.

Americans with Disabilities Act (ADA) The act requiring employers to make reasonable accommodations for disabled employees; it prohibits discrimination against disabled persons.

application form The form that provides information on education, prior work record, and skills.

application service provider An online vendor that uses its own servers and systems to manage tasks for employers, such as recruitment or training. In recruitment, they compile application information, prescreen applicants, and help the employer rank applicants and set interview appointments.

arbitration The most definitive type of third-party intervention, in which the arbitrator often has the power to determine and dictate the settlement terms.

authority The right to make decisions, direct others' work, and give orders.

authorization cards In order to petition for a union election, the union must show that at least 30% of employees may be interested in being unionized. Employees indicate this interest by signing authorization cards.

balanced scorecard Refers to a process for assigning financial and nonfinancial goals to the chain of activities required for achieving the company's strategic aims, and for continuously monitoring results.

bargaining unit The group of employees the union will be authorized to represent.

behavior modeling A training technique in which trainees are first shown good management techniques in a film, are then asked to play roles in a simulated situation, and are then given feedback and praise by their supervisor.

behavior modification Using contingent rewards or punishment to change behavior.

benefits Indirect financial payments given to employees. They may include health and life insurance, vacation, pension, education plans, and discounts on company products, for instance.

bona fide occupational qualification (BFOQ) Requirement that an employee be of a certain religion, sex, or national origin where that is reasonably necessary to the organization's normal operation. Specified by the 1964 Civil Rights Act.

boycott The combined refusal by employees and other interested parties to buy or use the employer's products.

burnout The total depletion of physical and mental resources caused by excessive striving to reach an unrealistic work-related goal.

business necessity Justification for an otherwise discriminatory employment practice, provided there is an overriding legitimate business purpose.

career The occupational positions a person has had over many years.

career development The lifelong series of activities that contribute to a person's career exploration, establishment, success, and fulfillment.

career management A process for enabling the employees to better understand and develop their career skills and interests, and to use the skills and interests most effectively both within the company and, if necessary, after they leave the firm.

career planning The deliberate process through which someone becomes aware of personal skills, interests, knowledge, motivations, and other characteristics; and establishes action plans to attain specific goals.

case study method A development method in which the manager is presented with a written description of an organizational problem to diagnose and solve.

central tendency The tendency to rate all employees about average.

channel assembly Having a supplier or distributor perform some of the steps required to create the company's product or service.

citations Summons informing employers and employees of the regulations and standards that have been violated in the workplace.

Civil Rights Act of 1964, Title VII Law that makes it unlawful practice for an employer to discriminate against any individual with respect to hiring, compensation, terms, conditions, or privileges of employment because of race, color, religion, sex, or nation.

Civil Rights Act of 1991 (CRA 1991) This act places burden of proof back on employers and permits compensatory and punitive damages.

closed shop A form of union security in which the company can hire only union members. This was outlawed in 1947 for interstate commerce, but still exists in some industries (such as printing).

coaching Educating, instructing, and training subordinates.

coaching/understudy method An experienced worker or supervisor trains the employee on the job.

co-determination The right to a voice in setting company policies; workers generally elect representatives to the supervisory board.

collective bargaining The process through which representatives of management and the union meet to negotiate a labor agreement.

compensable factors Fundamental, compensable elements of a job, such as skills, effort, responsibility, and working conditions.

competency model A graphic model that consolidates, usually in one diagram, a precise overview of the competencies (the knowledge, skills, and behaviors) someone would need to do a job well.

competitive advantage The basis for differentiation over competitors and thus for hoping to claim certain customers.

competitive strategy Identifies how to build and strengthen the business's long-term competitive position in the marketplace.

computer-based training Trainees use a computer-based system to interactively increase their knowledge or skills.

content validity A test that is *content valid* is one in which the test contains a fair sample of the tasks and skills actually needed for the job in question.

controlled experimentation Formal methods for testing the effectiveness of a training program, preferably with before-and-after tests and a control group.

corporate strategy Identifies the sorts of businesses that will comprise the company and the ways in which these businesses relate to each other.

criterion validity A type of validity based on showing that scores on the test (*predictors*) are related to job performance (*criterion*).

critical incident method Keeping a record of uncommonly good or undesirable examples of an employee's work-related behavior and reviewing it with the employee at predetermined times.

defined benefit plan A plan that contains a formula for specifying retirement benefits.

defined contribution plan A plan in which the employer's contribution to employees' retirement or savings funds is specified.

digital dashboard Presents the manager with desktop graphs and charts, so he or she gets a picture of where the company has been and where it's going, in terms of each activity in the strategy map.

discipline A procedure that corrects or punishes a subordinate for violating a rule or procedure.

discrimination Taking specific actions toward or against the person based on the person's group.

dismissal Involuntary termination of an employee's employment with the firm.

disparate impact An unintentional disparity between the proportion of a protected group applying for a position and the proportion getting the job.

disparate treatment An intentional disparity between the proportion of a protected group and the proportion getting the job.

diversity Having a workforce comprised of two or more groups of employees with various racial, ethnic, gender, cultural, national origin, handicap, age, and religious backgrounds.

downsizing Refers to the process of reducing, usually dramatically, the number of people employed by the firm.

economic strike A strike that results from a failure to agree on the terms of a contract that involve wages, benefits, and other conditions of employment.

Employee Assistance Program (EAP) A formal employer program for providing employees with counseling and/or treatment programs for problems such as alcoholism, gambling, or stress.

employee compensation All forms of pay or rewards going to employees and arising from their employment.

employee orientation A procedure for providing new employees with basic background information about the firm.

Employee Retirement Income Security Act (ERISA) Signed into law by President Ford in 1974 to require that pension rights be vested, and protected by a government agency, Pension Benefits Guarantee Corporation.

employee stock ownership plan (ESOP) A corporation contributes shares of its own stock to a trust to purchase company stock for employees. The trust distributes the stock to employees upon retirement or separation from service.

employment (or personnel) planning The process of formulating plans to fill the employer's future openings, based on (1) projecting open positions, and (2) deciding whether to fill these with inside or outside candidates.

Equal Employment Opportunity Commission (EEOC) The commission, created by Title VII, empowered to investigate job discrimination complaints and sue on behalf of complainants.

Equal Pay Act of 1963 An amendment to the Fair Labor Standards Act designed to require equal pay for women doing the same work as men.

ethics The study of standards of conduct and moral judgment; also the standards of right conduct.

ethnocentric A management philosophy that leads to the creation of home market-oriented staffing decisions.

executive support systems Provide top managers with information for making decisions on matters such as 5-year plans.

exit interviews Interviews conducted by the employer immediately prior to the employee leaving the firm with the aim of better understanding what the employee thinks about the company.

expatriates Non-citizens of the country in which they are working.

expectancy A person's expectation that his or her effort will lead to performance.

fact finder In labor relations, a neutral party who studies the issues in a dispute and makes a public recommendation for a reasonable settlement.

Fair Labor Standards Act Congress passed this act in 1938 to provide for minimum wages, maximum hours, overtime pay, and child labor protection. The law has been amended many times and covers most employees.

flexible benefits plan Individualized plans allowed by employers to accommodate employee preferences for benefits.

functional strategies Identifies the basic courses of action that each department will pursue in order to help the business attain its competitive goals.

gainsharing plan An incentive plan that engages employees in a common effort to achieve productivity objectives and share the gains.

gender harassment A form of hostile environment harassment that appears to be motivated by hostility toward individuals who violate gender ideals.

gender-role stereotypes The tendency to associate women with certain (frequently non-managerial) jobs.

geocentric A staffing policy that seeks the best people for key jobs throughout the organization, regardless of nationality.

good-faith bargaining A term that means both parties are communicating and negotiating and that proposals are being matched with counterproposals, with both parties making every reasonable effort to arrive at agreements. It does not mean that either party is compelled to agree to a proposal.

Griggs v. Duke Power Company Supreme Court case in which the plaintiff argued that his employer's requirement that coal handlers be high-school graduates was unfairly discriminatory. In finding for the plaintiff, the Court ruled that discrimination need not be overt to be illegal, that employment practices must be related to job performance, and that the burden of proof is on the employer to show that hiring standards are job related.

guaranteed fair treatment Employer programs aimed at ensuring that all employees are treated fairly, generally by providing formalized, well-documented, and highly publicized vehicles through which employees can appeal any eligible issues.

high-performance work system An integrated set of human resources policies and practices that together produce superior employee performance.

host country nationals Citizens of the country in which the multinational company has its headquarters.

HR audit An analysis by which an organization measures where it currently stands and determines what it has to accomplish to improve its HR function.

HR Scorecard Measures the HR function's effectiveness and efficiency in producing employee behaviors needed to achieve the company's strategic goals.

human resource information systems Interrelated components working together to collect, process, store, and disseminate information to support decision making, coordination, control, analysis, and visualization of an organization's human resource management activities.

human resource management The process of acquiring, training, appraising, and compensating employees, and of attending to their labor relations, health and safety, and fairness concerns.

human resource metric The quantitative measure of some human resource management yardstick such as employee turnover, hours of training per employee, or qualified applicants per position.

illegal bargaining items Items in collective bargaining that are forbidden by law; for example, the clause agreeing to

hire "union members exclusively" would be illegal in a right-to-work state.

improvisation A form of management training in which the trainees learn skills such as openness and creativity by playing games that require that they improvise answers and solutions.

incentive plan A compensation plan that ties pay to performance.

information system The interrelated people, data, technology, and organizational procedures a company uses to collect, process, store, and disseminate information.

in-house development centers A company-based facility for exposing current or prospective managers to exercises to develop improved management skills.

instrumentality The perceived relationship between successful performance and obtaining the reward.

insubordination Willful disregard or disobedience of the boss's authority or legitimate orders.

international human resource management The human resource management concepts and techniques employers use to manage the human resource challenges of their international operations.

Internet-based purchasing Internet-based purchasing that automatically monitors the customer's needs online and produces the necessary products, shipping documents, and bills.

interview A procedure designed to solicit information from a person's oral responses to oral inquiries.

job analysis The procedure for determining the duties and skill requirements of a job and the kind of person who should be hired for it.

job description A list of a job's duties, responsibilities, reporting relationships, working conditions, and supervisory responsibilities—one product of a job analysis.

job evaluation A formal and systematic comparison of jobs to determine the worth of one job relative to another.

job posting Posting notices of job openings on company bulletin boards as a recruiting method.

job rotation A management training technique that involves moving a trainee from department to department to broaden his or her experience and identify strengths and weaknesses.

job specification A list of a job's "human requirements," that is, the requisite education, skills, personality, and so on—a product of a job analysis.

Landrum-Griffin Act A law aimed at protecting union members from possible wrongdoing on the part of their unions.

layoff A situation in which employees are told there is no work for them but that management intends to recall them when work is again available.

lifelong learning Provides employees with continuing learning experiences over their tenure with the firm, with the aim of ensuring they have the opportunity to obtain the knowledge and skills they need to do their jobs effectively.

line manager A manager who is authorized to direct the work of subordinates and responsible for accomplishing the organization's goals.

locals Employees that work for the company abroad and are citizens of the countries where they are working, also known as **host country nationals**.

lockout A refusal by the employer to provide opportunities to work.

management assessment centers A facility in which management candidates are asked to make decisions in hypothetical situations and are scored on their performance.

management development Any attempt to improve current or future management performance by imparting knowledge, changing attitudes, or increasing skills.

management game A development technique in which teams of managers compete by making computerized decisions regarding realistic but simulated situations.

management information systems Help managers make better decisions by producing standardized, summarized reports on a regular basis.

management process The five basic functions of planning, organizing, staffing, leading, and controlling.

manager Someone who is responsible for accomplishing the organization's goals, and who does so by managing the efforts of the organization's people.

managing To perform five basic functions: planning, organizing, staffing, leading, and controlling.

mandatory bargaining items Items in collective bargaining that a party must bargain over if they are introduced by the other party—for example, pay.

mediation Labor relations intervention in which a neutral third party tries to assist the principals in reaching agreement.

merit pay (merit raise) Any salary increase awarded to an employee based on his or her individual performance.

mission statement Spells out who the company is, what it does, and where it's headed.

national emergency strikes Strikes that might "imperil the national health and safety."

National Labor Relations Board (NLRB) The agency created by the Wagner Act to investigate unfair labor practice charges and to provide for secret-ballot elections and majority rule in determining whether or not a firm's employees want a union.

negligent hiring Hiring workers with criminal records or other such problems without proper safeguards.

Norris-LaGuardia Act This law marked the beginning of the era of strong encouragement of unions and guaranteed to each employee the right to bargain collectively "free from interference, restraint, or coercion."

Occupational Safety and Health Act The law passed by Congress in 1970 "to assure so far as possible every working man and woman in the nation safe and healthful working conditions and to preserve our human resources."

Occupational Safety and Health Administration (OSHA) The agency created within the Department of Labor to set safety and health standards for almost all workers in the United States.

Office of Federal Contract Compliance Programs (OFCCP) The office responsible for implementing executive orders and ensuring compliance of federal contractors.

offshoring Having local employees abroad do jobs that the firm's domestic employees previously did in-house.

organization A group consisting of people with formally assigned roles who work together to achieve the organization's goals.

organizational culture The characteristic values, traditions, and behaviors a company's employees share.

organizational development (OD) A development method aimed at changing the attitudes, values, and beliefs of employees so that employees can improve the organization.

outplacement counseling A systematic process by which a terminated person is trained and counseled in the techniques of self-appraisal and securing a new position.

Patient Protection and Affordable Care Act (PPACA) The act contains various provisions, for instance expanding Medicaid eligibility, subsidizing health insurance premiums, and encouraging businesses to provide health care benefits.

performance analysis Verifying that there is a performance deficiency and determining whether that deficiency should be rectified through training or through some other means (such as transferring the employee).

performance appraisal Evaluating an employee's current and/or past performance relative to his or her performance standards.

performance management The process through which companies ensure that employees are working toward organizational goals. It includes practices through which the manager defines the employee's goals and work, develops the employee's skills and capabilities, evaluates the person's goal-directed behavior, and then rewards him or her in a fashion consistent with the company's and the person's needs.

personnel replacement charts Company records showing present performance and promotability of inside candidates for the firm's most important positions.

piecework A system of incentive pay tying pay to the number of items processed by each individual worker.

polycentric A management philosophy oriented toward staffing positions with local talent.

portability Making it easier for employees who leave the firm prior to retirement to take their accumulated pension funds with them.

preferential shop A type of union security in which union members get preference in hiring, but the employer can still hire nonunion members.

Pregnancy Discrimination Act (PDA) An amendment to Title VII of the Civil Rights Act that prohibits sex discrimination based on "pregnancy, childbirth, or related medical conditions."

profit-sharing plan A plan whereby most employees share in the company's profits.

protected class Persons such as older workers and women protected by equal opportunity laws including Title VII.

qualifications inventories Manual or computerized records listing employees' education, career and development interests, languages, special skills, and so on to be used in identifying inside candidates for promotion.

ranking method The simplest method of job evaluation that involves ranking each job relative to all other jobs, usually based on a job's overall difficulty.

ratio analysis A forecasting technique that involves analyzing and extrapolating the ratio of a dependent variable, such as sales persons required, with an independent variable, such as sales.

reliability The characteristic that refers to the consistency of scores obtained by the same person when retested with the identical or equivalent tests.

right to work The public policy in a number of states that prohibits union security of any kind.

salary (or compensation) survey A survey aimed at determining prevailing pay rates. Provides specific wage rates for specific jobs.

Scanlon plan An incentive plan developed in 1937 by Joseph Scanlon and designed to encourage cooperation, involvement, and sharing of benefits.

scatter plot A graphical method used to help identify the relationship between two quantitative variables.

sensitivity training A method for increasing employees' insights into their own behavior through candid discussions in groups led by special trainers.

severance pay A one-time payment employers provide when terminating an employee.

sexual harassment Harassment on the basis of sex that has the purpose or effect of substantially interfering with a person's work performance or creating an intimidating, hostile, or offensive work environment.

staff manager A manager who assists and advises line managers.

stock option The right to purchase a stated number of shares of company stock at a set price at some time in the future.

strategic human resource management Linking HRM policies and practices with strategic goals and objectives in order to improve business performance.

strategic management The process of identifying and executing the organization's mission by matching its capabilities with the demands of its environment.

strategic plan The company's plan for how it will match its internal strengths and weaknesses with external opportunities and threats in order to maintain a competitive advantage.

strategic planning The manager formulates specific strategies to take the company from where it is now to where he or she wants it to be.

strategy The company's long-term plan for how it will balance its internal strengths and weaknesses with its external opportunities and threats to maintain a competitive advantage.

strategy map A graphical tool that summarizes the chain of activities that contribute to a company's success.

strategy-based metrics Metrics that specifically focus on measuring the activities that contribute to achieving a company's strategic aims.

structured situation interview A series of job-relevant questions with predetermined answers that interviewers ask of all applicants for the job.

supplier partnering Having a limited number of suppliers, so as to build relationships that improve quality and reliability, rather than just to improve costs.

supply chain Refers to all of a company's suppliers, manufacturers, distributors, and customers, and to the interactions among them.

supply chain management The integration of the activities that procure materials, transform them into intermediate goods and final product, and deliver them to customers.

survey feedback A method that involves surveying employees' attitudes and providing feedback to facilitate problems being solved by the managers and employees.

sympathy strike A strike that takes place when one union strikes in support of another union's strike.

Taft-Hartley Act (Labor Management Relations Act) A law prohibiting union unfair labor practices and enumerating the rights of employees as union members. It also enumerates the rights of employers.

talent management The end-to-end process of planning, recruiting, developing, managing, and compensating employees throughout the organization.

task analysis A detailed study of a job to identify the skills required so that an appropriate training program may be instituted.

team building Improving the effectiveness of teams through the use of consultants and team-building meetings.

terminate at will The idea, based in law, that the employment relationship can be terminated at will by either the employer or the employee for any reason.

termination interview The interview in which an employee is informed of the fact that he or she has been dismissed.

test validity The accuracy with which a test, interview, and so on measures what it purports to measure or fulfills the function it was designed to fill.

third-country nationals Citizens of a country other than the parent or host country.

Title VII of the 1964 Civil Rights Act The section of the act that says an employer cannot discriminate on the basis of race, color, religion, sex, or national origin with respect to employment.

training The process of teaching new employees the basic skills they need to perform their jobs.

transaction-processing systems Provide the company's managers and accountants with detailed information about short-term, daily activities, such as accounts payables, tax liabilities, and order status.

transparency Giving supply chain partners easy access to information about details like demand, inventory levels, and status of inbound and outbound shipments, usually through a Web-based portal.

trend analysis Study of a firm's past employment needs over a period of years to predict future needs.

unfair labor practice strike A strike aimed at protesting illegal conduct by the employer.

union salting A union organizing tactic by which workers who are employed by a union as undercover union organizers are hired by unwitting employers.

union shop A form of union security in which the company can hire nonunion people but they must join the union after a prescribed period of time and pay dues. (If they do not, they can be fired.)

unsafe acts Behaviors that potentially cause accidents.

unsafe conditions The mechanical and physical conditions that cause accidents.

valance The perceived value a person attaches to the reward.

vested The proportion of the employer's contribution to the employee's pension plan that is guaranteed to the employee and which the employee can therefore take when he or she leaves.

vestibule/simulated training A method in which trainees learn on the actual or on simulated equipment they would use on the job, but are actually trained off the job.

virtual classroom Special collaboration software used to enable multiple remote learners, using their PCs or laptops, to participate in live audio and visual discussions, communicate via written text, and learn via content such as PowerPoint slides.

Vocational Rehabilitation Act of 1973 The act requiring certain federal contractors to take affirmative action for disabled persons.

voluntary (permissible) bargaining items Items in collective bargaining for which bargaining is neither illegal nor mandatory—neither party can be compelled to negotiate over those items.

wage curve Shows the relationship between the relative value of the job and the average wage paid for this job.

Wagner Act A law that banned certain types of unfair labor practices and provided for secret-ballot elections and majority rule for determining whether or not a firm's employees want to unionize.

wildcat strike An unauthorized strike occurring during the term of a contract.

workaholic People who feel driven to always be on time and meet deadlines.

workers' compensation Provides income and medical benefits to work-related accident victims or their dependents regardless of fault.

workplace flexibility Arming employees with the information technology tools they need to get their jobs done wherever the employees are.

works councils Formal, employee-elected groups of worker representatives that meet monthly with managers to discuss topics ranging, for instance, from no-smoking policies to layoffs.

wrongful discharge An employee dismissal that does not comply with the law or does not comply with the contractual arrangement stated or implied by the firm via its employment application forms, employee manuals, or other promises.

Name/Organization Index

Subject Index

Note: Headings in bold indicate key terms. Page references with "f" indicate figures: those with "t" indicate tables.

Retirement benefits, 234–236
 cash balance pension plans, 235
 domestic partner benefits, 236
 ERISA, 235
 pension plans, 234–235
 in small businesses, 364–365
 social security, 234
 vesting, 236
Retirement counseling, 433
Reward systems
 fair treatment and, 263
 small business, 362–365
Right to work, 285
 laws, 288
Rorschach test, 122, 122f

S

Safety and health. *See* Employee safety and health
Safety committees, 329
Safety inspections, 316–318, 329
 See also Occupational Safety and Health
  Administration (OSHA)
Safety policy, 329, 329f
Safety training
 for Hispanics, 326–327
 Internet-based, 326
Salary (or compensation) surveys,
  217–218, 218f
Salespeople, incentives for, 224
Sample metrics, 14
Sarbanes-Oxley Act (SOX), 14, 223, 227, 263
Scanlon plan, 228
Scatter plot, 88–89, 89f
Scholastic Aptitude Test, 122
Screening systems in employee testing and
  selection, 145
Seasonal layoffs, 321
Security programs, 337–338
Segmenting employees
 in employee compensation, 217
 in performance appraisals, 206
Self-Directed Search (SDS) test, 429
Self-promotion, 134
Self-ratings, 191
Self-reporting
 personality tests, 127, 128
 screening instruments for alcoholism, 331
Senior professional in HR (SPHR)
 certification, 4, 14
Sensitivity training, 174
Service jobs, 8
Severance pay, 231
Sexual harassment
 causes of, 29–30
 court decisions, 27
 defining, EEOC guidelines for, 26
 employee liability in claims, 30
 hostile environment created by coworkers or
  nonemployees, 27
 hostile environment created by supervisors,
  26–27
 manager/employer liability in claims,
  27–28, 30
 online form for filing report of, 28–29f
 proving, 26–27
 quid pro quo, 26
Sexual orientation, 32
Short-term incentives, 221
*SHRM Human Resource Curriculum
 Guidebook,* 19
Sick leave, 230–231
SIMPLE IRA plan, 362–363
Simulated learning, 164
Single parents as job candidates, 101–102
Situational judgment tests, 130
Skill-based pay, 222
Skills matrix for profiles in talent management,
  86–87, 87f
Skinner's behavior modification/
  reinforcement, 245

Small businesses
 appraisal and compensation in, 356
 benefits and rewards in, 360–363
 challenges of, 350–351
 communications in, 363
 EEO compliance and, 352–354
 employee selection in, 354–356, 358–359
 fairness in family businesses, 363–364
 forms used in, 366–367
 HR procedures in, managing, 366–367
 human resource information system (HRIS) in,
  370–372
 importance of HRM to, 351
 Internet and government tools used to support,
  352–358
 leveraging small size, 328–364
 planning and recruiting in, 354
 professional employer organizations used by,
  364–365
 safety and health in, 356, 357–358
 systems and procedures in, managing, 366–367
 training in, 356, 359–360, 359t
 vs. large firm HR, 350–351
Smoking in the workplace, 335
Socialization, 156
Social networking sites, 138–139
Social security, 234
Society for Human Resource Management (SHRM)
 audit tools, 410
 benchmarking services, 410, 412f
 disaster plan survey, 338
 HR certification and, 14
 HR-to-employee ratios, 411f
 Human Capital Benchmarking Study, 350
 managerial development seminars, 168, 171
 outsourcing survey, 415–417, 415t
 recruitment practice survey, 99
 sample metrics, 411f
 *SHRM Human Resource Curriculum
  Guidebook,* 19
 smoking in the workplace survey, 337
 training solutions offered by, 356
Special purposes training, 167–168
 diversity training, 168
 lifelong learning, 167–168
 teamwork and empowerment, 168
 training abroad, 168
Staffing, in management process. *See* Employee
  testing and selection; International HRM staffing;
  Recruitment
Staff managers, 2
 defined, 3
 HR cooperation and, 4
 HRM aspects of, 3
 vs. line managers, 3–4
Standards for Educational and Psychological Testing
  (APA), 24
Standards of performance, 84
Stanford-Binet test, 126
State EEO laws, 32–33
Stereotyping, 40
Stock options, 227
Strategic audits, 409
Strategic fit, achieving, 75
Strategic human resource management
 competitive strategies in, 75
 defined, 54
 example of (Einstein Medical), 68–69
 example of (Portman Ritz-Carlton,
  Shanghai), 54
 importance of, to managers, 54–56
 in mergers and acquisitions, 69–71
 in strategic planning, 63–69
Strategic management, 56
Strategic management process, 56–63
 competitive advantage created by, 61–62
 computerized business planning software
  used in, 59
 leveraging and, 58
 steps in, 56–59, 56f

 in strategic HRM, 62–63
 types of strategies in, 59–61, 60f
Strategic management tools, 65–68, 67f
 balanced scorecard, 66
 digital dashboards, 66–67
 strategy map, 65, 65f
Strategic plan
 defined, 56
 translating into HR policy and practice, 67, 68f
Strategic planning, 63–69
 defined, 56
 HR's involvement in, extent of, 63t
 HR's strategy execution role in, 64
 HR's strategy formulation role in, 64–65
 in strategic HRM, 63–69
 strategic management tools used in, 65–68
Strategic Role Assessment matrix, 206, 206f
Strategy
 competitive, in strategic HRM, 75
 defined, 56
Strategy-based metrics, 413
Strategy implementation, 59
Strategy map, 65, 65f, 67f, 413
Streaming desktop video, 13t
Stress and the Manager (Albrecht), 333
Strictness/leniency problem, 202
Strikes, 300
Strong-Campbell Interest Inventory, 128
Structured situation interview, 149–150
Succession planning systems, 87, 91
Sun Learning eXchange, 161
Supplemental pay benefits. *See* Pay for time not
  worked
Supply chain management, 422
Survey feedback, 174
SWOT analysis, 58, 59, 413
 chart, 58f
Sympathy strike, 300

T

Taft-Hartley Act, 287–288
Talent management
 active-management segmented approach to, 206
 application forms used in, 102–104
 building blocks of, 80–81, 80f
 in compensation allocations, 217
 defined, 11, 79–80
 differential development assignments in, 172–173
 employee interviews and, 137, 138t
 implications for HR managers, 11
 job analysis in, conducting, 81–85
 in performance appraisal and management,
  205–206
 predictive workforce monitoring in, 91
 process, 79–81
 profiles in, role of, 85–87, 137, 138t
 recruiting job candidates and, 92–102
 Strategic Role Assessment matrix used in,
  206, 206f
 workforce planning and, 87–91
Tangible employment action, 26
Task analysis, 158
Task Analysis Record Form, 359–360, 359t
Team building, 175
Team incentive plans, 226, 243–244
Teams abroad, 398
Teamwork training techniques, 168
Technology
 advances in HRM, 8, 12, 13t
 health care benefits and, 234
 training and, 157
Telecommuters as job candidates, 99
Temporary workers, 96–97
Terminate at will, 269–270
Termination from job. *See* **Dismissal**
Termination interview, 272–273
Terrorism, 338, 382
Testing in employee selection. *See* Employee testing
  and selection
Test of Mechanical Comprehension, 126, 126f